# THE BIGGEST MOVIE & TV QUIZ BOOK EVER!

# THE BIGGEST MOVIE & TV QUIZ BOOK EVER!

**Packed with over 16,500 questions!**

CARLTON BOOKS

THIS IS A CARLTON BOOK



Published by Carlton Books Limited 2002
20 Mortimer Street
London
W1T 3JW



A CIP catalogue for this book is available from the British Library.

ISBN 1 84222 740 8

Movie questions set by Dr Jeremy Sims
TV questions set by The Puzzle House

Printed in Great Britain

# Contents

# INTRODUCTION

Welcome to the ultimate movie and TV quiz book. Going to see a movie and watching television are two of the things that unite us all. There aren't many of them, either. Alcohol is another one, barring the occasional tee-totaller. So it is perfectly natural that this book came into being. Frankly, the human psyche demanded it. Divided into two halves – movie quizzes and TV quizzes – you'll find more than 16,750 questions covering a wide variety of subjects related to movies and television.

Whether your first experience of the cinema was the first talkie or *Toy Story*, there's lots to enjoy among these pages. So much has happened since the early days of the movies that there's plenty to quiz you on. Many different subjects and interests are catered for. Are action movies your speciality? Is your knowledge of classic movie moments second to none? Or are you an all-round mine of information? If you answered yes to at least one of these questions, then this book is for you. You'll find 7,750 questions all about the first hundred years of movie history.

Everyone watches TV at least sometimes, and most of us watch it a lot more than that. Where else can you get the same breadth of experience and depth of emotion over such a wide range of areas in just one evening? It's impossible. For better or worse, TV has become a vital and entrenched fixture of modern life. It has the added benefit of being a topic that everyone knows something about, so it's an ideal subject to quiz people on, particularly after they've had a couple of pints. Inside you'll find more than 9,000 questions covering a stunning range of programmes and programme-related areas.

Both the movie quizzes and TV quizzes are divided into three main sections – easy, medium and hard questions. For those of a nervous disposition, begin with the easy questions and work your way on to the hard ones when you've got the hang of things. The questions in each of the quizzes are also themed, so you can choose specialist subjects or more general topics.

We know that you, the reader of this book, would never dream of taking a sly peek at an answer if you weren't sure what the correct answer was. Well, not everyone is as honest as you are. That is why the answers to the questions are on a different page from the questions themselves. We tell you where to find the answers underneath the quiz number and topic heading. You won't have far to look. The correct answers will be just a few pages before or after the questions.

Running a quiz that just involves family and friends is usually a simple affair. All you really need is a copy of this book. However, at the back of the book you'll also find a comprehensive set of guidelines on how to prepare for and run a successful quiz of your own down your local pub, and some handy answer sheet templates to photocopy and give out to contestants. Running a pub quiz can be a lot of hard work, but it's also very rewarding, even if not usually particularly lucrative. There is one important guideline you should always remember when running a quiz of course, and that is never, ever, under any circumstances, give out your own pens.

More importantly than that though – seriously for a minute – when you are going to be running a quiz, prepare properly beforehand. Don't just take this book along and read out of it (because apart from anything else, some other wise guy might have bought a copy, too, and be checking the answers). Note down all the questions and all the answers, and make sure you've got them all ready in the order you want to ask them. The whole event will disintegrate into chaos if you're fumbling around for the questions, and – even worse – hesitating over the answers. If an answer makes you think "hang on a moment, is that right?" then double-check it to make sure that it is not only correct, but it is the *only* correct answer. While every possible effort has been undertaken to make absolutely sure that every answer is accurate, there is a slight possibility that an error may have crept in, and the answer is wrong. Nothing is more humiliating than telling people who are right that they are wrong in front of a lot of witnesses who will remember it and tease you about it mercilessly for the next three years. If you've made sure of your answers, you'll be absolutely 100% safe, not just 99.9% safe.

At a public quiz people don't want to be made to look stupid. It's a night out, remember. They've probably had a hard day at the office and the last thing they need is an evening of supposed relaxation where they're made to look as though they know nothing at all. They want to have fun, so start with easy questions to get everyone in the mood. Only when you've lulled them into a false sense of security should you step up the pressure by adding the medium and finally the hard questions.

So there you go. Take your book in hand, wade in and have fun. After all, that's what it's all about.

# MOVIE QUIZZES

# CONTENTS

## *LEVEL 1:* THE EASY QUESTIONS

There are those who say that any question is easy if you know the answer. Well maybe. In this section most people will be able to come up with most of the answers without too much difficulty. The questions are about well-known films and famous names. There are no trick questions. The questions are short and snappy. The answers are brief and simple

Use these questions in an organized quiz in the early rounds so that everyone will get something right. There is nothing worse than announcing the score in the first round and finding Team 1 got zero. They'll all want to go home and will never come back again. Give them plenty of easy questions to get them in the mood. The pressure comes later!

An easy question certainly won't ask you the name of the third extra on the left on the deck of the Titanic. However, if you didn't even know that there was a movie called *Titanic*, then there will certainly be some questions in this section that you simply won't be able to answer. Broadly speaking, we assume most people would consider these questions to be straightforward!

Finally a word of warning. Don't always say the first thing that comes into your head, however easy the question may seem. If you can't answer one of the difficult questions in the final section of this book most of your fellow contestants will be not at all surprised, and probably relieved. If you get a really easy question wrong because you were too impulsive, the embarrassment factor goes off the scale!

## *QUIZ 1* POT LUCK 1 ........ LEVEL 1

*Answers – see page 15*

1 Which film centre is also known as Tinseltown?
2 Which writer was 'in Love' in the 1998 movie?
3 In which movie based on a Jane Austen novel did Gwyneth Paltrow play Emma Woodhouse?
4 What follows the names of Harry Connick and Robert Downey?
5 Who played the lead role in *The African Queen* after David Niven turned it down?
6 Who sang the title song of *Who's That Girl*?
7 In which decade was *Star Wars* first released?
8 Who played the villain in the 90s movie *Silence of the Lambs*?
9 Who won the Best Actor Oscar for *One Flew over the Cuckoo's Nest*?
10 In which decade was *Goldfinger* released?
11 How is Demetria Guynes better known?
12 Who won the Best Director Oscar for *Annie Hall*?
13 From which country did Mikhail Barishnikov defect to the USA?
14 In which country was Britt Ekland born?
15 In which eastern bloc country was the movie *Reds* set?
16 In which decade was *Mission: Impossible* released?
17 Who was Paul Newman's wife whom he directed in *Rachel, Rachel*?
18 What did T stand for in *E.T.*?
19 How is former Bond girl, Mrs Ringo Starr, Barbara Goldbach better known?
20 Which Apollo mission was the subject of a movie starring Tom Hanks?
21 Which comedian Bob has hosted the Oscars ceremony over 20 times?
22 Rupert Everett starred in 'The Madness of' which king?
23 Burt Bacharach was a former accompanist for which actress Marlene?
24 Which movie did the song 'Fame' come from?
25 Which Phoebe of TV mini-series *Lace* married actor Kevin Kline?

**Answers Pot Luck 2** (see Quiz 3)
**1** India. **2** Thompson. **3** 3 hours. **4** Mike Newell. **5** *The Boxer.* **6** Marlon Brando. **7** 1930s. **8** Cage. **9** Boxing. **10** Julia Roberts. **11** *The Godfather.* **12** Oldman. **13** Quentin. **14** Brad Pitt. **15** Sister. **16** Curtis. **17** Mitty. **18** *Jaws.* **19** Winona. **20** Reynolds. **21** Stone. **22** 1980s. **23** Harlow. **24** *Green.* **25** Elton John.

## *QUIZ 2* 1930s ........ LEVEL 1

*Answers – see page 16*

1 *Anna Christie* was the first talkie for which Swedish star?
2 *The Blue Angel* with Marlene Dietrich was shot in English and which other language?
3 Which 'modern' film was Chaplin's last silent movie?
4 In *Stagecoach* which actor John played the Ringo Kid?
5 Which 1939 movie featured a Yellow Brick Road?
6 Which dancers appeared in *The Story of Vernon and Irene Castle*?
7 *Mr Smith Goes to* where in the title of the 1939 movie?
8 Which Laurence played Heathcliff to Merle Oberon's Cathy in *Wuthering Heights*?
9 What were Katharine Hepburn and Cary Grant *Bringing Up* in the 1938 comedy?
10 Which King was a successful ape?
11 Which Clark Gable film, the name of a city, was about a Californian earthquake at the beginning of the 20th century?
12 *The Adventures of* which English hero was the title of a 1938 movie with Errol Flynn?
13 What type of character did James Cagney play in *Angels with Dirty Faces*?
14 *Thoroughbreds Don't Cry* teamed Judy Garland with which Mickey?
15 Which Busby did the choreography for *Footlight Parade*?
16 Which *Hotel* was the title of a Garbo movie?
17 Which zany brothers made *Animal Crackers* in 1930?
18 In which city is *The Hunchback of Notre Dame* set?
19 Bela Lugosi starred as the first sound version of which character?
20 Where was it *All Quiet* in the movies in 1930?
21 The movie *Scarface* was based on the life of which gangster?
22 Which 1939 movie was about a schoolmaster called Mr Chipperfield?
23 What was the heroine of *Gone with the Wind* called?
24 Boris Karloff starred in one of the first horror movies about which Mary Shelley character?
25 What completes the title of the Mae West movie, *She Done Him* ____?

**Answers Animation** (see Quiz 4)
**1** Gibson. **2** Gromit. **3** Disney. **4** *The Lion King*. **5** Williams. **6** The Beast. **7** Rowan Atkinson. **8** Jane. **9** Bugs Bunny. **10** 1940s. **11** Phil Collins. **12** Dalmatians. **13** *Jungle Book*. **14** 1960s. **15** Cat. **16** *Antz*. **17** The Aristocats. **18** *101 Dalmatians*. **19** Donald. **20** 1930s. **21** Bugs Bunny. **22** 1990s. **23** *Jungle Book*. **24** Irons. **25** *Toy Story*.

## *QUIZ 3* POT LUCK 2 ........ LEVEL 1

*Answers – see page 13*

1 Which Asian country is home to 'Bollywood'?
2 Which Emma starred in *Sense and Sensibility*?
3 To the nearest hour, how long does *Titanic* last?
4 Who directed *Four Weddings and a Funeral*?
5 In which 1997 movie did Daniel Day Lewis play a boxer?
6 Who won the Best Actor Oscar for *On the Waterfront*?
7 In which decade of the 20th century was Joan Collins born?
8 Which Nicolas starred in *Face/Off*?
9 Is *Raging Bull* about American football, boxing or bull-fighting?
10 *My Best Friend's Wedding* and *Sleeping with the Enemy* featured which actress?
11 The character Sonny Corleone was in which sequence of movies?
12 *Air Force One* starred which Gary?
13 What is the first name of the *Pulp Fiction* director?
14 Which actor links *Se7en, Sleepers* and *Thelma and Louise*?
15 What relation is Shirley MacLaine to Warren Beatty?
16 Which Tony starred in *Some Like It Hot*?
17 'The Secret Life of' which Walter formed a movie title?
18 Which early Spielberg blockbuster featured a shark?
19 Which Ms Ryder had her big break in *Beetlejuice*?
20 Which 70s actor Burt was *Cosmopolitan*'s first male nude centrefold?
21 Which Oliver won the Best Director Oscar for *Born on the Fourth of July*?
22 In which decade was *Batman* with Michael Keaton released?
23 Which famous Jean tested for the role of Scarlett O'Hara?
24 Which colour completes the film title, *How ___ Was My Valley*?
25 Which pop singer wrote the music for Disney's *The Lion King*?

**Answers Pot Luck 1** (see Quiz 1)
**1** Hollywood. **2** Shakespeare. **3** *Emma.* **4** Junior. **5** Humphrey Bogart. **6** Madonna. **7** 1970s. **8** Anthony Hopkins. **9** Jack Nicholson. **10** 1960s. **11** Demi Moore. **12** Woody Allen. **13** USSR – Latvia. **14** Sweden. **15** USSR. **16** 1990s. **17** Joanne Woodward. **18** Terrestrial. **19** Barbara Bach. **20** 13. **21** Hope. **22** George. **23** Dietrich. **24** *Fame.* **25** Cates.

## *QUIZ 4* ANIMATION ........ LEVEL 1

*Answers – see page 14*

1 Which Mel was the voice of Captain Smith in *Pocahontas*?
2 Who did Nick Park create as Wallace's faithful hound?
3 Who worked with Pixar to make *Toy Story*?
4 Which movie has the cub Simba and his evil uncle Scar?
5 Which Robin was the voice of the genie in *Aladdin*?
6 Who appeared with Beauty in the 1991 Disney movie?
7 Which alter ego of Mr Bean was the voice of Zazu in *The Lion King*?
8 Which Tarzan mate did Minnie Driver provide the voice for in *Tarzan*?
9 Who featured in *Knighty Knight Bugs* in 1958?
10 In which decade was *Fantasia* released?
11 Who provided the music for the Disney *Tarzan* film?
12 Pongo and Perdita were which types of black-and-white dog in the 1961 Disney movie?
13 Which 'Book' movie featured a jazz-loving bear, Baloo?
14 In which decade was *Jungle Book* released?
15 What type of creature was Felix, an early animation character?
16 Anne Bancroft provided a voice in which 1998 movie about insects?
17 Which felines were the stars of a 1970 Disney classic?
18 In which canine caper was there a 'Twilight Bark'?
19 Which cartoon duck was usually dressed in blue and white?
20 In which decade was *Snow White and the Seven Dwarfs* released?
21 Which Bunny did Mel Blanc provide the voice for?
22 In which decade was *The Lion King* released?
23 Which film featured the song 'The Bare Necessities'?
24 Which English actor Jeremy was the voice of Scar in *The Lion King*?
25 Which movie featured Buzz Lightyear and Mr Potato Head?

**Answers 1930s** (see Quiz 2)
**1** Greta Garbo. **2** German. **3** *Modern Times.* **4** Wayne. **5** *The Wizard of Oz.* **6** Fred Astaire & Ginger Rogers. **7** *Washington.* **8** Olivier. **9** *Baby.* **10** King Kong. **11** *San Francisco.* **12** *Robin Hood.* **13** Gangster. **14** Rooney. **15** Berkeley. **16** *Grand.* **17** Marx Brothers. **18** Paris. **19** Dracula. **20** *On the Western Front.* **21** Al Capone. **22** *Goodbye Mr Chips.* **23** Scarlett O'Hara. **24** Frankenstein. **25** *Wrong.*

## *QUIZ 5* MUSIC ON FILM ........ LEVEL 1

*Answers – see page 19*

1 Which Hugh Grant/Julia Roberts movie set in London featured 'She'?
2 Who first sang 'Somewhere over the Rainbow'?
3 Gene Autry was usually billed as a singing what?
4 Which Newman/Redford movie featured, 'Raindrops Keep Falling on My Head'?
5 John Barry is linked with the music for films about which celebrated secret agent?
6 'Colours of the Wind' was from which movie about a native North American heroine?
7 'When You Wish upon a Star' was from which film about a puppet?
8 Which Mrs was a character and the theme song in *The Graduate*?
9 'Can You Feel the Love Tonight' came from which Disney movie?
10 'Whole New World' was heard in which Disney hit about a genie?
11 'Bright Eyes' from *Watership Down* was about which animals?
12 Which 'Top' 80s movie had the hit song 'Take My Breath Away'?
13 'Up Where We Belong' was used in which movie with Richard Gere and Debra Winger?
14 Which French–Canadian sang the theme from *Titanic*?
15 Who sang 'You Must Love Me' from *Evita*?
16 Which 'Cowboy' movie provided the hit 'Everybody's Talkin'' for Nilsson?
17 Which Oscar-winner featured 'My Heart Will Go On'?
18 Who wrote the music for *Evita*?
19 'The Streets of Philadelphia' from which movie won Best Song Oscar?
20 Which Shirley sang the title song for the 007 movie *Goldfinger*?
21 What type of 'River' was the theme from *Breakfast at Tiffany's*?
22 Scott Joplin's music for *The Sting* is played on which musical instrument?
23 Which 'Melody', a hit for The Righteous Brothers, featured in *Ghost*?
24 How is composer and Oscar-winner Hoagland Howard Carmichael better known?
25 Which Welshman Tom sang the theme song for 007's *Thunderball*?

**Answers Arnold Schwarzenegger** (see Quiz 7)
**1** Austria. **2** Iron. **3** Conan. **4** *The Terminator*. **5** Red. **6** DeVito. **7** Total. **8** George Bush. **9** Los Angeles. **10** Her husband. **11** *Conan the Barbarian*. **12** Preston. **13** Maria. **14** Cameron. **15** Pregnant. **16** Austrian Oak. **17** *Terminator 2*. **18** *True Lies*. **19** 'The Last'. **20** 1940s. **21** Kindergarten. **22** Computers. **23** J.F. Kennedy. **24** Planet Hollywood. **25** Jeff Bridges.

## *QUIZ 6* POT LUCK 3 ........ LEVEL 1

*Answers – see page 20*

1 *Top Gun* and *City of Angels* featured which actress?
2 The character Vincent Vega appeared in which movie?
3 Which Susan starred in *The Witches of Eastwick*?
4 In 1998 who separated from her husband Bruce Willis?
5 In which decade was the remake of *Godzilla* released after the 1955 movie?
6 Who played Jack in *Titanic*?
7 In which decade does *The Talented Mr Ripley* take place?
8 Who played the title role in *Citizen Kane*?
9 Which Matt starred in *Wild Things*?
10 Which word links a 'Hawk' and a 'Wolf' to give two film titles?
11 Who played Rosemary in *Rosemary's Baby*?
12 Was *Beverley Hills Cop* first released in the 1960s, 70s or 80s?
13 *Ghostbusters* and *Alien* featured which actress?
14 Who played the police captain in *Casablanca*?
15 Which actress links *The Silence of the Lambs* and *Taxi Driver*?
16 Which superhero gets involved with Cat Woman?
17 Who starred in the *Lethal Weapon* series of films?
18 What is the name of Jamie Lee Curtis's actor father?
19 Which fruit would complete this title, *The ____ of Wrath*?
20 Which Jamie starred in *Halloween*?
21 Does *Mary Poppins* last for 140, 200 or 240 minutes?
22 Who won the Best Director Oscar for *Titanic*?
23 In which decade was *Rain Man* released?
24 Which group had a giant hit with the movie-linked song 'Take My Breath Away'?
25 In which decade of the 20th century was Sean Connery born?

**Answers Horror** (see Quiz 8)
**1** Kenneth Branagh. **2** The Devil. **3** *Bram Stoker's Dracula.* **4** *Scream 2.* **5** William Peter Blatty. **6** Bela. **7** Invisible. **8** King. **9** Dracula. **10** Cruise. **11** Spiders. **12** Kubrick. **13** The creature. **14** *Halloween.* **15** Spacek. **16** Elm Street. **17** 1970s. **18** Mia Farrow. **19** Victor. **20** In London. **21** *The Birds.* **22** Anthony Perkins. **23** Anthony Hopkins. **24** Pfeiffer. **25** Hammer.

## *QUIZ 7* ARNOLD SCHWARZENEGGER ........ LEVEL 1

*Answers – see page 17*

1 In which European country was he born?
2 What was he 'Pumping' in the 1977 documentary film about himself?
3 What was the name of 'the Barbarian' he played in 1982?
4 Which smash hit movie gave him the line 'I'll be back'?
5 What colour went before 'Sonja' in his 1985 movie?
6 Which Danny was his co-star in *Twins*?
7 What type of 'Recall' was his 1990 movie?
8 In 1990 which Republican President made him chairman of the Council on Physical Fitness?
9 In which Californian city was *The Terminator* set?
10 Which muscleman relative of Jayne Mansfield did he play in the TV biopic?
11 What was *Conan the Destroyer* the sequel to?
12 Which Kelly co-starred in *Twins*?
13 Which journalist Ms Shriver did he marry?
14 Which James, later famous for *Titanic*, directed *The Terminator*?
15 What very unmasculine condition was he in *Junior*?
16 In weightlifting circles he was billed as what type of Austrian tree?
17 Which *Terminator* film was subtitled 'Judgment Day'?
18 What sort of 'Lies' did he make for James Cameron in 1994?
19 What sort of 'Action Hero' was he in 1993?
20 In which decade was he born?
21 What sort of 'Cop' was he in 1990?
22 In *True Lies* Schwarzenegger is a salesman of what?
23 He married the niece of which late US President?
24 Which 'Planet' restaurant chain did he back?
25 Who was Schwarzenegger's male co-star in *Stay Hungry*?

**Answers Music on Film** (see Quiz 5)
**1** *Notting Hill.* **2** Judy Garland. **3** Cowboy. **4** *Butch Cassidy and the Sundance Kid.* **5** Bond films. **6** *Pocahontas.* **7** *Pinocchio.* **8** Robinson. **9** *The Lion King.* **10** *Aladdin.* **11** Rabbits. **12** *Top Gun.* **13** *An Officer and a Gentleman.* **14** Celine Dion. **15** Madonna. **16** *Midnight Cowboy.* **17** *Titanic.* **18** Andrew Lloyd Webber. **19** *Philadelphia.* **20** Bassey. **21** 'Moon River'. **22** Piano. **23** 'Unchained Melody.' **24** Hoagy Carmichael. **25** Jones.

## *QUIZ 8* HORROR ········· LEVEL 1

*Answers – see page 18*

1 Who directed Kenneth Branagh in *Mary Shelley's Frankenstein*?
2 Who, according to the movie, fathered *Rosemary's Baby*?
3 In which Dracula movie did Anthony Hopkins play Professor van Helsing?
4 What was the sequel to *Scream* called?
5 Who wrote the screenplay of William Peter Blatty's *The Exorcist*?
6 What was the first name of Dracula actor Lugosi?
7 What sort of 'Man' was Claude Rains in 1933?
8 Which Stephen's first novel *Carrie* was a successful 70s movie?
9 Who was Transylvania's most famous vampire?
10 Which Tom played a vampire with Brad Pitt in *Interview with the Vampire: The Vampire Chronicles*?
11 Which creepy-crawlies are the subject of *Arachnophobia*?
12 Which Stanley made *The Shining* with Jack Nicholson?
13 What part did Boris Karloff play in the pre-World War II *Frankenstein*?
14 Which 1978 movie shares its name with the spooky 31st October?
15 Which Sissy played the title role in *Carrie*?
16 On which street was the 'Nightmare' in the 80s movie series?
17 In which decade was *The Exorcist* first released?
18 Who was the female star of *Rosemary's Baby*?
19 What was Frankenstein's first name in the Kenneth Branagh version?
20 Where was the 'American Werewolf' in the 1981 movie with David Naughton?
21 Which Hitchcock movie featured feathered attackers?
22 Who directed and starred in *Psycho 3* in 1986?
23 Which British actor won an Oscar for *The Silence of the Lambs*?
24 Which Michelle co-starred with Jack Nicholson in *Wolf*?
25 Which British studios were famous for their horror movies?

**Answers Pot Luck 3** (see Quiz 6)
**1** Meg Ryan. **2** *Pulp Fiction.* **3** Sarandon. **4** Demi Moore. **5** 1990s. **6** Leonardo DiCaprio. **7** 1950s. **8** Orson Welles. **9** Dillon. **10** Sea. **11** Mia Farrow.
**12** 80s. **13** Sigourney Weaver. **14** Claude Rains. **15** Jodie Foster. **16** Batman.
**17** Mel Gibson. **18** Tony Curtis. **19** *Grapes.* **20** Lee Curtis. **21** 140 minutes.
**22** James Cameron. **23** 1980s. **24** Berlin. **25** 1930s.

## *QUIZ 9* POT LUCK 4 ........................ LEVEL 1

*Answers – see page 23*

1 Which detective has been portrayed on screen over 200 times?
2 Which 1988 film did rock star Phil Collins star in?
3 Which Ewan starred in *Emma*?
4 *Batman Forever* and *To Die For* featured which actress?
5 Which *Home Alone* star was the 20th century's highest paid child in the movies?
6 Who played the young Obi Wan Kenobi in *Star Wars Episode I: The Phantom Menace*?
7 Which Anthony played *Zorba the Greek*?
8 Who sang 'I Will Always Love You' in her film, *The Bodyguard*?
9 Which film legend Mack inspired the musical *Mack and Mabel*?
10 Which Buzz appeared in *Toy Story*?
11 Which veteran actor Richard was Dr Hammond in *Jurassic Park*?
12 Which James starred in the original *Harvey*?
13 Which singer Diana starred in *Lady Sings the Blues*?
14 Which French sex symbol became an animal rights campaigner?
15 Which children's toys are linked with 'Guys' in the title of a film based on a musical?
16 In which TV soap did Larry Hagman find fame after appearing on the big screen?
17 In which decade was *Return of the Jedi* released?
18 Which actor links *The Magnificent Seven* and *The King and I*?
19 Val Kilmer played Jim Morrison in the movie about which rock band?
20 Which Robin starred in *Mrs Doubtfire*?
21 Which actor links *Mission: Impossible, A Few Good Men* and *Days of Thunder*?
22 What was the name of the movie based on TV's *The X-Files*?
23 Which Glenda won the Best Actress Oscar for *Women in Love*?
24 In which decade of the 20th century was Jamie Lee Curtis born?
25 What was the Bond theme for *A View to a Kill* called?

**Answers Late Greats** (see Quiz 11)
**1** Car. **2** Gish. **3** Marvin. **4** Rex Harrison. **5** Gable. **6** Niven. **7** England. **8** Pub. **9** Clark Gable. **10** Vivien Leigh. **11** Richard Burton. **12** Charlie Chaplin & Paulette Goddard. **13** Rock Hudson. **14** Laurence Olivier. **15** Gardner. **16** Davis. **17** Davis. **18** W.C. Fields. **19** Cary Grant. **20** Nose. **21** Jackie Gleason. **22** Stewart. **23** *Citizen Kane* **24** Dean. **25** Betty Grable.

## *QUIZ 10* 1980s STARS ........ LEVEL 1

*Answers – see page 24*

1 Which pop superstar did Sean Penn marry in 1985?
2 Which ex Mrs Sonny Bono played Loretta Castorini in *Moonstruck*?
3 When Billy Crystal was Harry, who was Meg Ryan?
4 Which 24-year-old Michael played teenager Marty in *Back to the Future*?
5 Which husband of Demi Moore played John McLane in *Die Hard*?
6 Which Kirstie appeared in *Star Trek II*?
7 Which tough guy actor has the nickname Sly?
8 Which Melanie was a 'Working Girl' for Harrison Ford?
9 Who played Tom Cruise's autistic brother in *Rain Man*?
10 Which Patrick practised 'Dirty Dancing' with Jennifer Grey?
11 Which Glenn's 'Attraction' looked 'Fatal' to Michael Douglas in 1987?
12 Which successful US talk show hostess appeared in *The Color Purple*?
13 Who changed her name from Susan Weaver before appearing in movies such as *Ghostbusters*?
14 In *Born on the Fourth of July*, Tom Cruise played a veteran from which war?
15 Which Canadian Leslie found big-screen fame as Lieutenant Frank Drebin?
16 Which Richard was the *American Gigolo*?
17 Which Mel played the title role in *Mad Max II*?
18 Which Kevin played opposite Meryl Streep in *Sophie's Choice*?
19 Which animal was a star with Clint Eastwood in *Any Which Way You Can*?
20 What did Elliott call his pet alien in the 80s Spielberg movie?
21 What sort of busters were Dan Aykroyd and Bill Murray?
22 Which Michael was in *Romancing the Stone* in 1984?
23 What was the name of the cartoon rabbit in the title of the movie with Bob Hoskins?
24 Michael Keaton starred as which caped crusader in 1989?
25 Which 007 joined Harrison Ford in *Indiana Jones and the Last Crusade*?

**Answers Pot Luck 5** (see Quiz 12)
**1** Danny Boyle. **2** 1950s. **3** *Kitty*. **4** 85 minutes. **5** Ingrid Bergman. **6** Winona Ryder. **7** Diamonds. **8** Madness. **9** *A Return to Oz*. **10** Tina Turner. **11** *Gone with the Wind*. **12** Oldman. **13** Nazis. **14** *The Full Monty*. **15** Dolly Parton. **16** Audrey Hepburn. **17** Michelle Pfeiffer. **18** *Sophie's Choice*. **19** Stockholm. **20** Michael Jackson. **21** Diane Keaton. **22** Whoopi Goldberg. **23** 1960s. **24** Peter Sellers. **25** 1930s.

## *QUIZ 11* LATE GREATS ........ LEVEL 1

*Answers – see page 21*

1 In what type of crash did James Dean meet his death?
2 Which Lillian was dubbed The First Lady of the Silent Screen?
3 Which Lee turned down George C. Scott's role in *Patton*?
4 Who won the Best Actor Oscar for *My Fair Lady*?
5 Which Clark's last movie was *The Misfits*?
6 Which David's autobiography was called *The Moon's a Balloon*?
7 Where was Jessica Tandy born?
8 In what type of building did Oliver Reed die?
9 Who died 12 days after finishing *The Misfits*?
10 Who won the Best Actress Oscar for *Gone with the Wind*?
11 Which Welsh actor directed and starred in *Dr Faustus* in 1968?
12 Which husband and wife starred in *The Great Dictator* in 1940?
13 Who was Bogart talking to when he said, 'You look very soft for a rock'?
14 Which British actor won an Oscar for *Hamlet* in 1948?
15 Which Ava was Oscar-nominated for *Mogambo*?
16 Which Bette tested for the role of Scarlett O'Hara?
17 Which Sammy starred in *Sweet Charity*?
18 How was William Claude Fields known to cinema goers?
19 Jennifer Grant is the only daughter of which great from the heyday of Hollywood?
20 Which part of him did Jimmy Durante insure for $100,000?
21 How was John Gleason known in movies?
22 Which James died in 1997 aged 89?
23 What was Orson Welles's first film, in 1941?
24 Which doomed James starred in *Rebel Without a Cause*?
25 How was Elizabeth Ruth Grable better known?

**Answers Pot Luck 4** (see Quiz 9)
**1** Sherlock Holmes. **2** *Buster*. **3** McGregor. **4** Nicole Kidman. **5** Macaulay Culkin. **6** Ewan McGregor. **7** Quinn. **8** Whitney Houston. **9** Mack Sennett. **10** Lightyear. **11** Attenborough. **12** Stewart. **13** Ross. **14** Brigitte Bardot. **15** Dolls. **16** *Dallas*. **17** 1980s. **18** Yul Brynner. **19** The Doors. **20** Williams. **21** Tom Cruise. **22** *The X-Files*. **23** Jackson. **24** 1950s. **25** 'A View to a Kill'.

## *QUIZ 12* POT LUCK 5 ........ LEVEL 1

*Answers – see page 22*

1 Which Danny directed *Trainspotting*?
2 In which decade of the 20th century was Kevin Costner born?
3 Which girl's first name completes the film title, ____ *Foyle*?
4 Did *Ace Ventura, Pet Detective* run for 65, 85 or 155 minutes?
5 Who got the lead in *Casablanca* after Hedy Lamarr turned it down?
6 Which actress links *Bram Stoker's Dracula* and *Beetlejuice*?
7 What, according to Monroe's song, are 'a girl's best friend'?
8 Which ailment is mentioned in the title of a movie about King George III?
9 What was the sequel to *The Wizard of Oz* called?
10 Which female pop star featured in *Mad Max Beyond Thunderdome*?
11 Scarlett O'Hara was heroine of which epic film?
12 Which Gary starred in *The Fifth Element*?
13 Which political group is central to the plot of *The Sound of Music*?
14 Which 90s movie told of a group of stripping Sheffield steelworkers?
15 Which blonde country star had a cameo role in *The Beverly Hillbillies*?
16 Which Audrey starred in *My Fair Lady*?
17 Who played the female lead in *Grease 2*?
18 In which movie did Meryl Streep play a Polish holocaust survivor?
19 Greta Garbo was born in which European capital city?
20 Martin Scorsese directed the video *Bad* for which pop superstar?
21 Which Diane was in *The First Wives' Club*?
22 *The Color Purple* and *Sister Act 2* featured which actress?
23 In which decade was *The Graduate* released?
24 Which Peter played *Inspector Clouseau*?
25 Did Shirley Temple first win an Oscar in the 1930s, 50s or 70s?

**Answers 1980s Stars** (see Quiz 10)
**1** Madonna. **2** Cher. **3** Sally. **4** J. Fox. **5** Bruce Willis. **6** Alley. **7** Sylvester Stallone. **8** Griffith. **9** Dustin Hoffman. **10** Swayze. **11** Close. **12** Oprah Winfrey. **13** Sigourney Weaver. **14** Vietnam. **15** Nielsen. **16** Gere. **17** Gibson. **18** Kline. **19** Orang Utan. **20** E.T. **21** Ghostbusters. **22** Douglas. **23** Roger. **24** Batman. **25** Sean Connery.

## *QUIZ 13* OSCARS – BEST FILMS ........ LEVEL 1

*Answers – see page 27*

1 Which musical set in New York won 10 awards in 1961?
2 'Dances with' what was the first winner of the 1990s?
3 The chauffeur was 'Driving Miss' whom in 1989?
4 Who was 'in Love' in 1998 to take Best Film honours?
5 *Chariots of Fire* was about events at which 1924 sporting event?
6 What was 'Confidential' in the movie with Kim Basinger?
7 Which musical Mary had 13 nominations and five awards in 1964?
8 Judi Dench played which queen in *Shakespeare in Love*?
9 Which 'List' won in 1993?
10 *The English Patient* tells of a desert explorer during which war?
11 Which continent was in the title of an 80s winner with Meryl Streep?
12 Which pacifist leader of India was the subject of a 1982 biopic?
13 What was the name of the sequel to *The Godfather* which won two years after the original?
14 Which 'Hunter' was the 1979 winner?
15 What was the name of the musical based on a Dickens novel about the boy who asked for more?
16 In which country was *Gigi* set?
17 Who was the 1984 winner *Amadeus* about?
18 Which 80s film is about The Dragon Throne?
19 Which 'Connection' was Best Picture of 1971?
20 *Platoon* was set during which Asian conflict?
21 *The Greatest Show on Earth* was about what type of entertainment?
22 *The Sting* won Best Picture during which decade?
23 The most successful winner of the 90s had the shortest name: what?
24 Who was 'versus Kramer' in 1979?
25 In which European country was *Cabaret* set during the 1930s?

**Answers 1940s** (see Quiz 15)
**1** Hitchcock. **2** *Pinocchio*. **3** *The Outlaw*. **4** St Louis. **5** Old Lace. **6** Horses. **7** Christmas. **8** Hayworth. **9** Easter. **10** The Ambersons. **11** Elephant. **12** *The Philadelphia Story*. **13** *Green*. **14** Maltese. **15** Kane. **16** 34th Street. **17** Red. **18** *Casablanca*. **19** Vienna. **20** Sailors. **21** Philip. **22** Hitler. **23** *Bambi*. **24** Walt Disney. **25** Coronets.

## *QUIZ 14* POT LUCK 6 ............ LEVEL 1

*Answers – see page 28*

1 Which Geena starred in *A League of their Own*?
2 In which country was Leslie Nielsen born?
3 Which Helen was the only American nominated for Best Actress Oscar in 1998?
4 Which actor links *Batman, A Few Good Men* and *Wolf*?
5 Steven Spielberg made 'Close Encounters of' which kind?
6 Which much-quoted actress wrote an autobiography called *Goodness Had Nothing to Do with It*?
7 Which whale was played by Keiko in a 90s movie?
8 *Top Gun* was about which of the armed services?
9 Was *Bambi* first released in the 1920s, 40s or 60s?
10 Which Frank starred in the 50s movie *From Here to Eternity*?
11 What is Nicolas Cage's real surname?
12 Real-life character Lee Harvey Oswald appears in which Oliver Stone movie?
13 Which word completes the film title, *I Am a ____ from a Chain Gang*?
14 Which character was voiced by Robin Williams in *Aladdin*?
15 Which James Bond has an actor son called Jason?
16 *Total Recall* and *Casino* both featured which actress?
17 Who played opposite Ginger Rogers 10 times?
18 Which pop star Tina did Angela Bassett play in the 1993 biopic?
19 In which decade was *Batman Forever* released?
20 Who won the Best Actor Oscar for *The Godfather*?
21 Which actress Natalie did Robert Wagner marry twice?
22 In which decade of the 20th century was Michelle Pfeiffer born?
23 Which mode of transport completes the film title, *Night ____ To Munich*?
24 Which Kevin played Bottom in the 1990s *A Midsummer Night's Dream*?
25 Which Mark starred in *The Empire Strikes Back*?

**Answers Paul Newman** (see Quiz 16)
**1** Blue. **2** Taylor. **3** 1960s. **4** Scorsese. **5** Robert Redford. **6** *Towering Inferno.* **7** Chicago. **8** 1960s. **9** Poitier. **10** Drug overdose. **11** Woodward. **12** *The Glass Menagerie.* **13** Andrews. **14** Motor racing. **15** Billy the Kid. **16** Jimmy Carter. **17** Butch Cassidy. **18** Summer. **19** *The Sting.* **20** Fast. **21** Luke. **22** Salad dressing. **23** Bridge. **24** Best Actor. **25** 1970s.

## *QUIZ 15* 1940s ........ LEVEL 1

*Answers – see page 25*

1 *Rebecca* was the first Hollywood movie for which director Alfred?
2 Which Disney movie featured a wooden puppet?
3 Which 1943 movie was outlawed for six years because of Jane Russell's attributes?
4 The 1944 Judy Garland movie says 'Meet Me in' which town?
5 What went with 'Arsenic' in the comedy with Cary Grant?
6 *National Velvet* centred on what type of animals?
7 *It's a Wonderful Life* is set at which festive time of year?
8 Which Rita played the title role in *Gilda*?
9 At what time of year was the 'Parade' which starred Fred Astaire and Judy Garland?
10 Which 'Magnificent' family was the subject of a 40s movie directed by Orson Welles?
11 What sort of animal was Dumbo?
12 Which 'Story' with Cary Grant and Katharine Hepburn had the name of a US state in its title?
13 Which colour completes the title of 1941 Oscar winner, *How ____ Was My Valley*?
14 What was the nationality of the 'Falcon' in the 1941 movie with Humphrey Bogart and Peter Lorre?
15 Which 'Citizen' was a debut for Orson Welles?
16 On which street was there a 'Miracle' in a 1947 film?
17 What colour were the dancing shoes in the movie with Moira Shearer?
18 Which movie has the line, 'Here's lookin' at you kid'?
19 In which Austrian city is *The Third Man* set?
20 What type of servicemen were on leave in *On the Town*?
21 Which private detective Marlowe is the subject of *The Big Sleep*?
22 Which dictator did Chaplin play and mock in *The Great Dictator*?
23 Which Disney movie was the tale of a young fawn?
24 Who was the most famous director of *Fantasia*?
25 What went with 'Kind Hearts' in the movie with Alec Guinness?

**Answers Oscars – Best Films** (see Quiz 13)
**1** *West Side Story*. **2** Wolves. **3** Daisy. **4** Shakespeare. **5** Olympic Games. **6** LA. **7** *Mary Poppins*. **8** Elizabeth I. **9** *Schindler's List*. **10** World War II. **11** (Out of) Africa. **12** Gandhi. **13** *The Godfather Part II*. **14** *The Deer Hunter*. **15** *Oliver!* **16** France. **17** Mozart. **18** *The Last Emperor*. **19** *The French Connection*. **20** The Vietnam War. **21** Circus. **22** 1970s. **23** *Titanic*. **24** Kramer. **25** Germany.

## *QUIZ 16* PAUL NEWMAN ........ LEVEL 1

*Answers – see page 26*

1 What colour are Paul Newman's eyes?
2 Which Elizabeth was his co-star in *Cat on a Hot Tin Roof*?
3 In which decade was he Oscar-nominated for *The Hustler*?
4 Which Martin directed him in *The Color of Money*?
5 Who was his co-star in *Butch Cassidy and the Sundance Kid*?
6 In which 70s disaster movie did he play the architect of a skyscraper?
7 In which city is *The Sting* set?
8 In which decade was *Butch Cassidy* first released?
9 Which actor Sidney is co-partner in his production company First Artists?
10 He founded the Scott Newman Foundation in memory of his son who died from what?
11 Which actress Joanne did Paul Newman marry in 1958?
12 What 'Menagerie' did he direct in 1987?
13 Which singer Julie was his co-star in *Torn Curtain* in 1966?
14 Which speed sport is he involved in, which he used in 1969 in *Winning*?
15 Which western hero Billy did he play in *The Left-Handed Gun*?
16 In 1978 which Democratic US President appointed him a US delegate to the UN Conference on Nuclear Disarmament?
17 In *Butch Cassidy and the Sundance Kid*, which part did he play?
18 Which 'Long Hot' season was the title of a 1958 movie?
19 In which movie did he play conman Henry Gondorff?
20 How was his character Eddie Felson described?
21 Which 'Cool Hand' character did he play in 1967?
22 What type of salad product did he market for charity?
23 He and his wife played 'Mr and Mrs' who in 1990?
24 Which Oscar did he win for *The Color of Money*?
25 In which decade did he team up again with Redford for *The Sting*?

**Answers Pot Luck 6** (see Quiz 14)
**1** Davis. **2** Canada. **3** Hunt. **4** Jack Nicholson. **5** The Third Kind. **6** Mae West. **7** Willy. **8** The Air Force. **9** 1940s. **10** Sinatra. **11** Coppola. **12** *JFK*. **13** *Fugitive*. **14** The Genie. **15** Sean Connery. **16** Sharon Stone. **17** Fred Astaire. **18** Tina Turner. **19** 1990s. **20** Marlon Brando. **21** Wood. **22** 1950s. **23** *Train*. **24** Kline. **25** Hamill.

## *QUIZ 17* POT LUCK 7 ........ LEVEL 1

*Answers – see page 31*

1 *Mrs Doubtfire* and *Jumanji* both featured which actor?
2 Which Danny starred in *LA Confidential*?
3 *Gregory's Two Girls* was the sequel to which film?
4 Which Michael played Marty in *Back to the Future*?
5 Which musical set in gangland New York won 11 Oscars in the 60s?
6 Which Henry wrote the score for *The Pink Panther*?
7 Peter Lawford was the brother-in-law of which late US president?
8 In the film's title, which word describes Clint Eastwood's character Harry?
9 Who wrote the musical score for *Star Wars*?
10 Who was billed in his first movie as Arnold Strong?
11 Forties movie *The Outlaw* featured which Jane?
12 Which actress links *Ghost* and *The Juror*?
13 Which musical about Danny and Sandy was re-released in the 90s?
14 Which Nicolas starred in *Leaving Las Vegas*?
15 Who was Vincente Minnelli's famous daughter?
16 Which word completes the film title, *A Room with a* ____?
17 *Land Girls* starred which Anna?
18 Which Meg starred in *When Harry Met Sally*?
19 Madonna bought a burial plot next to where which blonde icon is buried?
20 In which decade of the 20th century was Al Pacino born?
21 Which Ralph starred in the film version of *The Avengers*?
22 According to the film title, what should you do to your wagon?
23 Which Annette was Warren Beatty's first wife?
24 In which decade was *Some Like It Hot* released?
25 Did *Babe* run for 52, 92 or 182 minutes?

**Answers Pot Luck 8** (see Quiz 19)
**1** Redford. **2** Dustin Hoffman. **3** The Spice Girls. **4** Wayne's. **5** Piano. **6** Tom Hanks. **7** Black. **8** Tarzan. **9** Mulder & Scully. **10** *10*. **11** Patrick Swayze. **12** Sutherland. **13** Jacques Tati. **14** *Robin Hood: Prince of Thieves*. **15** 1930s. **16** Red. **17** Sergeant Bilko. **18** Glenn Close. **19** Ryan O'Neal. **20** Dinosaurs. **21** Bette Midler. **22** American. **23** 1970s. **24** 'The Living Daylights'. **25** Demi Moore.

## *QUIZ 18* BLOCKBUSTERS ........ LEVEL 1

*Answers – see page 32*

1 Which 'Park' was a blockbuster of the 1990s?
2 Who played Jack in *Titanic*?
3 What was the nationality of Oskar Schindler in Spielberg's movie?
4 Which shark-infested movie was the first to take $100 million at the box office?
5 In which movie was someone told to "phone home"?
6 What sort of 'Menace' was Episode I in the *Star Wars* movies?
7 What mythical sea creature did Daryl Hannah play in *Splash!*?
8 Who played Schindler in *Schindler's List*?
9 Which song was used for the hugely successful *The Full Monty*?
10 What was the most expensive film made in the 20th century?
11 What was the last Bond movie of the 20th century?
12 Who played Dan Gallagher in *Fatal Attraction*?
13 Which musical was made about Eva Peron?
14 How was the 'Mission' described in the 1996 release with Tom Cruise?
15 For which role was Faye Dunaway Oscar-nominated in *Bonnie and Clyde*?
16 Mel Gibson's movie *Gallipoli* was set during which war?
17 Which 'King' grossed the fourth highest sum in the US in the 1990s?
18 What did E stand for in *E.T.*?
19 Which singer played Rachel Marron in *The Bodyguard*?
20 Who won the Best Director Oscar for *Schindler's List*?
21 Which 'Day' was released just before the 4th of July in the US?
22 'Tomorrow is another day' is the last line of which movie?
23 In which movie did Warren Beatty say, 'We rob banks'?
24 *The Empire Strikes Back* was the sequel to which blockbusting film?
25 Which David won the Best Director Oscar for *The Bridge over the River Kwai*?

**Answers Famous Firsts** (see Quiz 20)
**1** *The Jazz Singer.* **2** Andy. **3** Disney **4** Venice. **5** Godzilla. **6** *Dirty Harry.* **7** Wray. **8** *Snow White and the Seven Dwarfs.* **9** Chan. **10** Bombay. **11** Technicolor. **12** Widescreen (Cinemascope). **13** Smell. **14** *Toy Story.* **15** *The Deer Hunter.* **16** *Great Expectations.* **17** *Bugsy Malone.* **18** Fiennes. **19** 1920s. **20** 'White Christmas'. **21** Robert Redford. **22** Warner. **23** *The Jazz Singer.* **24** Hepburn. **25** Paris.

## *QUIZ 19* POT LUCK 8 .................... LEVEL 1

*Answers – see page 29*

1 Which Robert starred in *The Horse Whisperer*?
2 Who won the Best Actor Oscar for *Rain Man*?
3 Which pop group starred in *Spiceworld*?
4 Whose 'World' was a 1992 film with Mike Myers and Dana Carvey?
5 *Shine* is about a musician playing which instrument?
6 Which actor links *Forrest Gump, You've Got Mail* and *A League of their Own*?
7 Which colour goes before 'Narcissus' and 'mail' to form film titles?
8 Johnny Weissmuller portrayed which jungle hero?
9 Who are the two main characters in *The X-Files*?
10 Which Bo Derek film had a number as the title?
11 Who starred opposite Jennifer Gray in *Dirty Dancing*?
12 Which Donald played Hawkeye in the film *M*A*S*H*?
13 Who starred in and directed *Monsieur Hulot's Holiday*?
14 Which movie used the song 'Everything I Do (I Do it for You)'?
15 In which decade of the 20th century was Jack Nicholson born?
16 Which colour links 'Shoes' and 'Dust' in film titles?
17 Which sergeant created by Phil Silvers featured in a 90s movie?
18 Which actress links *Fatal Attraction* and *101 Dalmatians*?
19 What is the name of Tatum O'Neal's actor father?
20 Which creatures dominated *Jurassic Park*?
21 *The First Wives' Club, Ruthless People* and *Hocus Pocus* all feature which actress?
22 A werewolf in London and a man in Paris were both of what nationality?
23 In which decade was *The Godfather* released?
24 What was the Bond theme for *The Living Daylights* called?
25 Who played opposite Patrick Swayze in *Ghost*?

**Answers Pot Luck 7** (see Quiz 17)
**1** Robin Williams. **2** Danny DeVito. **3** *Gregory's Girl*. **4** Michael J. Fox. **5** *West Side Story*. **6** Mancini. **7** John F. Kennedy. **8** Dirty. **9** John Williams. **10** Arnold Schwarzenegger. **11** Russell. **12** Demi Moore. **13** *Grease*. **14** Cage. **15** Liza Minnelli. **16** *View*. **17** Friel. **18** Ryan. **19** Marilyn Monroe. **20** 1940s. **21** Fiennes. **22** *Paint Your Wagon*. **23** Bening. **24** 1950s. **25** 92 minutes.

## *QUIZ 20* FAMOUS FIRSTS ........ LEVEL 1

*Answers – see page 30*

1 What was the first talkie?
2 In the first *Toy Story*, which child owns the toys?
3 Which film company opened the first ever theme park?
4 Where in Italy did the first film festival take place?
5 Which monster lizard, first seen in 1955, was in a 1997 blockbuster?
6 What was the first movie in which Eastwood was Harry Callahan?
7 Which Fay was the first scream queen, in *King Kong*?
8 What was Disney's first feature film – with eight people in the title?
9 Which oriental detective Charlie first appeared on screen in 1926?
10 Where were India's first studios, giving rise to the name 'Bollywood'?
11 What was the first two-colour system used in movie making?
12 *The Robe* was the first movie with what type of screen?
13 *The Scent of Mystery* was the first movie with sight, sound and what?
14 Which 1995 'Story' was the first computer-animated film?
15 What was the first major movie about the Vietnam War?
16 Which 1946 Oscar-winning Dickens film gave Alec Guinness his major movie debut?
17 Which movie with an all-child cast was Alan Parker's directorial debut?
18 Which Ralph played Steed in the first Avengers movie to hit the big screen?
19 In which decade were the Oscars first presented?
20 Which Christmas classic was first heard in *Holiday Inn*?
21 Who was Oscar-nominated for his directorial debut in *Ordinary People*?
22 Which Brothers made the first talkie?
23 In which movie did Al Jolson say, 'You ain't heard nothin' yet'?
24 Which Katharine won the first BAFTA Best Actress award?
25 In which French city was the first movie in Europe shown?

**Answers Blockbusters** (see Quiz 18)
**1** *Jurassic Park.* **2** Leonardo DiCaprio. **3** German. **4** *Jaws.* **5** *E.T.* **6** *The Phantom Menace.* **7** Mermaid. **8** Liam Neeson. **9** 'You Sexy Thing'. **10** *Titanic.* **11** *The World Is Not Enough.* **12** Michael Douglas. **13** *Evita.* **14** Impossible. **15** Bonnie. **16** World War I. **17** *The Lion King.* **18** Extra. **19** Whitney Houston. **20** Steven Spielberg. **21** *Independence Day.* **22** *Gone with the Wind.* **23** *Bonnie and Clyde.* **24** *Star Wars.* **25** Lean.

## *QUIZ 21* THE SILENT YEARS ........ LEVEL 1

*Answers – see page 35*

1 What sort of films did the Keystone Company make?
2 Samuel Goldfish changed his name to what after founding a film company?
3 In which state did William Fox found his film production company in 1912?
4 Which 'Little Lord' was played by Mary Pickford, who also played his mother?
5 Which movie about the little boy who asked for more starred Jackie Coogan?
6 In which decade did Chaplin make *The Kid*?
7 How many 'Horsemen of the Apocalypse' were there in the Valentino movie?
8 In which decade of the 20th century was Keystone founded?
9 Which Gloria found fame in *The Danger Girl* in 1916?
10 'The Taming of' what was the only movie to star Douglas Fairbanks and Mary Pickford together?
11 Ford Sterling led which Kops?
12 What was the first name of Langdon of *Tramp Tramp Tramp* fame?
13 Which regal first name did director/producer/writer Vidor have?
14 Which Fred's tours to the US brought Chaplin from England?
15 Pathe Weekly showed what on their reels?
16 Which Brothers released their first major feature in 1915?
17 Which Rudolph shot to stardom in *The Sheik*?
18 Who was forced out of Goldwyn Pictures in 1922?
19 Cecil B. de Mille's *King of Kings* was about whom?
20 *Birth of a Nation* was the first movie screened at which presidential home?
21 Which Cecil made the spectacular *Ten Commandments*?
22 Who made *The Gold Rush*?
23 Lon Chaney starred as which Phantom in 1925?
24 Which D.W. made *Birth of a Nation*?
25 Which 'Singer' marked the end of the silent era?

**Answers Elizabeth Taylor** (see Quiz 23)
**1** England. **2** Grand National. **3** Cleopatra. **4** Fisher. **5** *The Taming of the Shrew.* **6** Agatha Christie. **7** 8. **8** Richard Burton. **9** Flintstone. **10** AIDS. **11** Jackson. **12** American. **13** Virginia Woolf. **14** Perfume. **15** Violet. **16** *The Simpsons.* **17** Carrie Fisher. **18** Rooney. **19** *Cat on a Hot Tin Roof.* **20** Richard Burton. **21** *Little Women.* **22** 1940s. **23** *Jane Eyre.* **24** Tracy. **25** Clowns.

## *QUIZ 22* POT LUCK 9 ........ LEVEL 1

*Answers – see page 36*

1 Which Woody starred in *Natural Born Killers*?
2 Which 007 starred in *The Lawnmower Man*?
3 What is the first name of FBI agent Starling in *The Silence of the Lambs*?
4 In which country was Jean-Claude Van Damme born?
5 In which TV soap did Joan Collins and John Forsythe find fame after appearing on the big screen?
6 Did *Aladdin* run for 60, 90 or 130 minutes?
7 Which Diane played Steve Martin's wife in *Father of the Bride*?
8 Which *Grease* star danced with Princess Diana at the White House?
9 Which Julie links *Darling* in the 1960s and *Afterglow* in the 90s?
10 In which decade of the 20th century did James Stewart die?
11 Which actor was tennis star John McEnroe's first father in law?
12 The character Harry Lime appears in which spy thriller?
13 What was Crocodile Dundee's homeland?
14 *The Sunshine Boys* starred which Walter?
15 Which western star John first acted as 'Duke Morrison'?
16 In which decade was *Psycho* released?
17 In a movie title, which word goes before 'of the Lost Ark'?
18 Which actress links *Se7en* and *Sliding Doors*?
19 Which Kim likened Hollywood to the Mafia?
20 *Three Kings*, with George Clooney, takes place during which war?
21 In which decade of the 20th century was Liam Neeson born?
22 In which 1976 movie did Sylvester Stallone play a boxer?
23 What type of snack completes the film title *Animal* ____?
24 Which famous Loretta tested for the role of Scarlett O'Hara?
25 Who sang 'Fame' in *Fame*?

**Answers Unforgettables** (see Quiz 24)
**1** Davis. **2** *High Society*. **3** *Paint Your Wagon*. **4** Swanson. **5** Oliver Reed. **6** Richard Burton. **7** Humphrey Bogart & Lauren Bacall. **8** Mae West. **9** Henry Fonda. **10** Dietrich. **11** Elvis Presley. **12** Jeanette Macdonald. **13** Charlie Chaplin. **14** Durante. **15** John Wayne. **16** Transylvania. **17** Legs. **18** 1970s. **19** Rex Harrison. **20** Joan Crawford. **21** Spencer Tracy. **22** Car. **23** Laurence Olivier. **24** First. **25** Kelly.

## *QUIZ 23* ELIZABETH TAYLOR ........................................ LEVEL 1

*Answers – see page 33*

1 In which country was Elizabeth Taylor born?
2 Which horse race was her movie *National Velvet* about?
3 Which Egyptian queen did she play in the 1960s?
4 Which singer Eddie did she marry after her third husband was killed?
5 Which Shakespeare play, with Taylor as the volatile Katherine, did Taylor and Burton bring to the big screen?
6 Who wrote the whodunnit on which her 1980 movie *The Mirror Crack'd* was based?
7 Which number followed 'Butterfield' in her first Oscar-winning movie?
8 Which husband did she fall in love with on the set of *Cleopatra*?
9 Which Fred's mother-in-law was she when she played Pearl Slaghoople in 1994?
10 In 1993 she received an award at the Oscars ceremony for her work with sufferers from what?
11 On which pop star Michael's estate did she marry for the eighth time?
12 What was the nationality of her parents?
13 'Who's Afraid of' whom was the title of her second Oscar-winner?
14 What type of beauty product did she launch towards the end of the 20th century?
15 What colour are her famous eyes?
16 She was the voice of Baby Maggie in which cartoon series?
17 Which star of *Star Wars* was her one-time step-daughter?
18 Which Mickey was her co-star in *National Velvet*?
19 In which movie based on a Tennessee Williams play was she the 'cat' Maggie?
20 Which actor did Elizabeth Taylor marry twice?
21 Which 'Little' film was based on the classic by Louisa May Alcott?
22 In which decade did she make her very first movie?
23 In which movie about Charlotte Bronte's most famous heroine did she appear in 1944?
24 Which Spencer played the title role in *Father of the Bride*?
25 In *A Little Night Music* she sang 'Send in the' what?

**Answers The Silent Years** (see Quiz 21)
**1** Comedy. **2** Goldwyn. **3** California. **4** Fauntleroy. **5** *Oliver Twist.* **6** 1920s. **7** Four. **8** Second decade (1912). **9** Swanson. **10** The Shrew. **11** Keystone. **12** Harry. **13** King. **14** Karno. **15** News. **16** Warner Brothers. **17** Valentino. **18** Sam Goldwyn. **19** Jesus Christ. **20** The White House. **21** B. de Mille. **22** Charlie Chaplin. **23** Phantom of the Opera. **24** Griffith. **25** *The Jazz Singer.*

## *QUIZ 24* UNFORGETTABLES ........ LEVEL 1

*Answers – see page 34*

1 Which Bette said, 'Until you're known in my profession as a monster, you're not a star'?
2 What was Grace Kelly's last film, with Frank Sinatra and Bing Crosby?
3 In which 1961 movie did Lee Marvin have a singing role?
4 Which Gloria played Norma Desmond in *Sunset Boulevard*?
5 Which famous hell-raising actor wrote an autobiography called *Reed All About It*?
6 Which Welshman's real name was Richard Jenkins?
7 Which husband and wife starred in *Key Largo* in 1948?
8 Which film star wrote the novel *Constant Sinner*?
9 Who played the father of real-life daughter Jane in *On Golden Pond* in 1981?
10 Which Marlene found fame with *The Blue Angel*?
11 Who played two parts in *Kissin' Cousins* in 1964?
12 Who played opposite Nelson Eddy eight times?
13 Robert Downey Jr was Oscar-nominated for playing which unforgettable star of the silent screen?
14 Which Jimmy's nickname was Schnozzle?
15 Who played The Ringo Kid in the classic western *Stagecoach*?
16 Where was Bela Lugosi born?
17 Which part of her did Cyd Charisse insure for $5 million?
18 In which decade of the 20th century was River Phoenix born?
19 Which British actor won an Oscar for *My Fair Lady*?
20 Whose autobiography was called *A Portrait of Joan*?
21 Who died 15 days after finishing *Guess Who's Coming to Dinner*?
22 In what type of crash did Jayne Mansfield meet her death?
23 Who directed and starred in *Hamlet* in 1948?
24 In which World War did Humphrey Bogart receive a facial injury which gave him his trademark sneer?
25 Which Gene discovered Leslie Caron?

**Answers Pot Luck 9** (see Quiz 22)
**1** Harrelson. **2** Pierce Brosnan. **3** Clarice. **4** Belgium. **5** *Dynasty*. **6** 90 minutes. **7** Keaton. **8** John Travolta. **9** Christie. **10** 1990s. **11** Ryan O'Neal. **12** *The Third Man*. **13** Australia. **14** Matthau. **15** Wayne. **16** 1960s. **17** *Raiders*. **18** Gwyneth Paltrow. **19** Basinger. **20** Gulf War. **21** 1950s. **22** *Rocky*. **23** *Crackers*. **24** Young. **25** Irene Cara.

## *QUIZ 25* POT LUCK 10 ........ LEVEL 1

*Answers – see page 39*

1 Who, in the movie title, is the 'International Man of Mystery'?
2 Who directed *Forrest Gump*?
3 Which song won Best Song Oscar for *Breakfast at Tiffany's*?
4 What word links a 'Book' and 'Asphalt' to form two film titles?
5 Which Jane starred in *Barbarella*?
6 Which British movie is about the 1924 Olympics?
7 What's the name of the chief villain of *The Lion King*?
8 Which Emma wrote the screenplay for *Sense and Sensibility*?
9 Which boxer appeared in *The Greatest*?
10 *Love Me Tender* was the first film for which rock 'n' roll star?
11 Which actor links *True Lies, Total Recall* and *Twins*?
12 The character Richard Hannay appears in a film about how many steps?
13 Who played Dolly in the 60s movie *Hello Dolly*?
14 Which creatures were 'in the Mist' in the title of the Sigourney Weaver movie?
15 Was *Ghostbusters* first released in the 1960s, 70s or 80s?
16 Which hard man English football player appeared in *Lock, Stock and Two Smoking Barrels*?
17 In which decade of the 20th century was Dennis Quaid born?
18 Which wife of Kenneth Branagh has also been Oscar nominated?
19 Who did Timothy Dalton play in *Licence to Kill*?
20 Which word completes the film title, ____ *Largo*?
21 Who played the Fay Wray role in the remake of King Kong?
22 Which Tom starred in *A Few Good Men*?
23 Who created the accident prone Mr Bean?
24 Which Tom won the Best Actor Oscar for *Philadelphia* in 1993?
25 In which decade was *You Only Live Twice* released?

**Answers Superstars** (see Quiz 27)
**1** Sean Connery **2** Meryl Streep. **3** Henry Fonda. **4** Clooney. **5** Marilyn Monroe. **6** Madonna. **7** Sophia Loren. **8** John Wayne. **9** Leonardo DiCaprio. **10** Olivia Newton-John. **11** Paul Newman. **12** Nicolas Cage. **13** Tom Cruise & Nicole Kidman. **14** *Rocky* **15** Katharine Hepburn. **16** 1940s. **17** Julie Andrews. **18** *Carlito's Way*. **19** West Germany. **20** *G.I. Jane*. **21** Cher. **22** *Se7en*. **23** Picasso. **24** *The Color Purple*. **25** *Dick Tracy*.

## *QUIZ 26* HARRISON FORD ........ LEVEL 1

*Answers – see page 40*

1 What is Harrison Ford's real name?
2 Which 007 played his father in *Indiana Jones and the Last Crusade*?
3 Which Steven directed Ford in *Raiders of the Lost Ark*?
4 Which Kate was his co-star in *Indiana Jones and the Temple of Doom*?
5 In which sci-fi movie did he first find fame?
6 Which Melanie was a co-star in *Working Girl*?
7 In which movie did he play Richard Kimble in a film version of the TV series?
8 What sort of 'Graffiti' was the title of a 1973 movie?
9 In which decade did he star in *Witness*?
10 In which decade was Ford born?
11 In which California city was *Blade Runner* set?
12 What is the occupation of Indiana Jones?
13 What was 'Presumed' in the title of the 1990 movie?
14 In which decade did he star in the first *Star Wars* movie?
15 Which 1997 film was the name of a special aircraft?
16 'Clear and Present' what was the title of Ford's 1994 movie?
17 Which Annette co-starred with him in *Regarding Henry*?
18 Who directed him as Col Lucas in *Apocalypse Now*?
19 What relation to Harrison Ford is scriptwriter Melissa Mathison?
20 In *Air Force One* he plays the role of a man in which office?
21 In what sort of 'Games' did he play ex-CIA agent Jack Ryan in 1992?
22 How many 'Nights' go with the 'Six Days' in a movie title?
23 What was the first *Star Wars* sequel in which he starred?
24 Which Bonnie plays Ford's wife in *Presumed Innocent*?
25 Which 'Solo' part did he play in the *Star Wars* movies?

**Answers Pot Luck 11** (see Quiz 28)
**1** *Eyes Wide Shut.* **2** Hawke. **3** Grasshoppers. **4** Pierce Brosnan. **5** 80 minutes. **6** Ireland. **7** Attenborough. **8** 1950s. **9** Popeye. **10** Uma Thurman. **11** The Vietnam War. **12** Willis. **13** Kramer (*Kramer versus Kramer*). **14** *Apollo 13.* **15** Dog. **16** Guinness. **17** Jerry Lewis. **18** Faye Dunaway. **19** Wayne. **20** Anna. **21** *Alien.* **22** Michelle Pfeiffer. **23** 1960s. **24** Charlie Chaplin. **25** Gerry and the Pacemakers.

## *QUIZ 27* SUPERSTARS ........ LEVEL 1

*Answers – see page 37*

1 Which 007 has a tattoo with 'Scotland Forever' on it?
2 Who links *Silkwood* and *The French Lieutenant's Woman*?
3 Who died shortly after finishing *On Golden Pond*?
4 Which George, a superstar of the small screen, had a big-screen flop with *The Peacemaker*?
5 Whose real first names were Norma Jean?
6 Which singer/actress's surname is Ciccone?
7 How is Sofia Scicolone better known?
8 Who was dying of cancer when he made *The Shootist* about a gunman dying of cancer?
9 Whose boat sank while making *The Beach* after becoming a star in *Titanic*?
10 Which blonde reached superstar status after playing Sandy in *Grease*?
11 Who played opposite Joanne Woodward 11 times?
12 Whose real name is Nicholas Coppola?
13 Which husband and wife starred in *Eyes Wide Shut* in 1999?
14 In which 1976 movie did Sylvester Stallone play a boxer?
15 Who first starred with Spencer Tracy in *Woman of the Year*?
16 In which decade of the 20th century was Michael Douglas born?
17 Who won the Best Actress Oscar for *Mary Poppins*?
18 In which movie did Al Pacino play Carlito Brigante?
19 Where in Europe was Bruce Willis born?
20 In which 'G.I.' movie did Demi Moore shave her head?
21 Who played Winona Ryder's eccentric mother in *Mermaids*?
22 Brad Pitt's affair with Gwyneth Paltrow began on the set of which movie?
23 Which painter did Anthony Hopkins play on screen in 1996?
24 What was Whoopi Goldberg's first film, in 1985?
25 Which cartoon character did Warren Beatty play in a 1990 movie?

**Answers Pot Luck 10** (see Quiz 25)
**1** Austin Powers. **2** Robert Zemeckis. **3** 'Moon River'. **4** Jungle. **5** Fonda. **6** *Chariots of Fire.* **7** Scar. **8** Thompson. **9** Muhammad Ali. **10** Elvis Presley. **11** Arnold Schwarzenegger. **12** 39 (*The Thirty-Nine Steps*). **13** Barbra Streisand. **14** Gorillas. **15** 1980s. **16** Vinnie Jones. **17** 1950s. **18** Emma Thompson. **19** James Bond. **20** *Key.* **21** Jessica Lange. **22** Cruise. **23** Rowan Atkinson. **24** Hanks. **25** 1960s.

## *QUIZ 28* POT LUCK 11 ............ LEVEL 1

*Answers – see page 38*

1 What was the last movie made by Stanley Kubrick?
2 Which Ethan starred in the 1998 *Great Expectations*?
3 What type of insects were posing the greatest threat in *A Bug's Life*?
4 Who replaced Timothy Dalton as James Bond?
5 Did *Toy Story* last 45, 80 or 240 minutes?
6 Where was 1990s James Bond, Pierce Brosnan, born?
7 Which Richard won the Best Director Oscar for *Gandhi*?
8 In which decade of the 20th century was Kirstie Alley born?
9 Robin Williams played which cartoon sailor?
10 *The Avengers* and *Dangerous Liaisons* both featured which actress?
11 *The Deer Hunter* was about which war?
12 Which Bruce starred in *The Jackal*?
13 Who did Kramer take to court?
14 Ed Harris played the mission controller in which Tom Hanks film?
15 Is Gromit a person, a dog or a sheep?
16 Which Sir Alec starred in *Star Wars*?
17 Which zany comedian often co-starred with Dean Martin in the 50s?
18 Who played a lead role in *Bonnie and Clyde* after Jane Fonda turned it down?
19 Which John won the Best Actor Oscar for *True Grit*?
20 Which woman's name links the King of Siam and Karenina?
21 'In space no one can hear you scream' was the cinema poster line for which Sigourney Weaver movie?
22 Which actress links *Batman Returns, One Fine Day* and *Scarface*?
23 In which decade was *Butch Cassidy and the Sundance Kid* released?
24 Who played the Little Tramp in *The Kid*?
25 Which Liverpool band appeared in the movie *Ferry Cross the Mersey*?

**Answers Harrison Ford** (see Quiz 26)
**1** Harrison Ford. **2** Sean Connery. **3** Spielberg. **4** Capshaw. **5** *Star Wars.* **6** Griffith. **7** *The Fugitive.* **8** American. **9** 1980s. **10** 1940s. **11** Los Angeles. **12** Archaeologist. **13** Innocent. **14** 1970s. **15** *Air Force One.* **16** Danger. **17** Bening. **18** Francis Ford Coppola. **19** Wife. **20** US President. **21** *Patriot Games.* **22** Seven. **23** *The Empire Strikes Back.* **24** Bedelia. **25** Hans Solo.

## QUIZ 29 1950s ........ LEVEL 1

*Answers – see page 43*

1 Bette Davis starred in a film 'All About' whom?
2 What sort of 'Holiday' was had by Gregory Peck and Audrey Hepburn?
3 James Dean was 'East of' where in 1955?
4 In which principality, a favourite with millionaires, was *To Catch a Thief* with Grace Kelly set?
5 Which movie named after a US state includes 'Oh What a Beautiful Morning'?
6 How long did Phileas Fogg have to go round the world in?
7 'The African' what was a 1951 movie with Bogart and Hepburn?
8 Which 1959 Charlton Heston movie is famous for its chariot races?
9 Which massacre takes place at the start of *Some Like It Hot*?
10 Which tragic diary was filmed in 1959?
11 'The Bridge on' which Asian river was a big hit of the 50s?
12 In a 1951 film, where was 'An American in', as played by Gene Kelly?
13 Which 'Place' was a top 50s film which later became a top soap with Ryan O'Neal and Mia Farrow?
14 Whose dress is blown up by the air from a subway grating in *The Seven Year Itch*?
15 What was 'A Streetcar Named' in the Brando and Vivien Leigh movie?
16 What 'light' was Chaplin's last US movie, made in 1952?
17 Which James appeared in *Vertigo* and *Rear Window*?
18 Which story set in Never Never Land was made by Disney in 1953?
19 How many 'Leagues under the Sea' were in the title of the 1954 movie with Kirk Douglas?
20 What were the 'Stockings' made from in the title of the 1957 movie?
21 What type of animal is Harvey in the movie of the same name?
22 What was *Les Vacances de Monsieur Hulot* called in English?
23 What did you Dial for Murder in Hitchcock's classic?
24 How many brides were there 'for Seven Brothers' in 1954?
25 Where were 'Strangers' in the title of a 1951 Hitchcock movie?

**Answers 1960s Stars** (see Quiz 31)
**1** Steve McQueen. **2** *Lawrence of Arabia*. **3** Sean Connery. **4** Shirley MacLaine. **5** Richard Burton. **6** Janet Leigh. **7** Mia Farrow. **8** Ann-Margret. **9** Audrey Hepburn. **10** Barbra Streisand. **11** Nicholson. **12** *Midnight Cowboy*. **13** Michael Crawford. **14** Kirk Douglas. **15** John Wayne. **16** Yul Brynner. **17** Lemmon & Matthau. **18** James Bond. **19** Andress. **20** Julie Christie. **21** Mills. **22** Marilyn Monroe. **23** The Beatles. **24** Lancaster. **25** Paul Newman.

## *QUIZ 30* POT LUCK 12 ........ LEVEL 1

*Answers – see page 44*

1 Where in America was Leonardo DiCaprio born?
2 Which Dan starred in *The Blues Brothers*?
3 A 90s movie title was 'The Bridges of' which county?
4 The song 'Circle of Life' features in which animated movie?
5 Who played the title role in *Gandhi*?
6 Who played herself in *Dear Brigitte* in 1965?
7 Which actor links *Face/Off* and *Grease*?
8 The Japanese attack on where is central to *From Here to Eternity*?
9 Who played Truman in *The Truman Show*?
10 *Postcards from the Edge* was based on the life of which Carrie?
11 Which Ms Smith played the Mother Superior in Whoopi Goldberg's *Sister Act*?
12 Which 1997 movie equalled *Ben Hur*'s record haul of Oscars?
13 Who played the Caped Crusader in *Batman Forever*?
14 Which Melanie married Antonio Banderas?
15 Robert De Niro sang about New York in which film?
16 Which Jane was one of the first movie stars to produce fitness videos?
17 Who was Kenneth Branagh's wife whom he directed in *Much Ado About Nothing* in 1993?
18 What was the Bond theme for *For Your Eyes Only* called?
19 What is Bruce Willis' profession in *The Sixth Sense*?
20 Which James was the knife thrower in *The Magnificent Seven*?
21 In which decade was *The Sting* released?
22 Which word completes the film title, *In ___ We Serve*?
23 In which decade of the 20th century was Julie Andrews born?
24 Who directed *Evita*?
25 Which Jeff starred in *Tron*?

**Answers Weepies** (see Quiz 32)
**1** USA. **2** Blind. **3** Barbra Streisand. **4** Cancer. **5** *Romeo and Juliet*. **6** Turner. **7** Jack. **8** Brief. **9** Binoche. **10** Danes. **11** Antonio Banderas. **12** *The Horse Whisperer*. **13** Clint Eastwood. **14** Deeply. **15** Omar Sharif. **16** *Kramer versus Kramer*. **17** *William Shakespeare's Romeo and Juliet*. **18** Tyler Moore. **19** *Tess of the d'Urbervilles*. **20** Meryl Streep. **21** Geraldine. **22** 1990s. **23** Dustin Hoffman. **24** Cinderella. **25** *Love Story*.

## *QUIZ 31* 1960s STARS ........ LEVEL 1

*Answers – see page 41*

1 Whose movies included *The Great Escape* and *Bullitt*?
2 Peter O'Toole played the title role in which movie set in the sands of the Middle East?
3 Which 007 played opposite Tippi Hedren in *Marnie*?
4 Which sister of Warren Beatty starred with Jack Lemmon in *The Apartment*?
5 Who was Elizabeth Taylor's husband on and off screen in *Who's Afraid of Virginia Woolf*?
6 Which star of *Psycho* is the mother of Jamie Lee Curtis?
7 Which sometime partner of Woody Allen starred in *Rosemary's Baby*?
8 Whose real name is Ann-Margret Olsson?
9 Which star of *My Fair Lady* was born in Belgium?
10 Which singing superstar was the Funny Girl in the title of the movie?
11 Which Jack found fame in *Easy Rider*?
12 Which 'Cowboy' was played by Jon Voight in 1969?
13 Which future star of *Phantom of the Opera* appeared in *Hello Dolly*?
14 Which actor father of *Fatal Attraction*'s Michael starred in *Spartacus*?
15 Which star of westerns starred in, produced and directed *The Alamo*?
16 Which *The King and I* star was 'the old Cajun' in *The Magnificent Seven*?
17 Which Jack and Walter played *The Odd Couple*?
18 George Lazenby played whom in *On Her Majesty's Secret Service*?
19 Which Ursula's first major English language film was *Dr No*?
20 Which long-haired blonde starred in *Darling*, for which she won an Oscar?
21 Which Hayley played both twins in *The Parent Trap*?
22 Which blonde's last movie was *The Misfits*, written by Arthur Miller?
23 Which pop group starred in *A Hard Day's Night*?
24 Which Burt frolicked in the surf with Deborah Kerr in *From Here to Eternity*?
25 Who starred as Fast Eddie Felson in *The Hustler*, a role he was to reprise 25 years later in *The Color of Money*?

**Answers 1950s** (see Quiz 29)
**1** Eve. **2** Roman. **3** Eden. **4** Monaco. **5** *Oklahoma!*. **6** 80 Days. **7** Queen. **8** *Ben Hur*. **9** St Valentine's Day Massacre. **10** *The Diary of Anne Frank*. **11** The River Kwai. **12** Paris. **13** *Peyton Place*. **14** Marilyn Monroe's. **15** Desire. **16** *Limelight*. **17** Stewart. **18** *Peter Pan*. **19** Twenty Thousand. **20** Silk. **21** Rabbit. **22** *Monsieur Hulot's Holiday*. **23** M. **24** Seven Brides. **25** On a Train.

## *QUIZ 32* WEEPIES ........ LEVEL 1

*Answers – see page 42*

1 In which country does the action of *The Horse Whisperer* take place?
2 What disability does Al Pacino have in *Scent of a Woman*?
3 Which singer starred in and directed *The Prince of Tides*?
4 In *Terms of Endearment* Debra Winger is dying from which disease?
5 Which doomed lovers were played by Leonard Whiting and Olivia Hussey in 1968?
6 Which Lana was the star of *Imitation of Life*?
7 What was the name of Leonardo DiCaprio's character in *Titanic*?
8 What type of 'Encounter' occurred between Celia Johnson and Trevor Howard in the movie classic?
9 Which Juliette nursed the 'English Patient'?
10 Which Claire starred in *Little Women* and *Romeo and Juliet*?
11 Which husband of Melanie Griffith starred opposite Tom Hanks in *Philadelphia*?
12 Which Nicholas Evans novel was *The Horse Whisperer* based on?
13 Who falls for Meryl Streep in *The Bridges of Madison County*?
14 What follows 'Truly, Madly' in the Anthony Minghella weepie?
15 Who played the title role in *Dr Zhivago*?
16 Which movie had the ad line, 'There are three sides to this love story'?
17 The 1996 version of *Romeo and Juliet* mentioned its writer's name in the title; what was it called?
18 Which Mary, famous for her TV roles, starred opposite Donald Sutherland in *Ordinary People*?
19 Which Thomas Hardy novel was *Tess* based on?
20 Who played Mrs Kramer in the 1979 weepie?
21 Which daughter of Charlie Chaplin starred in *Dr Zhivago*?
22 In which decade was *Ghost* released?
23 Who won the Best Actor Oscar for *Kramer versus Kramer*?
24 *Ever After* was a remake of which fairy story?
25 Ryan O'Neal's affair with Ali McGraw began on the set of which movie?

**Answers Pot Luck 12** (see Quiz 30)
**1** Hollywood. **2** Aykroyd. **3** Madison County. **4** *The Lion King*. **5** Ben Kingsley. **6** Brigitte Bardot. **7** John Travolta. **8** Pearl Harbor. **9** Jim Carrey. **10** Fisher. **11** Maggie Smith. **12** *Titanic*. **13** Val Kilmer. **14** Griffith. **15** *New York, New York*. **16** Fonda. **17** Emma Thompson. **18** 'For Your Eyes Only'. **19** Child psychologist. **20** Coburn. **21** 1970s. **22** *Which*. **23** 1930s. **24** Alan Parker. **25** Bridges.

## *QUIZ 33* POT LUCK 13 ........ LEVEL 1

*Answers – see page 47*

1 *Maverick* and *Freaky Friday* both featured which actress?
2 Which character battles against The Joker?
3 Which star of *Sliding Doors* split with fiancé Brad Pitt in 1997?
4 Who wrote most of the songs for *Saturday Night Fever*?
5 *Philadelphia* became the first mainstream Hollywood movie to focus on which disease?
6 Which Shirley sang the Bond song 'Diamonds Are Forever'?
7 In a Disney film title, which animal did Pete own?
8 Which actress links *Batman and Robin* and *Pulp Fiction*?
9 Was *King Kong* first released in the 1930s, 50s or 70s?
10 Which Bruce is the voice of Mikey in *Look Who's Talking*?
11 Which blonde French actress's real name is Camille Javal?
12 Which Disney movie was based on the life of a native American?
13 Who met husband-to-be Richard Burton on the set of *Cleopatra*?
14 The cop Popeye Doyle first appeared in which classic thriller?
15 In which decade of the 20th century was Richard Attenborough born?
16 Which Ernest starred in *The Wild Bunch*?
17 To the nearest hour, how long does *Lady and the Tramp* last?
18 According to the film title, Lawrence was 'of' which country?
19 Who played the lead role in *Fatal Attraction* after Debra Winger turned it down?
20 In which decade was *E.T.* released?
21 Which actor was in *A River Runs Through It*, *Meet Joe Black* and *Legends of the Fall*?
22 What colour is Queen Victoria, according to the film title?
23 Who sang 'A Groovy Kind of Love' in *Buster*?
24 Which Robert won the Best Actor Oscar for *Raging Bull*?
25 Marlene Dietrich was born in which European capital?

**Answers Pot Luck 14** (see Quiz 35)
**1** Affleck. **2** Jack Nicholson. **3** Cher. **4** Emily Watson. **5** Johnson. **6** Scorsese. **7** Michael Caine. **8** Prince. **9** Straw. **10** Austria. **11** *Toy Story*. **12** Basinger. **13** *Sue*. **14** Richard Burton. **15** *Columbo*. **16** Fonda. **17** Little (*The Little Foxes* and *The Little Mermaid*). **18** 1950s. **19** Andress. **20** Venice. **21** Mel Gibson. **22** Cat (*The Cat and the Canary* and *Cat on a Hot Tin Roof*). **23** Duchovny. **24** *Stand By Me*. **25** 1960s.

## *QUIZ 34* BEHIND THE CAMERA ........ LEVEL 1

*Answers – see page 48*

1 Which Sam said, 'A producer shouldn't get ulcers, he should give them'?
2 In which country was Stanley Kubrick born?
3 Which English producer David was head of Columbia for two years in the 80s?
4 What was Bob Fosse's contribution to *Cabaret* and *All That Jazz*?
5 What was the first name of producer Thalberg who has given his name to a special movie award?
6 Which Winner appeared in *You Must Be Joking* as well as directing?
7 Which actor directed *Star Trek V: The Final Frontier*?
8 Which letter was used to show the superior film when there was a cinema double-feature?
9 Which soft-drinks company once owned Columbia Pictures?
10 What was the name of MGM's lion?
11 *The Peacemaker* was the first release from which Spielberg stable?
12 Which man and dog were the creation of Briton Nick Park?
13 Who did Martin Scorsese direct in *Raging Bull* and *Taxi Driver*?
14 Which actor Leonard stayed behind the camera for *Three Men and a Baby*?
15 Which Mrs Minnelli, Judy, did Vincente direct in *The Pirate*?
16 What name is given to the hinged board which shows the film's details during shooting?
17 Who was Oscar-nominated for his debut as director of *Dances with Wolves*?
18 What precedes 'Star' in the name of the studio which made *Men in Black*?
19 In which of his own movies did Cecil B. de Mille appear in 1950?
20 Which George links *Star Wars* and *Raiders of the Lost Ark*?
21 What is the first name of director Zemeckis of *Back to the Future*?
22 Which member of Dire Straits wrote the music for *Local Hero*?
23 Buena Vista was set up to distribute which studio's films?
24 What geographical symbol did Paramount use as its logo?
25 What is the name of Garry Marshall's sister who is also a film director?

**Answers Child Stars** (see Quiz 36)
**1** Macaulay Culkin. **2** Donald. **3** *Mary Poppins.* **4** Natalie Wood. **5** The Artful Dodger. **6** 1930s. **7** Drew Barrymore. **8** New York. **9** Durbin. **10** *The Piano.* **11** Elliott. **12** Judy Garland. **13** *Little Women.* **14** Pickford. **15** Jodie Foster. **16** Ryan O'Neal. **17** James. **18** Lassie. **19** 1970s. **20** Coogan. **21** Seven. **22** *E.T.* **23** *Kramer versus Kramer.* **24** Rooney. **25** Hawke.

## QUIZ 35 POT LUCK 14 .................... LEVEL 1

*Answers – see page 45*

1 Which Ben co-wrote *Good Will Hunting*?
2 Who won the Best Actor Oscar for *As Good as it Gets*?
3 How is Oscar-winning actress, former Mrs Sonny Bono, better known?
4 Which actress was BAFTA nominated for *Angela's Ashes*?
5 Which Celia starred in the tearjerker *Brief Encounter*?
6 Which director Martin did Isabella Rossellini marry?
7 Who was born Maurice Micklewhite?
8 Which pop star's first film was *Purple Rain*?
9 Dustin Hoffman was in a movie about what kind of 'Dogs'?
10 In which country was Arnold Schwarzenegger born?
11 Which 'Story' was the first ever completely computer-animated movie?
12 Which Kim did Alec Baldwin marry?
13 Which name completes the film title, *Peggy ___ Got Married*?
14 Elizabeth Taylor was twice married to which Welsh actor?
15 In which TV cop series did Peter Falk find fame after appearing on the big screen?
16 Which Henry won the Best Actor Oscar for *On Golden Pond*?
17 In film titles, what sizes are foxes and a mermaid?
18 In which decade of the 20th century was Sharon Stone born?
19 Which Ursula co-starred with Elvis in *Fun in Acapulco*?
20 *Don't Look Now* is set in which Italian city?
21 Which actor links *Mad Max* and *Braveheart*?
22 Which animal links a canary and a tin roof in film titles?
23 Which David starred in *The X-Files*?
24 Which movie did the song 'Stand By Me' come from?
25 In which decade was *West Side Story* released?

**Answers Pot Luck 13** (see Quiz 33)
**1** Jodie Foster. **2** Batman. **3** Gwyneth Paltrow. **4** The Bee Gees. **5** AIDS. **6** Bassey. **7** Dragon. **8** Uma Thurman. **9** 1930s. **10** Willis. **11** Brigitte Bardot. **12** *Pocahontas*. **13** Elizabeth Taylor. **14** *French Connection*. **15** 1920s. **16** Borgnine. **17** 1 hour. **18** Arabia. **19** Glenn Close. **20** 1980s. **21** Brad Pitt. **22** Brown (*Mrs Brown*). **23** Phil Collins. **24** De Niro. **25** Berlin.

## *QUIZ 36* CHILD STARS ........ LEVEL 1

*Answers – see page 46*

1 Who found fame when he was left *Home Alone*?
2 Which O'Connor was a child star before being a huge success in *Singin' in the Rain*?
3 In which musical movie did Karen Dotrice appear as a child with a superhuman nanny?
4 Which child star later played Maria in the musical *West Side Story*?
5 Jack Wild played which cheeky role in *Oliver!*?
6 In which decade did Shirley Temple win a Special Oscar for her outstanding contribution to movies?
7 Which star of *E.T.* wrote an autobiography called *Little Girl Lost*?
8 In *Home Alone 2* Macaulay Culkin is lost where?
9 Which Deanna was a contemporary of Judy Garland?
10 Anna Paquin won an Oscar with Holly Hunter for which movie?
11 What was the name of Henry Thomas's character in *E.T.*?
12 Who co-starred with Mickey Rooney 10 times on screen?
13 Which movie based on Louisa M. Alcott's novel starred a young Elizabeth Taylor?
14 Which Mary was the 'world's sweetheart' and made her first movie aged 16 in 1909?
15 Who played the gangster's moll in *Bugsy Malone* before later becoming a multiple Oscar winner?
16 Who played the father of Tatum in *Paper Moon*?
17 Which member of the Fox family, brother of Edward, was known as William when he was a child star?
18 Who was asked to 'Come Home' in Elizabeth Taylor's 1943 movie?
19 In which decade of the 20th century was Drew Barrymore born?
20 Which Jackie was immortalized in Chaplin's *The Kid*?
21 How many Von Trapp children were there in *The Sound of Music*?
22 In which movie did Drew Barrymore find fame as Gertie?
23 Justin Henry was Oscar-nominated for which movie where his parents Meryl Streep and Dustin Hoffman are to divorce?
24 Which Mickey married eight times?
25 Which Ethan starred in *Explorer* before his 20th birthday?

**Answers Behind the Camera** (see Quiz 34)
**1** Goldwyn. **2** USA. **3** Puttnam. **4** Choreography. **5** Irving. **6** Michael. **7** William Shatner. **8** A. **9** Coca Cola. **10** Leo. **11** Dreamworks. **12** Wallace & Gromit. **13** Robert De Niro. **14** Nimoy. **15** Garland. **16** Clapperboard. **17** Kevin Costner. **18** Tri. **19** *Sunset Boulevard*. **20** Lucas. **21** Robert. **22** Mark Knopfler. **23** Disney. **24** Mountain. **25** Penny.

## *QUIZ 37* POT LUCK 15 ........ LEVEL 1

*Answers – see page 51*

1 Was *The Ten Commandments'* running time nearer to 60, 100 or 220 minutes?
2 *Shakespeare in Love* and *A Perfect Murder* both feature which actress?
3 According to a movie title, 'Only Angels Have' what?
4 Which word follows 'Never Say Never' in a Sean Connery movie title?
5 What is the name of Michael Douglas's actor father?
6 Which star actor was in *Apollo 13, Sleepless in Seattle* and *Big*?
7 Who sang the theme song for *Titanic*?
8 Which word follows 'Dirty Rotten' in a Steve Martin movie title?
9 War veteran Ron Kovic features in which movie?
10 Which Barbra starred with Nick Nolte in *The Prince of Tides*?
11 Who sang the title song of *Help!*?
12 Which famous Carole tested for the role of Scarlett O'Hara?
13 In which decade of the 20th century was Rowan Atkinson born?
14 Which Melanie starred in *Working Girl*?
15 According to the film title, how many 'Degrees of Separation' are there?
16 Which Elliott featured in *M*A*S*H*?
17 Which director had a long custody battle for his children with Mia Farrow?
18 *The Empire Strikes Back* was a sequel to which blockbuster?
19 Which actor Martin was assigned to assassinate Brando in *Apocalypse Now*?
20 Which actress links *Pretty Woman* and *Hook*?
21 Dancer Eugene Curran Kelly became known under which name?
22 In *Mary Poppins*, what job does Mary take?
23 Which Jonathan starred in *Evita*?
24 Which spread can complete the film title, *A Taste of* ____?
25 *Lady and the Tramp* were what type of animals?

**Answers Westerns** (see Quiz 39)
**1** Kilmer. **2** Civil War. **3** Clint Eastwood. **4** Cat. **5** Cooper. **6** Marvin. **7** Mitchum. **8** Bob Dylan. **9** *Paint Your Wagon.* **10** 1960s. **11** Horse operas. **12** Autry. **13** Van Cleef. **14** *True Grit.* **15** Clint Eastwood. **16** Stanwyck. **17** Freeman. **18** Newman. **19** 1950s. **20** Costner. **21** *Shane.* **22** Hackman. **23** Wayne. **24** *The Magnificent Seven.* **25** Marvin.

## *QUIZ 38* OSCARS – BEST ACTORS ........ LEVEL 1

*Answers – see page 52*

1 Which 'Raging' animal won for Robert De Niro in 1980?
2 In which movie did Anthony Hopkins play Hannibal Lecter?
3 Which street made Michael Douglas an 80s winner?
4 Who was the only actor to win two Best Actor Oscars in the 1990s?
5 Which body part is in the title of a Daniel Day-Lewis winning movie?
6 Which Gary is one of only a handful of actors to win Best Actor twice?
7 Which fields made a Best Supporting winner of Haing S. Ngor?
8 Which 007 was Best Supporting Actor in *The Untouchables*?
9 Which 70s Mafia movies both won three nominations for Best Supporting Actor?
10 Best Actor winners in 1990 and 1991 came from which kingdom?
11 Which man made Dustin Hoffman a 1988 winner?
12 Which Henry was the oldest Best Actor winner of the 20th century?
13 Which two Jacks were 70s winners in the Best Actor category?
14 What is the nationality of 1998 winner Roberto Benigni?
15 In 1992 Al Pacino won for 'Scent of a' what?
16 What is the middle initial of Best Actor Scott who won for *Patton*?
17 Which simple fellow with a heart of gold won Tom Hanks a second Oscar?
18 Which Paul won for *The Color of Money*?
19 Which James was nominated for *The Godfather*?
20 Which Robin won Best Supporting Actor for *Good Will Hunting*?
21 Geoffrey Rush won for *Shine*, a biopic about what type of musician?
22 Which Kevin was Best Supporting Actor in *A Fish Called Wanda*?
23 Nicolas Cage was 'Leaving' where in his 1995 winning role?
24 Who, with the name of the American capital in his name, won Best Supporting Actor for *Glory*?
25 Which Tom Hanks winning portrayal was a ping-pong star?

**Answers Pot Luck 16** (see Quiz 40)
**1** Gary Shandling. **2** China. **3** *Falcon Crest.* **4** Myers. **5** Christie. **6** Diaz. **7** Samuel L. Jackson. **8** They dress as women. **9** Kate Winslet. **10** Kline. **11** *Raging Bull.* **12** Accept it. **13** *Aladdin.* **14** Eye patch. **15** Costner. **16** *West.* **17** Never. **18** Park. **19** Wayne. **20** Indiana Jones. **21** Hackman. **22** *Daughter.* **23** Warren Beatty. **24** 1960s. **25** Reynolds.

## *QUIZ 39* WESTERNS ........ LEVEL 1

*Answers – see page 49*

1 Which Val starred in *Tombstone*?
2 During which American war was *Dances with Wolves* set?
3 Which spaghetti western icon was 'The Good' in *The Good, The Bad and The Ugly*?
4 Which animal name precedes 'Ballou' in the Jane Fonda western spoof?
5 Which Gary won the Best Actor Oscar for *High Noon*?
6 Which Lee won the Best Actor Oscar playing opposite Jane Fonda?
7 Which Robert co-starred with John Wayne in *El Dorado*?
8 Which 60s folk singer had a minor role in *Pat Garrett and Billy the Kid*?
9 'I Was Born under a Wandrin' Star' comes from which western?
10 In which decade did spaghetti westerns first hit the screens?
11 Westerns were referred to as what type of operas?
12 Which Gene was dubbed the Singing Cowboy?
13 Which Lee found fame in spaghetti westerns?
14 In which 'True' western did John Wayne famously wear an eye patch?
15 Who won the Best Director Oscar for *Unforgiven*?
16 Which Barbara, star of *Forty Guns*, was one of the few female members of the National Cowboy Hall of Fame?
17 Which Morgan appeared with Clint Eastwood in *Unforgiven*?
18 Which blue-eyed Paul starred in *Hud*?
19 In which decade was *High Noon* released?
20 Which Kevin won the Best Director Oscar for *Dances with Wolves*?
21 'Come back, Shane' is the last line of which movie?
22 Which Gene won an Oscar as the sheriff in *Unforgiven*?
23 Which western legend John's final movie was *The Shootist*?
24 Which movie was a remake of *Seven Samurai*?
25 Which Lee starred in *The Man Who Shot Liberty Valance*?

**Answers Pot Luck 15** (see Quiz 37)
**1** 220 minutes. **2** Gwyneth Paltrow. **3** Wings. **4** Again. **5** Kirk Douglas. **6** Tom Hanks. **7** Celine Dion. **8** Scoundrels. **9** *Born on the Fourth of July*. **10** Streisand. **11** The Beatles. **12** Lombard. **13** 1950s. **14** Griffith. **15** Six. **16** Gould. **17** Woody Allen. **18** *Star Wars*. **19** Sheen. **20** Julia Roberts. **21** Gene Kelly. **22** Nanny. **23** Pryce. **24** *Honey*. **25** Dogs.

## *QUIZ 40* POT LUCK 16 ........ LEVEL 1

*Answers – see page 50*

1 Which US comic star Gary featured in the 90s *Doctor Dolittle*?
2 Which country links 'town' and 'Syndrome' in movie titles?
3 In which TV soap did Jane Wyman find fame after appearing on the big screen?
4 Which Mike starred in *Wayne's World*?
5 Which 60s star Julie was Oscar-nominated in 1998?
6 *There's Something About Mary* featured which Cameron?
7 Which actor links *Jurassic Park* and *Coming to America*?
8 In *Some Like It Hot*, what disguise do Curtis and Lemmon adopt?
9 Which actress appeared on the cinema poster for *Titanic*?
10 Which Kevin featured in *A Fish Called Wanda*?
11 In which 1980 movie did Robert De Niro play a boxer?
12 What did George C. Scott refuse to do with his Oscar for *Patton*?
13 The song 'A Whole New World' comes from which animated movie?
14 What did John Wayne wear on his face in *True Grit*?
15 Which Kevin won a Best Director Oscar for *Dances with Wolves*?
16 Which direction completes the film title *Once Upon a Time in the* ____?
17 How many times did Greta Garbo marry?
18 Which Nick won an Oscar for *The Wrong Trousers*?
19 Which John starred in *Stagecoach*?
20 Which Mr Jones was a character in *Raiders of the Lost Ark*?
21 Which Gene won the Best Actor Oscar for *The French Connection*?
22 Which family member completes the film title, *Ryan's* ____?
23 Who directed *Dick Tracy*?
24 In which decade of the 20th century was Nicolas Cage born?
25 Which Debbie starred in *Singin' in the Rain*?

**Answers Oscars – Best Actors** (see Quiz 38)
**1** Bull. **2** *The Silence of the Lambs.* **3** *Wall Street.* **4** Tom Hanks. **5** (My Left) Foot. **6** Cooper. **7** *The Killing Fields.* **8** Sean Connery. **9** *The Godfather* & *The Godfather Part II.* **10** United Kingdom. **11** *Rain Man.* **12** Fonda. **13** Lemmon & Nicholson. **14** Italian. **15** Woman. **16** C. **17** Forrest Gump. **18** Newman. **19** Caan. **20** Williams. **21** Pianist. **22** Kline. **23** Las Vegas. **24** Denzel Washington. **25** Forrest Gump.

## *QUIZ 41* CLASSICS ........ LEVEL 1

*Answers – see page 55*

1 Which movie had the ad line, 'They're young, they're in love and they kill people'?
2 What sort of race was a main feature of *Ben Hur*?
3 Who won the Best Actor Oscar for *It Happened One Night*?
4 Which movie begins with the line, 'Yes, this is Sunset Boulevard, Los Angeles, California'?
5 In which decade was *The Sound of Music* released?
6 What was the profession of Mr Chips, in *Goodbye, Mr Chips*?
7 In which city was *Breakfast at Tiffany's* set?
8 'I Could Have Danced All Night' comes from which musical movie?
9 'Rosebud' was a significant word in which classic movie?
10 In *The Wizard of Oz* what sort of animal is Dorothy's pet, Toto?
11 In which decade was *Top Hat* with Astaire and Rogers released?
12 Which blonde was originally destined for *Move Over Darling* before Doris Day stepped in?
13 Which James won Best Actor Oscar for *The Philadelphia Story*?
14 Who sings the opening song in *The Sound of Music*?
15 What is the town in question in *On the Town*?
16 Which movie had the ad line, 'You are cordially invited to George and Martha's for dinner'?
17 'Louis, I think this is the beginning of a beautiful friendship' is the last line of which movie?
18 In which decade was *The Wizard of Oz* first released?
19 In which movie did Dustin Hoffman say, 'Mrs Robinson, you're trying to seduce me, aren't you?'?
20 Who won the Best Actor Oscar for *The King and I*?
21 Which Basil played Sherlock Holmes in *The Hound of the Baskervilles*?
22 Which British actor won an Oscar for *Gandhi*?
23 'Raindrops Keep Fallin' on My Head' won an Oscar when it was used in which movie in 1969?
24 Which movie is set in Rick's bar in North Africa?
25 In which decade was *Gone with the Wind* first released?

**Answers 1960s** (see Quiz 43)
**1** *Romeo and Juliet.* **2** World War I. **3** Plants. **4** Jane. **5** Pink. **6** Italy. **7** Simon & Garfunkel. **8** *Bonnie and Clyde.* **9** 2001. **10** Katharine Hepburn. **11** Liberty Valance. **12** Cactus. **13** Seven. **14** Russia. **15** Rome. **16** *The Birds.* **17** San Francisco. **18** Shower. **19** *Cleopatra.* **20** Julie Andrews. **21** Tiffany's. **22** One Million. **23** *The Apartment.* **24** World War II. **25** Russia (*From Russia with Love*).

## *QUIZ 42* POT LUCK 17 ........ LEVEL 1

*Answers – see page 56*

1 Who was described as the 'Prince of Thieves' in the title of a 90s blockbuster?
2 Which Anthony starred in *Silence of the Lambs*?
3 Does *South Pacific* last nearly 1, 2 or 3 hours?
4 Which actress links *Sleepless in Seattle* and *You've Got Mail*?
5 Was *Alien* first released in the 1960s, 70s or 80s?
6 Which Jessica became the then-oldest Oscar winner for *Driving Miss Daisy*?
7 Which Burt starred in *Smokey and the Bandit*?
8 For which role is Bela Lugosi best remembered?
9 Which famous US family did Arnold Schwarzenegger marry into?
10 The song 'Who Will Buy' features in which musical movie?
11 In which decade was *Forrest Gump* released?
12 Which city was Macaulay Culkin lost in, in *Home Alone 2*?
13 Who co-wrote and starred in the *Rambo* films?
14 Which singer/actress won the Best Actress Oscar for *Cabaret*?
15 Which Redgrave was nominated for an Oscar in 1999?
16 At what Fahrenheit temperature do books burn in the film title?
17 In which decade of the 20th century was Alec Baldwin born?
18 Catherine Zeta Jones comes from which country?
19 Which Jack starred in *Some Like It Hot*?
20 Which wife of Richard Burton has also been Oscar-nominated?
21 Upon which day of the week does 'Night Fever' occur?
22 Which silent screen heartthrob starred in *The Sheik*?
23 What was the Bond theme for *Live and Let Die* called?
24 In which decade was *Twins* released?
25 Which soap did Hollywood actress Demi Moore star in?

**Answers Pot Luck 18** (see Quiz 44)
**1** Goldie Hawn. **2** Holland. **3** *Top Gun*. **4** Mel Gibson. **5** Cop. **6** Gary Oldman. **7** *Kojak*. **8** Shatner. **9** Before. **10** Foster. **11** Anthony Hopkins. **12** A Fish. **13** Superman. **14** Mia Farrow. **15** Twelve (*The Dirty Dozen*). **16** Chesney Hawkes. **17** 1960s. **18** Fisher. **19** Branagh. **20** Ball. **21** Gary. **22** Nicolas Cage. **23** 1970s. **24** Carrey. **25** *House*.

## *QUIZ 43* 1960s ........ LEVEL 1

*Answers – see page 53*

1 *West Side Story* was based on which Shakespeare play about star-crossed lovers?
2 *Lawrence of Arabia* was set during which world conflict?
3 In *The Day of the Triffids*, what were Triffids?
4 Which 'Baby' was played by Bette Davis in 1962?
5 What colour 'Panther' was a film with Peter Sellers?
6 *A Fistful of Dollars* was the first western to be successful in the USA which was made where?
7 Which duo sang the songs on the soundtrack of *The Graduate*?
8 Which Faye Dunaway/Warren Beatty movie would have been called *Parker and Barrow* if the characters' surnames had been used?
9 Which year was in the title of 'A Space Odyssey' released in 1968?
10 *Guess Who's Coming to Dinner?* was the last film to star Spencer Tracy opposite whom?
11 'The Man Who Shot' whom starred James Stewart and Lee Marvin?
12 What 'Flower' gave Goldie Hawn her first big screen hit?
13 How many 'Magnificent' heroes were there in the 1960s classic?
14 Where was *Doctor Zhivago* set?
15 In which capital city was *La Dolce Vita* set?
16 Which Hitchcock movie featured aggressive feathered friends?
17 *Bullitt* featured a famous car chase in which city?
18 Where in the motel was Janet Leigh when she met her death in *Psycho*?
19 Which movie about a queen of Egypt starred Elizabeth Taylor and Richard Burton?
20 *The Americanization of Emily* was the first non-singing film for which actress who had previously made *Mary Poppins*?
21 'Breakfast at' which jewellers' was the title of an Audrey Hepburn film?
22 How many 'Years BC' were there in the movie with Raquel Welch?
23 Which Jack Lemmon/Shirley MacLaine film is the name of a place to live?
24 *The Longest Day* was about the Allied invasion in which war?
25 Which Iron Curtain country was in the title of the second Bond movie?

**Answers Classics** (see Quiz 41)
**1** *Bonnie and Clyde.* **2** Chariot. **3** Clark Gable. **4** *Sunset Boulevard.* **5** 1960s. **6** Teacher. **7** New York. **8** *My Fair Lady.* **9** *Citizen Kane.* **10** Dog. **11** 1930s. **12** Marilyn Monroe. **13** Stewart. **14** Julie Andrews. **15** New York. **16** *Who's Afraid of Virginia Woolf?.* **17** *Casablanca.* **18** 1930s. **19** *The Graduate.* **20** Yul Brynner **21** Rathbone. **22** Ben Kingsley. **23** *Butch Cassidy and the Sundance Kid.* **24** *Casablanca.* **25** 1930s.

## *QUIZ 44* POT LUCK 18 ........ LEVEL 1

*Answers – see page 54*

1 What is Goldie Hawn's real name?
2 Which Linda starred in the *Terminator* movies?
3 Which movie did the song 'Take My Breath Away' come from?
4 *Lethal Weapon*, *Ransom* and *Maverick* all feature which actor?
5 In the *Die Hard* movies what is the job of the Bruce Willis character?
6 Who played the Count in *Bram Stoker's Dracula*?
7 In which TV cop series did movie actor Telly Savalas find fame?
8 Which William starred in *Star Trek: The Motion Picture*?
9 Was Disney's *Snow White* released before, after or during World War II?
10 Which Jodie starred in *Bugsy Malone*?
11 Who played C. S. Lewis in *Shadowlands*?
12 Which creature was 'Called Wanda' in a movie title?
13 Which superhero battles against Lex Luther?
14 Who went on to *Hannah and Her Sisters* from TV's *Peyton Place*?
15 Lee Marvin headed a 'Dirty' cast of how many in a 60s movie?
16 Who sang the title song of *The One and Only*?
17 In which decade of the 20th century was Helena Bonham-Carter born?
18 Which Carrie starred in *The Empire Strikes Back*?
19 Which Kenneth was dubbed 'the new Olivier'?
20 Which actress Lucille did Desi Arnaz marry twice?
21 Frank J. Cooper took on which first name in Hollywood?
22 Which actor links *The Rock*, *Moonstruck* and *Leaving Las Vegas*?
23 In which decade was *Grease* released?
24 Which Jim starred in *The Mask*?
25 Which word completes the film title, *The Old Dark* ___?

**Answers Pot Luck 17** (see Quiz 42)
**1** Robin Hood. **2** Anthony Hopkins. **3** 3 hours. **4** Meg Ryan. **5** 1970s. **6** Tandy. **7** Reynolds. **8** Dracula. **9** The Kennedy family. **10** *Oliver!* **11** 1990s. **12** New York. **13** Sylvester Stallone. **14** Liza Minnelli. **15** Lynn. **16** 451 (*Fahrenheit 451*). **17** 1950s. **18** Wales. **19** Lemmon. **20** Elizabeth Taylor. **21** Saturday. **22** Rudolph Valentino. **23** 'Live and Let Die'. **24** 1980s. **25** *General Hospital.*

## *QUIZ 45* CLINT EASTWOOD ........................................ LEVEL 1

*Answers – see page 59*

1 What was the nickname of the westerns he made in Italy?
2 What type of ape features in *Every Which Way But Loose*?
3 *In the Line of Fire* is about a security agent haunted by his failure to prevent which US President's assassination?
4 Who directed him in *Unforgiven*?
5 'A Fistful of' what was the title of his first Italian-made western?
6 He played opposite Meryl Streep in 'The Bridges of' which county?
7 With which Kevin did he co-star in *A Perfect World*?
8 'Escape from' which prison was the title of a 1979 movie?
9 In which decade was Clint Eastwood born?
10 *Any Which Way You Can* was the sequel to what?
11 Whose 'Bluff' was the title of a 60s movie?
12 In which TV series was he famous in the 50s and 60s?
13 What went with 'The Good' and 'The Bad' in the 1966 movie?
14 Eastwood won an Oscar for *Unforgiven* in what category?
15 Which Sondra was Eastwood's co-star in *Every Which Way But Loose* and his partner off screen?
16 Which Tyne of *Cagney and Lacey* fame appeared in the Dirty Harry movie *The Enforcer*?
17 In which decade was his first spaghetti western made?
18 He was elected to which role in Carmel, California in 1986–88?
19 In which western musical starring Lee Marvin did he sing in 1969?
20 *Bird* was about Charlie Parker, famous for what type of music?
21 'Play Misty for' whom was the name of the first movie he directed?
22 What was his nickname in the spaghetti westerns?
23 Which Gene was his co-star in *Unforgiven*?
24 What was the surname of 'The Outlaw – Josey'?
25 Which 'Dirty' character did he play in 1971?

**Answers Pot Luck 19** (see Quiz 47)
**1** Friday. **2** 1960s. **3** Julia Roberts. **4** *What's New Pussycat?* **5** Frank Sinatra. **6** *Crocodile Dundee.* **7** *Terminator 2.* **8** Humphrey Bogart. **9** Nicole Kidman. **10** Fried green tomatoes (*Fried Green Tomatoes at the Whistle Stop Café*). **11** In Space. **12** Hepburn. **13** Places. **14** Golf. **15** Moranis. **16** The Marx Brothers. **17** Samuel L. Jackson. **18** *Northwest.* **19** 1970s. **20** Cher. **21** *Morning.* **22** 1910s. **23** 3 hours. **24** Hoffman. **25** The weather.

## *QUIZ 46* WHO'S WHO? ........................................ LEVEL 1

*Answers – see page 60*

1 Which former 007 appeared in *Spiceworld: The Movie*?
2 How is John Cheese better known?
3 Which Elizabeth won the Best Actress Oscar for *Butterfield 8*?
4 Which actress Janet is Jamie Lee Curtis's mother?
5 Cate Blanchett played English queen Elizabeth, but where does she hail from?
6 In which continent was Richard E. Grant born?
7 Which cosmetics house did Madonna advertise in the late 1990s?
8 What was the name of the town where Winona Ryder was born?
9 What is the name of Laura Dern's father?
10 Who said, 'Having a double barrelled name makes it hell to sign autographs'?
11 What is Liam Neeson's real first name?
12 In which decade of the 20th century was Julia Roberts born?
13 How is *M*A*S*H* actor Elliott Goldstein better known?
14 Which Sean played the condemned man in *Dead Man Walking*?
15 How is Virginia Davis of *Thelma and Louise* better known?
16 How was Farrah Fawcett known during her marriage to actor Lee Majors?
17 Which brother of Ralph Fiennes starred in *Shakespeare in Love*?
18 Who won the Best Actor Oscar for *Ben Hur*?
19 Which French actress said, 'The more I see of men, the more I like dogs'?
20 Actress Nancy Davis married which actor and US President?
21 Which member of the Fonda family starred in *Single White Female* in 1992?
22 Which country shares its name with actor Gooding who starred in *Jerry Maguire*?
23 Which singer and pianist appeared in *Spiceworld: The Movie*?
24 How is Britt-Maria Eklund better known?
25 What was Barbra Streisand's first film, in 1966?

**Answers Directors** (see Quiz 48)
**1** Cameron. **2** Coppola. **3** Anthony. **4** *The Dirty Dozen*. **5** Blake Edwards. **6** 1930s. **7** Czechoslovakia. **8** Mel Gibson. **9** Vadim. **10** Charlie Chaplin. **11** *Apocalypse Now*. **12** Charlie Chaplin. **13** Alfred Hitchcock. **14** *M*A*S*H*. **15** Rosemary's. **16** Stone. **17** Cubby Broccoli. **18** Bo Derek. **19** Capra. **20** Mendes. **21** Woody Allen. **22** Federico. **23** Huston. **24** Steven Spielberg. **25** Frank.

## *QUIZ 47* POT LUCK 19 ........ LEVEL 1

*Answers – see page 57*

1 Which day of the week links 'Thirteenth' and 'Freaky' in movie titles?
2 In which decade of the 20th century was Brooke Shields born?
3 Which star actress was in *The Pelican Brief, Six Days Seven Nights* and *Stepmom*?
4 Which Woody Allen film title includes a reference to a feline?
5 Which singer played the tough guy captain in *Von Ryan's Express*?
6 Which 80s film was the most profitable in Australian history?
7 Which sequel had the subtitle 'Judgment Day'?
8 Who played the lead in *Casablanca* after George Raft turned it down?
9 Which actress links *Eyes Wide Shut* and *Practical Magic*?
10 What kind of fruit can you get at the Whistle Stop Café, according to the film title?
11 Where was Gary Oldman 'Lost' in the 1998 hit movie?
12 Which movie veteran Katharine was the first actress to win four Oscars?
13 Which word follows 'Trading' in an Eddie Murphy movie title?
14 Bing Crosby had just finished a round of what when he died?
15 Which Rick starred in *Honey, I Shrunk the Kids*?
16 Which brothers starred in *Monkey Business*?
17 *Patriot Games, Pulp Fiction* and *Sphere* all feature which actor?
18 Which direction completes this film title, *North By* ____?
19 In which decade was *One Flew Over the Cuckoo's Nest* released?
20 Which singer/actress won the Best Actress Oscar for *Moonstruck*?
21 Which time period completes the film title, *Saturday Night and Sunday* ____?
22 In which decade of the 20th century was Lucille Ball born?
23 To the nearest hour, how long does *The Sound of Music* last?
24 Which Dustin starred in *Tootsie*?
25 What did Nicole Kidman forecast in *To Die For*?

**Answers Clint Eastwood** (see Quiz 45)
**1** Spaghetti westerns. **2** Orang Utan. **3** J.F. Kennedy. **4** He did. **5** Dollars. **6** Madison County. **7** Costner. **8** Alcatraz. **9** 1930s. **10** *Every Which Way But Loose.* **11** Coogan's. **12** *Rawhide.* **13** The Ugly. **14** Best Director. **15** Locke. **16** Daly. **17** 1960s. **18** Mayor. **19** *Paint Your Wagon.* **20** Jazz. **21** Me. **22** The Man with No Name. **23** Hackman. **24** Wales. **25** Harry.

## *QUIZ 48* DIRECTORS ........ LEVEL 1

*Answers – see page 58*

1 On accepting a Golden Globe for *Titanic*, which James said, 'Does this prove that size does matter?'?
2 Which Francis Ford is the uncle of actor Nicolas Cage?
3 What is the first name of Minghella, who made *The English Patient*?
4 Which 'Dirty' film led Robert Aldrich to founding his own studio?
5 Which director's real name is William Blake McEdwards?
6 In which decade of the 20th century was Woody Allen born?
7 In which country was Milos Forman born?
8 Who won the Best Director Oscar for *Braveheart*?
9 Which director Roger did Brigitte Bardot marry?
10 Which superstar of the silent screen was the subject of a biopic directed by Richard Attenborough in 1992?
11 In which of his own movies did Francis Ford Coppola appear in 1979?
12 Who directed and starred in *The Great Dictator* in 1940?
13 Who said, 'If I made *Cinderella* the audience would be looking for a body in the coach'?
14 Robert Altman directed which movie about a Mobile Army Hospital in Korea, later a TV series?
15 Whose 'Baby' was the Hollywood debut for Roman Polanski, in a movie which starred Mia Farrow?
16 Which Oliver directed *Platoon*?
17 How was Albert Broccoli better known?
18 Who was John Derek's wife whom he directed in *Bolero* in 1984?
19 Which Frank won the Best Director Oscar for *It Happened One Night*?
20 Which Sam won a Golden Globe for *American Beauty*?
21 Who took his film surname form his real name, Allen Stewart Konigsberg?
22 What was the first name of Italian director Fellini?
23 Which John won Best Director Oscar for *The Treasure of the Sierra Madre*?
24 Who funded the Survivors of the Shoah Visual History Foundation after making a Holocaust movie?
25 What was the first name of Hollywood director Capra, of *It's a Wonderful Life* fame?

**Answers Who's Who?** (see Quiz 46)
**1** Roger Moore. **2** John Cleese. **3** Taylor. **4** Leigh. **5** Australia. **6** Africa. **7** Max Factor. **8** Winona. **9** Bruce. **10** Helena Bonham Carter. **11** William. **12** 60s. **13** Elliott Gould. **14** Penn. **15** Geena Davis. **16** Farrah Fawcett-Majors. **17** Joseph. **18** Charlton Heston. **19** Brigitte Bardot. **20** Ronald Reagan. **21** Bridget. **22** Cuba. **23** Jools Holland. **24** Britt Ekland. **25** *Funny Girl*.

## *QUIZ 49* LIVING LEGENDS ........ LEVEL 1

*Answers – see page 63*

1 Which Katharine's book was subtitled *How I Went to Africa with Bogart, Bacall and Huston and Almost Lost My Mind*?
2 Which Robert turned down Dustin Hoffman's role in *The Graduate*?
3 In which movie did Tom Hanks say, 'Life is like a box of chocolates'?
4 Which Deborah rolled in the sand with Burt Lancaster in *From Here to Eternity*?
5 In which decade was Jack Nicholson born?
6 Which band's music made *Saturday Night Fever* a success?
7 Which English 007 said, 'You're not a star till they can spell your name in Vladivostok'?
8 Which double Oscar-winner became a Dame in 2000 partly for her work with AIDS sufferers?
9 Which Christopher's autobiography was called *Still Me*?
10 Which Peter said, 'My idea of heaven is moving from one smoke filled room to another'?
11 Who won the Best Actress Oscar for *Funny Girl*?
12 Who made a fortune out of a recipe for salad dressing?
13 Which Scots star was at the top of the money-making lists of 1966?
14 Which painter Vincent did Kirk Douglas play in *Lust for Life*?
15 Which lady was the US's top money-maker with Rock Hudson in 1962?
16 Who changed his name after seeing an advertising hoarding for *The Caine Mutiny*?
17 Which Katharine tested for the role of Scarlett O'Hara?
18 Omar Sharif's affair with Barbra Streisand began on the set of which movie?
19 Which Michael's autobiography was called *What's It All About?*?
20 What was Julie Andrews's first film, in 1964?
21 How is Doris Kapelhoff better know?
22 Where was Bob Hope born?
23 Which cartoon character did Robin Williams play?
24 Who directed and starred in *Yentl* in 1983?
25 Which tough guy's real name is Charles Buchinski?

**Answers Fred Astaire** (see Quiz 51)
**1** Frederick. **2** Ginger Rogers. **3** Sister. **4** *Top Hat.* **5** Garland. **6** *Towering Inferno.* **7** *Finian's Rainbow.* **8** Dance. **9** Feathers. **10** Rio. **11** Hayworth. **12** Once. **13** Dramatic role. **14** 1890s. **15** *Sergeant Pepper's Lonely Hearts Club Band.* **16** Legs. **17** 1980s. **18** Gene. **19** Tails. **20** Bing Crosby. **21** Fleet. **22** Divorcee. **23** *Swing Time.* **24** 1930s. **25** Audrey.

## *QUIZ 50* POT LUCK 20 ........ LEVEL 1

*Answers – see page 64*

1 Who partners Turner in a Tom Hanks movie?
2 Which Jim starred in *The Truman Show*?
3 How often are the Oscars presented?
4 Which star actress was in *Dangerous Minds, Wolf* and *One Fine Day*?
5 Which word completes the film title, *Since You Went* ____?
6 Which Bill starred in *Ghostbusters*?
7 What is the first name of Mr Hytner who directed *The Crucible* and *The Madness of King George*?
8 According to the movie title, what do 'Gentlemen Prefer'?
9 Which British actor Jeremy was an Oscar winner with *Reversal of Fortune*?
10 In which decade was *Thelma and Louise* released?
11 Which Tom was male lead in *Jerry Maguire*?
12 Which word follows 'Jumpin' Jack' in a Whoopi Goldberg movie title?
13 What did Dumbo do immediately before his ears grew so big?
14 Which actress Debra served in the Israeli army?
15 In which decade of the 20th century was Clint Eastwood born?
16 Which Caped Crusader was the subject of one of the top 80s films?
17 Which actor links *Platoon, Donnie Brascoe* and *Nick of Time*?
18 How many gunfighters were hired in the 'Magnificent' film of 1960?
19 Who was Warren Beatty's wife whom he directed in *Bugsy* in 1991?
20 Which word completes the film title, *The Rocky Horror Picture* ____?
21 'Evergreen' won an Oscar when it was used in which movie in 1976?
22 Which Tom won the Best Actor Oscar for *Forrest Gump*?
23 In which decade was *The Spy Who Loved Me* released?
24 Who directed *The Commitments*?
25 Charlie Chaplin was famous for wearing what type of hat?

**Answers Pot Luck 21** (see Quiz 52)
**1** *Ice Storm.* **2** 150 minutes. **3** Colbert. **4** 1960s. **5** Crystal. **6** Motorcycle. **7** Sharon Stone. **8** *Titanic.* **9** Cagney. **10** Honor. **11** Sarandon. **12** Paris. **13** Hanna & Barbera. **14** Tchaikovsky. **15** Kiefer Sutherland. **16** Gere. **17** In the Stone. **18** Fred Flintstone. **19** Cher. **20** King. **21** Tom Cruise. **22** Judy Garland. **23** 1930s. **24** James Garner. **25** 'From Russia with Love'.

## *QUIZ 57* POT LUCK 23 ........ LEVEL 1

*Answers – see page 71*

1 Which early 1990s Disney animal cartoon is set in Africa?
2 Who played Princess Leia in *Star Wars*?
3 Which *ER* star played Batman in the 1997 movie?
4 Which Michael Douglas film has the word 'Wall' in the title?
5 In which TV detective series did James Garner find fame after appearing on the big screen?
6 Which silent movie actor was nicknamed the 'Great Stone Face'?
7 Which Patricia wrote the book on which *The Talented Mr Ripley* was based?
8 Which Claire starred in the 90s *Romeo and Juliet*?
9 Who sang 'Call Me' in *American Gigolo*?
10 Which word goes before 'Proposal' in a Demi Moore movie title?
11 What is another name for a horse opera?
12 Which computer company with a fruit logo bought Pixar?
13 What sort of video disc is a DVD?
14 The medium Oda Mae Brown appears in which movie?
15 'Up Where We Belong' was the theme music to which 80s film?
16 Who played Baron von Trapp in *The Sound of Music*?
17 In which decade of the 20th century was Michael J. Fox born?
18 Which keyboard instrument gave its name to a film with Holly Hunter?
19 Which name completes the film title, *Star Trek: The Wrath Of* ____?
20 Which first name goes before 'Valentine' to make a movie title?
21 Which director Blake did Julie Andrews marry?
22 Which Michelle starred in *The Witches of Eastwick*?
23 Which 'Rider' was Clint Eastwood's next western after *The Outlaw Josey Wales*?
24 Which word follows 'Sibling' in a Carrie Fisher movie title?
25 In which movie did Dustin Hoffman play 'Dorothy'?

**Answers Judy Garland** (see Quiz 59)
**1** 'Over the Rainbow'. **2** Fred Astaire. **3** Vincente Minnelli. **4** 1920s. **5** Ziegfeld. **6** Mason. **7** Dorothy. **8** Gable. **9** Rooney. **10** *The Wizard of Oz*. **11** Bogarde. **12** St Louis. **13** Frances. **14** 1960s. **15** Liza Minnelli. **16** *Annie Get Your Gun*. **17** Ira. **18** Star. **19** Shirley Temple. **20** Kelly. **21** *Babes in Arms*. **22** Nuremberg. **23** *Easter Parade*. **24** Lorna. **25** 1960s.

## *QUIZ 58* 1970s ........ LEVEL 1

*Answers – see page 72*

1 Which romantic Rudolph did Rudolph Nureyev play on film in 1977?
2 Which 'Story' had the ad line, 'Love means never having to say you're sorry'?
3 Willy Wonka was in charge of what type of factory?
4 The movie *Rocky* was about what type of sportsman?
5 Which dance was 'The Last in Paris' with Marlon Brando?
6 In which decade was *Grease* set?
7 Which cult sci-fi series came to the big screen with *The Motion Picture* in 1979?
8 Which puppets including Kermit and Miss Piggy had their own big screen hit?
9 Which instrumentalist was 'on the Roof' in 1971?
10 Which night of the week suffered 'Night Fever'?
11 Which US city was named twice in the 1977 hit with Robert De Niro?
12 What followed 'What's Up' in the title of the move with Barbra Streisand and Ryan O'Neal?
13 Which gangster movie was based on Mario Puzo's novel?
14 Where did the action of *The Poseidon Adventure* take place?
15 What nationality of 'Graffiti' was directed by George Lucas in 1973?
16 In which country was *The Three Musketeers* set?
17 Which fruit was 'Clockwork' in 1971?
18 Which King's court was included – loosely – in *Monty Python and the Holy Grail*?
19 Which precious gems were in the title of the 1971 Bond movie?
20 How were 'Saddles' described in the 1974 movie with Gene Wilder?
21 What was the sequel to *The Godfather* called?
22 Which Korean War movie spawned a TV series which lasted 11 years?
23 Whose 'Daughter' starred Robert Mitchum and Sarah Miles?
24 Which Warren Beatty movie had the title of a hair-care item as its title?
25 Which 'Connection' starred Gene Hackman?

**Answers Pot Luck 24** (see Quiz 60)
**1** Nick Park. **2** 1950s. **3** Hercule Poirot. **4** Thompson. **5** Nicholson. **6** Julie Andrews. **7** *Bismarck*. **8** Cliffhanger. **9** Robin Williams. **10** 33⅓. **11** Alfred Hitchcock. **12** Dry ice. **13** Reed. **14** Moore. **15** Goldwyn. **16** Jeff Goldblum. **17** *M*A*S*H*. **18** 1960s. **19** Michael Caine. **20** The cold (*The Spy Who Came in from the Cold*). **21** Ginger Rogers. **22** *Walking*. **23** Mozart. **24** Arnold Schwarzenegger. **25** 'Over the Rainbow'.

## *QUIZ 59* JUDY GARLAND ........................................................ LEVEL 1

*Answers – see page 69*

1 Which Garland song from *The Wizard of Oz* won an Oscar?
2 Which dancer replaced Gene Kelly in *Easter Parade* after he hurt his ankle?
3 Which husband of Garland's, of Italian descent, directed her in *Meet Me in St Louis*?
4 In which decade was she born?
5 Which 'Girl' was in the title of a 1941 movie?
6 Which James was Garland's co star in *A Star Is Born*?
7 What was the name of her famous character in *The Wizard of Oz*?
8 To which Clark did she sing 'You Made Me Love You' in *Broadway Melody of 1938*?
9 With which Mickey did she first star in 1937?
10 For which famous movie did she receive a special juvenile Oscar?
11 Which Dirk was her co-star in *I Could Go On Singing*?
12 Where did Judy sing 'Meet Me' in the 1944 movie?
13 What was her first name when she was part of the Gumm Sisters Kiddie Act?
14 In which decade did she make her last film?
15 What is the name of her daughter with Vincente Minnelli?
16 On which movie about the wild west's Annie Oakley was she replaced by Betty Hutton in 1950?
17 Which Gershwin wrote the lyrics of Garland's classic 'The Man That Got Away' from *A Star Is Born*?
18 In *Babes in Arms* Garland sang 'You Are My Lucky' what?
19 Which child star did she replace in *The Wizard of Oz*?
20 Which Gene debuted with her in *For Me and My Gal* in 1942?
21 *Babes on Broadway* was a sequel to which movie also with Mickey Rooney?
22 'Judgment at' where, the location for war crime trials, was a 1961 dramatic role for Garland?
23 Which 'Parade' was a 1948 hit musical for her?
24 What is the name of her daughter with producer Sid Luft?
25 In which decade of the 20th century did Judy Garland die?

**Answers Pot Luck 23** (see Quiz 57)
**1** *The Lion King*. **2** Carrie Fisher. **3** George Clooney. **4** *Wall Street*. **5** *The Rockford Files*. **6** Buster Keaton. **7** Highsmith. **8** Danes. **9** Blondie. **10** Indecent. **11** Western. **12** Apple. **13** Digital. **14** *Ghost*. **15** *An Officer and a Gentleman*. **16** Christopher Plummer. **17** 1960s. **18** The piano. **19** *Khan*. **20** Shirley. **21** Edwards. **22** Pfeiffer. **23** *Pale Rider*. **24** Rivalry. **25** *Tootsie*.

## *QUIZ 60* POT LUCK 24 ........ LEVEL 1

*Answers – see page 70*

1 Who directed *A Close Shave*?
2 In which decade of the 20th century was Carrie Fisher born?
3 Which sleuth features in Agatha Christie's *Murder on the Orient Express*?
4 Which Emma won the Best Actress Oscar for *Howard's End*?
5 Which Jack starred in *Wolf*?
6 Who was the female lead in *Mary Poppins*?
7 Which word completes the film title, *Sink the* ____?
8 What name is given to a situation in film where a suspense scene is temporarily left unresolved?
9 Which actor links *The Birdcage* and *Patch Adams*?
10 What number completes the title, *Naked Gun* ____*: The Final Insult*?
11 Who directed *To Catch a Thief* and *North by Northwest*?
12 What sort of ice was used to give a misty effect in movie making?
13 Which Oliver played Bill Sikes in *Oliver!*?
14 Which Dudley portrayed Arthur?
15 What does the G stand for in MGM studios?
16 Who played the wisecracking mathematician in *Jurassic Park*?
17 The character Trapper John featured in which war-based movie?
18 In which decade was *True Grit* released?
19 Who played the lead in *Alfie* after Laurence Harvey turned it down?
20 According to the film title, where did the spy come in from?
21 Who danced in high heels in the Astaire/Rogers movies?
22 What completes the film title, *Dead Man* ___?
23 *Amadeus* told the story of which classical composer?
24 Which star actor was in *Junior* and *Terminator 2: Judgment Day*?
25 Which song from *The Wizard of Oz* won an Oscar?

**Answers 1970s** (see Quiz 58)
**1** Valentino. **2** *Love Story*. **3** Chocolate. **4** Boxer. **5** Tango. **6** 1950s. **7** *Star Trek*. **8** The Muppets. **9** Fiddler. **10** Saturday. **11** New York. **12** Doc. **13** *The Godfather*. **14** At sea. **15** American. **16** France. **17** Orange. **18** Arthur. **19** Diamonds (*Diamond Are Forever*). **20** Blazing. **21** *The Godfather Part II*. **22** *M*A*S*H*. **23** *Ryan's Daughter*. **24** *Shampoo*. **25** *The French Connection*.

## *QUIZ 61* STARS OF THE 21ST CENTURY ........ LEVEL 1

*Answers – see page 75*

1 What was Leonardo DiCaprio's first major movie after *Titanic*?
2 Where does Robert Carlyle hail from?
3 Which major US university did Matt Damon attend?
4 Which star of *The Talented Mr Ripley* was engaged to Brad Pitt?
5 What type of 'Voice' did Jane Horrocks have in the 1998 movie?
6 Which actor links *The Phantom Menace* and *Trainspotting*?
7 What sort of 'Inspector' did Matthew Broderick become?
8 Which Kate found fame in *Sense and Sensibility* when only 20?
9 Which Ms Moore was Ralph Fiennes's co-star in *The End of the Affair*?
10 Which Jennifer provided a voice in *Antz* and starred in *Anaconda*?
11 In which movie did Mena Suvari star with Kevin Spacey?
12 What is the first name of British actress Ms Swinton who appears in *The Beach*?
13 Tom Hanks, Tim Allen and Kelsey Grammer were heard but not seen in which cartoon sequel?
14 Which Jennifer from *Friends* was one of the voices in *The Iron Giant*?
15 Which TV star Alex divorced Ralph Fiennes in 1997?
16 Which Annette starred in *American Beauty*?
17 What day of the week was *Sleepy Hollow*'s Christina Ricci's name in the *Addams Family* movies?
18 Which Jeanne's movies include *Sliding Doors* and *Mickey Blue Eyes*?
19 Which English actor played opposite Gwyneth Paltrow in *The Talented Mr Ripley*?
20 Which Matthew married Sarah Jessica Parker in 1997?
21 Who was the star and executive producer of *Onegin*?
22 Which Anna played opposite Ewan McGregor in *Rogue Trader*?
23 What was Leonardo DiCaprio's first film released in the 21st century?
24 Which star of *There's Something About Mary* was described as 'something of a Jean Harlow of the 90s'?
25 If Jodie Foster was Anna, who was Chow Yun-Fat?

**Answers Pot Luck 25** (see Quiz 63)
**1** *Titanic.* **2** Macaulay Culkin. **3** Vietnam. **4** Bill Clinton. **5** The Marx Brothers. **6** Location. **7** *Corner.* **8** *Shadowlands.* **9** Sequel. **10** 1980s. **11** Dreyfuss. **12** A miracle (*The Miracle of Morgan's Creek*). **13** Betty Grable. **14** *West Side Story.* **15** Volcano eruption. **16** *American Beauty.* **17** Crawford . **18** Children. **19** Pig. **20** Bjorn Borg. **21** *Habit.* **22** 1960s. **23** Under an hour (30 mins). **24** Tom Jones. **25** Fonda.

## *QUIZ 62* MARILYN MONROE ........ LEVEL 1

*Answers – see page 76*

1 What were her real first names?
2 The title of her 1953 movie was 'How to Marry' who?
3 In which film which mentioned blondes did she play Lorelei Lee?
4 In the 1957 movie Olivier played 'The Prince'; who was Monroe?
5 *Some Like It Hot*, about the aftermath of the St Valentine's Day Massacre, is set in which decade?
6 Monroe had a minor role in a Bette Davis movie, 'All About' whom?
7 To which US President did she famously sing 'Happy Birthday'?
8 Which Billy directed her in *The Seven Year Itch*?
9 Which classic Beatles album features Marilyn Monroe – among many others – on the cover?
10 In *Some Like It Hot* which stringed musical instrument does she play?
11 Which Ethel was her leading co-star in *There's No Business Like Show Business*?
12 What was the official cause of her death?
13 What type of sportsman was her second husband, Joe Di Maggio?
14 Which Jack and Tony were her co-stars in *Some Like It Hot*?
15 Which star of *Evita* has a tattoo of Marilyn Monroe on her body?
16 What was her first name as Miss Kane in *Some Like It Hot*?
17 Which brunette Jane was her co-star in *Gentlemen Prefer Blondes*?
18 What sort of 'Business' was the title of a 1952 movie?
19 Which 1953 movie took its name from some Canadian falls?
20 What was the name of the Elton John song about Marilyn Monroe?
21 Which 1955 Monroe movie featured Tom Ewell?
22 What were 'a Girl's Best Friend' in the title of one her songs?
23 Which playwright Arthur was her third and last husband?
24 With which King of Hollywood did she make her last completed film – which was also his final movie?
25 In which decade did Marilyn Monroe die?

**Answers 1930s Stars** (see Quiz 64)
**1** Marlene Dietrich. **2** Mae West. **3** Greta Garbo. **4** G. **5** One. **6** James. **7** Weissmuller. **8** Pickford. **9** W.C.. **10** Eddy. **11** Shirley Temple. **12** Cooper. **13** Hardy. **14** Laughton. **15** Tyrone Power. **16** Judy Garland. **17** Hedy Lamarr. **18** None. **19** Clark Gable. **20** The Marx Brothers. **21** Blonde. **22** Claudette Colbert. **23** Stanwyck. **24** Crawford. **25** Vivien Leigh.

## *QUIZ 63* POT LUCK 25 ........ LEVEL 1

*Answers – see page 73*

1 Which film earned James Cameron a 1997 Oscar?
2 *Home Alone* made which child into a worldwide star?
3 *Platoon* was about which a war in which country?
4 Who was US President when *Air Force One* was released?
5 Which brothers featured in *Animal Crackers*?
6 What name is given to a filming site away from the studio?
7 Which word completes the film title, *The Shop Around the* ____?
8 What is the name of the film about the writer C. S. Lewis?
9 What name is given to a movie which follows up on events of a previous film?
10 In which decade was *The Empire Strikes Back* released?
11 Which Richard starred in *American Graffiti*?
12 What happened at Morgan's Creek, according to the film title?
13 Who insured her legs for a million dollars in the 1940s?
14 Which musical based on *Romeo and Juliet* was a 60s Oscar winner?
15 What natural disaster is at the heart of *Dante's Peak*?
16 What won the Best Film Oscar at the first ceremony of the new Millennium?
17 Which Joan starred in *Whatever Happened to Baby Jane?*?
18 Bugsy Malone features what particular type of performers?
19 What sort of farm animal was Babe?
20 Which Swedish tennis star appeared in *Racquet* in 1979?
21 Which word completes the film title, *Sister Act 2: Back in the* ____?
22 In which decade of the 20th century was Jodie Foster born?
23 Does *A Close Shave* last under an hour, one hour or two hours?
24 Which Tom sang 'It's Not Unusual' in *Mars Attacks!*?
25 Dad Henry and children Jane and Peter are from which family?

**Answers Stars of the 21st Century** (see Quiz 61)
**1** *The Beach*. **2** Scotland. **3** Harvard. **4** Gwyneth Paltrow. **5** Little. **6** Ewan McGregor. **7** Gadget. **8** Winslet. **9** Julianne. **10** Lopez. **11** *American Beauty*. **12** Tilda. **13** *Toy Story 2*. **14** Aniston. **15** Kingston. **16** Bening. **17** Wednesday. **18** Tripplehorne. **19** Jude Law. **20** Broderick. **21** Ralph Fiennes. **22** Friel. **23** *The Beach*. **24** Cameron Diaz. **25** The King.

## *QUIZ 64* 1930s STARS ........ LEVEL 1

*Answers – see page 74*

1 Which German-born actress was the star of *The Blue Angel*?
2 Which scandal-seeking blonde appeared in *I'm No Angel* and *She Done Him Wrong*?
3 Which Swedish star's first spoken line was, 'Gimme a visky with a ginger ale on the side'?
4 Which middle initial did Edward Robinson use?
5 How many Marx Brothers remained silent on screen?
6 Which first name was shared by actors Stewart and Cagney?
7 Which Johnny took the title role in *Tarzan the Ape Man*?
8 Which Mary, a founder of United Artists, retired in 1933?
9 Actor Fields appeared in *Six of a Kind;* what were his initials?
10 Which Nelson partnered Jeanette Macdonald for the first time in *Naughty Mariette*?
11 Which child star topped the list of US money-makers in 1935?
12 Which Gary appeared in *Mr Deeds Goes to Town*?
13 Did Laurel or Hardy or both of them have a moustache?
14 Which Charles played Quasimodo in *The Hunchback of Notre Dame*?
15 What was Tyrone Power's father called?
16 Which star of *The Wizard of Oz* was born Frances Gumm?
17 Hedy Kiesler found fame swimming nude in a Czech movie; how was she renamed in Hollywood?
18 How many Oscars did Chaplin win in the 1930s?
19 Which star of *Gone with the Wind* was dubbed the King of Hollywood?
20 Margaret Dumont made seven films with which comedy brothers?
21 What colour was Jean Harlow's hair?
22 Which actress with the initials C.C. was Clark Gable's co-star in *It Happened One Night*?
23 Which 30s actress Barbara found fame in the 80s soap *The Colbys*?
24 Which Joan was the subject of a 1970s biography *Mommie Dearest*?
25 Which actress said 'Tomorrow is another day' at the end of *Gone with the Wind*?

**Answers Marilyn Monroe** (see Quiz 62)
**1** Norma Jean. **2** A Millionaire. **3** *Gentlemen Prefer Blondes.* **4** The Showgirl. **5** 1920s. **6** Eve. **7** Kennedy. **8** Wilder. **9** *Sergeant Pepper's Lonely Hearts Club Band.* **10** Ukelele. **11** Merman. **12** Drugs overdose. **13** Baseball player. **14** Lemmon & Curtis. **15** Madonna. **16** Sugar. **17** Russell. **18** *Monkey Business.* **19** *Niagara.* **20** 'Candle in the Wind'. **21** *The Seven Year Itch.* **22** Diamonds. **23** Miller. **24** Clark Gable – *The Misfits.* **25** 1960s.

## *QUIZ 65* POT LUCK 26 ........ LEVEL 1

*Answers – see page 79*

1 Which star actor was in *As Good as it Gets* and *The Shining*?
2 The original 'Candle in the Wind' was about which movie icon?
3 Which Jim starred in *Ace Ventura, Pet Detective*?
4 What do the male leads do in both *Mrs Doubtfire* and *Tootsie*?
5 Which actress links *Sister Act* and *Ghost*?
6 What sort of store does Hugh Grant own in *Notting Hill*?
7 *Air Force One* starred which Glenn?
8 In which decade was *Aladdin* released?
9 Who played the lead roles in *Butch Cassidy and the Sundance Kid*?
10 Which Terence starred in *The Adventures of Priscilla, Queen of the Desert*?
11 Which word follows 'Presumed' in a Harrison Ford movie title?
12 What name is given to a movie which shows events which happened before a previously known story?
13 Which Kevin starred in *Waterworld*?
14 Which role did Mark Hamill play in *Star Wars*?
15 Which early rocker Bill was in the movie *Rock around the Clock*?
16 Who shared the title with Thelma in the 1991 movie?
17 Who won the Best Actress Oscar for *Sophie's Choice*?
18 *Indecent Proposal* and *A Few Good Men* both feature which actress?
19 What sort of movie did a scream queen appear in?
20 Which James starred in *The Philadelphia Story*?
21 In which decade was *The Omen* released?
22 Which movie did the song 'Night Fever' come from?
23 Which word completes the movie title *Honey, I Shrunk The* ____?
24 In which decade of the 20th century was Winona Ryder born?
25 Which Tom starred in *A League of their Own*?

**Answers Heroes & Villains** (see Quiz 67)
**1** Keach. **2** Canada. **3** Arnold Schwarzenegger. **4** Oskar. **5** Pesci. **6** Lee Harvey Oswald. **7** *The Birds*. **8** Telly Savalas. **9** Shaw. **10** 1970s. **11** Pearl Harbor. **12** Bates. **13** Paris. **14** Jeremy Irons. **15** *The Silence of the Lambs*. **16** Ivy (Uma Thurman). **17** Caan. **18** Jack Nicholson. **19** Stephen King. **20** John Travolta. **21** The Penguin. **22** *The Terminator*. **23** Sophia Loren. **24** Jodie Foster. **25** Woody Allen.

## *QUIZ 66* ANIMAL MOVIES ........ LEVEL 1

*Answers – see page 80*

1 What was the name of Gene Autry's 'Wonder Horse'?
2 Who played Cruella De Vil in the real-life version of *101 Dalmatians*?
3 Which animal played the title role in *Babe*?
4 What type of animal was Rin Tin Tin?
5 What was Dumbo?
6 Which Doctor could 'talk to the animals'?
7 What was unusual about Clarence the Lion's eyes?
8 What did Fritz and Felix have in common?
9 What was Roy Rogers's horse called?
10 Which 70s blockbuster was about a man-eating shark?
11 What breed of lugubrious dog featured in *Turner and Hooch*?
12 *International Velvet* was about what type of animal?
13 What types of animal were to be found in Jurassic Park?
14 What sort of creatures were Leonardo, Michelangelo, Raphael and Donatello?
15 In which decade was the real-life version of *101 Dalmatians* released?
16 What sort of creature was Tarka?
17 What type of animal was Gentle Ben?
18 Cheta was a chimp in which jungle movie series?
19 What name went after 'Free' in the movie about a whale?
20 Which composer shared a name with a St Bernard dog in the movies?
21 In *101 Dalmatians* Cruella De Vil wanted the puppies in order to make what?
22 What sort of animals were the stars of *Born Free*?
23 Which film featured Mufasa the lion?
24 Which animal featured in the Sherlock Holmes story which has been filmed most?
25 What breed of dog was Lassie?

**Answers Pot Luck 27** (see Quiz 68)
**1** John Travolta. **2** Paltrow. **3** Fatal. **4** 1980s. **5** Ben E. King. **6** Silver. **7** Gibson. **8** *Dances with Wolves.* **9** Palin. **10** Hepburn. **11** *Evita.* **12** Loose. **13** Kane. **14** Drew Barrymore. **15** Sinbad. **16** Liza Minnelli. **17** Harrison Ford. **18** Bankhead. **19** Nancy. **20** Ivy. **21** Anderson. **22** Francis Ford Coppola. **23** *The Colbys.* **24** 1950s. **25** 4 hours.

## *QUIZ 67* HEROES & VILLAINS ........ LEVEL 1

*Answers – see page 77*

1 Which Stacy spent nine months in Britain's Reading Gaol?
2 Leslie Nielsen was a member of which country's air force?
3 Which bodybuilder was Mr Freeze in *Batman and Robin*?
4 What was the first name of Schindler in the movie with Liam Neeson?
5 Which Joe tries to burgle Macaulay Culkin when he's *Home Alone*?
6 Which real-life villain did Gary Oldman play in *JFK*?
7 What are the villains in the 1963 movie with Tippi Hedren and Rod Taylor?
8 In *On Her Majesty's Secret Service* which smooth-headed TV detective played Blofeld?
9 Which Robert was the cheating gangster in *The Sting*?
10 In which decade did Christopher Reeve first play superhero Superman?
11 Burt Lancaster joined the US army after which major action in the Pacific?
12 Which Kathy played the villainous Annie in *Misery*?
13 Brigitte Bardot was awarded the freedom of which French city?
14 Which British actor played Claus von Bulow in *Reversal of Fortune*?
15 Mega-villain Hannibal Lecter appeared in which 1990s movie?
16 Who was 'Poison' in *Batman and Robin*?
17 Which James played Sonny Corleone in *The Godfather*?
18 Who was the villainous Joker in *Batman* in 1989?
19 Who wrote the novel on which *The Green Mile* was based?
20 Who played the Clintonesque character in *Primary Colors*?
21 Which villain did Danny DeVito play in a Batman movie?
22 In which movie did Arnold Schwarzenegger first say, 'I'll be back'?
23 Which Italian actress was jailed in 1962 for tax evasion?
24 John Hinckley shot Ronald Reagan because of his obsession with which former child star?
25 Which film director married the adopted daughter of his former partner?

**Answers Pot Luck 26** (see Quiz 65)
**1** Jack Nicholson. **2** Marilyn Monroe. **3** Carrey. **4** Dress in drag. **5** Whoopi Goldberg. **6** Bookshop. **7** Close. **8** 1990s. **9** Paul Newman and Robert Redford. **10** Stamp. **11** Innocent. **12** Prequel. **13** Costner. **14** Luke Skywalker. **15** Haley. **16** Louise. **17** Meryl Streep. **18** Demi Moore. **19** Horror. **20** Stewart. **21** 1970s. **22** *Saturday Night Fever*. **23** *Kids*. **24** 1970s. **25** Hanks.

## *QUIZ 68* POT LUCK 27 ........ LEVEL 1

*Answers – see page 78*

1 Which star actor was in *Pulp Fiction* and *Look Who's Talking*?
2 Which Gwyneth starred in *Emma*?
3 Which word goes before 'Attraction' in a Michael Douglas movie title?
4 In which decade was *Who Framed Roger Rabbit?* released?
5 Who sang the title song of 'Stand By Me'?
6 Which metal links 'Bullet' and 'Streak' to give two film titles?
7 Which Mel went classical and appeared as Hamlet?
8 In which film did a character named John Dunbar appear?
9 *A Fish Called Wanda* featured which Michael?
10 Which Katharine had both an on- and off-screen relationship with Spencer Tracy?
11 The song 'You Must Love Me' came from which movie?
12 In a Clint Eastwood title, which word follows 'Every Which Way But'?
13 Orson Welles' first film was about which 'Citizen'?
14 *Batman Forever, The Wedding Singer* and *Wayne's World 2* all feature which actress?
15 Which name completes the film title, *The Seventh Voyage of* ____?
16 Who played Sally Bowles in *Cabaret*?
17 Which Mr Ford starred in *The Empire Strikes Back*?
18 Which famous Tallulah tested for the role of Scarlett O'Hara?
19 Which woman's name connects with 'Sid' to give a film title?
20 Which plant was Uma Thurman's character named after in *Batman and Robin*?
21 Which Gillian starred in *The X-Files*?
22 Who directed the movie *Bram Stoker's Dracula*?
23 In which TV soap did Charlton Heston find fame after appearing on the big screen?
24 In which decade of the 20th century was Patrick Swayze born?
25 To the nearest hour, how long does the 60s movie *Cleopatra* last?

**Answers Animal Movies** (see Quiz 66)
**1** Champion. **2** Glenn Close **3** Pig. **4** Dog. **5** Elephant. **6** Dolittle. **7** He was cross-eyed. **8** They were cats. **9** Trigger. **10** *Jaws.* **11** Bloodhound. **12** Horses. **13** Dinosaurs. **14** Turtles. **15** 1990s. **16** Otter. **17** Bear. **18** *Tarzan.* **19** Willy. **20** Beethoven. **21** Coat. **22** Lions. **23** *The Lion King.* **24** Hound (of the Baskervilles). **25** Collie.

## *QUIZ 69* 1950s STARS ........ LEVEL 1

*Answers – see page 83*

1. Which aunt of George Clooney starred in *White Christmas*?
2. Who died in his car before his movie *Rebel Without a Cause* was released?
3. Which swashbuckling star, never far away from scandal, died in 1959?
4. Which blonde singer/actress first starred opposite Rock Hudson in *Pillow Talk*?
5. Which singer famous for his blue eyes starred in *From Here to Eternity*?
6. Who famously sang 'The Man that Got Away' in *A Star Is Born*?
7. Which Christopher first played Dracula in 1958?
8. Who, with Lady, was in the second most successful 50s movie?
9. Which Ben won most Oscars in the 1950s?
10. Which Jack was Oscar-nominated for *Some Like It Hot*?
11. Which Danny played Hans Christian Andersen in the 50s biopic?
12. Which star of horror movies starred in *The Fly*?
13. Which Kim appeared opposite James Stewart in *Vertigo*?
14. What was the nationality of Maurice Chevalier who starred in *Gigi*?
15. Which singer, real name Dino Crocetti, starred with John Wayne in *Rio Bravo*?
16. Who was the most famous blonde in *Gentlemen Prefer Blondes*?
17. Which Elizabeth was the *Cat on a Hot Tin Roof*?
18. Which Gregory won an Oscar for *To Kill a Mockingbird*?
19. What does Gene Kelly carry while he is *Singin' in the Rain*?
20. Which 50s star became Princess Grace of Monaco?
21. Which singer joined Frank Sinatra to be in *High Society*?
22. In which country was Sophia Loren born?
23. Which Doris played Calamity Jane?
24. Who did Charlton Heston play in *The Ten Commandments*?
25. Which pop idol appeared in *Jailhouse Rock*?

**Answers Pot Luck 28** (see Quiz 71)
**1** *All the President's Men.* **2** Hopkins. **3** 1950s. **4** *Buster.* **5** Bacall. **6** Johnny Depp. **7** *The Lost World.* **8** Kelly. **9** Norman Bates. **10** Carnal. **11** Chimney sweep. **12** Steve Martin. **13** Oprah Winfrey. **14** Emma Thompson. **15** Edinburgh. **16** Picnic. **17** *The Wizard of Oz.* **18** Zorro. **19** *Funny Girl.* **20** Johnny. **21** To Town. **22** *Carousel.* **23** England. **24** Bryan Adams. **25** 1980s.

## *QUIZ 70* OSCARS – WHO'S WHO? ........ LEVEL 1

*Answers – see page 84*

1 Who won Best Director for *Braveheart* which Mel Gibson starred in?
2 Who played the title role in *Evita* whose only Oscar was for the song 'You Must Love Me'?
3 Who was the youngest Oscar nominee at the year 2000 ceremony?
4 Who won Best Actress for *Kitty Foyle* after finding fame as Fred Astaire's dancing partner?
5 Who won a Special Oscar for Outstanding Contribution aged six?
6 Which cat and mouse won Best Short Cartoon in 1943?
7 Which Bob received an honorary award in 1952 for his contribution to comedy?
8 Who played Maria von Trapp in the highest-grossing Oscar-winning musical of the 1960s?
9 'The Madness of' which king earned a nomination for Alan Bennett?
10 Who refused to attend the Oscar ceremony to receive his Best Actor award for *The Godfather*?
11 For playing which Shirley was Pauline Collins Oscar-nominated?
12 Who won Best Supporting Actress for one of the Kramers?
13 Mickey Rooney won an honorary award in 1982 for two, three, four or five decades of movie making?
14 Who starred with Gromit in *A Close Shave*?
15 Which Extra Terrestrial won a Best Visual Effects award for its creators?
16 What sort of worker's daughter gave Sissy Spacek a 1980 Oscar?
17 In which decade did John Williams win for the score of *Star Wars*?
18 Who was Oscar-nominated for his first movie *Citizen Kane*?
19 Ingrid Bergman was a winner for 'Murder on' which luxury train?
20 Which moustache-wearing Marx won an honorary award in 1973?
21 Which George, famous for *Star Wars*, won a special award in 1991?
22 Which Steven directed *Schindler's List*?
23 Which Quentin contributed to the original screenplay of *Pulp Fiction*?
24 Whose 'Ragtime Band' was nominated in 1938?
25 Which shark movie won a music Oscar for composer John Williams?

**Answers 1980s** (see Quiz 72)
**1** *Arthur.* **2** Chelsea. **3** Private. **4** *Return of the Jedi.* **5** Wall Street. **6** Eastwick. **7** American. **8** China. **9** Lethal. **10** French. **11** Twins. **12** Vietnam. **13** *Superman II.* **14** Australia. **15** Three. **16** *9 to 5.* **17** Conan. **18** Twice. **19** Beverley Hills. **20** Cambodia (Kampuchea). **21** Blues Brothers. **22** Prizzi's. **23** Bull. **24** Susan. **25** The Empire.

## *QUIZ 71* POT LUCK 28 ........ LEVEL 1

*Answers – see page 81*

1 Reporters Woodward and Bernstein featured in which movie?
2 Which Anthony starred in *The Elephant Man*?
3 In which decade was *Room at the Top* released?
4 Which movie did the song 'A Groovy Kind of Love' come from?
5 Which Lauren was married to Humphrey Bogart?
6 *Edward Scissorhands* and *What's Eating Gilbert Grape?* both feature which actor?
7 What was Steven Spielberg's follow-up to *Jurassic Park* called?
8 Which Gene starred in *Singin' in the Rain*?
9 What is the name of the psychopath in *Psycho*?
10 Which word goes before 'Knowledge' in a Jack Nicholson movie title?
11 What was the profession of Dick van Dyke in *Mary Poppins*?
12 Which actor links *Parenthood* and *Father of the Bride*?
13 Which chat show presenter was Oscar-nominated for *The Color Purple*?
14 Who was the female star of *Junior*?
15 In which city was *Trainspotting* set?
16 In the movie title, what was held 'at Hanging Rock'?
17 Which musical movie features a dog called Toto?
18 Which hero left a trademark letter Z behind him?
19 Fanny Brice is a character in which 60s Barbra Streisand movie?
20 In a Michelle Pfeiffer movie title, who partnered Frankie?
21 Where does Mr Deeds go, according to the film title?
22 The song 'You'll Never Walk Alone' features in which musical movie?
23 In which country was Cary Grant born?
24 Who sang 'Everything I Do (I Do it for You)' in *Robin Hood: Prince of Thieves*?
25 In which decade was *Arthur* released?

**Answers 1950s Stars** (see Quiz 69)
**1** Rosemary Clooney. **2** James Dean. **3** Errol Flynn. **4** Doris Day. **5** Frank Sinatra. **6** Judy Garland. **7** Lee. **8** The Tramp. **9** *Ben Hur*. **10** Lemmon. **11** Kaye. **12** Vincent Price. **13** Novak. **14** French. **15** Dean Martin. **16** Marilyn Monroe. **17** Taylor. **18** Peck. **19** Umbrella. **20** Grace Kelly. **21** Bing Crosby. **22** Italy. **23** Day. **24** Moses. **25** Elvis Presley.

## *QUIZ 72* 1980s ............ LEVEL 1

*Answers – see page 82*

1 What was the name of the Dudley Moore movie where he played womanizer Arthur Bach?
2 Which daughter of Bill Clinton shares her name with Jane Fonda's character in *On Golden Pond*?
3 What rank was Goldie Hawn as army recruit Judy Benjamin?
4 The film originally called *Revenge of the Jedi* was changed to what?
5 On which famous financial New York thoroughfare does the movie with Michael Douglas and Charlie Sheen take place?
6 Where were 'The Witches' in the film with Michelle Pfeiffer and Cher?
7 What nationality 'Gigolo' was Richard Gere in 1980?
8 *The Last Emperor* is set in which now-communist Asian country?
9 What type of 'Weapon' did Mel Gibson wield in the movie with Danny Glover?
10 Which 18th century revolution was the setting for *Dangerous Liaisons*?
11 What close relations were Arnold Schwarzenegger and Danny De Vito in the 1988 hit movie?
12 Which country follows 'Good Morning' in the title of the Robin Williams movie?
13 What was the sequel to *Superman* called?
14 Crocodile Dundee comes to New York from which country?
15 How many men looked after the baby in the Tom Selleck hit of 1987?
16 Which hours were Jane Fonda and Dolly Parton working in 1980?
17 Who was 'the Barbarian' played by Arnold Schwarzenegger in 1981?
18 'The Postman Always Rings' how many times in the Jack Nicholson/Jessica Lange movie?
19 Where did Eddie Murphy's Detroit cop operate in the 1984 movie?
20 *The Killing Fields* were in which South-East Asian country?
21 What sort of 'Brothers' were Dan Aykroyd and John Belushi in 1980?
22 Which family's 'Honor' is the subject of a John Huston movie with Jack Nicholson and John's daughter Anjelica?
23 Jake La Motta's story was told in 'Raging' what?
24 A hit man is 'Desperately Seeking' whom in 1985?
25 What 'Strikes Back' in the sequel to *Star Wars*?

**Answers Oscars – Who's Who?** (see Quiz 70)
**1** Mel Gibson. **2** Madonna. **3** Haley Joel Osment. **4** Ginger Rogers. **5** Shirley Temple. **6** Tom & Jerry. **7** Hope. **8** Julie Andrews. **9** George. **10** Marlon Brando. **11** Valentine. **12** Meryl Streep. **13** Five. **14** Wallace. **15** *E.T.* **16** *The Coal Miner's Daughter*. **17** 1970s. **18** Orson Welles. **19** Orient Express. **20** Groucho. **21** Lucas. **22** Spielberg. **23** Tarantino. **24** Alexander's. **25** *Jaws*.

## *QUIZ 73* POT LUCK 29 ........ LEVEL 1

*Answers – see page 87*

1 What colour was Uma Thurman's hair in *Pulp Fiction*?
2 In which decade was *Doctor Zhivago* released?
3 Which Rob starred in *Wayne's World*?
4 Who is the central character in *Good Will Hunting*?
5 *Face/Off, Snake Eyes* and *Honeymoon in Vegas* all feature which actor?
6 W. C. Dunkenfield kept his first two initials to become who?
7 Which Hitchcock-directed movie had 'Window' in the title?
8 Which John starred in *The Blues Brothers*?
9 In a musical movie, which number links brides and brothers?
10 Which 1998 movie featured a giant lizard and Matthew Broderick?
11 Which actor was the father of Jeff and Beau Bridges?
12 Which actress Jane married CNN chief Ted Turner?
13 In which animated film does Shere Khan appear?
14 How many millimetres was the standard film gauge width?
15 What was the nationality of Ingrid Bergman?
16 *Lady Sings the Blues* told the life of which Billie?
17 Which Ralph was an *English Patient* Oscar nominee?
18 In which decade was *Indiana Jones and the Last Crusade* released?
19 Who was the male lead in *Casablanca*?
20 Which Hepburn had a cameo role in Spielberg's *Always*?
21 Which Antonio starred in *Evita*?
22 Does *The Color Purple* last between 1 and 2, 2 and 3, or 3 and 4 hours?
23 Who played the lead role in *Lawrence of Arabia* after Albert Finney turned it down?
24 *Look Who's Talking Too* was a sequel to which movie?
25 In which decade of the 20th century was Kurt Russell born?

**Answers Robert Redford** (see Quiz 75)
**1** Baseball. **2** Johnson. **3** Ross. **4** Ordinary. **5** Las Vegas. **6** Three. **7** Utah. **8** *Butch Cassidy and the Sundance Kid.* **9** Africa. **10** California. **11** Streisand. **12** 1970s. **13** Horse. **14** Nixon. **15** 1930s. **16** Demi. **17** Personal. **18** Tyler Moore. **19** The Sundance Kid. **20** *Washington Post.* **21** *The Great Gatsby.* **22** Blond. **23** Park. **24** *Quiz Show.* **25** Eagles.

## *QUIZ 74* FAMOUS NAMES ........ LEVEL 1

*Answers – see page 88*

1 Which Michael won the Best Actor Oscar for *Wall Street*?
2 Who did Stanley Kaufmann say should be called Barbra Strident?
3 What is the name of Casey Affleck's actor brother?
4 Who was Shirley MacLaine named after?
5 Which surname was shared by dad Lloyd and sons Beau and Jeff?
6 Which 'Poison' plant name did Uma Thurman have in *Batman and Robin*?
7 Which Richard played the Spice Girls' manager in *Spiceworld: The Movie*?
8 Who played his namesake Woody Boyd in *Cheers*?
9 How is Mary Elizabeth Spacek better known?
10 Who did Al Pacino play in *Frankie and Johnny*?
11 What was the name of Jane Fonda's actor father?
12 Which Elizabeth – as famous for her frocks as for her films – starred in *Austin Powers, International Man of Mystery*?
13 How is Edward Bridge Danson III better known?
14 Which Daniel won an Oscar for *My Left Foot* in 1989?
15 What is the name of the actress daughter of actor Bruce Dern?
16 Which Danny, of *Junior* and *Twins* fame, married Rhea Perlman?
17 In which decade of the 20th century was Tom Cruise born?
18 What colour did Yul Brynner wear for the last 40 years of his life, to make shopping easier?
19 Who did Vanessa Redgrave play in the biopic *Agatha*?
20 What was the first name of Abbott, of Abbott and Costello fame?
21 Which Rebecca was the nanny from hell in *The Hand that Rocks the Cradle*?
22 In which country was Catherine Deneuve born?
23 How is Alicia Foster better know?
24 Which surname is shared by actors Rosanna, Patricia, David and Alexis?
25 At what sport did Arnold Schwarzenegger excel?

**Answers Pot Luck 30** (see Quiz 76)
**1** Steven Spielberg. **2** Scott Thomas. **3** 1970s. **4** Elvis Presley. **5** Mary Shelley. **6** Dalmatians. **7** Humphrey Bogart. **8** Meg Ryan. **9** Dr Dolittle. **10** B. **11** The Riddler. **12** *Romeo and Juliet.* **13** *Nashville.* **14** Al Pacino. **15** *The Boston Strangler.* **16** 2001. **17** Keaton. **18** Itch. **19** Body builder. **20** Prisoner (*The Prisoner of Zenda*). **21** 1960s. **22** *Mad Max Beyond The Thunderdome.* **23** John Travolta. **24** Nanny. **25** Barrymore.

## *QUIZ 75* ROBERT REDFORD ........ LEVEL 1

*Answers – see page 85*

1 Robert Redford won a university scholarship in which American sport?
2 Which Jeremiah was the subject of a 1972 film?
3 Which Katharine was a co-star in *Butch Cassidy*?
4 What sort of 'People' were in the title of his directorial debut in 1980?
5 In which gambling capital is *Indecent Proposal* set?
6 How many 'Days of the Condor' were in the title of the 1975 film?
7 In which state, capital Salt Lake City, is his Sundance Institute?
8 In which movie with Paul Newman did Redford first find fame?
9 He was 'Out of' where in the 1985 movie with Meryl Streep?
10 Redford was born in Santa Monica in which west-coast state?
11 Which Barbra played opposite Redford in *The Way We Were*?
12 In which decade did he make *The Candidate*?
13 Which animal is named in the 'Whisperer' title of his 1998 success?
14 In *All the President's Men* which President is being referred to?
15 In which decade of the Depression was *The Sting* set?
16 To which Moore did he make an *Indecent Proposal* in 1993?
17 In 1996 Redford was 'Up Close and' what in the movie?
18 Which Mary did he direct in *Ordinary People*?
19 In *Butch Cassidy and the Sundance Kid* which part did Redford play?
20 In *All the President's Men* the journalists worked for which Washington newspaper?
21 Which 1974 movie saw him as Jay Gatsby?
22 What colour is Redford's hair?
23 Redford was 'Barefoot in the' what in the movie with Jane Fonda based on a Neil Simon play?
24 What sort of 'Show 'earned him an Oscar-nomination in 1994?
25 Which 'Legal' birds were in the title of his 1986 movie?

**Answers Pot Luck 29** (see Quiz 73)
**1** Black. **2** 1960s. **3** Lowe. **4** Will Hunting. **5** Nicolas Cage. **6** W. C. Fields. **7** *Rear Window*. **8** Belushi. **9** Seven (*Seven Brides for Seven Brothers*). **10** *Godzilla*. **11** Lloyd Bridges. **12** Fonda. **13** *Jungle Book*. **14** 35. **15** Swedish. **16** Holliday. **17** Fiennes. **18** 1980s. **19** Humphrey Bogart. **20** Audrey. **21** Banderas. **22** 2 and 3. **23** Peter O'Toole. **24** *Look Who's Talking*. **25** 1950s.

## *QUIZ 76* POT LUCK 30 ........ LEVEL 1

*Answers – see page 86*

1 Who directed *Schindler's List*?
2 Which Kristin starred in *The Horse Whisperer*?
3 In which decade was *Moonraker* released?
4 Who sang the title song of *Jailhouse Rock*?
5 Which writer created the character Frankenstein?
6 In a movie title there were 101 what?
7 Who won the Best Actor Oscar for *The African Queen*?
8 Which star actress was in *When Harry Met Sally*, *Courage Under Fire* and *French Kiss*?
9 The song 'Talk to the Animals' features in which movie?
10 Which initial featured in Cecil de Mille's name?
11 In *Batman Forever* which villain was played by Jim Carrey?
12 Which 90s film of a Shakespeare play starred Leonardo DiCaprio?
13 Which 70s film was also the name a Tennessee town famous for its music?
14 Which Al won Best Actor Oscar for *Scent of a Woman*?
15 The character Albert DeSalvo appeared in which murder movie?
16 What year was 'A Space Odyssey' for Stanley Kubrick?
17 Which Michael starred in *Batman Returns*?
18 Marilyn Monroe starred in 'The Seven Year' what?
19 What did Arnold Schwarzeneger play in *Stay Hungry*?
20 In a movie title, what type of person was found in Zenda?
21 In which decade of the 20th century was Keanu Reeves born?
22 Which mid 80s film did rock star Tina Turner star in?
23 *Saturday Night Fever*, *Get Shorty* and *Phenomenon* all feature which actor?
24 What was the profession of Mrs Doubtfire?
25 Which Drew starred in *E.T.*?

**Answers Famous Names** (see Quiz 74)
**1** Douglas. **2** Barbra Streisand. **3** Ben. **4** Shirley Temple. **5** Bridges. **6** Ivy. **7** E. Grant. **8** Woody Harrelson. **9** Sissy Spacek. **10** Johnny. **11** Henry. **12** Hurley. **13** Ted Danson. **14** Day-Lewis. **15** Laura Dern. **16** DeVito. **17** 1960s. **18** Black. **19** Agatha Christie. **20** Bud. **21** De Mornay. **22** France. **23** Jodie Foster. **24** Arquette. **25** Weightlifting.

## *QUIZ 77* BOX OFFICE SUCCESSES ........ LEVEL 1

*Answers – see page 91*

1 What was the highest grossing film of the 1990s?
2 Who wrote the first *Rocky* movie as well as starring in it?
3 Which member of the Sheen family was Bud Fox in *Wall Street*?
4 Which 1977 smash hit was re-released 20 years later?
5 *Goodfellas* was about which organization?
6 *Babe* was the tale of a pig which wanted to be a what?
7 Which Cecil directed *The Greatest Show on Earth*?
8 Which British Bob found himself with a cartoon rabbit co-star in 1988?
9 Which Tom Hanks movie was the fourth most successful in the US in 1994?
10 Which 'Day' took $104.3 million in its first week in 1996?
11 Which Spielberg war movie was the most successful of the 1990s?
12 The *Men in Black* operated in which city?
13 Who wrote the George Lucas-directed *Star Wars*?
14 Which movie about the Kennedy assassination has just three letters in its title?
15 Which film set in Africa was Disney's most successful ever when it was released in 1994?
16 R2-D2 and C-3PO were in which film series?
17 *The Longest Day* was about which landings?
18 Which 1930s movie has been showing in Atlanta ever since it was released?
19 What colour suit did John Travolta wear in the disco in *Saturday Night Fever*?
20 Which character looks back in *Titanic*?
21 Lara's Theme was from which movie set in Russia?
22 Which Robert Altman movie was a smash, though set in the dark days of the Korean War?
23 Which movie included 'A Spoonful of Sugar' and 'Feed the Birds'?
24 Which Newman/Redford hit used Scott Joplin ragtime tunes?
25 Sensurround was used to add impact to which natural disaster movie?

**Answers Pot Luck 31** (see Quiz 79)
**1** Jerry Hall. **2** Travolta. **3** *Meaning.* **4** *The Mask of Zorro.* **5** *Notting Hill.* **6** Lange. **7** Newman. **8** Joe. **9** Newton-John. **10** Eddie Murphy. **11** 30s. **12** The Marx Brothers. **13** 1960s. **14** 1990s **15** Drew Barrymore. **16** Sunrise. **17** Sean Connery. **18** Mel Brooks. **19** The Oscars. **20** Meryl Streep. **21** France. **22** Rose. **23** Shot him (*The Man Who Shot Liberty Valance*). **24** Nimoy. **25** 1960s.

## *QUIZ 78* SCI-FI ........ LEVEL 1

*Answers – see page 92*

1 Which actor Reeves starred in *Bill and Ted's Excellent Adventure*?
2 What sort of creatures run amok in *Jurassic Park*?
3 *E.T.* arrived in a suburb of which Californian city?
4 Where were Gary Oldman and William Hurt 'Lost' in 1998?
5 Which Bruce faced *Armageddon* in 1998?
6 Which 1998 movie featured TV's Mulder and Scully?
7 What sort of giant reptile was Godzilla?
8 Which special day in the USA was the subject of a 1996 movie with Will Smith?
9 Which Judge was played by Sylvester Stallone in 1995?
10 Which Rick 'Shrunk the Kids'?
11 'Close Encounters of' which kind were a 1977 Spielberg success?
12 What was the name of the Princess in *Star Wars*?
13 'The Planet of' which creatures starred Charlton Heston in 1968?
14 The time-travelling hero of the *Highlander* movies came from which part of the UK?
15 *Aliens* was the sequel to which 1979 movie?
16 Which pop superstar David starred in *Labyrinth*?
17 In which decade was *Jurassic Park* released?
18 Which 1985 Terry Gilliam movie takes its name from a South American country famous for its coffee?
19 Which 'Runner' starred Harrison Ford?
20 Which Barrymore played Gertie in *E.T.*?
21 Which Lois is played by Margot Kidder in *Superman*?
22 Tommy Lee Jones and Will Smith were 'Men in' what colour?
23 In which 'Motion Picture' did Mr Spock get a big-screen outing?
24 What colour is Superman's cape in the movies with Christopher Reeve?
25 Which Matthew played Dr Niko Tatopoulos in *Godzilla*?

**Answers 1970s Stars** (see Quiz 80)
**1** Bo Derek. **2** Reynolds. **3** Carrie Fisher. **4** Clint Eastwood. **5** Mental hospital. **6** *Jaws 2*. **7** Ross. **8** Lee. **9** Sutherland. **10** Harvey. **11** McQueen. **12** Marlon Brando. **13** Dustin Hoffman. **14** Woody Allen. **15** Superman. **16** Taxi. **17** Newton-John **18** Tatum O'Neal. **19** Martin. **20** Australia **21** De Niro. **22** Sigourney Weaver. **23** Monty Python. **24** Michael Douglas. **25** Moore.

## *QUIZ 79* POT LUCK 31 ........ LEVEL 1

*Answers – see page 89*

1 Which former partner of Mick Jagger appeared in *Batman*?
2 Which John starred in *Face/Off*?
3 Which word completes the film title, *Monty Python's the ____ of Life*?
4 Which Zorro film was released in 1998?
5 What was Richard Curtis's next Hugh Grant movie after *Four Weddings and a Funeral*?
6 Which Jessica starred in *Tootsie*?
7 Which Randy wrote the music for *James and the Giant Peach*?
8 Who was 'Versus the Volcano' in a Meg Ryan movie?
9 Which Olivia, star of *Grease*, appeared in the less successful *Xanadu*?
10 *The Nutty Professor* and *Doctor Dolittle* both feature which actor?
11 Was Irving Thalberg in his 20s, 30s or 40s when he died in the 1930s?
12 Which brothers enjoyed *A Night at the Opera*?
13 In which decade of the 20th century was Meg Ryan born?
14 In which decade was *Terminator 2: Judgment Day* released?
15 Which actress links *E.T.* and *Scream*?
16 Which word follows 'Tequila' in a Michelle Pfeiffer movie title?
17 Which former 007 played a Scottish villain in *The Avengers*?
18 Who directed *Blazing Saddles*?
19 What is the popular name of the annual awards presented by the Academy of Motion Picture Arts and Sciences?
20 Who played the female lead in *Sophie's Choice*?
21 In *The Pink Panther*, Peter Sellers is an inspector in which country?
22 Ingrid Bergman and Judy Garland have had what type of flower named after them?
23 What did the man do to Liberty Valance, according to the film title?
24 Which Leonard starred in *Star Trek: The Motion Picture*?
25 In which decade was *Bullitt* released?

**Answers Box Office Successes** (see Quiz 77)
**1** *Titanic.* **2** Sylvester Stallone. **3** Charlie. **4** *Star Wars.* **5** The Mafia. **6** Sheepdog. **7** B. de Mille. **8** Hoskins. **9** *Forrest Gump.* **10** *Independence Day.* **11** *Saving Private Ryan.* **12** New York. **13** George Lucas. **14** *JFK.* **15** *The Lion King.* **16** *Star Wars.* **17** D-Day Landings. **18** *Gone with the Wind.* **19** White. **20** Rose. **21** *Dr Zhivago.* **22** *M*A*S*H.* **23** *Mary Poppins.* **24** *The Sting.* **25** *Earthquake.*

## *QUIZ 80* 1970s STARS ........ LEVEL 1

*Answers – see page 90*

1 Which actress starred in *10* with Dudley Moore?
2 Which Burt was a 70s hit star but filed for bankruptcy 20 years later?
3 Which daughter of Eddie Fisher and Debbie Reynolds found fame in *Star Wars*?
4 Which star of spaghetti westerns appeared as *The Outlaw Josey Wales*?
5 In what type of hospital is *One Flew over the Cuckoo's Nest* set?
6 What was the sequel to *Jaws* called?
7 Which Supreme Diana starred in *Lady Sings the Blues*?
8 Which horror movie star Christopher played Scaramanga in *The Man with the Golden Gun*?
9 Which Donald, father of Kiefer, played opposite Julie Christie in *Don't Look Now*?
10 What is the first name of Mr Keitel who played Charlie in *Mean Streets*?
11 Which Steve starred opposite future real-life wife Ali McGraw in *Getaway*?
12 Who played the head of the Corleone family in *The Godfather*?
13 Which actor suffers in the dentist's chair in *Marathon Man*?
14 Which bespectacled American directed and starred in *Annie Hall*?
15 Which cartoon character was played by Christopher Reeve?
16 What type of 'Driver' was Robert De Niro in 1976?
17 Which Olivia played Sandy in *Grease*?
18 Which child star was dubbed 'Tantrum' O'Neal?
19 Which member of the Sheen family starred in *Apocalypse Now* in '79?
20 In which country was US-born Mel Gibson brought up?
21 Which New Yorker Robert famously said, 'You talkin' to me?'?
22 Who was the lead actress in *Alien*?
23 Which comedy team which included John Cleese made the *Life Of Brian*?
24 Which son of actor Kirk starred in *The China Syndrome*?
25 Which Roger was the most frequent James Bond in the 70s?

**Answers Sci-Fi** (see Quiz 78)
**1** Keanu. **2** Dinosaurs. **3** Los Angeles. **4** Space. **5** Willis. **6** *The X-Files*. **7** Lizard. **8** *Independence Day*. **9** Dredd. **10** Moranis. **11** The Third Kind. **12** Leia. **13** The Apes. **14** Scotland. **15** *Alien*. **16** Bowie. **17** 1990s. **18** *Brazil*. **19** *Blade Runner*. **20** Drew. **21** Lane. **22** Black. **23** *Star Trek*. **24** Red. **25** Broderick.

## *QUIZ 81* POT LUCK 32 ........ LEVEL 1

*Answers – see page 95*

1 Which Anne starred in the 1998 *Great Expectations*?
2 *The Witches of Eastwick* and *Up Close and Personal* both feature which actress?
3 Which Shirley won an Oscar at the age of five?
4 In which show is Mr Burbank a popular character?
5 Which word follows 'Last Action' in a Sharon Stone movie title?
6 What is the nationality of Brigitte Nielsen, Sylvester Stallone's second wife?
7 Which Joe starred in *Home Alone*?
8 What is the name of the male cub in *The Lion King*?
9 Marni Nixon dubbed whose singing voice in *My Fair Lady*?
10 Which word follows 'Dog Day' in an Al Pacino movie title?
11 Which Gary starred in *High Noon*?
12 Which crime writer did Vanessa Redgrave play in *Agatha*?
13 Which Richard starred in *Close Encounters of the Third Kind*?
14 The song 'If I Were a Rich Man' features in which musical movie?
15 In which decade was *Raiders of the Lost Ark* released?
16 Commandant Goeth appears in which movie?
17 Which superhero gets involved with Lois Laine?
18 Which actress links *The Rose* and *Get Shorty*?
19 *Braveheart* was set in which country?
20 Which Donald starred in *Halloween*?
21 Who played the lead role in *My Fair Lady* after Cary Grant refused it?
22 Which actress co-launched the Planet Hollywood restaurant chain?
23 Which word completes the film title *The Shawshank* ____?
24 In which decade of the 20th century was Roger Moore born?
25 Which Sally featured in *Forrest Gump*?

**Answers Musicals** (see Quiz 83)
**1** Argentina. **2** Travolta. **3** Gene. **4** Penguins. **5** Pink Floyd. **6** *West Side Story.* **7** *Grease.* **8** *The Rocky Horror Picture Show.* **9** *Paint Your Wagon.* **10** Louis Armstrong. **11** John Travolta. **12** Yellow. **13** Omar Sharif. **14** The Beatles. **15** *Calamity Jane.* **16** *Mary Poppins.* **17** *The King and I.* **18** New York. **19** Harrison. **20** Maurice Chevalier. **21** Austria. **22** *Funny Girl.* **23** Ross. **24** Show Business. **25** The Bee Gees.

## *QUIZ 82* CHARLIE CHAPLIN ............ LEVEL 1

*Answers – see page 96*

1 Chaplin said all he needed to make a movie was a park, a policeman and a pretty what?
2 What type of hat did the Little Tramp wear?
3 Which company famous for its crazy cops was Chaplin invited to join?
4 What was the first name of Mr Karno, with whose troupe Chaplin first went to the USA?
5 What was Chaplin's middle name, shared by Winston Churchill?
6 Which Mack first employed Chaplin in the movies?
7 Chaplin's debut movie was called 'Making a' what?
8 Which United company did he found in 1919 with three other stars of the silent movie era?
9 Which 'Rush' did he film in 1925?
10 Which actress Paulette did he marry in 1933?
11 Of his four wives, how many were in their teens when he married them?
12 Where was Chaplin referring to when he said 'I'd never go back there if Jesus Christ was President.'?
13 What was the name of the biopic directed by Richard Attenborough?
14 'A Countess from' where was the title of a 60s Chaplin movie?
15 Who wrote most of the musical score for *City Lights*?
16 *The Great Dictator* was made during which conflict?
17 Which Buster teamed up with Chaplin in *Limelight*?
18 What relation is actress Geraldine Chaplin to Charlie?
19 In which decade of the 20th century did Chaplin die at the age of 88?
20 Which 'Modern' film was a satire on the industrialization of society?
21 In which British city was Chaplin born?
22 Which name is shared by his half-brother and his son – both performers?
23 Which member of his family played the part of his mother in the 1992 movie about his life?
24 What did the Tramp carry and twirl in his hand?
25 His fourth wife Oona O'Neill was the daughter of which playwright?

**Answers Pot Luck 33** (see Quiz 84)
**1** Arnold Schwarzenegger. **2** The Muppets. **3** Foster. **4** *America*. **5** New York. **6** 'Colors of the Wind'. **7** *Waterworld*. **8** Field. **9** Lon Chaney. **10** A London tube train. **11** Barbra Streisand. **12** Francis Ford Coppola. **13** King Arthur. **14** Dead. **15** TV journalist. **16** In Paris. **17** Brooks. **18** 1960s. **19** Astaire. **20** Marilyn Monroe. **21** Nicholson. **22** 'Goldeneye'. **23** The Righteous Brothers. **24** 1970s. **25** The Flintstones.

## *QUIZ 83* MUSICALS ........ LEVEL 1

*Answers – see page 93*

1 In which country does the action of *Evita* take place?
2 Which John starred in *Grease* in 1978?
3 Which Kelly directed *Hello Dolly*?
4 Which Antarctic creatures feature in *Mary Poppins*?
5 Which 'Pink' band made the movie *The Wall*?
6 In which movie based on *Romeo and Juliet* did Richard Beymer play Tony?
7 Which movie featured the song 'Greased Lightning'?
8 In which 'Picture Show' does Frank N. Furter appear?
9 In which western musical did Lee Marvin sing 'Wandrin' Star'?
10 Which jazz trumpeter nicknamed Satchmo appeared in *High Society*?
11 Who played Tony Manero in *Saturday Night Fever*?
12 What colour submarine was a Beatles classic?
13 Which bridge-playing actor played Mr Arnstein in *Funny Girl*?
14 Which 60s pop band's second movie was *Help!*?
15 'Secret Love' won Best Song Oscar from which 'Calamity' film?
16 'Chim Chim Cheree' came from which movie about a super-nanny?
17 Which musical was banned in Thailand for most of the latter half of the 20th century?
18 *West Side Story* takes place on the west side of which city?
19 Which Rex reprised his Broadway role as Professor Higgins in the movie *My Fair Lady*?
20 Which French star wrote an autobiography called *I Remember It Well*?
21 *The Sound of Music* was set in which country?
22 Which 1968 film with Barbra Streisand was about Fanny Brice?
23 Which Diana played Dorothy in *The Wiz*?
24 According to Irving Berlin's musical 'There's No Business Like' what?
25 Which pop brothers wrote the music for *Saturday Night Fever*?

**Answers Pot Luck 32** (see Quiz 81)
**1** Bancroft. **2** Michelle Pfeiffer. **3** Temple. **4** *The Truman Show.* **5** Hero. **6** Danish. **7** Pesci. **8** Simba. **9** Audrey Hepburn's. **10** Afternoon. **11** Cooper. **12** Agatha Christie. **13** Dreyfuss. **14** *Fiddler on the Roof.* **15** 1980s. **16** *Schindler's List.* **17** Superman. **18** Bette Midler. **19** Scotland. **20** Pleasance. **21** Rex Harrison. **22** Demi Moore. **23** *Redemption.* **24** 1920s. **25** Field.

## *QUIZ 84* POT LUCK 33 ........ LEVEL 1

*Answers – see page 94*

1 *Eraser, The Terminator* and *Last Action Hero* all feature which actor?
2 Which band of puppets featured in their own *Christmas Carol*?
3 Which Jodie starred in *Silence of the Lambs*?
4 Which country completes the film title, *Once Upon a Time in* ___?
5 In which city was Robert De Niro a sinister *Taxi Driver*?
6 Which song won Best Song Oscar for *Pocahontas*?
7 In which ill-fated movie did Kevin Kostner play Mariner?
8 Which Sally featured in *Smokey and the Bandit*?
9 Which horror film actor was nicknamed 'the man of a thousand faces'?
10 In *Sliding Doors* the sliding doors were part of what?
11 Who got her first starring role in *Funny Girl*?
12 Who won the Best Director Oscar for *The Godfather, Part II*?
13 The film musical *Camelot* involves which King?
14 In a movie title which word goes in front of 'Poets' Society'?
15 What was the profession of Schwarzenegger's wife?
16 In a movie title, where did the 'Last Tango' take place?
17 Which director Mel did Anne Bancroft marry?
18 In which decade of the 20th century was Eddie Murphy born?
19 Which famous movie Fred is on the cover of *Sergeant Pepper*?
20 Who was the most famous blonde in *Gentlemen Prefer Blondes*?
21 Which Jack starred in *A Few Good Men*?
22 What was the Bond theme for *Goldeneye* called?
23 Who sang 'Unchained Melody' in *Ghost*?
24 In which decade was *Love Story* released?
25 Which family lives in Bedrock?

**Answers Charlie Chaplin** (see Quiz 82)
**1** Girl. **2** Bowler. **3** Keystone. **4** Fred. **5** Spencer. **6** Sennett. **7** Living. **8** United Artists. **9** *The Gold Rush.* **10** Goddard. **11** All four. **12** America. **13** *Chaplin.* **14** Hong Kong. **15** Chaplin himself. **16** World War II. **17** Keaton. **18** Daughter. **19** 1970s. **20** *Modern Times.* **21** London. **22** Sydney. **23** His daughter Geraldine. **24** Cane. **25** Eugene O'Neill.

## *QUIZ 85* OSCARS – BEST ACTRESSES ........ LEVEL 1

*Answers – see page 99*

1 Which Katharine won most Best Actress Oscars in the 20th century?
2 Which Gwyneth dissolved in tears at the 1998 ceremony?
3 Which Jessica was the oldest Best Actress of the 20th century?
4 What was the first 1990s movie which made Jodie Foster a winner?
5 Which pop star won with *Moonstruck*?
6 Whose 'Choice' made Meryl Streep a 1982 winner?
7 Which Kathy played the crazed fan from hell in *Misery*?
8 Which British politician Glenda won two Oscars?
9 Which child star won a special award in 1934 aged six?
10 Which daughter of Ryan O'Neal was the first 10-year-old to win a Best Supporting award in her own right?
11 Which daughter of Judy Garland won for *Cabaret* in 1972?
12 In which decade did Louise Fletcher win for *One Flew Over the Cuckoo's Nest*?
13 Which Jane won twice in the 70s for *Klute* and *Coming Home*?
14 Was Katharine Hepburn in her 50s, 60s, 70s or 80s when she won for *On Golden Pond*?
15 Which star of *Sister Act* was Best Supporting Actress for *Ghost*?
16 In *Dead Man Walking* what was Susan Sarandon's profession?
17 How many times was Jodie Foster Best Supporting Actress in the 90s?
18 Who won for her title role in *Mary Poppins*?
19 Which Ellen was a winner for *Alice Doesn't Live Here Any More*?
20 Which musical instrument gave Holly Hunter a 1993 award?
21 What colour 'Sky' was the title of Jessica Lange's 1994 winner?
22 What is the nationality of Juliette Binoche, a winner for *The English Patient*?
23 Who got a Best Actress Oscar in the 90s without speaking?
24 Which member of the Huston dynasty won Best Supporting role for *Prizzi's Honor*?
25 For which movie did Vivien Leigh win Best Actress and Hattie McDaniel win Best Supporting Actress?

**Answers Pot Luck 34** (see Quiz 87)
**1** Gwyneth Paltrow. **2** Foster. **3** 1960s. **4** A nun. **5** Francis Ford Coppola. **6** Humphrey Bogart. **7** Bank clerk. **8** Bridget. **9** Elizabeth I. **10** Pierce Brosnan. **11** *Annie Get Your Gun.* **12** Archaeologist. **13** Instinct. **14** Tatum O'Neal. **15** Turtles. **16** Madonna. **17** Willis. **18** Jodie Foster. **19** 1960s. **20** Her hair. **21** Stephen Fry. **22** His valet. **23** James Cagney. **24** George Clooney. **25** *Wax.*

## *QUIZ 86* STARS OF THE SILENT YEARS ........................ LEVEL 1

*Answers – see page 100*

1 How was Alonzo Chaney, the man with a thousand faces, better known?
2 Which Mary was one of the first female film stars?
3 Which child star Jackie starred with Chaplin in *The Kid*?
4 Where was Rudolph Valentino born?
5 What was the first name of British-born actor Colman?
6 What was the surname of Pearl who appeared in *The Perils of Pauline*?
7 What was larger-than-life Roscoe Arbuckle's nickname?
8 What was the first name of actor Von Stroheim?
9 Although born in Canada, Mary Pickford was known as which country's sweetheart?
10 What was the surname of John, Ethel and Lionel?
11 How was Joseph Francis Keaton better known?
12 Which United company did Chaplin, Griffith, Fairbanks and Pickford found?
13 What type of star was Rin Tin Tin?
14 Which John partnered Garbo on and off screen?
15 Which Clara was called the 'It' Girl?
16 Which Charlie was discovered by Mack Sennett?
17 Which part of the skyscraper tower did Harold Lloyd hang from in the famous *Safety Last*?
18 Which Mack helped set up the Keystone Company?
19 Which master of animation founded Laugh O Gram Films in 1922?
20 What was the first name of the high-living actress Miss Normand?
21 Which Joan made her screen debut in 1925?
22 Who was born Greta Louisa Gustaffson?
23 Which Douglas made his screen debut in 1915?
24 Which Stan and Ollie graduated to sound after success in the silent era?
25 What was the first name of Miss Gish who starred in *The White Sister*?

**Answers 1990s** (see Quiz 88)
**1** Will. **2** *Ace Ventura.* **3** Fortune. **4** Louise. **5** Robin Hood. **6** Dracula. **7** Swayze. **8** Dogs. **9** *Jurassic Park.* **10** Indecent. **11** Seattle. **12** World War II. **13** *Peter Pan.* **14** Roberts. **15** Antonio Banderas. **16** Innocent. **17** Elizabeth. **18** *Terminator 2.* **19** President Kennedy. **20** *Look Who's Talking Too.* **21** Addams family. **22** Scissorhands. **23** Tomatoes. **24** The Edge. **25** *The Doors.*

## *QUIZ 55* POT LUCK 22 .................................................... LEVEL 1

*Answers – see page 65*

1 Which Juliette starred in *Natural Born Killers*?
2 Which word completes the film title *Single White* ___?
3 Which Gwyneth starred in the 1998 *Great Expectations*?
4 The song 'Oh What a Beautiful Morning' features in which musical movie?
5 Which actor links *Beverly Hills Cop, Harlem Nights* and *Boomerang*?
6 Which Gregory starred in *The Omen*?
7 Which 70s Agatha Christie movie was about a murder on a train?
8 Which number completes the film title *Slaughterhouse* ___?
9 Which Sylvester starred in *Judge Dredd*?
10 Which friend of Fred Flintstone was played by Rick Moranis?
11 *City Slickers* starred which Billy?
12 Which Richard starred in *An Officer and a Gentleman*?
13 In which decade was Disney's *Jungle Book* released?
14 Which *Grease* and *Saturday Night Fever* actor is a qualified pilot?
15 Which word follows 'The Age of' in a Michelle Pfeiffer movie title?
16 Which Diane starred in *The Godfather*?
17 Whose black bra made £4,600 at auction in 1997?
18 Which Annie features in a Woody Allen movie title?
19 Which Holly won the Best Actress Oscar for *The Piano*?
20 What metal are 'Magnolias' made from, according to the film title?
21 In which decade of the 20th century was Richard Gere born?
22 How many Mr Olympia titles did Arnold Schwarzenegger win – five, seven or nine?
23 Which star actress was in *Mermaids, Little Women* and *Alien:Resurrection*?
24 How was Ruth Elizabeth Davis better known?
25 Which Kevin starred in *Wild Things*?

**Answers Film Companies** (see Quiz 53)
**1** Goldwyn. **2** Disney. **3** Radio. **4** 20th Century Fox. **5** Cohn. **6** Pickford. **7** Chaplin. **8** *E.T.*. **9** Warner Brothers (to make Time Warner). **10** British Lion. **11** Rupert Murdoch. **12** Burt Lancaster. **13** George Harrison. **14** Spielberg. **15** Warner Brothers. **16** Horror. **17** Metro. **18** Lion. **19** *Toy Story*. **20** Sony. **21** Hughes. **22** Louis. **23** Ealing. **24** Zanuck. **25** Four.

## *QUIZ 56* 1940s STARS ........ LEVEL 1

*Answers – see page 66*

1 The Margarita cocktail was named after which Rita, as it was her real first name?
2 In which country was Cary Grant born?
3 Which dancing partner of Fred Astaire won an Oscar for *Kitty Foyle*?
4 Which comedian was Bing Crosby paired with in the *Road* movies?
5 Which Spencer was both Jekyll and Hyde in the 1941 movie?
6 Which Fonda appeared in *The Grapes of Wrath*?
7 If Humphrey Bogart played Rick, who played Ilsa in a 40s classic?
8 Which future politician became president of the Screen Actors Guild?
9 Which western star was nicknamed Duke?
10 Who teamed with Abbott to make them a top money-making duo of the 40s?
11 Which Bette's tombstone said, 'She did it the hard way'?
12 Which Porter did Cary Grant play in *Night and Day*?
13 Which Carole, then Mrs Clark Gable, died in a plane crash in 1942?
14 What sort of organic items did Carmen Miranda wear on her head?
15 Which James, more famous for gangster roles, played George M. Cohan in *Yankee Doodle Dandy*?
16 In which country was Ingrid Bergman born?
17 Who married Lauren Bacall after making *To Have and Have Not* with her?
18 Which dancer, famous for *Top Hat*, appeared with Bing Crosby in *Holiday Inn*?
19 Which Elizabeth played aspiring jockey Velvet Brown in *National Velvet*?
20 What type of role does Bing Crosby play in *The Bells of St Mary's*?
21 Which Katharine played Tracy Lord in *The Philadelphia Story*?
22 Which first name was shared by Mitchum and Taylor?
23 Rita Hayworth was best known for having what colour hair?
24 Which Mickey was the top money-maker as the decade opened?
25 Which part of her did Betty Grable insure for a multimillion-dollar sum?

**Answers World Cinema** (see Quiz 54)
**1** Mussolini. **2** Scotland. **3** China. **4** Valentine's Day. **5** World War II. **6** Italy. **7** Australia. **8** Vadim. **9** *The Piano*. **10** France. **11** Rank. **12** Melina. **13** India. **14** Bernardo Bertolucci. **15** Jim. **16** *Elizabeth*. **17** Ireland. **18** Brigitte Bardot. **19** Sweden. **20** Sophia Loren. **21** Japan. **22** Hedy Lamarr. **23** Rome. **24** Sweden. **25** Renny.

## *QUIZ 87* POT LUCK 34 ........ LEVEL 1

*Answers – see page 97*

1 Which star actress was in *Hook, Great Expectations* and *Emma*?
2 Which Jodie starred in *Nell*?
3 In which decade of the 20th century was Demi Moore born?
4 In *Sister Act* what was Whoopi Goldberg disguised as?
5 Who directed *Apocalypse Now*?
6 *Bogey's Baby* was a biography of the wife of which movie star?
7 In *The Mask* the central character worked as what type of clerk?
8 Which Fonda is Peter's daughter?
9 Which Queen appears in *Shakespeare in Love*?
10 Which James Bond actor starred in *Dante's Peak*?
11 Which musical was sharpshooter Annie Oakley the subject of?
12 What is the profession of Indiana Jones in the adventure movies?
13 Which word follows 'Basic' in a Michael Douglas movie title?
14 Which actress became Mrs John McEnroe in the 1980s?
15 What type of creatures were Donatello, Raphael, Michaelangelo and Leonardo?
16 Which singer/actress married Sean Penn in 1985?
17 Which Bruce starred in *The Fifth Element*?
18 Who won the Best Actress Oscar for *The Silence of the Lambs*?
19 In which decade was *My Fair Lady* released?
20 What did Demi Moore have removed to make *G.I. Jane*?
21 Who played the title role in the 1997 movie *Wilde*?
22 Which member of Arthur's staff was played by John Gielgud in *Arthur*?
23 Who won the Best Actor Oscar for *Yankee Doodle Dandy*?
24 Who starred in *Batman and Robin* after finding fame in TV's *ER*?
25 Which word completes the film title, *Mystery of the ____ Museum*?

**Answers Oscars – Best Actresses** (see Quiz 85)
**1** Hepburn. **2** Paltrow. **3** Tandy. **4** *The Silence of the Lambs*. **5** Cher. **6** Sophie's. **7** Bates. **8** Jackson. **9** Shirley Temple. **10** Tatum O'Neal. **11** Liza Minnelli. **12** 1970s. **13** Fonda. **14** 70s. **15** Whoopi Goldberg. **16** Nun. **17** Never. **18** Julie Andrews. **19** Burstyn. **20** *The Piano*. **21** Blue. **22** French. **23** Holly Hunter (*The Piano*). **24** Anjelica. **25** *Gone with the Wind*.

## *QUIZ 88* 1990s ............ LEVEL 1

*Answers – see page 98*

1 Which 'Good' person was 'Hunting' in the movie with Matt Damon?
2 Which 'Pet Detective' movie was Jim Carrey's big break?
3 Jeremy Irons starred in 'Reversal of' what?
4 Who hits the road with Thelma in the 1991 movie?
5 Which hero was 'Prince of Thieves' in the Kevin Costner movie?
6 Which Bram Stoker story was filmed by Francis Ford Coppola in 1992?
7 Which Patrick was the murder victim in *Ghost*?
8 Which animal follows 'Reservoir' in the title of the movie with Harvey Keitel?
9 Which 'Park' was home to dinosaurs in 1993?
10 What type of 'Proposal' did Robert Redford make to Demi Moore?
11 Where was Tom Hanks 'Sleepless' in the romantic movie?
12 The action of *Saving Private Ryan* takes place during which war?
13 *Hook* was based on which J.M. Barrie children's story?
14 Which Julia was the *Pretty Woman* of the film with Richard Gere?
15 Which Spanish star was Che in *Evita* opposite Madonna in 1996?
16 In 1990 Harrison Ford is 'Presumed' what in the 1990 thriller?
17 Which English queen won awards for Cate Blanchett in 1999?
18 Which 1991 *Terminator* film had the subtitle 'Judgment Day'?
19 Who was the subject of the movie *JFK*?
20 What was the first sequel to *Look Who's Talking*?
21 Which ghoulish family had their own movie after first appearing in a cartoon strip?
22 What type of hands did Edward have in the movie with Johnny Depp?
23 What were 'Fried Green' at the Whistle Stop Café?
24 Where were 'Postcards From' in the title of the 1990 movie?
25 What was the name of the 1991 movie about The Doors and its lead singer Jim Morrison?

**Answers Stars of The Silent Years** (see Quiz 86)
**1** Lon Chaney. **2** Pickford. **3** Coogan. **4** Italy. **5** Ronald. **6** White. **7** Fatty Arbuckle. **8** Erich. **9** America's. **10** Barrymore. **11** Buster Keaton. **12** United Artists. **13** Dog. **14** Gilbert. **15** Bow. **16** Chaplin. **17** Clock face. **18** Sennett. **19** Walt Disney. **20** Mabel. **21** Crawford. **22** Greta Garbo. **23** Fairbanks. **24** Laurel and Hardy. **25** Lilian.

## *QUIZ 89* POT LUCK 35 ········ LEVEL 1

*Answers – see page 103*

1 In which decade was *Home Alone* released?
2 What was Boris Karloff's role in *Frankenstein*?
3 Which Denise starred in *Wild Things*?
4 *Misery* is based on the novel by which writer?
5 Which word completes the film title, *Sense and* ____?
6 What is the first name of Mrs Peel in *The Avengers*?
7 Which Alec featured in *Working Girl*?
8 Which Oscar-winner based in India set a record for most extras?
9 *Saving Private Ryan* and *Philadelphia* both feature which actor?
10 Who won the Best Actress Oscar for *Klute*?
11 Which middle initial did director Alan Pakula use?
12 Michael Palin is the voice of which rodent in *The Wind in the Willows*?
13 Who are the stars of *A Grand Day Out*?
14 What were the first names of *Abbott and Costello*?
15 In which decade of the 20th century was Rob Lowe born?
16 The song 'Get Me to the Church on Time' features in which musical movie?
17 Which famous Lana tested for the role of Scarlett O'Hara?
18 According to the film title, what happened on 34th Street?
19 Who played the lead in *The Graduate* after Robert Redford refused it?
20 Which Donald starred in *Singin' in the Rain*?
21 *Enter the Dragon* was the first US kung fu film of which Mr Lee?
22 Charlie Chaplin was a founder of which United film studio?
23 In which decade was *M*A*S*H* released?
24 Which John starred in *A Fish Called Wanda*?
25 Which word completes the film title, *See No Evil, Hear No* ____?

**Answers Pot Luck 36** (see Quiz 91)
**1** Jack Nicholson. **2** Martin. **3** Vanities. **4** Landau. **5** Chocolates. **6** 1990s. **7** Hepburn. **8** *Staircase.* **9** Winger. **10** *The Wrong Trousers.* **11** Glover. **12** King. **13** Russell. **14** 1940s. **15** Cruise. **16** File. **17** Spielberg. **18** Demi Moore. **19** Batman. **20** River Phoenix. **21** Sarandon. **22** Chicago. **23** Day. **24** *Lady.* **25** Fisher.

## *QUIZ 90* COMEDY ........ LEVEL 1

*Answers – see page 104*

1 Which movie featured Jim Carrey as Truman Burbank?
2 Which comic star Ellen starred in *Doctor Dolittle* with Eddie Murphy?
3 Which Austin was the 'International Man of Mystery'?
4 Which Mr was the subject of the 'Ultimate Disaster Movie', with Rowan Atkinson?
5 In which 1997 movie did Jim Carrey promise to tell the truth for a whole day?
6 In which Yorkshire steel town was *The Full Monty* set?
7 Which zany Jerry made the 60s version of *The Nutty Professor*?
8 Which cartoon family from Bedrock hit the big screen in 1994?
9 Who found fame as Charles in *Four Weddings and a Funeral*?
10 Which day was the subject of a 1993 movie with Bill Murray and Andie MacDowell?
11 What job does Mrs Doubtfire take on to look after 'her' own children?
12 Who received $8 million for making the sequel to *Sister Act, Sister Act 2*?
13 In 1963 what sort of precious gem was 'The Pink Panther'?
14 Whose 'World' starred Mike Myers and Dana Carvey?
15 What sort of reptiles were Donatello and Leonardo?
16 Which Morgan was *Driving Miss Daisy* in 1989?
17 The *Sliding Doors* of Gwyneth Paltrow's movie are on which type of train?
18 Who was Michelle Pfeiffer 'Married to' in the movie with Matthew Modine?
19 Who played the title role in *Tootsie*?
20 Which star of *Cabaret* appeared with Dudley Moore in *Arthur*?
21 Which country singer appeared in *9 to 5*?
22 Which 'Brothers' played by John Belushi and Dan Aykroyd were Jake and Elwood?
23 Which 1979 Woody Allen movie shares its name with a rich part of New York?
24 Which Jack was one half of *The Odd Couple*?
25 'A Funny Thing Happened on the Way to' where in 1966?

**Answers Film Festivals** (see Quiz 92)
**1** France. **2** Berlin. **3** *Pulp Fiction.* **4** Sliding. **5** Gene. **6** Cannes. **7** Redford. **8** Golden Palm. **9** Edinburgh. **10** *Spiceworld: The Movie.* **11** *Rain Man.* **12** Hitler invaded Poland. **13** *Michael Collins.* **14** 1960s. **15** Grand Prix. **16** Europe. **17** *Barton Fink.* **18** Collins. **19** May. **20** Grant. **21** Golden. **22** Stoppard. **23** *Pulp Fiction.* **24** Venice. **25** Burke.

## QUIZ 91 POT LUCK 36 ........ LEVEL 1

*Answers – see page 101*

1 *A Few Good Men* and *One Flew Over the Cuckoo's Nest* featured which actor?
2 The 90s version of *Sergeant Bilko* featured which Steve?
3 Which word follows 'The Bonfire of the' in a Bruce Willis movie title?
4 Which Martin featured in *The X-Files*?
5 Forrest Gump declared that life was like a box of what?
6 In which decade was *Groundhog Day* released?
7 Which Audrey starred in *Breakfast at Tiffany's*?
8 Which word completes the film title, *The Spiral* ____?
9 Which Debra starred in *An Officer and a Gentleman*?
10 Which trousers won Nick Park an Oscar?
11 Which Danny starred in *The Color Purple*?
12 Which word title links 'Creole' and 'The Fisher' in movie titles?
13 *Backdraft* starred which Kurt?
14 In which decade of the 20th century was Goldie Hawn born?
15 Which Tom starred in *The Firm*?
16 In a movie title which word goes after 'The Ipcress'?
17 Which Steven directed *Saving Private Ryan*?
18 Which star actress was in *G.I. Jane*, *Striptease* and *Disclosure*?
19 Which character battles against The Penguin?
20 Who was the late brother of Joaquin Phoenix, known in some movies as Leaf?
21 Which Susan won the Best Actress Oscar for *Dead Man Walking*?
22 *The Sting* took place in which gangster city?
23 Which Doris starred in romantic films with Rock Hudson?
24 Which word completes the film title, *The* ____ *Vanishes*?
25 Which Carrie featured in *When Harry Met Sally*?

**Answers Pot Luck 35** (see Quiz 89)
**1** 1990s **2** The monster. **3** Richards. **4** Stephen King. **5** *Sensibility*. **6** Emma. **7** Baldwin. **8** *Gandhi*. **9** Tom Hanks. **10** Jane Fonda. **11** J. **12** Rat. **13** Wallace and Gromit. **14** Bud, Lou. **15** 1960s. **16** *My Fair Lady*. **17** Turner. **18** A Miracle. **19** Dustin Hoffman. **20** O'Connor. **21** Bruce. **22** United Artists. **23** 1970s. **24** Cleese. **25** *Evil*.

## QUIZ 92 FILM FESTIVALS ........ LEVEL 1

*Answers – see page 102*

1 Which country hosts the Cannes Film Festival?
2 Which German festival gives an award of a Golden Bear?
3 Which 'Fiction' movie won a prize at Cannes in 1994?
4 What sort of 'Doors' won Peter Howitt a screenwriter award in 1998?
5 Which Kelly was a winner with *Invitation to the Dance* in 1956?
6 Which festival was the subject of a book called *Hollywood on the Riviera*?
7 Which Robert founded the Sundance Festival?
8 What does Palme d'Or mean in the award from the Cannes Film festival?
9 Which Scottish city hosts a film festival and an arts festival in August?
10 Which Spice Girls movie was launched at the Cannes Film Festival?
11 Which Dustin Hoffman/Tom Cruise movie won a Golden Bear in 1989?
12 Why was the first Cannes Film Festival abandoned in 1939?
13 Which 'Michael' won a Golden Lion for Neil Jordan in 1996?
14 In which decade was the Cannes Film Festival disrupted due to nationwide demonstrations in France?
15 Which term, often used in motor racing, was used as the name of the main prize at Cannes just after World War II?
16 Which continent has awards called Felixes?
17 Which movie with 'Barton' in the title found success at Cannes?
18 Which Michael did Liam Neeson play in the title role of Neil Jordan's movie which won in Venice in 1996?
19 In which month of the year does the Cannes Festival take place?
20 Which Hugh won Best Actor at Venice for his debut movie *Maurice*?
21 What colour Lion is the name of the award at Venice?
22 Which Tom won in Venice for *Rosencrantz and Guildenstern Are Dead*?
23 Which Quentin Tarantino film won a Palme d'Or in 1994?
24 Which Italian city famous for its canals hosts a film festival?
25 Which Kathy won for *Nil by Mouth* at Cannes in 1998?

**Answers Comedy** (see Quiz 90 )
**1** *The Truman Show*. **2** DeGeneres. **3** Powers. **4** Bean. **5** *Liar Liar*. **6** Sheffield. **7** Lewis. **8** The Flintstones. **9** Hugh Grant. **10** Groundhog Day. **11** Nanny. **12** Whoopi Goldberg. **13** Diamond. **14** *Wayne's World*. **15** Turtles. **16** Freeman. **17** Underground. **18** The Mob **19** Dustin Hoffman. **20** Liza Minnelli. **21** Dolly Parton. **22** Blues Brothers. **23** *Manhattan*. **24** Lemmon. **25** The Forum.

## *QUIZ 93* JODIE FOSTER ........ LEVEL 1

*Answers – see page 107*

1 In which decade was Jodie Foster born?
2 Which Richard was her co star in *Sommersby*?
3 Who spoke her lines in the French film *Moi, Fleur Bleue*?
4 In which city was her film *Taxi Driver* set?
5 For which movie did she win her first 90s Oscar?
6 In which decade did she win her first ever Oscar for *The Accused*?
7 Which Liam was her co-star in *Nell*?
8 In which 1994 gambling movie did she star with James Garner?
9 In which movie with only children in the cast did she play a gangster's moll?
10 Which Martin directed her with Robert de Niro in *Taxi Driver*?
11 Who won the Best Actor Oscar when Foster won for *The Silence of the Lambs*?
12 In which Californian city was she born?
13 Who owns the production company Egg which made *Nell*?
14 Which 'Freaky' day was in the title of a 1977 Disney film?
15 Which Cybill appeared with Foster in *Taxi Driver* as campaign worker Betsy?
16 What is the name of Foster's first son?
17 What did she advertise as a child as The Coppertone Girl?
18 What is her real first name?
19 Which President suffered an assassination attempt by a stalker obsessed by Foster?
20 In which country did she advertise Honda cars, where they were first made?
21 In which movie did she win an Oscar as federal agent Clarice Starling?
22 Who 'Doesn't Live Here Any More' according to her 1974 movie?
23 In which film did she play Anna in a *King and I*-style remake?
24 Which 'Little Man' saw her major feature film directing debut?
25 In which Woody's film *Shadows and Fog* did she have a cameo role?

**Answers 1990s Stars** (see Quiz 95)
**1** Affleck. **2** Spanish. **3** *The Truman Show*. **4** Costner. **5** Whoopi Goldberg. **6** Drew. **7** Mike Myers. **8** Leonardo DiCaprio. **9** Madonna. **10** Five. **11** Kate Winslet. **12** Pitt. **13** Animals. **14** Canada. **15** Gerard. **16** Hugh Grant. **17** Jodie Foster. **18** Robin Williams. **19** Anderson. **20** The Mohicans. **21** Depp. **22** Tom Cruise's. **23** Alec. **24** English. **25** Keanu.

## *QUIZ 94* POT LUCK 37 ........ LEVEL 1

*Answers – see page 108*

1 Which word follows 'Pale' in a Clint Eastwood movie title?
2 Which Jack starred in *The Witches of Eastwick*?
3 In which decade was *The Birds* released?
4 Who played the lead role in *The King and I* after James Mason turned it down?
5 Who played the baddie Pierce Brosnan was up against in *The World is Not Enough*?
6 Which colour completes the film title *The Solid ___ Cadillac*?
7 Who was Adele Austerlitz's famous brother?
8 *The Sunshine Boys* starred which George?
9 What sort of column did Hedda Hopper write about Hollywood?
10 Which blonde country star appeared in *The Best Little Whorehouse in Texas*?
11 Which important person is held to ransom in *Air Force One*?
12 Which actress took the lead in *The Avengers*?
13 Which word completes the film title *A Star Is ___*?
14 For which film did Julie Andrews win her first Oscar?
15 Which Hollywood star was nicknamed 'The Look'?
16 The Von Trapp family featured in which musical movie?
17 Who played Tinkerbell in *Hook*?
18 Which Burt starred in the 50s movie *From Here to Eternity*?
19 What is the name of the chief male character in *The Avengers*?
20 Who sang the title song of *A Hard Day's Night*?
21 Who plays Deloris in *Sister Act*?
22 In the film title, what goes with 'Kind Hearts'?
23 In which decade of the 20th century was Melanie Griffith born?
24 Who starred in *Private Benjamin* after finding fame in TV's *Laugh In*?
25 *Mermaids* and *Edward Scissorhands* featured which actress?

**Answers Pot Luck 38** (see Quiz 96)
**1** The Big. **2** Kate Winslet. **3** Foot (*My Left Foot*). **4** Tom Cruise. **5** *The Graduate.* **6** Gwyneth Paltrow. **7** 20s. **8** The Mob. **9** *The Sound of Music.* **10** Judi Dench. **11** London. **12** Spaghetti. **13** Gotham. **14** Jeff Bridges. **15** *Dr No.* **16** St Bernard. **17** Spielberg. **18** 1980s. **19** *Mermaids.* **20** *Kiss.* **21** *The Bodyguard.* **22** Georgia. **23** Carlyle. **24** Gangsters. **25** Ingrid Bergman.

## *QUIZ 95* 1990s STARS ........ LEVEL 1

*Answers – see page 105*

1 Which Ben co-wrote and starred in *Good Will Hunting* with Matt Damon?
2 What is the nationality of Antonio Banderas?
3 Which 'Show' was a big hit for Jim Carrey?
4 Which Kevin played John Dunbar in *Dances with Wolves*?
5 Which African-American actress played the medium in *Ghost*?
6 Which member of the Barrymore acting dynasty appeared in *The Wedding Singer*?
7 Who played the spoof spy Austin Powers in the late 1990s movies?
8 Which heart-throb played Romeo opposite Claire Danes in *Romeo and Juliet*?
9 Which future star of *Evita* played Breathless Mahoney in *Dick Tracy*?
10 How many Spice Girls star in *Spiceworld: The Movie*?
11 Who played Rose in the blockbuster *Titanic*?
12 Which Brad became engaged to Jennifer Aniston after breaking off his engagement to Gwyneth Paltrow?
13 Eddie Murphy as Dr Doolittle could talk to whom in the 1998 hit?
14 In which part of North America was Dan Aykroyd born?
15 What is the first name of French actor Depardieu?
16 Liz Hurley was the long-time partner of which *Four Weddings and a Funeral* star?
17 Who played the female FBI agent in *The Silence of the Lambs*?
18 Who played the title role in *Mrs Doubtfire*?
19 Which Gillian played Scully in the movie version of *The X-Files*?
20 Daniel Day-Lewis is the 'Last of' which people in the 1992 movie?
21 Which Johnny was nearly 30 when he played teenager Gilbert in *What's Eating Gilbert Grape?*?
22 Whose 'Mission' was 'Impossible' in 1996?
23 Who is oldest of the Baldwin brothers, who married Kim Basinger?
24 American Gwyneth Paltrow adopted what national accent for *Sliding Doors* and *Emma*?
25 What is Keanu Reeves's real first name?

**Answers Jodie Foster** (see Quiz 93)
**1** 1960s. **2** Gere. **3** She did. **4** New York. **5** *The Silence of the Lambs.* **6** 1980s. **7** Neeson. **8** *Maverick.* **9** *Bugsy Malone.* **10** Scorsese. **11** Anthony Hopkins. **12** Los Angeles. **13** Jodie Foster. **14** Friday. **15** Shepherd. **16** Charles. **17** Suntan lotion. **18** Alicia. **19** Reagan. **20** Japan. **21** *The Silence of the Lambs.* **22** Alice. **23** *Anna and the King.* **24** Tate. **25** Allen.

## *QUIZ 96* POT LUCK 38 ........ LEVEL 1

*Answers – see page 106*

1 In movie titles which two words go in front of 'Chill', 'Heat' and 'Lebowski'?
2 Which leading actress was Oscar-nominated for *Titanic*?
3 Which left part of the body is named in the title of a movie with Daniel Day-Lewis?
4 *Rain Man, The Firm* and *Cocktail* all feature which actor?
5 Middle-aged seductress Mrs Robinson features in which movie?
6 Who won the Best Actress Oscar for *Shakespeare in Love*?
7 In which decade of the 20th century was Audrey Hepburn born?
8 Who was Michelle Pfeiffer 'Married to' in a movie title?
9 The song 'Climb Every Mountain' features in which musical movie?
10 Which English actress was the first to play M in the Bond movies?
11 Bob Hope was born in which European capital city?
12 What's the Italian food often linked with westerns?
13 In which city does the action of *Batman* take place?
14 What's the name of the actor brother of Beau Bridges?
15 What was the first Bond movie with Sean Connery?
16 What breed of dog is Beethoven?
17 Which director Steven did Amy Irving marry?
18 In which decade was *Wall Street* released?
19 Which movie featured 'The Shoop Shoop Song'?
20 Which word completes the film titles, ____ *Me Deadly* and ____ *Me Kate*?
21 Which film saw Whitney Houston's acting debut?
22 *Gone with the Wind* is set in which American state?
23 Which Robert starred in *The Full Monty*?
24 What is the main 'occupation' of the characters in *Bugsy Malone*?
25 Who was the female lead in *Casablanca*?

**Answers Pot Luck 37** (see Quiz 94)
**1** Rider. **2** Nicholson. **3** 1960s. **4** Yul Brynner. **5** Robert Carlyle. **6** *Gold.* **7** Fred Astaire. **8** Burns. **9** Gossip. **10** Dolly Parton. **11** US President. **12** Uma Thurman. **13** *Born.* **14** *Mary Poppins.* **15** Lauren Bacall. **16** *The Sound of Music.* **17** Julia Roberts. **18** Lancaster. **19** Steed. **20** The Beatles. **21** Whoopi Goldberg. **22** Coronets. **23** 50s. **24** Goldie Hawn. **25** Winona Ryder.

## QUIZ 97 HEADLINE MAKERS ........ LEVEL 1

*Answers – see page 111*

1 In which city did Hugh Grant make the headlines for 'lewd conduct'?
2 Where was Elizabeth Taylor born?
3 Who died two days after finishing *Giant*?
4 Which Julie's voice was damaged after a minor op went wrong?
5 Michael J. Fox hit the headlines after disclosing he was suffering from which disease?
6 Which Sidney was the first black actor to top the money making list?
7 In *All the President's Men* Redford and Hoffman play journalists investigating which break-in?
8 Which Mr Moore scored 10 before disclosing he had an incurable disease?
9 Which Sharon had the famous leg-crossing scene in *Basic Instinct*?
10 Which 'Heavenly' Michael Cimino movie nearly destroyed United Artists?
11 Who hit the headlines by receiving $8.5 million for the sequel to *Sister Act*?
12 Who starred in a TV remake of *Rear Window* after becoming paralysed after a fall from a horse?
13 In the1940s which Flynn was acquitted of assault charges on his yacht?
14 Which star of *Saturday Night Fever* famously danced with Diana, Princess of Wales at a White House reception?
15 Which Liz went to a premiere in a dress held together by safety pins?
16 Which Richard married and divorced supermodel Cindy Crawford?
17 Which husband and wife starred in *Shanghai Surprise* in 1986?
18 Which silent star sold his Hollywood home to move to Switzerland in 1953?
19 Which Jack played The Joker in a Batman movie?
20 In what type of crash did Grace Kelly meet her death?
21 The relationship between Richard Burton and Elizabeth Taylor began on the set of which movie?
22 Which Julia married Lyle Lovett after leaving Kiefer Sutherland at the altar?
23 Which cosmetics house did Liz Hurley advertise?
24 Which daughter of Henry was known as Hanoi Jane for her anti-Vietnam War actions?
25 Warren Beatty's affair with Madonna began on the set of which movie?

**Answers Pot Luck 39** (see Quiz 99)
**1** 1990s. **2** Aykroyd. **3** Marilyn Monroe. **4** Quiet. **5** De Niro. **6** World War II. **7** Jodie Foster. **8** *Mission: Impossible.* **9** *Entrapment.* **10** *The Wizard of Oz.* **11** Daniel Day-Lewis. **12** Bruce Willis. **13** A woman. **14** Ship. **15** Canada. **16** 50s. **17** LeBlanc. **18** Dredd. **19** Meet Me. **20** Nicolas Cage. **21** None. **22** 1970s. **23** The Bee Gees. **24** Roberts. **25** Green.

## *QUIZ 98* THE 21ST CENTURY ........ LEVEL 1

*Answers – see page 112*

1 Where was *The Beach* made?
2 In which country was *Angela's Ashes* set?
3 Which member of the Arquette family appeared in *Stigmata*?
4 Johnny Depp starred in what type of 'Hollow'?
5 What sort of 'Collector' was played by Denzel Washington?
6 What was the first Bond movie showing in the new millennium?
7 Who was Bicentennial Man?
8 What sort of 'Sense' did Bruce Willis have in the screen ghost story?
9 In which north of England city was *East Is East* set?
10 What colour 'Streak' features in the title of the Martin Lawrence movie?
11 Which Tommy was the pursuer in *Double Jeopardy*?
12 Which Mr was 'Talented' in the movie with Matt Damon?
13 Which Ralph Fiennes movie had the ad line, 'The end was just the beginning'?
14 Which 'Orchard' came to the big screen with Charlotte Rampling and Alan Bates?
15 Where was 'The House' in the movie directed by William Malone?
16 Which *Scream* movie appeared at the start of Y2K?
17 What was the sequel to *Toy Story*?
18 Which Martin directed *Bringing Out the Dead*?
19 Which G & S were the subjects of *Topsy Turvy*?
20 *Music of the Heart* was about what type of musician?
21 Which Emily plays Angela in *Angela's Ashes*?
22 Which Matt and Ben starred in *Dogma*?
23 Which Kevin starred in *American Beauty*?
24 Who was Johnny Depp's co-star in *Sleepy Hollow*?
25 What type of 'Giant' was the name of an animated movie hit?

**Answers Action** (see Quiz 100)
**1** *Dr No.* **2** Leonardo DiCaprio. **3** Fiennes. **4** Batman. **5** Pryce. **6** Pierce Brosnan. **7** Tornado. **8** 1970s. **9** Kidman. **10** *Braveheart.* **11** Jamie Lee Curtis. **12** *The Fugitive.* **13** Seymour. **14** D-Day landings. **15** 1990s. **16** James Bond. **17** Ursula Andress. **18** Izzard **19** A POW camp. **20** Burton. **21** Telly Savalas **22** Three. **23** Arthur. **24** Pizza. **25** Pierce Brosnan.

## *QUIZ 99* POT LUCK 39 ........ LEVEL 1

*Answers – see page 109*

1 In which decade was *Misery* released?
2 Which Dan starred in *Ghostbusters*?
3 Who was the lead actress in *Some Like It Hot*?
4 According to the film title, it was all what on the Western Front?
5 Which Robert starred in the 1998 *Great Expectations*?
6 During which war was *Land Girls* set?
7 Which star actress was in *Contact*, *The Accused* and *Sommersby*?
8 The spy Ethan Hunt appears in which movie with a Mission?
9 In which 1999 film did Sean Connery star with Catherine Zeta Jones?
10 A cowardly lion appears in which musical movie?
11 Who played Hawkeye in the 90s movie *The Last of the Mohicans*?
12 Who went on to the *Die Hard* movies from TV's *Moonlighting*?
13 In *Tootsie* what does the Dustin Hoffman character pretend to be to get a part in a soap?
14 *The Poseidon Adventure* is about a disaster on what type of vehicle?
15 In which country on the American continent was Donald Sutherland born?
16 In which decade of the 20th century was Michael Keaton born?
17 Which Matt starred in *Lost in Space*?
18 Which Judge from *2000 AD* comic appeared on film in 1995?
19 In a movie title, what will you do to me in St Louis?
20 Which actor was in *Con Air*, *City of Angels* and *It Could Happen to You*?
21 How many Oscar nominations did Madonna get for *Evita*?
22 In which decade was *Cabaret* released?
23 Who sang 'Night Fever' in *Saturday Night Fever*?
24 Which Julia starred in *Pretty Woman*?
25 Which colour goes before 'Card' and 'Pastures' in film titles?

**Answers Headline Makers** (see Quiz 97)
**1** Los Angeles. **2** England. **3** James Dean. **4** Andrews. **5** Parkinson's Disease. **6** Poitier. **7** Watergate. **8** Dudley. **9** Stone. **10** *Heaven's Gate*. **11** Whoopi Goldberg. **12** Christopher Reeve. **13** Errol. **14** John Travolta. **15** Hurley. **16** Gere. **17** Sean Penn & Madonna. **18** Charlie Chaplin. **19** Nicholson. **20** Car. **21** *Cleopatra*. **22** Roberts. **23** Estee Lauder. **24** Jane Fonda. **25** *Dick Tracy*.

## *QUIZ 100* ACTION ............ LEVEL 1

*Answers – see page 110*

1 Which Bond movie was shown in Japan as *No Need for a Doctor*?
2 Which star of *Titanic* was King Louis XIV in *The Man in the Iron Mask*?
3 Which Ralph starred as Steed in *The Avengers*?
4 Which comic-book character was played by George Clooney of *ER* fame in 1997?
5 Which Jonathan, a star of *Evita*, played villain Elliott Carver in *Tomorrow Never Dies*?
6 Which 90s 007 starred as Harry Dalton in *Dante's Peak*?
7 What type of natural disaster is the setting for *Twister*?
8 In which decade did the action of *Apollo 13* take place?
9 Which Mrs Cruise, Nicole, starred in *Batman Forever*?
10 Which 1995 Mel Gibson movie told the story of Scot, William Wallace?
11 Which daughter of Tony Curtis played Arnold Schwarzenegger's wife in *True Lies*?
12 In which movie – from the classic TV series of the same name – did Harrison Ford play Richard Kimble?
13 Which British-born Jane was Roger Moore's first Bond girl in *Live and Let Die*?
14 Which Landings feature in the action of *Saving Private Ryan*?
15 In which decade was *The Lost World: Jurassic Park* released?
16 Which role did Timothy Dalton play in *The Living Daylights*?
17 Who played the Bond girl in *Dr No*?
18 Which comedian Eddie appeared in *The Avengers*?
19 *The Great Escape* was an escape from what?
20 Which Richard, husband of Elizabeth Taylor, starred in *Where Eagles Dare*?
21 Which TV Kojak played Blofeld in *On Her Majesty's Secret Service*?
22 How many 'Days of the Condor' feature in the title of the 70s Robert Redford movie?
23 *Excalibur* featured action at the court of which legendary King?
24 What type of Italian food was a Turtles' favourite?
25 Who succeeded Timothy Dalton as 007 in *GoldenEye*?

**Answers The 21st Century** (see Quiz 98)
**1** Thailand. **2** Ireland. **3** Patricia. **4** *Sleepy Hollow.* **5** Bone. **6** *The World Is Not Enough.* **7** Robin Williams. **8** Sixth. **9** Manchester. **10** Blue. **11** Lee Jones. **12** Ripley. **13** *The End of the Affair.* **14** *The Cherry Orchard.* **15** On Haunted Hill. **16** *Scream 3.* **17** *Toy Story 2.* **18** Scorsese. **19** Gilbert & Sullivan. **20** Violinist. **21** Watson. **22** Damon & Affleck. **23** Spacey. **24** Christina Ricci. **25** *The Iron Giant.*

## *QUIZ 101* OSCAR TRIVIA ........ LEVEL 1

*Answers – see page 114*

1 What colour is an Oscar?
2 In which decade were the Oscars first presented?
3 What was the last movie of the 1990s to win more than nine Oscars?
4 Which theme park founder won 20 Oscars?
5 In which season does the Oscars ceremony usually take place?
6 At which home of the film industry was the first Oscar ceremony held?
7 Which rodent won Walt Disney a Special Award in 1932?
8 Which Mickey won a 1938 Oscar for 'bringing the spirit of youth to the screen'?
9 Which Maggie won an Oscar for playing an Oscar-nominee in *California Suite*?
10 Whose Oscar sold for $510,000 for her role in *Gone with the Wind*?
11 Which Vanessa won Best Supporting Actress for *Julia*, even though she played the title role?
12 In *Sleuth*, there were two characters; how many were nominated?
13 Which 'Color' in 1985 had 11 nominations and not a single win?
14 What relation were winners Olivia de Havilland and Joan Fontaine?
15 How many times did Alfred Hitchcock win an Oscar for which he was nominated?
16 What relation was Oscar-winner Walter to Oscar-winner John Huston?
17 Which wife of Paul Newman has also been Oscar-nominated?
18 Which song from *The Wizard of Oz* won the Best Song Oscar?
19 Richard Burton was Oscar-nominated in three successive years; how many times did he win?
20 'The Cool Cool Cool' of which part of the day won a songwriting Oscar for Hoagy Carmichael?
21 In *Who's Afraid of Virginia Woolf*, there were four characters; how many were Oscar-nominated?
22 Which Anthony Hopkins and Jodie Foster film won for them both?
23 'Days of Wine and Roses' won best song, from which movie?
24 Which Civil War movie was the last winner before the outbreak of World War II?
25 How many actors shared the Best Actor Award in 1932?

**Answers Partnerships** (see Quiz 103)
**1** Ginger Rogers. **2** Gershwin. **3** Spencer Tracy. **4** Demi Moore. **5** Garth. **6** Streisand. **7** Helen Mirren. **8** *Dangerous Liaisons*. **9** Nicole Kidman. **10** Nelson. **11** Chaplin. **12** Bruce Willis & Demi Moore. **13** Paul Newman & Joanne Woodward. **14** Richard Burton & Elizabeth Taylor. **15** Lauren Bacall. **16** Oldman. **17** Michael Douglas. **18** Wayne. **19** Kline. **20** Griffith. **21** Frank Sinatra. **22** *Crocodile Dundee*. **23** Brother, Eric. **24** Brooks. **25** Kenneth Branagh & Emma Thompson.

## *QUIZ 102* POT LUCK 40 ........ LEVEL 1

*Answers – see page 115*

1 Which word goes in front of 'Morning, Vietnam' and 'Will Hunting' in film titles?
2 *Air Force One* starred which Harrison?
3 About which film was it said, 'It's light years ahead'?
4 Which Matt co-wrote *Good Will Hunting*?
5 *Interview with the Vampire, Twelve Monkeys* and *The Devil's Own* all feature which actor?
6 Which Michelle playted Titania in the 1990s *A Midsummer Night's Dream*?
7 What is the first name of Macaulay Culkin's character in *Home Alone*?
8 In which decade was *Heat* released?
9 Which Gene starred in *The French Connection*?
10 The character Eliza Doolittle appears in which musical movie?
11 Which name completes the title *Whatever Happened to Baby ____*??
12 Who played Obi-Wan Kenobi in the *Star Wars* trilogy?
13 The song 'Tonight' features in which musical movie?
14 Which poison goes with 'Old Lace'?
15 What was Best Picture when Tom Hanks won Best Actor Oscar for *Forrest Gump*?
16 Who went on to star in *Entrapment* after appearing on UK TV's *The Darling Buds of May*?
17 Which famous Norma tested for the role of Scarlett O'Hara?
18 Which Michelle starred in *Wolf*?
19 Did Clark Gable die during the1950s, 1960s or 1970s?
20 Who directed *Alien*?
21 Which Helen won the Best Actress Oscar for *As Good as it Gets*?
22 In which decade was *Thunderball* released?
23 The character Mrs Doubtfire supposedly came from which country?
24 Who sang the title song of *Three Coins in the Fountain*?
25 In which decade of the 20th century was Deborah Kerr born?

**Answers Oscar Trivia** (see Quiz 101)
**1** Gold. **2** 1920s. **3** *Titanic.* **4** Walt Disney. **5** Spring. **6** Hollywood. **7** Mickey Mouse. **8** Rooney. **9** Smith. **10** Vivien Leigh. **11** Redgrave. **12** Two. **13** *The Color Purple.* **14** Sisters. **15** Never. **16** Father. **17** Joanne Woodward. **18** 'Over the Rainbow'. **19** Never. **20** Evening. **21** Four. **22** *The Silence of the Lambs.* **23** *Days of Wine and Roses.* **24** *Gone with the Wind.* **25** Two.

## *QUIZ 103* PARTNERSHIPS ........................................ LEVEL 1

*Answers – see page 113*

1 Who was the screen partner of the dancer whose real name was Frederick Austerlitz?
2 Which brothers George and Ira wrote the music for 'Someone to Watch Over Me'?
3 Who played opposite Katharine Hepburn 10 times?
4 Who was the actress who launched Planet Hollywood with actors Willis, Schwarzenegger and Stallone?
5 Who is Wayne's sidekick in *Wayne's World*?
6 Which Barbra did actor James Brolin marry in 1998?
7 Which star of *Prime Suspect* was Liam Neeson's co star in *Excalibur*?
8 Michelle Pfeiffer's affair with John Malkovich began on the set of which movie?
9 Which wife of Tom Cruise has also been Oscar-nominated?
10 What was the first name of actor Eddy who had an on-screen partnership with Jeanette MacDonald?
11 Paulette Goddard was the co-star and third wife of which Charlie?
12 Who are the parents of Rumer, Scout and Tallulah Willis?
13 Which husband and wife starred in *Mr and Mrs Bridge* in 1994?
14 Which husband and wife were Oscar-nominated together in 1966?
15 Humphrey Bogart's affair with which actress started in real life while they were making *To Have and Have Not*?
16 Which Gary was married to Uma Thurman?
17 Who announced his engagement to Catherine Zeta Jones in 2000?
18 Which John first starred with Maureen O'Hara in *Rio Grande*?
19 Which Kevin did Phoebe Cates marry in 1989?
20 Which actress Melanie did Don Johnson marry twice?
21 Which singer/actor was the first husband of Mia Farrow?
22 The relationship between Paul Hogan and Linda Koslowski began on the set of which movie?
23 Julia Roberts make her screen debut opposite which family member?
24 Which Mel did Anne Bancroft marry in 1964?
25 Which husband and wife were the subject of the biography *Ken and Em*?

**Answers Pot Luck 40** (see Quiz 102)
**1** Good. **2** Ford. **3** *Toy Story*. **4** Damon. **5** Brad Pitt. **6** Pfeiffer. **7** Kevin. **8** 1990s. **9** Hackman. **10** *My Fair Lady*. **11** *Jane*. **12** Alec Guinness. **13** *West Side Story*. **14** Arsenic. **15** *Forrest Gump*. **16** Catherine Zeta Jones. **17** Shearer. **18** Pfeiffer. **19** 1960s. **20** Ridley Scott. **21** Hunt. **22** 1960s. **23** Scotland. **24** Frank Sinatra. **25** 20s.

## *LEVEL 2: THE MEDIUM QUESTIONS*

Things are hotting up. The easy questions are behind you and you will have to test those brain cells just a little bit more with this section.

Once again it is questions on worldwide cinema and famous people which make up most of this level. Highly complex and mind-blowingly obscure questions are still to come! There will be a fair number of the-answer's-on-the-tip-of-my-tongue type questions as well. You can remember who won the Best Supporting Actress Oscar for *Shakespeare in Love* just after the event but can you remember who won it a couple of years later? This is how the questions are getting that little bit harder.

In most public quizzes the majority of your questions will be at this level. You've had the easy questions to get them in the mood and the difficult questions are just around the corner. If you are setting topic sections in groups of ten for a general audience, perhaps give two easy questions, two difficult ones and six medium ones. You should know your audience. If you have quiz rookies then increase the number of easy questions. If they're real quiz experts then reduce the number of medium questions and increase the difficulty quotient. The more quizzes you run the more experienced you will become and the balance of levels will become simpler to estimate.

A quick word of advice about the Pot Luck sections here. Genuine movie buffs can bone up on their specialist subjects but with the Pot Luck sections they have no idea at all what is going to be thrown at them. They may be experts on the films of Arnold Schwarzenegger but ask them a question on weepies and they could be stumped. Use these sections frequently!

## *QUIZ 1* POT LUCK 1 ........ LEVEL 2

*Answers – see page 119*

1 Who turned down Eddie Murphy's role in *Beverly Hills Cop*?
2 Who directed *Thelma and Louise*?
3 How is Caryn Johnson better known?
4 In which decade was *Mr Smith Goes to Washington* released?
5 *Indiana Jones and the Last Crusade* and *Speakers* both feature which actor?
6 Who won the Best Actor Oscar for *La Vita E Bella* (*Life is Beautiful*)?
7 Which Madeleine starred in *The Last of the Mohicans*?
8 To the nearest hour, how long does *The Birds* last?
9 Which Elisabeth starred in *Leaving Las Vegas*?
10 Which poet's life story is told in *Tom and Viv*?
11 What was the name of Tom Hanks's character in *Saving Private Ryan*?
12 What is actress Drew Barrymore's real first name?
13 Who played Anita in *West Side Story*?
14 What nationality does Juliette Binoche play in *The English Patient*?
15 What was the name of Tom Hanks's character in *Big*?
16 Who directed *The Piano* and *The Portrait of a Lady*?
17 *International Velvet* and *Dreamscape* both featured which actor?
18 Which song won Best Song Oscar for *The Man Who Knew Too Much*?
19 Anthony Minghella won his first Best Director Oscar for which movie?
20 Who won the Best Actress Oscar for *The Accused*?
21 *Goodfellas* was released in which decade?
22 Which Jenny starred in *Logan's Run*?
23 Who directed *The Truman Show*?
24 Who played George III's consort in *The Madness of King George*?
25 Which baseball star did Marilyn Monroe marry in 1954?

**Answers Partnerships** (see Quiz 3)
**1** *Eyes Wide Shut*. **2** Ewan McGregor. **3** Renny Harlin. **4** Martin Scorsese. **5** Joanne Whalley-Kilmer. **6** *The Misfits*. **7** Ethan Hawke. **8** Tom & Jerry. **9** Tom Cruise. **10** Kelly Preston. **11** Jane Seymour. **12** Kristin Scott Thomas. **13** Rhea Perlman. **14** Charles Bronson. **15** *One Night in the Tropics*. **16** Demi Moore. **17** Jeff & Beau Bridges. **18** Ava Gardner. **19** Whitney Houston. **20** Bogart & Bacall. **21** Paul Simon. **22** Orson Welles. **23** Gwyneth Paltrow. **24** *Camelot*. **25** Diandra.

## *QUIZ 2* 1930s ........ LEVEL 2

*Answers – see page 120*

1 In which movie did Errol Flynn say, 'It's injustice I hate, not the Normans'?
2 What was the Marx Brothers' first film for MGM?
3 Who found fame in *Public Enemy*?
4 Which subject of the 90s movie *Gods and Monsters* directed *Frankenstein*?
5 Which movie was about Longfellow Deeds?
6 Which famous Robert Louis Stevenson personality was the subject of a 1932 movie with Fredric March?
7 The star of many Tarzan movies had been an accomplished Olympian in which sport?
8 Who played Elizabeth I in *Elizabeth and Essex* opposite Errol Flynn?
9 In which movie did Bela Lugosi say, 'Listen to them, children of the night. What music they make'?
10 Who choreographed *Forty-Second Street*?
11 In which 1934 Oscar-winning movie did Clark Gable famously say, 'Behold the walls of Jericho'?
12 Which movie made a star of Claude Rains, though he was only seen for a few moments?
13 Which 'Bride' was Elsa Lanchester in a 1935 classic?
14 Who did Charles Laughton play in *Mutiny on the Bounty*?
15 Which studio filmed *Goodbye Mr Chips* in England?
16 Which British star of *Gone with the Wind* was 'The Scarlet Pimpernel'?
17 Which city was terrorized by *King Kong*?
18 To the nearest hour, how long does *Monkey Business* last?
19 Who starred as 'Camille'?
20 Who was the French star of *Love Affair* in 1939?
21 In which movie did Chaplin satirize the mechanical society?
22 Which youthful duo starred in *Babes in Arms*?
23 How was song-and-dance director William Berkeley Enos better known?
24 Which British-born director made *Sabotage*?
25 In which 1934 movie did Astaire and Rogers dance 'The Continental'?

**Answers Pot Luck 2** (see Quiz 4)
**1** Anthony Perkins. **2** William. **3** Crowe. **4** Victor Fleming. **5** Tatiana Romanova. **6** Denys Finch-Hatton. **7** Ming the Merciless. **8** 1970s. **9** Bean. **10** Los Angeles. **11** Jason Gould (her real-life son). **12** 139 minutes. **13** Malcolm McDowell. **14** John Lasseter. **15** Bowie. **16** *The Avengers*. **17** Three. **18** Howard Keel. **19** Dr Evil. **20** Tomlinson. **21** Tony Curtis. **22** Tony Scott. **23** Claudette Colbert. **24** 1940s. **25** Joe Pesci.

## *QUIZ 3* PARTNERSHIPS ........ LEVEL 2

*Answers – see page 117*

1 In which 1999 movie wer Harvey Keitel and Jennifer Jason Leigh replaced by Tom Cruise and Nicole Kidman?
2 Who did Danny Boyle direct in both *Trainspotting* and *Shallow Grave*?
3 Which director was Geena Davis's third husband?
4 Harvey Keitel is particularly known for his work with which director?
5 How did Joanne Whalley style herself during her 1988–1996 marriage?
6 Marilyn Monroe divorced Arthur Miller a week after the premiere of which movie?
7 Who was Uma Thurman's on- and off-screen partner in *Gattaca*?
8 Fred Quimby was partly responsible for bringing which duo to the big screen?
9 Mimi Rogers was the first wife of which superstar of the 80s and 90s?
10 Which star of *Twins* married John Travolta?
11 Which wife of director James Keach was a Bond girl in *Live and Let Die*?
12 Which star of *The Horse Whisperer* married a French doctor?
13 Who married Danny DeVito during a break on *Cheers*?
14 Which tough guy played opposite Jill Ireland 12 times?
15 What was Abbot and Costello's first feature film?
16 Who played the mother of her daughter Rumer in *Striptease* in 1996?
17 Which brothers appeared in *The Fabulous Baker Boys*?
18 Which wife of Frank Sinatra was Oscar-nominated at the same time as him?
19 Which singer/actress was Mrs Bobby Brown?
20 *Dark Passage* featured which couple?
21 Who married Debbie Reynolds's daughter in 1983?
22 Which director did Rita Hayworth marry?
23 Who was Brad Pitt's on- and off-screen partner while they were making *Se7en*?
24 Vanessa Redgrave's affair with Franco Nero began on the set of which musical movie?
25 What was the name of Mrs Michael Douglas who divorced him in 1995?

**Answers Pot Luck 1** (see Quiz 1)
**1** Sylvester Stallone. **2** Ridley Scott. **3** Whoopi Goldberg. **4** 1930s. **5** River Phoenix. **6** Roberto Benigni. **7** Stowe. **8** 2 hours. **9** Shu. **10** T.S. Eliot. **11** Captain John Miller. **12** Andrew. **13** Rita Moreno. **14** Canadian. **15** Josh. **16** Jane Campion. **17** Christopher Plummer. **18** 'Whatever Will Be, Will Be' ('Que Sera, Sera'). **19** *The English Patient.* **20** Jodie Foster. **21** 1990s. **22** Agutter. **23** Peter Weir. **24** Helen Mirren. **25** Joe DiMaggio.

## *QUIZ 4* POT LUCK 2 ........ LEVEL 2

*Answers – see page 118*

1 *Desire under the Elms* and *Psycho III* both feature which actor?
2 What is the first name of Brad Pitt, who uses his middle name in the movies?
3 Which Russell starred in *LA Confidential*?
4 Who won the Best Director Oscar for *Gone with the Wind*?
5 What was the name of the Bond girl in *From Russia with Love*?
6 What was the name of Robert Redford's character in *Out of Africa*?
7 What was the name of the villain in *Flash*?
8 In which decade was *Mean Streets* released?
9 Which Sean starred in *GoldenEye*?
10 Where does Rowan Atkinson's *Bean* take place?
11 Who played Barbra Streisand's son in *The Prince of Tides*?
12 Within twenty minutes, how long does *Apocalypse Now* last?
13 Who did Stanley Kubrick cast in the lead role in *A Clockwork Orange*?
14 Who directed *Toy Story*?
15 Which David starred in *Labyrinth*?
16 A character named Sir August de Wynter appeared in which film?
17 How many Oscars did Woody Allen win for *Annie Hall*?
18 Who played opposite Betty Hutton in *Annie Get Your Gun*?
19 Who is the bad character in *Austin Powers: International Man of Mystery*?
20 Which David featured in *Mary Poppins*?
21 Who played Albert DeSalvo in *The Boston Strangler*?
22 Who directed *Top Gun*?
23 Who won the Best Actress Oscar for *It Happened One Night*?
24 In which decade was Disney's *Pinocchio* released?
25 *Home Alone* and *Lethal Weapon 3* both feature which actor?

**Answers 1930s** (see Quiz 2)
**1** *The Adventures of Robin Hood.* **2** *A Night at the Opera.* **3** James Cagney. **4** James Whale. **5** *Mr Deeds Goes to Town.* **6** *Dr Jekyll and Mr Hyde.* **7** Swimming. **8** Bette Davis. **9** *Dracula.* **10** Busby Berkeley. **11** *It Happened One Night.* **12** *The Invisible Man.* **13** Bride of Frankenstein. **14** Captain Bligh. **15** MGM. **16** Leslie Howard. **17** New York. **18** 1 hour (78 mins). **19** Greta Garbo. **20** Charles Boyer. **21** *Modern Times.* **22** Mickey Rooney & Judy Garland. **23** Busby Berkeley. **24** Alfred Hitchcock. **25** *The Gay Divorcee.*

## *QUIZ 5* ANIMALS ON SCREEN ........ LEVEL 2

*Answers – see page 123*

1 Who or what was Andre in the film of the same name?
2 What sort of whale was Willy?
3 Which movie saw a creature threatening Amity off the Long Island coast?
4 What was the sequel to *Beethoven* called?
5 On whose novel was *101 Dalmatians* based?
6 Which creatures predominate in *Deep Blue Sea*?
7 Which actress founded the Born Free Foundation after appearing in the movie?
8 What sort of animal was the star of *Gus*?
9 In which film does Tom Hanks use the help of a dog to solve a murder?
10 Which veteran, and former child star, was one of the voices in the 80s *The Fox and the Hound*?
11 What sort of star was Rhubarb?
12 Which *X-Files* star played a villain in *Beethoven*?
13 Which animals were the stars of *Ring of Bright Water*?
14 What was Tom Mix's horse called?
15 The first dog to play which big-screen star was really called Pal?
16 What was the name of the basketball-playing golden retriever in *Air Bud* in 1997?
17 How many horses did Gene Autry have called Champion?
18 In which musical does Bill have a dog called Bullseye?
19 What type of animal was Digby in the Peter Sellers movie?
20 What breed of dog was K9 in the John Belushi movie?
21 How many dogs and cats make *The Incredible Journey*?
22 Which little girl had a dog as a nanny, called Nana?
23 What sort of animal featured in *My Friend Flicka*?
24 What was the cat called in *Breakfast at Tiffany's*?
25 What was the sequel to *The Incredible Journey* called?

**Answers Pot Luck 3** (see Quiz 7)
**1** William. **2** Motor Racing. **3** William Holden. **4** Ang Lee. **5** 1940s. **6** Liotta. **7** Burns. **8** Bob Hoskins. **9** Louisiana. **10** Kevin Bacon. **11** 2 hours. **12** John and Anjelica Huston. **13** Sean Penn. **14** *The Wedding Singer*. **15** Lee. **16** Ethel Merman. **17** Mozart. **18** Preston. **19** Scott Hicks. **20** West Germany. **21** *A Bill of Divorcement*. **22** 1980s. **23** McDormand. **24** William Wyler. **25** Ward.

## *QUIZ 6* JOHN WAYNE ........ LEVEL 2

*Answers – see page 124*

1 What was his nickname?
2 In which classic western did he play the Ringo Kid?
3 Which sport did he play competitively when he was at college?
4 Which wife of Charlie Chaplin was his co-star in *Reap the Wild Wind*?
5 What was the first movie in which he starred with Maureen O'Hara?
6 Which singer was his drunken assistant in *Rio Bravo*?
7 What type of sportsman did he pay in *The Quiet Man*?
8 Which Hollywood great was his female co-star in *The Shootist*?
9 In which movie did he famously say, 'Truly this man was the son of God'?
10 Which role did he play in *The Alamo*?
11 In which 1975 movie did he reprise his role from *True Grit*?
12 What was his real name?
13 He starred in and directed *The Green Berets* during which war?
14 What was the first movie for which he received an Oscar?
15 Which movie earned him his first Oscar nomination?
16 Which TV western series did he introduce the first episode of on camera?
17 Which legendary ruler did he play in *The Conqueror*?
18 What was the name of his first major movie?
19 Which director gave him the role in *She Wore a Yellow Ribbon*?
20 In which city was *Brannigan* set?
21 On what occasion was his last public appearance?
22 What was his directorial debut?
23 In which movie did he play Civil War veteran Ethan Edwards?
24 *El Dorado* was a virtual remake of which 1959 hit movie?
25 What was the name of his final movie?

**Answers Oscars – Best Actors** (see Quiz 8)
**1** George Burns. **2** *Wall Street.* **3** *The English Patient.* **4** Ben Kingsley. **5** Jude Law. **6** Priest. **7** Emil Jannings. **8** Manservant. **9** Daniel Day-Lewis. **10** *The People versus Larry Flint.* **11** None. **12** Rex Harrison. **13** *Midnight Cowboy.* **14** None. **15** *Wall Street.* **16** George III. **17** *Amistad.* **18** *Chinatown.* **19** James Dean. **20** Daniel Day-Lewis. **21** Marlon Brando. **22** *The Elephant Man.* **23** Don Corleone. **24** *Schindler's List.* **25** Rex Harrison.

## *QUIZ 7* POT LUCK 3 ........ LEVEL 2

*Answers – see page 121*

1 What is Liam Neeson's real first name?
2 At what sport did Paul Newman excel?
3 Who won the Best Actor Oscar for *Stalag 17*?
4 Who directed *Sense and Sensibility*?
5 In which decade was the epic *Samson and Delilah* released?
6 Which Ray starred in *Field of Dreams*?
7 What is Harry's surname in *When Harry Met Sally*?
8 Who played Smee in *Hook*?
9 In which state is *The Green Mile* set?
10 Which actor links *Tremors* and *Flatliners*?
11 To the nearest hour, how long does *The Blues Brothers* last?
12 Which father and daughter respectively directed and starred in *Prizzi's Honor*?
13 *Taps* and *We're No Angels* featured which actor?
14 In which film did a character named Robbie Hart appear?
15 Which Bernard featured in *Moonraker*?
16 Whose real name was Ethel Zimmerman?
17 Which composer did Tom Hulce play in a 1984 Milos Forman film?
18 What is the last name of Bill from *Bill and Ted's Excellent Adventure*?
19 Who directed *Shine*?
20 In which country was Bruce Willis born?
21 What was Katharine Hepburn's first film, in 1932?
22 In which decade was *Raging Bull* released?
23 Which Frances starred in *Fargo*?
24 Who won the Best Director Oscar for *Ben Hur*?
25 Which Stephen did John Hurt play in *Scandal*?

**Answers Animals On Screen** (see Quiz 5)
**1** Seal. **2** Orca (Killer Whale). **3** *Jaws.* **4** *Beethoven's Second.* **5** Dodie Smith. **6** Sharks. **7** Virginia McKenna. **8** Mule. **9** *Turner and Hooch.* **10** Mickey Rooney. **11** Cat. **12** David Duchovny. **13** Otters. **14** Tony. **15** Lassie. **16** Buddy. **17** Three. **18** *Oliver!.* **19** Dog. **20** German Shepherd. **21** Two dogs, one cat. **22** Wendy (*Peter Pan*). **23** Horse. **24** Cat. **25** *Homeward Bound: The Incredible Journey.*

## *QUIZ 8* OSCARS – BEST ACTORS ........ LEVEL 2

*Answers – see page 122*

1 Who was 80 when he won for *The Sunshine Boys*?
2 What was Michael Douglas's first nomination as performer?
3 For which movie did Ralph Fiennes receive his second nomination?
4 How is 1982 winner, Krishna Bahji, better known?
5 Which 1999 Oscar nominee played Lord Alfred Douglas in *Wilde*?
6 What was Bing Crosby's profession in *Going My Way*?
7 Who won the first Oscar for Best Actor?
8 What was John Gielgud's profession in the movie *Arthur* for which he won an award?
9 When Brenda Fricker first won as Best Actress which winner played her son?
10 For which movie did Woody Harrelson receive his first nomination?
11 What is the total number of Oscars won by Errol Flynn, Peter Cushing and Richard Burton?
12 Who was nominated for *Cleopatra* but won a year later as Professor Higgins?
13 Jon Voight's first nomination was for which X-rated movie?
14 How many Oscars did Sean Connery win for James Bond?
15 What was Michael Douglas's first win as Actor?
16 Which King gave Nigel Hawthorne a nomination?
17 For which Spielberg movie was Anthony Hopkins nominated in 1997?
18 What was the second of Jack Nicholson's three nominations between 1973 and 1975?
19 Who was the first actor to be awarded two posthumous Oscars?
20 Which 80s winner and 90s nominee is the son of Jill Balcon and a poet laureate?
21 Whose first award was for playing Terry Malloy in a 50s classic?
22 For which movie did John Hurt receive a nomination after *Midnight Express*?
23 Who did Robert De Niro play in *The Godfather Part II*?
24 Which Spielberg movie gave Liam Neeson his first nomination?
25 Which Brit won Best Actor in a musical the same year that Julie Andrews won for *Mary Poppins*?

**Answers John Wayne** (see Quiz 6)
**1** Duke. **2** *Stagecoach*. **3** (American) Football. **4** Paulette Goddard. **5** *Rio Grande*. **6** Dean Martin. **7** Boxer. **8** Lauren Bacall. **9** *The Greatest Story Ever Told*. **10** Davy Crockett. **11** *Rooster Cogburn*. **12** Marion Morrison. **13** Vietnam. **14** *True Grit*. **15** *Sands of Iwo Jima*. **16** *Gunsmoke*. **17** Genghis Khan. **18** *The Big Trail*. **19** John Ford. **20** London. **21** 1979 Oscar ceremony. **22** *The Alamo*. **23** *The Searchers*. **24** *Rio Bravo*. **25** *The Shootist*.

## *QUIZ 9* POT LUCK 4 ........ LEVEL 2

*Answers – see page 127*

1 Who directed *Scream*?
2 How is Joyce Frankenberg better known?
3 In which decade was *Gigi* released?
4 Which Linda starred in *Dante's Peak*?
5 Who won the Best Actress Oscar for *Misery*?
6 In which film did Roger Moore first play 007?
7 What was the name of Tommy Lee Jones's character in *Men in Black*?
8 Who won the Best Director Oscar for *The Apartment*?
9 Used in *Breakfast at Tiffany's*, 'Moon River' is the theme music from which film?
10 Who was 'La Lollo'?
11 Who co-starred with Meryl Streep in *A Cry in the Dark*?
12 Who received her first Oscar nomination for *Silkwood*?
13 Which song won Best Song Oscar for *The Towering Inferno*?
14 In which film did a character named Johnny Castle appear?
15 Who replaced George Segal in Blake Edwards's comedy *10*?
16 Who directed Anthony Hopkins in *Shadowlands*?
17 What was Marilyn Monroe's last film?
18 Who plays the title role in *Michael Collins*?
19 To the nearest hour, how long does *The Bodyguard* last?
20 Which actor links the films *Alice* and *Malice*?
21 Who directed *Romeo + Juliet*?
22 In which decade was *Willy Wonka and the Chocolate Factory* released?
23 Who won the Best Actor Oscar for *Leaving Las Vegas*?
24 Which Toni starred in *Emma*?
25 Who played the Bond girl in *Live and Let Die*?

**Answers Robin Williams** (see Quiz 11)
**1** *Mork & Mindy*. **2** Sally Field. **3** Robert De Niro. **4** 1980s. **5** Nixon. **6** Pierce Brosnan. **7** *The World According to Garp*. **8** Popeye. **9** Kenneth Branagh. **10** *Mrs Doubtfire*. **11** Lawyer. **12** Jeff. **13** The genie. **14** Peter Pan. **15** Shelley Duvall. **16** Aberdeen. **17** *Jumanji*. **18** Disc jockey. **19** *Moscow on the Hudson*. **20** Gilliam. **21** *Good Morning, Vietnam*. **22** *Dead Poets Society*. **23** Levinson. **24** *Cadillac Man*. **25** 1960s.

## *QUIZ 10* CLASSICS ........ LEVEL 2

*Answers – see page 128*

1 In which classic did Paul Heinreid play Victor Laszlo?
2 Which animal sings 'We're off to see the wizard, the wonderful Wizard of Oz' with Dorothy and co.?
3 In which movie did Trevor Howard play Alec Harvey?
4 What was deemed the cinema's first epic?
5 Which 50s movie told of Moses leading the children of Israel to the Promised Land?
6 'All right, Mr de Mille, I'm ready for my close-ups now' is the last line of which movie?
7 In which movie did Debra Winger begin with, 'Anyone here named Loowis?'?
8 Was Debbie Reynolds 18, 20 or 22 when she made *Singin' in the Rain*?
9 Which inventor did Michael Redgrave play in *The Dam Busters*?
10 Which of the stars of *The Philadelphia Story* donated his salary for the movie to war relief?
11 Who was Spade in *The Maltese Falcon*?
12 In *The Third Man* who had Joseph Cotten come to Vienna to meet?
13 Which movie had the ad line, 'Meet Benjamin. He's a little worried about his future'?
14 *A Man for All Seasons* is about whom?
15 Which 1946 Frank Capra movie with James Stewart became a Christmas classic?
16 Who did Marlene Dietrich play in *The Blue Angel*?
17 Who does James Cagney play in *White Heat*?
18 Which movie opens with the line, 'What can you say about a 25-year-old girl who died'?
19 Which member of the Corleone family did Al Pacino play in the *Godfather* trilogy?
20 In which movie did Rita Hayworth remove a glove to 'Put the Blame on Mame'?
21 What was Lauren Bacall's first film, in 1943?
22 In *Genevieve* who or what was Genevieve?
23 Which movie did Elvis Presley make next after *King Creole*?
24 Who played opposite Lana Turner in the original *The Postman Always Rings Twice*?
25 In which 1954 movie did Marlon Brando play a boxer?

**Answers Pot Luck 5** (see Quiz 12)
**1** Stephen King. **2** Paul Newman. **3** Kozlowski. **4** Hugh Montenegro and his Orchestra and Chorus. **5** George Clooney. **6** Elia Kazan. **7** Bill Murray. **8** *Rain Man.* **9** Stander. **10** Donald O'Connor. **11** Lee Marvin. **12** Rick Moranis. **13** Archie Leach. **14** 1950s. **15** *The Prince and the Showgirl.* **16** Kenneth Branagh. **17** Franco Zeffirelli. **18** 2 hours. **19** Groucho. **20** 'Nobody Does It Better'. **21** Robert Redford. **22** Bette Davis. **23** Cusack. **24** Bob Geldof. **25** 1930s.

## *QUIZ 11* ROBIN WILLIAMS ........................................ LEVEL 2

*Answers – see page 125*

1 In which TV series did Robin Williams find fame in the 70s/80s?
2 Who played his ex-wife in *Mrs Doubtfire*?
3 Who was his male co-star in *Awakenings*?
4 In which decade did he make his first major movie?
5 In *Good Morning, Vietnam*, which President does Cronauer alias Williams impersonate?
6 Which 007 starred in *Mrs Doubtfire*?
7 Which 80s movie saw co-star Glenn Close win an Oscar nomination?
8 Which cartoon character did he play in a 1980 Robert Altman movie?
9 Which then-husband of Emma Thompson directed *Dead Again*?
10 In which movie does he play Daniel Hilliard?
11 What is the occupation of the grown-up Peter Pan in *Hook*?
12 Which member of the Bridges family was a co-star in *The Fisher King*?
13 Whose voice did he provide in *Aladdin*?
14 Who did he play in *Hook*?
15 Who played Olive to his Popeye?
16 Where in Scotland is the 'nanny' from in *Mrs Doubtfire*?
17 In which film was he 'released' from a board game after 26 years?
18 What was his job in *Good Morning, Vietnam*?
19 In which early film did he play a Russian saxophonist?
20 Which former Python Terry directed him in *The Fisher King*?
21 Which movie gave him his first Oscar nomination?
22 In which movie did he play an unorthodox prep school teacher?
23 Which Barry directed him in *Good Morning, Vietnam*?
24 In which film is he a car salesman held hostage by a jealous husband?
25 The 80s *Good Morning, Vietnam* featured songs from which decade on its soundtrack?

**Answers Pot Luck 4** (see Quiz 9)
**1** Wes Craven. **2** Jane Seymour. **3** 1950s. **4** Hamilton. **5** Kathy Bates. **6** *Live and Let Die*. **7** K. **8** Billy Wilder. **9** *Days of Wine and Roses*. **10** Gina Lollobrigida. **11** Sam Neill. **12** Cher. **13** 'We May Never Love Like This Again'. **14** *Dirty Dancing*. **15** Dudley Moore. **16** Richard Attenborough. **17** *The Misfits*. **18** Liam Neeson. **19** 2 hours. **20** Alec Baldwin. **21** Baz Luhrmann. **22** 1970s. **23** Nicolas Cage. **24** Collette. **25** Jane Seymour.

## *QUIZ 12* POT LUCK 5 ........ LEVEL 2

*Answers – see page 126*

1 On whose book was the River Phoenix film *Stand By Me* based?
2 Who won the Best Actor Oscar for *The Color of Money*?
3 Which Linda starred in *Crocodile Dundee*?
4 Who recorded the title song of *The Good, the Bad and the Ugly*?
5 Who starred opposite Nicole Kidman in *The Peacemaker*?
6 Who won the Best Director Oscar for *On the Waterfront*?
7 *Tootsie* and *Scrooged* both feature which actor?
8 A character named Charlie Babbitt appeared in which film?
9 Which Lionel featured in *New York, New York*?
10 Who played Cosmo Brown in *Singin' in the Rain*?
11 Which actor's split from long-time partner Michelle introduced the word 'palimony'?
12 *Ghostbusters* and *Parenthood* both feature which actor?
13 Who did John Cleese play in *A Fish Called Wanda*?
14 In which decade was *Bus Stop* released?
15 In which film was Laurence Olivier teamed with Marilyn Monroe?
16 Which actor links *In the Bleak Mid-Winter* and *Othello*?
17 Who directed Mel Gibson in *Hamlet*?
18 To the nearest hour, how long does *Alien* last?
19 Which Marx brother was born Julius?
20 What was the Bond theme for *The Spy Who Loved Me* called?
21 Who directed *A River Runs Through It*?
22 Who won the Best Actress Oscar for *Dangerous*?
23 Which John starred in *Con Air*?
24 Which singer appeared in *The Wall*?
25 In which decade was *Pygmalion* released?

**Answers Classics** (see Quiz 10)
**1** *Casablanca.* **2** Lion. **3** *Brief Encounter.* **4** *Birth of a Nation.* **5** *The Ten Commandments.* **6** *Sunset Boulevard.* **7** *Shadowlands.* **8** 20. **9** Barnes Wallis. **10** Cary Grant. **11** Humphrey Bogart. **12** Harry Lime. **13** *The Graduate.* **14** Thomas More. **15** *It's a Wonderful Life.* **16** Lola Lola. **17** Cody Jarrett. **18** *Love Story.* **19** Michael. **20** *Gilda.* **21** *To Have and Have Not.* **22** Car. **23** *GI Blues.* **24** John Garfield. **25** *On the Waterfront.*

## *QUIZ 13* CARTOONS ........ LEVEL 2

*Answers – see page 131*

1 Who was the voice of the dragon in *Mulan*?
2 Which 1997 movie featured the voices of Meg Ryan and John Cusack?
3 What was the first full-length animated movie to be Oscar-nominated for Best Film?
4 Whose songs feature in *Toy Story*?
5 Where do the characters live in *Who Framed Roger Rabbit??*
6 Which 1945 Gene Kelly movie featured an animation sequence by Hanna and Barbera?
7 Which movie features Jiminy Cricket and Figaro?
8 *The Land Before Time* features an orphaned what?
9 Which 1995 movie saw Robin Williams being rescued from a board game?
10 Hakuna Matata is in which movie?
11 What are the Siamese cats called in *Lady and the Tramp*?
12 What was the name of the wicked uncle in *The Lion King*?
13 What is the name of the dinosaur in *Toy Story*?
14 *The Return of Jafar* was the sequel to which movie?
15 Which classic film has a rabbit called Thumper?
16 Which director provided a voice in *Antz*?
17 Which star of *Friends* provides a voice in *The Iron Giant*?
18 Who was the voice of John Smith in *Pocahontas*?
19 Who was the voice of Jessica in *Who Framed Roger Rabbit??*
20 Which studio, famous for musicals, did Hanna and Barbera work for in the 40s?
21 Which 1999 movie featured the voices of Minnie Driver and Tony Goldwyn?
22 Which duo's first movie was in *Puss Gets the Boot*?
23 Lea Salonga sang on the soundtrack of *Aladdin* after making her name in which musical?
24 In *The Lion King* what sort of animal was Shenzi?
25 What is the name of 'the king of the swingers' in Disney's *Jungle Book*?

**Answers Pot Luck 6** (see Quiz 15)
**1** Johnny Depp. **2** Lithgow. **3** 87 minutes. **4** Jonathan Demme. **5** 1940s. **6** Lane. **7** Brad Pitt. **8** Barry Levinson. **9** *The Deer Hunter*. **10** *Scream*. **11** 1970s. **12** Moorehead. **13** Sharon and Susan. **14** Groucho Marx. **15** *Crocodile Dundee*. **16** Kelly McGillis. **17** Dan Aykroyd. **18** Mel Gibson. **19** Holly Goodhead. **20** Broderick. **21** Mrs Pearce. **22** Jack Lemmon. **23** *Blind Date*. **24** Katharine Hepburn. **25** 1950s.

## *QUIZ 14* 1980s STARS ........................................ LEVEL 2

*Answers – see page 132*

1 What sort of accent does Meryl Streep have in *Out of Africa*?
2 Who was described as the Buster Keaton of Hong Kong?
3 Which star of *Chariots of Fire* and *Gandhi* died of AIDS in 1990?
4 Where does Rutger Hauer hail from?
5 Which Oscar-winner from *Ordinary People* was married to Debra Winger for three years?
6 What was Diane Keaton's next Oscar nomination after *Annie Hall*?
7 Kevin Kline appeared in the movie of which Gilbert & Sullivan opera which he had starred in on Broadway?
8 What sort of musician was Sigourney Weaver in *Ghostbusters*?
9 Which outspoken talk-show hostess made her movie debut in *Hairspray*?
10 Which widow of Kurt Cobain was a star of *Sid and Nancy*?
11 In which film did Jack Nicholson say, 'Here's Johnny'?
12 Which star of TV's *Cheers* is famous on the big screen for *Look Who's Talking*?
13 Who won the National Society of Film Critics award in the US for playing the ghoul in *Beetlejuice*?
14 Who was the aerobics instructor in *Perfect*?
15 Who gained notoriety for her 'you like me, you really like me' Oscar acceptance speech in 1984?
16 Who had his wife as co-star in *Shanghai Surprise*?
17 Which father and son appeared in *Wall Street*?
18 Who played Loretta Lynn in *Coal Miner's Daughter*?
19 For which movie was Julie Walters Oscar-nominated on her film debut?
20 Which husband and wife starred in *DOA* in 1988?
21 Who played two parts in *Dead Ringers* in 1988?
22 In which movie did Debra Winger play an angel?
23 Who played Sid Vicious in *Sid and Nancy*?
24 Which writer did Jack Nicholson play in *Reds*?
25 Who married Melanie Griffith twice?

**Answers Dustin Hoffman** (see Quiz 16)
**1** *Kramer versus Kramer*. **2** Two. **3** *Papillon*. **4** Journalist. **5** Broderick. **6** *The Merchant of Venice*. **7** Jessica Lange. **8** 1930s. **9** Nichols. **10** *Little Big Man*. **11** Los Angeles. **12** *Billy Bathgate*. **13** *The Graduate*. **14** *Tootsie*. **15** Willy Loman. **16** Raymond. **17** *Midnight Cowboy*. **18** *Marathon Man*. **19** *Ishtar*. **20** Carl Bernstein. **21** *Agatha*. **22** Lenny Bruce. **23** Sean Connery. **24** *Dick Tracy*. **25** Captain Hook in *Hook*.

## *QUIZ 15* POT LUCK 6 ........ LEVEL 2

*Answers – see page 129*

1 Which movie star had 'Winona Forever' tattoed on his arm?
2 Which John starred in *Cliffhanger*?
3 Within fifteen minutes, how long does *The Blair Witch Project* last?
4 Who won the Best Director Oscar for *The Silence of the Lambs*?
5 In which decade of the 20th century was Chevy Chase born?
6 Which Diane featured in *Rumble Fish*?
7 Who played JD in *Thelma and Louise*?
8 Who directed *Rain Man*?
9 Which Michael Cimino film about Vietnam won five Oscars in the 70s?
10 In which film did a character named Gale Weathers first appear?
11 In which decade was *Chinatown* released?
12 Which Agnes appeared in *Citizen Kane* and *Jane Eyre*?
13 What are the names of the twins in *The Parent Trap*?
14 Margaret Dumont was which comedian's most famous film stooge?
15 In which 80s action comedy did the character Sue Charlton appear?
16 Who was Tom Cruise's leading lady in *Top Gun*?
17 Which actor links *The Couch Trip* and *Sergeant Bilko*?
18 Which actor's middle names are Columcille Gerard?
19 What was the name of the Bond girl in *Moonraker*?
20 Which Matthew starred in *The Cable Guy*?
21 Who is Professor Higgins's housekeeper in *My Fair Lady*?
22 Who won the Best Actor Oscar for *Save the Tiger*?
23 What was Bruce Willis's first film, in 1987?
24 Who won the Best Actress Oscar for *Morning Glory*?
25 In which decade was *Around the World in Eighty Days* released?

**Answers Cartoons** (see Quiz 13)
**1** Eddie Murphy. **2** *Anastasia.* **3** *Beauty and the Beast.* **4** Randy Newman. **5** Toontown. **6** *Anchors Aweigh.* **7** *Pinocchio.* **8** Dinosaur. **9** *Jumanji.* **10** *The Lion King.* **11** Si & Am. **12** Scar. **13** Rex. **14** *Aladdin.* **15** *Bambi.* **16** Woody Allen. **17** Jennifer Aniston. **18** Mel Gibson. **19** Kathleen Turner. **20** MGM. **21** *Tarzan.* **22** Tom & Jerry. **23** *Miss Saigon.* **24** Hyena. **25** King Louie.

## *QUIZ 16* DUSTIN HOFFMAN ........................ LEVEL 2

*Answers – see page 130*

1 Which 70s weepie saw Meryl Streep as his co-star?
2 How many 20th century Oscars did he win?
3 In which movie did he play a prisoner on Devils' Island?
4 What was his occupation in *All the President's Men*?
5 Which Matthew played his son in *Family Business*?
6 Which Shakespeare play did he appear in on Broadway and in London in 1989 and 1990 respectively?
7 Who was his female co-star in *Tootsie*?
8 In which decade was he born?
9 Which Mike directed him in *The Graduate*?
10 In which western did he age from 12 to 121?
11 In which city was he born?
12 In which 1991 movie did he play gangster Dutch Schultz?
13 For which movie did he receive his first Oscar nomination?
14 Which movie saw him as a female soap star?
15 Which character did he play on stage in *Death of a Salesman*?
16 What was his character called in *Rain Man*?
17 In which movie did he play Ratso Rizzo?
18 For which 1976 role did he famously keep himself awake for seven days to look the part?
19 For which flop did he team up with Warren Beatty?
20 What was the name of his character in *All the President's Men*?
21 In which 1979 biopic did he receive mixed reviews?
22 Who did he portray in *Lenny*?
23 Which superstar played his father in *Family Business*?
24 In which Warren Beatty movie did he play Mumbles in 1990?
25 Which character was he in a 1991 film based on a children's classic?

**Answers 1980s Stars** (see Quiz 14)
**1** Danish. **2** Jackie Chan. **3** Ian Charleson. **4** Holland. **5** Timothy Hutton. **6** *Reds.* **7** *Pirates of Penzance.* **8** Cellist. **9** Ricki Lake. **10** Courtney Love. **11** *The Shining.* **12** Kirstie Alley. **13** Michael Keaton. **14** Jamie Lee Curtis. **15** Sally Field. **16** Sean Penn. **17** Martin & Charlie Sheen. **18** Sissy Spacek. **19** *Educating Rita.* **20** Dennis Quaid & Meg Ryan. **21** Jeremy Irons. **22** *Made in Heaven.* **23** Gary Oldman. **24** Eugene O'Neill. **25** Don Johnson.

## *QUIZ 17* LATE GREATS ........ LEVEL 2

*Answers – see page 135*

1 Who described himself as Mr Average Joe American?
2 Which silent star's name was an anagram of 'Arab death'?
3 Who was the sister of Olivia De Havilland?
4 About whom did Elia Kazan say, 'He was sad and sulky. You kept expecting him to cry'?
5 Whose biography was called *Blonde Venus*?
6 Which 30s star famous for his dislike of children said, 'I am free of all prejudices, I hate everybody equally'?
7 How many times did Alan Hale play Little John in a Robin Hood movie?
8 Which director was the subject of *Gods and Monsters*, played on screen by Sir Ian McKellen?
9 Who said, 'There are two reasons I'm in showbusiness and I'm standing on both of them'?
10 What colour was Danny Kaye's hair before Goldwyn made him dye it blond?
11 Who said, 'Astaire represents the aristocracy when he dances. I represent the proletariat'?
12 Whose photo in a swimsuit was pinned to the atomic bomb dropped on Bikini?
13 Who did Goldwyn mean when he said, 'It took longer to make one of Mary's contracts than to make one of Mary's pictures'?
14 In *Casablanca* which British actor said, 'I'm only a poor corrupt official'?
15 Which Tex sang the title song from *High Noon*?
16 Which creator of *Star Trek* was executive producer on the early *Star Trek* movies?
17 Who was the mother of actress Isabella Rossellini?
18 Which French actor's body was exhumed in 1997 because of a paternity suit?
19 Who died shortly after finishing *Network*?
20 In which decade did Jean Harlow die?
21 Whose marriage to Ava Gardner lasted just seven months?
22 Anthony Perkins died during the making of which movie?
23 Who played opposite Olivia De Havilland eight times?
24 Where was Audrey Hepburn born?
25 Whose autobiography was called *Back in the Saddle Again*?

**Answers 1940s** (see Quiz 19)
**1** Little John. **2** Rita Hayworth. **3** Jo. **4** Betty Grable. **5** Aldous Huxley. **6** *It's a Wonderful Life.* **7** Larry Parks. **8** *Brigadoon.* **9** *Miracle on 34th Street.* **10** Maxim De Winter. **11** James Cagney. **12** Gene Autry. **13** *Casablanca.* **14** Charles Foster. **15** Bra. **16** Heinreid. **17** Spencer Tracy. **18** Betty Grable. **19** Bing Crosby. **20** *Pimpernel Smith.* **21** *Great Expectations.* **22** World War I. **23** *The Magnificent Ambersons.* **24** Judy Garland. **25** Jennifer Jones.

## *QUIZ 18* POT LUCK 7 ........ LEVEL 2

*Answers – see page 136*

1 What was the name of Nicolas Cage's character in *Con Air*?
2 In which decade was *Driving Miss Daisy* released?
3 Which movie star released a single called 'A Distant Star' in 1986?
4 Which suave actor turned down Robert Preston's role in *The Music Man*?
5 Which Elizabeth starred in *Big*?
6 Who won the Best Actor Oscar for *Dr Jekyll and Mr Hyde*?
7 What is Richard Gere's middle name?
8 Who was the youngest Marx brother?
9 What is Schindler's nationality in *Schindler's List*?
10 Who did Louise Fletcher play in *One Flew over the Cuckoo's Nest*?
11 For which film did Gregory Peck win his first Oscar?
12 Which Kevin featured in *Se7en*?
13 Who was Paul Newman's second wife?
14 Who played Renton in *Trainspotting*?
15 Which film features the song 'Brush Up Your Shakespeare'?
16 In which decade was *El Dorado* released?
17 Which actress is Mrs Carlo Ponti?
18 Who sang the Bond theme 'From Russia with Love'?
19 Who won the Best Actress Oscar for *Jezebel*?
20 What was the name of Jack Nicholson's character in *Prizzi's Honor*?
21 Which Shelley starred in *The Brady Bunch Movie*?
22 Who played the devious US Senator in *GI Jane*?
23 Which type of disability affects Tom Cruise and Susan Hampshire?
24 In the 1980s who bought the screen rights to *Dick Tracy* and made a film from it?
25 Who is Mrs Danny DeVito?

**Answers Pot Luck 8** (see Quiz 20)
**1** *Fatal Attraction*. **2** Hunt. **3** Michael Caine. **4** 1960s. **5** Jennifer Jones. **6** Tiffany Case. **7** Jonathan Demme. **8** James Mason. **9** *Return of the Jedi*. **10** Callow. **11** Woody Allen. **12** Burt Reynolds. **13** Walter Matthau. **14** Marianne Faithfull. **15** *Liar Liar*. **16** 'I Just Called to Say I Love You'. **17** Preston. **18** Jessica Lange. **19** 1970s. **20** Burt Lancaster. **21** Mayer. **22** Redgrave. **23** Lee Marvin. **24** John Schlesinger. **25** Bening.

## *QUIZ 19* 1940s ........ LEVEL 2

*Answers – see page 133*

1 Which Merry Man did Alan Hale play in *The Adventures of Robin Hood*?
2 Which redhead played Virginia Brush in *Strawberry Blonde*?
3 Which sister did June Allyson play in *Little Women*?
4 Which blonde replaced Alice Faye in *Down Argentina Way*?
5 Which author of *Brave New World* wrote screenplays for *Pride and Prejudice* and *Jane Eyre*?
6 In which movie did Henry Travers play an angel?
7 Who played Al Jolson in *The Jolson Story*?
8 What was the first musical hit in 1947 of Lerner and Loewe, which became a movie hit seven years later?
9 In which classic movie did Edward Gwenn play Kris Kringle?
10 Who did Laurence Olivier play in *Rebecca*?
11 Who played George M. Cohan in *Yankee Doodle Dandy*?
12 Which cowboy was high up in the money-making lists in 1940?
13 Which movie had the line, 'We'll always have Paris'?
14 What were Citizen Kane's first names?
15 Which garment did Howard Hughes develop for Jane Russell in *The Outlaw*?
16 Which Paul was one of Bette Davis's co-stars in *Now Voyager*?
17 Who played two parts in *Dr Jekyll and Mr Hyde* in 1941?
18 Who was the star of the 40s version of *Million Dollar Legs*?
19 Who was Father O'Malley to Ingrid Bergman's Sister Benedict in 1945?
20 What was the Leslie Howard version of *The Scarlet Pimpernel* called?
21 Which Dickens novel was successfully adapted for the big screen by David Lean in 1946?
22 *Sergeant York* was about a hero from which conflict?
23 Which Orson Welles movie was given its final edit without his approval?
24 Who was Fred Astaire's co-star in *Easter Parade*?
25 Which real-life Jennifer starred in *Portrait of Jennie*?

**Answers Late Greats** (see Quiz 17)
**1** Gary Cooper. **2** Theda Bara. **3** Joan Fontaine. **4** James Dean. **5** Marlene Dietrich. **6** W.C. Fields. **7** Three. **8** James Whale. **9** Betty Grable. **10** Red. **11** Gene Kelly. **12** Betty Grable. **13** Mary Pickford. **14** Claude Rains. **15** Ritter. **16** Gene Roddenberry. **17** Ingrid Bergman. **18** Yves Montand. **19** Peter Finch. **20** 1930s. **21** Artie Shaw. **22** *Psycho V*. **23** Errol Flynn. **24** Belgium. **25** Gene Autry.

## *QUIZ 20* POT LUCK 8 ........ LEVEL 2

*Answers – see page 134*

1 A character named Dan Gallagher appears in which film?
2 Which Helen starred in *As Good as it Gets*?
3 How is Maurice Micklewhite better known?
4 In which decade was *Planet of the Apes* released?
5 Who won the Best Actress Oscar for *The Song of Bernadette*?
6 What was the name of the Bond girl in *Diamonds Are Forever*?
7 Who directed *Philadelphia*?
8 *A Star Is Born* and *The Verdict* featured which actor?
9 Jabba the Hutt is a villain in which 1983 movie sequel?
10 Which Simon featured in *Four Weddings and a Funeral*?
11 Which actor links *Hannah and Her Sisters* and *Mighty Aphrodite*?
12 Which actor's first two wives were Judy Carne and Loni Anderson?
13 Who played Oscar Madison in *The Odd Couple*?
14 Who was Alain Delon's *Girl on an Motorcycle* in 1968?
15 A character named Fletcher Reede appeared in which film?
16 Which song won Best Song Oscar for *The Woman in Red*?
17 Which Kelly featured in *Jerry Maguire*?
18 Who played opposite Dustin Hoffman in *Tootsie*?
19 In which decade was *Annie Hall* released?
20 Who won the Best Actor Oscar for *Elmer Gantry*?
21 What did the second M stand for in MGM?
22 Which Lynn featured in *Shine*?
23 *Cat Ballou* and *Paint Your Wagon* both featured which actor?
24 Who won the Best Director Oscar for *Midnight Cowboy*?
25 Which Annette starred in *The American President*?

**Answers Pot Luck 7** (see Quiz 18)
**1** Cameron Poe. **2** 1980s. **3** Anthony Hopkins. **4** Cary Grant. **5** Perkins. **6** Frederic March. **7** Tiffany. **8** Zeppo. **9** Austrian. **10** Nurse Ratchet. **11** *To Kill a Mockingbird.* **12** Spacey. **13** Joanne Woodward. **14** Ewan McGregor. **15** *Kiss Me Kate.* **16** 1960s. **17** Sophia Loren. **18** Matt Monro. **19** Bette Davis. **20** Charley Partanna. **21** Long. **22** Anne Bancroft. **23** Dyslexia. **24** Warren Beatty. **25** Rhea Perlman.

## *QUIZ 21* STARS OF THE 21ST CENTURY .............................. LEVEL 2

*Answers – see page 139*

1 Which actress was Oscar-nominated for *The End of the Affair*?
2 What nationality are Jennifer Lopez's parents?
3 Who was Valerie Edmond's male co-star in *One More Kiss*?
4 Which actress voices Jessie in *Toy Story 2*?
5 Which actor links *Sleepy Hollow* and *Starship Troopers*?
6 Who links the films *Now and Then* and *American Beauty*?
7 Who does Virginie Ledoyden play in *The Beach*?
8 Who starred opposite Johnny Depp in *Devil's Advocate*?
9 Who played the law officer in *Double Jeopardy*?
10 Who plays Toni Collette's son in *The Sixth Sense*?
11 Which actress links *Romeo + Juliet* and *Little Women*?
12 What name links *Stigmata* and *Scream 3*?
13 Who has been Oscar-nominated for *Being John Malkovich*?
14 Who was 'the next best thing' for Madonna in the movie of the same name?
15 Which actor links *The Beach* and *Angela's Ashes*?
16 Which actress links *Elizabeth* and *The Talented Mr Ripley*?
17 Who voices the Rooster in *Chicken Run*?
18 Which actress links *Pleasantville* and *Dangerous Liaisons*?
19 Who links *Trainspotting* and *Star Wars: The Phantom Menace*?
20 Which actress links *Leon* and *Star Wars: The Phantom Menace*?
21 Who played the young temptress in *American Beauty*?
22 Who links *Picture Perfect* and *The Iron Giant*?
23 What was the name of DiCaprio's character in *The Beach*?
24 Who was Oscar-nominated for *The Talented Mr Ripley*?
25 Which actress links *The Ice Storm* and *The Opposite of Sex*?

**Answers Pot Luck 9** (see Quiz 23)
**1** Najimy. **2** Boxing. **3** Elizabeth Mastrantonio. **4** Ingrid Bergman. **5** Steve Martin. **6** Chris Columbus. **7** Sean Archer. **8** *Children of a Lesser God.*
**9** Rachmaninov. **10** 1950s. **11** Franklin Schaffner. **12** *Singin' in the Rain.* **13** *Air Force One.* **14** Lucy Honeychurch. **15** Alfred Hitchcock. **16** *Gigi.* **17** Richard E. Grant. **18** Steve McQueen. **19** *The Color Purple.* **20** Peter Benchley. **21** Donald Pleasence. **22** Jeremy Irons. **23** Cox. **24** 1980s. **25** Maximilian Schell.

## *QUIZ 22* CHILD STARS ............ LEVEL 2

*Answers – see page 140*

1 What is Macaulay Culkin's brother called who starred in *Father of the Bride*?
2 Which former child star became Mrs Andre Agassi?
3 Who played the Artful Dodger in *Oliver!*?
4 In which movie, remade in 1998, did Hayley Mills sing 'Let's Get Together'?
5 Whose autobiography was called *Little Girl Lost*?
6 Who played the possessed child in *The Exorcist*?
7 Which Oscar winner from *As Good as it Gets* was a child star on US TV?
8 In which Bruce Willis movie did Haley Joe Osment star?
9 Mark Lester played the title role in which 60s musical?
10 How many movies had Macaulay Culkin made before *Home Alone*?
11 Was Judy Garland 13, 15 or 17 when she played Dorothy in *The Wizard of Oz*?
12 In which 1993 dinosaur film did Joseph Mazello star?
13 Lisa Jakub ended up having her father disguised as a nanny in which movie?
14 Rumer Willis appeared with Mum in *Striptease*; who is she?
15 Which child star appeared in *Mermaids*, aged 10, and moved on to *The Ice Storm*?
16 Was Jodie Foster 12, 14 or 16 when she starred in *Taxi Driver*?
17 Who was Macaulay Culkin's first wife?
18 Who said, 'I was a 16-year-old boy for 30 years'?
19 Former child star Richard Beymer starred in which 60s musical opposite Natalie Wood?
20 In which country was Deanna Durbin born?
21 Which star of *Chasing Amy* started acting at the age of eight?
22 What was Hayley Mills's first film, in 1959?
23 How many times did Judy Garland marry?
24 Who played two parts in *The Prince and the Pauper* in 1977?
25 Who played opposite Judy Garland 10 times?

**Answers Directors** (see Quiz 24)
**1** Finland. **2** Cecil B. de Mille. **3** Charlton Heston. **4** Christopher Guest. **5** *Cry Freedom.* **6** *Heaven's Gate.* **7** *Pulp Fiction.* **8** Kenneth Branagh. **9** Alan Parker. **10** Julie Andrews. **11** Ireland. **12** Blount. **13** Geena Davis. **14** John. **15** Cuba. **16** Kirk. **17** Kenneth Branagh. **18** Roman Polanski. **19** *Poetic Justice.* **20** *Jurassic Park.* **21** Antonio Banderas. **22** Robert Wise. **23** *The Horse Whisperer.* **24** Frank Sinatra. **25** *Bruno.*

## *QUIZ 23* POT LUCK 9 ........ LEVEL 2

*Answers – see page 137*

1 Which Kathy featured in *Sister Act*?
2 At what sport did Robert De Niro excel?
3 Which Mary starred in *The Abyss*?
4 Who won the Best Actress Oscar for *Gaslight*?
5 *The Muppet Movie* and *The Man with Two Brains* link which actor?
6 Who directed *Mrs Doubtfire*?
7 What was the name of John Travolta's character in *Face/Off*?
8 William Hurt and Marlee Matlin's relationship began on the set of which movie?
9 Which classical composer's music features in *Brief Encounter*?
10 In which decade was *An Affair to Remember* released?
11 Who won the Best Director Oscar for *Patton*?
12 Which classic musical charts the careers of Lockwood and Lamont?
13 In which film did the character President James Marshall appear?
14 What was the name of Helena Bonham Carter's character in *A Room with a View*?
15 Who directed the 1938 version of *The Lady Vanishes*?
16 For which film was Vincente Minnelli awarded his only Oscar?
17 Who played Seward in the 90s *Bram Stoker's Dracula*?
18 *The Blob* and *Le Mans* both featured which actor?
19 Sisters named Celie and Nettie appeared in which film?
20 Who wrote the book on which *Jaws* was based?
21 Who played Heinrich Himmler in *The Eagle Has Landed*?
22 Which British actor won an Oscar for *Reversal of Fortune*?
23 Which Courtney starred in *Ace Ventura, Pet Detective*?
24 In which decade was *Airplane!* released?
25 Who won the Best Actor Oscar for *Judgment at Nuremberg*?

**Answers Stars of the 21st Century** (see Quiz 21)
**1** Julianne Moore. **2** Puerto Rican. **3** Gerry Butler. **4** Joan Cusack. **5** Casper Van Dien. **6** Thora Birch. **7** Francoise. **8** Charlize Theron. **9** Tommy Lee Jones. **10** Haley Joel Osment. **11** Claire Danes. **12** Arquette (Patricia and David). **13** Spike Jonze. **14** Rupert Everett. **15** Robert Carlyle. **16** Cate Blanchett. **17** Mel Gibson. **18** Reese Witherspoon. **19** Ewan McGregor. **20** Natalie Portman. **21** Mena Suvari. **22** Jennifer Aniston. **23** Richard. **24** Jude Law. **25** Christina Ricci.

## *QUIZ 24* DIRECTORS ........ LEVEL 2

*Answers – see page 138*

1 Where does Renny Harlin hail from?
2 About which producer/director did his brother say, 'Cecil always bites off more than he can chew, then chews it'?
3 Who directed and starred in *Antony and Cleopatra* in 1973?
4 Which director did Jamie Lee Curtis marry?
5 Which movie did Richard Attenborough direct about a journalist's escape from South Africa?
6 Which flop was Michael Cimino's next film after *The Deer Hunter*?
7 In which of his own movies did Quentin Tarantino appear in 1994?
8 Which British director's autobiography was called *In the Beginning*?
9 Who directed *Angela's Ashes*?
10 Which movie star is Blake Edwards married to?
11 John Ford was from a family which originally came from which country?
12 What did the B stand for in Cecil B. de Mille's name?
13 Who was Renny Harlin's wife when he directed her in *The Long Kiss Goodnight*?
14 Which Boulting brother was the director?
15 Director Tomas Gutierrez Alea hails from which island?
16 Which Douglas made his directorial debut in *Posse*?
17 Who directed his then mother-in-law in *Much Ado About Nothing* in 1993?
18 Which director, whose mother perished in Auschwitz, subsequently fled the USA on an assault charge?
19 What was John Singleton's follow-up to *Boyz N the Hood*?
20 Which movie was Spielberg editing by satellite while filming *Schindler's List*?
21 Whose directorial debut was *Crazy in Alabama*?
22 Who replaced William Wyler as director of *The Sound of Music*?
23 What was Robert Redford's first attempt at directing himself?
24 Which singer/actor's only foray behind the camera was in *None But the Brave*?
25 What was Shirley MacLaine's first film in full charge as director?

**Answers Child Stars** (see Quiz 22)
**1** Kieran. **2** Brooke Shields. **3** Jack Wild. **4** *The Parent Trap*. **5** Drew Barrymore. **6** Linda Blair. **7** Helen Hunt. **8** *The Sixth Sense*. **9** *Oliver!*. **10** Three. **11** 17. **12** *Jurassic Park*. **13** *Mrs Doubtfire*. **14** Demi Moore. **15** Christina Ricci. **16** 14. **17** Rachel Miner. **18** Mickey Rooney. **19** *West Side Story*. **20** Canada. **21** Ben Affleck. **22** *Tiger Bay*. **23** Five. **24** Mark Lester. **25** Mickey Rooney.

## QUIZ 25 MUSICALS ........ LEVEL 2

*Answers – see page 143*

1 Which song won an Oscar for *Evita*, although it did not feature in the original stage show?
2 When Mary Poppins lands to take over the Banks household, what does she carry in her right hand?
3 Who was Fred Astaire's partner in *The Band Wagon*?
4 Which 80s movie has the song 'I Had The Time of My Life'?
5 Which fading movie star is played by Jean Hagen in *Singin' in the Rain*?
6 Which *Mary Poppins* song won the Academy Award?
7 Who played Eva's lover Magaldi in *Evita*?
8 Which musical featured the song 'Hopelessly Devoted to You'?
9 Who directed the musical *New York, New York*?
10 In which musical did Albert Finney play Daddy Warbucks?
11 Which Nellie sang 'I'm Gonna Wash That Man Right Out of My Hair'?
12 Which member of Procul Harum sang about the 'Rainbow Tour' in *Evita*?
13 Who climbed the walls singing 'Make 'em Laugh' in *Singin' in the Rain*?
14 'The Rhythm of Life' came from which musical?
15 What is the plant's catchphrase in *Little Shop of Horrors*?
16 Which musical ends with the line, 'Where the devil are my slippers'?
17 Which musical was a remake of *The Philadelphia Story*?
18 How many Oscars did *West Side Story* win?
19 What is the song played at the end of *The Sound of Music*?
20 Who was the Famous Five's manager in *Spiceworld*?
21 In which 50s musical did Fred Astaire dance on the walls and ceiling of a hotel?
22 Who won an Oscar for his role as Master of Ceremonies in *Cabaret*?
23 In *My Fair Lady* Jeremy Brett sings 'On the Street Where You Live' as which character?
24 Who sang 'Did You Ever' in *High Society*?
25 In which musical did Judy Garland sing 'Have Yourself a Merry Little Christmas'?

**Answers Marlon Brando** (see Quiz 27)
**1** Motorcycles. **2** *A Streetcar Named Desire.* **3** Mexico. **4** Cannes. **5** 1920s. **6** Vito Corleone. **7** *On the Waterfront.* **8** Manslaughter. **9** *The Wild One.* **10** *Brando: Songs My Mother Never Taught Me.* **11** Frank Sinatra. **12** *Guys and Dolls.* **13** *A Dry White Season.* **14** *The Men.* **15** *Last Tango in Paris.* **16** *One Eyed Jacks.* **17** Tahiti. **18** Vivien Leigh. **19** *On the Waterfront.* **20** *A Countess from Hong Kong.* **21** Francis Ford Coppola. **22** *A Streetcar Named Desire.* **23** *The Teahouse of the August Moon.* **24** *The Godfather.* **25** Mark Antony.

## *QUIZ 26* POT LUCK 10 ........ LEVEL 2

*Answers – see page 144*

1 A character named Dr Sherman Klump appeared in which film?
2 Which actress links *Torn Curtain* and *Star!*?
3 In which decade was *Porky's* released?
4 Which actor had siblings called Leaf, Rainbow, Summer and Liberty?
5 Who won the Best Director Oscar for *A Man for All Seasons*?
6 Which film musical features Nellie Forbush?
7 Which Denise featured in *Starship Troopers*?
8 What was the name of the Bond girl in *Octopussy*?
9 In which city does the action of *Godzilla* take place?
10 In which decade of the 20th century was Geena Davis born?
11 Which Mary featured in *Independence Day*?
12 Who won the Best Actress Oscar for *Mildred Pierce*?
13 Who played General Ben Vandervoort in *The Longest Day*?
14 To the nearest hour, how long does *Spartacus* last?
15 In which movie was Whoopi Goldberg the voice of hyena Shenzi?
16 Which writer directed *Rosencrantz and Guildenstern Are Dead* in 1990?
17 The character Martin Riggs appeared in which film?
18 Which actor is the grandson of producer Michael Balcon?
19 *Local Hero* is set on the west coast of which country?
20 *Planet of the Apes* and *The Poseidon Adventure* featured which actor?
21 Which redhead sang 'Bewitched, Bothered and Bewildered' in *Pal Joey*?
22 Which Sam featured in *The Hunt for Red October*?
23 In which decade was *The Bells of St Mary's* released?
24 *Top Gun* and *Cat Chaser* both feature which actress?
25 What's Arnold Schwarzenegger's job in *Total Recall*?

**Answers Pot Luck 11** (see Quiz 28)
**1** Pugsley. **2** Milos Forman. **3** O'Hara. **4** Paul Henreid. **5** 1980s. **6** *Moonstruck*. **7** Biehn. **8** Nancy Sinatra. **9** Kevin Costner. **10** Charles Russell. **11** Herself. **12** Switzerland. **13** Vivien Leigh. **14** Robert Loggia. **15** Bruce Lee. **16** 1960s. **17** Saturday (Night Fever). **18** Videodrome. **19** *Breakfast At Tiffany's*. **20** Sophia Loren. **21** *Cape Fear*. **22** William Hurt. **23** Rob Bowman. **24** *Dark City*. **25** Daniel Day-Lewis.

## *QUIZ 27* MARLON BRANDO ........ LEVEL 2

*Answers – see page 141*

1 What modes of transport dominate *The Wild One*?
2 Which Oscar-nominated movie had Brando previously done as a play on Broadway?
3 Where was *Viva Zapata* set?
4 At which European film festival did he win with *On the Waterfront*?
5 In which decade was he born?
6 Which character did he play in *The Godfather*?
7 For which movie did he receive his first Oscar?
8 His son Christian was jailed on what charge?
9 Which movie had the ad line, 'That streetcar man has a new desire'?
10 What was his autobiography called?
11 Which singer was earmarked for Brando's role in *On the Waterfront*?
12 In which musical did he play Sky Masterson?
13 For which 1989 movie did he receive an Oscar nomination?
14 In which movie did he make his screen debut?
15 For which 70s Bernardo Bertolucci film was he Oscar-nominated?
16 Which movie saw his directorial debut?
17 Near which South Sea island is his home Tetiaroa?
18 Who played Blanche opposite Brando in *A Streetcar Named Desire*?
19 In which movie did he famously say, 'I coulda had class. I coulda been a contender'?
20 Which Chaplin movie did he make in 1967?
21 Who directed Brando in *The Godfather*?
22 For which movie did he receive his first Oscar nomination?
23 In which 1956 movie did he play a Japanese interpreter?
24 He sent a native American Indian to pick up his Oscar for which film?
25 Which role earned him a 1953 Oscar nomination in *Julius Caesar*?

**Answers Musicals** (see Quiz 25)
**1** 'You Must Love Me'. **2** Umbrella. **3** Cyd Charisse. **4** *Dirty Dancing*. **5** Lina Lamont. **6** 'Chim Chim Cheree'. **7** Jimmy Nail. **8** *Grease*. **9** Martin Scorsese. **10** *Annie*. **11** Forbush (*South Pacific*). **12** Gary Brooker. **13** Donald O' Connor. **14** *Sweet Charity*. **15** 'Feed Me'. **16** *My Fair Lady* **17** *High Society*. **18** 10. **19** 'Climb Every Mountain'. **20** Richard E. Grant. **21** *Royal Wedding*. **22** Joel Grey. **23** Freddie Eynsford-Hill. **24** Bing Crosby & Frank Sinatra. **25** *Meet Me in St Louis*.

## *QUIZ 28* POT LUCK 11 ........................................ LEVEL 2

*Answers – see page 142*

1 What was the name of Jimmy Workman's character in *The Addams Family*?
2 Who won the Best Director Oscar for *Amadeus*?
3 Which Catherine featured in *Home Alone*?
4 Who played Victor Laszlo in *Casablanca*?
5 In which decade was *Blade Runner* released?
6 Cher won her first Oscar for which film?
7 Which Michael featured in *The Terminator*?
8 Who sang the Bond theme from 'You Only Live Twice'?
9 Who starred as Eliot Ness in *The Untouchables* in 1987?
10 Who directed *The Mask*?
11 Who did Julie Christie play in the 1975 film *Nashville*?
12 In which country did Charlie Chaplin spend the final years of his life?
13 Who won the Best Actress Oscar for *A Streetcar Named Desire*?
14 *An Officer and a Gentleman* and *Big* both feature which actor?
15 How is Lee Yuen Kam better known in western movies?
16 In which decade was *The Longest Day* released?
17 Tony Manero was a character in a movie about which day?
18 Which 1982 film did rock star Debbie Harry star in?
19 In which film did a character named Paul Varjak appear?
20 *El Cid* and *The Millionairess* both featured which actress?
21 In which film did a character named Max Cody appear?
22 Who won the Best Actor Oscar for *Kiss of the Spider Woman*?
23 Who directed *The X-Files*?
24 What was Charlton Heston's first film, in 1950?
25 Which actor is the son of a British Poet Laureate?

**Answers Pot Luck 10** (see Quiz 26)
**1** *The Nutty Professor.* **2** Julie Andrews. **3** 1980s. **4** River Phoenix. **5** Fred Zinnemann. **6** *South Pacific.* **7** Richards. **8** Octopussy. **9** New York. **10** 1950s. **11** McDonnell. **12** Joan Crawford. **13** John Wayne. **14** 3 hours. **15** *The Lion King.* **16** Tom Stoppard. **17** *Lethal Weapon.* **18** Daniel Day-Lewis. **19** Scotland. **20** Roddy McDowall. **21** Rita Hayworth. **22** Neill. **23** 1940s. **24** Kelly McGillis. **25** Construction worker.

## *QUIZ 29* ACTION ........................................ LEVEL 2

*Answers – see page 147*

1 In which movie did Robert Duvall say, 'I love the smell of napalm in the morning'?
2 In *Tomorrow Never Dies*, who played M?
3 Which singer appeared in *Mad Max Beyond Thunderdome*?
4 What was the third *Die Hard* movie called?
5 Which French city was the location for *French Connection II*?
6 What was the name of Sean Connery's villain in *The Avengers*?
7 Who was Harrison Ford's male co-star in *The Devil's Own*?
8 Which tunnel is the location for a helicopter pursuit in *Mission: Impossible*?
9 What was Serpico's first name, as played by Al Pacino?
10 Ian Fleming's Jamaican home gave its name to which Bond movie?
11 Which actor plays the head of the crew in *Armageddon*?
12 Which 007 starred in *Dante's Peak*?
13 What came number three in Oliver Stone's Vietnam trilogy?
14 Which 70s movie with Jack Lemmon was about a cover-up over a nuclear accident?
15 In *Day of the Jackal* who was the leader who was to be assassinated?
16 What was the name of Eddie Murphy's character in *48 Hours*?
17 *Courage under Fire* was about which conflict?
18 Who was the star of *Last Action Hero*?
19 Who sang the Bond theme from *For Your Eyes Only*?
20 What was Leonardo Di Caprio's first film after *Titanic*?
21 Where was *Apocalypse Now* filmed?
22 Who played the pregnant police chief in *Fargo*?
23 Which movie had the ad line, 'They came too late and stayed too long'?
24 *Patriot Games* was the sequel to which movie?
25 Who played Danny Velinski in *The Great Escape*?

**Answers Pot Luck 12** (see Quiz 31)
**1** 3 hours. **2** 1980s. **3** Julie Andrews. **4** Judd. **5** Paul Robeson. **6** Warren Beatty. **7** Tom Mullen. **8** Julia Roberts. **9** Honor Blackman. **10** Emily Lloyd. **11** 1920s. **12** *One Flew over the Cuckoo's Nest.* **13** Robertson. **14** Edward G. Robinson. **15** Moore. **16** *The Rock.* **17** Colin Firth. **18** Tippi Hedren. **19** Jon Voight. **20** 1950s. **21** Alan Rickman. **22** Arthur Hiller. **23** Modine. **24** Audrey Hepburn. **25** Christopher Lloyd.

## *QUIZ 30* OSCARS – WHO'S WHO? ............ LEVEL 2

*Answers – see page 148*

1 Who received her first Best Actress nomination for *The English Patient*?
2 Who was the female singer on 'Hopelessly Devoted (to You)' from a winning soundtrack?
3 Which screenwriter was nominated for *Four Weddings and a Funeral*?
4 Who was Oscar-nominated for the music for *Angela's Ashes*?
5 What nationality is director Ang Lee?
6 In which movie did Al Pacino play Frank Slade?
7 For which Cher/Meryl Streep movie did Nora Ephron receive her first nomination?
8 How many nominations had Helen Hunt received before winning for *As Good as it Gets*?
9 Who first sang 'The Way We Were' in the movie of the same name?
10 In 1981 who shouted 'The British are coming' at the Oscars ceremony?
11 Who has sung two 1990s Oscar-winning songs?
12 Which Brit made the animated Oscar-winner in 1993 and 1995?
13 Who shared a best screenplay Oscar for *Pygmalion*?
14 What was the nationality of the actor who won for *Life Is Beautiful*?
15 Who directed Gary Cooper to an Oscar in *Sergeant York*?
16 Who earned a nomination for the theme song from *9 to 5*?
17 Who, in addition to Cher, won an Oscar for *Moonstruck*?
18 Who designed the Oscar?
19 Which actress criticized the US government over Haiti before announcing the nominees at the 1992 Oscar ceremony?
20 Who has hosted the Oscars ceremony most often?
21 Which two British stars were nominated for *Gods and Monsters*?
22 Who was Oscar-nominated for *Twelve Monkeys*?
23 Who was 80 when she won an Oscar?
24 Who received a Special Award for *Pollyanna* aged 13?
25 Which Italian director received an honorary award in 1995?

**Answers Stars of the 50s** (see Quiz 32)
**1** Gene Kelly. **2** Claire Bloom. **3** Jean Hagen (as Lina Lamont). **4** Mario Lanza. **5** Christopher Lee. **6** Ethel Merman. **7** Kim Novak. **8** James Dean. **9** Jayne Mansfield. **10** Pal Joey. **11** Alistair Sim. **12** Harry. **13** Fred Astaire. **14** World War I. **15** *North by Northwest.* **16** Brigitte Bardot. **17** Yul Brynner. **18** Paul Newman & Joanne Woodward. **19** Richard Burton. **20** Pearl Bailey. **21** *Roman Holiday.* **22** James Stewart. **23** *Witness for the Prosecution.* **24** Burl Ives. **25** Gene Kelly.

## *QUIZ 31* POT LUCK 12 ........ LEVEL 2

*Answers – see page 145*

1 To the nearest hour, how long does *Braveheart* last?
2 In which decade was *Trading Places* released?
3 How is Julia Wells better known?
4 Which Ashley featured in *Heat*?
5 In the 1930s who sang 'Old Man River' in *Showboat*?
6 Who won the Best Director Oscar for *Reds*?
7 What was the name of Mel Gibson's character in *Ransom*?
8 Who married Lyle Lovett instead of Kiefer Sutherland?
9 Who played the Bond girl in *Goldfinger*?
10 *Wish You Were Here* and *The Real Thing* featured which actress?
11 Was *The Untouchables* with Kevin Costner set in the 1920s, 40s or 60s?
12 In which film did a character named Randie P. McMurphy appear?
13 Which Cliff featured in *Three Days of the Condor*?
14 Which screen gangster was born Emmanuel Goldenberg in Rumania in 1893?
15 Which Julianne starred in *The Lost World: Jurassic Park*?
16 A character named John Mason appeared in which film?
17 Who played Kristin Scott Thomas's husband in *The English Patient*?
18 Who was the blonde female star in *Marnie* and *The Birds*?
19 Who won the Best Actor Oscar for *Coming Home*?
20 In which decade was *The Greatest Show on Earth* released?
21 Who played the villain in *Robin Hood: Prince of Thieves*?
22 Who directed *Love Story*?
23 Which Matthew starred in *Married to the Mob*?
24 Who won the Best Actress Oscar for *Roman Holiday*?
25 *Who Framed Roger Rabbit?* and *Back to the Future III* featured which actor?

**Answers Action** (see Quiz 29)
**1** *Apocalypse Now.* **2** Judi Dench. **3** Tina Turner **4** *Die Hard with a Vengeance.* **5** Marseilles. **6** Sir August De Wynter. **7** Brad Pitt. **8** Channel Tunnel. **9** Frank. **10** *GoldenEye.* **11** Bruce Willis. **12** Pierce Brosnan. **13** *Platoon.* **14** *The China Syndrome.* **15** Charles de Gaulle. **16** Reggie Hammond. **17** Gulf War. **18** Arnold Schwarzenegger. **19** Sheena Easton **20** *The Man in the Iron Mask.* **21** The Philippines. **22** Frances McDormand. **23** *The Wild Bunch.* **24** *The Hunt for Red October.* **25** Charles Bronson.

## *QUIZ 32* STARS OF THE 50s ........ LEVEL 2

*Answers – see page 146*

1 In *An American in Paris* who said, 'That's quite a dress you almost have on'?
2 Which unknown was chosen by Chaplin to star with him in *Limelight*?
3 In *Singin' in the Rain*, who said, 'we feel all our hard work ain't been in vain for nothin'!'?
4 How was Alfredo Cocozza who starred in *The Great Caruso* better known?
5 Who was the monster in *The Curse of Frankenstein*?
6 Which lady with a massive voice was the star of *Call Me Madam*?
7 Who was the blonde James Stewart had to follow in *Vertigo*?
8 Who died while filming *Giant* in 1955?
9 Which blonde starred in *Will Success Spoil Rock Hunter??*
10 In which movie did Rita Hayworth sing 'Bewitched, Bothered and Bewildered'?
11 Who played Scrooge in the classic movie, with George Cole as his younger self?
12 'The Trouble with' whom was a movie debut for Shirley MacLaine?
13 Which dancer did Danny Kaye replace in *White Christmas*, a remake of *Holiday Inn*?
14 *The African Queen* is about events in which war?
15 Which Hitchcock/Cary Grant film has its climax on Mount Rushmore?
16 Who was described as France's most ogled export in 1956?
17 Which Russian-born star played the Pharaoh in *The Ten Commandments*?
18 Which husband and wife first appeared together in *The Long Hot Summer*?
19 Which Welsh actor wins Jesus' robe in a dice game in *The Robe*?
20 Whose autobiography was called *The Raw Pearl*?
21 For what was Audrey Hepburn Oscar-nominated on her film debut?
22 Who played Glenn Miller in *The Glenn Miller Story*?
23 In which movie did Tyrone Power have his final completed role?
24 Who played Big Daddy in *Cat on a Hot Tin Roof*?
25 Which dancer discovered Leslie Caron?

**Answers Oscars – Who's Who?** (see Quiz 30)
**1** Kristin Scott Thomas. **2** Olivia Newton-John (*Grease*). **3** Richard Curtis. **4** John Williams. **5** Taiwanese. **6** *Scent of a Woman*. **7** *Silkwood*. **8** None. **9** Barbra Streisand. **10** Colin Welland. **11** Madonna. **12** Nick Park. **13** George Bernard Shaw. **14** Italian. **15** Howard Hawks. **16** Dolly Parton. **17** Olympia Dukakis. **18** Cedric Gibbons. **19** Susan Sarandon. **20** Bob Hope. **21** Lynn Redgrave & Ian McKellen. **22** Brad Pitt. **23** Jessica Tandy. **24** Hayley Mills. **25** Antonioni.

## *QUIZ 33* HORROR ........ LEVEL 2

*Answers – see page 151*

1 In which state does the action of *The Blair Witch Project* take place?
2 How old was Regan MacNeil when she was possessed in *The Exorcist*?
3 What is the name of the film in *Scream 2* based on the murders in *Scream*?
4 Who plays Sergeant Neil Howie in *The Wicker Man*?
5 What is John Cassavetes's occupation in *Rosemary's Baby*?
6 What type of bird is the first to attack Melanie in *The Birds*?
7 Who played Dr Seward in *Bram Stoker's Dracula*?
8 Who wrote the score for *Psycho*?
9 What does Mike throw into the river in *The Blair Witch Project*?
10 What is the name of the lead character in *Night of the Living Dead*?
11 Who plays 'Leatherface' in the film *The Texas Chainsaw Massacre*?
12 Who produced *Poltergeist*?
13 Who was the star of *The House of Wax*?
14 Who directed *Psycho III*?
15 In which horror movie did Johnny Depp make his debut?
16 What is the name of Danny's imaginary friend in *The Shining*?
17 In which movie does Anjelica Houston say, 'Don't torture yourself, Gomez. That's my job'?
18 Which Mrs Charles Laughton played the title role in *The Bride of Frankenstein*?
19 Who directed *The Evil Dead*?
20 In which state is *Halloween* set?
21 Brad Pitt stayed in Peter Cushing's house while making which movie?
22 Who has the double role in *Mary Reilly*, based on *Dr Jekyll and Mr Hyde*?
23 Upon whose novel is *Carrie* based?
24 What was the first Sherlock Holmes Hammer horror movie in colour?
25 What was the name of Richard Dreyfuss's character in *Jaws*?

**Answers Heroes & Villains** (see Quiz 35)
**1** Alan Rickman. **2** Arnold Schwarzenegger. **3** *The Shining*. **4** Gary Oldman. **5** Bela Lugosi. **6** Joe Pesci. **7** The Rat Pack. **8** *On Her Majesty's Secret Service*. **9** O.J. Simpson. **10** Quentin Tarantino. **11** Two. **12** Liam Neeson. **13** Roman Polanski. **14** (Tea with) Mussolini. **15** Jon Voight. **16** *The Gladiator*. **17** Jean Claude van Damme. **18** Christopher Walken. **19** Norman Bates (*Psycho*). **20** Alec Guinness. **21** Sigourney Weaver. **22** Mae West. **23** Peter Lawford. **24** Rommel. **25** Erich von Stroheim.

## *QUIZ 34* POT LUCK 13 ........ LEVEL 2

*Answers – see page 152*

1 In which film does a character named Rod Tidwell appear?
2 The song 'Unchained Melody' was revived by featuring in which movie?
3 Which Alan featured in the 1991 movie *Hamlet*?
4 Who won the Best Director Oscar for *Forrest Gump*?
5 Who played Susie Diamond in *The Fabulous Baker Boys*?
6 Who won the Best Actress Oscar for *The Three Faces of Eve*?
7 Who played Cruella De Vil's sidekick Jasper in *101 Dalmatians*?
8 Which veteran starred with Burt Lancaster in *Tough Guys* in 1986?
9 What was the name of the Keir Dullea character in *2001: A Space Odyssey*?
10 In which decade was *Romancing the Stone* released?
11 Who directed *Lethal Weapon*?
12 Which early screen comedian's real name was Louis Cristillo?
13 Which soap did Hollywood star Alec Baldwin star in?
14 In which film did Clint Eastwood first play 'The man with no name'?
15 Who was the US teacher in *To Sir with Love*?
16 In which decade was *Fahrenheit 451* released?
17 Who played King Arthur in the film musical *Camelot*?
18 *Dracula* and *The Man with the Golden Gun* both featured which actor?
19 From 1990 to 1997 every movie that got the Best Picture Oscar also got an Oscar in which other category?
20 *Dances with Wolves* concerns a soldier from which war?
21 Who played Doug Roberts in *The Towering Inferno*?
22 *2010* and *Memphis Belle* both feature which actor?
23 Who won the Best Actor Oscar for *The Private Life of Henry VIII*?
24 What was the Bond girl's name in *The Man with the Golden Gun*?
25 Which Burt appeared in *Bean –The Ultimate Disaster Movie*?

**Answers Meryl Streep** (see Quiz 36)
**1** Clint Eastwood. **2** *Silkwood.* **3** Jeremy Irons. **4** Linda. **5** Karen Blixen. **6** Taken by a dingo. **7** *Dancing at Lughnasa.* **8** *Julia.* **9** Australian. **10** Alan Alda. **11** Carrie Fisher. **12** *The River Wild.* **13** *The French Lieutenant's Woman.* **14** Evita. **15** John Cazale. **16** Bruce Willis. **17** *Manhattan.* **18** *The Deer Hunter.* **19** Jack Nicholson. **20** *Sophie's Choice.* **21** Shirley Maclaine. **22** *Silkwood.* **23** *Kramer versus Kramer.* **24** Robert De Niro. **25** Goldie Hawn.

## *QUIZ 35* HEROES & VILLAINS ........ LEVEL 2

*Answers – see page 149*

1 Who was the villainous Sheriff in *Robin Hood: Prince of Thieves*?
2 Which tough guy directed *Christmas in Connecticut*?
3 Which movie featured Jack Torrance?
4 Which actor kidnapped Harrison Ford in *Air Force One*?
5 Which horror star did Martin Landau play in *Ed Wood*?
6 Which star of *Goodfellas* was a child star on radio?
7 *The Clan*, with Sinatra, Martin & Co. was also known as what?
8 In which movie did Diana Rigg play Mrs 007?
9 Which sportsman-turned-actor whose journey in a white truck was real-life drama had the nickname 'The Juice'?
10 Whose first major movie as director was *Reservoir Dogs*?
11 How many Batman films did Michael Keaton appear in?
12 Who played outlaw Rob Roy in the 90s film of the same name?
13 Who was Sharon Tate married to at the time of her murder?
14 Which villain's name appeared in the title of a 1999 film with Cher and Maggie Smith?
15 Who won an Oscar for *Coming Home* after missing out for *Midnight Cowboy*?
16 Oliver Reed died during the making of which movie?
17 Who was nicknamed 'The Muscles from Brussels'?
18 Who was in *Batman Returns* 14 years after playing the crazed POW in *The Deer Hunter*?
19 Which Hitchcock villain said, 'A boy's best friend is his mother'?
20 Who played Colonel Nicholson in *Bridge on the River Kwai* after Bogart and Olivier rejected it?
21 Who is associated with the role of Ripley in *Aliens*?
22 Which 30s sex symbol replied to 'I've heard so much about you' with 'You can't prove a thing!'?
23 Which member of the Rat Pack was a Kennedy brother-in-law?
24 Who did James Mason play in *The Desert Fox*?
25 Which screen villain was born Hans Erich Maria Stroheim von Nordenwall?

**Answers Horror** (see Quiz 33)
**1** Maryland. **2** 12. **3** *Stab.* **4** Edward Woodward. **5** Actor. **6** Seagull. **7** Richard E. Grant. **8** Bernard Herrmann. **9** The map. **10** Barbara. **11** Gunner Hansen. **12** Steven Spielberg. **13** Vincent Price. **14** Anthony Perkins. **15** *A Nightmare on Elm Street.* **16** Tony. **17** *The Addams Family.* **18** Elsa Lanchester. **19** Sam Raimi. **20** Illinois. **21** *Interview with the Vampire.* **22** John Malkovich. **23** Stephen King. **24** *The Hound of the Baskervilles.* **25** Hooper.

## *QUIZ 36* MERYL STREEP ........ LEVEL 2

*Answers – see page 150*

1 Who was her co-star in *The Bridges of Madison County*?
2 Which of her films was about a nuclear nightmare?
3 Who was her English co-star in *The French Lieutenant's Woman*?
4 What was the name of her character in *The Deer Hunter*?
5 Which Danish author did she play in *Out of Africa*?
6 In *A Cry in the Dark* how did she say her baby had died in the Australian outback?
7 In which 90s movie did she master an Irish accent?
8 In which movie with Vanessa Redgrave and Jane Fonda did she make her screen debut?
9 What was the nationality of her character in *A Cry in the Dark*?
10 Which *M*A*S*H* star was her co-star in *The Seduction of Joe Tynan*?
11 Her role in *Postcards from the Edge* was based on the life of which actress who wrote the book?
12 What was her first action film in 1994?
13 In which film did she play an actress and the Victorian character she plays?
14 Which musical role eluded her in the mid-90s after she had impressed with her singing in *Postcards from the Edge*?
15 *The Deer Hunter* was the last film for which actor who was her then partner?
16 Who was her male co-star in *Death Becomes Her*?
17 In which Woody Allen film did she appear in 1979?
18 Which 70s movie about Vietnam won her her first Oscar nomination?
19 Who was her co-star in *Ironweed*?
20 In which movie did she win an Oscar for her portrayal of a Polish holocaust victim?
21 Who played her mother in *Postcards from the Edge*?
22 In which movie did she play a factory worker opposite Cher?
23 Which divorce drama won her her first Oscar?
24 Who was her co-star in the unsuccessful *Falling in Love* in 1984?
25 Which blonde actress was her co-star in *Death Becomes Her*?

**Answers Pot Luck 13** (see Quiz 34)
**1** *Jerry Maguire.* **2** *Ghost.* **3** Bates. **4** Robert Zemeckis. **5** Michelle Pfeiffer. **6** Joanne Woodward. **7** Hugh Laurie. **8** Kirk Douglas. **9** Dave Bowman. **10** 1980s. **11** Richard Donner. **12** Lou Costello. **13** *The Doctors.* **14** *A Fistful of Dollars.* **15** Sidney Poitier. **16** 1960s. **17** Richard Harris. **18** Christopher Lee. **19** Best Director. **20** American Civil War. **21** Paul Newman. **22** John Lithgow. **23** Charles Laughton. **24** Mary Goodnight. **25** Reynolds.

## *QUIZ 37* POT LUCK 14 ........ LEVEL 2

*Answers – see page 155*

1 *King Kong* and *Cape Fear* both featured which actress?
2 Who played the journalist loosely based on Carl Bernstein in *Heartburn*?
3 Which Ben featured in *The Truth about Cats and Dogs*?
4 In which decade was *Oklahoma!* first released?
5 What was the name of Will Smith's character in *Independence Day*?
6 Who won the Best Actress Oscar for *Darling*?
7 Which poet's name was the middle name of James Dean?
8 Which Kevin featured in *A Few Good Men*?
9 Who played Jack Lemmon's daughter in *Grumpy Old Men*?
10 In which decade of the 20th century was Sally Field born?
11 A character named John Doherty appeared in which film?
12 Who played Susan Sarandon's husband in *Lorenzo's Oil*?
13 Who won the Best Director Oscar for *The Sound of Music*?
14 Who played Rudyard Kipling in *The Man Who Would Be King*?
15 Who beat Meryl Streep for the lead role in *The Horse Whisperer*?
16 Which animals feature in *Oliver and Company*?
17 *The Killers* and *Field of Dreams* both feature which actor?
18 Who directed *LA Confidential*?
19 How were producers Harry, Albert, Sam and Jack known collectively?
20 In which category did Joel Gray win an Oscar for *Cabaret*?
21 Which Michelle featured in *Tomorrow Never Dies*?
22 Who directed *Labyrinth*?
23 Who played the wistful widowed father in *Sleepless in Seattle*?
24 In which decade was *Witness* released?
25 Who won the Best Actor Oscar for *The Lost Weekend*?

**Answers The Silent Years** (see Quiz 39)
**1** 12. **2** Samuel Goldfish. **3** United Artists. **4** *The Mark of Zorro*. **5** Irving Thalberg. **6** Pickfair. **7** Keystone. **8** William. **9** Universal. **10** Mabel Normand. **11** Potemkin. **12** Clara Bow. **13** Roscoe. **14** William Randolph Hearst. **15** Censorship and self-regulation of the movie industry. **16** Very large eyes. **17** Mack Sennett. **18** Glasses. **19** Buster Keaton. **20** Pauline. **21** New York. **22** Edison. **23** Keystone. **24** Davis. **25** Adolph Zukor.

## *QUIZ 38* BLOCKBUSTERS ........ LEVEL 2

*Answers – see page 156*

1 *Titanic* overtook which movie as the most costly ever made?
2 On whose books was *Mary Poppins* based?
3 Upon which day do the characters in *Independence Day* launch a nuclear attack on the alien mother ship?
4 Who plays Alfred in *Batman*?
5 What number in the series of Bond films is *GoldenEye*?
6 Against which king is Mel Gibson fighting in *Braveheart*?
7 In what year is *Apollo 13* set?
8 What is the name of Andy's sister in *Toy Story*?
9 What is Harry Tasker's fake job in *True Lies*?
10 What is the last sin to be executed in *Se7en*?
11 Who voiced Shenzi in *The Lion King*?
12 What speed must the bus keep above to stop it from exploding in *Speed*?
13 Who was the female lead in *Raiders of the Lost Ark*?
14 Where do Fred and Barney work in *The Flintstones*?
15 In which state is *Nell* set?
16 Which character is played by Gary Sinise in *Forrest Gump*?
17 Which character did Ben Kingsley play in *Schindler's List*?
18 In which city is *The Firm* set?
19 In which movie did Bette Davis say, 'Fasten your seatbelts. It's going to be a bumpy night'?
20 What nationality is Holly Hunter's character in *The Piano*?
21 In *Jurassic Park* the DNA of which creature is mixed with dinosaur DNA?
22 What city is *Judge Dredd* set in?
23 Who kills Vincent in *Pulp Fiction*?
24 What is the last image we see in *Forrest Gump*?
25 Who is the evil kid next door in *Toy Story*?

**Answers Pot Luck 15** (see Quiz 40)
**1** Chewbacca. **2** Warren Beatty. **3** Wrestling. **4** 1980s. **5** White. **6** John Ford. **7** Babcock. **8** Vivien Leigh. **9** Christopher Lambert. **10** *Independence Day*. **11** 'Streets of Philadelphia'. **12** Nora Ephron. **13** Susan George. **14** Cameron Crowe. **15** Ingrid Bergman. **16** Al Pacino. **17** Judy Garland. **18** 1940s. **19** *Splendor in the Grass*. **20** Ben Kingsley. **21** Dennis Quaid. **22** *The Sting*. **23** Mel Gibson. **24** Anne Bancroft. **25** Brolin.

## *QUIZ 39* THE SILENT YEARS ........ LEVEL 2

*Answers – see page 153*

1 How many reels were there in D.W. Griffith's *Birth of a Nation*?
2 Who founded Goldwyn Pictures with Archibald & Edgar Selwyn in 1916?
3 The quote, 'The lunatics have taken over the asylum' referred to the founding of which company, by actors?
4 What was Douglas Fairbanks's first movie in his famous swashbuckling role?
5 Who was in charge of production when MGM was first formed?
6 What was the name of the home Douglas Fairbanks shared with Mary Pickford?
7 Which company founded in 1912 was famous for its slapstick comedies?
8 What was the first name of Fox of 20th Century Fox fame?
9 Which company did Carl Laemmle found in 1912?
10 Who was the most famous female star of Mack Sennett's Keystone movies?
11 Which 'Battleship' was the subject of a 20s movie by Eisenstein?
12 Who acquired her nickname after starring in the movie *It*?
13 What was Fatty Arbuckle's real first name?
14 On which newspaper tycoon's yacht was director Thomas Ince murdered?
15 What was the Hays Office set up to do after the death of starlet Virginia Rappe?
16 Which of Eddie Cantor's physical attributes was particularly unusual?
17 Who founded Keystone in 1912?
18 Which accessory was Harold Lloyd's trademark?
19 Who directed and starred in *The General* in 1929?
20 In 1914 Pearl White starred in 'The Perils of' whom?
21 In which US city did *Birth of a Nation* open in 1915?
22 Which prolific US inventor co-founded the Motion Picture Patents Company?
23 Which studio was famous for its Bathing Beauties?
24 Which star Mildred did Harold Lloyd marry?
25 Who founded the Famous Players Film Company?

**Answers Pot Luck 14** (see Quiz 37)
**1** Jessica Lange. **2** Jack Nicholson. **3** Chaplin. **4** 1950s. **5** Captain Steven Hiller. **6** Julie Christie. **7** Byron. **8** Bacon. **9** Daryl Hannah. **10** 1940s. **11** *Thunderbolt and Lightfoot.* **12** Nick Nolte. **13** Robert Wise. **14** Christopher Plummer. **15** Kristin Scott Thomas. **16** Cats and dogs. **17** Burt Lancaster. **18** Curtis Hanson. **19** Warner Brothers. **20** Best Supporting Actor. **21** Yeoh. **22** Jim Henson. **23** Tom Hanks. **24** 1980s. **25** Ray Milland.

## *QUIZ 40* POT LUCK 15 ........ LEVEL 2

*Answers – see page 154*

1 What was the name of Peter Mayhew's character in *Star Wars*?
2 Who turned down Al Pacino's role in *The Godfather*?
3 At what sport did Kirk Douglas excel?
4 In which decade was *Field of Dreams* released?
5 Mickey Mouse's gloves are what colour?
6 Who won the Best Director Oscar for *The Grapes of Wrath*?
7 Which Barbara featured in *Far and Away*?
8 Who won an Oscar as Blanche in *A Streetcar Named Desire*?
9 *Subway* and *Highlander* both featured which actor?
10 A character named President Whitmore appears in which film?
11 Which song from *Philadelphia* won an Oscar?
12 Which writer directed *Sleepless in Seattle*?
13 Who played Dustin Hoffman's wife in *Straw Dogs*?
14 Who directed *Jerry Maguire*?
15 In the 1940s who was shunned by Hollywood when she left her husband for Roberto Rossellini?
16 Who won the Best Actor Oscar for *Scent of a Woman*?
17 Who was the most famous member of the Gumm Sisters Kiddie Act?
18 In which decade was *Song of the South* released?
19 What was Warren Beatty's first film, in 1961?
20 *Testimony* and *Schindler's List* both featured which actor?
21 Who played Jerry Lee Lewis in *Great Balls of Fire*?
22 For which film did Robert Redford win his first Oscar nomination?
23 Who played Fletcher Christian in *The Bounty* in 1984?
24 Who won the Best Actress Oscar for *The Miracle Worker*?
25 Which James featured in *Westworld*?

**Answers Blockbusters** (see Quiz 38)
**1** *Waterworld.* **2** P.L. Travers. **3** July 4th. **4** Michael Gough. **5** 17th. **6** Edward I. **7** 1970. **8** Emily. **9** Computer salesman. **10** Wrath. **11** Whoopi Goldberg. **12** 50 mph (80 km/h). **13** Karen Allen. **14** Slate gravel quarry. **15** North Carolina. **16** Lieutenant Dan Taylor. **17** Itzhak Stern. **18** Memphis. **19** *All About Eve.* **20** Scottish. **21** Frog. **22** Mega City One. **23** Butch (Bruce Willis). **24** A feather. **25** Sid.

## QUIZ 41 1950s ...... LEVEL 2

*Answers – see page 159*

1 Who plays the neighbour James Stewart suspects of murder in *Rear Window*?
2 Which composer was Oscar-nominated for *On the Waterfront* seven years before making *West Side Story*?
3 What is the 'Green Fire' in the title of the movie with Grace Kelly and Stewart Granger?
4 Which Brando movie was banned in the UK for 15 years?
5 In which movie did Marilyn Monroe sing 'That Old Black Magic'?
6 Who played Captain Ahab in *Moby Dick*?
7 Who was Judy Garland's British co-star in *A Star Is Born*?
8 Which daughter of Hitchcock appeared in *Strangers on a Train*?
9 In *Guys and Dolls* where does Sarah go with Sky to find 12 sinners?
10 Who played Eloise Kelly in *Mogambo*?
11 Norman Maine in *A Star Is Born* is based on which silent movie star?
12 What was Tony Curtis and Cary Grant's only movie together?
13 Who played Al Capone in *Al Capone*?
14 Which movie was about the island which won a George Cross in World War II?
15 What was Elvis Presley's third movie?
16 *The Forbidden Planet* was loosely based on which Shakespeare play?
17 In which city is *Limelight* set?
18 Who played Jesse James in *Kansas Raiders*?
19 *White Christmas* was a partial remake of which classic?
20 In which movie did Gloria Swanson say, 'I am big. It's the pictures that got small'?
21 What was the sequel to the first *Godzilla* movie called?
22 Who played Moses in *The Ten Commandments*?
23 What was James Stewart's profession in *Rear Window*?
24 What name did Jack Lemmon adopt when disguised in drag in *Some Like It Hot*?
25 To the nearest twenty minutes, how long does *Ben Hur* last?

**Answers Behind the Camera** (see Quiz 43)
**1** Jim Threapleton. **2** *Charlie's Angels*. **3** Alec Baldwin. **4** John Dykstra. **5** Cecil Beaton. **6** Alan Bennett. **7** *A Room with a View*. **8** Kenneth Branagh. **9** Cubby Broccoli. **10** Coco Chanel. **11** Warhol. **12** Roddy Doyle. **13** Demi Moore. **14** Todd AO. **15** Roy. **16** Nora Ephron. **17** Elton John. **18** Stephen King. **19** *Taxi Driver*. **20** Balmain. **21** Jodie Foster. **22** David Wark. **23** Frank McCourt. **24** Selznick Independent Pictures. **25** *Close Encounters of the Third Kind*.

## QUIZ 42 POT LUCK 16 ........ LEVEL 2

*Answers – see page 160*

1 In which decade was *The Shining* released?
2 How is Bernard Schwarz better known?
3 What was the name of Brad Pitt's character in *Se7en*?
4 Who played the man in the wheelchair in Hitchcock's *Rear Window*?
5 Who directed *Independence Day*?
6 Which Juliette featured in *The English Patient*?
7 Which song won Best Song Oscar for *Evita*?
8 Who played the sadistic sheriff in Eastwood's *Unforgiven*?
9 Who won the Best Director Oscar for *All About Eve*?
10 *Clean and Sober* and *Batman Returns* both featured which actor?
11 The Bogart and Bacall relationship began on the set of which movie?
12 Who played Christy Brown's mother in *My Left Foot*?
13 Who won the Best Actress Oscar for *Room at the Top*?
14 Who was married to Debbie Reynolds and Elizabeth Taylor?
15 Who directed *Jackie Brown*?
16 What did the W stand for in W.C. Fields's name?
17 Which musical gangster movie features 'bullets' of whipped cream?
18 What was the name of the villain in *Diamonds Are Forever*?
19 In which decade was Disney's *Peter Pan* released?
20 Which horror writer directed the film *Maximum Overdrive*?
21 Who won the Best Actor Oscar for *The Goodbye Girl*?
22 *Kiss of the Spider Woman* and *The Addams Family* both feature which actor?
23 Who played the surprise guest in *Guess Who's Coming to Dinner*?
24 Which Yale graduate was known as the King of the Horror Movie?
25 Which Kenneth featured in *What's Up, Doc?*?

**Answers Space & Sci-Fi** (see Quiz 44)
**1** *Apollo 13*. **2** Superman. **3** Rollerball. **4** *Star Trek*. **5** George Lucas. **6** Ewan McGregor. **7** Bees. **8** Ray Bradbury. **9** Robby. **10** Saul David. **11** Red Leader. **12** 1997. **13** Hoth. **14** The Eiffel Tower. **15** A V-8. **16** Shepperton studios. **17** California. **18** Walter Seltzer. **19** Douglas Trumbull. **20** James Earl Jones. **21** *The Sentinel*. **22** Otis. **23** Michael Hutchence. **24** Cave. **25** J.

## *QUIZ 43* BEHIND THE CAMERA ........ LEVEL 2

*Answers – see page 157*

1 Which director did Kate Winslet marry?
2 What was Drew Barrymore's debut as producer?
3 Which Mr Kim Basinger became a partner in Eldorado Pictures?
4 Who was the computer-controlled Dykstraflex camera named after?
5 Who designed the stunning costumes in *Gigi* and *My Fair Lady*?
6 Which British playwright was Oscar-nominated for *The Madness of King George*?
7 What was Merchant Ivory's first film, an adaptation of an E.M. Forster novel?
8 Who set up the Shakespeare Film Company in 1998?
9 Who was producer of the first James Bond movies and *Chitty Chitty Bang Bang*?
10 Which French fashion designer designed for several films in the 30s and 40s, including *La Marseillaise*?
11 Joe Dallesandro found fame in which Andy's movies?
12 Who was the original author on whose novel *The Commitments* was based?
13 Who starred in and also co-produced *Now and Then....*?
14 Which wide-screen system was promoted by Mike Todd?
15 Which Boulting brother was the producer?
16 Who wrote *Sleepless in Seattle*?
17 Which singer produced *Women Talking Dirty*?
18 Who wrote the novel on which *The Shawshank Redemption* was based?
19 In which of his own movies did Martin Scorsese appear in 1976?
20 Which French designer Pierre founded his own couture house in the 50s and contributed to over 70 movies?
21 Who directed and starred in *Little Man Tate* in 1991?
22 What did the D.W. stand for in D.W. Griffith's name?
23 On whose book is *Angela's Ashes* based?
24 What was David O. Selznick's independent production company called?
25 Which 70s sci-fi blockbuster got Frank Warner a Special Award for sound effects editing?

**Answers 1950s** (see Quiz 41)
**1** Raymond Burr. **2** Leonard Bernstein. **3** Emeralds. **4** *The Wild One.* **5** *Bus Stop.* **6** Gregory Peck. **7** James Mason. **8** Patricia. **9** Havana. **10** Ava Gardner. **11** John Gilbert. **12** *Operation Petticoat.* **13** Rod Steiger. **14** *The Malta Story.* **15** *Jailhouse Rock.* **16** *The Tempest.* **17** London. **18** Audie Murphy. **19** *Holiday Inn.* **20** *Sunset Boulevard.* **21** *Godzilla Raids Again.* **22** Charlton Heston. **23** Photographer. **24** Daphne. **25** 212 minutes.

## *QUIZ 44* SPACE & SCI-FI ........................ LEVEL 2

*Answers – see page 158*

1 Which film has the line, 'Houston, we have a problem'?
2 Who had a father called Jor-El?
3 What sport did James Caan play as Jonathan E?
4 Which sci-fi series did De Forrest Kelly star in?
5 Who did Spielberg describe as 'Walt Disney's version of a mad scientist'?
6 Who replaced Alec Guinness in *The Phantom Menace*?
7 What type of creature carries the disease in *The X-Files*?
8 Who wrote the novel *Fahrenheit 451*?
9 What is the name of the robot in *Forbidden Planet*?
10 Who produced *Logan's Run*?
11 Who is Luke Skywalker's squadron commander in the final battle in *Star Wars*?
12 In what year is *Escape from New York* set?
13 What planet were the rebels on before Darth Vader destroyed their base in *The Empire Strikes Back*?
14 For which monument is an H-bomb intended in *Superman II*?
15 What does Mel Gibson drive in the film *Mad Max*?
16 In which British studios was *Alien* filmed?
17 In which state does the *Invasion of the Body Snatchers* take place?
18 Who produced *The Omega Man*?
19 Who created the special effects for *Star Trek: The Motion Picture*?
20 Who was the voice of Darth Vader in the *Star Wars* trilogy?
21 *2001: A Space Odyssey* is based on which Arthur C. Clarke story?
22 What is the name of Lex Luthor's henchman in *Superman*?
23 Which member of INXS appeared in *Dogs in Space* in 1986?
24 In what sort of dwelling does Ben Kenobi live?
25 What is the name of Will Smith's character in *Men in Black*?

**Answers Pot Luck 16** (see Quiz 42)
**1** 1980s. **2** Tony Curtis. **3** David Mills. **4** James Stewart. **5** Roland Emmerich. **6** Binoche. **7** 'You Must Love Me'. **8** Gene Hackman. **9** Joseph L. Mankiewicz. **10** Michael Keaton. **11** *To Have and Have Not.* **12** Brenda Fricker. **13** Simone Signoret. **14** Eddie Fisher. **15** Quentin Tarantino. **16** William. **17** *Bugsy Malone.* **18** Ernst Stavro Blofeld. **19** 1950s. **20** Stephen King. **21** Richard Dreyfuss. **22** Raul Julia. **23** Sidney Poitier. **24** Vincent Price. **25** Mars.

## *QUIZ 45* POT LUCK 17 ........ LEVEL 2

*Answers – see page 163*

1 Which star of *Look Who's Talking Too* was a TV regular on 'Cheers'?
2 Who sang the Bond theme from *GoldenEye*?
3 *Mermaids* and *Hook* featured which actor?
4 Who won the Best Director Oscar for *Lawrence of Arabia*?
5 Which Dianne featured in *Edward Scissorhands*?
6 A character named Sister Helen Prejean appeared in which film?
7 Which Jon featured in *Mission: Impossible*?
8 Who directed *The Ice Storm*?
9 Who played the title role in *Goldfinger*?
10 In which decade was *From Here To Eternity* released?
11 Which British actor won an Oscar for *My Left Foot*?
12 In which film did a character named Farmer Hoggett appear?
13 How was Hollywood's Joan de Beauvoir de Havilland better known?
14 Who won Best Supporting Actor Oscar for *Ryan's Daughter*?
15 Who was the first Jane to Johnny Weissmuller's *Tarzan*?
16 Who achieved notoriety by directing *Women In Love* in 1969?
17 Dietrich appeared in the German *The Blue Angel*, but who starred in the US version?
18 Who won the Best Actress Oscar for *I Want To Live*?
19 Which was the first animated film in the 90s for which Tim Rice won an Oscar?
20 *The Third Man* and *My Fair Lady* featured which British actor?
21 Which star of *The Godfather* bought an island called Tetiaroa?
22 In which film did a character named Oliver Barrett IV first appear?
23 In which film did Reynolds, Kelly and O'Connor sing 'Good Morning'?
24 *Lovesick* and *Santa Claus* featured which actor?
25 In which decade was *Dead Poets Society* released?

**Answers 1930s Stars** (see Quiz 47)
**1** Bert Lahr. **2** Lucille Ball. **3** Charles Boyer. **4** The Dionne Quins. **5** Carole Lombard. **6** Alice Faye. **7** Australian. **8** Tallulah Bankhead. **9** Claudette Colbert. **10** Peter Lorre. **11** Laurel & Hardy. **12** Jean Harlow. **13** *The Private Life of Henry VIII*. **14** Gypsy Rose Lee. **15** Mickey Rooney. **16** Myrna Loy. **17** Jimmy Durante. **18** Paulette Goddard. **19** Bela Lugosi. **20** White. **21** John Gilbert. **22** W.C. Fields. **23** Mary Pickford. **24** Joan Crawford. **25** Gary Cooper.

## *QUIZ 46* MEMORABLE MOVIE MOMENTS ........................................ LEVEL 2

*Answers – see page 164*

1 What was the last film personally produced by Walt Disney?
2 Which vehicle chased Cary Grant in *North by Northwest*?
3 Which movie persuaded everyone to 'Phone home'?
4 Which lizard first appeared in the Japanese movie *Gojira*?
5 Who painted the Picasso picture used in *Titanic* which was owned by Kate Winslet's character Rose?
6 Which 90s musical saw the most costume changes of any movie?
7 Which *Gone with the Wind* character has her baby while Atlanta is burning?
8 In which movie did Burt Lancaster have his most memorable scene with Deborah Kerr?
9 In which Joan Fontaine/Laurence Olivier movie does Mrs Van Hopper stub out her cigarette in the face cream?
10 Which Oliver Reed/Alan Bates movie was the first to feature male nudity?
11 Which movie with David Niven and Cantinflas boasted an all-star cast?
12 Which 30s horror classic had the ad line, 'A love story that lived for a thousand years'?
13 Who played the Jewish accountant in *Schindler's List*?
14 In which 90s movie is Clarice on the trail of Buffalo Bill?
15 Which actor played the mad scientist who created Edward Scissorhands?
16 Which movie introduced words such as 'Cowabunga' into the juvenile vocabulary?
17 Where does the most memorable scene in *When Harry Met Sally* take place?
18 Which movie about the Cambodian war introduced the expression for scenes of wartime atrocities?
19 Which movie did John Hurt make which required him to spend hours each day in make-up?
20 In which movie was Clint Eastwood first in danger of being upstaged by Clyde?
21 Which boy is on stage with Carrie in the gory finale to the movie?
22 Who plays the forger who goes blind in *The Great Escape*?
23 On which date does the movie *Independence Day* begin?
24 Where does *The Fantastic Voyage* take place?
25 What does Rita Hayworth peel off as she sings 'Put the Blame on Mame' in *Gilda*?

**Answers Pot Luck 18** (see Quiz 48)
**1** *Nutcracker Suite.* **2** Chris Columbus. **3** Meg Ryan. **4** Sutherland. **5** Cop. **6** (Sir) Anthony Hopkins. **7** John Carpenter. **8** *Braveheart.* **9** Peter Finch. **10** *Popeye.* **11** 1960s. **12** Twiggy. **13** Coco. **14** Gordon Macrae. **15** Sir Anthony Hopkins. **16** James Garner. **17** Barry Levinson. **18** *The Seven Year Itch.* **19** Margaret Rutherford. **20** *Dirty Harry.* **21** John Malkovich. **22** Diana Rigg. **23** Jane Fonda. **24** Macchio. **25** 1940s.

## *QUIZ 47* 1930s STARS ........ LEVEL 2

*Answers – see page 161*

1 Who said, 'After *The Wizard of Oz* I was typecast as a lion, and there aren't many parts for lions'?
2 Which former Goldwyn Girl went on to TV superstardom as comedienne and producer?
3 Which French actor did not say, 'Come with me to the Casbah' in *Algiers*?
4 Which quintet were the star of *Five of a Kind*?
5 How was Jane Peters better known?
6 Which blonde sang the title song in *Alexander's Ragtime Band*?
7 In 1942 Errol Flynn changed to US citizenship from what?
8 Which star of the 20s and 30s said, 'I'm as pure as the driven slush'?
9 Who played Cleopatra in de Mille's 1934 classic?
10 Who starred as the murderer in *M*?
11 Which comedy duo were the stars of *Way Out West*?
12 In *Hell's Angels* which blonde asked if she could slip into something more comfortable?
13 In which movie did Charles Laughton say, 'Am I a king or a breeding bull?'?
14 Which famous striptease artist was born Louise Hovick?
15 Which child star played Puck in *A Midsummer Night's Dream*?
16 Who was dubbed the Queen of Hollywood in the 30s?
17 Whose catchphrase was 'Everyone wants to get into de act!'?
18 How was Marion Levy, a.k.a. Mrs Chaplin, better known?
19 Who played Igor in *Son of Frankenstein* in 1939?
20 What colour suit and boots did Tom Mix famously wear?
21 Who was Garbo's co-star in *Queen Christina*?
22 Which noted enemy of 'animals and children' played Mr Micawber in *David Copperfield*?
23 Which silent movie star announced her retirement in 1933?
24 Which Lucille changed her name to Joan and found fame playing strong roles?
25 Who links *Beau Geste, City Streets* and *The Lives of a Bengal Lancer*?

**Answers Pot Luck 17** (see Quiz 45)
**1** Kirstie Alley. **2** Tina Turner. **3** Bob Hoskins. **4** David Lean. **5** Wiest. **6** *Dead Man Walking*. **7** Voight. **8** Ang Lee. **9** Gert Frobe. **10** 1950s. **11** Daniel Day Lewis. **12** *Babe*. **13** Joan Fontaine. **14** John Mills. **15** Maureen O'Sullivan. **16** Ken Russell. **17** Dietrich. **18** Susan Haywood. **19** *Aladdin*. **20** Wilfrid Hyde-White. **21** Marlon Brando. **22** *Love Story*. **23** *Singin' In the Rain*. **24** Dudley Moore. **25** 1980s.

## *QUIZ 48* POT LUCK 18 ........ LEVEL 2

*Answers – see page 162*

1 Which Tchaikovsky ballet piece features in Disney's *Fantasia*?
2 Who directed *Home Alone*?
3 Which actress played Jim Morrison's girlfriend in *The Doors*?
4 Which Donald featured in *Disclosure*?
5 What was Michael Douglas's profession in *Basic Instinct*?
6 *Magic* and *Desperate Hours* both feature which actor?
7 Who directed the 70s movie *Halloween*?
8 Which 90s film was about William Wallace?
9 Who won the Best Actor Oscar for *Network*?
10 What was Robin Williams's first film, in 1980?
11 In which decade was *Sink the Bismarck* released?
12 Who played the female lead role in *The Boyfriend* in 1971?
13 What was the name of Irene Cara's character in *Fame*?
14 Who played Curly in the 1955 musical *Oklahoma!*?
15 Which knighted Welsh actor was born on New Year's Eve?
16 Which star of *Maverick* played Brett Maverick in the TV series?
17 Who won the Best Director Oscar for *Rain Man*?
18 The character Richard Sherman is in which time-linked film?
19 Which Dame played Agatha Christie's Miss Marple in four 60s whodunnits?
20 A serial killer named Scorpio appears in which film?
21 Who played the Vicomte de Valmont in *Dangerous Liaisons*?
22 Who played the first Mrs James Bond?
23 Who won the Best Actress Oscar for *Coming Home* in 1978?
24 Which Ralph featured in *My Cousin Vinny*?
25 In which decade was *Bambi* released?

**Answers Memorable Movie Moments** (see Quiz 46)
**1** *The Happiest Millionaire.* **2** Plane. **3** *E.T.* **4** Godzilla. **5** They used the original. **6** *Evita.* **7** Melanie. **8** *From Here to Eternity.* **9** *Rebecca.* **10** *Women in Love.* **11** *Around the World in Eighty Days.* **12** *The Mummy.* **13** Ben Kingsley. **14** *Silence of the Lambs.* **15** Vincent Price. **16** *Teenage Mutant Ninja Turtles.* **17** Restaurant. **18** *The Killing Fields.* **19** *The Elephant Man.* **20** *Every Which Way But Loose.* **21** Tommy. **22** Donald Pleasence. **23** 2nd July. **24** In a scientist's bloodstream. **25** Glove.

## *QUIZ 49* FAMOUS FIRSTS ........ LEVEL 2

*Answers – see page 167*

1 Which Bond film was released on the same day as the Beatles' first single?
2 Which Latvian ballet dancer made his movie debut in *The Turning Point*?
3 Who was chief artist on the very first Mickey Mouse cartoon?
4 What was Michael Jackson's first movie?
5 How was 'famous first' Asa Yoelson better known?
6 What was Hitchcock's first talkie?
7 Which ground-breaking animation film was developed by Silicon Graphics Inc.?
8 Which movie pioneer said, 'I moved the whole world on to a 20-foot screen'?
9 What was Hitchcock's first film in colour?
10 Which Shakespeare play was the first British movie to win a BAFTA, in 1948?
11 What was Tatum O'Neal's first movie, which won her an Oscar?
12 What was the first movie shown in Cinemascope?
13 Which Richard Burton/Elizabeth Taylor movie was Mike Nichols's directorial debut and won him an Oscar nomination?
14 Which James's screen debut was in a Pepsi commercial?
15 Which Janet was the first Best Actress Oscar winner?
16 Which Irish novelist opened Dublin's first cinema?
17 In which movie did Elizabeth Taylor first act with Richard Burton?
18 Mike Nichols won the first director's BAFTA for which Dustin Hoffman classic?
19 Glenn Close made her film debut as whose mother in *The World According to Garp*?
20 In which movie did pop star Tommy Steele make his Hollywood debut?
21 What was the first movie shown at the White House?
22 *Broken Arrow* was the first western made from which perspective?
23 Who was the first British winner of a Best Actress BAFTA for *The Prime of Miss Jean Brodie*?
24 Whose made his screen debut aged 13 with father John in *Tiger Bay*?
25 Which 'Express' was Spielberg's debut as a feature film director?

**Answers Who's Who?** (see Quiz 51)
**1** Ralph Fiennes. **2** Granddaughter. **3** Air Force. **4** Fred Flintstone. **5** Eric. **6** George Clooney. **7** Joseph Fiennes. **8** Jason Gould. **9** William Hurt. **10** Susan Sarandon. **11** Jacqueline Du Pré. **12** Sonny. **13** Faye Dunaway. **14** Morgan Freeman. **15** John Thaw. **16** Diane Ladd. **17** Nine. **18** Milan. **19** Bruce Willis. **20** Yardley. **21** Timothy Leary. **22** Jane Wyman. **23** Janet. **24** Ewan McGregor. **25** Gertrude Lawrence.

## *QUIZ 50* POT LUCK 19 .................... LEVEL 2

*Answers – see page 168*

1 In which film did King Jaffe Joffer appear?
2 Which Alan featured in *Die Hard*?
3 In which decade was *Rebecca* released?
4 In which movie did Winona Ryder play Cher's daughter?
5 Who won the Best Director Oscar for *One Flew over the Cuckoo's Nest*?
6 Which actor married US journalist Maria Shriver, one of the Kennedy clan?
7 Which character did Anthony Hopkins play in *Legends of the Fall*?
8 To the nearest hour, how long does *Dances with Wolves* last?
9 'King of the Cowboys' Leonard Slye was better known as whom?
10 Who directed *Goodfellas*?
11 A character named Rooster Cogburn first appeared in which film?
12 Who played Dolly in the 60s *Hello Dolly*?
13 In which decade was *A Streetcar Named Desire* released?
14 Which James was Professor Lindenbrook in *Journey to the Centre of the Earth*?
15 Who won the Best Actress Oscar for *Children of a Lesser God*?
16 *Anna and the King of Siam* and *Cleopatra* featured which Rex?
17 Who played Blofeld in *On Her Majesty's Secret Service*?
18 In which decade of the 20th century was Danny Glover born?
19 Which pop veteran featured in *The Man Who Fell to Earth*?
20 Who was Roger Moore's first Bond girl?
21 At what sport did Warren Beatty excel?
22 Who won the Best Actor Oscar for *Captains Courageous*?
23 Which conductor is Woody Allen's father in law?
24 Who directed *The Full Monty*?
25 Who played Lieutenant Schaffer in *Where Eagles Dare*?

**Answers Box Office Successes** (see Quiz 52)
**1** Maize. **2** Demolitions expert. **3** Detective. **4** John Ford. **5** Elvis. **6** Boston. **7** Goldfish. **8** *Ben Hur*. **9** Miranda Richardson. **10** 85. **11** Desert explorer. **12** Lester. **13** Alexis Arquette. **14** Qantas. **15** Peter Weir. **16** Jenny. **17** Tiberius. **18** Jerry Hall. **19** 3. **20** Dewey. **21** James Cameron. **22** *Revenge of the Jedi*. **23** Mike Todd. **24** Sofia Coppola. **25** *Licence Revoked*.

## *QUIZ 51* WHO'S WHO? ........ LEVEL 2

*Answers – see page 165*

1 Who starred in, and was executive producer of, *Onegin*?
2 What relation, if any, is Bridget Fonda to Henry?
3 Morgan Freeman was in which branch of the services before he became an actor?
4 Which comic-strip character did John Goodman play on screen?
5 What is the name of Julia Roberts's estranged brother?
6 Who replaced Val Kilmer as Batman?
7 Who found fame in *Shakespeare in Love* and *Elizabeth* in 1998?
8 What is the actor son of Barbra Streisand called?
9 Which actor links *Broadcast News* and *Lost in Space*?
10 Who was originally known as Susan Tomalin?
11 Who did Emily Watson play in *Hilary and Jackie*?
12 What is Al Pacino's nickname?
13 Who was in both the 60s and 90s versions of *The Thomas Crown Affair*?
14 Who played Red in the 90s version of *The Shawshank Redemption*?
15 In the 1992 biopic *Chaplin*, who played Fred Karno?
16 Who played the mother of real-life daughter Laura in *Wild at Heart*?
17 How many times did Zsa Zsa Gabor marry?
18 In which Italian city was Greta Scacchi born?
19 Which actor had a hit with 'Under the Boardwalk'?
20 Which cosmetics house did Helena Bonham Carter advertise?
21 Which hippie guru was Winona Ryder's godfather?
22 Who was the only actress to divorce a future US president?
23 Which Jackson starred in *Poetic Justice*?
24 Which *Phantom Menace* actor's uncle is fellow actor Denis Lawson?
25 Who did Julie Andrews play in *Star!*?

**Answers Famous Firsts** (see Quiz 49)
**1** *Dr No.* **2** Mikhail Baryshnikov. **3** Ub Iwerks. **4** *The Wiz.* **5** Al Jolson. **6** *Blackmail.* **7** *Toy Story.* **8** D.W. Griffith. **9** *Rope.* **10** *Hamlet.* **11** *Paper Moon.* **12** *The Robe.* **13** *Who's Afraid of Virginia Woolf?* **14** Dean. **15** Gaynor. **16** James Joyce. **17** *Cleopatra.* **18** *The Graduate.* **19** Robin Williams. **20** *The Happiest Millionaire.* **21** *Birth of a Nation.* **22** Indians'. **23** Maggie Smith. **24** Hayley Mills. **25** *Sugarland Express.*

## *QUIZ 52* BOX OFFICE SUCCESSES ........ LEVEL 2

*Answers – see page 166*

1 What type of crops grow in the field in which Mulder and Scully are chased across in *The X-Files*?
2 What is Harry Stamper's occupation in *Armageddon*?
3 What is Kevin Spacey's job in *LA Confidential*?
4 Which director links *Prizzi's Honor* and *The African Queen*?
5 Which famous rocker is said to have been an alien in *Men in Black*?
6 In which city is *Good Will Hunting* set?
7 In *Titanic*, what does Rose bring aboard the salvage boat, other than her luggage?
8 Which 50s film cost $4million, twice the maximum cost of the time?
9 Who plays Christina Ricci's stepmother in *Sleepy Hollow*?
10 How many changes of costume does Madonna have in *Evita*?
11 What is *The English Patient*'s occupation?
12 Which character is played by Kevin Spacey in *American Beauty*?
13 Which actor wears a single white glove in *The Wedding Singer*?
14 According to Charles in *Rain Man*, which airline has never had a crash?
15 Who directed *The Truman Show*?
16 What is the name of Tea Leoni's character in *Deep Impact*?
17 What does the 'T' stand for in James T. Kirk?
18 Who plays Alicia in *Batman*?
19 How many brothers did Private Ryan have?
20 Which character is played by David Arquette in *Scream 2*?
21 Who directed the first *Terminator* films?
22 What was *Return of the Jedi* originally called?
23 Which husband of Elizabeth Taylor produced *Around the World in Eighty Days* before his early death?
24 Who appeared in dad's *Godfather Part III*?
25 What was the original title of *Licence to Kill*?

**Answers Pot Luck 19** (see Quiz 50)
**1** *Coming to America*. **2** Rickman. **3** 1940s. **4** *Moonstruck*. **5** Milos Forman. **6** Arnold Schwarzenegger. **7** Colonel Ludlow. **8** 3 hours. **9** Roy Rogers. **10** Martin Scorsese. **11** *True Grit*. **12** Barbra Streisand. **13** 1950s. **14** Mason. **15** Marlee Matlin. **16** Harrison. **17** Telly Savalas. **18** 1940s. **19** David Bowie. **20** Jane Seymour. **21** American Football. **22** Spencer Tracy. **23** Andre Previn. **24** Peter Cattaneo. **25** Clint Eastwood.

## *QUIZ 53* POT LUCK 20 ........ LEVEL 2

*Answers – see page 171*

1 Which Jessica featured in *Play Misty for Me*?
2 How is Margaret Hyra better known?
3 In which decade was *All Quiet on the Western Front* released?
4 Who won the Best Actor Oscar for *Goodbye Mr Chips*?
5 What is Charlie Sheen's real name?
6 Omar Sharif is an expert at which card game?
7 Which Aidan featured in *Desperately Seeking Susan*?
8 Who played Scrooge in the 1951 *A Christmas Carol*?
9 A character named Harry Tasker appeared in which film?
10 Who won the Best Director Oscar for *Mr Deeds Goes to Town*?
11 Which actress links *High Noon* and *Rear Window*?
12 What was the name of Indiana Jones's sidekick in *The Temple of Doom*?
13 Who was Isabella Rossellini's mother?
14 Which song won Best Song Oscar for *The Sandpiper*?
15 The character named Charlie Croker is in which comedy/thriller film?
16 Which veteran actress said, 'I acted vulgar, Madonna *is* vulgar'?
17 Which surname was shared by John, Lionel, Ethel and Drew?
18 To the nearest hour, how long does *Doctor Zhivago* last?
19 Which actor's films include *Big Jim McLain, McLintock* and *McQ*?
20 Who directed *A Few Good Men*?
21 Which actress links *Love on the Dole* and *An Affair to Remember*?
22 In which decade was *The Driver* released?
23 What was the name of the villain in *Moonraker*?
24 Who won the Best Actress Oscar for *Guess Who's Coming to Dinner*?
25 In which film did a character named Horace Vendergelder appear?

**Answers Pot Luck 21** (see Quiz 55)
**1** *The Bodyguard.* **2** 1950s. **3** Walken. **4** Frank Sinatra. **5** *The Third Man.* **6** *Out of Africa.* **7** Jennifer Jones. **8** *Schindler's List.* **9** Betty Grable. **10** Maggie Smith. **11** Katz. **12** 1 hour. **13** Normandy. **14** *Dick Tracy.* **15** Mark Lester. **16** David Lynch. **17** Nicholson. **18** Los Lobos. **19** *The Search for Spock.* **20** Mike Nichols. **21** Boxing. **22** 1960s. **23** Ernest Hemingway. **24** *The Client.* **25** Tomlin.

## *QUIZ 54* KATHARINE HEPBURN ........ LEVEL 2

*Answers – see page 172*

1 In which decade was she born?
2 Which play, in which she played Tracy Lord, did she buy the film rights for and then sell to MGM?
3 Which John was her father in her first movie, *Bill of Divorcement*?
4 How many times was she Oscar-nominated in the 20th century?
5 Which American First Lady did she model herself on for *The African Queen*?
6 Which star of westerns was her co-star in *Rooster Cogburn*?
7 What was the name of her autobiography?
8 For which movie did she receive her first Oscar?
9 In which movie did she say, 'Nature, Mr Allnut, is what we are put in this world to rise above'?
10 In 1938 she was referred to as 'box office' what?
11 What part did Ludlow Ogden Smith play in her life?
12 For which 1962 Eugene O'Neill movie was she Oscar-nominated and a winner at the Cannes Film Festival?
13 For which film with Spencer Tracy did she win her second Oscar?
14 Which actor's aunt did she play in *Love Affair* in 1994?
15 How many films did she make with Spencer Tracy?
16 Which acerbic critic said, 'She ran the gamut of emotions from A to B'?
17 Who, with Cary Grant, was her male co-star in *The Philadelphia Story*?
18 With which star of the musical *Funny Girl* did she share an Oscar in 1968?
19 Who was her co-star in *Bringing Up Baby*?
20 Which 1933 movie, based on a novel by Louisa M. Alcott, did she star in?
21 Which French woman did she play in *The Lion in Winter*?
22 For which film did she win her third Oscar?
23 In which 1951 movie did she play a spinster opposite Humphrey Bogart?
24 For which film with Henry Fonda did she win her fourth Oscar?
25 In which US state was she born?

**Answers Music On Film** (see Quiz 56)
**1** Richard Rodgers. **2** Burt Bacharach. **3** Shirley Bassey. **4** Quincy Jones. **5** Bill Haley and the Comets. **6** *South Park Bigger, Longer & Uncut.* **7** George Harrison. **8** 'You'll Be in My Heart'. **9** Burt Bacharach. **10** *Toy Story 2.* **11** Beethoven. **12** 'A Spoonful of Sugar'. **13** Harry Connick Jr. **14** Cole Porter. **15** Stephen Sondheim. **16** Ennio Morricone. **17** *The Deer Hunter.* **18** Donny Osmond. **19** James Horner. **20** *Let's Make Love.* **21** Eric Clapton. **22** Isaac Hayes. **23** A-ha. **24** Stephen Sondheim. **25** Leopold Stokowski.

## *QUIZ 55* POT LUCK 21 ........ LEVEL 2

*Answers – see page 169*

1 A character named Frank Farmer appeared in which film?
2 In which decade was *Father of the Bride* first released?
3 Which Christopher featured in *The Deer Hunter*?
4 Who won an Oscar as Maggio in *From Here to Eternity*?
5 'I never knew the old Vienna' is the first line of which movie?
6 Which film was about Danish author Karen Blixen?
7 Which actress links the 1950s *Carrie* and *Towering Inferno*?
8 Which movie gave Steven Spielberg his first Oscar?
9 Who was voted No. 1 pin-up by US soldiers in World War II?
10 Which English actress played an elderly Wendy in *Hook*?
11 Which Mike featured in *Pumping Iron*?
12 To the nearest hour, how long does *Dumbo* last?
13 *Saving Private Ryan* dealt with events in which part of France?
14 The relationship between Warren Beatty and Madonna began on the set of which movie?
15 Who played the title role in *Oliver!*?
16 Who directed *The Elephant Man*?
17 In *The Bridge on the River Kwai,* Alec Guinness was which Colonel?
18 Who sang the title song of *La Bamba*?
19 What is the subtitle of *Star Trek III*?
20 Who directed *The Birdcage*?
21 Before entering films which sport did Mickey Rourke practise?
22 In which decade was *If...* released?
23 Which author appeared in *The Old Man and the Sea*?
24 In which film did a character named Reggie Love appear?
25 Which Lily featured in *Nashville*?

**Answers Pot Luck 20** (see Quiz 53)
**1** Walter. **2** Meg Ryan. **3** 1930s. **4** Robert Donat. **5** Carlos Estevez. **6** Bridge. **7** Quinn. **8** Alastair Sim. **9** *True Lies.* **10** Frank Capra. **11** Grace Kelly. **12** Shortround. **13** Ingrid Bergman. **14** 'The Shadow of Your Smile'. **15** *The Italian Job.* **16** Marlene Dietrich. **17** Barrymore. **18** 3 hours. **19** John Wayne. **20** Rob Reiner. **21** Deborah Kerr. **22** 1970s. **23** Drax. **24** Katharine Hepburn. **25** *Hello Dolly.*

## *QUIZ 56* MUSIC ON FILM ........ LEVEL 2

*Answers – see page 170*

1 Who worked with Oscar Hammerstein II on *South Pacific* and *Oklahoma*?
2 Who was Oscar-nominated for *What's New Pussycat?*?
3 Who sang the Bond theme from *Moonraker*?
4 Who wrote the soundtrack for *The Italian Job*?
5 Who provided the music for *The Blackboard Jungle*?
6 'Blame Canada' came from which movie?
7 Which Beatle was responsible for the music in *Shanghai Surprise*?
8 Which *Tarzan* song was Oscar-nominated?
9 Who scored *Butch Cassidy and the Sundance Kid*?
10 'When She Loved Me' came from which animated movie?
11 Which classical composer's music did Malcolm McDowell like in *A Clockwork Orange*?
12 Which song is played over the opening credits in *Mary Poppins*?
13 Whose music features on the soundtrack of *When Harry Met Sally*?
14 Whose music was used in *Anything Goes* and *High Society*?
15 Who wrote the *West Side Story* lyrics to Leonard Bernstein's music?
16 Who wrote the music for *The Good, the Bad and the Ugly*?
17 'Cavatina' was the theme music for which 70s movie?
18 Who provided the songs in *Mulan*?
19 Who wrote the music for the Oscar-winning song from *Titanic*?
20 In which movie did Marilyn Monroe sing 'My Heart Belongs to Daddy'?
21 Which UK guitarist and singer wrote the soundtrack for *Rush*?
22 Who won an Oscar for *Shaft*?
23 Who sang the Bond theme from *The Living Daylights*?
24 Which composer provided the music for *Reds*?
25 Who led the Philadelphia Orchestra in *Fantasia*?

**Answers Katharine Hepburn** (see Quiz 54)
**1** 1900s. **2** *The Philadelphia Story*. **3** Barrymore. **4** Eight. **5** Eleanor Roosevelt. **6** John Wayne. **7** *Me*. **8** *Morning Glory*. **9** *The African Queen*. **10** Poison. **11** She married him. **12** *Long Day's Journey into Night*. **13** *Guess Who's Coming to Dinner?* **14** Warren Beatty's. **15** Nine. **16** Dorothy Parker. **17** James Stewart. **18** Barbra Streisand. **19** Cary Grant. **20** *Little Women*. **21** Eleanor of Aquitaine. **22** *The Lion in Winter*. **23** *The African Queen*. **24** *On Golden Pond*. **25** Connecticut.

## *QUIZ 57* 1940s STARS ........ LEVEL 2

*Answers – see page 175*

1 Which star of *Gone with the Wind* was shot down by German fighter planes in 1943?
2 Who was Olivia De Havilland's sister?
3 Who was the US's highest paid woman star of the 1940s?
4 Who played Elsa Bannister in *The Lady from Shanghai*?
5 How is Betty Thornberg, who starred in *Annie Get Your Gun*, better known?
6 Which star of *Brief Encounter* made her debut in *In Which We Serve*?
7 To the nearest two inches, how tall was Alan Ladd?
8 Who was famous for her long blonde hair which hung over one eye?
9 Who co-wrote and sang the songs in *Lady and the Tramp*?
10 Who was called 'The Hunk'?
11 Who played Bill Walker in *GI Joe*?
12 Which duo were reunited in 1949 after a 10-year gap in *The Barkleys of Broadway*?
13 Which redhead said, 'I never thought of myself as a sex symbol, more a comedienne who could dance'?
14 Ingrid Bergman's romance with which Italian director forced her to leave Hollywood for Europe?
15 Who played the title role in *Mr Skeffington* opposite Bette Davis?
16 Which Victor said, 'I'm no actor and I've 64 films to prove it'?
17 Which star of *Song of Bernadette* married David O. Selznick?
18 Which *Gone with the Wind* nominee's 40s films included *The Dark Mirror* and *The Snake Pit*?
19 Whose role in *Odd Man Out* took him to Hollywood?
20 Who was Bill Sikes when Alec Guinness starred as Fagin?
21 Whose death in 1942 persuaded Clark Gable to join the US Air Corps?
22 Which actress links Hitchcock's *Spellbound* and *The Bells of St Mary's*?
23 Which 40s star was famous for her sarong?
24 Who was described as 'Slinky! Sultry! Sensational!' in a promotion poster before *To Have and Have Not*?
25 Who was dubbed the 'Brazilian Bombshell'?

**Answers 1960s** (see Quiz 59)
**1** *Whatever Happened to Baby Jane?* **2** Helen Keller. **3** Jerry Lewis. **4** *Darling.* **5** Jackie Gleason. **6** Glenn Campbell. **7** Henry Fonda. **8** Givenchy. **9** Howard Hughes. **10** *Paint Your Wagon.* **11** Paris & New York. **12** Bolivia. **13** Sidney Poitier. **14** *Winning.* **15** Turin. **16** *Hud.* **17** *Oliver!.* **18** *Alfie.* **19** *Tom Jones.* **20** Charlton Heston. **21** 2 hours. **22** D-Day landings. **23** Ursula Andress. **24** *The Greatest Story Ever Told.* **25** *Hello Dolly.*

## *QUIZ 58* POT LUCK 22 ........ LEVEL 2

*Answers – see page 176*

1 What was Mel Gibson's job in the 1997 thriller *Conspiracy Theory*?
2 Which George turned down Bogart's role in *The Maltese Falcon*?
3 The character Catherine Tramell appeared in which movie?
4 Who won the Best Actor Oscar for *Patton*?
5 Which Arsenio featured in *Coming to America*?
6 Who starred opposite Mickey Rooney in *National Velvet* in 1944?
7 Which Karen featured in *Raiders of the Lost Ark*?
8 Who directed *Dead Man Walking*?
9 Who played the title role in *The Bachelor*?
10 Pearl Slaghoople is mother-in-law to which fictional character?
11 Which comedian played opposite Jane Russell in *The Paleface*?
12 Who played the Bond girl in *Never Say Never Again*?
13 Who is Pongo's mate in *101 Dalmatians*?
14 Which former child star became ambassador to Ghana and Czechoslovakia?
15 Which actress links *A Streetcar Named Desire* and *Planet of the Apes*?
16 Who won the Best Actress Oscar for *Mrs Miniver*?
17 What was the first Monty Python film for the cinema?
18 In which movie did Gregory Peck play James McKay?
19 To the nearest fifteen minutes, how long does *Fantasia* last?
20 A character named Rachel Marron appeared in which film?
21 In which decade was Disney's *Sleeping Beauty* released?
22 Which brothers starred in *Young Guns*?
23 *The Sting* and *Sneakers* both featured which actor?
24 Which Henry turned down Peter Finch's role in *Network*?
25 What was the name of Tommy Lee Jones's character in *The Fugitive*?

**Answers Superstars** (see Quiz 60)
**1** Demi Moore. **2** Richard Gere. **3** *Book.* **4** Alfredo James. **5** Julie Andrews. **6** *Daylight.* **7** Michael Douglas. **8** Canada. **9** Michelle Pfeiffer. **10** Uma Thurman. **11** *Pulp Fiction.* **12** Dolly Parton. **13** Brad Pitt. **14** Sharon Stone. **15** Brad Pitt. **16** Enzio. **17** 26. **18** Leonardo DiCaprio. **19** Eight. **20** *Taxi Driver.* **21** Michelle Pfeiffer. **22** Robin Williams. **23** Whoopi Goldberg. **24** Kathleen Turner. **25** Emma Thompson.

## *QUIZ 59* 1960s ........ LEVEL 2

*Answers – see page 173*

1 In which movie did Bette Davis and Joan Crawford play two old ladies with murder in mind?
2 Which blind and deaf lady was the subject of *The Miracle Worker*?
3 Who played two parts in *The Nutty Professor* in 1963?
4 In which movie did Dirk Bogarde say to Julie Christie, 'Your idea of fidelity is not having more than one man in bed at the same time'?
5 Who played Minnesota Fats in *The Hustler*?
6 Which gentle-voiced country singer appeared in *True Grit*?
7 Who played against type in *Once Upon a Time in the West*?
8 Which French fashion designer Hubert worked on *Breakfast at Tiffany's*?
9 Which eccentric recluse and film-maker was the basis for a character played by George Peppard in *The Carpetbaggers*?
10 What was the last of Lerner and Loewe's 60s musicals?
11 Between which two cities is *The Great Race* set?
12 In which South American country were Butch Cassidy and Sundance finally tracked down?
13 Who played the guest in *Guess Who's Coming to Dinner*?
14 Paul Newman has motor-raced professionally since starring in which movie?
15 In which city was *The Italian Job* filmed?
16 Which movie had the ad line, 'The man with the barbed wire soul'?
17 For which movie was Jack Wild Oscar-nominated on his film debut?
18 Which 1966 movie made Brit Michael Caine an international star?
19 In which of his own movies did Tony Richardson appear in 1963?
20 Who played Michelangelo in *The Agony and the Ecstasy*?
21 To the nearest hour, how long does *A Man for All Seasons* last?
22 Which event was *The Longest Day* about?
23 Which Bond girl appeared in *What's New Pussycat?*?
24 In which movie did Donald Pleasence play the devil?
25 Which musical movie featured the character Horace Vandergelder?

**Answers 1940s Stars** (see Quiz 57)
**1** Leslie Howard. **2** Joan Fontaine. **3** Betty Grable. **4** Rita Hayworth. **5** Betty Hutton. **6** Celia Johnson. **7** 5 feet 5 inches. **8** Veronica Lake. **9** Peggy Lee. **10** Victor Mature. **11** Robert Mitchum. **12** Fred Astaire & Ginger Rogers. **13** Rita Hayworth. **14** Roberto Rossellini. **15** Claude Rains. **16** Mature. **17** Jennifer Jones. **18** Olivia De Havilland. **19** James Mason. **20** Robert Newton. **21** His wife, Carole Lombard's. **22** Ingrid Bergman. **23** Dorothy Lamour. **24** Lauren Bacall. **25** Carmen Miranda.

## *QUIZ 60* SUPERSTARS ........ LEVEL 2

*Answers – see page 174*

1 Which star of *St Elmo's Fire* was the voice of Esmerelda in the cartoon *Hunchback of Notre Dame*?
2 Who published the book *Pilgrim* containing photos he had taken in Tibet?
3 What simple title did Whoopi Goldberg's autobiography have?
4 What are Al Pacino's real first names?
5 About whom did Christopher Plummer say, 'Working with her is like being hit over the head with a Valentine card'?
6 Which 1996 disaster movie starred Sylvester Stallone?
7 Michael Keaton shares his real name with another superstar; whom?
8 Where was Rick Moranis born?
9 Which actress links Susie in *The Fabulous Baker Boys* and Countess Ellen in *The Age of Innocence*?
10 Whose first two husbands were Gary Oldman and Ethan Hawke?
11 Which 90s movie got John Travolta's career back on track after a series of flops?
12 Which country star was in the list of top movie money-makers in 1981?
13 Who was Richard Gere's younger male co-star in *Seven Years In Tibet*?
14 Which star of *Basic Instinct* provided a voice in *Antz*?
15 In 1999 who in the US was voted 'the man you would most like to repopulate the world with after a Martian invasion'?
16 What is Sylvester Stallone's middle name?
17 How old was Barbra Streisand when she made her screen debut?
18 Who played Meryl Streep's son in *Marvin's Room*?
19 How many times did Elizabeth Taylor marry in the 20th century?
20 In which movie did Robert De Niro say, 'You talkin' to me?'?
21 Which star of *The Witches of Eastwick* was the voice of Tzipporah in *Prince of Egypt*?
22 Who has children called Zachary and Zelda?
23 Which film star wrote the novel *Alice*?
24 Whose first Oscar nomination was for *Peggy Sue Got Married*?
25 Which English actress was John Travolta's co-star in *Primary Colors*?

**Answers Pot Luck 22** (see Quiz 58)
**1** Cabbie. **2** Raft. **3** *Basic Instinct.* **4** George C. Scott. **5** Hall. **6** Elizabeth Taylor. **7** Allen. **8** Tim Robbins. **9** Chris O'Donnell. **10** Fred Flintstone. **11** Bob Hope. **12** Kim Basinger. **13** Perdita. **14** Shirley Temple. **15** Kim Hunter. **16** Greer Garson. **17** *And Now for Something Completely Different.* **18** *The Big Country.* **19** 115 minutes. **20** *The Bodyguard.* **21** 1950s. **22** Charlie Sheen, Emilio Estevez. **23** Robert Redford. **24** Fonda. **25** Sam Gerard.

## *QUIZ 61* POT LUCK 23 .................................................. LEVEL 2

*Answers – see page 179*

1 In which film did Michael Douglas declare that 'Greed is good'?
2 Within fifteen minutes, how long does *The Elephant Man* last?
3 Who played Bernardo in *The Magnificent Seven*?
4 Who won the Best Actor Oscar for *Sergeant York*?
5 Which John featured in *Carrie*?
6 Who was the voice of Jessica Rabbit in *Who Framed Roger Rabbit?*?
7 In which movie does Sugar Kane appear?
8 In which decade was *On the Town* released?
9 A character named Mitch McDeere appeared in which film?
10 Which director Roger links Bardot, Deneuve and Fonda?
11 Which actress links *Hannah and Her Sisters* and *Beaches*?
12 Which Oscar did Kevin Costner win for *Dances with Wolves*?
13 Which George featured in *Look Who's Talking*?
14 Within thirty minutes, how long does *Reservoir Dogs* last?
15 Which 1973 film did rock star Bob Dylan star in?
16 Which notorious 1943 movie had the advertising tag, 'Mean, moody, magnificent'?
17 *The Bostonians* and *Superman* featured which actor?
18 Who won the Best Director Oscar for *Gigi*?
19 In which film did a character named Madeleine Elster appear?
20 Who won the Best Actress Oscar for *Kitty Foyle*?
21 What was the name of Herbert Lom's character in *A Shot in the Dark*?
22 Who directed *Dead Poets Society*?
23 Which Steven featured in *Rambo: First Blood, Part II*?
24 In which decade was *Harvey* released?
25 Who won an Oscar as Margaret Schlegel in *Howard's End* in 1992?

**Answers Sequels & Remakes** (see Quiz 63)
**1** *The Godfather.* **2** *A Perfect Murder.* **3** *The Jewel of the Nile.* **4** *Anna and the King.* **5** *Indiana Jones and the Last Crusade.* **6** *Oliver's Story.* **7** *Cabaret.* **8** One. **9** *Another 48 Hours.* **10** *One Million Years BC.* **11** *Patriot Games.* **12** *The Return of Jafar.* **13** Deloris (*Sister Act II*). **14** *Return of the Jedi.* **15** Eric Clapton. **16** Val Kilmer. **17** One. **18** Clouseau. **19** *Alien³*. **20** Paul Hogan. **21** *The Lost World.* **22** 30. **23** New York. **24** *The Hustler.* **25** Ripley.

## *QUIZ 62* 1990s STARS ........ LEVEL 2

*Answers – see page 180*

1 Who played the White House PR guru in *Wag the Dog*?
2 Who played two parts in *The Man in the Iron Mask* in 1998?
3 What is the name of Susan Sarandon's character in *Dead Man Walking*?
4 In which movie did Gwyneth Paltrow first practise her English accent?
5 Who was Drew Barrymore's co-star in *The Wedding Singer*?
6 Who play the undercover cops in *Rush*?
7 Whose first movie was *Kiss Daddy Goodnight*?
8 Which musician did Geoffrey Rush play in *Shine*?
9 Which member of the Arquette family married the nephew of Francis Ford Coppola?
10 What was Antonio Banderas's follow-up to *Evita*?
11 Whose first major follow-up to *Another Country* was *My Friend's Wedding*?
12 Who was the SAS man who escaped from Alcatraz in *The Rock*?
13 In which movie did Al Pacino play the devil?
14 Who played two parts in *Meet Joe Black* in 1998?
15 What was the name of Robert Carlyle's character in *Trainspotting*?
16 Who played Anthony Hopkins's daughter in *The Mask of Zorro*?
17 What is the name of Morgan Freeman's detective in *Se7en*?
18 Which British actor played the villain in the third *Die Hard* movie?
19 In which movie did John Travolta play an angel?
20 Which husband and wife starred in *Too Much* in 1996?
21 In which movie did Susan Sarandon play Michaela Odone, the mother of a dying child?
22 Who played Leonardo DiCaprio's stepfather in *This Boy's Life*?
23 What is the name of Gwyneth Paltrow's character in *Shakespeare in Love*?
24 Who played Tina Turner in *What's Love Got to Do With It?*?
25 Which low-budget 1999 thriller starred Joseph Leonard?

**Answers Pot Luck 24** (see Quiz 64)
**1** Blanche. **2** Allen. **3** Shirley MacLaine. **4** 1940s. **5** Brigitte Bardot. **6** Caan. **7** *The Thomas Crown Affair*. **8** Annie Wilkes. **9** *The Fugitive*. **10** Chico. **11** Goldie Hawn. **12** Neil Simon. **13** Peggy Lee. **14** Petula Clark. **15** 1930s. **16** Harold Hill. **17** Jerome Robbins & Robert Wise. **18** Lauren Bacall. **19** Sean Bean. **20** 1930s. **21** *The Lion in Winter*. **22** *Kiss Me Kate*. **23** 115 minutes. **24** Keanu Reeves. **25** *Gone with the Wind*.

## *QUIZ 63* SEQUELS & REMAKES ........................................ LEVEL 2

*Answers – see page 177*

1 What was the first sequel to an Oscar-winner to win an Oscar?
2 Which 90s movie was a remake of *Dial M for Murder* with Grace Kelly?
3 What was the sequel to *Romancing the Stone*?
4 Which Jodie Foster movie was a remake of a 50s music classic with Deborah Kerr?
5 Which movie announced, 'The man with the hat is back. And this time he's bringing his dad'?
6 What was the follow up to *Love Story*?
7 Which 70s musical was based on *I Am a Camera*?
8 How many *Terminator* films were made before the one called *Judgment Day*?
9 What was the sequel to *48 Hours* called?
10 *When Dinosaurs Ruled the Earth* was the sequel to which Raquel Welch movie?
11 *Clear and Present Danger* was the sequel to which 'Games'?
12 Which follow-up to Disney's *Aladdin* was released soon after the original?
13 Which heroine came 'Back in the Habit'?
14 What was the second sequel to *Star Wars*?
15 Which guitarist nicknamed Slowhand provided the music for *Lethal Weapon* and its first two sequels?
16 Who succeeded Michael Keaton as Batman?
17 How many sequels to *Die Hard* did Bonnie Bedelia star in?
18 *A Shot in the Dark* was one of the sequels about which Inspector?
19 Which sequel was criticized with the comment, 'In space no one can hear you snore'?
20 Who wrote and starred in *Crocodile Dundee II*?
21 What was the sequel to *Jurassic Park* called?
22 To the nearest million dollars, how much did *Rambo III* lose?
23 Where was Kevin lost in *Home Alone II*?
24 *The Color of Money* recreated the main character from which film?
25 What was the name of the only crew member to survive in *Alien*?

**Answers Pot Luck 23** (see Quiz 61)
**1** *Wall Street.* **2** 124 minutes. **3** Charles Bronson. **4** Gary Cooper. **5** Travolta. **6** Kathleen Turner. **7** *Some Like it Hot.* **8** 1940s. **9** *The Firm.* **10** Roger Vadim. **11** Barbara Hershey. **12** Best Director. **13** Segal. **14** 99 mins. **15** *Pat Garret and Billy the Kid.* **16** *The Outlaw.* **17** Christopher Reeve. **18** Vincente Minnelli. **19** Vertigo. **20** Ginger Rogers. **21** Inspector Dreyfus. **22** Peter Weir. **23** Berkoff. **24** 1950s. **25** Emma Thompson.

## *QUIZ 64* POT LUCK 24 ........ LEVEL 2

*Answers – see page 178*

1 What was the name of Baby Jane's sister in *Whatever Happened to Baby Jane*?
2 Which Nancy featured in *Robocop*?
3 Who won the Best Actress Oscar for *Terms of Endearment*?
4 In which decade was *His Girl Friday* released?
5 How is Camille Javal better known?
6 Which James featured in *A Bridge Too Far*?
7 'The Windmills of Your Mind' won an Oscar when it was used in which movie?
8 What was the name of the lady 'gaoler' in *Misery*?
9 In which film did a character named Dr Richard Kimble appear?
10 Who was the oldest Marx brother?
11 Which actress links *Shampoo* and *Overboard*?
12 Who wrote the play on which *The Odd Couple* was based?
13 Who sings 'He's a Tramp' in *Lady and the Tramp*?
14 Who played opposite Peter O'Toole in the 1960s *Goodbye Mr Chips*?
15 In which decade of the 20th century was Christopher Lloyd born?
16 What was the name of Robert Preston's character in *The Music Man*?
17 Who won the Best Director Oscar for *West Side Story*?
18 Who was the female lead actress in the 1940s *The Big Sleep*?
19 Which movie star has '100% Blade' tattooed on his arm?
20 In which decade was *Hell's Angels* released?
21 What was Anthony Hopkins's first film, in 1968?
22 Which musical film is based on *The Taming of the Shrew*?
23 Within fifteen minutes, how long does *E.T.* last?
24 *River's Edge* and *The Night Before* both feature which actor?
25 In which classic did Olivia de Havilland play Melanie Wilkes?

**Answers 1990s Stars** (see Quiz 62)
**1** Anne Heche. **2** Leonardo DiCaprio. **3** Sister Helen Prejean. **4** *Emma.* **5** Adam Sandler. **6** Jennifer Jason Leigh & Jason Patric. **7** Uma Thurman. **8** David Helfgott. **9** Patricia (Mrs Nicolas Cage). **10** *The Mask of Zorro.* **11** Rupert Everett. **12** Sean Connery. **13** *The Devil's Advocate.* **14** Brad Pitt. **15** Begbie. **16** Catherine Zeta Jones. **17** Somerset. **18** Jeremy Irons. **19** Michael. **20** Antonio Banderas & Melanie Griffith. **21** *Lorenzo's Oil.* **22** Robert De Niro. **23** Viola De Lessops. **24** Angela Bassett. **25** *The Blair Witch Project.*

## *QUIZ 65* TOM HANKS ........................................ LEVEL 2

*Answers – see page 183*

1 In which film did he fall for a mermaid?
2 In which US state was he born?
3 In *Forrest Gump* he tours China playing which game?
4 In which movie was he the subject of a radio phone-in?
5 *Volunteers* is about volunteers in which corps?
6 In *Turner and Hooch,* who or what is his detective partner?
7 What is his real name in *Sleepless in Seattle*?
8 For which movie was he Oscar-nominated for playing a boy trapped in a man's body?
9 Who played his mother in *Philadelphia*?
10 In which decade is *That Thing You Do!* set?
11 Who played his partner in *Philadelphia*?
12 Whom did he play in *Apollo 13*?
13 In which movie did he play Captain John Miller?
14 What was his first Oscar-winner in the title role?
15 He met his wife Rita Wilson on the set of which movie?
16 In which movie did he play a lawyer dying from AIDS?
17 In what year did the real action of *Apollo 13* take place?
18 Whom did he marry after his divorce from Samantha Lewes?
19 Who plays the only lawyer willing to take on his case in *Philadelphia*?
20 Who was his co-star in *Splash*?
21 Which sport was featured in *A League of their Own*?
22 Who played Annie in *Sleepless in Seattle*?
23 Which 1996 movie saw him as director as well actor?
24 Who played his mother in *Forrest Gump*?
25 Which future Mrs Antonio Banderas was his co-star in *Bonfire of the Vanities*?

**Answers Pot Luck 25** (see Quiz 67)
**1** Roth. **2** 100 minutes. **3** Daniel Hillard. **4** 1960s. **5** *Postcards from the Edge.* **6** John Ford. **7** *Scent of a Woman.* **8** Gladys Knight. **9** Robert Wagner. **10** Sonja Henie. **11** Michael Crichton. **12** Charlie Allnutt. **13** Diane Keaton. **14** Jeff Bridges. **15** 1940s. **16** Tim Robbins. **17** Orson Welles. **18** *A River Runs Through It.* **19** Fox. **20** *Amistad.* **21** 2 hours. **22** Whoopi Goldberg. **23** John Landis. **24** Paul Scofield. **25** Marceau.

## QUIZ 66 UNFORGETTABLES ........ LEVEL 2

*Answers – see page 184*

1 Who was Frank Sinatra's second wife to be a professional actress?
2 Which actor, who died in 1997, was famous for his slow drawl and slow walk?
3 By what single name was Harris Glenn Milstead better known?
4 Which voluptuous blonde was Miss Photoflash 1952?
5 What was Bob Hope's theme song?
6 On what island did Oliver Reed die?
7 Where was Anthony Quinn born?
8 Leonard Slye was better known as which cowboy star?
9 Which husband of Ava Gardner said of her, 'a lady of strong passions, one of them rage'?
10 Which godfather of Jennifer Aniston was Oscar-nominated for *The Birdman of Alcatraz*?
11 Which king did Robert Shaw play in *A Man for All Seasons*?
12 Who was head of Universal at 21, MGM at 25 and died aged 37 in 1936?
13 Which of Spencer's famous co-stars said to him, 'I'm a little tall for you, Mr Tracy'?
14 Whose funeral in the USA in 1926 was a national event and prompted a number of suicides?
15 Lee Van Cleef found fame in what type of movies?
16 Otto Preminger was from which country before settling in the USA?
17 Who was originally billed as 'Oklahoma's Yodeling Cowboy'?
18 Which husband of Barbara Stanwyck had the real name of Spangler Arlington Brugh?
19 Which French writer/director's second wife was Jane Fonda?
20 Which wife of Roman Polanski was murdered by the Charles Manson Family?
21 How many times did Lana Turner marry?
22 William Powell was engaged to which blonde actress at the time of her untimely death?
23 Whose marriage to Ethel Merman lasted just three weeks?
24 Whose only Oscar nomination was for *Running on Empty* before his early death?
25 In a difficult dance sequence in *Top Hat*, Fred Astaire broke many what?

**Answers Children's Films** (see Quiz 68)
**1** Kermit & Miss Piggy. **2** Dustbin. **3** Jasmine. **4** Pongo & Perdita. **5** Rick Moranis. **6** *The Hunchback of Notre Dame*. **7** Robin Williams. **8** Gertie. **9** The garden. **10** Danny DeVito. **11** *Hook*. **12** Ralph. **13** California. **14** Harry Connick Jr **15** *Bugsy Malone*. **16** Baloo. **17** Blue. **18** Danny Kaye. **19** Rowan Atkinson. **20** *Jurassic Park*. **21** *Pig in the City*. **22** Woody. **23** Disney. **24** Gene Wilder. **25** Anne Bancroft.

## *QUIZ 67* POT LUCK 25 ........ LEVEL 2

*Answers – see page 181*

1 Which Tim featured in *Reservoir Dogs*?
2 Within fifteen minutes, how long does *Edward Scissorhands* last?
3 What was the name of Robin Williams's character in *Mrs Doubtfire*?
4 In which decade was the biker classic *Easy Rider* released?
5 The character named Suzanne Vale appeared in which film?
6 Who won the Best Director Oscar for *How Green Was My Valley*?
7 In which film did a character named Colonel Frank Slade appear?
8 Who sang the Bond theme from *Licence to Kill*?
9 Which actor was married twice to Natalie Wood?
10 Which Norwegian skater starred in *Thin Ice*?
11 Which writer directed *Westworld* in 1973?
12 What was the name of Humphrey Bogart's character in *The African Queen*?
13 Who won the Best Actress Oscar for *Annie Hall*?
14 *Starman* and *The Fisher King* starred which actor?
15 In which decade was *Rope* released?
16 *Bull Durham* and *Bob Roberts* featured which actor?
17 Who played Harry Lime in *The Third Man*?
18 In which movie did Brad Pitt play the character *Paul MacLean*?
19 Which animal is Robin Hood in the Disney film?
20 Which Spielberg film was about slavery?
21 To the nearest hour, how long does *The Last of the Mohicans* last?
22 Which actress links *Burglar* and *Ghost*?
23 Who directed *Coming to America*?
24 Who won the Best Actor Oscar for *A Man for All Seasons*?
25 Which Sophie featured in *Braveheart*?

**Answers Tom Hanks** (see Quiz 65)
**1** *Splash.* **2** California. **3** Ping Pong. **4** *Sleepless in Seattle.* **5** Peace Corps. **6** Dog. **7** Sam. **8** *Big.* **9** Joanne Woodward. **10** 1960s. **11** Antonio Banderas. **12** Jim Lovell. **13** *Saving Private Ryan.* **14** *Forrest Gump.* **15** *Volunteers.* **16** *Philadelphia.* **17** 1970. **18** Rita Wilson. **19** Denzel Washington. **20** Daryl Hannah. **21** Baseball. **22** Meg Ryan. **23** *That Thing You Do!.* **24** Sally Field. **25** Melanie Griffith.

## *QUIZ 68* CHILDREN'S FILMS ........ LEVEL 2

*Answers – see page 182*

1 Who were the Cratchits in *The Muppet Christmas Carol*?
2 Where does Beethoven hide when he first escapes from the puppy robbers' truck?
3 What is the name of the princess in *Aladdin*?
4 Who were responsible for setting up the 'Twilight Bark'?
5 Who plays the inventor in *Honey, I Shrunk the Kids*?
6 Kevin Kline provided a voice in which Disney movie set in France?
7 Who was the Prof in the remake of *The Absent Minded Professor*?
8 Who did Drew Barrymore play in *E.T.*?
9 Where does the professor dump the kids in *Honey, I Shrunk the Kids*?
10 Who starred in and directed *Matilda*?
11 In which 1991 children's movie did Glenn Close appear uncredited as a pirate?
12 Which Fiennes was a voice in *The Prince of Egypt*?
13 Where did 'The Karate Kid' move to?
14 Which musician who found fame with *When Harry Met Sally* contributes to *The Iron Giant*?
15 Which children's gangster movie marked Alan Parker's directorial debut?
16 Who teaches Mowgli 'The Bare Necessities of Life'?
17 At the Mad Hatter's tea party in *Alice in Wonderland* what colour is Alice's dress?
18 Who played the title role in *Hans Christian Andersen*?
19 Which British comedian was the voice of Zazu in *The Lion King*?
20 What was an adventure '65 million years in the making'?
21 What was the sequel to *Babe* called?
22 Who becomes a collector's item in *Toy Story 2*?
23 Which studio made the end-of-millennium *Tarzan*?
24 Which Gene played the owner of the factory in *Willy Wonka and the Chocolate Factory*?
25 Which Mrs Mel Brooks can be heard in *Antz*?

**Answers Unforgettables** (see Quiz 66)
**1** Mia Farrow. **2** James Stewart. **3** Divine. **4** Jayne Mansfield. **5** 'Thanks for the Memory'. **6** Malta. **7** Mexico. **8** Roy Rogers. **9** Mickey Rooney. **10** Telly Savalas. **11** Henry VIII. **12** Irving Thalberg. **13** Katharine Hepburn. **14** Rudolph Valentino. **15** Spaghetti westerns. **16** Austria. **17** Gene Autry. **18** Robert Taylor. **19** Roger Vadim. **20** Sharon Tate. **21** Seven. **22** Jean Harlow. **23** Ernest Borgnine. **24** River Phoenix. **25** Canes.

## *QUIZ 69* POT LUCK 26 ........ LEVEL 2

*Answers – see page 187*

1 A character named Dr Ellie Sattler appeared in which film?
2 *Rich and Famous* and *Top Gun* both feature which actress?
3 Which actress links *Meet Me in St Louis* and *Easter Parade*?
4 In a 1990 film which heroes lived in the sewers?
5 In which decade was *Monkey Business* first released?
6 In which film does Mark Renton appear?
7 Which actress links *Lady Jane* and *Howard's End*?
8 In which film did a character named Julian Kaye appear?
9 What was the name of the Bond girl in *Goldfinger*?
10 Who played Cal in *East of Eden*?
11 Who won the Best Director Oscar for *My Fair Lady*?
12 A character named Maggie Pollitt appeared in which 1950s film?
13 Within fifteen minutes, how long does *The English Patient* last?
14 Which Gary featured in *Lethal Weapon*?
15 Who directed *Casablanca*?
16 Which Julie featured in *Shampoo*?
17 Which movie did the song 'Call Me' come from?
18 How was Natasha Gurdin better known?
19 Which movie gave Steven Spielberg his first Oscar nomination?
20 Which fairy tale became a movie with the song 'Bibbidy Bobbidy Boo'?
21 Who founded the Sundance Festival for independent film makers?
22 Which Ted featured in *Body Heat*?
23 In which decade was *Monty Python's Life of Brian* released?
24 Who won the Best Actor Oscar for *Going My Way*?
25 A character named Holly Golightly appeared in which film?

**Answers Tony Curtis** (see Quiz 71)
**1** 1920s. **2** Bernard. **3** New York. **4** Navy. **5** Five. **6** Saxophonist. **7** *The Last Tycoon*. **8** Ali Baba. **9** Painting. **10** *Houdini*. **11** Cary Grant. **12** Malibu. **13** *Tony Curtis*. **14** *Some Like It Hot*. **15** *Trapeze*. **16** Janet Leigh. **17** *Boeing Boeing*. **18** Albert De Salvo. **19** *The Defiant Ones*. **20** *Kid Andrew Cody & Julie Sparrow*. **21** Cary Grant. **22** Kelly Curtis. **23** Joe. **24** Kirk Douglas. **25** Natalie Wood.

## QUIZ 70 STARS OF THE SILENT YEARS ............ LEVEL 2

*Answers – see page 188*

1 In 1913 who did Fatty Arbuckle sign up with to make comedies?
2 Which Chaplin movie made a star of Jackie Coogan?
3 Who was the star of *Grandma's Boy*?
4 Who shot to stardom with *The Miracle Man*?
5 Who starred in *Sherlock Junior* and *The Navigator*?
6 Who did Garbo sign up with in 1925?
7 Which Louise was the star of *Lulu*?
8 Whose biography was subtitled *The Woman Who Made Hollywood*?
9 Which comedy star was arrested on charges of rape and manslaughter in 1920?
10 Who was the Mabel in the title of the Jerry Herman musical about her and Mack Sennett?
11 Where was Erich von Stroheim born?
12 Marion Davies was the protegée of which newspaper magnate?
13 Which deadpan comic made films with Fatty Arbuckle from 1917?
14 Which British-born comic starred in Mack Sennett's *Tillie's Punctured Romance*?
15 Which comedy group's debut was *The Cocoanuts*?
16 Who starred in the epic *The Wind*?
17 Which actress starred in D.W. Griffith's *The Violin Maker of Cremona* after being an extra just a few months before?
18 Who was considered the first vamp?
19 In which decade did Laurel team up with Hardy?
20 Which bespectacled comic was famous for his *Lucky Luke* two-reelers?
21 Who made his screen debut in *Making a Living* in 1914?
22 What relation was Dorothy to Lillian Gish?
23 Which frequent leading lady of Chaplin's starred with him in *The Kid*?
24 What was Mack Sennett's real first name?
25 Which four-legged star made his debut in *The Man from Hell's River*?

**Answers Pot Luck 27** (see Quiz 72)
**1** *White Hunter, Black Heart*. **2** Gregory Peck. **3** Goldblum. **4** Jake and Elwood. **5** Bette Midler. **6** Lauren Bacall. **7** O'Toole. **8** 1940s. **9** Louise Fletcher. **10** Wendy Torrance. **11** John Landis. **12** *South Pacific*. **13** Little Richard. **14** Ally Sheedy. **15** Heche. **16** *Flubber*. **17** Jenny. **18** James Cagney. **19** Mick Jackson. **20** Mickey Rooney. **21** Robert Redford. **22** Berkley. **23** 1960s. **24** Peter Banning. **25** *Young Guns*.

## *QUIZ 71* TONY CURTIS ........ LEVEL 2

*Answers – see page 185*

1 In which decade was Tony Curtis born?
2 What is his real first name?
3 In which city was he born?
4 In which branch of the services did he serve in World War II?
5 How many wives had he had by the end of the 20th century?
6 What type of instrumentalist was he in *Some Like It Hot*?
7 In which 70s movie were Robert De Niro and Robert Mitchum his co-stars?
8 Who was he 'Son of' in a 1952 film?
9 In which branch of the arts did he also achieve success in later life?
10 In which biopic did he star with Janet Leigh in 1953?
11 Which Hollywood great did he parody in *Some Like It Hot*?
12 On which famous beach is *Don't Make Waves* set?
13 What was the name of his autobiography?
14 In which movie does he end up with Marilyn Monroe in a motorboat?
15 Which 1956 movie was about the circus?
16 Which star of *Psycho* was he married to?
17 In which jet-age comedy did he star with Jerry Lewis in 1965?
18 What was the name of his character in *The Boston Strangler*?
19 Which movie with Sidney Poitier gave him his first Oscar nomination?
20 What was the name of the novel he wrote in 1977?
21 Who was his male co-star in *Operation Petticoat*?
22 Who is his other famous actress daughter along with Jamie Lee?
23 What was the name of his character in *Some Like It Hot*?
24 Who played the title role in *Spartacus* in which he starred?
25 Which late star was his co-star in *The Great Race*?

**Answers Pot Luck 26** (see Quiz 69)
**1** *Jurassic Park*. **2** Meg Ryan. **3** Judy Garland. **4** Teenage Mutant Ninja Turtles. **5** 1930s. **6** *Trainspotting*. **7** Helena Bonham Carter. **8** *American Gigolo*. **9** Pussy Galore. **10** James Dean. **11** George Cukor. **12** *Cat on a Hot Tin Roof*. **13** 155 minutes. **14** Busey. **15** Michael Curtiz. **16** Christie. **17** *American Gigolo*. **18** Natalie Wood. **19** *Close Encounters of the Third Kind*. **20** Cinderella. **21** Robert Redford. **22** Danson. **23** 1970s. **24** Bing Crosby. **25** *Breakfast at Tiffany's*.

## *QUIZ 72* POT LUCK 27 ........ LEVEL 2

*Answers – see page 186*

1 Which Clint Eastwood movie was based on the screenwriter Peter Viertel's experiences while shooting *The African Queen*?
2 Who won the Best Actor Oscar for *To Kill a Mockingbird*?
3 Which Jeff featured in *The Big Chill*?
4 What were the names of the 'Blues Brothers'?
5 *The Rose* and *Scenes from a Mall* starred which actress?
6 Which actress links *Misery* and *The Mirror Has Two Faces*?
7 Which Peter featured in *The Last Emperor*?
8 In which decade was *Great Expectations* first released?
9 Who won the Best Actress Oscar for *One Flew over the Cuckoo's Nest*?
10 What was the name of Shelley Duvall's character in *The Shining*?
11 Who directed *The Blues Brothers*?
12 In which film did a nurse named Nellie Forbush appear?
13 Who married Bruce Willis and Demi Moore?
14 *Short Circuit* and *Betsy's Wedding* featured which actress?
15 Which Anne featured in *Six Days, Seven Nights*?
16 What was the 90s remake of *The Absent Minded Professor* called?
17 What was the name of Robin Wright's character in *Forrest Gump*?
18 Which famous gangster actor was a founder of the Screen Actors' Guild?
19 Who directed *The Bodyguard*?
20 *National Velvet* and *Breakfast at Tiffany's* both featured which actor?
21 Who won the Best Director Oscar for *Ordinary People*?
22 Which Elizabeth featured in *Showgirls*?
23 In which decade was *Spartacus* released?
24 What was the name of Robin Williams's character in *Hook*?
25 Which 80s teenage western starred actors known as the Brat Pack?

**Answers Stars of the Silent Years** (see Quiz 70)
**1** Mack Sennett. **2** *The Kid.* **3** Harold Lloyd. **4** Lon Chaney. **5** Buster Keaton. **6** MGM. **7** Brooks. **8** Mary Pickford. **9** Fatty Arbuckle. **10** Normand. **11** Austria. **12** William Randolph Hearst. **13** Buster Keaton. **14** Charlie Chaplin. **15** The Marx Brothers. **16** Lillian Gish. **17** Mary Pickford. **18** Theda Bara. **19** 1920s. **20** Harold Lloyd. **21** Charlie Chaplin. **22** Sisters. **23** Edna Purviance. **24** Michael. **25** Rin Tin Tin.

## *QUIZ 73* HEADLINE MAKERS ........ LEVEL 2

*Answers – see page 191*

1 Who said in *The Times*, 'We take our commitment to each other very seriously' just before splitting up?
2 Who directed and starred in *Chinese Coffee*?
3 Which much-married actress was Miss Hungary 1936?
4 Who was paid $6 million to play 'The Saint' in 1996?
5 Who founded Maverick with Time Warner to make records and movies?
6 For which movie did Demi Moore become Hollywood's highest paid actress?
7 Who did Barbra Streisand replace Dudley Moore with in *The Mirror Has Two Faces*?
8 In which of his own movies did Roman Polanski appear in 1974?
9 What was Michael J. Fox's follow-up to *Back to the Future III*?
10 Who was Carrie Fisher's first husband?
11 Which movie did Jonathan Pryce make after *Carrington*?
12 Which singer/actor was deemed head of the 'Rat Pack'?
13 Which TV remake of a Hitchcock movie did Christopher Reeve make after his riding accident?
14 Which female member of the Fiennes family is famous as a director?
15 About whom did Howard Hughes say, 'There are two reasons why men will go to see her'?
16 Why will Winona Ryder never forget the name of the place she was born?
17 Leading lady Jean Peters retired from movies to marry which millionaire recluse?
18 How many times did Brigitte Bardot marry?
19 Which film star wrote the novel *Prime Time*?
20 Whose legs were insured for most, Fred Astaire's, Betty Grable's or Ginger Rogers's?
21 Which actress's official title is Lady Haden-Guest?
22 Who said the famous line, 'Win one for the Gipper', which he used in a different context in a later career?
23 Which Batman movie did Mrs Tom Cruise star in?
24 Which 60s model did Ken Russell cast in *The Boyfriend*?
25 Which star of *Friends* appeared in *Six Days Seven Nights*?

**Answers Studios & Companies** (see Quiz 75)
**1** 1950s. **2** Keystone. **3** Mountain. **4** Oliver. **5** Richard Burton. **6** New York. **7** *Alien Resurrection*. **8** Coca Cola. **9** Hammer. **10** Arnold Schwarzenegger. **11** *Saturday Night Live*. **12** Louis B. Mayer. **13** Fox; 20th Century Pictures. **14** Miramax. **15** MGM. **16** 20th Century Fox. **17** Pillow Talk. **18** *E.T.* **19** Hammer. **20** Gene Kelly. **21** Keystone. **22** David O. Selznick. **23** United Artists. **24** *Antz*. **25** *A Bug's Life*.

## QUIZ 74 POT LUCK 28 ........ LEVEL 2

*Answers – see page 192*

1 What was the name of Julia Roberts's character in *The Pelican Brief*?
2 Who won the Best Actress Oscar for *Alice Doesn't Live Here Any More*?
3 How is Ramon Estevez better known?
4 In which decade was *Adam's Rib* released?
5 In which film did the characters Doralee and Violet appear?
6 To the nearest hour, how long does *Marnie* last?
7 Who played the villain in the 80s movie *Flash Gordon*?
8 'For All We Know' won an Oscar when used in which movie in 1970?
9 Who starred opposite Liza Minnelli in *New York, New York*?
10 Who played the ageing Zorro in the 1998 movie?
11 How is Mary Cathleen Collins better known?
12 Who was Richard Hannay in the original *The Thirty-Nine Steps*?
13 Which veteran won an Oscar in 1981, two years after his daughter?
14 Which was the next 14-Oscar-nominated film after *All About Eve*?
15 *Where Eagles Dare* and *1984* starred which actor?
16 Who directed *Blade Runner*?
17 *The Man with the Golden Arm* and *Pal Joey* both featured which actor?
18 Who played the Bond girl in *Moonraker*?
19 To the nearest hour, how long does *The King and I* last?
20 Which comedies was Michael Balcon responsible for?
21 Who won the Best Director Oscar for *The Sting*?
22 Which Alec featured in *Beetlejuice*?
23 In which decade was *Peyton Place* released?
24 What was Kirk Douglas's first film, in 1946?
25 Which actress links *Logan's Run* and *The Cannonball Run*?

**Answers 1970s** (see Quiz 76)
**1** *Lady Sings the Blues.* **2** *The Devils.* **3** Four. **4** Carrie Fisher. **5** Robin Givens. **6** *Live and Let Die.* **7** *All the President's Men.* **8** Transylvania. **9** *Monty Python and the Holy Grail.* **10** *The Champ.* **11** Dustin Hoffman. **12** Tchaikovsky. **13** *Ryan's Daughter.* **14** *Vampira.* **15** *M*A*S*H.* **16** *Day for Night.* **17** Billie Holiday. **18** *Alien.* **19** *Prime Cut.* **20** *Tommy.* **21** Scott Joplin's. **22** Roger Moore. **23** *Ode to Billie Joe.* **24** *Play Misty for Me.* **25** *That's Entertainment.*

## *QUIZ 75* STUDIOS & COMPANIES ........ LEVEL 2

*Answers – see page 189*

1 In which decade did Hammer make the first of its Dracula series?
2 Which US company was famous for its slapstick comedy?
3 What was the logo of Paramount Pictures?
4 What did the O stand for in David O. Selznick's name?
5 Which Welsh actor first went to 20th Century Fox when he moved to Hollywood in the early 50s?
6 Where is the Actors' Studio which was founded in 1947?
7 Which sequel to *Alien* was made by Amalgamated Dynamics Inc. in 1997?
8 Which drinks company bought Columbia in 1982?
9 Which company's famous horror movies were made at Bray Studios?
10 Who starred in *Last Action Hero*, which was a flop for Columbia?
11 Which late-night US comedy show spawned movies such as *Wayne's World*?
12 Who was head of MGM for 25 years from 1925?
13 Which companies merged to make 20th Century Fox in 1935?
14 Which company did Disney acquire in 1993, which went on to make *Sliding Doors*?
15 Which company made *Singin' in the Rain*?
16 Which of the big five movie companies had Darryl F. Zanuck as its head, on and off, until the 60s?
17 What was the first singing comedy Doris Day made for Universal?
18 Which Spielberg movie was Universal's then biggest ever hit?
19 Which company made *When Dinosaurs Ruled the Earth*?
20 MGM lent Columbia which dancer for *Cover Girl*?
21 Which company foundered when Mack Sennett left for Paramount?
22 Who became head of RKO in 1931?
23 Which company made the first Bond movies?
24 Which computer-generated movie was made by Dreamworks in 1998?
25 What was Disney's answer to *Antz*?

**Answers Headline Makers** (see Quiz 73)
**1** Richard Gere & Cindy Crawford. **2** Al Pacino. **3** Zsa Zsa Gabor. **4** Val Kilmer. **5** Madonna. **6** *Striptease.* **7** George Segal. **8** *Chinatown.* **9** *Doc Hollywood.* **10** Paul Simon. **11** *Evita.* **12** Frank Sinatra. **13** *Rear Window.* **14** Martha. **15** Jane Russell. **16** Born in Winona, Minnesota. **17** Howard Hughes. **18** Five. **19** Joan Collins **20** Betty Grable's. **21** Jamie Lee Curtis. **22** Ronald Reagan. **23** *Batman Forever.* **24** Twiggy. **25** David Schwimmer.

## *QUIZ 76* 1970s ............ LEVEL 2

*Answers – see page 190*

1 For which movie was Diana Ross Oscar-nominated on her film debut?
2 Which Ken Russell movie was an adaptation of *The Devils of Loudun*?
3 How many years were there between *The French Connection* and *French Connection II*?
4 Who did Brian De Palma originally want for the title role in *Carrie*?
5 Which star of *The Wiz* married Mike Tyson?
6 What was Roger Moore's first Bond movie as 007?
7 Which Alan Pakula movie was about Watergate?
8 Where is Tim Curry's character from in *The Rocky Horror Picture Show*?
9 Which Monty Python movie was very loosely based on the Arthurian legend?
10 In which 1979 movie did Jon Voight play a boxer?
11 Who accidentally shot himself making *Little Big Man*?
12 Which composer did Richard Chamberlain play in *The Music Lovers*?
13 Which movie set in Ireland was David Lean's follow up to *Dr Zhivago*?
14 In which movie did David Niven play Dracula?
15 Which Korean War film gave Sally Kellerman an Oscar nomination?
16 In which of his own movies did Francois Truffaut appear in 1973?
17 *Lady Sings the Blues* was about which singer?
18 Which movie had the ad line, 'In space no one can hear you scream'?
19 In which movie did Sissy Spacek make her film debut?
20 Which rock opera did Ann Margret star in?
21 Whose piano rags were used in *The Sting*?
22 Who starred with Richard Harris and Richard Burton in *The Wild Geese*?
23 Which movie took its name and plot from a Bobbie Gentry song?
24 In which movie did Clint Eastwood play DJ Dave Garland?
25 Which movie was a compilation of MGM musicals?

**Answers Pot Luck 28** (see Quiz 74)
**1** Darby Shaw. **2** Ellen Burstyn. **3** Martin Sheen. **4** 1940s. **5** *9 to 5*. **6** 2 hours. **7** Max von Sydow. **8** *Lovers and Other Strangers*. **9** Robert de Niro. **10** Anthony Hopkins. **11** Bo Derek. **12** Robert Donat. **13** Henry Fonda. **14** *Titanic*. **15** Richard Burton. **16** Ridley Scott. **17** Frank Sinatra. **18** Lois Chiles. **19** 2 hours. **20** Ealing comedies. **21** George Roy Hill. **22** Baldwin. **23** 1950s. **24** *The Strange Love of Martha Ivers*. **25** Farah Fawcett.

## *QUIZ 77* POT LUCK 29 ........ LEVEL 2

*Answers – see page 195*

1 *Mad Max* was released in which decade?
2 At what sport did Liam Neeson excel?
3 Marlon Brando and who else turned down Robert Redford's role in *Butch Cassidy and the Sundance Kid*?
4 Which Tommy featured in *Batman Forever*?
5 Who won the Best Actor Oscar for *The Best Years of Our Lives*?
6 In which film did a character named Snake Plissken appear?
7 Who won the Best Director Oscar for *Out of Africa*?
8 Which actor links *Dragnet* and *A League of Their Own*?
9 Who played Melanie Wilkes in *Gone with the Wind*?
10 Who played Oscar's mother in *Wilde*?
11 In which decade was *Holiday Inn* released?
12 *Police Academy IV* and *Total Recall* both feature which actress?
13 Who married her co-star Alec Baldwin after they starred in *Too Hot to Handle*?
14 Who adapted Arthur Miller's *The Crucible* for the 90s film?
15 In which country was *The Good, the Bad and the Ugly* made?
16 Which animal is Little John in the Disney film *Robin Hood*?
17 What relation is Bridget Fonda to Jane?
18 Within fifteen minutes, how long does *National Velvet* last?
19 A character named Captain Ross appeared in which 1990s film?
20 Who won the Best Actress Oscar for *Coal Miner's Daughter*?
21 *Peggy Sue Got Married* and *The Rock* starred which actor?
22 Who directed *Barry Lyndon*?
23 Which Jonathan featured in *Star Trek: First Contact*?
24 Who played the Bond girl in *Octopussy*?
25 What was the name of Donald Sutherland's character in *Ordinary People*?

**Answers Pot Luck 30** (see Quiz 79)
**1** *Jaws.* **2** Linney. **3** 1940s. **4** Gene Hackman. **5** *The Dirty Dozen.* **6** Billy Wilder. **7** *Alien.* **8** *An Officer and a Gentleman.* **9** *On the Waterfront*. **10** Robert Zemeckis. **11** Georg. **12** Katharine Hepburn. **13** Sam. **14** Honey Rider. **15** *Edward Scissorhands.* **16** David Niven. **17** Hobson. **18** Amanda Donohoe. **19** *Snow White and the Seven Dwarfs.* **20** Rod Steiger. **21** Mexico. **22** 1950s. **23** Timothy Dalton. **24** *Unforgiven.* **25** 1940s.

## *QUIZ 78* OSCARS – BEST ACTRESSES ........ LEVEL 2

*Answers – see page 196*

1 What was the second of Meryl Streep's three nominations between 1981 and 1983?
2 Who was nominated for *Secrets and Lies*?
3 Which former Mrs Harvey Keitel was nominated for *Goodfellas*?
4 Which 80s winner has children called Chastity and Elijah Blue?
5 Who had a nomination for *The Wings of the Dove*?
6 For which movie did Mrs Antonio Banderas receive her first nomination?
7 Who was nominated for *Tumbleweeds*?
8 What was the name of Kate Winslet's character in *Titanic*?
9 Who was nominated for *Grifters* and *American Beauty*?
10 Which 60-something won in the 1990s after her second nomination in successive years?
11 Which one-time presidential candidate's cousin won for *Moonstruck*?
12 Who was the first English winner of the 1990s?
13 Sean Ferrer was the son of which 60s Best Actress?
14 For which movie did Holly Hunter win without speaking?
15 Who was the only female winner for *One Flew over the Cuckoo's Nest*?
16 For which movie was Glenn Close Oscar-nominated on her film debut?
17 Who won her first Oscar for *LA Confidential*?
18 Which Best Actress said, 'Women get all excited about nothing – then marry him'?
19 Marlee Matlin played someone coming to terms with deafness in which movie?
20 For which 1990s film was Julie Christie Oscar-nominated?
21 Who was Oscar-nominated for playing Tina Turner in the biopic?
22 What is the nationality of Brenda Fricker who won for *My Left Foot*?
23 Who was the older winner of the shared Best Actress Oscar in 1968?
24 Which TV personality was nominated for *The Color Purple*?
25 Who received her last Oscar for *The Trip to Bountiful*?

**Answers Living Legends** (see Quiz 80)
**1** Ghana. **2** *Klute*. **3** Charlton Heston. **4** Luciano Pavarotti. **5** Joan Plowright. **6** Sister. **7** Rocky & Rambo. **8** Rod Steiger. **9** Robin Williams. **10** Micheline. **11** Jane Wyman. **12** Egypt. **13** Dustin Hoffman. **14** Walter Matthau. **15** Jack Nicholson. **16** Howard Keel. **17** H. **18** Bob Hope. **19** *Planet of the Apes*. **20** Jason Robards. **21** Gregory Peck. **22** Spartan. **23** Robert De Niro. **24** Kirk Douglas. **25** Julie Andrews.

## *QUIZ 79* POT LUCK 30 ........ LEVEL 2

*Answers – see page 193*

1 *A Stillness in the Water* was eventually released as which ripping blockbuster?
2 Which Laura featured in *The Truman Show*?
3 In which decade was *The Grapes of Wrath* released?
4 Which actor links *Bonnie and Clyde* and *Superman*?
5 The character John Cassavetes appeared in which action film?
6 Who won the Best Director Oscar for *The Lost Weekend*?
7 The spacecraft Nostromo featured in which movie?
8 'Up Where We Belong' won an Oscar when used in which movie?
9 A character named Terry Malloy appeared in which gritty film?
10 Who directed *Back to the Future*?
11 In *The Sound of Music* what is Baron von Trapp's first name?
12 Who won the Best Actress Oscar for *On Golden Pond*?
13 What was the name of Patrick Swayze's character in *Ghost*?
14 What was the name of the Bond girl in *Dr No*?
15 In which film did a character named Kim Boggs appear?
16 Which actor's autobiography was called *The Moon's a Balloon*?
17 What was the name of the butler, played by John Gielgud, in *Arthur*?
18 Who played Lucy Irvine in *Castaway*?
19 Which Disney film got a special Academy Award for 'a significant screen innovation'?
20 Who won the Best Actor Oscar for *In the Heat of the Night*?
21 In which country is the village where the action of *The Magnificent Seven* takes place?
22 In which decade of the 20th century was Bill Murray born?
23 Which James Bond played Heathcliff in the 1970 *Wuthering Heights*?
24 The character Will Munny appeared in which film?
25 In which decade was Orson Welles's *Jane Eyre* released?

**Answers Pot Luck 29** (see Quiz 77)
**1** 1970s. **2** Boxing. **3** Warren Beatty. **4** Lee Jones. **5** Fredric March. **6** *Escape from New York.* **7** Sydney Pollack. **8** Tom Hanks. **9** Olivia de Havilland. **10** Vanessa Redgrave. **11** 1940s. **12** Sharon Stone. **13** Kim Basinger. **14** Arthur Miller. **15** Italy. **16** Bear. **17** Niece. **18** 125 minutes. **19** *A Few Good Men.* **20** Sissy Spacek. **21** Nicolas Cage. **22** Stanley Kubrick. **23** Frakes. **24** Maud Adams. **25** Calvin.

## QUIZ 80 LIVING LEGENDS ........ LEVEL 2

*Answers – see page 194*

1 In the 1970s Shirley Temple was made US Ambassador to which West African country?
2 Jane Fonda's affair with Donald Sutherland began on the set of which movie?
3 Who said, 'It's hard living up to Moses'?
4 Which tenor's only movie was *Yes Giorgio* in 1982?
5 How is Lady Olivier, star of *Tea with Mussolini*, better known?
6 What relation to Francis Ford Coppola is actress Talia Shire?
7 Which two characters did Sylvester Stallone say were 'money-making machines that could not be switched off'?
8 Which one-time husband of Claire Bloom appeared in *Mars Attacks*?
9 Starting with *Good Morning, Vietnam*, who made seven films which took over $100m at the US box office?
10 What is the first name of Mrs Sean Connery?
11 Who, when asked why she divorced Ronald Reagan, said, 'He talked too much'?
12 Where was Omar Sharif born?
13 Which superstar played Sean Connery's son in *Family Business*?
14 Who starred as a 'grumpy old man' with Jack Lemmon?
15 Which star was born in Neptune, New Jersey, in 1937?
16 Which musical star of *Annie Get Your Gun* and *Kiss Me Kate* also found TV fame in *Dallas*?
17 Which letter does Paul Newman say all his best movies begin with?
18 Who won three Special Oscars in over 60 years, partly for work entertaining US troops?
19 In which movie did Charlton Heston say, 'Take your paws off me, you dirty ape'?
20 Who was Lauren Bacall's second husband?
21 Who was Ambrose Pierce to Jane Fonda's schoolteacher in *Old Gringo*?
22 What was the name of Stallone's character in *Demolition Man*?
23 Who directed and starred in *A Bronx Tale* in 1993?
24 Whose autobiography was called *The Ragman's Son*?
25 Which film star wrote the novel *The Last of the Really Great Whangdoodles*?

**Answers Oscars – Best Actresses** (see Quiz 78)
**1** *Sophie's Choice*. **2** Brenda Blethyn. **3** Lorraine Bracco. **4** Cher. **5** Helena Bonham Carter. **6** *Working Girl*. **7** Janet McTeer. **8** Rose. **9** Annette Bening. **10** Judi Dench. **11** Olympia Dukakis. **12** Emma Thompson. **13** Audrey Hepburn. **14** *The Piano*. **15** Louise Fletcher. **16** *The World According to Garp*. **17** Kim Basinger. **18** Cher. **19** *Children of a Lesser God*. **20** *Afterglow*. **21** Angela Bassett. **22** Irish. **23** Katharine Hepburn. **24** Oprah Winfrey. **25** Geraldine Page.

## *QUIZ 81* WESTERNS ........ LEVEL 2

*Answers – see page 199*

1 Which Irishman plays English Bob in *Unforgiven*?
2 Which western film title links Randolph Scott and Daniel Day-Lewis?
3 Which member of the Brat Pack played Billy the Kid in *Young Guns*?
4 Which western superstar's son directed him in *The Train Robbers*?
5 Which brothers played Frank and Jesse James in *Long Riders*?
6 Kris Kristofferson and John Hurt were graduates from where in *Heaven's Gate*?
7 'For a minute there I thought we were in trouble' is the last line of which movie?
8 Who narrated *How the West Was Won*?
9 Which star played the title role in *Billy the Kid Returns* in 1939?
10 Which country was the location for *A Fistful of Dollars*?
11 Who was the Quaker bride of Gary Cooper in *High Noon*?
12 Who sang the title song for *Gunfight at the OK Corral*?
13 Who was the subject of the autobiographical *To Hell and Back*?
14 *Pale Rider* was a remake of which classic western?
15 What was the third of Sergio Leone's trio of spaghetti westerns?
16 Who directed the Civil War sequences of *How the West Was Won*?
17 Who was Clint Eastwood's co-star on and off screen in *Bronco Billy*?
18 What was the 50s remake of *Destry Rides Again* called?
19 In which movie did John Wayne play Tom Dunson?
20 Who played Sheriff Garrett in *Pat Garrett and Billy the Kid*?
21 Who was the star of *Jeremiah Johnson*?
22 What is the name of Gene Hackman's sheriff in *Unforgiven*?
23 In which western did Jodie Foster play a poker player?
24 In which 1953 classic did Alan Ladd face Jack Palance?
25 Which Huston played Wyatt Earp in *Law and Order* in the 30s?

**Answers 1960s Stars** (see Quiz 83)
**1** *Charade.* **2** Lulu. **3** Lee Marvin. **4** Mia Farrow. **5** Vincent Price. **6** Doris Day & Rock Hudson. **7** Dennis Hopper. **8** *Becket.* **9** Gregory Peck. **10** Anthony Perkins. **11** Jon Voight. **12** Rita Moreno. **13** Julie Christie. **14** Jane Fonda. **15** James Coburn. **16** Peppard. **17** *Romeo and Juliet.* **18** Mother Abbess. **19** Marianne Faithfull. **20** Omar Sharif. **21** Dyan Cannon. **22** Carroll Baker. **23** Natalie Wood. **24** Sidney Poitier. **25** Doris Day.

## *QUIZ 82* POT LUCK 31 ........ LEVEL 2

*Answers – see page 200*

1 Characters named Gertie and Elliot appeared in which film?
2 In which decade was *National Velvet* first released?
3 What was the first name of Schindler of *Schindler's List*?
4 What is the name of the Eddie Murphy character in the *Beverly Hills Cop* films?
5 Within fifteen minutes, how long does *My Fair Lady* last?
6 Robin Williams's *The Birdcage* was a remake of which film?
7 Who won the Best Actress Oscar for *Suspicion*?
8 Which Helen featured in *Twister*?
9 What is the name of Audrey Hepburn's cat in *Breakfast at Tiffany's*?
10 *Hot Shots!* and *Honey, I Blew Up the Kids* starred which actor?
11 Who directed *Babe*?
12 Which actress was Oscar-nominated for *Starting Over*?
13 Which Miriam tested for the role of Scarlett O'Hara?
14 *Young Blood* and *Dirty Dancing* both feature which actor?
15 Who won the Best Director Oscar for *The Best Years of Our Lives*?
16 Heinrich Harrer is a character in a film with which country in the title?
17 Who sang the Bond theme from *The Spy Who Loved Me*?
18 Which actor links *Witness* and *Predator 2*?
19 In *Singin' in the Rain* who danced with Gene Kelly in the Broadway Ballet scene?
20 To the nearest hour, how long does *The Apartment* last?
21 Which British actor won an Oscar for *A Man for All Seasons*?
22 Which Bond girl starred with Elvis Presley in *Fun in Acapulco*?
23 Which Sean featured in *The Avengers*?
24 In which decade was Disney's *Lady and the Tramp* released?
25 Who won the Best Actor Oscar for *Shine*?

**Answers World Cinema** (see Quiz 84)
**1** Deneuve. **2** *Life Is Beautiful*. **3** Gerard Depardieu. **4** Australia. **5** Fellini. **6** Benigni . **7** Brenda Blethyn. **8** Ingmar Bergman. **9** France . **10** Rome (*Roma*). **11** Farces. **12** Charles Aznavour. **13** Sophia Loren. **14** *Il Postino*. **15** *Blow Up*. **16** Jeremy Irons. **17** Jeanne Moreau. **18** *Seven Samurai*. **19** 1900s. **20** *Emmanuelle*. **21** Australia. **22** Fernando Rey. **23** Rome. **24** Gerard Depardieu. **25** *Eight and a Half*.

## *QUIZ 83* 1960s STARS ........ LEVEL 2

*Answers – see page 197*

1 In which movie with Audrey Hepburn did Cary Grant take a shower – fully clothed?
2 Which Scottish pop star sang the title song from *To Sir with Love*?
3 Who played two parts in *Cat Ballou* in 1965?
4 Which future wife of Frank Sinatra failed an audition to play one of the children in *The Sound of Music*?
5 Which horror movie star found fame in *The House of Usher*?
6 Which duo topped the money-making list of movie stars after starring in a string of light comedies together?
7 Who co-starred with Peter Fonda in *Easy Rider*?
8 For which movie was Richard Burton Oscar-nominated for playing an Archbishop of Canterbury?
9 Who starred in *To Kill a Mockingbird* and *The Guns of Navarone*?
10 Who made his directorial debut with the second sequel to *Psycho*?
11 Who was Dustin Hoffman's male co-star in *Midnight Cowboy*?
12 Who was Anita in *West Side Story*?
13 Who starred opposite Peter Finch and Alan Bates in *Far from the Madding Crowd* in 1967?
14 Who was directed by her then husband in the futuristic *Barbarella*?
15 Who was the star of *Our Man Flint*?
16 Which George was the star of *The Blue Max*?
17 Leonard Whiting and Olivia Hussey were the unknowns chosen by Franco Zeffirelli to make which movie?
18 Peggy Wood was Oscar-nominated for which role in *The Sound of Music*?
19 Which one-time girlfriend of Mick Jagger was *The Girl on a Motorcycle*?
20 Who appeared in two major David Lean movies, *Lawrence of Arabia* and *Dr Zhivago*?
21 Which Mrs Cary Grant starred in *Bob and Carol and Ted and Alice*?
22 Whose autobiography was called *Baby Doll*?
23 Which former child star was born Natasha Gurdin?
24 Who was the first black actor to top the poll of movie money-earners?
25 Who was the star of *That Touch of Mink*?

**Answers Westerns** (see Quiz 81)
**1** Richard Harris. **2** *The Last of the Mohicans.* **3** Emilio Estevez. **4** Michael Wayne (son of John). **5** James & Stacy Keach. **6** Harvard. **7** *Butch Cassidy and the Sundance Kid.* **8** Spencer Tracy. **9** Roy Rogers. **10** Mexico. **11** Grace Kelly. **12** Frankie Laine. **13** Audie Murphy. **14** *Shane.* **15** *The Good, the Bad and the Ugly.* **16** John Ford. **17** Sondra Locke. **18** *Destry.* **19** *Red River.* **20** James Coburn. **21** Robert Redford. **22** Sheriff Daggett. **23** *Maverick.* **24** *Shane.* **25** Walter

## *QUIZ 84* WORLD CINEMA ........ LEVEL 2

*Answers – see page 198*

1 What did Catherine Dorleac change her surname to?
2 Which 1998 movie written by and starring Roberto Benigni won the Grand Jury prize at Cannes?
3 Who played the title role in the 1990 *Cyrano De Bergerac*?
4 Where was *Muriel's Wedding* made?
5 Who directed the 60s hit *La Dolce Vita*?
6 Which Roberto found success in his native Italy with *Johnny Stecchino*?
7 Who won Best Actress at Cannes for *Secrets and Lies*?
8 Which Swedish director won the Palme de Palme D'or at the 50th Cannes Film Festival?
9 Which country did Dirk Bogarde move to in the 60s, which made him a star of many European movies?
10 About which city did Federico Fellini make a 1972 movie?
11 Georges Feydeau was a writer of what type of plays, many of which were made into movies?
12 Which Armenian-born French singer starred in Truffaut's *Shoot the Pianist*?
13 Which actress is Mrs Carlo Ponti?
14 Which 1994 movie was about a postman on an Italian island?
15 What was Michelangelo Antonioni's first English-language film, in 1966?
16 Which English actor played the title role in the US/French movie *Kafka*?
17 Who was the female star of *Jules et Jim*?
18 *The Magnificent Seven* was based on which Japanese classic?
19 In which decade does the action of *Picnic at Hanging Rock* take place?
20 Which 1974 movie went on to make Sylvia Kristel an international star?
21 *Strictly Ballroom* came from which country?
22 How was Fernando Arambillet of *French Connection* fame better known?
23 In which city was *La Dolce Vita* set?
24 Which French actor starred in *The Return of Martin Guerre*?
25 Which number was the name of an Oscar-nominated Fellini movie?

**Answers Pot Luck 31** (see Quiz 82)
**1** *E.T.* **2** 1940s. **3** Oskar. **4** Axel Foley. **5** 170 minutes. **6** *La Cage aux Folles*. **7** Joan Fontaine. **8** Hunt. **9** Cat. **10** Lloyd Bridges. **11** Chris Noonan. **12** Candice Bergen. **13** Hopkins. **14** Patrick Swayze. **15** William Wyler **16** Tibet (*Seven Years in Tibet*). **17** Carly Simon. **18** Danny Glover. **19** Cyd Charisse. **20** 2 hours. **21** Paul Scofield. **22** Ursula Andress. **23** Connery. **24** 1950s. **25** Geoffrey Rush.

## *QUIZ 85* POT LUCK 32 ........ LEVEL 2

*Answers – see page 203*

1 How is Allen Konigsberg better known?
2 Which Robert featured in *Austin Powers: International Man of Mystery*?
3 Who won the Best Actor Oscar for *Hamlet* in 1948?
4 *High Society* was a musical remake of which film?
5 Which pianist is the subject of *Shine*?
6 Which actor links *The Great Escape* and *Victor/Victoria*?
7 What was the first name of Demi Moore's character in *Ghost*?
8 In which decade was *A Day at the Races* released?
9 In real life Clint Eastwood became mayor of which town?
10 To the nearest hour, how long does *Napoleon* last?
11 'Say You, Say Me' won an Oscar when it was used in which movie?
12 Who died during the filming of *Dark Blood* in 1993?
13 Who directed *Arsenic and Old Lace*?
14 Which movie was going to be called *The Bride and the Wolf*?
15 The relationship between Steve McQueen and Ali MacGraw began on the set of which movie?
16 Who played contrasting roles of a mechanic in *Mona Lisa*, and Falstaff in *Henry V*?
17 Who was the Doctor in the original musical film *Doctor Dolittle*?
18 Who starred with Bette Davis in *Whatever Happened to Baby Jane?*?
19 Who is Leslie Nielsen in the *Naked Gun* films?
20 Which Eddie turned down Al Jolson's role in *The Jazz Singer*?
21 *The Birds* and *Cocoon* featured which actress?
22 Who won the Best Director Oscar for *Tom Jones* in 1963?
23 In which decade was *Wuthering Heights*, starring Laurence Olivier, released?
24 Who played the villain in the 70s movie *Diamonds are Forever*?
25 *JFK* and *Cool Runnings* starred which actor?

**Answers Oscar Trivia** (see Quiz 87)
**1** *The Rains Came.* **2** Academy of Motion Picture Arts and Sciences. **3** Nine. **4** *Coming Home.* **5** *Midnight Cowboy.* **6** 13. **7** *The Sting.* **8** Woodstock. **9** 19th. **10** *The Madness of King George.* **11** *Chariots of Fire.* **12** *Arthur.* **13** Burma. **14** Elizabeth Taylor. **15** 13.5 inches. **16** Haing S. Ngor. **17** 12. **18** Roosevelt Hotel. **19** Eight. **20** David Niven. **21** Diane Ladd & Laura Dern. **22** Six. **23** Christopher Hampton. **24** He died after the film was made. **25** Ben Kingsley.

## *QUIZ 86* STEVE McQUEEN ........ LEVEL 2

*Answers – see page 204*

1 In which decade was he born?
2 Which movie gave him his first lead role in 1958?
3 What colour were his eyes?
4 Who was his male co-star in *Papillon*?
5 What is his occupation *The Towering Inferno*?
6 Who was his co-star in *The Thomas Crown Affair*?
7 Which branch of the services did he join before going AWOL?
8 What was his first movie, in 1958?
9 What was his job in *Bullitt*?
10 What job did he have on *An Enemy of the People* in addition to acting?
11 In which country did he die?
12 In *The Getaway*, where did he and Ali McGraw get away to?
13 How did he attempt to escape in *The Great Escape*?
14 What was Bullitt's first name in the 1968 hit movie?
15 Which movie was about a famous motor race?
16 Which co-star from *The Getaway* did he marry?
17 In which 1960 classic western was he one of a group of gunmen?
18 Who was his first wife?
19 What was his documentary *On Any Sunday* about?
20 How many children did he have by his first wife?
21 For which 1966 film was he Oscar-nominated?
22 On which island is *Papillon* set?
23 What was the name of his last film?
24 Which film about a millionaire bank robber was a 1968 success?
25 In which decade did he die?

**Answers Pot Luck 33** (see Quiz 88)
**1** Abba. **2** Baseball. **3** 2 hours. **4** Ron Howard. **5** 1940s. **6** Duvall. **7** Jessica Tandy. **8** *Goodfellas*. **9** James Cagney. **10** Michael Cimino. **11** Jamie Lee Curtis. **12** Cyd Charisse. **13** Doug Quaid. **14** Marlon Brando. **15** Albert Finney. **16** Hayley Mills. **17** *Thank God It's Friday*. **18** Bronson. **19** The Sex Pistols. **20** 1950s. **21** *48 Hours*. **22** Glenda Jackson. **23** Stephen King. **24** Lea Thompson. **25** Steenburgen.

## *QUIZ 87* OSCAR TRIVIA ........ LEVEL 2

*Answers – see page 201*

1 For which movie was the first special effects Oscar awarded?
2 Who owns the Oscar once it has been awarded?
3 How many Oscars did *The English Patient* win?
4 What was the second of Jane Fonda's three nominations between 1977 and 1979?
5 What was the first X-rated film to win an Oscar?
6 How many nominations did *Mary Poppins* have?
7 For which movie did Marvin Hamlisch receive his first nomination?
8 Which pop festival was the subject of a documentary which won an Oscar in 1970?
9 *Topsy Turvy* is set during which century?
10 Which movie had the ad line, 'First he lost America. Now he's losing his mind'?
11 Which movie's title was a quote from Blake's 'Jerusalem'?
12 The hit song 'The Best That You Can Do' came from which movie?
13 In what country is *Bridge on the River Kwai* set?
14 Who won the only Oscar for *Butterfield 8*?
15 Within one inch, how tall is an Oscar?
16 Who was the only Cambodian winner of the 1980s?
17 How many 20th-century Oscar nominations did Meryl Streep have?
18 At which hotel were the first Oscar ceremonies held?
19 *Raging Bull* won two Oscars, but how many nominations did it receive?
20 Who was hosting the 1974 ceremony when it was interrupted by a streaker?
21 Who were the first mother and daughter to be nominated for the same film?
22 How many Oscars did *Oliver!* win?
23 Which dramatist won for *Dangerous Liaisons*?
24 Why did Peter Finch not collect his Oscar for *Network*?
25 Who won Best Actor for his first major role in 1982?

**Answers Pot Luck 32** (see Quiz 85)
**1** Woody Allen. **2** Wagner. **3** Laurence Olivier. **4** *The Philadelphia Story*. **5** David Helfgott. **6** James Garner. **7** Molly. **8** 1930s. **9** Carmel. **10** 5 hours. **11** *White Nights*. **12** River Phoenix. **13** Frank Capra. **14** *Moonstruck*. **15** *The Getaway*. **16** Robbie Coltrane. **17** Rex Harrison. **18** Joan Crawford. **19** Frank Drebin. **20** Cantor. **21** Jessica Tandy. **22** Tony Richardson. **23** 1930s. **24** Charles Gray. **25** John Candy.

## *QUIZ 88* POT LUCK 33 ........ LEVEL 2

*Answers – see page 202*

1 Muriel is a fan of which band in *Muriel's Wedding*?
2 At what sport did Billy Crystal excel?
3 To the nearest hour, how long does *Pretty Woman* last?
4 Who directed *Apollo 13*?
5 In which decade was Disney's *Dumbo* released?
6 Which Robert featured in *Apocalypse Now*?
7 Who was the oldest ever Oscar-winner when she won best actress in 1989?
8 In which film did a character named Henry Hill appear?
9 Who played George M. Cohan in *Yankee Doodle Dandy*?
10 Who won the Best Director Oscar for *The Deer Hunter*?
11 *My Girl* and *Forever Young* starred which actress?
12 How was Tula Ellice Finklea better known?
13 What was the name of the Schwarzenegger character in *Total Recall*?
14 Which tough guy played Sky Masterson in *Guys and Dolls*?
15 Which actor links *Annie* and *Miller's Crossing*?
16 Who was awarded a miniature Oscar for her role in *Pollyanna*?
17 The song 'Last Dance' came from which movie?
18 Which Charles thought his face was 'like a rock quarry that somebody has dynamited'?
19 Which band appeared in the movie *The Great Rock 'n' Roll Swindle*?
20 In which decade was *The Robe* released?
21 What was Eddie Murphy's first film, in 1982?
22 Who won the Best Actress Oscar for *A Touch of Class*?
23 Which writer directed *Maximum Overdrive* in 1986?
24 *Back to the Future* and *Space Camp* featured which actress?
25 Which Mary featured in *What's Eating Gilbert Grape*??

**Answers Steve McQueen** (see Quiz 86)
**1** 1930s. **2** *The Blob.* **3** Blue. **4** Dustin Hoffman. **5** Fire officer. **6** Faye Dunaway. **7** Marines. **8** *Somebody Up There Likes Me.* **9** Detective. **10** Executive Producer. **11** Mexico. **12** Mexico. **13** Motorcycle. **14** Frank. **15** *Le Mans.* **16** Ali McGraw. **17** *The Magnificent Seven.* **18** Neile Adams. **19** Motorcycle racing. **20** Two. **21** *The Sand Pebbles.* **22** Devil's Island. **23** *The Hunter.* **24** *The Thomas Crown Affair.* **25** 1980s.

## QUIZ 89 1980s ........ LEVEL 2

*Answers – see page 207*

1 Which McGann brother co-starred with Richard E. Grant in *Withnail and I*?
2 What was Timothy Dalton's last movie as 007?
3 Who was *The Jazz Singer* in the 1980 movie?
4 In *Scarface*, where did Tony Montana come from?
5 *Coal Miner's Daughter* was about which singer?
6 Whose *Empire of the Sun* was the basis of the hit movie made by Spielberg?
7 In which movie did Sean Connery play monk William of Baskerville?
8 Which future star of *LA Law* was Oliver Reed's co-star in *Castaway*?
9 Which outrageous French fashion designer designed for *The Cook, the Thief, His Wife and Her Lover*?
10 Which Beatle was producer on *Withnail and I*?
11 In which movie based on an Agatha Christie story did Rock Hudson star with Elizabeth Taylor?
12 For playing which composer was Tom Hulce Oscar-nominated in 1984?
13 What was the working title of *Ghostbusters*?
14 Which Woody Allen movie was Sharon Stone's debut?
15 What was the name of Glenn Close's character in *Fatal Attraction*?
16 Whose big break came as Lydia in *Beetlejuice*?
17 Who played Sonny Corleone in the first sequel to *The Godfather*?
18 Which Jack Lemmon movie was about US involvement in the overthrow of Allende's government in Chile?
19 For which movie was Marlee Matlin Oscar-nominated on her film debut?
20 Who played Annette Desoto in *Steel Magnolias*?
21 In which movie did Jessica Lange play an angel?
22 Which actress played two parts in *The French Lieutenant's Woman* in 1981?
23 Which writer did Daniel Day-Lewis play in *My Left Foot*?
24 In which movie did Helena Bonham Carter find fame as Lucy Honeychurch?
25 Who played Joan Crawford in *Mommie Dearest*?

**Answers Comedies** (see Quiz 91)
**1** Seven. **2** Maggie Smith. **3** *Tootsie.* **4** Manhattan. **5** Paris. **6** Adam Sandler. **7** *Some Like It Hot.* **8** Connie Booth. **9** *A Night in Casablanca.* **10** *American Pie.* **11** Steve Martin. **12** *The Runaway Bride.* **13** James Caan. **14** *The Pink Panther Strikes Again.* **15** Leslie Nielsen. **16** Goldie Hawn. **17** Kevin Kline. **18** Seahaven. **19** Alan Alda. **20** Mike Myers. **21** *Fierce Creatures.* **22** Bruce Willis. **23** Marty McFly. **24** Burns. **25** Lee Evans.

## *QUIZ 90* POT LUCK 34 ........ LEVEL 2

*Answers – see page 208*

1 What is the name of Indiana Jones's father?
2 Who directed *Aliens*?
3 *Jack and Sarah* and *Shakespeare in Love* both starred which actress?
4 Which Bill featured in *While You Were Sleeping*?
5 Who played Kenneth Branagh's wife in *Peter's Friends*?
6 Who or what are Tom, Dick and Harry in *The Great Escape*?
7 Who did Johnny Depp play in *LA Without a Map*?
8 The character Ray Kinsella appeared in which film about 'Dreams'?
9 Who won the Best Director Oscar for *Cabaret*?
10 In which decade was *Sabotage* released?
11 Which movie did the song 'The One and Only' come from?
12 Who was the leading actor in Hitchcock's *Rear Window*?
13 Mia Farrow starred in 'The Purple Rose of' where?
14 Which song from *Dick Tracy* won an Oscar?
15 Who won the Best Actress Oscar for *Anastasia* in 1956?
16 What was the name of the Bond girl in *Never Say Never Again*?
17 '(I've Had) The Time of My Life' won an Oscar when it was used in which movie in 1987?
18 To the nearest hour, how long does *Saving Private Ryan* last?
19 Who directed *Four Weddings and a Funeral*?
20 *Great Expectations* and *The Swiss Family Robinson* both featured which John?
21 Who starred opposite Julia Roberts in *My Best Friend's Wedding*?
22 Which author appeared in *Creepshow*?
23 In which decade was *Rio Bravo* released?
24 Which Jenny featured in *An American Werewolf in London*?
25 What were the first names of Hanna & Barbera?

**Answers Kevin Costner** (see Quiz 92)
**1** Los Angeles. **2** *The Bodyguard.* **3** 1920s. **4** Gary. **5** Morgan Freeman. **6** Eliot Ness. **7** Sioux. **8** Mary Elizabeth Mastrantonio. **9** Clint Eastwood. **10** Robert De Niro. **11** Advertising. **12** 1950s. **13** Oliver Stone. **14** *Bull Durham.* **15** Whitney Houston. **16** Baseball. **17** *Dances with Wolves.* **18** Diana, Princess of Wales. **19** Jim Garrison. **20** *Waterworld.* **21** Wyatt Earp. **22** *Robin Hood.* **23** The corpse. **24** Steve McQueen. **25** *Dances with Wolves.*

## *QUIZ 91* COMEDIES ........ LEVEL 2

*Answers – see page 205*

1 How many characters does Eddie Murphy play in *The Nutty Professor*?
2 Who played the head of the convent in *Sister Act*?
3 In which of his own movies did Sydney Pollack appear in 1982?
4 Where are the spooks running wild in *Ghostbusters*?
5 In *Home Alone* where have the family gone for the Christmas vacation?
6 Who played singer Robbie Hart in *The Wedding Singer*?
7 'Nobody's perfect' is the last line of which movie?
8 Who played the witch in *Monty Python and the Holy Grail*?
9 Which Marx Brothers movie has an amusing comparison with the Ingrid Bergman/Humphrey Bogart wartime classic?
10 Which 1999 movie shared its name with a Don Maclean classic song?
11 Who wrote and starred in *Bowfinger*?
12 Which 1999 movie re-teamed Richard Gere and Julia Roberts?
13 Who played Hugh Grant's prospective father-in-law in *Mickey Blue Eyes*?
14 What was the name of the fourth Pink Panther film?
15 Who played the title role in Mel Brooks's spoof *Dracula: Dead and Loving It*?
16 Which member of 'The First Wives Club' has the blondest hair?
17 Who played Otto in *A Fish Called Wanda*?
18 What is the name of the idyllic community in *The Truman Show*?
19 Which star of TV's *M*A*S*H* appeared in Woody Allen's *Manhattan Murder Mystery*?
20 Who played Dr Evil in the Austin Powers movie?
21 Which movie was 'an equal not a sequel' to *A Fish Called Wanda*?
22 Who was the voice of Mikey in *Look Who's Talking*?
23 What part did Michael J. Fox play in *Back to the Future*?
24 What was Harry's surname in *When Harry Met Sally*?
25 Which British comic appeared in *There's Something About Mary*?

**Answers 1980s** (see Quiz 89)
**1** Paul. **2** *The Living Daylights.* **3** Neil Diamond. **4** Cuba. **5** Loretta Lynn. **6** J.G. Ballard. **7** *The Name of the Rose.* **8** Amanda Donohoe. **9** Jean Paul Gaultier. **10** George Harrison. **11** *The Mirror Crack'd.* **12** Mozart. **13** *Ghostsmashers.* **14** *Stardust Memories.* **15** Alex Forrest. **16** Winona Ryder. **17** James Caan. **18** *Missing.* **19** *Children of a Lesser God.* **20** Daryl Hannah. **21** *All That Jazz.* **22** Meryl Streep. **23** Christy Brown. **24** *A Room with a View.* **25** Faye Dunaway.

## *QUIZ 92* KEVIN COSTNER ........ LEVEL 2

*Answers – see page 206*

1 He was born in which city?
2 In which movie did he play Frank Farmer?
3 In which decade did *The Untouchables* take place?
4 Which former pop star Kemp co-stars in *The Bodyguard*?
5 Who was his Moorish sidekick in *Robin Hood: Prince of Thieves*?
6 What was the name of his character in *The Untouchables*?
7 Which tribe features in *Dances with Wolves*?
8 Who was Maid Marian to his Robin Hood in 1991?
9 Who was his co-star and director in *A Perfect World*?
10 Who played Al Capone in his movie *The Untouchables*?
11 Which career did he start out in?
12 In which decade was he born?
13 Who directed him in *JFK*?
14 In which 1988 film did he co-star with Tim Robbins?
15 Who was his female co-star in *The Bodyguard*?
16 *Field of Dreams* was about which sport?
17 Which 1990 movie did he act in, direct and produce?
18 Who was he reputedly in conversation with to make a sequel to *The Bodyguard*?
19 What was the name of his District Attorney in *JFK*?
20 Which 1995 movie is reputedly the biggest flop ever made?
21 Which western hero did he play in 1994?
22 Which English hero did he play in ____ *Prince of Thieves*?
23 Which role did he famously have in the opening sequence of *The Big Chill*?
24 Which 70s star was earmarked for Costner's *Bodyguard* role?
25 In which movie does he play the role of John Dunbar?

**Answers Pot Luck 34** (see Quiz 90)
**1** Dr Henry Jones. **2** James Cameron. **3** Dame Judi Dench. **4** Pullman. **5** Rita Rudner. **6** Escape tunnels. **7** Himself. **8** *Field of Dreams*. **9** Bob Fosse. **10** 1930s. **11** *Buddy's Song*. **12** James Stewart. **13** Cairo. **14** 'Sooner or Later'. **15** Ingrid Bergman. **16** Domino. **17** *Dirty Dancing*. **18** 3 hours. **19** Mike Newell. **20** Mills. **21** Rupert Everett. **22** Stephen King. **23** 1950s. **24** Agutter. **25** William & Joseph.

## *QUIZ 93* POT LUCK 35 ........ LEVEL 2

*Answers – see page 211*

1 In *The Seven Year Itch* what colour was Monroe's skirt, blown around by air from a grating?
2 The relationship between Tom Cruise and Nicole Kidman began on the set of which movie?
3 In which decade of the 20th century was Christian Slater born?
4 Which actor links *St Elmo's Fire* and *Young Guns*?
5 What was the name of Richard Gere's character in *Pretty Woman*?
6 In which decade was *The Apartment* released?
7 Who won the Best Actor Oscar for *Boys' Town*?
8 Which Harry is the lead character in *The Ipcress File*?
9 Which song from *Mary Poppins* won an Oscar?
10 In which city is *Bullitt* set?
11 What was the sequel to *Grumpy Old Men* called?
12 The character John Keating was in which Robin Williams film?
13 Who said, 'People think I was born in top hat and tails'?
14 Who played Watson to Rathbone's Holmes in *The Hound of the Baskervilles*?
15 In which decade was *The Bridge on the River Kwai* released?
16 In which film did a lady named Tess Trueheart appear?
17 Who was known as the 'It' girl?
18 Who directed *The Alamo*?
19 For what did Walt Disney win a Special Award in 1931/2?
20 Who won the Best Actress Oscar for *The Country Girl*?
21 To the nearest hour, how long does *Ryan's Daughter* last?
22 What was the name of Arnold Schwarzenegger's character in *Twins*?
23 *The Towering Inferno* and *Superman III* both feature which suave actor?
24 Who sang the Bond theme from *Live and Let Die*?
25 In which film did a character named Vicky Vale appear?

**Answers 1970s Stars** (see Quiz 95)
**1** Steve McQueen. **2** Roy Scheider. **3** Simon MacCorkindale. **4** Audrey Hepburn. **5** Kurt Russell. **6** Richard Chamberlain. **7** Donald Sutherland. **8** George C. Scott. **9** *Tommy*. **10** *The Rocky Horror Picture Show*. **11** Oliver Reed. **12** Robert Mitchum. **13** Joel Gray. **14** Martin Sheen. **15** Al Pacino. **16** Bruce Lee. **17** Charles Bronson. **18** *First Blood*. **19** Louis Malle. **20** *Moonraker*. **21** Diane Keaton. **22** Jill Ireland. **23** Talia Shire. **24** Bo Derek. **25** Christopher Lee.

## *QUIZ 94* FAMOUS NAMES .......... LEVEL 2

*Answers – see page 212*

1 What did Johnny Depp change his 'Winona Forever' tattoo to when his relationship with Ms Ryder finished?
2 What is Bonnie Bedelia's real famous surname?
3 Which famous cartoon voice's autobiography was called *That's All Folks!*?
4 What was the name of James Cagney's sister?
5 Who did George Clooney replace as Batman?
6 What is Matt Damon's middle name?
7 What name does the J stand for in Michael J. Fox's name?
8 Whose autobiography was called *Dear Me*?
9 Which famous name did Nancy Davis marry?
10 Rebecca De Mornay was educated at which progressive English school?
11 Who played the mother of real-life daughter Mia in *Hannah and Her Sisters* in 1986?
12 Jamie Lee Curtis was born just before her father was about to shoot which movie?
13 What was Danny DeVito's profession prior to acting?
14 Who played Jerry Lee Lewis in *Great Balls of Fire*?
15 Which comic-strip character did Michelle Pfeiffer play on screen?
16 Where was Julie Christie born?
17 What are Meryl Streep's two real first names?
18 Whose autobiography was called *Absolutely Mahvelous*?
19 In which movie did Clint Eastwood say, 'Go ahead punk. Make my day'?
20 On which special day of the year was Sissy Spacek born?
21 Where was Richard E. Grant born?
22 Who played JD in *Thelma and Louise* after William Baldwin pulled out?
23 What relation is Helena Bonham Carter to former British PM Herbert Asquith?
24 Jeff Goldblum's affair with Laura Dern began on the set of which movie?
25 In which movie did Holly Hunter play an angel?

**Answers Pot Luck 36** (see Quiz 96)
**1** Hutton. **2** Ruth. **3** 1980s. **4** Oliver Stone. **5** *Pretty Woman.* **6** *Body Heat.* **7** 105 minutes. **8** Glenn Close. **9** *Dick Tracy.* **10** Britt Ekland. **11** Mike Nichols. **12** Four. **13** 'Dance of the Hours'. **14** Simon. **15** *Jailhouse Rock.* **16** 1930s. **17** *Mad City.* **18** 'When You Wish Upon a Star'. **19** Gene Wilder. **20** *The Towering Inferno.* **21** Glen Campbell. **22** Katharine Hepburn. **23** Wolfgang Peterson. **24** Richard Dreyfuss. **25** *Wild at Heart.*

## QUIZ 95 1970s STARS ........ LEVEL 2

*Answers – see page 209*

1 Who was Ali McGraw's third husband?
2 Who played the lead role in Bob Fosse's *All That Jazz*?
3 Which husband of Susan George starred in *Death on the Nile*?
4 Who was Marian to Sean Connery's Robin in *Robin and Marian*?
5 Who played Elvis Presley in *Elvis: The Movie*?
6 Which TV doctor played Tchaikovsky in *The Music Lovers*?
7 Which *Klute* co-star of Jane Fonda was a member of her anti-war troupe during the Vietnam conflict?
8 Who said he would not accept an Oscar if given one, as the ceremony was a meat parade?
9 In which 70s movie did Elton John appear?
10 Which movie with Tim Curry had wacky songs such as 'Time Warp'?
11 Who was Vanessa Redgrave's hell-raising co-star in *The Devils*?
12 Who was Philip Marlowe in *Farewell My Lovely* in the latter part of his career?
13 Who played the MC of the Kit Kat Club in *Cabaret*?
14 Who played the youth on a killing spree in *Badlands* opposite Sissy Spacek?
15 Who played the first-time bank robber in *Dog Day Afternoon*?
16 Which martial arts hero died suddenly in 1973 aged 33?
17 Which star of *Death Wish* was known in France as *le sacre monstre*?
18 What was Stallone's first Rambo movie?
19 Which French film director did Candice Bergen marry in 1980?
20 What was Roger Moore's last 70s movie as 007?
21 Whose roles included Kay Corleone in *The Godfather* and the heroine of *Looking for Mr Goodbar*?
22 Which Mrs Bronson said, 'I'm in so many Charles Bronson films because no one else will work with him'?
23 Who played Rocky's girlfriend in the first *Rocky* movie?
24 Who played the object of Dudley Moore's fantasies in *10*?
25 Which horror movie star played the villain in *The Man with the Golden Gun*?

**Answers Pot Luck 35** (see Quiz 93)
**1** White. **2** *Days of Thunder*. **3** 1960s. **4** Emilio Estevez. **5** Edward Lewis. **6** 1960s. **7** Spencer Tracy. **8** Palmer. **9** 'Chim Chim Cheree'. **10** San Francisco. **11** *Grumpier Old Men*. **12** *Dead Poets Society*. **13** Fred Astaire. **14** Nigel Bruce. **15** 1950s. **16** *Dick Tracy*. **17** Clara Bow. **18** John Wayne. **19** The creation of Mickey Mouse. **20** Grace Kelly. **21** 3 hours. **22** Julius Benedict. **23** Robert Vaughn. **24** Wings. **25** *Batman*.

## *QUIZ 96* POT LUCK 36 ........................................ LEVEL 2

*Answers – see page 210*

1 Which Lauren featured in *American Gigolo*?
2 What is the first name of Bette Davis, who used her middle name in the movies?
3 In which decade was *The Abyss* released?
4 Who directed the 1996 movie *Nixon*?
5 A character named Vivian Ward appeared in which film?
6 What was Kathleen Turner's first film, in 1981?
7 Within fifteen minutes, how long does *The X-Files* last?
8 *Hook* and *Mars Attacks!* starred which actress?
9 'Sooner or Later (I Always Get My Man)' won an Oscar when it was used in which movie in 1990?
10 Who played the Bond girl in *The Man with the Golden Gun*?
11 Who won the Best Director Oscar for *The Graduate*?
12 How many times did Humphrey Bogart marry?
13 Which Ponchielli piece features in Disney's *Fantasia*?
14 Which Neil wrote *California Suite*?
15 In which film did Elvis play Vince Everett?
16 In which decade was *Scarface* released?
17 In which movie is John Travolta a museum security guard who loses his job?
18 Which song from *Pinocchio* won an Oscar?
19 *Bonnie and Clyde* and *The Woman in Red* both feature which actor?
20 Which disaster movie featured the character Michael O'Hallorhan?
21 Which country singer was in *True Grit*?
22 Who won the Best Actress Oscar for *The Lion in Winter*?
23 Who directed *Air Force One*?
24 Which actor links *Stakeout* and *Always*?
25 In which film did a character named Lula Pace Fortune appear?

**Answers Famous Names** (see Quiz 94)
**1** 'Wino Forever'. **2** Culkin. **3** Mel Blanc. **4** Jeanne. **5** Val Kilmer. **6** Paige. **7** Nothing. **8** Peter Ustinov. **9** Ronald Reagan. **10** Summerhill. **11** Maureen O'Sullivan. **12** *Some Like It Hot*. **13** Hairdresser. **14** Dennis Quaid. **15** Catwoman. **16** India. **17** Mary Louise. **18** Billy Crystal. **19** *Sudden Impact*. **20** Christmas Day. **21** Swaziland. **22** Brad Pitt. **23** Great granddaughter. **24** *Jurassic Park*. **25** *A Life Less Ordinary*.

## *QUIZ 97* ORSON WELLES ........ LEVEL 2

*Answers – see page 215*

1 What was Orson Welles's first movie?
2 In which decade was he born?
3 Which H.G. Wells dramatization caused panic when Welles's production convinced people that aliens were invading?
4 Which film about an American family was a follow up to *Citizen Kane*?
5 Which character from a Charlotte Bronte novel did he play in 1944?
6 Which glamorous redhead did he marry in 1943?
7 Which 'Scottish play' did he release in 1948?
8 What was the name of his character in *The Third Man*?
9 Which newspaper magnate tried to endanger the release of *Citizen Kane*?
10 Who directed him in *The Third Man*?
11 Which Shakespeare play did he make in Morocco with himself in the title role?
12 Within three years, how old was Welles when he made *Citizen Kane*?
13 In which film about Sir Thomas More did he appear in 1966?
14 Which movie did Welles and Rita Hayworth finish immediately before she filed for divorce?
15 Which studio released his first movie?
16 What did he describe as the biggest toy train set a boy ever had?
17 How many Oscars did *Citizen Kane* win?
18 In *Citizen Kane*, what is the tycoon's dying word?
19 Where was Welles working before he went to Hollywood?
20 Which 'Journey' did he film in 1942?
21 Which Bond film did he appear in with David Niven as 007?
22 In which decade did he die?
23 He said he started at the top and worked where?
24 In which European city was *The Third Man* set?
25 Which German actress said of him, 'People should cross themselves when they say his name'?

**Answers Pot Luck 37** (see Quiz 99)
**1** Matt Dillon. **2** Wrestling. **3** Elvis Presley. **4** Steve Oedekerk. **5** Ricci. **6** Metro. **7** Clint Eastwood. **8** 1930s. **9** Garrett Breedlove. **10** 95 minutes. **11** Alec Guinness. **12** John Connor. **13** Geena Davis. **14** *City Slickers*. **15** *Help!* **16** Maggie Smith. **17** *The King and I*. **18** Sara. **19** Jane Russell. **20** John Huston. **21** The Monkees. **22** 2 hours. **23** Sir Carol Reed. **24** Bruce Willis. **25** 1970s.

## *QUIZ 98* 1990s ........ LEVEL 2

*Answers – see page 216*

1 What is Catherine Zeta Jones's job in *Entrapment*?
2 Which beach is shown in the opening sequence of *Saving Private Ryan*?
3 In which movie does Sean Penn play Matthew Poncelet?
4 Where was *Turtle Beach* filmed?
5 *Brassed Off* takes place in which mining town?
6 Which movie about a US President and a teenage girl was released around the time of the Lewinsky scandal?
7 *Ten Things I Hate About You* was based on which Shakespeare play?
8 Who played Woody Allen's wife in *Mighty Aphrodite*?
9 In which movie did Kathy Burke play opposite Meryl Streep and Emma Thompson?
10 What are the three students called in *The Blair Witch Project*?
11 Which 1995 movie was based on a *200 AD* comic strip character?
12 Where was *The Rock* set?
13 Which Queen is the subject of *Mrs Brown*?
14 What is the name of John Travolta's president in *Primary Colors*?
15 What was 'an equal not a sequel' to *Four Weddings and a Funeral*?
16 Who plays Charles van Doren in *Quiz Show*?
17 In which movie did Leonardo DiCaprio play Meryl Streep's rebellious son?
18 What was the name of Uma Thurman's character in *Pulp Fiction*?
19 What is the surname of the Jim Carrey character who is part of his own popular TV show?
20 What was the Richard Gere/Julia Roberts follow up to *Pretty Woman*?
21 Which director was played by Ian McKellen in *Gods and Monsters*?
22 Which roles did Leonardo DiCaprio play in *The Man in the Iron Mask*?
23 Who played the title role in *Onegin*?
24 In which movie did Al Pacino play Vincent Hanna?
25 In what month of what year does the action of *Apollo 13* take place?

**Answers Oscars – Best Films** (see Quiz 100)
**1** *Romeo and Juliet.* **2** *Goodfellas.* **3** Cornwall and Monte Carlo. **4** *The Silence of the Lambs.* **5** *Forrest Gump.* **6** Brother. **7** Sioux. **8** World War II. **9** *Gandhi.* **10** *Shakespeare in Love.* **11** *Chariots of Fire.* **12** 1920s. **13** Pennsylvania. **14** *Cabaret.* **15** *My Fair Lady.* **16** Balboa. **17** *In the Heat of the Night.* **18** *Let It Be.* **19** *Dances with Wolves.* **20** Ralph & Joseph Fiennes. **21** 1950s. **22** *Forrest Gump.* **23** Frank Sinatra. **24** *Driving Miss Daisy.* **25** *All About Eve.*

## *QUIZ 99* POT LUCK 37 ........ LEVEL 2

*Answers – see page 213*

1 Which actor links *The Outsiders* and *Rumble Fish*?
2 At what sport did Tom Cruise excel?
3 Who turned down Kris Kristofferson's role in *A Star Is Born*?
4 Who directed *Ace Ventura: When Nature Calls*?
5 Which Christina featured in *The Addams Family*?
6 What did the first M stand for in MGM?
7 Which movie star released an album called *Cowboy Favorites* in 1959?
8 In which decade was *The Thin Man* released?
9 Who did Jack Nicholson play in *Terms of Endearment*?
10 Within fifteen minutes, how long does *Wayne's World* last?
11 Which British actor won an Oscar for *Bridge on the River Kwai*?
12 What was the name of Edward Furlong's character in *Terminator 2*?
13 *Fletch* and *Beetlejuice* starred which actress?
14 In which film did a character named Mitch Robbins appear?
15 What was the Beatles' second film?
16 Who won the Best Actress Oscar for *The Prime of Miss Jean Brodie*?
17 In which film musical is Mrs Anna Leonowens a lead character?
18 What is the name of the heroine of *A Little Princess*?
19 Who played Rio in *The Outlaw*?
20 *The Maltese Falcon* was whose directorial debut?
21 Which band appeared in the movie *Head*?
22 To the nearest hour, does *Air Force One* last 1, 2 or 3 hours?
23 Who won the Best Director Oscar for *Oliver!*?
24 *Sunset* and *Death Becomes Her* both feature which actor?
25 In which decade was *Catch-22* released?

**Answers Orson Welles** (see Quiz 97)
**1** *Citizen Kane*. **2** 1910s. **3** *War of the Worlds*. **4** *The Magnificent Ambersons*. **5** Mr Rochester. **6** Rita Hayworth. **7** *Macbeth*. **8** Harry Lime. **9** William Randolph Hearst. **10** Carol Reed. **11** *Othello*. **12** 25. **13** *A Man for All Seasons*. **14** *The Lady from Shanghai*. **15** RKO. **16** Film studio. **17** Nine. **18** 'Rosebud'. **19** New York. **20** *Journey into Fear*. **21** *Casino Royale*. **22** 1980s (1985). **23** Down. **24** Vienna. **25** Marlene Dietrich.

## *QUIZ 100* OSCARS – BEST FILMS ............ LEVEL 2

*Answers – see page 214*

1 *Shakespeare in Love* told the story behind the making of which play?
2 Which movie had the ad line, 'Three decades of life in the Mafia'?
3 In which two locations is *Rebecca* set?
4 Which movie had the line, 'I wish we could chat longer, but I'm having an old friend for dinner'?
5 After which film's success was a book of quotes by its hero published?
6 What relation is Tom Cruise to Dustin Hoffman in *Rain Man*?
7 Which tribe is the subject of *Dances with Wolves*?
8 *Mrs Miniver* was set during which conflict?
9 Which 20th century winner had most extras?
10 What was the first Best Film Joseph Fiennes appeared in?
11 Which film was about a Jew and a Scotsman in 1924?
12 In which decade does the action of *Out of Africa* take place?
13 The friends in *The Deer Hunter* are from which state?
14 Which winning film was about Sally Bowles?
15 Which musical *Pygmalion* won in 1964?
16 What was Rocky's surname in *Rocky*?
17 Which Sidney Poitier movie won in 1967?
18 What was the only Beatles movie to receive a nomination?
19 What was the first western to win a Best Picture Oscar after a 60-year gap?
20 Which two brothers appeared in Best Films in the 1990s?
21 In which decade was *Marty* a winner?
22 What was the first 90s Best Film to have 13 nominations?
23 Which singing superstar was one of 44 cameos in *Around the World in Eighty Days*?
24 In which Best Film did Morgan Freeman play a chauffeur called Hoke?
25 Which Best Picture was about Margo Channing?

**Answers 1990s** (see Quiz 98)
**1** Insurance Investigator. **2** Omaha. **3** *Dead Man Walking.* **4** Thailand. **5** Grimley. **6** *Wag the Dog.* **7** *The Taming of the Shrew.* **8** Helena Bonham Carter. **9** *Dancing at Lughnasa.* **10** Michael, Heather & Joshua. **11** *Judge Dredd.* **12** Alcatraz. **13** Victoria. **14** Jack Stanton. **15** *Notting Hill.* **16** Ralph Fiennes. **17** *Marvin's Room.* **18** Mia Wallace. **19** (Truman) Burbank. **20** *The Runaway Bride.* **21** James Whale. **22** Louis XIV & his twin Philippe. **23** Ralph Fiennes. **24** *Heat.* **25** April 1970.

## *QUIZ 101* SEAN CONNERY ........ LEVEL 2

*Answers – see page 219*

1 Which country did he represent in the Mr Universe contest?
2 What was the name of his first wife?
3 In which branch of the armed forces did he serve?
4 In which 90s film did he play Sir August De Wynter?
5 What is the name of his actor son?
6 Which king did he play in *Robin Hood: Prince of Thieves*?
7 In which movie of an Agatha Christie classic did he appear in 1974?
8 Where in Scotland was he born?
9 In 1951 he appeared in the chorus of which famous Rodgers & Hammerstein musical?
10 In which Hitchcock movie did he star in 1964?
11 Whose names does he have on a tattoo?
12 Who was his female co-star in *The Russia House*?
13 In how many Bond films did he appear in the 60s?
14 In which 80s film did he play Harrison Ford's father?
15 In which 70s film did he play a legendary English hero?
16 Who was his co-star in *Goldfinger*?
17 In which 007 movie did he return in 1983?
18 Which 1990 film was based on a John Le Carré novel?
19 What is his real first name?
20 What was his only Bond movie of the 70s?
21 In which movie did he play a medieval detective?
22 What was he a commander of in *The Hunt for Red October*?
23 What is the name of the second Mrs Connery?
24 Which Welsh actress was his co-star in *Entrapment*?
25 In which 80s film did he play an Irish cop?

**Answers Pot Luck 38** (see Quiz 102)
**1** *Back to the Future III*. **2** Turner. **3** Solitaire. **4** *Smokey and the Bandit*. **5** 1950s. **6** James Cameron. **7** Logan. **8** 150 minutes. **9** Never. **10** Jim Garrison. **11** *Prince of Eygpt*. **12** John Wayne. **13** *Les Girls*. **14** Laura Dern. **15** Elizabeth Taylor. **16** Sonny Corleone. **17** Bernstein. **18** *Love Story*. **19** 1950s. **20** *Blade Runner*. **21** *Beauty and the Beast*. **22** Danny DeVito. **23** Kathy Bates. **24** 1940s. **25** William Wyler.

## *QUIZ 102* POT LUCK 38 ........ LEVEL 2

*Answers – see page 217*

1 Which *Back to the Future* film returns to the Wild West?
2 Which Kathleen featured in *The Accidental Tourist*?
3 What was the name of the Bond girl in *Live and Let Die*?
4 The relationship between Burt Reynolds and Sally Field began on the set of which movie?
5 *Sunset Boulevard* was released in which decade?
6 Who directed *The Abyss*?
7 What is the last name of Ted from *Bill and Ted's Excellent Adventure*?
8 Is *West Side Story* nearer to 90, 120 or 150 minutes?
9 How many times had James Coburn been Oscar nominated before he won for *Affliction*?
10 What was the name of Kevin Costner's character in *JFK*?
11 'When You Believe' won an Oscar when it was used in which movie in 1998?
12 Who played Genghis Khan in *The Conqueror*?
13 A character named Barry Nichols appeared in which 1950s film?
14 *Blue Velvet* and *Jurassic Park* both starred which actress?
15 Who won the Best Actress Oscar for *Who's Afraid of Virginia Woolf?*?
16 Who did James Caan play in *The Godfather*?
17 Who was Woodward's fellow reporter in *All the President's Men*?
18 A character named Jenny Cavilleri appeared in which film?
19 In which decade does the action of *Grease* take place?
20 In which film does a character named Rick Deckard appear?
21 Characters named Gaston and Belle appeared in which film?
22 Which actor links *Taxi* and *War of the Roses*?
23 Who played the villain in the movie *Misery*?
24 In which decade was Disney's *Cinderella* released?
25 Who won the Best Director Oscar for *Mrs Miniver*?

**Answers The 21st Century** (see Quiz 103)
**1** *House on Haunted Hill.* **2** Limerick. **3** Mike Leigh. **4** Ashley Judd. **5** *Sleepy Hollow.* **6** Ambulance Drivers. **7** American Football. **8** *The Wonder Boys.* **9** *Toy Story 2.* **10** Scotland. **11** *The Sixth Sense.* **12** Angela. **13** Cab driver. **14** Blue. **15** Evil Emperor Zurg. **16** New York City. **17** Madonna. **18** Robin Williams. **19** *The Mikado.* **20** *The Big Tease.* **21** Anthony Minghella. **22** Carolyn. **23** Andy's. **24** To escape from their run. **25** Daffy.

## *QUIZ 103* THE 21st CENTURY ........ LEVEL 2

*Answers – see page 218*

1 Which horror movie was a remake of a 1958 hit?
2 Where in Ireland is *Angela's Ashes* set?
3 Who was Oscar-nominated for the screenplay of *Topsy Turvy*?
4 Who plays the fugitive in *Double Jeopardy*?
5 Which Washington Irving ghost story starred Tim Burton and Johnny Depp?
6 What sort of drivers are the subject of *Bringing Out the Dead*?
7 *Any Given Sunday* is about which sport?
8 In which movie did Michael Douglas play an unkempt, thrice-married professor?
9 Which new millennium movie included the voices of Tom Hanks and Tim Allen?
10 Where is Valerie Edmond's childhood home in *One More Kiss*?
11 Which movie with Haley Joel Osment was Oscar-nominated?
12 What is the name of Mena Suvari's character in *American Beauty*?
13 What is the occupation of the serial killer in *The Bone Collector*?
14 What colour shirt is Bruce Willis wearing in *The Sixth Sense*?
15 Who is Buzz Lightyear's father in *Toy Story 2*?
16 Where does Johnny Depp's character travel from to reach Sleepy Hollow?
17 Who starred in *The Next Best Thing*?
18 Who was 'Bicentennial Man'?
19 *Topsy Turvy* is about the making of which Gilbert and Sullivan opera?
20 Which Craig Ferguson movie was about a hairdressing championship?
21 Which director adapted *The Talented Mr Ripley* for the big screen?
22 What is the name of Kevin Spacey's wife in *American Beauty*?
23 Whose bedroom do the toys inhabit in *Toy Story 2*?
24 What is the chickens' main aim in *Chicken Run*?
25 Which character gives Leonardo DiCaprio the map in *The Beach*?

**Answers Sean Connery** (see Quiz 101)
**1** Scotland. **2** Diane Cilento. **3** Navy. **4** *The Avengers*. **5** Jason. **6** Richard I. **7** *Murder on the Orient Express*. **8** Edinburgh. **9** *South Pacific*. **10** *Marnie*. **11** Mum & Dad. **12** Michelle Pfeiffer. **13** Five. **14** *Indiana Jones and the Last Crusade*. **15** *Robin and Marian*. **16** Honor Blackman. **17** *Never Say Never Again*. **18** *The Russia House*. **19** Thomas. **20** *Diamonds Are Forever*. **21** *The Name of the Rose*. **22** Submarine. **23** Micheline. **24** Catherine Zeta Jones. **25** *The Untouchables*.

## *LEVEL 3:* THE HARD QUESTIONS

These are the hard questions – and do we mean hard! When we were telling you about the easy questions we suggested you use them so that everyone can answer something. This is the section for those who have found it fairly straightforward so far and need something very challenging indeed. Alternatively, if you're one of those people with an amazing memory for the most obscure bits of information, this could just be the section for you.

You will still find questions on famous movie folk and major movies but this is where we also ask you about the lesser-known happenings in this fascinating industry. The questions may not be straightforward. You may need several bits of information to come up with the correct answer. You may have part of the information but not all of it. There was no limit to our cunning when this section was compiled!

It does happen that when you have a quiz for a prize or prizes you end up with a tie. We suggest that this is the section of the book you use to come up with a tie-breaker. The real subject experts may not be fazed by some of the specialist sections, mind-numbingly difficult though they are, so maybe use a few Pot Luck questions as tie-breakers. In this way you will know they won't have boned up in advance.

If you are reading this book for your own entertainment and are answering most of the questions in this supremely difficult section then congratulate yourself. John Wayne said, 'Motion pictures are for amusement.' We hope that this quiz book about motion pictures will give you many hours of amusement as well.

## *QUIZ 1* WHO'S WHO? ........ LEVEL 3

*Answers – see page 223*

1 Who said, 'You can't get spoiled if you do your own ironing'?
2 How is Edna Gilhooley better known?
3 What was the name of the band Johnny Depp played in before turning to acting?
4 At which university did Richard E. Grant study?
5 In which city was Edward G. Robinson born?
6 Who said he would prefer 'animal' on his passport to 'actor'?
7 Who said, 'I look like a quarry someone has dynamited'?
8 How is Francoise Sorya Dreyfus better known?
9 Who was dubbed the '80s Errol Flynn' by *Vanity Fair* magazine?
10 Which star actor was born on exactly the same day as the late Laurence Harvey?
11 Who said, 'I stopped making pictures because I don't like taking my clothes off'?
12 Who played Woody Guthrie in *Bound for Glory*?
13 Which director did Theresa Russell marry?
14 Whose marriage to Michelle Phillips lasted just eight days?
15 Which film star wrote the novel *Adieu Volidia*?
16 About which of his co-stars did Anthony Hopkins say, 'She's serious about her work but doesn't take herself seriously'?
17 What is Michael J. Fox's middle name?
18 Who starred in *Prom Night* and *Terror Train*?
19 Whom did Harrison Ford replace as Indiana Jones in *Raiders of the Lost Ark*?
20 Which actress's father was one of the Dalai Lama's first American Buddhist monks?
21 Which actor played drums in a band called Scarlet Pride?
22 Which actor is Sissy Spacek's cousin?
23 What does Tim Roth have tattooed on his arm?
24 What is Shirley MacLaine's real name?
25 Who played Francis Bacon in *Love Is the Devil*?

**Answers Humphrey Bogart** (see Quiz 3)
**1** DeForest. **2** Surgeon. **3** Leviathan. **4** *Broadway's Like That.* **5** Alexander Woollcott. **6** 28. **7** Mary Philips. **8** Captain Queeg. **9** Warner Brothers. **10** Duke Mantee. **11** John Huston. **12** *Virginia City*. **13** George Raft. **14** Leslie Howard. **15** *The Treasure of the Sierra Madre.* **16** *Casablanca.* **17** General Sternwood (Charles Waldron). **18** *To Have And Have Not.* **19** *The Maltese Falcon.* **20** Santana Pictures. **21** *High Sierra.* **22** Katharine Hepburn. **23** *The Harder they Fall.* **24** Vivian Sherwood Rutledge. **25** *The Big Sleep.*

## *QUIZ 2* POT LUCK 1 ........ LEVEL 3

*Answers – see page 224*

1. What room number does Norman Bates put Janet Leigh in?
2. What is the profession of Nicole Kidman's father?
3. Which movie star released an album called *Love's Alright* in 1993?
4. Who won the Best Director Oscar for *Kramer versus Kramer*?
5. Which Ann featured in *The Accused*?
6. Within five minutes, how long does *Zulu* last?
7. What was the name of Bruce Willis's character in *Armageddon*?
8. In what year did Tom Cruise and Nicole Kidman supposedly land in Oklahoma in the film *Far and Away*?
9. Which actor links *The Paper* and *The Scarlet Letter*?
10. Who said, 'Universal signed me as a contract player – which is a little lower than working in the mail room'?
11. What colour scarf is Scrooge given in *The Muppets' Christmas Carol*?
12. How old was David Lean when he made *A Passage to India*?
13. Who wrote the screenplay for *The Seven Year Itch* with Billy Wilder?
14. Which 1971 film did pop star James Taylor star in?
15. Which 90s movie featured the voices of Gary Shandling, Chris Reubens and Paul Rock?
16. Which movie gave Carlo Rambaldi a Special Award in 1976 for visual effects?
17. Which Amy featured in *The Accidental Tourist*?
18. Who played the Bond girl in *Diamonds Are Forever*?
19. Within ten minutes, how long does the 1970s version of *Carrie* last?
20. In which movie did Clark Gable play Gay Langland?
21. Who won the Best Actor Oscar for *The Way of All Flesh*?
22. Who was originally set to play Indiana Jones before Harrison Ford?
23. Who directed *Wolf*?
24. How many *Road* films did Crosby, Hope and Lamour make?
25. Which Michael starred in *The Abyss*?

**Answers Horror** (see Quiz 4)
**1** Bela Lugosi. **2** Summer Isle. **3** Corey Haim. **4** TV horror film host. **5** Bodega Bay. **6** *Return of the Fly*. **7** The Arctic. **8** Lon Chaney. **9** Manhattan. **10** George A. Romero. **11** Property developer. **12** Stephen Hopkins. **13** His body is struck by lightning. **14** Billy. **15** *Seizure*. **16** Ellen Burstyn. **17** Daryl Hannah. **18** John Williams. **19** 110 minutes. **20** Friday the 13th. **21** The right hand of Christopher Hart. **22** He did not speak. **23** Ants. **24** Joseph Losey. **25** Neil Jordan.

## *QUIZ 3* HUMPHREY BOGART ........ LEVEL 3

*Answers – see page 221*

1 What was his middle name?
2 What was the occupation of his father?
3 On which ship was he serving in World War I when he injured his lip, giving him his characteristic tough look?
4 In which short did he make his screen debut?
5 Which reviewer described his acting as 'what is usually and mercifully described as inadequate'?
6 How many feature films did he make between 1936 and 1940?
7 Who did he marry after Helen Menken?
8 For which character was he Oscar-nominated in *The Caine Mutiny*?
9 Which studio was he working for at the outbreak of World War II?
10 What was the name of the killer he played in *The Petrified Forest*?
11 Who collaborated with W.R. Burnett to write the hit *High Sierra*?
12 In which Errol Flynn western did he play a Mexican bandit?
13 Who turned down the Sam Spade role in *The Maltese Falcon*?
14 Who insisted he get the screen role in *The Petrified Forest* which he had played on Broadway?
15 In which movie did he play Fred C. Dobbs?
16 In which movie did he say, 'I stick my neck out for nobody'?
17 Whose daughter is Philip Marlowe hired to protect in *The Big Sleep*?
18 *The Breaking Point* was a remake of which Bogart movie?
19 Which film starred Bogart in John Huston's directorial debut?
20 Which company did he form in 1947?
21 In which movie did he play Mad Dog Earle?
22 Which of his co-stars said, 'There was no bunkum with Bogart'?
23 What was the name of the film released shortly before his death?
24 What role did Mrs Bogart play in *The Big Sleep*?
25 In which movie did he say, 'I don't mind if you don't like my manners. I don't like them myself'?

**Answers Who's Who?** (see Quiz 1)
**1** Meryl Streep. **2** Ellen Burstyn. **3** The Kids. **4** Cape Town. **5** Bucharest. **6** Mickey Rourke. **7** Charles Bronson. **8** Anouk Aimee. **9** Kevin Kline. **10** George Peppard. **11** Debbie Reynolds. **12** David Carradine. **13** Nicholas Roeg. **14** Dennis Hopper. **15** Simone Signoret. **16** Emma Thompson. **17** Andrew. **18** Jamie Lee Curtis. **19** Tom Selleck. **20** Uma Thurman. **21** Ewan McGregor. **22** Rip Torn. **23** The birthdates of his children. **24** Shirley Maclean Beaty. **25** Derek Jacobi.

## *QUIZ 4* HORROR ........ LEVEL 3

*Answers – see page 222*

1 Which actor was known professionally for a time as Ariztid Olt?
2 What is the name of the island that *The Wicker Man* is set upon?
3 Who played Sam in *The Lost Boys*?
4 What is Peter Vincent's occupation in *Fright Night*?
5 Where does Mitch live in *The Birds*?
6 What was the name of the 1959 sequel to *The Fly*?
7 Where is the action set in 50s classic *The Thing*?
8 Which actor was originally chosen to play Bela Lugosi's role in the 1931 film *Dracula*?
9 Where does Mia Farrow live in *Rosemary's Baby*?
10 Who directed *Night of the Living Dead*?
11 What is the father's occupation in *Poltergeist*?
12 Who directed *A Nightmare on Elm Street 5: The Dream Child*?
13 How is Jason brought back to life in *Friday the Thirteenth Part VI –Jason Lives*?
14 Who receives Gizmo as a gift in *Gremlins*?
15 Which low-budget horror movie did Oliver Stone direct in 1974?
16 Which star of *The Exorcist* is also known by the name Edna Rae?
17 Who starred in *The Final Terror* with then flat-mate Rachel Ward?
18 Who wrote the score for *Jaws*?
19 Within fifteen minutes, how long does *Scream* last?
20 On which day in America did *Bram Stoker's Dracula* open?
21 Who or what plays Thing in *The Addams Family*?
22 What is unusual about Christopher Lee's role in *Dracula – Prince of Darkness*?
23 What creatures were the stars of *Them!*?
24 Who made *The Damned* for Hammer?
25 Who directed *Interview with the Vampire: The Vampire Chronicles*?

**Answers Pot Luck 1** (see Quiz 2)
**1** Room 1. **2** Psychologist. **3** Eddie Murphy. **4** Robert Benton. **5** Hearn. **6** 135 minutes. **7** Harry Stamper. **8** 1892. **9** Robert Duvall. **10** Clint Eastwood. **11** Red. **12** 75. **13** George Axelrod. **14** *Two Lane Blacktop*. **15** *Dr Dolittle*. **16** *King Kong*. **17** Wright. **18** Jill St John. **19** 98 mins. **20** *The Misfits*. **21** Emil Jannings. **22** Tom Selleck. **23** Mike Nichols. **24** Seven. **25** Biehn.

## *QUIZ 5* POT LUCK 2 ........ LEVEL 3

*Answers – see page 227*

1 Which movie star was born on the same day as Quincy Jones?
2 A character named Melvin Udall appeared in which film?
3 Which Martin featured in *All the President's Men*?
4 Within five minutes, how long does *Yellow Submarine* last?
5 Which actor links *Another Country* and *Dance with a Stranger*?
6 Who directed *Batman*?
7 Who was elected President of the Screen Actors Union in 1947 and again in 1959?
8 Which Paul featured in *American Graffiti*?
9 On which Hawaiian island was *Jurassic Park* filmed?
10 After 'Best Boy' appears on the end credits of *Airplane II: The Sequel*, who appears as 'Worst Boy'?
11 A character named Jack Crabb appeared in which film?
12 Who played Thing in *The Addams Family*?
13 Who voiced Jasmine in the film *Aladdin*?
14 In which year was *Destry Rides Again* released?
15 Who was quoted as saying, 'Great talent is an accident of birth'?
16 Which movie is shown in the film *I Love You to Death*?
17 Who played Tony Moretti in the film *Action Jackson*?
18 Within ten minutes how long does *Sophie's Choice* last?
19 Who was Jim Carrey's make-up man for *The Mask*?
20 Who won the Best Actress Oscar for *Seventh Heaven*?
21 A character named Luis Molina appears in which film?
22 Which soap did Hollywood star Christian Slater star in?
23 Which Bill featured in *American Gigolo*?
24 Who was first choice for Sigourney Weaver's *Gorillas in the Mist* role?
25 Who won the Best Director Oscar for *From Here to Eternity*?

**Answers Oscars – Who's Who?** (see Quiz 7)
**1** Poldek Pfefferberg (who told his story to Thomas Keneally). **2** Ralph Bellamy. **3** Elmer Bernstein. **4** Gary Busey. **5** Donfeld. **6** Alec Guinness. **7** Steven Spielberg. **8** George Sanders (*All About Eve*). **9** Cuba Gooding Jr (*Jerry Maguire*). **10** John Corigliano. **11** *Bugsy*. **12** Yves Montand (Simone Signoret). **13** The Shadows (John Farrar). **14** Mammy in *Gone with the Wind* (Hattie McDaniel). **15** Judy Holliday. **16** Margaret Herrick. **17** Johnny Carson. **18** Sophia Loren. **19** Ruth Gordon. **20** Edmund Goulding. **21** Alice Brady's. **22** Holly Hunter. **23** *The Pride of the Yankees*. **24** Ivan Jandl. **25** Richard Williams.

## *QUIZ 6* 1930s ........ LEVEL 3

*Answers – see page 228*

1 Which movie was advertised as 'Garbo laughs'?
2 What was Johnny Weissmuller's first Tarzan movie called?
3 Which Russian-born choreographer worked on *The Goldwyn Follies*?
4 Who famously had a grapefruit squashed in her face by Cagney in *Public Enemy*?
5 In which movie did Marlene Dietrich sing 'See What the Boys in the Back Room Will Have'?
6 Who played Catherine the Great in *The Scarlet Empress*?
7 In which movie did Claudette Colbert say, 'The moment I saw you, I had an idea you had an idea'?
8 In which movie did Errol Flynn make his screen debut?
9 *The Country Doctor* was a movie about whose birth?
10 Which actress who appeared in *Anna Christie* wrote an autobiography called *The Life Story of an Ugly Duckling*?
11 Who played Sherlock Holmes in *The Sleeping Cardinal*?
12 Who was Janet Gaynor's most frequent partner of the 20s and 30s?
13 What was advertised as 'Garbo talks'?
14 If Leslie Howard is Professor Higgins, who is Eliza Doolittle?
15 In which of his own movies did King Vidor appear in 1934?
16 Which husband and wife were Oscar-nominated together in 1931?
17 Which movie had the ad line, 'He treated her rough and she loved it'?
18 Who played David Garrick to Anna Neagle's Peg Woffington in *Peg of Old Drury Lane* in 1935?
19 What was the first of Spencer Tracy's three Oscar nominations between 1936 and 1938?
20 Who played the title role in *Rembrandt* in 1936?
21 Which brother of Harold Lloyd was injured making *Scarface* in 1932?
22 Who played Captain Ahab in *Moby Dick*?
23 What were Mae West's two hits of 1933?
24 What did Miscah Auer impersonate in *My Man Godfrey*?
25 By what name did John Carradine star in movies between 1930 and 1935?

**Answers Pot Luck 3** (see Quiz 8)
**1** Book editor. **2** Barry McGuigan. **3** John Ford. **4** Jessica Lange. **5** Crewson. **6** *Godzilla*. **7** 83 mins. **8** Dabney Coleman. **9** Shelley Duvall (in *Popeye*). **10** Eddie Murphy. **11** Seven. **12** 'The Power of Love'. **13** New Jersey. **14** Baseball. **15** Hedaya. **16** Howard Zieff. **17** 138. **18** Ralph Fiennes. **19** Frank Coraci. **20** Patsy Kensit. **21** Johnny Rico. **22** Sound effects on *Robocop*. **23** 101 minutes. **24** Ron Howard. **25** Callow.

## *QUIZ 7* OSCARS – WHO'S WHO? ........ LEVEL 3

*Answers – see page 225*

1 Spielberg said he accepted for *Schindler's List* on whose behalf?
2 Which honorary winner's autobiography was called *When the Smoke Hits the Fan*?
3 Which composer was nominated for *The Man with the Golden Arm*?
4 Which nominee has been a member of Carp and a drummer with the Rubber Band?
5 Who was a nominee for costume for *Days of Wine and Roses*?
6 Who won an honorary award in 1979 for 'advancing the art of screen acting'?
7 Who did Amy Irving marry shortly after being nominated for *Yentl*?
8 Who won Best Supporting Actor the year Josephine Hull won Best Supporting Actress for *Harvey*?
9 Who did James Woods lose out to as Best Supporting Actor for *Ghosts from the Past*?
10 Who was nominated for music for *The Red Violin*?
11 What was Ben Kingsley's next nomination after his first win?
12 Who was the husband of the 1959 Best Supporting Actress?
13 The composer of the only nominated song from *Grease* was a member of which pop band?
14 The first black actress to win was honoured for which role?
15 Who won when Gloria Swanson was nominated for *Sunset Boulevard*?
16 Who supposedly named the Oscar, saying it looked like her uncle?
17 Who is the second most frequent host of the Oscars ceremony?
18 Who was the first performer to win an Oscar for a performance entirely in a foreign language?
19 Who was the Oscar winner in *Rosemary's Baby*?
20 Who in 1932 was the first director to see his film win Best Picture but not have a nomination himself?
21 In 1938, whose Oscar for *In Old Chicago* was received by an impostor and stolen?
22 Who was nominated for Best Actress and Best Supporting Actress in 1993?
23 What was the second of Gary Cooper's three nominations between 1941 and 1943?
24 Who won a Special Award for *The Search* aged nine?
25 Who won a Special Achievement Award for *Who Framed Roger Rabbit*??

**Answers Pot Luck 2** (see Quiz 5)
**1** Michael Caine (14.3.33). **2** *As Good As It Gets.* **3** Balsam. **4** 85 minutes. **5** Rupert Everett. **6** Tim Burton. **7** Ronald Reagan. **8** LeMat. **9** Kauai. **10** Adolph Hitler. **11** *Little Big Man.* **12** Christopher Hart. **13** Linda Larkin. **14** 1939. **15** Woody Allen. **16** *Bridge on the River Kwai.* **17** Robert Davi. **18** 157 minutes. **19** Jim Cannon. **20** Janet Gaynor. **21** *Kiss of the Spider Woman.* **22** *Ryan's Hope.* **23** Duke. **24** Jessica Lange. **25** Fred Zinnemann.

## *QUIZ 8* POT LUCK 3 .......... LEVEL 3

*Answers – see page 226*

1 What is the job of the Jack Nicholson character in *Wolf*?
2 Who coached Daniel Day-Lewis for his role in *The Boxer*?
3 Who won the Best Director Oscar for *The Informer*?
4 Who won the Best Actress Oscar for *Blue Sky*?
5 Which Wendy featured in *Air Force One*?
6 In which film did a character named Dr Niko Tatopoulos appear?
7 To the nearest five minutes, how long does *Snow White and the Seven Dwarfs* last?
8 Which actor played the womanizing boss in *9 to 5*?
9 Who played Robin Williams's wife in his first movie?
10 Which actor said, 'I've got a filthy mouth but it's my only sin'?
11 In how many films did Roger Moore play 007 altogether?
12 What was the theme tune to *Back to the Future*?
13 In which state was John Travolta born?
14 At what sport did William Baldwin excel?
15 Which Dan featured in *Alien: Resurrection*?
16 From whom did Penny Marshall take over the direction of *Jumpin' Jack Flash*?
17 Within 20, how many actors are named on the credits for the film *Gandhi*?
18 Which actor links *Wuthering Heights* and *Quiz Show*?
19 Who directed *The Wedding Singer*?
20 Which pop wife appeared in *The Great Gatsby* aged four?
21 What was the name of Casper Van Dien's character in *Starship Troopers*?
22 For what did Stephen Flick win a Special Award in 1987?
23 Within five minutes, how long does *The Wizard of Oz* last?
24 Who directed *Backdraft*?
25 Which Simon featured in *Ace Ventura: When Nature Calls*?

**Answers 1930s** (see Quiz 6)
**1** *Ninotchka.* **2** *Tarzan the Ape Man.* **3** George Balanchine. **4** Mae Clarke. **5** *Destry Rides Again.* **6** Marlene Dietrich. **7** *Midnight.* **8** *In the Wake of the Bounty.* **9** The Dionne Quins. **10** Marie Dressler. **11** Arthur Wortner. **12** Charles Farrell. **13** *Anna Christie.* **14** Wendy Hiller. **15** *Our Daily Bread.* **16** Alfred Lunt & Lynne Fontaine. **17** *Red Dust.* **18** Cedric Hardwicke. **19** *San Francisco.* **20** Charles Laughton. **21** Gaylord. **22** John Barrymore. **23** *She Done Him Wrong, I'm No Angel.* **24** Gorilla. **25** John Peter Richmond.

## *QUIZ 9* MUSIC ON FILM ........ LEVEL 3

*Answers – see page 231*

1 Who composed the score for the 1995 movie *August*?
2 Who wrote the title song for *When the Wind Blows*?
3 Who sang the theme song for *North to Alaska*?
4 Who was Oscar-nominated for music for *The Cider House Rules*?
5 The Oscar-nominated 'Save Me' came from which movie?
6 Which three people successively sang the title song in *Someone to Watch Over Me*?
7 In which movie did jazz saxophonist Charlie Barnet play his hit recording of 'Cherokee'?
8 For which movie did Bernard Herrmann receive his first Oscar?
9 Who wrote the music for *Lawrence of Arabia*?
10 Which Shostakovich piece was used in *Eyes Wide Shut*?
11 Whose recording of 'Why Do Fools Fall in Love' featured on the soundtrack of *American Graffiti*?
12 Who wrote the score for *The Asphalt Jungle*?
13 Who provided the score for *Never on Sunday*?
14 Which music plays in the background in *10*?
15 Whose songs were on the soundtrack of *Philadelphia*?
16 Who wrote the songs for *Lady and the Tramp*?
17 Who was Oscar-nominated for the original score for *The Talented Mr Ripley*?
18 Who contributed a song for his 1957 film *Fire Down Below*?
19 'It Might Be You' comes from which movie?
20 Who wrote the songs for *Shanghai Surprise*?
21 Which famous son appeared as Michael Jackson's friend in *Moonwalker*?
22 *Don't Look Back* is an account of whose tour of Britain?
23 Whose zither music is haunting part of *The Third Man*?
24 Who wrote the score for *Double Indemnity*?
25 Which piece of music accompanies the prehistoric section of *Fantasia*?

**Answers Pot Luck 4** (see Quiz 11)
**1** Blue. **2** Ian McDiarmid. **3** Gene Wilder. **4** Paul Simon. **5** Penelope Spheeris. **6** 158 minutes. **7** Warner Baxter. **8** *Night Shift*. **9** Harrison Ford. **10** Computer salesman. **11** *US Marshals*. **12** *Licence to Kill*. **13** James L. Brooks. **14** England. **15** Mandy Patinkin. **16** Harris. **17** *Just a Gigolo*. **18** Charles Shaughnessy. **19** Ben Kingsley. **20** Morgan Freeman. **21** Golic. **22** 140 minutes. **23** Brolin. **24** Mary Pickford. **25** Jack Colton.

## *QUIZ 10* TOM CRUISE ........ LEVEL 3

*Answers – see page 232*

1 Star of *Born on the Fourth of July*, when is his birthday?
2 What does he have in common with Robert De Niro and Charlie Chaplin?
3 What is his full real name?
4 What is the name of his character in *Days of Thunder*?
5 Who sang the title song of his first movie?
6 How old was he when he had his first movie role?
7 On which novel was *Taps* based?
8 Which 1999 movie was the last for its director?
9 Who directed him in the 1983 'brat pack' movie with Matt Dillon, Rob Lowe and others?
10 For which movie immediately after *Mission: Impossible* was he Oscar-nominated?
11 Who or what won an Oscar for *Top Gun*?
12 He received his first Oscar nomination for playing which role?
13 With which star of *Risky Business* did he have an off-screen romance?
14 Which 1986 movie won an Oscar for his co-star?
15 What is his job in the film which won his co-star Dustin Hoffman an Oscar?
16 Who was his wife prior to Nicole Kidman?
17 In which part of which state was he born?
18 Where did he spend a year before deciding to become an actor?
19 Which writer whose book a film was based on said, 'He's no more my Vampire Lestat than Edward G. Robinson is Rhett Butler'?
20 What 'award' did he win at high school?
21 What was his second film?
22 For which TV show did he make his directorial debut?
23 What was his next film after *Rain Man*?
24 What was the first movie he produced and starred in?
25 What was the first film he starred in with Nicole Kidman after their marriage?

**Answers Disaster Movies** (see Quiz 12)
**1** 264. **2** Hart Bochner. **3** Alfred Newman. **4** Ronald Neame. **5** Roger Simmons. **6** Alfred E. Green. **7** Jerry Bruckheimer. **8** On the beach. **9** Salvage hunter. **10** Industrial Light and Magic. **11** Ron Howard. **12** Elizabeth Hoffman. **13** 158 mins. **14** Jonathon Hensleigh. **15** Philip Lathrop. **16** Arthur Herzog. **17** Corey Allen. **18** New York to New Jersey tunnel. **19** Laurence Rosenthal. **20** McCallum. **21** Spencer Tracy. **22** Max Catto. **23** Special effects. **24** Michael M. Mooney's. **25** Fox & MGM (*Towering Inferno*).

## *QUIZ 11* POT LUCK 4 ........ LEVEL 3

*Answers – see page 229*

1 The ghostly sisters seen by Danny wear what colour dresses in *The Shining*?
2 Who played the villain in *Return of the Jedi*?
3 Which movie star released a single called 'Pure Imagination' in 1970?
4 Which singer featured in *Annie Hall*?
5 Who directed *Wayne's World*?
6 Within five minutes, how long does *Where Eagles Dare* last?
7 Who won the Best Actor Oscar for *In Old Arizona*?
8 What was Michael Keaton's first film, in 1982?
9 Which actor links *Regarding Henry* and *Heroes*?
10 What does Helen think husband Harry does for a living in *True Lies*?
11 A character named Mark Sheridan appeared in which film?
12 What was Timothy Dalton's last film as James Bond?
13 Who won the Best Director Oscar for *Terms of Endearment*?
14 In which country was the whole of *Full Metal Jacket* filmed?
15 Who played Sam Francisco in the film *Alien Nation*?
16 Which Ed featured in *Apollo 13*?
17 What was Marlene Dietrich's last movie?
18 What was the name of Robert Mitchum's character in *Ryan's Daughter*?
19 Who said, 'I love British cinema like a doctor loves his dying patient'?
20 Which actor links *Street Smart* and *Glory*?
21 Which character did Paul McGann play in the film *Alien*$^3$?
22 Within fifteen minutes, how long does *Apollo 13* last?
23 Which James starred in *The Amityville Horror*?
24 Who won the Best Actress Oscar for *Coquette*?
25 What was the name of Michael Douglas's character in *Romancing the Stone*?

**Answers Music On Film** (see Quiz 9)
**1** Anthony Hopkins. **2** David Bowie. **3** Johnny Horton. **4** Rachel Portman. **5** *Magnolia*. **6** Sting, Gene Ammons & Roberta Flack. **7** *Jam Session*. **8** *All That Money Can Buy*. **9** Maurice Jarre. **10** Jazz Suite No. 2. **11** Frankie Lymon's. **12** Miklos Rozsa. **13** Monos Hadjidakis. **14** Ravel's *Bolero*. **15** Bruce Springsteen & Neil Young's. **16** Peggy Lee & Sonny Burke. **17** Gabriel Yared. **18** Jack Lemmon. **19** *Tootsie*. **20** George Harrison. **21** Sean Lennon. **22** Bob Dylan's. **23** Anton Karas's. **24** Miklos Rozsa. **25** Stravinsky's *Rite of Spring*.

## *QUIZ 12* DISASTER MOVIES ........ LEVEL 3

*Answers – see page 230*

1 What is the body count of *Die Hard 2* said to be?
2 Who played Ellis in *Die Hard*?
3 Who wrote the score for *Airport*?
4 Who directed *The Poseidon Adventure*?
5 Which character is the technical expert responsible for the *Towering Inferno*?
6 Who directed the 50s movie *Invasion USA*?
7 Who produced *Armageddon*?
8 Where does the character Jenny die in *Deep Impact*?
9 What is the occupation of the character played by Bill Paxton in *Titanic*?
10 Which company provided the computer-generated images for *Twister*?
11 Who directed *Apollo 13*?
12 Who plays the grandmother of the Mayor's children in *Dante's Peak*?
13 Within ten minutes, how long does *Towering Inferno* run?
14 Who wrote *Die Hard with a Vengeance*?
15 Who was Oscar-nominated for *Earthquake*?
16 *The Swarm* is based on a novel written by whom?
17 Who directed *Avalanche*?
18 Where is *Daylight* set?
19 Who wrote the score for *Meteor*?
20 Which David featured in *A Night to Remember*?
21 Which actor received an Oscar nomination for *San Francisco*?
22 Who wrote the novel that *The Devil at Four O'Clock* is based on?
23 For what did *Krakatoa, East of Java* receive an Oscar nomination?
24 Upon whose novel is *The Hindenburg* based?
25 Which two studios made the movie based on *The Tower* and *The Glass Inferno*?

**Answers Tom Cruise** (see Quiz 10)
**1** 3rd July. **2** Left-handed. **3** Thomas Cruise Mapother IV. **4** Cole. **5** Lionel Richie ('Endless Love'). **6** 18. **7** *Father Sky*. **8** *Eyes Wide Shut* (Stanley Kubrick). **9** Francis Ford Coppola. **10** *Jerry Maguire*. **11** Song ('Take My Breath Away'). **12** Ron Kovic (*Born on the Fourth of July*). **13** Rebecca De Mornay. **14** *The Color of Money*. **15** Salesman. **16** Mimi Rogers. **17** Syracuse, New York. **18** Franciscan monastery. **19** Anne Rice (*Interview with the Vampire*). **20** Least Likely to Succeed. **21** *Taps*. **22** *Fallen Angels*. **23** *Cocktail*. **24** *Mission: Impossible*. **25** *Far and Away*.

## *QUIZ 13* CARY GRANT ........ LEVEL 3

*Answers – see page 235*

1 What was his middle name?
2 Under which star sign was he born?
3 Which studio did he sign with when he first went to Hollywood?
4 What was the first movie where he was cast opposite Marlene Dietrich?
5 For which film was he nominated for his second Oscar?
6 With whose troupe did he go to America in 1920?
7 Which short saw his screen debut?
8 What did the studio want to change his name to when he first arrived at Paramount?
9 Which 1948 movies both featured the then Mrs Cary Grant?
10 Which of his co-stars mimicked him in the subsequent film he made?
11 Which of his movies was a remake of *The More the Merrier*?
12 He was a director of which cosmetics company after his retirement from the big screen?
13 After 1958 what percentage of the takings did he receive in lieu of salary in his films?
14 His second wife was heiress to which empire?
15 For which movie did he donate his salary to war relief?
16 Who was the only winner of an Oscar for *Suspicion*, in which he starred?
17 In which film did he say, 'Insanity runs in my family. It practically gallops'?
18 Mae West's invitation to Cary Grant to 'come up some time and see me' came from a movie based on which play?
19 Who played his wife in the first movie for which he was Oscar-nominated?
20 Who won Best Actor for the year Grant was given a special Oscar?
21 In 1937–38 he was under joint contract to which studios?
22 Who was the mother of his only child?
23 Who did he play in *Night and Day*?
24 What was his first film for Hitchcock?
25 Which wife survived him?

**Answers Walt Disney** (see Quiz 15)
**1** Alfred Hitchcock. **2** *Flowers and Trees.* **3** Kansas City. **4** *Saludos Amigos; The Three Caballeros.* **5** *The Skeleton Dance.* **6** Alfred & Elma Milotte. **7** Made training films. **8** Laugh O Grams. **9** Julie Andrews (*Mary Poppins*). **10** Sagittarius.
**11** One large Oscar and seven small ones. **12** *Jungle Book.* **13** Leopold Stokowski.
**14** *Treasure Island.* **15** *Plane Crazy; Gallopin' Gaucho.* **16** Dippy Dawg.
**17** *Victory Through Air Power.* **18** *Alice in Cartoonland.* **19** *Jungle Cat.* **20** 29.
**21** Son-in-law. **22** *Oswald the Lucky Rabbit.* **23** Hayley Mills. **24** *The Happiest Millionaire.* **25** His daughter Diane.

## *QUIZ 14* POT LUCK 5 .................................................................... LEVEL 3

*Answers – see page 236*

1 How many dollars did Eve Marie Saint tip the waiter to seat Cary Grant near her in *North by Northwest*?
2 Within fifteen minutes, how long does *Bambi* last?
3 Which Steve featured in *Armageddon*?
4 A character named Robert Kincaid appeared in which film?
5 Who directed *Awakenings*?
6 Within five minutes, how long does *When Harry Met Sally* last?
7 Who would not be billed below Paul Newman, so refused the part of Sundance?
8 For what did W. Howard Greene and Harold Rosson win a Special Award in 1936?
9 Which actor was born Ivo Livi in 1921?
10 Which singer appeared in *Eat the Rich*?
11 Jimi Hendrix's 'Foxy Lady' featured in which 90s movie?
12 Which actor links *Impromptu* and *Bitter Moon*?
13 Which character was played by Josh Charles in the film *Dead Poets Society*?
14 Which Laurie featured in *Assault on Precinct 13*?
15 In the 1990s who won the Best Actress Oscar the year before Helen Hunt?
16 In which year did Alfred Hitchcock die?
17 Who directed *The Usual Suspects*?
18 In the 1980s who said, 'The baby's...only problem is he looks like Edward G Robinson'?
19 Richard Williams won a Special Award in 1988 for animation direction on what?
20 Who played Paris Carver in *Tomorrow Never Dies*?
21 Which British actor said, 'Teeth are a vitally important part of an actor's equipment'?
22 A character named Dr Zira appeared in which film?
23 Within ten minutes how long does *Amadeus* last?
24 Who played the professional exterminator in *Arachnophobia*?
25 Which British actor married a former Miss Guyana in 1973?

**Answers Partnerships** (see Quiz 16)
**1** Prince. **2** *Anchors Aweigh.* **3** Deanna Durbin. **4** Nicholas Roeg. **5** Three months. **6** Bruce Willis & Demi Moore. **7** *The Man Who Would Be King.* **8** Uma Thurman. **9** Sean Penn. **10** *Desk Set.* **11** Nancy Allen. **12** *Notorious.* **13** *The Naples Connection.* **14** *This Gun for Hire.* **15** Six. **16** Gary Oldman & Chloe Webb. **17** Dolly Parton. **18** James Caan. **19** *Losing Isaiah.* **20** William Powell. **21** Joanne Woodward, Nell Potts. **22** Simian Films. **23** Nanette Fabray. **24** Harry James. **25** *Adam's Rib.*

## *QUIZ 15* WALT DISNEY ............ LEVEL 3

*Answers – see page 233*

1 Who said, 'Disney has the best casting. If he doesn't like an actor he just tears him up'?
2 In which 1932 film did he experiment with colour?
3 Where did he first meet Ub Iwerks?
4 Which movies were made as a result of a government goodwill tour of South America?
5 What was the first of the *Silly Symphonies* called?
6 A meeting with which photographers brought about the *True Life* nature films?
7 What was Disney's job during World War II?
8 What did Disney and Iwerks call their first cartoons?
9 Which actress won an Oscar for the last major film he made before his death?
10 What was his star sign?
11 Which special Oscar award did he receive for *Snow White and the Seven Dwarfs*?
12 Which animated film was he working on at the time of his death?
13 Who, with Disney, received a special Oscar for *Fantasia*?
14 What was the first of his all-live-action movies?
15 What were the first two silent Mickey Mouse cartoons called?
16 What was Goofy originally called?
17 Which morale-boosting movie did Disney make in 1943?
18 In 1923 what was the name of the animated live-action cartoons he produced with his brother Roy and Ub Iwerks?
19 What was the last film in the series which began with *Seal Island*?
20 How many Oscars did Disney win in his lifetime?
21 Which relative of Walt became chief executive of Disney in 1983?
22 Which series did Walt launch with Roy in 1927?
23 Which British child star did he bring to Hollywood in the late 50s?
24 Which musical was he working on at the time of his death?
25 Who wrote a biography of Disney, published in 1958?

**Answers Cary Grant** (see Quiz 13)
**1** Alexander. **2** Capricorn. **3** Paramount. **4** *Blonde Venus.* **5** *None But the Lonely Heart.* **6** Bob Pender's. **7** *Singapore Sue.* **8** Cary Lockwood. **9** *Mr Blandings Build His Dream House; Every Girl Should Be Married.* **10** Tony Curtis (*Some Like It Hot*). **11** *Walk Don't Run.* **12** Fabergé. **13** 75%. **14** Woolworths. **15** *The Philadelphia Story.* **16** Joan Fontaine. **17** *Arsenic and Old Lace.* **18** *Diamond Lil.* **19** Irene Dunne. **20** John Wayne. **21** RKO & Columbia. **22** Dyan Cannon. **23** Cole Porter **24** *Suspicion.* **25** Barbara Harris.

## *QUIZ 16* PARTNERSHIPS ........ LEVEL 3

*Answers – see page 234*

1 Who was Kristin Scott Thomas's first co-star in 1986?
2 What was the first movie which teamed Gene Kelly with Frank Sinatra?
3 Who shared a 1938 Special Oscar with Mickey Rooney?
4 Which director did Theresa Russell marry?
5 For how long was James Caan married to Sheila Ryan?
6 Which married couple acted together in *Mortal Thoughts*?
7 In which movie did Mrs Michael Caine appear with him?
8 Which Mrs Ethan Hawke appeared in *Gattaca*?
9 Which husband of Robin Wright directed her in *The Crossing Guard*?
10 What was Spencer Tracy and Katharine Hepburn's penultimate film together?
11 How was Mrs Brian De Palma, star of *Dressed to Kill*, better known?
12 What was Cary Grant's second film with Hitchcock as director?
13 In which 80s movie did Mr and Mrs Harvey Keitel star?
14 What was Alan Ladd's first western opposite Veronica Lake?
15 How many real wives did the most famous Tarzan have?
16 Who played the title roles in *Sid and Nancy*?
17 Which singer/actress was Mrs Carl Dean?
18 Who co-starred with Bette Midler in *For the Boys*?
19 What was the first movie Samuel L. Jackson starred in with his wife?
20 Who played opposite Myrna Loy 13 times?
21 Which mother and daughter were in the title roles in *Rachel Rachel*?
22 Which production company was set up by Hugh Grant and Liz Hurley?
23 Who was the female triplet in the famous baby dance routine in *The Band Wagon*?
24 Which bandleader did Betty Grable marry in 1943?
25 What was the sixth Spencer Tracy/Katharine Hepburn movie?

**Answers Pot Luck 5** (see Quiz 14)
**1** Five. **2** 69 minutes. **3** Buscemi. **4** *The Bridges of Madison County*. **5** Penny Marshall. **6** 95 minutes. **7** Steve McQueen. **8** Colour cinematography. **9** Yves Montand. **10** Paul McCartney. **11** *Wayne's World*. **12** Hugh Grant. **13** Knox Overstreet. **14** Zimmer. **15** Frances McDormand. **16** 1980. **17** Bryan Singer. **18** Woody Allen. **19** *Who Framed Roger Rabbit?* **20** Teri Hatcher. **21** Peter Cushing. **22** *Planet of the Apes*. **23** 158 minutes. **24** John Goodman. **25** Michael Caine.

## *QUIZ 17* POT LUCK 6 ........ LEVEL 3

*Answers – see page 239*

1 Who said in 1985, 'When I grow up I still want to be a director'?
2 What was the name of Bruce Willis's character in *Twelve Monkeys*?
3 Within five minutes, how long does *Sleeping Beauty* last?
4 Which Cary featured in *Close Encounters of the Third Kind*?
5 What is the first name of Oliver Reed, who used his middle name in the movies?
6 Which Brian featured in *Cocoon*?
7 Who won the Best Actress Oscar for *The Divorcee*?
8 Which movie starts, 'I owe everything to George Bailey'?
9 Which actor was originally set to play Robert Redford's role in *Indecent Proposal*?
10 Who won the Best Director Oscar for *Marty*?
11 The song 'All The Way' came from which movie?
12 Which 1980 movie visited Sherwood Forest and the Titanic?
13 Which 1966 film did rock star Roy Orbison star in?
14 Which actor links *The Big Easy* and *Punchline*?
15 In which year did Orson Welles die?
16 Which writer directed *Tough Guys Don't Dance* in 1987?
17 In which film did a character named Roberta Glass appear?
18 'It Goes Like It Goes' won an Oscar when it was used in which movie in 1979?
19 Which Jon featured in *The Color of Money*?
20 Steve Martin was born in which American state?
21 In which movie did Clark Gable play Vic Norton?
22 What part does director Steve Miner play in *Friday the Thirteenth, Part 3*?
23 Who directed *Twister*?
24 In which film does a character named Freeman Lowell appear?
25 Which had the longest running time – *Dirty Dancing, Men in Black* or *The Color Purple*?

**Answers Goldie Hawn** (see Quiz 19)
**1** Scorpio. **2** Peter Sellers. **3** *Good Morning World.* **4** Washington DC. **5** *The Sugarland Express.* **6** *Deceived.* **7** Juliet. **8** Left-handed. **9** Ingrid Bergman. **10** Fred Astaire. **11** Isabella Rossellini. **12** *The One and Only Genuine Original Family Band.* **13** *The Duchess and the Dirtwater Fox.* **14** Mel Gibson. **15** Steven Spielberg. **16** Librarian. **17** *In the Wild.* **18** Goldy Jeanne Hawn. **19** Meryl Streep. **20** Wyatt. **21** *Cactus Flower.* **22** *Sophie's Choice.* **23** Her film characters. **24** Gus Trikonis. **25** *Cactus Flower.*

## QUIZ 18 FAMOUS FIRSTS ............ LEVEL 3

*Answers – see page 240*

1 What was the first mainstream film to use the word 'virgin'?
2 What was the first Royal Command Performance film?
3 Which airline showed the first in-flight movie?
4 How old was Mae West when she made her movie debut?
5 What was Fritz Lang's first Hollywood film?
6 What did Kevin Kline play on the piano in his first movie, *Sophie's Choice*?
7 What was John Boorman's US directing debut?
8 Who was the first actor to receive $1 million for a single picture?
9 VistaVision was first used in which classic movie?
10 What was the first movie shown in Aromarama?
11 What was Milos Forman's first US movie?
12 What was the first movie to feature Dracula?
13 Which movie was the first to have Sensurround?
14 In which movie did Chow Yun-Fat make his US debut?
15 What was the first western to win an Oscar for best film?
16 What was the first film that teamed Mickey Rooney and Judy Garland?
17 What was Selznick's first movie from his own independent company?
18 Who was the first American to join the Young Vic company on an American tour?
19 What was the first production from the west allowed in Beijing's Forbidden City?
20 What was Shirley MacLaine's first movie?
21 What was Hitchcock's first film for an independent producer?
22 Who was the first US singer/actor to entertain the troops in Korea?
23 What was the first in-flight movie?
24 In which movie did Harrison Ford make his screen debut as a messenger boy?
25 What were the names of the first two film magazines in the US?

**Answers Pot Luck 7** (see Quiz 20)
**1** Mel Gibson. **2** Raquel Welch. **3** 'I Got You Babe' by Sonny and Cher. **4** *Nil By Mouth*. **5** Greene. **6** *Dante's Peak*. **7** *The Young and the Restless*. **8** Scott Carey. **9** 88 minutes. **10** Dog. **11** Mel Brooks. **12** *The Swan*. **13** Reese's Pieces. **14** True. **15** Jodi Benson. **16** Jeff Goldblum. **17** Cab driver. **18** William Friedkin. **19** Dustin Hoffman. **20** *Total Recall*. **21** Veronica Quaife. **22** Foley. **23** George Arliss. **24** Michael Schultz. **25** 1 hour (1 hour 11 mins).

## *QUIZ 19* GOLDIE HAWN ........................................ LEVEL 3

*Answers – see page 237*

1 Under what star sign was she born?
2 Which Goon was her co-star in her movie produced by John Boulting?
3 What was her first TV series?
4 Where was she born?
5 Which film was advertised as 'The true story of a girl who took on all of Texas and almost won'?
6 In which 1991 movie did she play an uncharacteristically serious role?
7 She made her professional debut in which role?
8 What does she have in common with Judy Garland and Marilyn Monroe?
9 Who was the female star of her first Oscar-nominated film?
10 Who did she say was the only person who had ever made her speechless?
11 Which daughter of Ingrid Bergman was a fellow co-star along with Meryl Streep?
12 What was her very first movie – for Disney?
13 Which movie had the advertising line, 'If the rustlers didn't get you...the hustlers did!'?
14 Who was her co-star in 1990 in a cast with David Carradine?
15 Who directed her in *The Sugarland Express*?
16 What was her occupation in *Foul Play*?
17 Which TV documentary did she make about elephants?
18 How was she billed in her very first film?
19 Who was she originally tipped to play opposite in *Thelma and Louise*?
20 What is the name of her son by the actor she met on the set of *The One and Only Genuine Original Family Band*?
21 For which movie did she receive her first Oscar nomination?
22 For which movie was she turned down in preference to Meryl Streep, who won an Oscar for the role?
23 Who or what are all her pets named after?
24 Who did she divorce to marry husband No. 2?
25 Which movie saw her debut as producer?

**Answers Pot Luck 6** (see Quiz 17)
**1** Steven Spielberg. **2** James Cole. **3** 75 minutes. **4** Guffrey. **5** Robert. **6** Dennehy. **7** Norma Shearer. **8** *It's a Wonderful Life.* **9** Warren Beatty. **10** Delbert Mann. **11** *The Joker Is Wild.* **12** *Time Bandits.* **13** *The Fastest Guitar Alive.* **14** John Goodman. **15** 1985. **16** Norman Mailer. **17** *Desperately Seeking Susan.* **18** Norma Rae. **19** Turturro. **20** Texas. **21** *The Hucksters.* **22** A newscaster. **23** Jan De Bont. **24** *Silent Running.* **25** *The Color Purple.*

## *QUIZ 20* POT LUCK 7 ........................ LEVEL 3

*Answers – see page 238*

1 Which actor links *Tim* and *The Rest of Daniel*?
2 Which actress released the 1987 single 'This Girl's Back in Town'?
3 What song is playing every time Bill Murray wakes up on *Groundhog Day*?
4 Which film was Gary Oldman's directorial debut?
5 Which Graham featured in *Dances with Wolves*?
6 A character named Harry Dalton appeared in which film?
7 Which soap did Tom Selleck star in?
8 Who did Grant Williams play in *The Incredible Shrinking Man*?
9 Within five minutes, how long does *Sleeper* last?
10 Which animal mask does George Peppard steal in *Breakfast at Tiffany's*?
11 Who was quoted in *Newsweek* as saying, 'I only direct in self-defence'?
12 What was the last film Grace Kelly made before becoming a princess?
13 What type of sweets are used in the trail that E.T. follows in *E.T.*?
14 Which Rachel featured in *The Craft*?
15 Who voiced Ariel in *The Little Mermaid*?
16 Which actor links *California Split* and *Vibes*?
17 What is John Travolta's occupation in *Look Who's Talking*?
18 Who won the Best Director Oscar for *The French Connection*?
19 Who was offered the role of Rambo in *First Blood*, but turned it down?
20 In 1990 Eric Brevig won a Special Award for visual effects on which film?
21 What was the name of Geena Davis's character in *The Fly*?
22 Which Jeremy featured in *Dante's Peak*?
23 Who won the Best Actor Oscar for *Disraeli*?
24 Who directed *Car Wash*?
25 To the nearest hour, how long does the 30s movie *Frankenstein* last?

**Answers Famous Firsts** (see Quiz 18)
**1** Otto Preminger's *The Moon Is Blue.* **2** *A Matter of Life and Death.* **3** Imperial Airways. **4** 40. **5** *Fury.* **6** Schumann's 'Scenes From Childhood'. **7** *Point Blank.* **8** Marlon Brando. **9** *White Christmas.* **10** *Behind the Great Wall.* **11** *Taking Off.* **12** *Nosferatu.* **13** *Earthquake.* **14** *The Replacement Killers.* **15** *Cimarron.* **16** *Love Finds Andy Hardy.* **17** *Little Lord Fauntleroy.* **18** Richard Gere. **19** *The Last Emperor.* **20** *Trouble with Harry.* **21** *Rope.* **22** Al Jolson. **23** *The Lost World.* **24** *Dead Heat on a Merry Go Round.* **25** *Photoplay; Motion Picture Story Magazine.*

## *QUIZ 21* REMAKES ........ LEVEL 3

*Answers – see page 243*

1 *Sommersby* was a remake of which Depardieu classic?
2 What was the only movie Hitchcock remade?
3 Who was the male star of the fourth version of *Daddy Long Legs*?
4 Who starred in a 1981 remake of a 1946 film noir with Lana Turner?
5 Who won an Oscar for the 1950 George Cukor movie remade in 1993 with Melanie Griffith?
6 Which 1997 film was a remake of Les Compères?
7 Whose final movie was a remake with sound of *The Unholy Three*?
8 *Move Over Darling* reworked which 40s classic with Cary Grant?
9 Which Warren Beatty movie was a remake of *Here Comes Mr Jordan*?
10 A 30s classic with Clark Gable and Claudette Colbert was remade as *You Can't Run Away from It* starring whom?
11 *Singapore Woman* was a remake of which Bette Davis Oscar-winner?
12 In which movie did Bette Midler recreate a Barbara Stanwyck role?
13 Who directed *Love Affair* and its remake *An Affair to Remember*?
14 Who played the wedding organizer in the 1991 remake of a 50s Spencer Tracy classic?
15 *The Badlanders* was a western remake of which Sterling Hayden movie which had a young Monroe in the cast?
16 *Silk Stockings* was the musical remake of which classic?
17 Which Humphrey Bogart movie was a remake of *Bordertown*?
18 What was the Julia Roberts remake of *Dr Jekyll and Mr Hyde* called?
19 Where was the 70s remake of *Invasion of the Body Snatchers* set?
20 Who played the Hayley Mills role in the 90s version of a 1961 movie about twins?
21 Which 60s movie was a remake of Bob Hope's *The Paleface*?
22 *One Sunday Afternoon* was remade twice, once with the same title and once as what?
23 Velvet Brown as a child was played by Elizabeth Taylor, but who was the adult 30 years later?
24 What was the remake of *Kid Galahad* which did not star Elvis?
25 How was *Sentimental Journey* remade with Lauren Bacall?

**Answers Pot Luck 8** (see Quiz 23)
**1** Yul Brynner. **2** Red. **3** Marie Dressler. **4** Peanut stall. **5** Frank Borzage. **6** Cromwell. **7** *The Jazz Singer*. **8** David Levinson. **9** *Give My Regards to Broad Street*. **10** *Silent Running*. **11** *The Living Daylights*. **12** Robinson. **13** 'Under the Sea'. **14** Terry Hayes. **15** Dirk Bogarde. **16** 1980. **17** John Cleese. **18** 1930s. **19** 105 minutes. **20** Dysart. **21** F. Murray Abraham. **22** A mood ring. **23** Bree Daniels. **24** Terry Gilliam. **25** Oates.

## QUIZ 22 STARS OF THE 21st CENTURY ........................................ LEVEL 3

*Answers – see page 244*

1 Which actress links *Cookie* and *Angela's Ashes*?
2 Who played Sal in *The Beach*?
3 What was *Now and Then* star Thora Birch's first movie?
4 Who played the role of the lyricist in *Topsy Turvy*?
5 Who links *Independence Day* and *The Iron Giant*?
6 Who played Bonnie in *The Craft*?
7 Which actress links *Circle of Friends* and *GoldenEye*?
8 Who stars as Valerie Edmonds's 'old flame' in *One More Kiss*?
9 Who tries to eat Stuart Little?
10 Who played Wendy in *The Ice Storm*?
11 Who played Yul Brynner's role in the remake of *The King andI*?
12 Who links *Boogie Nights* and *The Myth of Fingerprints*?
13 What character did the actress who appeared in *The Mask* play in *My Best Friend's Wedding*?
14 Which actress played Glenn Close's role in the remake of *Dangerous Liaisons*?
15 Who played Glenn Gulia in *The Wedding Singer*?
16 Who links *The World is Not Enough* and *Wild Things*?
17 Which actress links *Mrs Doubtfire* and *Miracle on 34th Street*?
18 Who starred as Ray Liotta's daughter in *Corrina, Corrina*?
19 What role does ex-rapper Marky Mark play in *Three Kings*?
20 Who plays Sidney's boyfriend in *Scream 2*?
21 Who took Sir John Mills's role of Pip in the 90s adaptation of *Great Expectations*?
22 Who plays Maude in *The Big Lebowski*?
23 Which actress won a Golden Globe for *Boys Don't Cry*?
24 Where was Charlize Theron born?
25 Which actor starred in *Varsity Blues*?

**Answers 1950s Stars** (see Quiz 24)
**1** Ace in the Hole. **2** Eight. **3** Bette Davis. **4** Mae Clarke. **5** Nat King Cole. **6** 19. **7** Ira Grossel. **8** Mrs Nancy Reagan. **9** *Picnic.* **10** Rhonda Fleming. **11** Stanley Kowalski (*A Streetcar Named Desire*). **12** Cyd Charisse. **13** Maria Vargas. **14** Tab Hunter. **15** *Separate Tables.* **16** Agnes Moorehead: **17** Preacher Harry Powell. **18** The chimp. **19** MacDonald Carey. **20** *Darby O'Gill and the Little People.* **21** Ava Gardner. **22** Vincent Winters. **23** Rosemary Clooney. **24** Ben Johnson. **25** Peter Lorre.

## *QUIZ 23* POT LUCK 8 ........ LEVEL 3

*Answers – see page 241*

1 Which great actor died on the same day as fellow star Orson Welles?
2 What colour is Deborah Kerr's suit in the final scene of *An Affair to Remember*?
3 Who won the Best Actress Oscar for *Min and Bill*?
4 What sort of stall does Chico have in *Duck Soup*?
5 Who won the Best Director Oscar for *Seventh Heaven*?
6 Which James starred in *Babe*?
7 What movie is shown within the film *Goodfellas*?
8 Who did Jeff Goldblum play in *Independence Day*?
9 What was the name of the last film that Ralph Richardson ever made?
10 *Armageddon, Scream 2, Silent Running* – which has the shortest running time?
11 In which film did Caroline Bliss replace Lois Maxwell as Miss Moneypenny?
12 Which Amy featured in *Mean Streets*?
13 Which song won Best Song Oscar for *The Little Mermaid*?
14 Who wrote the screenplay for *Mad Max Beyond Thunderdome*?
15 Which actor's memoirs include the volume *Snakes and Ladders*?
16 In which year did Peter Sellers die?
17 Who voiced Cat R. Ward in *An American Tail: Fievel Goes West*?
18 In which decade was *Morocco* released?
19 Within five minutes, how long does *Shine* last?
20 Which Richard featured in *The Hospital*?
21 Who won the Best Actor Oscar for *Amadeus*?
22 What kind of ring does Vada have in *My Girl*?
23 What was the name of Jane Fonda's character in *Klute*?
24 Who directed *Twelve Monkeys*?
25 Which Warren featured in *Badlands*?

**Answers Remakes** (see Quiz 21)
**1** *The Return of Martin Guerre.* **2** *The Man Who Knew Too Much.* **3** Fred Astaire. **4** Jessica Lange & Jack Nicholson (*The Postman Always Rings Twice*). **5** Judy Holliday (*Born Yesterday*). **6** *Father's Day.* **7** Lon Chaney. **8** *My Favorite Wife.* **9** *Heaven Can Wait.* **10** June Allyson & Jack Lemmon. **11** *Dangerous.* **12** *Stella.* **13** Leo McCarey. **14** Martin Short (*Father of the Bride*). **15** *The Asphalt Jungle.* **16** *Ninotchka.* **17** *They Drive by Night.* **18** *Mary Reilly.* **19** San Francisco. **20** Lindsay Lohan. **21** *The Shakiest Gun in the West.* **22** *The Strawberry Blonde.* **23** Nanette Newman. **24** *The Wagons Roll at Night.* **25** *The Gift of Love.*

## *QUIZ 24* 1950s STARS ............ LEVEL 3

*Answers – see page 242*

1 In which movie did Kirk Douglas say, 'I'm a thousand-a-day man, Mr Boot. You can have me for nothing'?
2 What number juror was Henry Fonda in *Twelve Angry Men*?
3 Who played Catherine the Great in *John Paul Jones*?
4 Which actress was the inspiration for Monroe's Lorelei Lee in *Gentlemen Prefer Blondes*?
5 Which singer appeared in *St Louis Blues* as W.C. Handy?
6 Ava Gardner married three times, but how many wives did her husbands have between them?
7 What was Jeff Chandler's real name?
8 What was the most famous married name of the actress who was born Anne Frances Robbins?
9 In which movie did William Holden say, 'I gotta get somewhere. I just gotta'?
10 Who played Cleopatra in *Serpent of the Nile*?
11 Which Broadway role did Brando recreate on screen in 1951?
12 How was Tula Ellice Finklea better known?
13 Which role did Ava Gardner play in *The Barefoot Contessa*?
14 Which 50s teenage idol's real name was Andrew Arthur Kelm?
15 What was the third of Deborah Kerr's three nominations between 1956 and 1958?
16 Who played Elizabeth I in *The Story of Mankind*?
17 Who did Robert Mitchum play in *The Night of the Hunter*?
18 Which Ronald Reagan co-star in *Bedtime for Bonzo* died before the movie premiere?
19 Who played Jesse James in *The Great Missouri Raid*?
20 In which 50s film did Sean Connery sing?
21 Who played Julie in *Showboat*, though her singing voice was dubbed?
22 Who won a Special Oscar for *The Little Kidnappers* aged six?
23 Who was the only star of *White Christmas* to live until the end of the 20th century?
24 Who won a World Champion Cowboy title in 1953?
25 Who was Nero in *The Story of Mankind*?

**Answers Stars of the 21st Century** (see Quiz 22)
**1** Emily Lloyd. **2** Tilda Swinton. **3** *Purple People Eater*. **4** Jim Broadbent. **5** Harry Connick Jr. **6** Neve Campbell. **7** Minnie Driver. **8** Gerry Butler **9** Snowball the Cat. **10** Christina Ricci. **11** Chow Yun-Fat. **12** Julianne Moore. **13** Kimmy (Cameron Diaz). **14** Sarah Michelle Geller. **15** Matthew Glave. **16** Denise Richards. **17** Mara Wilson. **18** Tina Majorino. **19** Troy Barlow. **20** Jerry O'Connell. **21** Ethan Hawke. **22** Julianne Moore. **23** Hilary Swank. **24** South Africa. **25** James van der Beer.

## *QUIZ 25* ROMANCE .......... LEVEL 3

*Answers – see page 247*

1 From which play was *Casablanca* adapted?
2 Who plays Charlotte Vale's mother in *Now, Voyager*?
3 Where do Jenny and Oliver first meet in *Love Story*?
4 Who plays the subway ghost in *Ghost*?
5 Within fifteen minutes, how long does *Brief Encounter* last?
6 On whose novel is *The English Patient* based?
7 To which country does Kathleen Turner travel to save her sister in *Romancing the Stone*?
8 In what year is *Ryan's Daughter* set?
9 How much money does Holly Golightly receive for going to the 'powder room' in *Breakfast at Tiffany's*?
10 Which film is *An Affair to Remember* a remake of?
11 Which character does Humphrey Bogart play in the 1954 film *Sabrina*?
12 What is Jennie's last name in the film *Portrait of Jennie*?
13 Where is Beau's ranch in the film *Bus Stop*?
14 Who is Doctor Zhivago's childhood sweetheart?
15 Where is *Romeo and Juliet* set in the 1996 film?
16 Who owns the hotel that Jennifer Grey visits in *Dirty Dancing*?
17 What is Sandra Bullock's job in *While You Were Sleeping*?
18 Which fictional character was 'incapable of love, or tenderness or decency'?
19 On whose novel is *The Bridges of Madison County* based?
20 By what age would Julianne and Michael marry each other if they were not already married in the film *My Best Friend's Wedding*?
21 Who plays Fiona's brother in *Four Weddings and a Funeral*?
22 What's the name of the character that Monroe rents an apartment from in *The Seven Year Itch*?
23 What is the name of the youngest Dashwood sister in *Sense and Sensibility*?
24 Who was lined up for Bogart's role in *Casablanca*?
25 In which country did Amy Jolly seek romance?

**Answers Behind the Camera** (see Quiz 27)
**1** Orson Welles. **2** Marlon Brando. **3** *Things to Do in Denver when You're Dead.* **4** *The Other Half of the Sky.* **5** Robert Evans. **6** Jack Warner. **7** Nagisa Oshima. **8** *Shakespeare in Love.* **9** Howard Hawks (*The Big Sleep*). **10** Mike Leigh. **11** George Cukor. **12** Brian De Palma. **13** James Cameron. **14** James Whale. **15** Darryl F. Zanuck. **16** The street where he grew up – Mundy Lane. **17** Ace: *Iron Eagle III.* **18** Cher. **19** Marlon Brando. **20** Mel Brooks. **21** *The Hand.* **22** Jack Fisk. **23** Martin Scorsese. **24** Louis Malle. **25** *Everything You Always Wanted to Know About Sex... But Were Afraid to Ask.*

## *QUIZ 26* POT LUCK 9 ........................................ LEVEL 3

*Answers – see page 248*

1 What colour was the dress that Scarlett O'Hara made from her curtains?
2 What was Marlon Brando's first film, in 1950?
3 Within five minutes, how long does *Se7en* last?
4 Who directed the film *Body of Evidence*?
5 Which Jon featured in *Miller's Crossing*?
6 Who won the Best Actor Oscar for *The Champ*?
7 Who directed *Total Recall*?
8 In which film did a character named Leeloo appear?
9 What is Ted's middle name in *Bill & Ted's Excellent Adventure*?
10 Who did Joan Collins describe as, 'Short, myopic, not good looking'?
11 Which Pam starred in *Jackie Brown*?
12 Who was set to play Sofia Coppola's role in *The Godfather, Part III*, but pulled out on doctor's advice?
13 In which film did a pilot named Klaatu appear?
14 Who wrote the screenplay for the film *Billy Bathgate*?
15 Within fifteen minutes, how long does *Planet of the Apes* last?
16 Who directed *An Affair to Remember*?
17 Which Fiona featured in *The Avengers*?
18 In which film did Marisa Tomei make her debut?
19 Who wrote the screenplay for *The Bodyguard*?
20 For what did Ben Burtt win a Special Award in 1981?
21 What was the name of Spencer Tracy's character in *Father of the Bride*?
22 The song 'Secret Love' came from which movie?
23 Which Joan featured in *The Ice Storm*?
24 What movie is playing on a car radio in *The Flight of the Navigator*?
25 Who won the Best Director Oscar for *Cavalcade*?

**Answers Superstars** (see Quiz 28)
**1** 154. **2** 12 years. **3** Julie Andrews. **4** Robert Redford. **5** Shepherd. **6** Anthony Hopkins. **7** Charles Bronson. **8** Tony Curtis. **9** Lauren Bacall. **10** Holly Hunter. **11** Sylvester Stallone. **12** Alec Baldwin. **13** Philadelphia. **14** Meryl Streep. **15** Kim Basinger. **16** Harrison Ford. **17** Alec Guinness. **18** Syracuse Symphony Orchestra. **19** Lindsay Wagner. **20** *The Ugly American*. **21** Dan Aykroyd. **22** Julia Roberts. **23** Kim Basinger. **24** Michael Keaton. **25** Grimaldi.

## *QUIZ 27* BEHIND THE CAMERA ........ LEVEL 3

*Answers – see page 245*

1 Which director wrote the novel *Mr Arkadin*?
2 About which of his performers did Bernardo Bertolucci say, 'an angel of a man, a monster of an actor'?
3 What was Gary Fleder's directorial debut?
4 Which Oscar-nominated documentary did Shirley MacLaine co-direct in 1975?
5 Whose autobiography was called *The Kid Stays in the Picture*?
6 Which mogul said of Clark Gable, 'What the hell am I going to do with a guy with ears like that?'?
7 Who directed *Merry Christmas Mr Lawrence*?
8 What was John Madden's follow up to *Mrs Brown*?
9 Who directed the second Bogart and Bacall movie?
10 Who said, 'Given the choice of Hollywood or poking steel pins in my eyes, I'd prefer steel pins'?
11 Who was the last man to direct Garbo?
12 Which director did Nancy Allen marry?
13 Who was the director of the second *Alien* movie?
14 Who first directed Boris Karloff as Frankenstein?
15 Which production executive is in the American Croquet Hall of Fame?
16 What did Denzel Washington name his film company after?
17 What was John Glen's first feature after directing five Bond movies?
18 About whom did Peter Bogdanovich say, 'Working with her is like being in a blender with an alligator'?
19 Who took over directing *One Eyed Jacks* when Stanley Kubrick was sacked?
20 Which actor's company funded *The Elephant Man*?
21 Which low-budget horror movie did Oliver Stone direct in 1981?
22 Which production designer did Sissy Spacek meet on the set of *Badlands* and then marry?
23 Who directed the sequel to *The Hustler*?
24 Which French director said, 'It takes a long time to learn simplicity'?
25 What was Woody Allen's third movie as actor/director?

**Answers Romance** (see Quiz 25)
**1** *Everybody Comes to Rick's*. **2** Gladys Cooper. **3** In the library. **4** Vincent Schiavelli. **5** 86 minutes. **6** Michael Ondaatje. **7** Colombia. **8** 1916. **9** $50. **10** *Love Affair*. **11** Linus Larrabee. **12** Appleton. **13** Montana. **14** Tonya. **15** Venice Beach. **16** Max Kellerman. **17** Subway-ticket seller. **18** Rebecca de Winter (*Rebecca*). **19** Robert James Waller. **20** 28. **21** Simon Callow. **22** Richard Sherman. **23** Margaret. **24** Ronald Reagan. **25** Morocco (Dietrich character).

## *QUIZ 28* SUPERSTARS ........ LEVEL 3

*Answers – see page 246*

1 Within five points either way, what is Sharon Stone's IQ?
2 How much older than Harrison Ford was Sean Connery when he played his father?
3 About whom did Moss Hart say, 'She has that wonderful British strength. It makes you wonder why they lost India'?
4 Who founded the Institute of Resource Management to increase co-operation between developers and environmentalists?
5 What does Marlon Brando have on his passport as his profession?
6 Who dubbed Olivier's voice for extra scenes added to the 1990 release of *Spartacus*?
7 Who is known in Italy as 'Il Brutto'?
8 After netting a weekend with which actor did the winner say she'd have preferred the second prize of a fridge?
9 Who played Barbra Streisand's mother in *The Mirror Has Two Faces*?
10 Joel and Ethan Coen wrote *Raising Arizona* with whom in mind?
11 Who said, 'I built my body to carry my brain around in'?
12 Who gave up the chance to star in the sequel to *Patriot Games* so he could play Stanley Kowalski on Broadway?
13 Sidney Poitier plays a cop from which state in *In the Heat of the Night*?
14 Who did Cher describe as 'an acting machine in the same sense that a shark is a killing machine'?
15 Who recorded a pop album called *The Color of Sex*?
16 Who was voted Film Star of the Century in the 100th issue of *Empire* magazine?
17 Whose autobiography was called *Blessings in Disguise*?
18 With which orchestra did Richard Gere play trumpet when he was 16?
19 Which actress was born on exactly the same day as Meryl Streep?
20 In which movie did Brando's sister Jocelyn appear with him?
21 Who made his directorial debut with *Nothing But Trouble*?
22 Who said, 'I'm too tall to be a girl. I'm between a chick and a broad'?
23 Which actress once pursued a singing career and was known as Chelsea?
24 Who played Dogberry in Kenneth Branagh's production of Much *Ado About Nothing*?
25 What was Grace Kelly's married name?

**Answers Pot Luck 9** (see Quiz 26)
**1** Green. **2** *The Men* **3** 107 minutes. **4** Uli Edel. **5** Polito. **6** William Beery. **7** Paul Verhoeven. **8** *The Fifth Element.* **9** Theodore. **10** James Dean. **11** Grier. **12** Winona Ryder. **13** *The Day the Earth Stood Still.* **14** Tom Stoppard. **15** 119 minutes. **16** Leo McCarey. **17** Shaw. **18** *The Flamingo Kid.* **19** Lawrence Kasdan. **20** Sound effects editing on *Raiders of the Lost Ark.* **21** Stanley T. Banks. **22** *Calamity Jane.* **23** Allen. **24** *Grease.* **25** Frank Lloyd.

## *QUIZ 29* POT LUCK 10 .......... LEVEL 3

*Answers – see page 251*

1 Which Anita featured in *Barbarella*?
2 Who won the Best Actress Oscar for *Norma Rae*?
3 What is the name of the third eldest child in *The Sound of Music*?
4 Who did Michael Douglas play in *The Wonder Boys*?
5 *Flipper* and *Almost an Angel* starred which actor?
6 Within five minutes, how long does *Schindler's List* last?
7 Which Peter featured in *Fargo*?
8 Who directed *Tomorrow Never Dies*?
9 Which author appeared in *All at Sea*?
10 In which film did a character named Herbert Bock appear?
11 Which Roy said, 'There's not much to acting as far as I'm concerned'?
12 'Call Me Irresponsible' won an Oscar when it was used in which movie in 1963?
13 Who was Gort the robot in *The Day the Earth Stood Still*?
14 Which Jennifer featured in *The Fabulous Baker Boys*?
15 Richard Edlund won a Special Award for what in *Return of the Jedi*?
16 Burt Reynolds was born in which American state?
17 Who was the first woman to win consecutive best actress Oscars?
18 What novel does Paul Sheldon write whilst under the 'care' of Annie Wilkes?
19 Which Melanie featured in *Missing*?
20 How long does the 60s movie *101 Dalmatians* last?
21 In which year was *Shadow of Doubt* released?
22 Who won the Best Actor Oscar for *Free Soul*?
23 In which film did a character named Gabe Walker appear?
24 Who won the Best Director Oscar for *Going My Way*?
25 Which Richard featured in *Misery*?

**Answers 1940s** (see Quiz 31)
**1** *Adam's Rib.* **2** *All That Money Can Buy.* **3** *Foreign Correspondent.* **4** *The Palm Beach Story.* **5** *Two Faced Woman.* **6** Victor Mature & Hedy Lamarr. **7** *The Great Lie.* **8** *Lady in the Dark.* **9** *All That Money Can Buy.* **10** *The Pride of the Yankees.* **11** William Bendix. **12** *Pot O' Gold.* **13** Glenn Ford. **14** Paganini. **15** *The Tempest.* **16** Charlotte Bronte. **17** *Kiss of Death.* **18** *Champion.* **19** 'World'. **20** Claude Jarman Jr. **21** *Highway 66.* **22** *The Bishop's Wife.* **23** Olivia de Havilland. **24** Waiting outside a phone box. **25** *Follow the Boys.*

## *QUIZ 30* STARS OF THE SILENT YEARS ........ LEVEL 3

*Answers – see page 252*

1 Whose marriage to Rudolph Valentino lasted just one day?
2 Who made his debut in *For France*?
3 Who were the stars of D.W. Griffith's *Broken Blossoms*?
4 Who was the star of the first feature to be made in 3D?
5 Who gave Clara Bow the title of the 'It Girl'?
6 Who was the star of D.W. Griffith's *The White Rose*?
7 In which movie did Rin Tin Tin make his debut?
8 What was the first sound movie made by Pickford and Fairbanks?
9 What was Mary Pickford's real name?
10 Fatty Arbuckle was arrested on charges of rape and manslaughter in 1920 after whose death?
11 Whose autobiography was called *An American Comedy*?
12 Who told Mary Pickford, 'You're too little and too fat but I may give you a job'?
13 What was Douglas Fairbanks's real name?
14 Who starred in 300 westerns as Bronco Billy but could hardly ride a horse?
15 Who was known as 'The Biograph Girl with the Curls'?
16 Who did Chaplin go to work for in 1915 – at $1,000 a week?
17 What was Mabel Normand's real surname?
18 Peter Noble's biography *Hollywood Scapegoat* was about whom?
19 Which silent-movie star did Betty Grable marry in 1937?
20 Which single movie did Lillian Gish direct?
21 Whose affair with an entire football team was revealed in a court case where she sued her secretary in 1931?
22 Which famous screamer's first movie was *Street of Sin* in 1928?
23 What was Mary Pickford's autobiography called?
24 Who did George Cukor describe as 'a beautiful nothing'?
25 Who played 'the man with a thousand faces' in a fifties biopic?

**Answers Pot Luck 11** (see Quiz 32)
**1** Prosky. **2** *Somerset.* **3** Bruce Willis. **4** Helen Hayes. **5** *Nell.* **6** Magee. **7** Richard White. **8** Anthony Hopkins. **9** Harrison Ford. **10** Shepard. **11** George Stevens. **12** Montana. **13** Sissy Spacek. **14** Nina. **15** *The River.* **16** Pee-Wee Herman. **17** Aiello. **18** Eric Stoltz. **19** Ron Howard. **20** Sound in *Fantasia.* **21** 120 minutes. **22** *Mean Streets.* **23** Fierstein. **24** Singapore. **25** Peter Markle.

## *QUIZ 31* 1940s ........ LEVEL 3

*Answers – see page 249*

1 Which movie had the ad line, 'The dangerous age for women is from three to seventy'?
2 In which movie did Walter Huston play the devil?
3 Which movie did Hitchcock make to encourage the US to enter World War II?
4 Which movie opens with the line, 'And so they lived happily ever after. Or did they?'?
5 Which movie did Garbo make immediately before retiring?
6 Who played the title roles in Cecil B de Mille's *Samson and Delilah*?
7 In which movie did Mary Astor say, 'If I didn't think you meant so well, I'd feel like slapping your face'?
8 In which film did Mischa Auer say, 'This is the end, the absolute end'?
9 Which William Dieterle movie was based on the Faust story?
10 What was the second of Gary Cooper's three Oscar nominations between 1941 and 1943?
11 Who played Babe Ruth in *The Babe Ruth Story*?
12 What did James Stewart say was the worst of all his movies?
13 Who had two teeth knocked out by Rita Hayworth during the making of *Gilda*?
14 Who did Stewart Granger play in *The Magic Bow*?
15 *Yellow Sky* was based on which Shakespeare play?
16 Which writer did Olivia de Havilland play in *Devotion*?
17 For which movie was Richard Widmark Oscar-nominated on his film debut?
18 In which 1949 movie did Kirk Douglas play a boxer?
19 What is the last word of *White Heat*?
20 Who won a Special Oscar for *The Yearling*, aged 12?
21 What was the working title of *The Grapes of Wrath*?
22 In which movie did Cary Grant play an angel?
23 Who played two parts in *The Dark Mirror* in 1946?
24 What is Hitchcock's cameo appearance in *Rebecca*?
25 In which 1944 movie did Orson Welles play himself?

**Answers Pot Luck 10** (see Quiz 29)
**1** Pallenberg. **2** Sally Field. **3** Louisa. **4** Grady Tripp. **5** Paul Hogan. **6** 185 minutes. **7** Stormare. **8** Roger Spottiswoode. **9** Jackie Collins. **10** *The Hospital.* **11** Roy Rogers. **12** *Papa's Delicate Condition.* **13** Lock Martin. **14** Tilly. **15** Visual effects. **16** Georgia. **17** Luise Rainer. **18** *Misery's Child.* **19** Mayron. **20** 79 minutes. **21** 1943. **22** Lionel Barrymore. **23** *Cliffhanger.* **24** Leo McCarey. **25** Farnsworth.

## *QUIZ 32* POT LUCK 11 ........ LEVEL 3

*Answers – see page 250*

1 Which Robert featured in *Dead Man Walking*?
2 Which soap did Hollywood star Ted Danson star in?
3 Which movie star released an album called *Heart of Soul* in 1990?
4 Who won the Best Actress Oscar for *Sin of Madelon Claudet*?
5 A character named Jerome Lovell appeared in which film?
6 Which Patrick featured in *Barry Lyndon*?
7 Who voiced Gaston in the film *Beauty and the Beast*?
8 *Bookworm* and *Surviving Picasso* both starred which actor?
9 Who said, 'I ask for the money I want, they pay it. It's that simple'?
10 Which Sam featured in *Days of Heaven*?
11 Who won the Best Director Oscar for *A Place in the Sun*?
12 *The Horse Whisperer* is set in which US state?
13 Who plays the brain in the film *The Man with Two Brains*?
14 What was the name of Juliet Stevenson's character in *Truly, Madly, Deeply*?
15 In 1984 Kay Rose won a Special Award for sound effects editing on which movie?
16 Who plays Penguin's father in the film *Batman Returns*?
17 Which Danny featured in *Moonstruck*?
18 Who plays Rocky Dennis in *Mask*?
19 Who directed *Ransom*?
20 For what did Walt Disney win a Special Award in 1941?
21 Within five minutes, how long does *Platoon* last?
22 A character named Johnny Boy appeared in which film?
23 Which Harvey featured in *Mrs Doubtfire*?
24 What was the destination in the first *Road* film?
25 Who directed the film *Bat 21*?

**Answers Stars of the Silent Years** (see Quiz 30)
**1** Jane Acker. **2** Erich von Stroheim. **3** Richard Barthelmess & Lillian Gish. **4** Noah Beery. **5** Elinor Glyn. **6** Ivor Novello. **7** *The Man from Hell's River.* **8** *The Taming of the Shrew.* **9** Gladys Smith. **10** Virginia Rappe. **11** Harold Lloyd's. **12** D.W. Griffith. **13** Douglas Ullman. **14** Gilbert M. Anderson. **15** Mary Pickford. **16** Essanay. **17** Fortescue. **18** Erich von Stroheim. **19** Jackie Coogan. **20** *Remodelling Her Husband.* **21** Clara Bow. **22** Fay Wray. **23** *Sunshine and Shadow.* **24** Louise Brooks. **25** James Cagney.

## *QUIZ 33* BLOCKBUSTERS ........ LEVEL 3

*Answers – see page 255*

1 Which movie is *Twelve Monkeys* based on?
2 Who raised Hawkeye in *The Last of the Mohicans*?
3 Within fifteen minutes, how long does *The Godfather, Part II* last?
4 Who wrote the screenplay for *Unforgiven*?
5 What is the Penguin's real name in *Batman Returns*?
6 Which movie begins with 'No man's life can be encompassed in one telling'?
7 What film does Kevin Costner take Whitney Houston to see in The *Bodyguard*?
8 Which John co-directed *Aladdin*?
9 Who wrote the screenplay for *Basic Instinct*?
10 What colour are Woody's eyes in *Toy Story*?
11 What relation is Maid Marian to the King in *Robin Hood: Prince of Thieves*?
12 What is Peter Pan's job after he grows up in *Hook*?
13 Which character is played by Al Pacino in *Dick Tracy*?
14 Which president does Anthony Hopkins played in *Amistad*?
15 What colour ribbon holds together Jenny's chocolates in *Forrest Gump*, when Tom Hanks is sitting at the bus stop?
16 What is the name of Sam's scheming co-worker in *Ghost*?
17 What movie is playing within *When Harry Met Sally*?
18 Who plays Edward Scissorhands' father?
19 Which 80s hit was a remake of *Trois Hommes et un Couffin*?
20 The first script of which movie was called *The Man who Came to Play*?
21 Which palace was used for Kenneth Branagh's *Hamlet*?
22 Which daughter of a *Sound of Music* star appeared in *Pulp Fiction*?
23 In which publication did the Addams Family first appear?
24 Who plays Kevin Costner's father in *Robin Hood: Prince of Thieves*?
25 In what year is *The Last of the Mohicans* set?

**Answers Pot Luck 12** (see Quiz 35)
**1** Steven Spielberg. **2** Garry Marshall. **3** Colin Firth. **4** Ice Hockey. **5** Robert Duvall. **6** Helen Tasker. **7** 94 minutes. **8** *Captain Carey*. **9** Charles. **10** Madison. **11** *Wild at Heart*. **12** Elia Kazan. **13** Bob Hoskins. **14** Arndt. **15** Winchester '73. **16** Wayne Szalinski. **17** Marie. **18** *Slamdance*. **19** *Ghostbusters*. **20** Delpy. **21** Lisa Bonet. **22** Architecture. **23** 87 minutes. **24** Richard Blaney. **25** Spencer.

## *QUIZ 34* THE MARX BROTHERS ........ LEVEL 3

*Answers – see page 256*

1 Who was the oldest Marx Brother?
2 What was the name of their 1925 Broadway hit?
3 Which movie did they make immediately after *Monkey Business*?
4 Which brother's real name was Adolph but was also known as Arthur?
5 What was their last film for Paramount?
6 Who was Harpo cast as in *The Story of Mankind*?
7 Whose autobiography was called *Memoirs of a Mangy Lover*?
8 In which movie did they reunite after World War II?
9 Who directed their first movie for MGM?
10 Who replaced Harpo in *Androcles and the Lion* in 1952?
11 Which Brother made the shortest appearance in *Love Happy*?
12 What was the last movie they made before the death of producer Irving Thalberg?
13 What were the real names of the two brothers who left the team early on?
14 What was Harpo's most celebrated prop?
15 Which brother played romantic relief in their first five films?
16 What was the name of Groucho's son who published biographies of his father?
17 What was the name of their mother, daughter of vaudeville artists?
18 In which silent movie did Harpo make his debut?
19 To whom did Groucho say, 'Excuse me, I thought you were a fella I once knew in Pittsburgh'?
20 *Duck Soup* features the Presidency of which state?
21 Which Marx brother lived longest?
22 What was their name when they consisted of Groucho, Chico, Harpo, Gummo, their mother and her sister?
23 In which movie did they make their final appearance as a team?
24 What were Harpo's memoirs called?
25 Who received the only Oscar nomination for *A Day at the Races*?

**Answers Famous Names** (see Quiz 36)
**1** Burt Reynolds. **2** Keith Carradine. **3** *Butch Cassidy and the Sundance Kid.* **4** Karuna. **5** David Hemmings. **6** *The Crow.* **7** Ellen McRae. **8** Brigitta. **9** Robert Shaw. **10** Billy Crystal. **11** University of Wisconsin. **12** Hugh Grant. **13** Friday. **14** Argentina. **15** Tiffany. **16** *Together for Days.* **17** Winona Ryder. **18** Jane Wyman (once Mrs Ronald Reagan). **19** Peter O'Toole. **20** Patrick Godfrey. **21** Andrew Blyth Barrymore. **22** Sally Field. **23** Bruce Willis. **24** Poppy (*Prime Cut*). **25** Esterhuysen.

## *QUIZ 35* POT LUCK 12 ........ LEVEL 3

*Answers – see page 253*

1 Who said, 'The most expensive habit in the world is celluloid'?
2 Who directed *Pretty Woman*?
3 Who played Tommy Judd in the film *Another Country*?
4 At what sport did Keanu Reeves excel?
5 Who won the Best Actor Oscar for *Tender Mercies*?
6 What was the name of Jamie Lee Curtis's character in *True Lies*?
7 Within ten minutes, how long does *Porky's* last?
8 'Mona Lisa' won an Oscar when it was used in which movie in 1950?
9 Which Josh featured in *Dead Poets Society*?
10 What is the name of the mermaid in *Splash*?
11 In which film does a character named Sailor Ripley appear?
12 Who won the Best Director Oscar for *Gentleman's Agreement*?
13 *The Long Good Friday* and *Zulu Dawn* both starred which actor?
14 Which Denis featured in *Basic Instinct*?
15 Lin McAdam, played by James Stewart, searched for which stolen gun of his fathers?
16 What was the name of Rick Moranis's character in *Honey, I Shrunk the Kids*?
17 What is the first name of Debra Winger, who uses her middle name in the movies?
18 Which 1988 film did rock star Adam Ant star in?
19 In which movie does Bill Murray say, 'OK, so she's a dog'?
20 Which Julie starred in *Before Sunrise*?
21 Who played Epiphany Proudfoot in the film *Angel Heart*?
22 Which subject did James Mason study at Cambridge?
23 Within five minutes, how long does *Pinocchio* last?
24 What was the name of Jon Finch's character in *Frenzy*?
25 Which John featured in *Presumed Innocent*?

**Answers Blockbusters** (see Quiz 33)
**1** *La Jetée*. **2** Chingachgook. **3** 200 minutes. **4** David Webb Peoples. **5** Oscar Cobblepot. **6** *Gandhi*. **7** *Yojimbo*. **8** Musker. **9** Joe Eszterhas. **10** Brown. **11** Cousin. **12** Attorney. **13** Big Boy Caprice. **14** John Quincy Adams. **15** Yellow. **16** Carl. **17** *Casablanca*. **18** Vincent Price. **19** *Three Men and a Baby*. **20** *The Deer Hunter*. **21** Blenheim. **22** Amanda Plummer. **23** *The New Yorker*. **24** Brian Blessed. **25** 1757.

## *QUIZ 36* FAMOUS NAMES ........ LEVEL 3

*Answers – see page 254*

1 Who said, 'My movies were the kind they showed in planes or prisons because nobody can leave'?
2 Which actor is the father of actress Martha Plimpton?
3 In which movie did Paul Newman say, 'Who are these guys?'?
4 What is Uma Thurman's middle name?
5 Which star actor was born on exactly the same day as Juliet Mills?
6 Brandon Lee, son of Bruce, died during the making of which movie?
7 How was Ellen Burstyn billed in the 1960s?
8 Which member of the Von Trapp family did Hugh Grant play while still at school?
9 Which film star wrote the novel *The Sun Doctor*?
10 Whose movie career began as a pregnant man in *Rabbit Test*?
11 Where did Willem Dafoe study before beginning his acting career?
12 Who did Robert Downey Jr describe as a 'self important, boring, flash-in-the-pan Brit.'?
13 On which day of the week was Tuesday Weld born?
14 Where was Olivia Hussey born?
15 What is Richard Gere's middle name?
16 What was Samuel L. Jackson's very first movie?
17 Which actress has siblings called Sunyata, Jubal and Yuri?
18 Who said, 'I recommend marriage highly to everyone but me'?
19 Whose autobiography was called *Loitering with Intent*?
20 Who played Leonardo da Vinci in *Ever After*?
21 What is Drew Barrymore's full name?
22 Who was originally earmarked for the Cher role in *Moonstruck*?
23 Which actor sang in a band called Loose Goose?
24 Sissy Spacek made her movie debut playing which character opposite Gene Hackman and Lee Marvin?
25 What does the E stand for in Richard E. Grant's name?

**Answers The Marx Brothers** (see Quiz 34)
**1** Chico. **2** *The Cocoanuts.* **3** *Horse Feathers.* **4** Harpo. **5** *Duck Soup.* **6** Isaac Newton. **7** Groucho's. **8** *A Night in Casablanca.* **9** Sam Wood. **10** Alan Young. **11** Groucho. **12** *A Day at the Races.* **13** Milton (Gummo) & Herbert (Zeppo). **14** Taxi horn. **15** Zeppo. **16** Arthur. **17** Minnie Schoenberg. **18** *Too Many Kisses.* **19** Greta Garbo. **20** Fredonia. **21** Groucho. **22** The Six Musical Mascots. **23** *Love Happy.* **24** *Harpo Speaks!* **25** Dave Gould (choreography).

## *QUIZ 37* SCI-FI ........ LEVEL 3

*Answers – see page 259*

1 What planet does Leslie Nielsen land on in *Forbidden Planet*?
2 Which actor said about which part, 'Take my name... I haven't a clue what it's meant to mean'?
3 Who provided the voice of Hal 9000?
4 What is the name of the monster in *Twenty Million Miles to Earth*?
5 Who played Lois Lane in the first Superman movie of the 1970s?
6 What is the name of Princess Leia's father?
7 Upon which planet does Barbarella live?
8 Who composed the music for *Planet of the Apes*?
9 Which studio released *The Day the Earth Stood Still*?
10 Who played the monster in *The War of the Worlds*?
11 Who plays Elliott's older brother in *E.T.*?
12 In what year was *Blade Runner: The Director's Cut* released?
13 What colour are Chewbacca's eyes in *Star Wars*?
14 What are the names of Dr John Hammond's grandchildren in *Jurassic Park*?
15 Upon what day does the film *Independence Day* begin?
16 How many years into the future is *Starship Troopers* set?
17 Which *Star Wars* role did Al Pacino reject?
18 What was Dr Niko Tatopoulos researching prior to Godzilla's appearance?
19 Within fifteen minutes, how long does *The Empire Strikes Back* last?
20 Who directed the third *Star Wars* movie?
21 What caused 'The Incredible Shrinking Man' to shrink?
22 What is the name of Major Don West's ship in *Lost in Space*?
23 *Invasion of the Body Snatchers* starts at a hospital in which city?
24 What is the name of the professor in *Twenty Thousand Leagues under the Sea*?
25 Which planet are the Robinson family sent to colonize in *Lost in Space*?

**Answers 1950s** (see Quiz 39)
**1** John Longden. **2** *Marguerite of the Night.* **3** F. Scott Fitzgerald. **4** Julie Harris. **5** Double Bass. **6** *Fort Algiers.* **7** Donald O'Connor. **8** 8,552. **9** Dan O'Herlihy. **10** *The Love Lottery.* **11** Anthony Quinn. **12** *Somebody Up There Likes Me.* **13** Audrey Hepburn. **14** Karl Malden. **15** *Forever Darling.* **16** *Paris Holiday.* **17** Charles Laughton & Elsa Lanchester. **18** Dirk Bogarde. **19** Paul Gauguin. **20** Marilyn Monroe & Jean Hagen. **21** *Witness for the Prosecution.* **22** William Holden. **23** Eli Wallach. **24** The atom bomb. **25** *The Tempest.*

## *QUIZ 38* POT LUCK 13 ............ LEVEL 3

*Answers – see page 260*

1 At which number do the Banks live in *Mary Poppins*?
2 Which Jim starred in *The Beverly Hillbillies*?
3 In which film does a character named William Somerset appear?
4 Who directed the 90s movie *The Nutty Professor*?
5 What movie is shown within the film *Field of Dreams*?
6 Within five minutes, how long does *Philadelphia* last?
7 *Casino Royale* and *The Assam Garden* starred which actress?
8 Who wrote, 'If you can drive a car, you can direct a movie'?
9 Who won the Best Director Oscar for *Letter to Three Wives*?
10 Which Mike featured in *Mad Max II*?
11 Who links the soundtracks of *Psycho* and *Taxi Driver*?
12 What advice did Mel Brooks give Burt Reynolds on directing?
13 The Nazi in *Marathon Man* had been hiding in which country?
14 Who directed *Clear and Present Danger*?
15 What was director Tony Richardson's final film?
16 What was the name of the American in *An American in Paris*?
17 In which year was *DOA* released?
18 Who won the Best Actress Oscar for *Network*?
19 Which song from *Papa's Delicate Condition* won an Oscar?
20 What was the name of Elizabeth Taylor's character in *Who's Afraid of Virginia Woolf*?
21 Within ten minutes, how long does *Pocahontas* last?
22 Who directed *City of Angels*?
23 Which song from *Song of the South* won an Oscar?
24 A character named Leonard Lowe appeared in which film?
25 Which John featured in *Beverly Hills Cop*?

**Answers Oscars – Best Films & Directors** (see Quiz 40)
**1** *In Old Arizona*. **2** Seven. **3** Sam Mendes. **4** William Wyler. **5** Woody Allen. **6** Lewis Gilbert. **7** John Huston. **8** Bob Fosse, *Cabaret*. **9** Jonathan Demme. **10** Image Movers. **11** *The Apartment*. **12** *Johnny Belinda*. **13** Four. **14** *Jerry Maguire*. **15** Irving Pichel. **16** *Slow Dancing in the Big City*. **17** *Rebecca*. **18** *They Shoot Horses Don't They?* **19** Gardener. **20** *A Nervous Romance*. **21** American Zoetrope. **22** Barry Levinson's. **23** William Friedkin's. **24** Bob Fosse. **25** Oliver Stone.

## *QUIZ 39* 1950s ........ LEVEL 3

*Answers – see page 257*

1 Who played Sherlock Holmes in *The Man with the Twisted Lip*?
2 In which movie did Yves Montand play the devil?
3 Which writer did Gregory Peck play in *Beloved Infidel*?
4 Who played Sally Bowles in *I Am a Camera*?
5 In *Strangers on a Train* what is Hitchcock seen carrying on to the train?
6 In which movie does Yvonne De Carlo sing 'I'll Follow You'?
7 Who played Keaton in *The Buster Keaton Story*?
8 To the nearest 100, how many animals were there in *Around the World in Eighty Days*?
9 Who played Crusoe in *The Adventures of Robinson Crusoe*?
10 In which 1954 movie did Humphrey Bogart play himself?
11 Who played the title role in *The Hunchback of Notre Dame*?
12 In which 1956 movie did Paul Newman play a boxer?
13 Who severely hurt her back making *The Unforgiven*?
14 Who dislocated Marlon Brando's shoulder making *A Streetcar Named Desire*?
15 In which movie did James Mason play an angel?
16 In which of his own movies did Preston Sturgess appear in 1958?
17 Which husband and wife were Oscar-nominated together in 1957?
18 Who played two parts in *Libel* in 1959?
19 Who did Anthony Quinn play on screen in *Lust for Life*?
20 Who played the gangsters' molls in *The Asphalt Jungle*?
21 In which movie did Tyrone Power have his final completed role?
22 Who played the innocent to Gloria Swanson's Norma Desmond in *Sunset Boulevard*?
23 Whose withdrawal from *From Here to Eternity* meant Frank Sinatra got the part?
24 *The Thing* was based on a fear of what?
25 *Forbidden Planet* was based on which Shakespeare play?

**Answers Sci Fi** (see Quiz 37)
**1** Altair 4. **2** Alec Guinness, Ben Obi Wan Kenobi. **3** Douglas Rain. **4** Ymir. **5** Margot Kidder. **6** Bail Organa. **7** Sorgo. **8** Jerry Goldsmith. **9** 20th Century Fox. **10** Charles Gemora. **11** Robert MacNaughton. **12** 1992. **13** Blue. **14** Lex and Timmy. **15** July 2nd. **16** 400. **17** Hans Solo. **18** Chernobyl earthworms. **19** 124 mins. **20** Richard Marquand. **21** A cloud of mist. **22** Jupiter 2. **23** San Francisco. **24** Pierre Aronnax. **25** Alpha Prime.

## *QUIZ 40* OSCARS – BEST FILMS & DIRECTORS ........ LEVEL 3

*Answers – see page 258*

1 What was the first western to be nominated for Best Film?
2 How many nominations did *The Insider* have?
3 Which director holds the record for most nominations by a first-time non-American director?
4 Who won his third Best Director for his third Best Picture in 1959?
5 Who directed the first two films for which Dianne Wiest won an award?
6 Who did Carol Reed replace on *Oliver!*?
7 Which winner was an amateur lightweight boxing champion in the early 20s?
8 Who was the only 70s director to win but not see his movie win Best Film?
9 Which 90s winning director is a former producer for New World Productions?
10 Which company did Robert Zemeckis found in 1997?
11 What was the last black-and-white picture to win Best Film before *Schindler's List*?
12 Which multi-nomination movie had the ad line, 'There was temptation in her helpless silence – then torment'?
13 Out of 12 nominations, how many awards did *The Song of Bernadette* win?
14 What was James L. Brooks's first nomination of the 90s?
15 Who was the unseen narrator of *How Green Was My Valley*?
16 What was John G. Avildsen's next movie after his first award?
17 In which movie did Judith Anderson say, 'You're overwrought, madam. I've opened a window for you....'?
18 Which Jane Fonda movie gave Sydney Polack his first nomination?
19 What was The Last Emperor's job in Mao's Republic?
20 What was the subtitle of *Annie Hall*?
21 Which studio did Coppola set up after the success of *The Godfather*?
22 Whose first wife was screenwriter Valerie Curtin?
23 Whose biography was called *Hurricane Billy*?
24 Who was nominated for a 70s movie based on his own life?
25 Who, on receiving his award said, 'I think you are really acknowledging the Vietnam veteran...'?

**Answers Pot Luck 13** (see Quiz 38)
**1** 17. **2** Varney. **3** *Se7en*. **4** Tom Shadyac. **5** *Harvey*. **6** 119 minutes. **7** Deborah Kerr. **8** John Landis. **9** Joseph L. Mankiewicz. **10** Preston. **11** Bernard Herrmann. **12** Fire someone on the first day. **13** Uruguay. **14** Phillip Noyce. **15** *Blue Sky*. **16** Jerry Mulligan. **17** 1950. **18** Faye Dunaway. **19** 'Call Me Irresponsible'. **20** Martha. **21** 81 mins. **22** Brad Silberling. **23** 'Zip-A-Dee-Doo-Dah'. **24** *Awakenings*. **25** Ashton.

## *QUIZ 41* POT LUCK 14 ........ LEVEL 3

*Answers – see page 263*

1 Which film star was born on the same day as Gymnast Olga Korbut?
2 Who designed The Riddler's costume in *Batman Forever*?
3 Who won the Best Director Oscar for *Rocky*?
4 Which movie featured 5,000 unpaid New Yorkers as extras?
5 What was Doris Day's first film, in 1948?
6 In which film does a character named Louis Dega appear?
7 Which Ralph featured in *The Bodyguard*?
8 Who played the villain in *Moonraker*?
9 Within five minutes, how long does *The Piano* last?
10 Who won the Best Actor Oscar for *The Informer*?
11 *King Kong* and *All That Jazz* starred which actress?
12 Who links *Forbidden Planet* made in 1956 and *Spy Hard* in 1996?
13 Who directed *My Best Friend's Wedding*?
14 What does Julie Andrews hold in her left hand on *The Sound of Music* movie poster?
15 What was the name of Alan Rickman's character in *Truly, Madly, Deeply*?
16 Where in America was Raquel Welch born?
17 Which film includes clips from *Dracula* and *Strangers on a Train*?
18 Who was the butler in *Princess Caraboo*?
19 Which Ron featured in *Reversal of Fortune*?
20 In which film does a character named Jim Stark appear?
21 Which writer directed *Dream Wife* in 1953?
22 How old was Sam Raimi when he directed *The Evil Dead*?
23 Who has a production company called Edited?
24 Which John featured in *The Pelican Brief*?
25 In which film does a character named Jane Spencer appear?

**Answers James Bond** (see Quiz 43)
**1** Ian Fleming. **2** *Goldfinger*. **3** *Casino Royale*. **4** Two. **5** Hamburg. **6** *GoldenEye*. **7** *Licence to Kill*. **8** *Dr No*. **9** *Never Say Never Again*. **10** Barbara Bach. **11** George Lazenby. **12** *Live and Let Die*. **13** 117 minutes. **14** Stoke Poges. **15** *Thunderball*. **16** *You Only Live Twice*. **17** *A View to a Kill*. **18** Spectre. **19** Auric. **20** *You Only Live Twice*. **21** *Dr No*. **22** Carver. **23** Ian Fleming's home in Jamaica. **24** 'No news is bad news'. **25** *A View to a Kill*.

## *QUIZ 42* FILM FESTIVALS .................... LEVEL 3

*Answers – see page 264*

1 For which movie did Shirley MacLaine win Best Actress at Berlin in 1971?
2 What won the International Jury Prize at the first Cannes festival?
3 Who took the Palme D'Or at Cannes in 1985 for *When Father Was Away on Business*?
4 What is the full name of the Best Film award at Venice?
5 Who shared Golden Lions in 1980 for *Gloria* and *Atlantic City*?
6 What was the nationality of the 1996 winner in Berlin?
7 In what year was the Palme D'Or inaugurated at Cannes?
8 How many prizes were given at Cannes in 1947 for all film genres?
9 Between which years was the Venice Film Festival suspended?
10 For which movie did Edward G. Robinson win at Cannes at the last festival of the 40s?
11 Which 1990s movie won a Golden Lion for Neil Jordan?
12 For which movie did Elodie Bouchez and Natacha Regnier share Best Actress at Cannes in 1998?
13 For which movie did Cher win Best Actress at Cannes in 1985?
14 Who won at Cannes the year before starring in *Evita*?
15 In what year after its inauguration was no Golden Bear given?
16 Which actress won in Venice in 1993 for *Three Colours: Blue*?
17 Who won Best Actress at Cannes for *Cal* and *The Madness of King George*?
18 Which two Brits won Best Actor and Actress at Cannes in 1965?
19 Who won the Best Actress award at Cannes in 1997?
20 How was Ingmar Bergman's Golden Bear winner *Smultonstallet* also known?
21 Which very English collection of stories was a winner in Berlin for Pasolini in 1972?
22 Who won Best Actress at Cannes for *La Reine Margot*?
23 Who won the inaugural Golden Bear award?
24 What were the short-lived European Film Awards called?
25 Who received the Golden Lion for *Rosencrantz and Guildenstern Are Dead*?

**Answers Pot Luck 15** (see Quiz 44)
**1** *As the World Turns.* **2** Daryl Hannah. **3** James Frawley. **4** Taylor. **5** 101 minutes. **6** *Don't Look Now.* **7** 1940s. **8** Patricia Neal. **9** Miller. **10** Burt Reynolds. **11** 141 minutes. **12** Adrian Cronauer. **13** *Aladdin.* **14** Ford. **15** *Cabaret.* **16** Alan J. Pakula. **17** *Drugstore Cowboy.* **18** Skerritt. **19** Leo McCarey. **20** Tom Topor. **21** Goldie Hawn. **22** Daniella Bianchi. **23** Tasmania (Australia). **24** *Planet of the Apes.* **25** Daniels.

## *QUIZ 43* JAMES BOND ........ LEVEL 3

*Answers – see page 261*

1 Who described James Bond as 'a blunt instrument wielded by a government department'?
2 Which 007 movie did Sean Connery make prior to *Marnie*?
3 Which Bond film did Deborah Kerr appear in?
4 How many Bond films were released during Ian Fleming's lifetime?
5 Where is the first hour of *Tomorrow Never Dies* set?
6 Which movie's villain was Xenia Onatopp?
7 Which movie first had the toothpaste with plastic explosive?
8 What is the only Bond movie not to have an action sequence before the credits?
9 In which movie did Rowan Atkinson (a.k.a. Mr Bean) make his big-screen debut?
10 Which Bond girl married a Beatle?
11 Which 007 backed the restaurant chain the Spy House?
12 Which movie had the electromagnetic watch with the spinning blade?
13 Within fifteen minutes, how long does *You Only Live Twice* last?
14 Which golf course featured in *Goldfinger*?
15 What was the most successful Bond film of the 70s and 80s in terms of cinema admissions?
16 What was the final Bond movie, as far as Ian Fleming was concerned?
17 May Day was the Bond girl in which film?
18 In the films, what replaced the Soviet organization Smersh which existed in the books?
19 What was Goldfinger's first name?
20 In which movie did Blofeld kidnap US and USSR spaceships to try and gain planetary control?
21 Which Bond movie opened during the Cuban missile crisis?
22 What is the name of the villain in the movie that preceded *The World Is Not Enough*?
23 What was *GoldenEye* named after?
24 What is the motto of the villain in *Tomorrow Never Dies*?
25 What was the last film where Lois Maxwell played Miss Moneypenny?

**Answers Pot Luck 14** (see Quiz 41)
**1** Debra Winger (16.5.55). **2** Jim Carrey. **3** John G. Avildsen. **4** *King Kong* remake. **5** *Romance on the High Seas.* **6** *Papillon.* **7** Waite. **8** Michael Lonsdale. **9** 120 minutes. **10** Victor McLaglen. **11** Jessica Lange. **12** Leslie Nielsen. **13** P.J. Hogan. **14** Guitar case. **15** Jamie. **16** Chicago. **17** *Innocent Blood.* **18** Kevin Kline. **19** Silver. **20** *Rebel Without a Cause.* **21** Sidney Sheldon. **22** 19. **23** Jack Lemmon. **24** Heard. **25** *Naked Gun: From the Files of Police Squad.*

## *QUIZ 44* POT LUCK 15 ........ LEVEL 3

*Answers – see page 262*

1 Which soap did Meg Ryan star in?
2 Which actress links *Blade Runner* and *Legal Eagles*?
3 Who directed *The Muppet Movie*?
4 Which Christine featured in *The Wedding Singer*?
5 Within ten minutes, how long does *The Mask* last?
6 A character named John Baxter appeared in which film?
7 The action of *The Godfather* starts in which decade?
8 Who won the Best Actress Oscar for *Hud*?
9 Which Larry featured in the 90s movie *The Nutty Professor*?
10 Which movie star released a single called 'I Like Having You Around' in 1974?
11 Within five minutes, how long does *The Pelican Brief* last?
12 Who did Robin Williams play in *Good Morning, Vietnam*?
13 Which 1990s movie concerned the city of Agrabah?
14 Which Steven featured in *When Harry Met Sally*?
15 Philosophy student Brian Roberts turns up in which movie?
16 Who directed *Klute* and *The Pelican Brief*?
17 Which film is based upon an unpublished novel by James Fogle, written whilst he was in prison?
18 Which Tom featured in *A River Runs Through It*?
19 Who won the Best Director Oscar for *The Awful Truth*?
20 Who wrote the screenplay for *The Accused*?
21 Which actress links *Dollars* and *Butterflies Are Free*?
22 Who played the Bond girl in *From Russia with Love*?
23 In which country was Errol Flynn born?
24 John Chambers won an Honorary Oscar Award in 1968 for make-up in which film?
25 Which William featured in *The Parallax View*?

**Answers Film Festivals** (see Quiz 42)
**1** *Desperate Characters.* **2** *The Battle of the Rails.* **3** Emir Kusturica. **4** Golden Lion of St Mark. **5** John Cassavetes & Louis Malle. **6** Taiwanese (Ang Lee). **7** 1955. **8** Six. **9** 1942 & 1946. **10** *House of Strangers.* **11** *Michael Collins.* **12** *Dream Life of Angels.* **13** *Mask.* **14** Jonathan Pryce. **15** 1970. **16** Juliette Binoche. **17** Helen Mirren. **18** Terence Stamp & Samantha Eggar. **19** Kathy Burke. **20** *Wild Strawberries.* **21** *The Canterbury Tales.* **22** Virna Lisi. **23** Gene Kelly. **24** Felixes. **25** Tom Stoppard.

## QUIZ 45 1960s STARS ........ LEVEL 3

*Answers – see page 267*

1 What was William Wyler's third movie with Audrey Hepburn?
2 Which role did John Wayne play in *North to Alaska*?
3 What was Marilyn Monroe's penultimate completed movie?
4 For which movie did Burt Lancaster win an Oscar for his second nomination?
5 Who did Robert Mitchum play in *The Sundowners*?
6 In which movie did Zero Mostel say, 'He who hesitates is poor'?
7 What was the first of Richard Burton's three Oscar nominations between 1964 and 1966?
8 Who inspired the David Hemmings role in Antonioni's *Blow Up*?
9 What was the sequel to *One Million Years BC*?
10 Who wrote the novel *A Christmas Story* the same year as starring in *Night of the Iguana*?
11 In which film of her father's did Anjelica Huston make her screen debut?
12 Sean Connery's first father-in-law was a world authority on what subject?
13 In *The Birds*, Hitchcock walks past Tippi Hedren with what?
14 Which then husband and wife starred in *The Illustrated Man*?
15 Who played Elizabeth I in *Seven Seas to Calais*?
16 Which actor 'killed' Ronald Reagan in his final film *The Killers*?
17 Which singer was Oscar-nominated for his role as a shell-shocked GI in *Captain Newman MD*?
18 Who did Alec Guinness play in *Lawrence of Arabia*?
19 Who played Bob & Ted, in *Bob and Carol and Ted and Alice*?
20 Julie Christie won an Oscar for *Darling* after which US actress turned the part down?
21 Who links *The Dirty Dozen* and *Rosemary's Baby*?
22 Who directed and starred in *Charlie Bubbles* in 1968?
23 Who is the only US actor in *King Rat*?
24 Who played the title role in *Dr No*?
25 Which Redgrave appeared in *A Man for All Seasons*?

**Answers Pot Luck 16** (see Quiz 47)
**1** Chocolate. **2** Barry Sonnenfeld. **3** Wood. **4** Mark Rutland. **5** Tatum O'Neal. **6** 110 minutes. **7** Barbara Hershey. **8** Morse. **9** 'Baby It's Cold Outside'. **10** John Book. **11** Walter & John Huston. **12** Brestoff. **13** Katherine Hepburn. **14** Richard Marquand. **15** *Jackie Brown*. **16** Art Carney. **17** *The Accidental Tourist*. **18** Joel Schumacher. **19** 1993. **20** 'Last Dance'. **21** Russo. **22** Richard Attenborough. **23** Moor Azeem. **24** 117 minutes. **25** Norman.

## *QUIZ 46* FILM COMPANIES & STUDIOS ........ LEVEL 3

*Answers – see page 268*

1 Who founded Lightstorm Entertainment with James Cameron?
2 Who has a company called Flower Productions?
3 Who became an independent producer after appearing as Jethro in *The Beverley Hillbillies*?
4 Who bought Vitagraph in 1925?
5 Who founded New World Pictures in 1970?
6 Who set up M & M Productions?
7 Which studio made the 1954 *Godzilla* movie?
8 Who founded the Oz Film Manufacturing Company in 1914?
9 Who was the only female founder member of First Artists?
10 What was Warner Brothers' follow-up talkie to *The Jazz Singer*?
11 Who announced a $65 million loss after the failure of *Meet Joe Black*?
12 In which film did Paramount introduce Vistavision?
13 Which record company bought Universal in 1952?
14 What were Pinewood Studios first used for at the start of World War II?
15 What was the most successful company that made B movies?
16 Who replaced Louis B. Mayer at MGM in 1951?
17 Which Moscow-born composer was head of RKO's music department from 1941 to 1952?
18 Which company asked Oliver Stone to make *Salvador*?
19 Menahem Golan and Yoram Globus took over which company in 1979?
20 What was First Artists' first movie after Steve McQueen joined the company?
21 What is Denzel Washington's film company called?
22 Which millionaire bought 20th Century Fox in 1981?
23 What was Fox's wide screen system pioneered in 1929 called?
24 Who set up the computer-effects company Digital Domain?
25 Who acquired Paramount in 1966?

**Answers John Ford** (see Quiz 48)
**1** Sean Aloysius O'Feeney. **2** Aquarius. **3** 12. **4** Member of the Ku Klux Klan. **5** *The Iron Horse; Four Sons.* **6** Monument Valley. **7** *The Battle of Midway; December 7th.* **8** Four. **9** Orson Welles. **10** 1973. **11** *The Tornado.* **12** *Three Bad Men.* **13** *How Green Was My Valley.* **14** Argosy Productions. **15** *She Wore a Yellow Ribbon.* **16** Mervyn LeRoy. **17** *Seven Women.* **18** *Mogambo.* **19** Peter Bogdanovich. **20** *The Quiet Man.* **21** *Drums Along the Mohawk.* **22** George O'Brien. **23** *The Quiet Man.* **24** Universal. **25** *Straight Shooting.*

## *QUIZ 47* POT LUCK 16 ........ LEVEL 3

*Answers – see page 265*

1 What type of sauce was used in the shower scene in *Psycho*?
2 Who directed *Men in Black*?
3 Which John featured in *War Games*?
4 What was the name of Sean Connery's character in *Marnie*?
5 Who was the youngest performer in the 20th century to win an Oscar open to adults?
6 Within ten minutes, how long does *Mission: Impossible* last?
7 Which actress links *Splitting Heirs* and *The Portrait of a Lady*?
8 Which David featured in *The Rock*?
9 Which song from *Neptune's Daughter* won an Oscar?
10 Who does Harrison Ford play in *Witness*?
11 Which father and son, actor and director, won Oscars for *The Treasure of the Sierra Madre*?
12 Which Richard featured in *Car Wash*?
13 Who played Tracy Lord in *The Philadelphia Story*?
14 Who directed *Return of the Jedi*?
15 What was Quentin Tarantino's third film as a director?
16 Who won the Best Actor Oscar for *Harry and Tonto*?
17 A character named Muriel Pritchett appears in which film?
18 Who directed *Batman Forever*?
19 In which year did Audrey Hepburn die?
20 Which song won Best Song Oscar for *Thank God It's Friday*?
21 Which James featured in *My Own Private Idaho*?
22 Who was Jane Seymour's first father-in-law?
23 What was the name of Morgan Freeman's character in *Robin Hood: Prince of Thieves*?
24 Within five minutes, how long does *Patriot Games* last?
25 Which Zack featured in *Romancing the Stone*?

**Answers 1960s Stars** (see Quiz 45)
**1** *How to Steal a Million.* **2** Big Sam. **3** *Let's Make Love.* **4** *Elmer Gantry.* **5** Paddy Carmody. **6** *The Producers.* **7** *Becket.* **8** David Bailey. **9** *When Dinosaurs Ruled the Earth.* **10** Richard Burton. **11** *A Walk with Love and Death.* **12** Tropical medicine (Diane Cilento's father). **13** Two dogs. **14** Rod Steiger & Claire Bloom. **15** Irene Worth. **16** Lee Marvin. **17** Bobby Darin. **18** Prince Feisal. **19** Elliott Gould & Robert Culp. **20** Shirley MacLaine. **21** John Cassavetes. **22** Albert Finney. **23** George Segal. **24** Joseph Wiseman. **25** Corin.

## *QUIZ 48* JOHN FORD ........ LEVEL 3

*Answers – see page 266*

1 What was John Ford's real name?
2 Under what star sign was he born?
3 How many older siblings did he have?
4 He appeared in *Birth of a Nation* as an extra, playing what?
5 Which two silent movies did he direct in 1924 and 1928?
6 Where, on the Arizona–Utah line, did he make nine movies?
7 Which two of his World War II documentaries won Oscars?
8 How many times did he win the New York Film Critics Award?
9 Who, when asked which US directors appealed to him most, said, 'The Old Masters. John Ford, John Ford and John Ford'?
10 In what year did Ford die?
11 What was his first two-reeler called?
12 Which 20s movie was about the Oklahoma land rush?
13 What did he win an Oscar for the year after *The Grapes of Wrath*?
14 Which company did he form with Merian C. Cooper?
15 What was the middle film of his so-called Cavalry Trilogy?
16 Who replaced him on the set of *Mister Roberts* after he reputedly argued with Henry Fonda?
17 What was his final feature film?
18 Which of his films was a remake of *Red Dust*?
19 Who made the documentary *Directed By John Ford*?
20 Which film starred John Wayne and was set in the Emerald Isle?
21 In which 1939 film did he direct Henry Fonda and co-star Claudette Colbert?
22 Which star of *The Iron Horse* did he direct again in *Salute*?
23 For which movie did he win an unprecedented fourth Oscar?
24 What was the first Hollywood studio he worked for?
25 What was his first feature film?

**Answers Film Companies & Studios** (see Quiz 46)
**1** Lawrence Kasanoff. **2** Drew Barrymore. **3** Max Baer Jr. **4** Warner Brothers. **5** Roger Corman. **6** Michael Caine. **7** Toho Studios. **8** Frank L. Baum. **9** Barbra Streisand. **10** *The Singing Fool.* **11** Universal. **12** *White Christmas.* **13** Decca. **14** Food storage. **15** Republic Studios. **16** Dore Schary. **17** Constantin Bakaleinikoff. **18** Hemdale. **19** Cannon Films. **20** *Pocket Money.* **21** Mundy Lane. **22** Marvin Davis. **23** Fox Grandeur. **24** James Cameron. **25** Gulf Western.

## *QUIZ 49* 1990s STARS ........ LEVEL 3

*Answers – see page 271*

1 Who sets out to trap Pierce Brosnan in *The Thomas Crown Affair*?
2 What is Jim Carrey's middle name?
3 Which English actress said, 'When you're called a character actress it's because you're too ugly to be called a leading lady'?
4 Where was Samuel L. Jackson born?
5 Who does Nicolas Cage play in *Face/Off*?
6 Who played Leonardo DiCaprio's mother in *This Boy's Life*?
7 Which 90s Oscar nominee made his debut aged five in *Pound*?
8 Which star of TV's *Taxi* starred in *Independence Day*?
9 Who replaced Mia Farrow in *Manhattan Murder Mystery*?
10 Which star of *Heavenly Creatures* was Oscar-nominated a year later?
11 Who directed and starred in *Hoffa* in 1992?
12 Which actress, also an accomplished artist, exhibited with Christian Fenouillat in 1994?
13 In which movie did Kate Winslet have her first nude scene?
14 What is Ralph Fiennes's middle name?
15 Who played John Lennon in *Backbeat*?
16 Which painter did Joss Ackland play in *Surviving Picasso*?
17 Which star of *Mouse Hunt* runs Little Mo Productions?
18 Which perfume house did Rupert Everett model for in adverts?
19 Who was Woody Allen's ex wife in *Deconstructing Harry*?
20 John Candy died during the making of which movie?
21 What was Whitney Houston's follow-up to *The Bodyguard*?
22 Which 90s Oscar nominee is a founder of the Atlanta-based Just Us Theatre Company?
23 Which aunt of Macaulay Culkin appeared in *Shadow of a Doubt*?
24 What was Hugh Grant's first movie to be made in Hollywood?
25 Who played Lyon Gaultier in the 90s movie *AWOL*?

**Answers Warren Beatty** (see Quiz 51)
**1** Henry Warren Beaty. **2** Aries. **3** Buck Henry. **4** Natalie Wood. **5** *Shampoo*. **6** Director (*Reds*). **7** 'Sooner or Later'. **8** Vivien Leigh. **9** Tess Trueheart. **10** Gene Hackman. **11** Diane Keaton. **12** *The Many Loves of Doby Gillis*. **13** *Shampoo*. **14** *The Pick Up Artist*. **15** *Butch Cassidy and the Sundance Kid*. **16** Paula Prentiss. **17** *Here Comes Mr Jordan*. **18** *Reds*. **19** Frank Sinatra. **20** Madonna. **21** Charles Boyer & Irene Dunne. **22** Elaine May. **23** Bugsy Siegel. **24** Kansas. **25** Woody Allen.

## *QUIZ 50* POT LUCK 17 ........ LEVEL 3

*Answers – see page 272*

1 *Jackie Brown* is based on whose bestseller, *Rum Punch*?
2 Which Diane featured in *The Wicker Man*?
3 Who directed *Lost in Space*?
4 Who starred with Terence Stamp in 60s movie *The Collector*?
5 Which actress links *Raising Arizona* and *Once Around*?
6 Within five minutes, how long does *Pale Rider* last?
7 Who was Daniel Day-Lewis's actress mother?
8 Who played Charlie's handsome colleague in *Roxanne*?
9 What was the name of Edward Woodward's character in *The Wicker Man*?
10 Who played Addy in the film *City Heat*?
11 Who won the Best Director Oscar for *The Divine Lady*?
12 In which land is *The Neverending Story* set?
13 Within ten minutes, how long does *Invasion of the Body Snatchers* last?
14 Which Paul featured in *Romeo + Juliet*?
15 What was the name of Anthony Hopkins's character in *The Elephant Man*?
16 Who directed *Butterfield 8*?
17 Who won the Best Director Oscar for *The Last Emperor*?
18 Who played Peter Falk's grandson in *The Princess Bride*?
19 Who played Bonnie Rayburn in the film *City Slickers*?
20 In which film did a character named Griffin Mill appear?
21 The song 'Swinging on a Star' came from which movie?
22 Who played opposite Elliott Gould in the 70s remake of *The Lady Vanishes*?
23 Which Carrie featured in *Pale Rider*?
24 Who won the Best Actress Oscar for *Two Women*?
25 Who directed *The Cable Guy*?

**Answers Late Greats** (see Quiz 52)
**1** Cartoonist & illustrator. **2** *Rio Lobos.* **3** Fatty Arbuckle. **4** Peggy Ashcroft. **5** Ginger Rogers. **6** *San Francisco.* **7** Peter Finch. **8** Henry Fonda. **9** Howard Hughes. **10** 'Old Cary Grant fine. How you?' **11** *Waterloo Bridge.* **12** Fred Karno. **13** Morgan. **14** Alan Ladd. **15** 1975. **16** Peter Sellers. **17** Tuberculosis. **18** Ludlow Ogden Smith's. **19** *Brainstorm.* **20** Pier Angeli. **21** *The Manchurian Candidate.* **22** *Something's Got to Give.* **23** Alice Faye. **24** Tolochenaz, Switzerland. **25** Anne of Cleves (Elsa Lanchester).

## *QUIZ 51* WARREN BEATTY ............ LEVEL 3

*Answers – see page 269*

1 What is his full real name?
2 Under what star sign was he born?
3 Who was his co-director in *Heaven Can Wait*?
4 Who was his co-star in his feature film debut?
5 Which of his movies was set on the eve of the 1968 election?
6 In what capacity did he win an Oscar for the movie based on *Ten Days that Shook the World*?
7 What song won Best Song Oscar in his movie with Madonna?
8 Who was his co-star in *The Roman Spring of Mrs Stone*?
9 Which character was his true love in *Dick Tracy*?
10 Who played his brother in his first Oscar-nominated movie?
11 Who was his female co-star in the movie where he played John Reed?
12 In which US TV series did he appear in the 50s?
13 Which movie gave him his second Oscar nomination?
14 He was executive producer on which movie in the same year that *Ishtar* flopped?
15 Which movie did he turn down to do *The Only Game in Town*?
16 Who was his co-star in *The Parallax View*?
17 His third movie with Julie Christie was a remake of which movie?
18 Which movie was advertised as 'Never since *Gone with the Wind* has there been a great romantic epic like it'?
19 Who did he replace on *The Only Game in Town*?
20 In whose documentary *Truth or Dare* did he feature in 1991?
21 Who were the original stars of *Love Affair*, which he remade in 1994?
22 Who directed the 80s comedy flop where he starred with Dustin Hoffman?
23 Who was the subject of the biopic where he met his wife?
24 Where was his first feature-length movie set?
25 Who said if he came back in another life he wanted to be Warren Beatty's fingertips?

**Answers 1990s Stars** (see Quiz 49)
**1** Rene Russo. **2** Eugene. **3** Kathy Burke. **4** Chatanooga, Tennessee. **5** Castor Troy. **6** Ellen Barkin. **7** Robert Downey Jr. **8** Judd Hirsch. **9** Diane Keaton. **10** Kate Winslet. **11** Danny DeVito. **12** Juliette Binoche. **13** *Jude*. **14** Nathaniel. **15** Ian Hart. **16** Matisse. **17** Lee Evans. **18** Yves St Laurent. **19** Kirstie Alley. **20** *Wagons East*. **21** *Waiting to Exhale*. **22** Samuel L. Jackson. **23** Bonnie Bedelia. **24** *Nine Months*. **25** Jean Claude van Damme.

## *QUIZ 52* LATE GREATS ........................................ LEVEL 3

*Answers – see page 270*

1 What was Gary Cooper's job before he became an actor?
2 Which movie was John Wayne working on when he won his Oscar for *True Grit*?
3 Which silent-movie star turned director using the pseudonym William Goodrich?
4 Who appeared in a 30s classic and was Oscar-nominated for her final film in 1984?
5 Which superstar did Lew Ayres marry after Lola Lane?
6 In which movie did Clark Gable play Blackie Norton?
7 How was William Mitchell better known?
8 Cartoonist Al Capp based Li'l Abner on which late actor?
9 Who said of Clark Gable, 'His ears made him look like a taxicab with both doors open'?
10 When a journalist wired Cary Grant's agent saying, 'How old Cary Grant?' what did Cary Grant himself reply?
11 What was Vivien Leigh's first movie after *Gone with the Wind*?
12 Which pioneer's catchphrase was 'Leave 'em wanting'?
13 What was the name of Ava Gardner's dog, to which she left a maid and a limo in her will?
14 Which actor was US diving champion in 1932?
15 In what year did Charlie Chaplin eventually receive a knighthood?
16 Which comedy actor was a former vice president of the London Judo Society?
17 How did Vivien Leigh die?
18 Whose marriage to Katharine Hepburn lasted just three weeks?
19 What was Natalie Wood's last movie?
20 Which Italian actress was the twin of Marisa Pavan?
21 Which movie did Sinatra make shortly after paying a ransom on his son's kidnap?
22 Marilyn Monroe died during the making of which movie which was never finished?
23 How was Anne Leppert better known?
24 Where is there a museum celebrating Audrey Hepburn's work as a UN Ambassador?
25 Which queen did Charles Laughton's real-life wife play in *The Private Life of Henry VIII*?

**Answers Pot Luck 17** (see Quiz 50)
**1** Elmore Leonard. **2** Cilento. **3** Stephen Hopkins. **4** Samantha Eggar. **5** Holly Hunter. **6** 115 minutes. **7** Jill Balcon. **8** Rick Rossovich. **9** Sergeant Neil Howie. **10** Jane Alexander. **11** Frank Lloyd. **12** Fantasia. **13** 80 minutes. **14** Sorvino. **15** Dr Frederick Treves. **16** Daniel Mann. **17** Bernardo Bertolucci. **18** Fred Savage. **19** Helen Slater. **20** *The Player.* **21** *Going My Way.* **22** Cybill Shepherd. **23** Snodgrass. **24** Sophia Loren. **25** Ben Stiller.

## *QUIZ 53* POT LUCK 18 ........ LEVEL 3

*Answers – see page 275*

1 How many rooms does the Bates Motel have?
2 What was the name of Jessica Tandy's character in *Fried Green Tomatoes at the Whistle Stop Café*?
3 Who won the Best Actor Oscar for *Story of Louis Pasteur*?
4 Who directed *A League of Their Own*?
5 Which Samantha featured in *Little Women*?
6 Does *Groundhog Day* last around 85, 100 or 120 minutes?
7 In which film did the character Major General Roy Urquhart appear?
8 A Charles Portis novel became which late 60s classic movie?
9 Which Richard featured in *Logan's Run*?
10 In which film did a sailor named Ned Land appear?
11 *No Minor Chords: My Days in Hollywood* was whose autobiography?
12 Which actress links *Mr North* and *The Witches*?
13 A character named Charles Horman appeared in which film?
14 Which film actor's voice was that on Michael Jackson's video *Thriller*?
15 What is the first name of Bruce Willis, who uses his middle name in the movies?
16 Within five minutes, how long does *9 to 5* last?
17 Which Martin featured *in Little Big Man*?
18 Whose memoirs of Limerick were made into a film with Emily Watson?
19 In which film does the character named Sean Thornton appear?
20 In 1984 which movie star released the pop single 'The Christmas Song'?
21 How is actor/director Nobby Clarke better known?
22 What movie is shown within the film *The Fabulous Baker Boys*?
23 A character named Doris Murphy appeared in which film?
24 Which Chris featured in *The Fifth Element*?
25 What's the name and number of the computer in *2001*?

**Answers Alfred Hitchcock** (see Quiz 55)
**1** Leytonstone. **2** Leo. **3** Title card illustrator. **4** *Elstree Calling.* **5** *The Lady Vanishes.* **6** Daphne Du Maurier (*Rebecca*). **7** St Ignatius College, London. **8** *The Lodger.* **9** James Allardice. **10** Alma Reville. **11** David O. Selznick. **12** Carole Lombard. **13** *The Case of Jonathan Drew.* **14** He won with his first! **15** Blondes. **16** Julie Andrews. **17** Bernard Herrmann. **18** *Frenzy.* **19** *Elstree Calling.* **20** *Suspicion* (Cary Grant). **21** Mount Rushmore. **22** Pierre Boileau & Thomas Narcejac. **23** *Rope.* **24** *Shadow of a Doubt.* **25** Madeleine Carroll.

## QUIZ 54 1960s ........ LEVEL 3

*Answers – see page 276*

1 Which movie had the ad line, 'Don't give away the ending; it's the only one we have'?
2 Who injured his leg making *Cat Ballou*, eventually requiring an amputation?
3 *A Fistful of Dollars* was based on which samurai classic?
4 Which composer did Dirk Bogarde play in *Song Without End*?
5 Who played Catherine the Great in *Great Catherine*?
6 Who turned down the Clark Gable role in *The Misfits* as he said he didn't understand it?
7 In which movie did Lon Chaney play the devil?
8 Who played Wyatt Earp in *Hour of the Gun*?
9 Which role did Ava Gardner play in *The Night of the Iguana*?
10 Who played Elizabeth I in *The Fighting Prince of Donegal*?
11 For which movie was Terence Stamp Oscar-nominated on his film debut?
12 Who played Jean Harlow in *Harlow*?
13 In *The Birds*, Hitchcock walks past Tippi Hedren with what?
14 Who played Sherlock Holmes in *A Study in Terror*?
15 In which movie did John Philip Law play an angel?
16 Who played two parts in *Fahrenheit 451* in 1966?
17 Which husband and wife were Oscar-nominated together in 1963?
18 *The Jackals* was based on which Shakespeare play?
19 In which of his own movies did John Huston appear in 1966?
20 In which 1962 movie did Anthony Quinn play a boxer?
21 'Shut up and deal' is the last line of which movie?
22 What is the nickname of 'The Man With No Name'?
23 Who turned down the role of Lara in *Dr Zhivago*?
24 What was the name of Jackie Gleason's character in *The Hustler*?
25 What was the third of Richard Burton's three Oscar nominations between 1964 and 1966?

**Answers Pot Luck 19** (see Quiz 56)
**1** *Cleopatra.* **2** Elizabeth Taylor. **3** Benjamin. **4** 1987. **5** Hera. **6** *Abbott and Costello Meet Frankenstein.* **7** *War Hunt.* **8** 120 minutes. **9** Goodall. **10** *A Star Is Born.* **11** Lewis Milestone. **12** Faye Dunaway. **13** *Legends of the Fall.* **14** Garfield. **15** Rebecca De Mornay. **16** *Airplane!* **17** 1980. **18** Judy Holliday. **19** Danny Cannon. **20** Robert Thorn. **21** 96 minutes. **22** *How I Won the War.* **23** Sam Bowden. **24** *Basic Instinct.* **25** 128 minutes.

## *QUIZ 55* ALFRED HITCHCOCK ........ LEVEL 3

*Answers – see page 273*

1 In which part of London was Hitchcock born?
2 What is his star sign?
3 What was his first job in the movie industry?
4 In which movie did he have his only pie-throwing scene?
5 What was the last hit movie he made in the UK before leaving for Hollywood?
6 Who wrote the novel on which his first Hollywood movie was based?
7 At which school was he enrolled at an early age?
8 What was the British title of the film he made that saw his first cameo appearance?
9 Who wrote the commentary for his *Alfred Hitchcock Presents* TV anthology series?
10 Who did he marry in 1926?
11 Which producer first signed him to work in the USA?
12 Who was the star of his 1941 romantic comedy?
13 How was *The Lodger* titled in the USA?
14 How many Hollywood films did he make before winning his first Oscar for Best Film?
15 Who did Hitchcock say made the best victims?
16 Who played the double agent's girlfriend in *Torn Curtain*?
17 Who wrote the score for the shower scene in *Psycho*?
18 Which hit film did he make in Britain after a 30-year gap in Hollywood?
19 Which of his early movies was based on *The Taming of the Shrew*?
20 What was his first movie to star the actor born Archibald Leach?
21 On which mountain was much of *North by Northwest* shot?
22 Whose novel was *Vertigo* based on?
23 What was his first movie in colour?
24 What was reputedly his own favourite among his films?
25 Who played the starring female role Hitchcock created for *The Thirty-Nine Steps*?

**Answers Pot Luck 18** (see Quiz 53)
**1** 12. **2** Ninny Threadgoode. **3** Paul Muni. **4** Penny Marshall. **5** Mathis. **6** 100. **7** *A Bridge Too Far*. **8** *True Grit*. **9** Jordan. **10** *20,000 Leagues Under the Sea*. **11** André Previn. **12** Anjelica Huston. **13** *Missing*. **14** Vincent Price. **15** Walter. **16** 110 minutes. **17** Balsam. **18** Frank McCourt's. **19** *The Quiet Man*. **20** Billy Crystal. **21** Bryan Forbes. **22** *It's a Wonderful Life*. **23** *A League of Their Own*. **24** Tucker. **25** HAL 9000.

## *QUIZ 56* POT LUCK 19 ........ LEVEL 3

*Answers – see page 274*

1 Producer Buddy Adler died during the making of which blockbuster movie?
2 Which movie star released a single called 'Wings in the Sky' in 1976?
3 Which Richard featured in *Catch 22*?
4 In which year did Fred Astaire die?
5 Who did Honor Blackman play in *Jason and the Argonauts*?
6 Which movie is shown in the film *Into the Night*?
7 What was Robert Redford's first film, in 1961?
8 Within fifteen minutes, how long does the 1990s *Emma* last?
9 Which Caroline featured in *Schindler's List*?
10 A character named Esther Blodgett appeared in which film?
11 Who won the Best Director Oscar for *Two Arabian Knights*?
12 Which actress links *Barfly* and *American Dreamers*?
13 *Legends of the Fall, Liar Liar, The Lion King* – which runs the longest?
14 Which Allen featured in *The Candidate*?
15 When Roger Vadim remade *And God Created Woman*, who played the role originally played by his first wife?
16 In which film did a character named Ted Striker appear?
17 In which year was *Time Bandits* released?
18 Who won the Best Actress Oscar for *Born Yesterday*?
19 Who directed *Judge Dredd*?
20 What was the name of Gregory Peck's character in *The Omen*?
21 Within five minutes, how long does *Night of the Living Dead* last?
22 Which 1967 film did rock star John Lennon star in?
23 Who did Nick Nolte play in *Cape Fear*?
24 In which film did a character named Beth Curran appear?
25 Within fifteen minutes, how long does *Ghost* last?

**Answers 1960s** (see Quiz 54)
**1** *Psycho.* **2** Jay C. Flippen. **3** *Yojimbo.* **4** Franz Liszt. **5** Jeanne Moreau. **6** Robert Mitchum. **7** *The Devil's Messenger.* **8** James Garner. **9** Maxine Falk. **10** Catherine Lacey. **11** *Billy Budd.* **12** Carroll Baker. **13** Two dogs. **14** John Neville. **15** *Barbarella.* **16** Julie Christie. **17** Rex Harrison & Rachel Roberts. **18** *The Tempest.* **19** *The Bible.* **20** *Requiem for a Heavyweight.* **21** *The Apartment.* **22** Blondie. **23** Jane Fonda. **24** Minnesota Fats. **25** *Who's Afraid of Virginia Woolf?*.

## *QUIZ 57* 1970s STARS ........ LEVEL 3

*Answers – see page 279*

1 Who did John Belushi play in his first movie?
2 Who was the only woman to have major billing for *A Bridge Too Far*?
3 Which 70s Best Actress Oscar nominee became co-artistic director of the Actors Studio after the death of Lee Strasberg?
4 Who became his country's top star of the 70s and was dubbed the Dutch Paul Newman?
5 Who directed and starred in *The Last Movie* in 1971?
6 Which Hitchcock film trailer saw the director floating in the Thames?
7 Which 70s star was the granddaughter of fashion designer Elsa Schiaparelli?
8 Who was Best Actress at Cannes for *An Unmarried Woman*?
9 Which movie featured Michael York, Jacqueline Bisset and Lauren Bacall?
10 Which future Oscar-winner made his debut as a car vandal in *Sunday Bloody Sunday*?
11 In which movie did Julie Christie first star opposite Warren Beatty?
12 In which movie did Robert De Niro play a dying baseball player?
13 What was Tom Selleck's first film, in 1970?
14 Who starred as the editor of the newspaper in question in *All the President's Men*?
15 Who made his directorial debut with *Hide in Plain Sight* in 1980?
16 What was Peter Ustinov's first film as Agatha Christie's Belgian detective?
17 Which ex circus performer was Oscar-nominated for his role in *The Heartbreak Kid*?
18 Who did Dudley Moore replace in *10*?
19 What was Sting's first movie?
20 In 1970 who won the LA Silver Annual Handball Tournament?
21 Who was the first director to cast Goldie Hawn in a straight film?
22 In which movie did Jane Fonda play Lilian Hellman?
23 Which star of *Bugsy Malone* was once Pamela Anderson's fiancé?
24 In which movie did Richard Dreyfuss have his first romantic lead?
25 Stacy Keach replaced whom in *Fat City*?

**Answers Pot Luck 20** (see Quiz 59)
**1** Gymnastics. **2** John McTiernan. **3** 14. **4** Morton. **5** *48 Hours*. **6** Ian Ogilvy. **7** Adam Ant. **8** 150. **9** *Guiding Light*. **10** Criena Rohan's. **11** Donat. **12** Julie Edwards (Julie Andrews). **13** Mia Farrow. **14** Red (National colour of Wales – Richard Burton). **15** 'I'm Easy'. **16** John Belushi. **17** Irving Berlin. **18** 105 minutes. **19** Natalie Wood. **20** Sidney Poitier. **21** 93 minutes. **22** Muldoon. **23** *Scent of a Woman*. **24** Jane Powell. **25** Sheila McCarthy.

## *QUIZ 58* CLARK GABLE ........ LEVEL 3

*Answers – see page 280*

1 What was his real first name?
2 Under what star sign was he born?
3 In which 1925 Von Stroheim movie did he appear?
4 Which of his wives was 14 years his senior?
5 Which movie studio turned him down in 1930?
6 In which movie, where he had second billing to Leslie Howard, did he make his name?
7 Which medals did he receive in World War II?
8 What was his first movie after the death of his third wife?
9 Who did he marry while making the movie where he played Rhett Butler?
10 Who directed him in his final movie?
11 In which movie did he star opposite the actress who 'wanted to be alone'?
12 Which studio 'borrowed' Gable for *It Happened One Night*?
13 Which production executive once screen tested him and said he looked like an ape?
14 Who was the mother of his only child, though he died before the child was born?
15 In which movie did he sing 'Puttin' on the Ritz'?
16 Who did he famously punch on the chin in *Night Nurse*?
17 In which two 1934 movies did he star with Myrna Loy?
18 Which movie had to be altered several times after his co-star died during filming?
19 On the set of which movie did he meet Carole Lombard?
20 Who was his first wife after he was widowed?
21 Which 1948 movie was a big-screen version of his Broadway play?
22 Who wrote the screenplay of his final movie?
23 His fourth wife was the widow of which actor?
24 In which movie did he play Peter Warne?
25 What was the name of his character in *Red Dust*?

**Answers Headline Makers** (see Quiz 60)
**1** *Calponia harrisonford.* **2** Mia Farrow. **3** Hugh Grant & Liz Hurley. **4** *The Island of Doctor Moreau.* **5** Mae West. **6** Bridget Fonda (as Mandy Rice-Davies). **7** Zsa Zsa Gabor. **8** Philip Glass. **9** Melanie Griffith. **10** Marvin Hamlisch. **11** Howard Hughes. **12** Jill Ireland. **13** John Garfield. **14** Andy Garcia. **15** *Doombeach.* **16** Hedy Lamarr. **17** 4454813. **18** *Ulee's Gold* (1997). **19** Irene Dunne. **20** Somalia. **21** Greta Scacchi. **22** Felipe De Alba. **23** Audie Murphy. **24** Celeste Holm. **25** Bob Hope.

## *QUIZ 59* POT LUCK 20 ........ LEVEL 3

*Answers – see page 277*

1 At what sport did Richard Gere excel?
2 Who directed *The Hunt for Red October*?
3 How many people are killed in the gangster movie *Dick Tracy*?
4 Which Joe featured in *Speed*?
5 In which film does a character named Jack Cates appear?
6 Who played Chagall in the film *Death Becomes Her*?
7 Which singer appeared in *Slam Dance*?
8 Within ten minutes, how long does *The Firm* last?
9 Which soap did Kevin Bacon star in?
10 Whose novel is the film *The Delinquents* based on?
11 Which Peter featured in *The China Syndrome*?
12 Under what name has the Oscar nominee for *Victor/Victoria* written books for children?
13 Which actress links *A Wedding* and *Blind Terror*?
14 Elizabeth Taylor's fifth husband was buried wearing which colour?
15 Which song won Best Song Oscar for *Nashville*?
16 The movie Wired was based on whose life story?
17 About whom did Jerome Kern say, he 'has no place in American music. He is American music'?
18 Within five minutes, how long does *My Best Friend's Wedding* last?
19 *Brainstorm* and *Meteor* both feature which actress?
20 Who won the Best Actor Oscar for *Lilies of the Field*?
21 Within fifteen minutes, how long does *Look Who's Talking* last?
22 Which Patrick featured in *Starship Troopers*?
23 A character named Charlie Simms appeared in which film?
24 Who played opposite Howard Keel in *Seven Brides for Seven Brothers*?
25 Who played Samantha Copeland in the film *Die Hard 2*?

**Answers 1970s Stars** (see Quiz 57)
**1** Bluto (*National Lampoon's Animal House*). **2** Liv Ullmann. **3** Ellen Burstyn. **4** Rutger Hauer. **5** Dennis Hopper. **6** *Frenzy*. **7** Marisa Berenson. **8** Jill Clayburgh. **9** *Murder on the Orient Express*. **10** Daniel Day-Lewis. **11** *McCabe and Mrs Miller*. **12** *Bang the Drum Slowly*. **13** *Myra Breckinridge*. **14** Jason Robards. **15** James Caan. **16** *Death on the Nile*. **17** Eddie Albert. **18** George Segal. **19** *Quadrophenia*. **20** Ryan O'Neal. **21** Steven Spielberg (*Sugarland Express*). **22** *Julia*. **23** Scott Baio. **24** *The Goodbye Girl*. **25** Marlon Brando.

## *QUIZ 60* HEADLINE MAKERS ........ LEVEL 3

*Answers – see page 278*

1 What name was given to the species of spider named after the star of the Indiana Jones movies?
2 Whose 1997 autobiography was called *What Falls Away*?
3 In 1996 whose mattress from their holiday home fetched £550 at auction?
4 What was Brando's last movie of the 20th century?
5 Who said, 'Don't forget dear, I invented censorship'?
6 Who said the infamous, 'Well he would, wouldn't he' line in *Scandal*?
7 Whose husbands include George Sanders and Conrad Hilton?
8 Which composer, along with Richard Gere, founded the Tibet House in Greenwich Village in 1988?
9 Who fell in love with at 14, and later married, her mother's co-star of *The Harrad Experiment*?
10 Who was the first person to win three Oscars in one night?
11 Which director designed the plane called the Spruce Goose?
12 Which star of *Breakheart Pass* and *Death Wish II* was a spokeswoman for the American Cancer Society in the 80s?
13 How was Julius Garfinkle better known when he was blacklisted during the McCarthy era?
14 Which star of *The Untouchables* had fled the Castro regime aged five?
15 What was Glenda Jackson's final movie before she embarked on a political career?
16 Which actress invented an anti-jamming device for the Allies which laid the foundations for secure military communications?
17 What suspect number did Hugh Grant have when he was arrested with Divine Brown on Sunset Strip?
18 For which movie did Peter Fonda receive his first Oscar nomination after finding fame in *Easy Rider*?
19 Which Hollywood star was appointed by President Eisenhower as an alternate delegate to the UN's 12th General Assembly?
20 Audrey Hepburn made a highly publicized visit to which country for UNICEF just before her final illness took hold?
21 Who needed hospital treatment making *Turtle Beach* when a coconut fell on her head?
22 Whose marriage to Zsa Zsa Gabor lasted just eight days?
23 Which actor was the US's most decorated soldier ever?
24 Which star of *Oklahoma!* was knighted by King Olaf of Norway, the country of her birth, in 1979?
25 Which comedy star gave his name to a golfing Desert Classic?

**Answers Clark Gable** (see Quiz 58)
**1** William. **2** Aquarius. **3** *The Merry Widow*. **4** Josephine Dillon. **5** MGM. **6** A *Free Soul*. **7** Distinguished Flying Cross & Air Medal. **8** *Adventure*. **9** Carole Lombard. **10** John Huston. **11** *Susan Lenox: Her Fall and Rise*. **12** Columbia. **13** Darryl F. Zanuck. **14** Kay Spreckels. **15** *Idiot's Delight*. **16** Barbara Stanwyck. **17** *Men in White; Manhattan Melodrama*. **18** *Saratoga* (with Jean Harlow). **19** *No Man of Her Own*. **20** Lady Sylvia Ashley. **21** *Command Decision*. **22** Arthur Miller. **23** Douglas Fairbanks. **24** *It Happened One Night*. **25** Dennis Carson.

## QUIZ 61 OSCAR TRIVIA ...... LEVEL 3

*Answers – see page 283*

1 What was Frank Capra's third Oscar in five years, in 1938?
2 Which movie had seven nominations but lost out to *Forrest Gump*?
3 Which movie broke all records by winning in all categories for which it was nominated in 1988?
4 Which 1964 Cary Grant movie won Oscars for writers Peter Stone and Frank Tarloff?
5 Who was Oscar-nominated for music for *American Beauty*?
6 Whose original screenplay was nominated for *The Sixth Sense*?
7 Which future Mrs Janusz Kaminski won an Oscar the same night he did in 1993?
8 What was the second of Brando's four consecutive nominations between 1951 and 1954?
9 Who was the first British actor to win Best Actor?
10 Who was the first Best Actress, British born of British parents?
11 Ingrid Bergman won for which film, marking her return from Hollywood exile?
12 Which 60s Oscar-winner was narrated by Michael MacLiammoir?
13 Who was the first actress of British parents who won an Oscar twice?
14 Who is the third most frequent host of the Oscars ceremony?
15 Which 1962 winner studied medicine at the University of California?
16 In which three categories did *E.T.* win?
17 Which Sammy Cahn Oscar-winning song had the longest title?
18 John Mollo won an Oscar in *Star Wars* in which category?
19 Who in 1989 was the first director since 1932 to see his film win Best Picture but not to have an Oscar nomination himself?
20 Who won a Special Award for *The Little Kidnappers* aged 10?
21 What was the first film to be nominated for Best Special Effects?
22 Who was nominated for *Pasha* in the 60s movie with Julie Christie and Omar Sharif?
23 What was the second of Gregory Peck's three nominations between 1945 and 1947?
24 For which character was Dustin Hoffman nominated in 1969?
25 Who was the only winner of an Oscar and a BAFTA for *Platoon*?

**Answers Box Office Successes** (see Quiz 63)
**1** Dodi Fayed. **2** *The Full Monty*. **3** Shelley Michelle. **4** Running for a bus. **5** Estelle Reiner. **6** Match. **7** Anthony Shaffer. **8** *Jaws: The Revenge*. **9** Charles Fleischer. **10** Miami. **11** 1938. **12** Kelly Macdonald. **13** Carl Denham (*King Kong*). **14** Henry Hill. **15** 39. **16** Kieran Culkin. **17** The Funky Chicken. **18** Martin Brest. **19** Matthew Modine. **20** P.J. Hogan. **21** Amon Goeth. **22** 112 minutes. **23** Wai Lin. **24** Steve Martin. **25** Teacher.

## *QUIZ 62* POT LUCK 21 ........ LEVEL 3

*Answers – see page 284*

1 Who directed *Groundhog Day*?
2 In which film does a character named Bud Fox appear?
3 In the 50s epic, what colour horses pull Ben Hur's chariot during the race?
4 Which Josh featured in *Teenage Mutant Ninja Turtles*?
5 Within five minutes, how long does *Mrs Doubtfire* last?
6 Who did Ray Milland play in *National Velvet*?
7 How many crew members were there in the Nostromo in *Alien*?
8 What movie is being watched in *Home Alone 2: Lost in New York*?
9 Which British actor won an Oscar for *Separate Tables*?
10 Within fifteen minutes, how long does *Lost in Space* last?
11 Which Nicholas featured in *Chariots of Fire*?
12 Who was the first non-professional actor to win an acting Oscar?
13 Which actress links *Drop Dead Fred* and *Soapdish*?
14 Which actor was originally set to play Tom Cruise's role in *Born on the Fourth of July*?
15 Which writer directed *Night Breed* in 1990?
16 Which 1988 film had the highest fee ever for a commissioned script?
17 Who played Brandi in the film *Boyz N the Hood*?
18 Which 1990 film had the highest ratio ever of stunt men to actors?
19 Who appears as a gravedigger in the film *LA Story*?
20 The song 'Buttons and Bows' came from which movie?
21 Which Ron featured in *Swingers*?
22 Who won the Best Actress Oscar for *The Rose Tattoo*?
23 A character named Joe Turner appeared in which film?
24 Who directed *Gremlins*?
25 Who played Lucy Westenra in the film *Bram Stoker's Dracula*?

**Answers The Silent Years** (see Quiz 64)
**1** *America.* **2** Pittsburgh. **3** *The Adventures of Kathlyn.* **4** Winsor McCay. **5** Bill Bitzer. **6** Archibald & Edgar Selwyn. **7** *Dream Street.* **8** *The Toll of the Sea.* **9** Columbia Pictures. **10** *The Power of Love.* **11** Santa Monica. **12** Thomas Ince. **13** *The Glorious Adventure.* **14** *Greed.* **15** Roxy Theater, New York. **16** Gilbert M. Anderson & George K. Spoor. **17** *A Study in Scarlet.* **18** Pathé Weekly. **19** *My Four Years in Germany.* **20** Electric Theatres. **21** *Tillie's Punctured Romance.* **22** *The Cure, Easy Street.* **23** Willis O'Brien. **24** *Birth of a Nation.* **25** Jack the Ripper.

## *QUIZ 63* BOX OFFICE SUCCESSES .......... LEVEL 3

*Answers – see page 281*

1 Which producer who tragically died in 1997 co-produced *Chariots of Fire*?
2 Which movie did *Titanic* overtake as a record UK earner?
3 Who was Julia Roberts's body double in the opening scene of *Pretty Woman*?
4 What is Hitchcock's cameo appearance in *North by Northwest*?
5 Who utters the famous line, 'I'll have what she's having' in *When Harry Met Sally*?
6 Who does Billy Zane play in *Back to the Future*?
7 Who adapted *Evil Under the Sun* for the big screen?
8 Which movie was Michael Caine filming so that he could not pick up his Oscar for *Hannah and Her Sisters*?
9 Who played Roger in *Who Framed Roger Rabbit?*?
10 Where is *Scarface* set?
11 In which year did Indiana Jones ride the Hindenburg in *Indiana Jones and the Last Crusade*?
12 Who plays Diane in *Trainspotting*?
13 Which character said, in which movie, 'It wasn't the airplanes. It was beauty killed the beast'?
14 Upon whose life is *Goodfellas* based?
15 How many different hats does Madonna wear in *Evita*?
16 Who plays Fuller in *Home Alone*?
17 What type of dance does Paul Barber say he can do in *The Full Monty*?
18 Who directed *Scent of a Woman*?
19 Who was Oscar-nominated for *Married to the Mob*?
20 Who directed *My Best Friend's Wedding*?
21 What character did Ralph Fiennes play in *Schindler's List*?
22 Within fifteen minutes, how long does *Goldfinger* last?
23 Which character does Michelle Yeoh play in *Tomorrow Never Dies*?
24 Who adapted the play *Cyrano de Bergerac* into the movie *Roxanne*?
25 What was Captain John Miller's job before he entered the army in *Saving Private Ryan*?

**Answers Oscar Trivia** (see Quiz 61)
**1** *You Can't Take it with You.* **2** *The Shawshank Redemption.* **3** *The Last Emperor.* **4** *Father Goose.* **5** Thomas Newman. **6** M. Night Shyamalan's. **7** Holly Hunter. **8** *Viva Zapata.* **9** George Arliss. **10** Julie Andrews. **11** *Anastasia.* **12** *Tom Jones.* **13** Olivia de Havilland. **14** Billy Crystal. **15** Gregory Peck. **16** Music; Sound; Visual Effects. **17** *Three Coins in the Fountain.* **18** Costume. **19** Bruce Beresford. **20** Jon Whitley. **21** *Only Angels Have Wings.* **22** Tom Courtenay. **23** *The Yearling.* **24** Ratso Rizzo (*Midnight Cowboy*). **25** Oliver Stone.

## *QUIZ 64* THE SILENT YEARS ........ LEVEL 3

*Answers – see page 282*

1 Which D.W. Griffith movie had the American Revolution as its subject?
2 Where did the first nickelodeon in the USA open?
3 What was the name of the first serial – in 13 parts – to be shown in cinemas?
4 Who created the cartoon *Gertie the Dinosaur* in 1914?
5 Who photographed *Birth of a Nation*?
6 Who founded Goldwyn Pictures with Samuel Goldfish?
7 Which movie did D.W. Griffith make in 1921 using synchronized sound on disc?
8 What was the first movie made in two-colour Technicolor?
9 What did the CBC Film Sales Corporation become in 1924?
10 What was the first feature to be made in 3D?
11 Where did Vitagraph open a studio in 1913?
12 Who set up Triangle Films with D.W. Griffith and Mack Sennett?
13 What was the first movie to be made in colour in England?
14 What was the epic *McTeague* called when it was finally released in 1923?
15 What was dubbed The Cathedral of the Motion Picture?
16 Who formed the Essanay company in Chicago?
17 What was the first Sherlock Holmes feature film, made in 1914, called?
18 What was the name of the first newsreel in the US?
19 What was Warner Brothers' first major feature?
20 What was the name of the first British cinema chain?
21 What was the name of Mack Sennett's first comedy feature?
22 What were Chaplin's first two two-reel comedies?
23 Who created the special effects for *The Lost World* which showed a dinosaur rampaging through London?
24 What was the first movie screened at the White House?
25 Who was Hitchcock's movie *The Lodger* about?

**Answers Pot Luck 21** (see Quiz 62)
**1** Harold Ramis. **2** *Wall Street.* **3** White. **4** Pais. **5** 125 minutes. **6** Don Birman. **7** Five. **8** *It's a Wonderful Life* (in Spanish). **9** David Niven. **10** 109 minutes. **11** Farrell. **12** Harold Russell (*Best Years of Our Lives*). **13** Carrie Fisher. **14** Al Pacino. **15** Clive Barker. **16** *Rain Man.* **17** Nia Long. **18** *The Rookie.* **19** Rick Moranis. **20** *The Paleface.* **21** Livingston. **22** Anna Magnani. **23** *Three Days of the Condor.* **24** Joe Dante. **25** Sadie Frost.

## *QUIZ 65* POT LUCK 22 ........ LEVEL 3

*Answers – see page 287*

1 What was the first movie to have a budget of $100 million?
2 Who directed *GoldenEye*?
3 Who won the Best Actor Oscar for *Watch on the Rhine*?
4 What colour hat is Andie MacDowell wearing in her first scene in *Four Weddings and a Funeral*?
5 Which Kevin featured in *Sleeping with the Enemy*?
6 In the film *Baby Boom* who played Dr Jeff Cooper?
7 Who played Biff Tannen in the film *Back to the Future*?
8 Who won the Best Director Oscar for *All Quiet on the Western Front*?
9 Within ten minutes, how long does *Mad Max* last?
10 Which movie star released the 1960s album *Everything I've Got*?
11 Which John featured in *1941*?
12 Which actress links *Candleshoe* and *The Little Girl Who Lives Down the Lane*?
13 A character named Robert Gold appeared in which film?
14 The father of which director was first flute of the NBC Symphony Orchestra under Toscanini?
15 Who directed *Escape from New York*?
16 The title of which 70s film was the date of the death of James Dean?
17 What is the name of 'The Horse Whisperer'?
18 Which song won Best Song Oscar for *Here Comes the Groom*?
19 How many days did it take John Hughes to write *The Breakfast Club*?
20 What unbilled role does Jack Nicholson play in *Broadcast News*?
21 Within five minutes, how long does *Monty Python's Life of Brian* last?
22 Which Henry featured in *Clear and Present Danger*?
23 A character named Loretta Castorini appeared in which film?
24 In which year was *San Francisco* released?
25 Who directed *Grease*?

**Answers Bette Davis** (see Quiz 67)
**1** Carl Laemmle, President of Universal. **2** *Cabin in Cotton.* **3** *Broken Dishes.* **4** *My Mother's Keeper.* **5** Empress Carlota Von Hapsburg. **6** *The Letter.* **7** George Cukor. **8** Peter Ustinov. **9** Bill Sampson. **10** Apple Annie (*Pocketful of Miracles*). **11** *Now Voyager.* **12** *The Petrified Forest.* **13** Goldwyn. **14** *The Private Lives of Elizabeth and Essex.* **15** *Whatever Happened to Baby Jane?* **16** Arthur Farnsworth. **17** American Film Institute's Lifetime Achievement Award. **18** George Arliss. **19** San Sebastian. **20** Catherine the Great. **21** *Old Acquaintance.* **22** Mildred the waitress. **23** *Hush Hush Sweet Charlotte.* **24** *The Lonely Life.* **25** ' She did it the hard way'.

## *QUIZ 66* 1980s STARS ........ LEVEL 3

*Answers – see page 288*

1 Who cast Cher in the play, then movie of *Come Back to the Five and Dime, Jimmy Dean, Jimmy Dean*?
2 How old was Richard Gere when he played a young recruit in *An Officer and a Gentleman*?
3 Which actress's husband designed the Olympic Gateway for the 1984 Los Angeles Olympics?
4 Who directed and starred in *The Four Seasons* in 1981?
5 For which 1985 film did Gerard Depardieu win Best Actor at Venice?
6 Which actor's voice was dubbed by Rich Little in *Curse of the Pink Panther* because he was so ill?
7 For which role was Willem Dafoe an Oscar-winner for *Platoon*?
8 Who did Faye Dunaway play in *Network*?
9 In the movie based on *Les Liaisons Dangereuses* who was Glenn Close?
10 As which character in *Frances* did Kevin Costner have one speaking line?
11 In which 80s movie did Sammy Davis Jr make a comeback?
12 Who played Mrs La Motta in *Raging Bull*?
13 Who did Schwarzenegger's co-star in *Twins* marry after the movie was finished?
14 Which Oscar-winner for *Cocoon* shared the Best Actor prize at Venice for *Things Change*?
15 Who came to international attention after appearing in Almodovar's *Women on the Verge of a Nervous Breakdown*?
16 Who played Bogey in *The Man with Bogart's Face*?
17 As which character did Kirstie Alley make her movie debut?
18 What was the name of Alan Rickman's character in *Die Hard*?
19 Who was the only female lead actress in Barry Levinson's directorial debut?
20 Who graduated from child to adult acting roles as Shirley Muldowney in *Heart Like a Wheel*?
21 Who plays the author of the book in *The Man Who Would Be King*?
22 In *Plenty* which British actress/comedienne was Meryl Streep's eccentric friend?
23 For which movie did Nicolas Cage have two teeth pulled out?
24 In *A Royal Love Story*, who played Princess Diana?
25 Who sang with Joan Jett on *Light of Day* in 1986?

**Answers Pot Luck 23** (see Quiz 68)
**1** River Phoenix (31.10.93). **2** Penny Marshall. **3** *How the West Was Won.* **4** Claude. **5** 100 minutes. **6** I Got Worms. **7** John Huston. **8** Bud Fox . **9** Edson. **10** Nicholas Kazan. **11** Steve Guttenberg. **12** *Along Came a Spider.* **13** *The Wind and the Lion.* **14** Whitfield. **15** Two hours. **16** Leo. **17** Alan Metter. **18** Dickey. **19** 'It Might As Well Be Spring'. **20** Mrs Canby. **21** Shirley Booth. **22** Roland Emmerich. **23** Anderson. **24** *Aria.* **25** *My Own Private Idaho.*

## *QUIZ 67* BETTE DAVIS ........................................ LEVEL 3

*Answers – see page 285*

1 Who said she had as much sex appeal as Slim Summerville?
2 In which movie did she say, 'I'd like to kiss ya but I just washed my hair!'?
3 In which show did she make her Broadway debut?
4 What was the name of the autobiography written by her daughter?
5 What role did she play in *Juarez*?
6 What was her third Oscar nomination in the run of five starting with *Jezebel*?
7 Which director fired her on her first professional engagement?
8 Who played the sleuth in the Agatha Christie movie she made?
9 Which role did her husband play in *All About Eve*?
10 Who did she play in her 1961 movie directed by Frank Capra?
11 In which movie did she say, 'Jerry, don't let's ask for the moon; we have the stars'?
12 Which movie did she make after receiving her first Oscar?
13 With which studio did she fail a screen test before signing for Universal?
14 What was the first movie in which she played a Tudor queen?
15 For which movie did she receive her tenth and final Oscar nomination?
16 By which husband was she widowed?
17 In 1977 she became the first woman to be honoured with which award?
18 Whose leading lady was she in *The Man Who Played God*?
19 Which film festival was she returning from when her terminal cancer claimed her life?
20 In *John Paul Jones* she played a cameo role as whom?
21 In which movie did she say, 'There comes a time in every woman's life where the only thing that helps is a glass of champagne'?
22 What was her name and her profession in *Of Human Bondage*?
23 Which was her next hit movie after her tenth Oscar nomination?
24 What was the name of her first autobiography?
25 What did she say would be put on her tombstone?

**Answers Pot Luck 22** (see Quiz 65)
**1** *True Lies*. **2** Martin Campbell. **3** Paul Lukas. **4** Navy Blue. **5** Anderson. **6** Sam Shepard. **7** Thomas F. Wilson. **8** Lewis Milestone. **9** 90 minutes. **10** Honor Blackman. **11** Belushi. **12** Jodie Foster. **13** *Darling*. **14** Francis Ford Coppola. **15** John Carpenter. **16** *September 30th 1955*. **17** Tom Booker. **18** 'In the Cool, Cool, Cool of the Evening'. **19** Three. **20** An anchorman. **21** 93 minutes. **22** Czerny. **23** *Moonstruck*. **24** 1936. **25** Randal Kleiser.

## *QUIZ 68* POT LUCK 23 ........ LEVEL 3

*Answers – see page 286*

1 Which actor died on the same day as film director Federico Fellini?
2 Who directed *Big*?
3 A character named Linus Rawlings appeared in which film?
4 What did the C stand for in W.C. Fields's name?
5 Within five minutes, how long does *Love Story* last?
6 What is the name of the shop that the two characters from *Dumb and Dumber* want to open?
7 Who said, 'I never killed an actor. Nearly lost a few'?
8 What was the name of Charlie Sheen's character in *Wall Street*?
9 Which Richard featured in *Do the Right Thing*?
10 Who wrote the screenplay for the film *At Close Range*?
11 *High Spirits* and *Diner* starred which actor?
12 What was the original title for the film *Arachnophobia*?
13 In which film did the splendidly named Mulay Ahmed Mohammed el Raisuli the Magnificent appear?
14 Which Mitchell featured in *My Cousin Vinny*?
15 To the nearest hour, how long does *LA Confidential* last?
16 What was the first name of Albert Finney's character in *Miller's Crossing*?
17 Who directed the film *Back to School*?
18 Which James featured in *Deliverance*?
19 Which song from *State Fair* won an Oscar?
20 Who did Kathy Bates play in the film *Arthur 2: On the Rocks*?
21 Who won the Best Actress Oscar for *Come Back, Little Sheba*?
22 Who directed *Godzilla*?
23 Which Jeff starred in *Clerks*?
24 Which film was Bridget Fonda's debut film?
25 In which film does a character named Mike Waters appear?

**Answers 1980s Stars** (see Quiz 66)
**1** Robert Altman. **2** 30. **3** Anjelica Huston. **4** Alan Alda. **5** *Police*. **6** David Niven. **7** Sergeant Elias. **8** Diana Christensen. **9** Marquise de Merteuil. **10** Luther Adler. **11** *Tap*. **12** Cathy Moriarty. **13** John Travolta. **14** Don Ameche. **15** Antonio Banderas. **16** Robert Sacchi. **17** Lt Saavik (*Star Trek II*). **18** Hans Gruber. **19** Ellen Barkin (*Diner*). **20** Bonnie Bedelia. **21** Christopher Plummer. **22** Tracey Ullman. **23** *Birdy*. **24** Catherine Oxenberg. **25** Michael J. Fox.

## *QUIZ 69* ACTION ........ LEVEL 3

*Answers – see page 291*

1 What was the name of the novel on which *Goodfellas* was based?
2 Which conflict is depicted in *Land and Freedom*?
3 Who does John Wayne play in *Sands of Iwo Jima*?
4 In which movie based on his own book did Audie Murphy play himself?
5 Who was the target in the 90s remake of *The Day of the Jackal*?
6 Which Hitchcock remake had 'Que Sera Sera' as its theme song?
7 Who drove the booby-trapped bus in *Speed*?
8 *You Only Live Once* was partly based on the life of which duo?
9 How many *Die Hard* movies were made before Samuel L. Jackson joined as Bruce Willis's sidekick?
10 Which women have an action-packed fight in *Destry Rides Again*?
11 Which Shakespeare play was turned into a gangland movie in *Men of Respect*?
12 In terms of admissions, what was the least successful Bond movie?
13 To the nearest hour, how long does *Dirty Harry* last?
14 Which '*Die Hard* on a plane' type movie was criticized as being as 'fresh as an in-flight meal'?
15 Who took next billing after Goldie Hawn in *Sugarland Express*?
16 Who plays the arch enemy in *French Connection II*?
17 Shaun Ryder's movie debut was in which movie?
18 Which race was the setting for *Cannonball*?
19 What were the two remakes of *The Asphalt Jungle* called?
20 Which movie opens with the line 'I believe in America'?
21 Who replaced Steve McQueen and Ali McGraw in a 90s remake of an action thriller?
22 Which two actors rejected *Bridge on the River Kwai* before Alec Guinness got the lead role?
23 Where did the boat chase take place in *Puppet on a Chain*?
24 Which character did Sylvester Stallone play in *Cop Land*?
25 Who directed the chariot race in *Ben Hur*?

**Answers Pot Luck 24** (see Quiz 71)
**1** *Rebecca*. **2** Meg Tilly. **3** Terry Gilliam. **4** Fats Domino. **5** 110. **6** Marley. **7** *Sunset Boulevard*. **8** George Stevens. **9** *Taps*. **10** Hulce. **11** 93 minutes. **12** Prahka Lasa. **13** Lerner. **14** Paul Hogan. **15** Kissy Suzuki. **16** Joel Coen. **17** *Hud*. **18** Nancy Travis. **19** Gene Hackman. **20** 1937. **21** David Warner. **22** Francis. **23** 129 minutes. **24** Tess Harper. **25** Adrian Lyne.

## *QUIZ 70* 1930s STARS ............................................ LEVEL 3

*Answers – see page 292*

1 What was John Barrymore's pet vulture called?
2 Who found fame in *Beau Brummel* opposite John Barrymore, who became her lover?
3 Who played Dr Kildare in a series of 30s films?
4 Who was Oscar-nominated for *Jezebel* and *White Banners*?
5 Who said, 'They used to photograph Shirley Temple through gauze. They should photograph me through linoleum'?
6 Who played the title role in *The Mighty Barnum*?
7 Jean Harlow died during the making of which movie?
8 Which former child star was one of the Three Smart Girls?
9 Who was fired as Norman Maine in the 1934 version of *A Star Is Born*?
10 Who was Hitler's favourite actress?
11 Which other Bennett sisters acted along with Constance?
12 Which comedienne's husbands included the promoter of the Todd AO wide screen system?
13 How was Etienne Pelissier de Bujac better known?
14 *The Prisoner of Zenda* was made from whose book?
15 How did *Gone with the Wind* star Butterfly McQueen meet her death?
16 Who played Bottom in *A Midsummer Night's Dream*?
17 Who said, 'I was shot to death in six films between 1931 and 1937'?
18 In which book did Sir Cecil Beaton describe his deep romance with Greta Garbo?
19 What was Carole Lombard's real name?
20 Which film star wrote the novel *Today Is Tonight*?
21 What did Irene Dunne receive her second Oscar nomination for?
22 Which actor directed the two movies which ended the career of John Gilbert?
23 In which movie did Jeanette MacDonald and Nelson Eddy first appear together?
24 What was the second of Spencer Tracy's three Oscar nominations between 1936 and 1938?
25 Who won the 400 yards freestyle gold at the 1932 Olympics?

**Answers Unforgettables** (see Quiz 72)
**1** Jean Harlow's. **2** *Father Goose.* **3** Dorothy Stratten. **4** Rudy Vallee. **5** Peggy Middleton. **6** Susan Blanchard. **7** Harrison Ford. **8** Kathryn Grayson. **9** *The Cat and the Canary.* **10** Ray Milland. **11** Tom Mix. **12** *Green Grow the Rushes.* **13** Gloria Swanson. **14** Dirk Bogarde. **15** Charles Farrell. **16** *Where's the Rest of Me?* **17** Calcutta (he was born in Omaha). **18** Drowned. **19** South Africa. **20** Orson Welles. **21** His pet Airedale dog. **22** *The Big Broadcast.* **23** James Stewart. **24** Sir Noel Coward. **25** Bing Crosby.

## *QUIZ 71* POT LUCK 24 ........ LEVEL 3

*Answers – see page 289*

1 What movie is showing within the film *Desperately Seeking Susan*?
2 Which actress was to play the role of Constanze in the film *Amadeus* before Elizabeth Berridge took over?
3 Who directed *The Fisher King*?
4 Which singer appeared in *Every Which Way You Can*?
5 Did *A Fish Called Wanda* last around 90, 110 or 130 minutes?
6 Which John featured in *Love Story*?
7 In which 1950 movie did Cecil B. de Mille appear on screen?
8 Which George won the Best Director Oscar for *Giant*?
9 What was Sean Penn's first film, in 1981?
10 Which Tom featured in *Mary Shelley's Frankenstein*?
11 Within ten minutes how long does *Honey, I Shrunk the Kids* last?
12 Which character in the film *All of Me* was played by Richard Libertini?
13 Which Michael featured in *Godzilla*?
14 Who wrote the screenplay for the film *Almost an Angel*?
15 What was the name of the Bond girl in *You Only Live Twice*?
16 Who directed *The Big Lebowski*?
17 In which film does a character named Lon Bannon appear?
18 Who was the main adult female actress in *Three Men and a Baby*?
19 *Bonnie and Clyde* and *Young Frankenstein* both featured which actor?
20 In which year was *Lost Horizon* with Ronald Colman released?
21 Who played the villain in the 80s movie *Time Bandits*?
22 What is the first name of 'Baby' Houseman in *Dirty Dancing*?
23 Within five minutes, how long does *The Lost World: Jurassic Park* last?
24 Who plays Rosa Lee in *Tender Mercies*?
25 Who directed *Flashdance*?

**Answers Action** (see Quiz 69)
**1** *Wiseguy*. **2** Spanish Civil War. **3** Sergeant Stryker. **4** *To Hell and Back*. **5** The First Lady. **6** *The Man Who Knew Too Much*. **7** Sandra Bullock. **8** Bonnie & Clyde. **9** Two. **10** Marlene Dietrich & Una Merkel. **11** *Macbeth*. **12** *The Man with the Golden Gun*. **13** 2 hours (102 mins). **14** *Passenger 57*. **15** Ben Johnson. **16** Fernando Rey. **17** *The Avengers*. **18** Trans American Grand Prix. **19** *The Badlanders; Cairo*. **20** *The Godfather*. **21** Alec Baldwin & Kim Basinger. **22** Noel Coward & Charles Laughton. **23** Amsterdam. **24** Freddy Heflin. **25** Andrew Marton.

## QUIZ 72 UNFORGETTABLES ........ LEVEL 3

*Answers – see page 290*

1 According to Jack Warner, Rin Tin Tin died with his head on whose lap?
2 What was Cary Grant's penultimate movie?
3 *The Killing of the Unicorn* was Peter Bogdanovich's book about the murder of which of his lovers?
4 Alice Faye was a singer in whose band?
5 What was Yvonne De Carlo's real name?
6 Which wife of Henry Fonda was a stepdaughter of Oscar Hammerstein II?
7 Which namesake of an 80s/90s star appeared in *The Mysterious Mrs M* in 1917?
8 How was Zelma Hedrick better known?
9 In which movie did Bob Hope say, 'I get goose pimples. Even my goose pimples get goose pimples'?
10 Which Welsh-born actor's autobiography was called *Wide Eyed in Babylon*?
11 Who was described as being as elegant on a horse as Fred Astaire on a dance floor?
12 What was Richard Burton's last UK film before turning to Hollywood?
13 Whose marriage to Wallace Beery lasted just three weeks?
14 Which film star wrote the novel *West of Sunset*?
15 Who played opposite Janet Gaynor 12 times?
16 What was Ronald Reagan's autobiography called?
17 Where did Marlon Brando's first press release say he had spent the first six months of his life?
18 How did Natalie Wood die?
19 Where was Basil Rathbone born?
20 Whose was the voice narrating Agatha Christie's *And Then There Were None*?
21 Who did John Wayne get his nickname 'Duke' from?
22 In which movie did Bob Hope find his theme tune?
23 Who collected Gary Cooper's final Oscar?
24 Which British writer, actor and director had two bit parts in D.W. Griffith's *Hearts of the World* in 1918?
25 Who died in 1977 stipulating that his sons could not touch a trust fund of money until they were 65?

**Answers 1930s Stars** (see Quiz 70)
**1** Maloney. **2** Mary Astor. **3** Lew Ayres. **4** Fay Bainter. **5** Tallulah Bankhead. **6** Wallace Beery. **7** *Saratoga*. **8** Deanna Durbin. **9** John Barrymore. **10** Greta Garbo. **11** Joan & Barbara. **12** Joan Blondell. **13** Bruce Cabot. **14** Anthony Hope. **15** Fire. **16** James Cagney. **17** Edward G. Robinson. **18** *The Happy Years*. **19** Jane Peters. **20** Jean Harlow. **21** *Theodora Goes Wild*. **22** Lionel Barrymore. **23** *Naughty Mariette*. **24** *Captains Courageous*. **25** Buster Crabbe.

## QUIZ 73 1970s ........ LEVEL 3

*Answers – see page 295*

1 Which movie had the ad line, 'You don't assign him to cases – you just turn him loose'?
2 Which former teen star made his debut in *Over the Edge*?
3 Who ate dog droppings in *Pink Flamingos*?
4 What was Mark Hamill's follow-up to *Star Wars*?
5 Which role did Al Pacino play in the 1975 Sidney Lumet movie?
6 *The Taking of Pelham One Two Three* is about the hijack of what?
7 Who played Valentino in *The World's Greatest Lover*?
8 In which state does the action start in *The Sting*?
9 Which movie had the ad line, 'The damnedest thing you ever saw'?
10 What's the name of the prostitute played by Jane Fonda in *Klute*?
11 Who played Sherlock Holmes in *The Seven Per Cent Solution*?
12 To the nearest hour, how long does *The Andromeda Strain* last?
13 What was the first film to use Dolby sound?
14 Who played Moses in *Moses*?
15 Who did Robert Mitchum play in *Ryan's Daughter*?
16 Who made the film of the biggest hippy festival ever?
17 Which flop prompted its producer to declare, 'It would have been cheaper to lower the Atlantic'?
18 In which movie did Burgess Meredith play the devil?
19 Who was Jugs in *Mother, Jugs and Speed*?
20 What was the first of Jack Nicholson's three nominations between 1973 and 1975?
21 Who was originally cast to play Evelyn Mulwray in *Chinatown* before she divorced the movie's producer?
22 In which 1972 movie did Stacey Keach play a boxer?
23 *Bound for Glory* was about which star?
24 Where and when was *The Man Who Would Be King* set?
25 Who played Carole Lombard in *Gable and Lombard*?

**Answers Pot Luck 25** (see Quiz 75)
**1** Murphy. **2** Arizona. **3** *The Inn of the Sixth Happiness*. **4** Luc Besson. **5** *Search for Tomorrow*. **6** 118 minutes. **7** Richard Adams. **8** Sylvester Stallone. **9** James Foley. **10** Cliff Robertson. **11** Nurse Costello. **12** *The Big Lebowski*. **13** Larry Hagman. **14** *Madam Sousatzka*. **15** Hall. **16** 126 minutes. **17** Oliver Stone. **18** Elliott. **19** 1954. **20** Sally Field. **21** *The Right Stuff*. **22** Jane Wyman. **23** Tom. **24** Sydney Pollack. **25** Emmerich.

## *QUIZ 74* JACK LEMMON ........................................................................ LEVEL 3

*Answers – see page 296*

1 What is his full real name?
2 Which character did he win his first Oscar for?
3 What was the name of the second Oscar-nominated film he made for Billy Wilder?
4 Who directed him in *Days of Wine and Roses*?
5 Under what star sign was he born?
6 Which director described him as somewhere between Chaplin and Cary Grant?
7 For which 1959 film was he Oscar-nominated and a BAFTA winner?
8 Which movie also featured Shirley MacLaine as Miss Kubelik?
9 Who did he play in *The Odd Couple*?
10 Who starred in and produced *The China Syndrome*?
11 What was billed as 'the greatest comedy ever made'?
12 Who won the Oscar for musical director in his film *Irma La Douce*?
13 What was the name of his character in *Avanti!*?
14 Who was the spouse in the movie whose title suggested how she could be dispensed with?
15 He was the son of a president of a company that made what?
16 What film was his directorial debut?
17 To which 1957 movie did he contribute a song?
18 For which two movies was he named Best Actor at Cannes?
19 Whose estranged father did he play in *Short Cuts*?
20 Where is his son missing, in *Missing*?
21 In which 1980 movie did he recreate his Broadway role as a dying playwright?
22 In which 1986 movie did he co-star with his wife and son?
23 Which movie was a remake of the French *L'Emmerdeur*?
24 In which movie did he play opposite Walter Matthau, who played Walter Burns?
25 At which film festival did he receive the Best Actor award for Glen*garry Glen Ross*?

**Answers Biopics** (see Quiz 76)
**1** Roshan Seth (Nehru). **2** J. Edgar Hoover (Bob Hoskins). **3** Walter Brennan. **4** Vincent van Gogh. **5** Missionary Gladys Aylward. **6** Iain Softley. **7** Beethoven. **8** Lionel Barrymore. **9** Billie Burke. **10** Calamity Jane. **11** Ruth Ellis (last woman to be hanged in Britain). **12** Lilian Roth. **13** Frank Loesser. **14** David Bowie. **15** Ambrose Bierce. **16** C.S. Lewis & Joy Gresham. **17** Anthony Hopkins (Nixon). **18** James Brolin. **19** *Bonnie and Clyde*. **20** Gary Busey. **21** The Dalai Lama. **22** Stephen Fry (Oscar Wilde). **23** Kafka. **24** Beethoven. **25** Phineas T. Barnum.

## *QUIZ 75* POT LUCK 25 ........ LEVEL 3

*Answers – see page 293*

1 Which Michael featured in *Manhattan*?
2 To which American state is Janet Leigh's car registered in *Psycho*?
3 What was Robert Donat's final film?
4 Who directed *The Fifth Element*?
5 Which soap did Kevin Kline star in?
6 Within five minutes, how long does *Logan's Run* last?
7 Who did Michael Douglas play in *The China Syndrome*?
8 Who is Q. Moonblood better known as on the credits of *First Blood*?
9 Who directed the film *After Dark, My Sweet*?
10 Who won the Best Actor Oscar for *Charly*?
11 What was the name of Julie Kavner's character in *Awakenings*?
12 In which movie does Jeff Bridges play The Dude?
13 *Superman* and *Nixon* both featured which actor?
14 For which movie did Shirley MacLaine win Best Actress at the Venice Film Festival in 1988?
15 Which Albert featured in *Malcolm X*?
16 Within ten minutes, how long does *Good Will Hunting* last?
17 Whose directing did Tom Cruise say was 'like seeing Bruce Springsteen live for the first time'?
18 Which Sam featured in *Tombstone*?
19 In which year was *Sabrina* first released?
20 Which movie star released an album called *The Star of the Flying Nun* in 1967?
21 In which film does a character named Chuck Yeager appear?
22 Who won the Best Actress Oscar for *Johnny Belinda*?
23 What was the name of Gabriel Byrne's character in *Miller's Crossing*?
24 Who directed *The Firm*?
25 Which Noah featured in *The Truman Show*?

**Answers 1970s** (see Quiz 73)
**1** *Dirty Harry*. **2** Matt Dillon. **3** Divine. **4** *Corvette Summer*. **5** Sonny Wortzik (*Dog Day Afternoon*). **6** Subway train. **7** Gene Wilder. **8** Illinois. **9** *Nashville*. **10** Bree Daniels. **11** Nicol Williamson. **12** Two hours (131 mins). **13** *A Clockwork Orange*. **14** Burt Lancaster. **15** Charles Shaughnessy. **16** Michael Wadleigh (*Woodstock*). **17** *Raise the Titanic*. **18** *The Sentinel*. **19** Raquel Welch. **20** *The Last Detail*. **21** Ali McGraw. **22** *Fat City*. **23** Woody Guthrie. **24** Afghanistan in the 1880s. **25** Jill Clayburgh.

## *QUIZ 76* BIOPICS ........................................................ LEVEL 3

*Answers – see page 294*

1 Who played the future Indira Gandhi's father in *Gandhi*?
2 Which role did the star of *Mona Lisa* and *Who Framed Roger Rabbit?* play in *Nixon*?
3 Who played Judge Roy Bean in *The Westerner*?
4 Who was the subject of *Lust for Life*?
5 Whose story was told in *Inn of the Sixth Happiness* with Ingrid Bergman?
6 Who directed the 1995 biopic about the Beatles' early days in Hamburg?
7 Who was the subject of *New Wine*, with Albert Basserman?
8 Who did Errol Flynn play in *Too Much Too Soon*?
9 What was the name of Mrs Florenz Ziegfeld, as played by Myrna Loy in the biopic?
10 Who did Ellen Barkin play in *Wild Bill*?
11 *Dance with a Stranger* was about whom?
12 Which singer did Susan Hayward play in *I'll Cry Tomorrow*?
13 Who wrote the songs in the Danny Kaye movie about Hans Christian Andersen?
14 Who played Andy Warhol in *Basquiat*?
15 Which writer did Gregory Peck play in *Old Gringo*?
16 Who are the two main characters in *Shadowlands*?
17 Who played the first US president to resign while in office?
18 Who played Clark Gable in *Gable and Lombard*?
19 Which movie opens with the line, 'Hey boy, what you doin' with my momma's car'?
20 Who played the title role of the rock singer who sang 'Peggy Sue'?
21 *Kundun* is Martin Scorsese's biography of whom?
22 Who played the title role in the 90s movie about the author of *The Importance of Being Earnest*?
23 Who was the subject of the movie in which Jeremy Irons starred after he won his first Oscar?
24 Which composer did Gary Oldman play in *Immortal Beloved*?
25 Who did Wallace Beery play in *A Lady's Morals* in 1930?

**Answers Jack Lemmon** (see Quiz 74)
**1** John Uhler Lemmon III. **2** Ensign Pulver (*Mister Roberts*). **3** *The Apartment.* **4** Blake Edwards. **5** Aquarius. **6** Billy Wilder. **7** *Some Like It Hot.* **8** *The Apartment.* **9** Felix Unger. **10** Michael Douglas. **11** *The Great Race.* **12** André Previn. **13** Hildy Johnson. **14** Virna Lisi (*How to Murder Your Wife*). **15** Doughnuts. **16** *Kotch.* **17** *Fire Down Below.* **18** *China Syndrome* & *Missing.* **19** Bruce Davison. **20** Chile. **21** *Tribute.* **22** *That's Life!* **23** *Buddy Buddy.* **24** *Avanti!* **25** Venice.

## *QUIZ 77* STEVEN SPIELBERG ........ LEVEL 3

*Answers – see page 299*

1 Which studio did he make his first professional movies with?
2 What was Amblin's logo?
3 Who gave Spielberg his first professional contract?
4 With whom did he found Dreamworks?
5 What was his 1989 movie a remake of?
6 What was the name of the police chief in his first blockbuster?
7 Who was his wife when he made *Always*?
8 Under what star sign was he born?
9 Who does he say he is always thinking of when he is directing?
10 In which 1980 movie did he have a cameo role?
11 On whose eyes were *E.T.*'s eyes based?
12 Who wrote the book on which his first Oscar-winner as director was based?
13 Which movie did he reissue as *The Special Edition* because he was initially dissatisfied with it?
14 Which Indiana Jones movie did Mrs Spielberg star in?
15 With which movie did he win an amateur contest aged 13?
16 On whose novel was his 1987 movie based?
17 What was his first film after *Close Encounters of the Third Kind*?
18 Which company did he form in 1984?
19 What was his 70s debut as a feature-film director?
20 Which animated features did he make prior to *Who Framed Roger Rabbit?*?
21 What was the second film which earned him a Best Director Oscar nomination?
22 Who wrote the book on which his first adult movie was based?
23 Which award did he win at the 1987 Oscar ceremony?
24 At which film festival was his first professional movie shown?
25 His sister won her first Oscar in what capacity for which movie?

**Answers Hollywood Heyday** (see Quiz 79)
**1** Doris Day. **2** *The Ghost Breakers*. **3** Joan Crawford. **4** David Niven. **5** *Major Barbara*. **6** Bing Crosby. **7** Ginger Rogers. **8** Spottiswoode Aitken. **9** *Private Worlds*. **10** Katharine Hepburn. **11** Jean Arthur. **12** Joseph Cotten. **13** Betty Grable. **14** Joan Crawford. **15** George Cukor. **16** *Monkey Business*. **17** Swedish. **18** Brigadier General. **19** Sri Lanka (Ceylon). **20** Charlotte Bronte. **21** Tallulah Bankhead. **22** Colin Clive. **23** Bing Crosby. **24** Peter Lorre. **25** June Allyson.

## *QUIZ 78* POT LUCK 26 ........ LEVEL 3

*Answers – see page 300*

1 What colour T-shirt is James Dean wearing in *Rebel Without a Cause* during the car race?
2 What is Private Benjamin's first name?
3 Who formed his own company, Bryna Productions, in 1955?
4 Which movie star released a single called 'Do It to Me' in 1979?
5 Who won the Best Actor Oscar for *A Double Life*?
6 Which Shelley featured in *Labyrinth*?
7 Who won the Best Director Oscar for *The Quiet Man*?
8 Which actress links *Cherry 2000* and *Close to Eden*?
9 The final car chase in *What's Up Doc* takes place in which city?
10 The songs 'On the Atchison', 'Topeka', and 'The Santa Fe' came from which movie?
11 Who played Sera in *Leaving Las Vegas*?
12 From 1936 to 1950 Judy Garland was with which studio?
13 Who wrote the screenplay for *Casualties of War*?
14 Onna White won a Special Award in 1968 for doing what in *Oliver!*?
15 Which Noah featured in *Shine*?
16 Who played Ronald Miller in the film *Can't Buy Me Love*?
17 To the nearest hour, how long does *The Graduate* last?
18 Which song won Best Song Oscar for *A Hole in the Head*?
19 What sort of car did Woody Allen have in *Sleeper*?
20 What is the first name of Robert Redford, who uses his middle name in the movies?
21 Who won the Best Actress Oscar for *The Heiress*?
22 *Star Wars* and *Kafka* both starred which actor?
23 Within five minutes, how long does *Jurassic Park* last?
24 Who directed *Face/Off*?
25 Which Kirsten featured in *Doctor Dolittle*?

**Answers Woody Allen** (see Quiz 80)
**1** Stewart. **2** Marshall Brickman. **3** *Zelig.* **4** *Getting Even; Without Feathers; Side Effects.* **5** *Don't Drink the Water.* **6** Orion. **7** Ralph Rosenblum. **8** Alvy Singer. **9** Meryl Streep (*Manhattan*). **10** *The New Yorker.* **11** Yale; Michael Murphy. **12** Bette Midler. **13** Mira Sorvino (*Mighty Aphrodite*). **14** *The Purple Rose of Cairo.* **15** *A Midsummer Night's Sex Comedy.* **16** Maureen O'Sullivan & Mia Farrow (*Hannah and Her Sisters*). **17** Louise Lasser. **18** *Husbands and Wives.* **19** Michael's Pub, New York. **20** *Interiors.* **21** Sagittarius. **22** *Stardust Memories.* **23** Jimmy Bond. **24** Satchel Paige. **25** Tony Lacey.

## *QUIZ 79* HOLLYWOOD HEYDAY ........ LEVEL 3

*Answers – see page 297*

1 Who was the only actress to be billed above James Cagney in 30 years of film-making?
2 In which movie did Bob Hope say, 'The girls call me pilgrim because every time I dance with one I make a little progress'?
3 Who was known during part of her career as Billie Cassin?
4 Which film star wrote the novel *Once Over Lightly*?
5 What was Deborah Kerr's first film?
6 Who said his epitaph should be, 'He was an average guy who could carry a tune'?
7 Whose first movie was *Campus Sweethearts* with Rudy Vallee?
8 Who played Dr Cameron in D.W. Griffith's *Birth of a Nation*?
9 What was Claudette Colbert's next Oscar nomination after her win with *It Happened One Night*?
10 Who won a bronze medal for skating aged 14 at Madison Square Garden?
11 Which actress, born Gladys Georgianna Greene, made her screen debut in John Ford's *Cameo Kirby*?
12 Who debuted in *Too Much Johnson* after starring on Broadway opposite Katharine Hepburn in *The Philadelphia Story*?
13 Sam Goldwyn changed which star's name to Frances Dean?
14 Which Hollywood star married the head of Pepsi Cola in 1956?
15 Which director was fired from the set of *Gone with the Wind* only ten days into production?
16 In which movie did the Marx Brothers hide in barrels of kippered herring?
17 What nationality is Warner Oland, a screen Charlie Chan?
18 Which rank did James Stewart reach in the US Air Force?
19 Where was Merle Oberon born?
20 Who did Olivia de Havilland play in *Devotion*?
21 Which star of Hitchcock's *Lifeboat* was a daughter of a Speaker of the US House of Representatives?
22 Who played Frankenstein in the 30s classic?
23 Whose autobiography was called *Call Me Lucky*?
24 Which movie star is named in Al Stewart's song 'The Year of the Cat'?
25 Who played a role in *Best Foot Forward* on Broadway in 1943 which she recreated in the movie two years later?

**Answers Steven Spielberg** (see Quiz 77)
**1** Universal. **2** Bicycle from *E.T.* **3** Sidney Sheinberg. **4** David Geffen & Jeffrey Katzenberg. **5** *A Guy Named Joe* (remade as *Always*). **6** Martin Brody. **7** Kate Capshaw. **8** Sagittarius. **9** The audience. **10** *The Blues Brothers.* **11** Einstein's. **12** Thomas Keneally. **13** *Close Encounters of the Third Kind.* **14** *Indiana Jones and the Temple of Doom.* **15** *Escape to Nowhere.* **16** J.G. Ballard (*Empire of the Sun*). **17** *1941*. **18** Amblin. **19** *The Sugarland Express.* **20** *An American Tail; The Land Before Time.* **21** *Raiders of the Lost Ark.* **22** Alice Walker (*The Color Purple*). **23** Irving G. Thalberg Award. **24** Atlanta. **25** Screenwriter, *Big.*

## *QUIZ 80* WOODY ALLEN ........ LEVEL 3

*Answers – see page 298*

1 What is his middle name?
2 With whom did he share his Oscar for the screenplay of *Annie Hall*?
3 In which movie did he play a human chameleon in 1983?
4 Which three books did he write in the 60s?
5 In the 60s what did he write for Broadway along with *Play it Again Sam*?
6 Which film studio did he join after leaving United Artists?
7 Who was the editor on his first film as director?
8 What was Allen's character called in his 1977 movie with Diane Keaton?
9 In his last film of the 70s, who played his ex-wife who had left him for another woman?
10 For which newspaper did he write comic essays in the 60s?
11 In *Manhattan*, what is the name of his best friend, and who plays him?
12 Who was his co-star in *Scenes from a Mall*?
13 Who won the Oscar for the 1995 movie for which he was nominated as writer?
14 For which 80s movie did he win the International Critics Prize at Cannes?
15 What was the name of his first film with Mia Farrow?
16 Which famous mother and daughter starred in his film for which Michael Caine won an Oscar?
17 Who was his wife when he made *What's Up, Tiger Lily?*?
18 Which film was released soon after his affair with his partner's adopted daughter was exposed?
19 Where did he perform for several decades as a jazz clarinetist?
20 What was his first straight drama called?
21 What is his star sign?
22 What was his last film for United Artists?
23 Which character did he play in a James Bond movie?
24 After whom did he name his natural son with Mia Farrow?
25 In *Annie Hall* what is the name of the pop singer played by Paul Simon?

**Answers Pot Luck 26** (see Quiz 78)
**1** White. **2** Judy. **3** Kirk Douglas. **4** Britt Ekland. **5** Ronald Colman. **6** Thompson. **7** John Ford. **8** Melanie Griffith. **9** San Francisco. **10** *The Harvey Girls*. **11** Elisabeth Shue. **12** MGM. **13** David Rabe. **14** Choreography. **15** Taylor. **16** Patrick Dempsey. **17** Two hours. **18** 'High Hopes'. **19** Volkswagen Beetle. **20** Charles. **21** Olivia de Havilland. **22** Sir Alec Guinness. **23** 127 minutes. **24** John Woo. **25** Wilson.

## *QUIZ 81* POT LUCK 27 ........ LEVEL 3

*Answers – see page 303*

1 At what sport did Chevy Chase excel?
2 In which film did the character named Kimberly Wells appear?
3 Who directed *The Empire Strikes Back*?
4 Which Matt featured in *The Driver*?
5 Which entertainer died on the same day as muppet maestro Jim Henson?
6 What was the name of Michael O'Keefe's character in *Caddyshack*?
7 Within five minutes, how long does *Jungle Book* last?
8 *Flash II* and *Village of the Damned* both starred which actor?
9 Which Jeremy features in *Saving Private Ryan*?
10 Who plays Miss Millie in the film *The Color Purple*?
11 Who changed Bernie for Tony in his first film, *Criss Cross*?
12 Which actor played Elliott in *E.T.*?
13 Who said, 'The characters I play have a need to be cuddled'?
14 Which British actor said, 'Eight times my heart stopped'?
15 Who wrote the screenplay for *Clean and Sober*?
16 Who played Gregory Peck's feeble neighbour in *To Kill a Mockingbird*?
17 Which Donald featured in *Escape from New York*?
18 Who won the Best Actress Oscar for *The Farmer's Daughter*?
19 A character named Laura Burney appeared in which film?
20 In which year was *Duel in the Sun* released?
21 Olympia Dukakis was a champion in what sport while at university?
22 Who did Kevin Dillon play in *The Doors*?
23 What is the name of Raquel Welch's actress daughter?
24 Within fifteen minutes, how long does *The Godfather* last?
25 Which star of *Pretty Woman* was born Jay Greenspan?

**Answers Oscars – Best Actors & Actresses** (see Quiz 83)
**1** Edmund Gwenn. **2** Barry Fitzgerald. **3** Robert Donat. **4** Five. **5** *Bonnie and Clyde*. **6** Sacheen Littlefeather. **7** *The Robe*. **8** Red Buttons. **9** *Rambling Rose*. **10** Patty Duke. **11** Daniel Day-Lewis. **12** *Broadcast News* (Holly Hunter). **13** *Dr Jekyll and Mr Hyde*. **14** Angelo Maggio (*From Here to Eternity*). **15** *The Search*. **16** Elisabeth Shue. **17** Humphrey Bogart. **18** *Thunderbolt and Lightfoot*. **19** *Heaven Knows Mr Allison*. **20** Judy Holliday. **21** *Double Indemnity*. **22** *The Spy Who Came in from the Cold*. **23** Ada McGrath. **24** James Dean. **25** *The Story of Adele H*.

## *QUIZ 82* CHILD STARS ........ LEVEL 3

*Answers – see page 304*

1 Which future TV comedian was the child clinging to Marie Dressler's skirts in *Tillie's Punctured Romance* in 1914?
2 How is former child star Suzanne Caputo better known?
3 Who starred in *Reunion* when they were two?
4 Which teen star was Stewart Granger's brother in *North to Alaska*?
5 About which seven-year-old did Paderewski say, 'Some day that boy might take my place'?
6 Roddy McDowall found fame as a child and adult actor, and in which other branch of the arts?
7 Which former child star appeared in *Carmen Jones* and *Porgy and Bess*?
8 In which movie did Liza Minnelli appear as a baby with her mother?
9 How was Anne Shirley known in her early days as a child star?
10 Which actor was torn between Meryl Streep and Dustin Hoffman in a 70s classic?
11 Who played Michael, the little boy that Mary Poppins was nanny to?
12 In which movie did the unknown Alan Barnes steal the show from a more famous Hayley Mills?
13 Whose debut was in *Uncle Buck*?
14 Who played the youngest Frank McCourt in *Angela's Ashes*?
15 Which star of Little Miss Thoroughbred received a 1945 Oscar for being 'outstanding as a child actress'?
16 Who played the brother in *The Railway Children*?
17 Who played the title role in David Lean's classic *Oliver Twist* and went on to be a TV producer?
18 Who played young Charlie in Richard Attenborough's *Chaplin*?
19 Whose marriage to Drew Barrymore lasted just six weeks?
20 Who played Gregory Peck's daughter in *To Kill a Mockingbird*?
21 Who won a Special Oscar for *The Window* aged 12?
22 Which star of *Captains Courageous* and *Kidnapped* went into advertising when his adult film career foundered?
23 What was Matthew Beard's nickname?
24 Who played Gene Tierney's daughter in the 1947 movie which also starred Rex Harrison and George Sanders?
25 Which former member of the *Our Gang* movies appeared in *That's Entertainment III* in her seventies?

**Answers Pot Luck 28** (see Quiz 84)
**1** Nora Ephron. **2** Bernard Herrman. **3** Meryl Streep. **4** Douglas McGrath. **5** *The Guns of Navarone.* **6** Nelson. **7** Woody Harrelson. **8** 135 minutes. **9** Marshall Will Kane. **10** Fiorentino. **11** *Giant.* **12** Bette Midler. **13** Roger Moore. **14** Rebecca Miller. **15** Marion. **16** Colicos. **17** Sally Field. **18** Wind In His Hair. **19** Nouri. **20** 1940s. **21** 2 hours. **22** 'Lullaby of Broadway'. **23** Archer. **24** *Reversal of Fortune.* **25** *Big Broadcast of 1938.*

## *QUIZ 83* OSCARS – BEST ACTORS & ACTRESSES .............................. LEVEL 3

*Answers – see page 301*

1 Who was 72 when he won for *Miracle on 34th Street*?
2 Who was the first person to be nominated as Best Actor and Best Supporting Actor for the same role?
3 The only major award *Gone with the Wind* did not win went to whom?
4 How many Oscar nominations did Shirley MacLaine have before the one with which she won for *Terms of Endearment*?
5 For which movie was Estelle Parsons nominated on her film debut?
6 Who accepted Brando's Oscar for him for *The Godfather*?
7 For which movie did Richard Burton get his second nomination?
8 Which actor, real name Aaron Chwatt, won for *Sayonara*?
9 What was Laura Dern's first nomination for?
10 Which teenager was a winner for *The Miracle Worker*?
11 Which winner became Arthur Miller's son-in-law?
12 For which movie did the winner from *The Piano* win her first nomination?
13 For which movie did Frederic March win the first of his two Oscars?
14 For which character did Frank Sinatra first win Best Supporting Actor?
15 For which movie was Montgomery Clift nominated on his film debut?
16 Which actress was nominated in the movie which won Nicolas Cage an award in 1995?
17 Who was a winner and deprived Brando for *A Streetcar Named Desire*?
18 For which movie did Jeff Bridges win his second supporting actor nomination?
19 What was the second of Deborah Kerr's three nominations between 1956 and 1958?
20 Who won when Bette Davis was nominated for *All About Eve*?
21 For which movie did Barbara Stanwyck lose out on a 1944 Oscar to Ingrid Bergman?
22 What was the second of Richard Burton's three nominations between 1964 and 1966?
23 For which character did Holly Hunter win Best Actress in 1993?
24 Who was the first actor to be nominated for two posthumous Oscars?
25 For which movie did Isabelle Adjani receive her first nomination?

**Answers Pot Luck 27** (see Quiz 81)
**1** Tennis. **2** *The China Syndrome.* **3** Irvin Kershner. **4** Clark. **5** Sammy Davis Jnr (16.5.90). **6** Danny. **7** 78 minutes. **8** Mark Hamill. **9** Davies. **10** Dana Ivey. **11** Tony Curtis. **12** Henry Thomas. **13** Dudley Moore. **14** Peter Sellers. **15** Tod Carroll. **16** Robert Duvall. **17** Pleasence. **18** Loretta Young. **19** *Sleeping with the Enemy.* **20** 1946. **21** Fencing. **22** John Densemore. **23** Tahnee Welch. **24** 175 minutes. **25** Jason Alexander.

## *QUIZ 84* POT LUCK 28 ........ LEVEL 3

*Answers – see page 302*

1 Who won an Oscar for her first screenplay, *Silkwood*?
2 Martin Scorsese dedicated *Taxi Driver* to the memory of which composer who finished the score just before he died?
3 Which movie star released a single called 'Amazing Grace' in 1984?
4 Who directed 90s movie *Emma*?
5 A character named Keith Mallory appeared in which film?
6 Which Barry featured in *The Shining*?
7 *Wildcats* and *Wag the Dog* both starred which actor?
8 Within five minutes, how long does *Jerry Maguire* last?
9 What was the name of Gary Cooper's character in *High Noon*?
10 Which Linda featured in *Men in Black*?
11 A character named Jett Rink appeared in which 50s film?
12 Which actress once 'packed pineapples at a local cannery in Honolulu'?
13 Which uncredited actor appears as Clouseau at the end of *The Curse of the Pink Panther*?
14 Who played Kay Otis in the film *Consenting Adults*?
15 Who did Karen Allen play in *Raiders of the Lost Ark*?
16 Which John featured in *The Postman Always Rings Twice*?
17 Who founded the company Fogwood Films?
18 Who was played by Rodney A. Grant in *Dances with Wolves*?
19 Which Michael starred in *Flashdance*?
20 In which decade was *Crossfire* released?
21 To the nearest hour, how long does *Blade Runner* last?
22 Which song from *Gold Diggers of 1935* won an Oscar?
23 Which Anne featured in *Fatal Attraction*?
24 In which film did a character named Claus von Bulow appear?
25 The song 'Thanks for the Memory' came from which movie?

**Answers Child Stars** (see Quiz 82)
**1** Milton Berle. **2** Morgan Brittany. **3** The Dionne Quins. **4** Fabian. **5** Liberace. **6** Photography. **7** Dorothy Dandridge. **8** *In the Good Old Summertime.* **9** Dawn O' Day. **10** Justin Henry (*Kramer versus Kramer*). **11** Matthew Garber. **12** *Whistle Down the Wind.* **13** Macaulay Culkin. **14** Joe Breen. **15** Peggy Ann Garner. **16** Gary Warren. **17** John Howard Davies. **18** Hugh Downer. **19** Jeremy Thomas. **20** Mary Badham. **21** Bobby Driscoll. **22** Freddie Bartholomew. **23** Stymie. **24** Natalie Wood (*The Ghost and Mrs Muir*). **25** Nanette Fabray.

## *QUIZ 85* 1980s ........ LEVEL 3

*Answers – see page 307*

1 Who are the two main characters who write to each other in *84 Charing Cross Road*?
2 What were the furry creatures called in *Gremlins*?
3 Which 1982 movie did Hugh Grant make while still at Oxford?
4 In which movie did Robert De Niro play the devil?
5 Within fifteen minutes, how long does *Arthur* last?
6 What was the name of the giant grizzly which starred in *Clan of the Cave Bear*?
7 Who did Faye Dunaway play in *Chinatown*?
8 What was Emilio Estevez's first movie as writer/director?
9 Who played Robinson Crusoe in *Crusoe*?
10 What was the occupation of Madame Sousatzka?
11 In which movie was Isabelle Adjani Oscar-nominated for playing Rodin's mistress?
12 What was the real name of the actress who played the title role in *Octopussy*?
13 Which movie is famous for the fact that all Kevin Costner's scenes were cut out of it?
14 Who played Frances Farmer in *Frances*?
15 In which 1984 movie did Liza Minnelli play herself?
16 Who played Mozart's rival in *Amadeus*?
17 What was the name of the brain in the jar in *The Man with Two Brains*?
18 Which film is being screened on TV during *Gremlins*?
19 Who played Richie Valens in *La Bamba*?
20 In which movie did Harry Dean Stanton play an angel?
21 What was the name of Kristin Scott's character in *A Handful of Dust*?
22 Which movie had the ad line, 'In Vietnam the wind doesn't blow – it sucks'?
23 Who was decapitated during the making of *Twilight Zone: The Movie*?
24 Which star of *Seinfeld* made an appearance in *Pretty Woman*?
25 In whose stately home was *Greystoke* filmed?

**Answers Pot Luck 29** (see Quiz 87)
**1** Billy. **2** *The Outsiders*. **3** Tobolowsky. **4** *Freejack*. **5** *Stir Crazy*. **6** Betty Thomas. **7** Sean Young. **8** Ramis. **9** Angela Lansbury. **10** 125 minutes. **11** Norman Taurog. **12** Preston Sturges. **13** Five. **14** Nelligan. **15** *A Fire over England*. **16** Judy Davis. **17** James Clavell. **18** *Always*. **19** *Blue Sky*. **20** Joe Eszterhas. **21** Charlton Heston. **22** Spike Lee. **23** *Awakenings*. **24** Olivia de Havilland. **25** Webb.

## *QUIZ 86* MUSICALS .................... LEVEL 3

*Answers – see page 308*

1 Which musical has the song, 'Why Can't a Woman Be More Like a Man'?
2 Who were the singing voices of Tony and Maria in *West Side Story*?
3 Who does Debbie Reynolds play in *Singin' in the Rain*?
4 Who wrote the score of the musical remake of *Ninotchka*?
5 June Allyson sang 'Thou Swell' in which movie?
6 In which 70s movie did 'Starsky' of *Starsky and Hutch* fame star?
7 Which character sings 'Sit Down You're Rockin' the Boat' in the Frank Loesser musical?
8 Who played the third sailor 'On the Town' with Frank Sinatra and Gene Kelly?
9 Which character did Stubby Kaye play in *Li'l Abner*?
10 Whose voice was dubbed by Marilyn Horne in *Carmen Jones*?
11 In *An American in Paris* the ex GI is in Paris to learn how to do what?
12 Which musical was the first to be shown in Todd AO?
13 In *Guys and Dolls* where does the double wedding take place?
14 In which 60s musical movie did Richard Attenborough sing?
15 Who played Peron's teenage mistress in *Evita*?
16 Who was the black female star of *Stormy Weather*?
17 Which character discovers the Von Trapps hiding in the abbey in *The Sound of Music*?
18 In what type of building does the opening scene of *Evita* take place?
19 Who choreographed the dance routines in *Half a Sixpence*?
20 Who played Barbra Streisand's husband in the follow-up to *Funny Girl*?
21 *Follow the Fleet* was based on which two Broadway plays?
22 In which Liza Minnelli musical is TV's Jane Krakowski from *Ally McBeal* one of the dancers?
23 Who wrote the score for the 1953 movie with Fred Astaire & Cyd Charisse?
24 Within fifteen minutes, how long does *Gigi* last?
25 What colour is Mary Poppins's sash when she's dancing with the penguins?

**Answers Animation** (see Quiz 88)
**1** Joan Cusack. **2** Art Babbitt. **3** Maurice Chevalier. **4** James Earl Jones. **5** *Plane Crazy*. **6** *Porky's Hare Hunt*. **7** *The Chain Gang*. **8** Joanna Lumley & Miriam Margolyes. **9** 1932. **10** Bach's Toccata & Fugue in D Minor. **11** John Lasseter. **12** Richard Williams. **13** 76 minutes. **14** MGM. **15** Universal. **16** Bob Hoskins. **17** Ralph Bakshi. **18** Don Bluth. **19** Michael J. Fox. **20** *Tin Toy*. **21** Columbia. **22** *Lady and the Tramp*. **23** *Fast and Furry Outs*. **24** Monstro. **25** Hans Zimmer.

## *QUIZ 87* POT LUCK 29 ........ LEVEL 3

*Answers – see page 305*

1 What was the name of the Kramers' son?
2 What was Rob Lowe's first film, in 1983?
3 Which Stephen featured in *Groundhog Day*?
4 Which 1992 film did rock star Mick Jagger star in?
5 Skip Donahue and Harry Monroe were characters in which film?
6 Who directed the 90s movie *Doctor Dolittle*?
7 Which actress was originally set to play the role of Vicki Vale before Kim Basinger took over in *Batman*?
8 Which Harold featured in *Ghostbusters*?
9 *National Velvet* and *Company of Wolves* starred which actress?
10 Within five minutes, how long does *Jaws* last?
11 Who won the Best Director Oscar for *Skippy* in 1931?
12 Which writer/director was the inventor of kissproof lipstick?
13 How many times was John Huston married?
14 Which Kate featured in *US Marshals*?
15 The relationship between Laurence Olivier and Vivien Leigh began on the set of which movie?
16 Who played Audrey Taylor in the film *Barton Fink*?
17 Which writer directed *To Sir, With Love* in 1967?
18 What was the last film Audrey Hepburn appeared in?
19 What was the last movie made by director Tony Richardson?
20 Who wrote the screenplay for the film *Basic Instinct*?
21 *Wayne's World 2* and *Hamlet* link which actor?
22 Who directed *Do the Right Thing*?
23 The character Dr Malcolm Sayer appeared in which film?
24 Who won the Best Actress Oscar for *To Each His Own*?
25 Which Chloe featured in *Twins*?

**Answers 1980s** (see Quiz 85)
**1** Helene Hanff & Frank Doel. **2** Mogwais. **3** *Privileged.* **4** *Angel Heart.* **5** 97 minutes. **6** Bart. **7** Evelyn Mulwray. **8** *Men at Work.* **9** Aidan Quinn. **10** Piano teacher. **11** *Camille Claudel.* **12** Maude Wikstrum (Maud Adams). **13** *The Big Chill.* **14** Jessica Lange. **15** *The Muppets Take Manhattan.* **16** F. Murray Abraham. **17** Anne Uumellmahaye. **18** *It's a Wonderful Life.* **19** Lou Diamond Phillips. **20** *One Magic Christmas.* **21** Brenda Last. **22** *Full Metal Jacket.* **23** Vic Morrow. **24** Jason Alexander. **25** Duke of Roxburghe.

## *QUIZ 88* ANIMATION ............ LEVEL 3

*Answers – see page 306*

1 Who is the voice of Jessie in *Toy Story 2*?
2 Who drew the wicked queen in *Snow White*?
3 Who sang the title song in *The Aristocats*?
4 Who was the voice of Mufasa in *The Lion King*?
5 The Mickey Mouse character first appeared in which cartoon, when he was briefly known as Mortimer?
6 In which movie did Bugs Bunny first appear?
7 Pluto made his big-screen debut in which movie?
8 Who voiced Spiker and Sponge in *James and the Giant Peach*?
9 In what year did Goofy appear in *Mickey's Review*?
10 With which piece of music does *Fantasia* open?
11 Who directed the first feature-length computer-generated film?
12 Who won an Oscar for animation for *Who Framed Roger Rabbit*??
13 Within fifteen minutes, how long does *Peter Pan* last?
14 Fred Quimby headed whose cartoon studio?
15 Which studio released *Oswald the Rabbit*?
16 Who was the voice of the Russian goose in *Balto*?
17 Who made the more adult animation, *Fritz the Cat*?
18 Whose production company released *An American Tail* in the 80s?
19 Who provided the voice of Chance in *Homeward Bound: The Incredible Journey*?
20 Which short movie did John Lasseter receive an Oscar for before he made *Toy Story*?
21 Which studio created *Color Rhapsodies*?
22 What was the only feature film in the 1950s devised by Disney from an original story?
23 In which movie did Road Runner have his first screen outing?
24 What is the name of the whale in *Pinocchio*?
25 Who wrote the score for *The Lion King*?

**Answers Musicals** (see Quiz 86)
**1** *My Fair Lady*. **2** Jimmy Bryant & Marni Nixon. **3** Kathy Seldon. **4** Cole Porter. **5** *Words and Music*. **6** *Fiddler on the Roof*. **7** Nicely Nicely Johnson. **8** Jules Munshin. **9** Marryin' Sam. **10** Dorothy Dandridge. **11** Paint. **12** *Oklahoma!*. **13** Times Square. **14** *Dr Dolittle*. **15** Andrea Corr. **16** Lena Horne. **17** Rolf. **18** Cinema. **19** Gillian Lynne. **20** James Caan. **21** *Shore Leave* & *Hit the Deck*. **22** *Stepping Out*. **23** Arthur Schwarz & Howard Dietz (*The Band Wagon*). **24** 116 minutes. **25** Red.

## *QUIZ 89* HEROES & VILLAINS ........ LEVEL 3

*Answers – see page 311*

1 Which movie did Kim Basinger back out of and lose a multi-million pound lawsuit as a result?
2 Who was the first actor ever to refuse an Oscar?
3 Which actor, who worked with the Resistance in Rome in World War II, made his first Hollywood appearance in *Little Women*?
4 Who walked out on her contract with 20th Century Fox after the failure of *Fallen Angel*?
5 Which Bond villain was identified by a Holocaust survivor as having saved her family from the Nazis?
6 Which actor, born Orson Whipple Hungerford III, was expelled from Spain in 1974?
7 Who was arrested in a Florida cinema in 1991 during a showing of *Naughty Nurses*?
8 Who was awarded a medal in 1938 by Goebbels and was appointed head of his film company Tobis?
9 Why did MGM sack Sinatra in 1949?
10 Which actor was the first glider pilot to land Allied troops behind Japanese lines in Burma?
11 Who received the Jean Hersholt Humanitarian Award during the 1977 Oscar ceremony?
12 Where was Leslie Howard returning from when he was shot down in World War II?
13 Who made his debut as a mugger in Woody Allen's *Bananas*?
14 Which cause does Paul Newman give the profits of his salad dressing business to?
15 Who set up the American Foundation for AIDS Research?
16 Which actress's daughter stabbed her boyfriend to death but was acquitted on grounds of protecting her mother?
17 What could 007 hero turned villain Sean Connery change in *The Avengers*?
18 Who did Gregory Peck play in *The Boys from Brazil*?
19 Who plays the villain alongside Quentin Tarantino in *From Dusk Till Dawn*?
20 Which actor famous for wholesome roles played the villain in *Double Indemnity*?
21 Which villain did Richard Widmark play in *Kiss of Death* in 1947?
22 Who played the first cinema vampire in *Nosferatu*?
23 Whose make-up turned Boris Karloff into one of the great screen performers of all time?
24 Where was Stacy Keach arrested in April 1984?
25 Who wrote *Mommie Dearest*?

**Answers Comedy** (see Quiz 91)
**1** *$3,000.* **2** *A Shot in the Dark.* **3** Nixon & Kennedy. **4** 98 minutes. **5** Sherman Klump. **6** Gonzo. **7** Car Salesman. **8** Leaf Phoenix. **9** A gopher. **10** Vincent Cadby. **11** Punxsutawney. **12** Alabama. **13** A bouncer. **14** Wyld Stallyns. **15** Elizabeth Taylor. **16** *Blazing Saddles.* **17** *The Bride and the Wolf.* **18** 1962. **19** Waco. **20** *A Day at the Races.* **21** Franck Eggelhoffer. **22** Fozziwig the rubber chicken factory owner. **23** *Kindergarten Cop.* **24** *Bedtime Story.* **25** Thora Birch.

## *QUIZ 90* POT LUCK 30 .......... LEVEL 3

*Answers – see page 312*

1 Which high flyer appeared in *The Boy in the Plastic Bubble*?
2 What is the last word of *Sleepy Hollow*?
3 Within five minutes, how long does *JFK* last?
4 Which Tony featured in *Ghost*?
5 Who directed *Deep Impact*?
6 What was the name of Audrey Hepburn's character in *The Nun's Story*?
7 In which film did a character named Stephen McCaffrey appear?
8 Edith Head contributed to some 1,000 movies, doing what?
9 *Four Rooms* and *A League of Their Own* starred which performer?
10 Who won the Best Actor Oscar for *All the King's Men* in 1949?
11 Which Paul featured in *Raiders of the Lost Ark*?
12 Who directed *Diamonds Are Forever*?
13 Who directed *Agnes Browne*?
14 Who played Pa Kent in the 1978 *Superman* movie?
15 Which soap did Hollywood star Tommy Lee Jones star in?
16 *The Year of Living Dangerously* was concerned with which year?
17 Which British actor won an Oscar for *A Double Life*?
18 In which year did David Niven die?
19 Which Paul featured in *The Full Monty*?
20 Who directed the film *Alive*?
21 Within fifteen minutes, how long does *Casablanca* last?
22 In which film did a character named C.R. MacNamara appear?
23 Which Barry featured in *Saturday Night Fever*?
24 Who won the Best Actress Oscar for *The Trip to Bountiful*?
25 Which 1943 film is Spielberg's 80s movie *Always* a remake of?

**Answers Oscars – Best of the Rest** (see Quiz 92)
**1** *The Turning Point.* **2** Luise Rainer. **3** Writer. **4** Peter Shaffer. **5** Costume design. **6** Francis Ford Coppola. **7** *The Bells of Saint Mary's; Say One For Me.* **8** *Ordinary People.* **9** *The English Patient; Shakespeare in Love.* **10** Carmine. **11** *Tom Jones.* **12** Three (Brando, Hoffman, Hanks). **13** Murdered on his way home from a rehearsal. **14** University of Hull. **15** Cinematography. **16** Douglas Fairbanks. **17** Sound effects. **18** *The Circus.* **19** Make-up. **20** *On the Waterfront; The Godfather; The Godfather Part II.* **21** 1937. **22** *The Last Command; The Way of All Flesh.* **23** Lewis Milestone. **24** Darryl Zanuck. **25** Three.

## *QUIZ 91* COMEDY ........ LEVEL 3

*Answers – see page 309*

1 What was *Pretty Woman* originally to have been called?
2 In which film did Peter Sellers first star as Clouseau?
3 Which presidents does Tom Hanks meet in *Forrest Gump*?
4 Within fifteen minutes, how long does *The Muppet Movie* last?
5 Who does Eddie Murphy play in the 90s remake of the Jerry Lewis comedy?
6 Who was the author in *The Muppet Christmas Carol*?
7 What is Ted Danson's job in *Made in America*?
8 Who plays Gary in the film *Parenthood*?
9 What type of animal drives Bill Murray mad in *Caddyshack*?
10 Who does Simon Callow play in *Ace Ventura: When Nature Calls*?
11 In which town is *Groundhog Day* set?
12 In which state is Vinny's cousin accused of murder in *My Cousin Vinny*?
13 What part does Meat Loaf play in *Wayne's World*?
14 What is the name of Bill & Ted's rock group in *Bill and Ted's Bogus Journey*?
15 Who played John Goodman's mother in law in *The Flintstones*?
16 In which film does railwayman Cleavon Little become sheriff?
17 What was *Moonstruck* originally to have been called?
18 In what year is *National Lampoon's Animal House* set?
19 Where was Steve Martin born?
20 'Marry me, Emily, and I'll never look at another horse' is the last line of which movie?
21 Which character does Martin Short play in the 90s film *Father of the Bride*?
22 Who did Fozzie Bear play in *The Muppet Christmas Carol*, and what was his job?
23 What was Arnold Schwarzenegger's first comedy movie of the 90s?
24 Which film was remade as *Dirty Rotten Scoundrels*?
25 Which actress links *Hocus Pocus* and *Now and Then*?

**Answers Heroes & Villains** (see Quiz 89)
**1** *Boxing Helena*. **2** George C. Scott. **3** Rossano Brazzi. **4** Alice Faye. **5** Gert Frobe (*Goldfinger*). **6** Ty Hardin. **7** Pee Wee Herman. **8** Emil Jannings. **9** He insulted boss Louis B. Mayer. **10** Jackie Coogan. **11** Charlton Heston. **12** Lisbon. **13** Sylvester Stallone. **14** Holiday camps for children with life-threatening diseases. **15** Elizabeth Taylor. **16** Lana Turner's daughter Cheryl. **17** The weather. **18** Joseph Mengele. **19** George Clooney. **20** Fred MacMurray. **21** Tommy Udo. **22** Max Schreck. **23** Jack Pierce. **24** Heathrow Airport. **25** Christina Crawford (daughter of Joan).

## *QUIZ 92* OSCARS – BEST OF THE REST ........ LEVEL 3

*Answers – see page 310*

1 Which 70s film had 11 nominations but won nothing?
2 Who was the first actress to win in consecutive years?
3 Out of 11 nominations *Becket* had one winner; in which category?
4 On whose play was F. Murray Abraham's Oscar-winning performance based?
5 In what capacity was Anna Biedrzycka Sheppard nominated for *Schindler's List*?
6 Who said, 'I probably have genius but no talent'?
7 Which two subsequent movies featured the lead character of *Going My Way*?
8 Which movie had the ad line, 'Everything is in its proper place except the past'?
9 In which two 90s Best Films did Colin Firth appear?
10 Which Coppola won an Oscar for *The Godfather Part II*?
11 What was the first movie to have three nominations for Best Supporting Actress?
12 Of all the actors with two wins, how many were still alive at the end of the 20th century?
13 How did the nominee director for *Rebel Without a Cause* meet his death?
14 Where did Anthony Minghella teach before being an Oscar winner?
15 In which category did Russell Carpenter win for *Titanic*?
16 Who was the first president of the Academy which presents the Oscars?
17 For what did Peter Berkos win a Special Award with *The Hindenburg*?
18 For which movie did Chaplin win his first Special Award?
19 In which category did William Turtle win a Special Award?
20 Which three films have received three nominations for *Best Supporting Actor*?
21 In what year was the Irving Thalberg award introduced?
22 For which two films was the first Best Actor given his award?
23 Who was the first person to win two awards for direction?
24 Who won the first Irving Thalberg award?
25 How many Oscars did Tim Rice win in the 1990s?

**Answers Pot Luck 30** (see Quiz 90)
**1** Buzz Aldrin. **2** Way ('And home is this way'). **3** 189 minutes. **4** Goldwyn. **5** Mimi Leder. **6** Gabrielle Van Der Mal. **7** *Backdraft.* **8** Costume design. **9** Madonna. **10** Broderick Crawford. **11** Freeman. **12** Guy Hamilton. **13** Anjelica Huston. **14** Glenn Ford. **15** *One Life to Live.* **16** 1965. **17** Ronald Colman. **18** 1983. **19** Barber. **20** Frank Marshall. **21** 102 minutes. **22** *One, Two, Three.* **23** Miller. **24** Geraldine Page. **25** *A Guy Named Joe.*

## *QUIZ 93* POT LUCK 31 ........................................ LEVEL 3

*Answers – see page 315*

1 Under what name does Janet Leigh sign in to the Bates Motel?
2 In which film does a character named Louise Bryant appear?
3 Which movie star was born on the same day as fellow star Marlon Brando?
4 To the nearest hour, did *Alfie* run 1, 2 or 3 hours?
5 Which Roger directed *Dante's Peak*?
6 Who won the Best Actress Oscar for *The Great Ziegfeld*?
7 What colour is Melanie's dress in *The Birds*?
8 Within fifteen minutes, how long does *Citizen Kane* last?
9 Which Chris featured in *The Princess Bride*?
10 A character named Prissy Bronte appeared in which film?
11 The song 'The Way You Look Tonight' came from which movie?
12 Who won the Best Director Oscar for *Bad Girl*?
13 Meryl Streep said you can't get spoiled if you do your own what?
14 Which John featured in the 80s version of *The Fly*?
15 Which movie star released a single called 'Lonely for a Girl' in 1965?
16 Who did Ralph Richardson play in *Time Bandits*?
17 What was the name of Deborah Kerr's character in *An Affair To Remember*?
18 Who directed the film *Air America*?
19 Which Robert featured in *Private Benjamin*?
20 For what did Les Bowie win a Special Award in 1978?
21 What movie is shown in the film *Hot Shots!*?
22 Within five minutes, how long does *Jackie Brown* last?
23 Who directed *The Craft*?
24 What was the name of Spencer Tracy's character in *Inherit the Wind*?
25 Which Matt featured in *Honey, I Shrunk the Kids*?

**Answers Writers** (see Quiz 95)
**1** William Nicholson. **2** Bob Hope & Danny Kaye. **3** *Delusions of Grandma.* **4** Dulwich College. **5** Alfred Uhry's. **6** Hans Christian Andersen. **7** Carl Woodward. **8** Billy Hayes's. **9** Spielberg. **10** Michael Crichton. **11** *The Lost World.* **12** Roger Avary. **13** Preston Sturges. **14** Henry Graham. **15** *Red Dragon* by Thomas Harris **16** Norman Mailer. **17** Neil Simon. **18** Harrison Ford (Melissa Mathison). **19** *Blue Collar.* **20** Winona Ryder. **21** Richard Stark. **22** Robin Ruzan. **23** Dan O'Bannon. **24** Nora Ephron & Carl Bernstein. **25** *The Age of Innocence.*

## *QUIZ 94* 1990s ........ LEVEL 3

*Answers – see page 316*

1 Who did Julia Roberts want for the part of Shakespeare in *Shakespeare in Love*, so turned down the movie herself?
2 Who played Margaret Schlegel's younger sister in *Howard's End*?
3 What did Jim Carrey have removed shortly after making *The Mask*?
4 *Backbeat* was about which pop star?
5 Which two Johns are Gwyneth Paltrow's prospective lovers in *Sliding Doors*?
6 Who played the unwitting drugs carriers in *Brokedown Palace*?
7 Where was Ms Heslop's home in *Muriel's Wedding*?
8 Who plays the prospective bride in *My Best Friend's Wedding*?
9 Who or what was *Andre* in the film of the same name?
10 What is the epidemic that breaks out in Spielberg's animated *Balto*?
11 What was Woody Allen's follow-up to *Everyone Says I Love You*?
12 Within fifteen minutes, how long does *Nell* last?
13 Who played Babe Ruth in *Babe*?
14 Which writer did Johnny Depp play in *Fear and Loathing in Las Vegas*?
15 What was the name of the gangster played by Ray Liotta in *Goodfellas*?
16 In *Quiz Show*, what is the quiz show called?
17 For which movie did Jamie Lee Curtis win her second Golden Globe Award?
18 *Devil's Candy* was written about the making of which movie?
19 *A Thousand Acres* was loosely based on which Shakespeare play?
20 Which father and son starred in *A Boy Called Hate*?
21 Who played Vincent van Gogh in *Vincent and Theo*?
22 River Phoenix died during the making of which movie?
23 Who did Al Pacino play in the 1990 movie with Warren Beatty and Madonna?
24 Who played two parts in *A Kiss Before Dying* in 1991?
25 Which movie had the ad line, 'The coast is toast'?

**Answers Pot Luck 32** (see Quiz 96)
**1** Eldred. **2** Cellist. **3** German. **4** *Apocalypse Now.* **5** Mie Hama. **6** 'You'll Never Know'. **7** Gary. **8** *Presumed Innocent.* **9** Michael Bay. **10** *Lady Jane.* **11** Jose Ferrer. **12** Judy Bernly. **13** 100 minutes. **14** 'All the Way'. **15** Schneider. **16** *Out of the Past.* **17** Meg Tilly. **18** Hutton. **19** 111 minutes. **20** Simon West. **21** Kitchen. **22** 1940s. **23** Michelle Pfeiffer. **24** Ronald Regan. **25** *The Unforgiven.*

## *QUIZ 95* WRITERS ........ LEVEL 3

*Answers – see page 313*

1 On whose play was *Shadowlands* based?
2 Who did Billy Wilder originally write *Some Like It Hot* for?
3 What was the name of the Carrie Fisher novel on which *Postcards from the Edge* was based?
4 Which school links P.G. Wodehouse, Raymond Chandler and A.E.W. Mason who all wrote for the movies?
5 On whose one-act play was *Driving Miss Daisy* based?
6 Whose work was the inspiration for *The Red Shoes*?
7 Who wrote *Wired* about John Belushi, which was later filmed?
8 Whose memoirs did Oliver Stone use to script *Midnight Express*?
9 Who did the director of *Home Alone* first work for when he began as a screenwriter?
10 Who was paid $10 million for the screen rights to his novel *Airframe*?
11 What is Arthur Conan Doyle's contribution to tales for the cinema other than Sherlock Holmes?
12 Who co-wrote *Pulp Fiction* with Quentin Tarantino?
13 Which writer turned director in *The Great McGinty*?
14 How is Graham Greene billed in his cameo role in *Day for Night*?
15 On which book by which author was *Manhunter* based?
16 Who wrote the novel on which Warner Brothers' *American Dream* was based?
17 Which playwright was Woody Harrelson's father-in-law until 1986?
18 Who is the husband of the writer of the screenplay for *E.T.*?
19 What was the directorial debut of Paul Schrader, who scripted *Taxi Driver*?
20 About whom did Arthur Miller say, 'She's as good as it gets'?
21 On whose novel was *Point Blank* based?
22 Which writer married Mike Myers?
23 Who scripted Ridley Scott's 1979 sci-fi movie with Sigourney Weaver?
24 Whose marriage is the subject of *Heartburn*?
25 Which Pullitzer Prize-winning novel by Edith Wharton was brought to the big screen by Martin Scorsese in 1993?

**Answers Pot Luck 31** (see Quiz 93)
**1** Marie Samuels. **2** *Reds.* **3** Doris Day (3.4.24). **4** 2 hours. **5** Roger Donaldson. **6** Luise Rainer. **7** Green. **8** 120 minutes. **9** Sarandon. **10** *Green Card.* **11** *Swingtime.* **12** Frank Borzage. **13** Ironing. **14** Boushel. **15** Oliver Reed. **16** The Supreme Being. **17** Terri McKay. **18** Roger Spottiswoode. **19** Webber. **20** Visual effects on *Superman.* **21** *Flight of the Intruder.* **22** 154 minutes. **23** Andrew Fleming. **24** Henry Drummond. **25** Frewer.

## *QUIZ 96* POT LUCK 32 ........ LEVEL 3

*Answers – see page 314*

1 What is the first name of Gregory Peck, who uses his middle name in the movies?
2 What is Sigourney Weaver's job in *Ghostbusters*?
3 What is the first language to be spoken in *The Lady Vanishes*?
4 A character named Lieutenant Willard appears in which film?
5 Who played the Bond girl in *You Only Live Twice*?
6 Which song from *Hello, Frisco, Hello* won an Oscar?
7 Which Lorraine featured in *Jaws*?
8 In which film does a character named Rusty Sabich appear?
9 Who directed *Armageddon*?
10 What was Helena Bonham Carter's first film, in 1984?
11 Who won the Best Actor Oscar for *Cyrano de Bergerac*?
12 What was the name of Jane Fonda's character in *9 to 5*?
13 To the nearest 10 minutes, how long does *The Italian Job* last?
14 Which song won Best Song Oscar for *The Joker Is Wild*?
15 Which Rob featured in *Judge Dredd*?
16 Which 1947 film is the 80s movie *Against All Odds* based upon?
17 Who played Agnes in the film *Agnes of God*?
18 *Ordinary People* featured which Timothy?
19 Within fifteen minutes, how long does *Dr No* last?
20 Who directed *Con Air*?
21 Which Michael featured in *Out of Africa*?
22 In which decade was *Mom and Dad* released?
23 *A Midsummer Night's Dream* and *Sweet Liberty* both star which actress?
24 Who links *Cowboys from Brooklyn, Tugboat Annie Sails Again* and *An Angel from Texas*?
25 A character named Rachel Zachery appears in which film?

**Answers 1990s** (see Quiz 94)
**1** Daniel Day-Lewis. **2** Helena Bonham Carter. **3** His gall bladder. **4** John Lennon. **5** Lynch & Hannah. **6** Kate Beckinsale & Claire Danes. **7** Porpoise Spit. **8** Cameron Diaz. **9** Seal. **10** Diphtheria. **11** *Deconstructing Harry*. **12** 113 minutes. **13** John Goodman. **14** Hunter S. Thompson. **15** Henry Hill. **16** *Twenty One*. **17** *True Lies*. **18** *The Bonfire of the Vanities*. **19** *King Lear*. **20** Scott & James Caan. **21** Tim Roth. **22** *Dark Blood*. **23** Big Boy Caprice. **24** Sean Young. **25** *Volcano*.

## *QUIZ 97* MEL GIBSON ........ LEVEL 3

*Answers – see page 319*

1 What is his star sign?
2 Whose voice was he in a 1995 Disney hit?
3 Where are the friends from in *Gallipoli*?
4 Which pop star wife starred in *Lethal Weapon 2*?
5 How was the sequel to *Mad Max* titled in the US?
6 Who played his mother in his first Shakespearean venture?
7 In which movie did he play Sissy Spacek's husband?
8 In which 1993 movie did he direct himself?
9 Where was *Air America* filmed?
10 Where did he study in Australia?
11 Which 1979 movie earned him the Australian equivalent of an Oscar?
12 What was his second movie directed by Peter Weir?
13 In which 1984 movie did he play a role previously played by Clark Gable and Marlon Brando?
14 Who was the subject of *Immortal Beloved*?
15 Which film was advertised as: 'From a place you may never have heard of, a story you'll never forget'?
16 Where was *Attack Force Z* set?
17 Who directed his first movie of a Shakespeare play?
18 What was the name of his character in *Lethal Weapon*?
19 What was the name of the 1993 biography by Roland Perry?
20 What is his production company called?
21 Where are the villains from in *Lethal Weapon 2*?
22 In which city was *Mrs Soffel* set?
23 In which city in which state was he born?
24 On which river was *The River* set?
25 Who played Gibson's murdered wife in *Braveheart*?

**Answers Pot Luck 33** (see Quiz 99)
**1** Demi Moore. **2** Evil Genius. **3** *Fried Green Tomatoes at the Whistle Stop Café.* **4** Susan. **5** Orange. **6** Molen. **7** Robert Wise. **8** Emily Lloyd. **9** 145 minutes. **10** 'Sweet Leilan'. **11** *Splash.* **12** *The Empire Strikes Back.* **13** Perez. **14** Frank Capra. **15** Nicholas Evans. **16** *Another World.* **17** Sound effects – *Star Wars.* **18** Romeo. **19** Sinise. **20** 188 minutes. **21** Joanna Lumley. **22** *The Conversation.* **23** Natasha Richardson. **24** Luise Rainer. **25** William Peter Blatty.

## *QUIZ 98* 1940s STARS ........ LEVEL 3

*Answers – see page 320*

1 What was the second of Ingrid Bergman's three Oscar nominations between 1943 and 1945?
2 What was the nickname of the house David Niven shared with Errol Flynn?
3 Which star of *Rebecca* was the first woman lawyer in Texas?
4 Whose autobiography was called *Intermission*?
5 In *Mildred Pierce* which actor famously said, 'Oh boy! I'm so smart it's a disease!'?
6 Who played Catherine the Great in *A Royal Scandal*?
7 How did the star of *Forever Amber* meet her death?
8 Rita Hayworth and Hedy Lamarr advertised which cosmetics house in the 40s?
9 Who was married to Dick Powell between 1945 and 1963?
10 Who played Cleopatra in Pascal's *Caesar and Cleopatra*?
11 How old was Sydney Greenstreet when he made his very first movie?
12 Who had a biography called *Divine Bitch*?
13 What was the first of Gregory Peck's three Oscar nominations between 1945 and 1947?
14 Who said, 'All they did at MGM was change my leading men and the water in my swimming pool'?
15 In which movie did Errol Flynn say, 'Now for Australia and a crack at those Japs'?
16 Which part did Henry Fonda play in *The Ox-Bow Incident*?
17 What was Glenn Ford's real first name?
18 Who played Judy McPherson in *Only Angels Have Wings*?
19 Stan Laurel married eight times, but to how many different women?
20 How did Veronica Lake die?
21 In which 1943 movie did Johnny Weissmuller play himself?
22 Bill Mead died during the making of which movie?
23 In which 1949 movie did Robert Ryan play a boxer?
24 What was the first of Ingrid Bergman's three nominations between 1943 and 1945?
25 Who won a Special Oscar for *Meet Me in St Louis* aged eight?

**Answers Classics** (see Quiz 100)
**1** Book shop. **2** Beethoven's Pastoral Symphony. **3** Swats a little boy with a newspaper. **4** *The Apartment.* **5** 1 hour (80 mins). **6** *The Third Man.* **7** *Holiday Inn* ('White Christmas'). **8** *Suspicion.* **9** South America. **10** Fred MacMurray & Jack Oakie. **11** Elwood P. Dowd. **12** *The Lodger.* **13** Walter Pidgeon. **14** *It Happened One Night.* **15** Rhett. **16** Dying sea captain. **17** *Road to Hong Kong.* **18** 1946. **19** Ub Iwerks. **20** Osgood Fielding III. **21** *Brief Encounter.* **22** *Grand Hotel.* **23** Cary Grant; William Holden. **24** *Going My Way.* **25** Art Babbitt.

## QUIZ 99 POT LUCK 33 ........ LEVEL 3

*Answers – see page 317*

1 Which actress has children called Scout and Rumer?
2 What was the name of the villain in *Time Bandits*?
3 A character named Evelyn Couch appeared in which film?
4 What was the name of Jill Eikenberry's character in *Arthur*?
5 What colour dress is Jane Banks wearing when we first meet her in *Mary Poppins*?
6 Which Jerry featured in *Rain Man*?
7 Who directed *The Andromeda Strain*?
8 *Cookie* and *Scorchers* both starred which actress?
9 To the nearest 10 minutes, how long does *Independence Day* last?
10 Which song from *Waikiki Wedding* won an Oscar?
11 What was the first film put out by the Disney subsidiary, Touchstone?
12 Brian Johnson won a Special Award in 1980 for visual effects on which movie?
13 Which Rosie featured in *Night on Earth*?
14 Who won the Best Director Oscar for *You Can't Take it with You*?
15 Who wrote the novel *The Horse Whisperer*?
16 Which soap did Hollywood star Morgan Freeman star in?
17 For what did Benjamin Burtt Jr win an Oscar Special Award in 1977?
18 What was the name of Joan Wilder's cat in *Romancing the Stone*?
19 Which Gary featured in *Ransom*?
20 Within fifteen minutes, how long does *Gandhi* last?
21 *Shirley Valentine* and *Curse of the Pink Panther* link which actress?
22 In which film does a character named Harry Caul appear?
23 Which daughter of Vanessa Redgrave featured in *Nell*?
24 Who won the Best Actress Oscar for *The Good Earth*?
25 Which writer directed *The Exorcist III* in 1990?

**Answers Mel Gibson** (see Quiz 97)
**1** Capricorn. **2** Captain John Smith (*Pocahonatas*). **3** Perth, Australia. **4** Patsy Kensit. **5** *The Road Warrior*. **6** Glenn Close. **7** *The River*. **8** *The Man Without a Face*. **9** Thailand. **10** National Institute of Dramatic Arts. **11** *Tim*. **12** *The Year of Living Dangerously*. **13** *The Bounty* (Fletcher Christian). **14** Beethoven. **15** *Gallipoli*. **16** Japan. **17** Franco Zeffirelli. **18** Martin Riggs. **19** *Lethal Hero*. **20** Icon Productions. **21** South Africa. **22** Pittsburgh. **23** Peekskill, New York. **24** Holston River, Tennessee. **25** Catherine McCormack.

## *QUIZ 100* CLASSICS ........ LEVEL 3

*Answers – see page 318*

1 In *Funny Face*, where is Audrey Hepburn working prior to becoming a model?
2 In *Fantasia* which piece of music accompanies the scenes set on Mount Olympus?
3 What is Hitchcock's cameo appearance in *Blackmail*?
4 Which movie opens with the line 'On November 1 1959, the population of New York City was 8,042,783'?
5 To the nearest hour, how long does *Rope* last?
6 In which movie did Trevor Howard play Major Calloway?
7 Which movie had the best-selling single ever until Elton John's 'Candle in the Wind' replaced it?
8 Francis Iles's *Before the Fact* was the basis for which Hitchcock film?
9 About which continent is Audrey Hepburn reading in the library in *Breakfast at Tiffany's*?
10 Who were the original male choices for the series which starred Hope, Crosby and Lamour?
11 What was the name of the 'owner' of the six-foot-tall rabbit Harvey?
12 What was the first Hitchcock movie with one of his cameo roles?
13 Who played Mr Miniver in the Greer Garson classic?
14 Which 30s classic was originally to have been called *Night Bus*?
15 Who wore most costumes in *Gone with the Wind* – Rhett, Melanie or Ashley?
16 What part did Walter Huston play in son John's first movie as director?
17 What was the seventh *Road* film?
18 In what year did Universal stop making Sherlock Holmes films with Basil Rathbone?
19 Who did most of the trick work for *The Birds*?
20 Which character amorously pursues Daphne in *Some Like It Hot*?
21 Which movie inspired Billy Wilder to make *The Apartment*?
22 *Hotel Berlin* was the sequel to what classic?
23 Who was first tipped for the role of Shears in *The Bridge on the River Kwai*, and who actually got it?
24 In which movie did Bing Crosby first play Father O'Malley?
25 Who drew the dance of the mushrooms in *Fantasia*?

**Answers 1940s Stars** (see Quiz 98)
**1** *Gaslight.* **2** Cirrhosis by the Sea. **3** Florence Bates (Mrs Van Hopper). **4** Anne Baxter. **5** Jack Carson. **6** Tallulah Bankhead. **7** Fire (Linda Darnell). **8** Max Factor. **9** June Allyson. **10** Vivien Leigh. **11** 61. **12** Susan Hayward. **13** *The Keys of the Kingdom.* **14** Esther Williams. **15** *Desperate Journey.* **16** Gil Carter. **17** Gwyllyn. **18** Rita Hayworth. **19** Four. **20** Hepatitis. **21** *Stage Door Canteen.* **22** *They Died With Their Boots On.* **23** *The Set Up.* **24** *For Whom the Bell Tolls.* **25** Margaret O'Brien.

## *QUIZ 101* WORLD CINEMA ........ LEVEL 3

*Answers – see page 323*

1 Who directed *Fratelli e Sorelle*?
2 Who died the day after completing *Il Postino*?
3 Which 1996 Patrice Leconte movie won a BAFTA and four Cesars?
4 Which 1960 Palme D'Or winner so exhausted its director that he did not make another movie for three years?
5 In which movie did Garbo make her Swedish debut as an extra?
6 What was the first Indian talkie called?
7 Who directed Sophia Loren for the first time in *The Gold of Naples*?
8 Who starred in Akira Kurosawa's *Seven Samurai*?
9 *Accatone* was which director's first movie?
10 Which Swedish actor went to Hollywood to appear in *The Greatest Story Ever Told*?
11 Who played Falstaff in *Chimes at Midnight,* which was made in Spain?
12 Who directed the classic Indian film *Pather Panchali*?
13 Who made *I Am Curious (Yellow)*?
14 Which is the only country in the world never to have imposed censorship for adult films?
15 Where was Simone Signoret born?
16 Which director wrote the novel *Les Enfants Terribles*?
17 Who played the philosophy teacher in Andre Techine's *Les Voleurs*?
18 Who collaborated with Bunuel to make *L'Age d'Or* in 1930?
19 Who directed *Les Enfants du Paradis*?
20 What was Louis Malle's first film after he returned to France from America, in 1992?
21 Which 1985 film was based on the John Osborne play *A Patriot for Me*?
22 Who was the Cambodian director of *Les Gens de la Rizière*?
23 Who was the only human in the Belgian movie *Romeo–Juliet*?
24 What is the name of the cat in *Chacun Cherche Son Chat*?
25 *None But the Brave* was a collaboration between the US and which other country?

**Answers Westerns** (see Quiz 103)
**1** Joe. **2** *Shenandoah.* **3** Johnny Mack Brown. **4** Joel McCrea. **5** *High Noon.* **6** William Boyd. **7** John Ford. **8** *How the West Was Won.* **9** Where the hero kisses his horse at the end but now worries about it. **10** *The Kentuckian.* **11** *The Wild Bunch.* **12** $1,000. **13** Robert Duvall. **14** *Tombstone.* **15** Cleavon Little. **16** Jerome Moross (*The Big Country*). **17** Kurt Russell. **18** The marshall throws his badge in the dust at the end. **19** Kevin Costner. **20** None. **21** *Bad Girls.* **22** *Butch Cassidy and the Sundance Kid.* **23** Matthew Garth. **24** Warner Baxter. **25** Monument Valley.

## *QUIZ 102* POT LUCK 34 ............................................ LEVEL 3

*Answers – see page 324*

1 What colour are the elevator doors in *The Shining*?
2 At what sport did Tommy Lee Jones excel?
3 Who won the Best Actor Oscar for *Marty*?
4 Who directed *Zulu*?
5 Which Jack featured in *Play Misty for Me*?
6 Which movie star released a single called 'Raisin' Heaven and Hell Tonight' in 1989?
7 A character named Reggie Hammond appeared in which film?
8 Within fifteen minutes, how long does *Jailhouse Rock* last?
9 Which actor died on the same day as fellow actor Raymond Massey?
10 Which Adam starred in *Full Metal Jacket*?
11 How many catsuits did Michelle Pfeiffer wear in *Batman Returns*?
12 Which song won Best Song Oscar for *The Poseidon Adventure*?
13 Who wrote the novel on which *Dances with Wolves* was based?
14 *Tim* and *Return to Oz* both starred which actress?
15 Who won the David Di Donatello award in Italy for *Amadeus*?
16 What movie is shown in the film *Hannah and her Sisters*?
17 Who played Alias in *Pat Garret and Billy the Kid*?
18 *Dark Journey* and *A Yank at Oxford* both starred which actress?
19 Who directed *Arthur*?
20 Who won the Best Actress Oscar for *Places in the Heart*?
21 In which film does a character named Gloria Wandrous appear?
22 Within five minutes, how long does *Gone with the Wind* last?
23 Which Fred featured in *The Player*?
24 In which decade was *Maytime* released?
25 What was the name of Robert Patrick's character in *Terminator 2: Judgment Day*?

**Answers The 21st Century** (see Quiz 104)
**1** *The Green Mile*. **2** *Shopping*. **3** New York. **4** Allan Corduner. **5** Blythe Danner. **6** My So-Called Life. **7** Gary Oldman. **8** *21 Jump Street*. **9** Wilhelm. **10** The Kids. **11** Tawny Madison. **12** Anna Friel. **13** *The Wonder Boys*. **14** Mike Figgis. **15** Om Puri. **16** Ndingombaba. **17** John Hannah. **18** 1985. **19** Michael Mann. **20** Johnny Lee Miller. **21** Melissa Joan Hart. **22** John Irving. **23** *Princess Ida*. **24** Winona Ryder. **25** Katie Holmes.

## *QUIZ 103* WESTERNS ................................................ LEVEL 3

*Answers – see page 321*

1 What is the name of 'The Man With No Name'?
2 Which James Stewart western had such a moving soliloquy it was released on record?
3 Who played Billy the Kid in the 1930 film of the same name?
4 Which star of westerns was married for 57 years to actress Frances Dee?
5 Which movie was based on *The Tin Star* by John W. Cunningham?
6 Who was Hopalong Cassidy's most famous alter ego?
7 Which director made *Cheyenne Autumn*?
8 What was the first western in Cinerama?
9 How did comic Milton Berle describe an adult western?
10 Which Burt Lancaster-directed movie was based on *The Gabriel Horn* by Felix Holt ?
11 Who were 'nine men who came too late and stayed too long'?
12 What was the reward in *Unforgiven*?
13 Who played Jesse James in *The Great Northfield Minnesota Raid*?
14 Which 90s western was a remake of *Gunfight at the OK Corral*?
15 What is the name of the first black sheriff in town in the western spoof *Blazing Saddles*?
16 Who wrote the theme tune for the 1958 western for which Burl Ives won an Oscar?
17 Who played Wyatt Earp in *Tombstone*?
18 Why did John Wayne say *High Noon* was un-American?
19 Which actor/director was described by a critic as having 'feathers in his hair and feathers in his head'?
20 How many Oscar-nominated westerns won between 1930 and 1990?
21 Who are Andie McDowell, Drew Barrymore, Madeleine Stow and Mary Stuart Masterson in the 1994 movie?
22 Which movie opens with the line 'Most of what follows is true'?
23 What was the name of John Wayne's ward in *Red River*?
24 Who first played the Cisco Kid in *Old Arizona*?
25 Which valley saw the climax of *Stagecoach*?

**Answers World Cinema** (see Quiz 101)
**1** Pupi Avati. **2** Massimo Troisi. **3** *Ridicule.* **4** *La Dolce Vita* (Fellini). **5** *A Fortune Hunter.* **6** *Alam Ara.* **7** Vittorio de Sica. **8** Toshiro Mifune. **9** Pasolini. **10** Max von Sydow. **11** Orson Welles. **12** Satyajit Ray. **13** Vilgot Sjöman. **14** Belgium. **15** Germany. **16** Jean Cocteau. **17** Catherine Deneuve. **18** Salvador Dali. **19** Marcel Carné. **20** *Damage.* **21** *Colonel Redl.* **22** Rithy Panh. **23** John Hurt (the rest were cats). **24** Gris Gris. **25** Japan.

## *QUIZ 104* THE 21st CENTURY ........ LEVEL 3

*Answers – see page 322*

1. Which Frank Darabont movie received an Oscar nomination at the beginning of the millennium?
2. What was Jude Law's first film?
3. From which American city did Annie MacLean work in *The Horse Whisperer*?
4. Who played the writer of the music in *Topsy Turvy*?
5. Who is Gwyneth Paltrow's mother?
6. What was the name of Claire Danes's TV series?
7. To whom was Uma Thurman married before Ethan Hawke?
8. In which TV series did Johnny Depp play a character named Tom Hanson?
9. What is Leonardo DiCaprio's middle name?
10. In which band did Johnny Depp play lead guitar?
11. Which character does Gwen DeMarco play in *Galaxy Quest*?
12. Which UK actress turned down a starring role in *Boys and Girls*?
13. Which movie is about professor Grady Tripp?
14. Who directed *Time Code 2000*?
15. Who plays the lead role in *East Is East*?
16. What is Eddie's last name in *Guest House Paradiso*?
17. Which actor links *Sliding Doors* and *Pandaemonium*?
18. In which year did Ethan Hawke make his screen debut?
19. Who directed *The Insider*?
20. Which actor is set to star in the film *Wasp Factory*?
21. Who stars in the teen movie *Drive Me Crazy*?
22. Who adapted *The Cider House Rules* for the big screen?
23. *Topsy Turvy* begins after the flop of which G & S opera?
24. Which actress stars in *Autumn in New York*?
25. Which actress links *Go* and TV series *Dawson's Creek*?

**Answers Pot Luck 34** (see Quiz 102)
**1** Red. **2** Polo. **3** Ernest Borgnine. **4** Cy Endfield. **5** Ging. **6** Patrick Swayze. **7** *48 Hours*. **8** 96 minutes. **9** David Niven (29.7.83). **10** Baldwin. **11** 63. **12** 'The Morning After'. **13** Michael Blake. **14** Piper Laurie. **15** Tom Hulce. **16** *Duck Soup*. **17** Bob Dylan. **18** Vivien Leigh. **19** Steve Gordon. **20** Sally Field. **21** *Butterfield 8*. **22** 222 minutes. **23** Ward. **24** 1930s. **25** T-1000.

# TV
# QUIZZES

# CONTENTS

# LEVEL 1: THE EASY QUESTIONS

The whole point of these questions is that they are, well, easy. As in not hard. That means that they shouldn't give you any problems, or indeed anyone else who has looked at a television set more than once in the last thirty years. If you get these questions right, that's really not much to be proud of. In fact, it's close to the truth that getting these questions wrong is something to be worried about. If you find yourself doing badly on these questions, there are many possible reasons. The first thing to check is that you're looking at the correct answer block. If you've made that mistake, it'll throw your results right out. Alternatively, you may be extremely drunk. If reading this short introduction is proving tricky, that could be the cause. Try again later. Another possible cause is that you might only be three or four years old – again, try again later, only make it much later. Finally, you may have been born in the wilds and have spent your life being raised by a friendly family of finches, in which case you can be forgiven for your ignorance. They're nice creatures, but they're really not much cop when it comes to Coronation Street.

So, when you're devising a quiz for people, you might like to soften them up with a few of these questions, preparing them for something nasty. If nothing else, it'll make sure that even the bloke in the corner who's so hammered he can't stand will get one or two points, and save face. Tomorrow, he may even be grateful enough to buy you a drink for being so considerate. It's worth a shot, so to speak...

# QUIZ 1 Children's TV 1

**Answers: see Quiz 2, page 330**

LEVEL 1

1. What is the name of Popeye's girlfriend?
2. Where do the Wombles live?
3. Which cartoon character yells "Yab-a-dab-a-doo"?
4. What kind of puppet animal is *Basil Brush*?
5. Herman was the Frankenstein-like father of which ghoulish family?
6. What is the real-life relationship between the children's comedy duo, *The Krankies*?
7. Which cartoon animal superhero has a pal called Spotty Man?
8. Who is Yogi Bear's smaller than the average bear pal?
9. Where would you find Ermintrude the cow and a rabbit called Dylan?
10. Which series featured International Rescue?
11. What is the name of the family *Paddington Bear* lives with?
12. What colour are Rupert Bear's checked trousers?
13. What is the symbol used by *Blue Peter*?
14. In *The Muppets*, what kind of animal is Fozzie?
15. How many human pals does *Scooby Doo* have?
16. What was the numberplate on *Postman Pat*'s van?
17. Who is Rod Hull's temperamental puppet friend?
18. What is the name of Keith Harris's duck friend who wishes he could fly?
19. What programme would you have been watching if "It's Friday....It's five o'clock ... and it's..."?
20. In *Batman*, which villain left riddles at the scenes of his crimes?
21. Which newspaper does Superman's alter ego Clark Kent write for?
22. What was the name of the Lone Ranger's horse?
23. What was Bagpuss?
24. What letter did Zorro cut with his sword at the beginning of each episode of his series?
25. What was the name of Fred Flinstone's pet dinosaur?
26. Name the *Flowerpot Men*.
27. Who is Sooty's canine sidekick?
28. What sort of creatures were *Pinky and Perky*?
29. Gomez and Mortitia are the husband and wife of which creepy TV family?
30. What is Casper?

ANSWERS

**News 1 (see Quiz 2)**

**1.** *News at Ten*. **2.** BBC1. **3.** Julia Somerville. **4.** 5.00pm. **5.** Selina Scott. **6.** Brian Moore. **7.** Australian. **8.** Martyn Lewis. **9.** *Newsnight*. **10.** Alan Whicker. **11.** Adie. **12.** David. **13.** Walden. **14.** Gay Byrne. **15.** Members of The Sex Pistols. **16.** QVC. **17.** Peter Jay. **18.** Horse racing. **19.** Coronation of Queen Elizabeth II. **20.** JICTAR. **21.** The creators of the personal computer. **22.** *Hooked*. **23.** Jancis Robinson. **24.** Graham Hancock. **25.** The Roman Catholic Church. **26.** Edward Heath. **27.** *Girls and Buoys*. **28.** Michael Palin. **29.** *Our World*. **30.** *The Family*.

## QUIZ 2 News 1

LEVEL 1

**Answers: see Quiz 1, page 329**

1. Which news programme does Trevor McDonald present?
2. On which channel is *Panorama?*
3. Who presented *TV Eye?*
4. What time does *Newsround* start?
5. Which ex-newsreader presented *The Clothes Show?*
6. Who was the ITV commentator for the 1998 Football World Cup Final?
7. What nationality is Clive James?
8. Who presented *Crime Beat?*
9. What is BBC2's evening news programme called?
10. Who presented *Whickers World?*
11. Which Kate is an international correspondent for BBC television?
12. Which Dimbleby presented *Question Time?*
13. Which Brian had a Sunday lunchtime political programme?
14. Who is the presenter of *The Late Show?*
15. Who swore while being interviewed by Bill Grundy?
16. Which is *The Shopping Channel?*
17. Who was the Chief Executive of the newly created *TV-AM?*
18. On which sport is John McCrillick a commentator?
19. Which royal event in 1953 had the largest television audience?
20. Which organisation researched ITV's viewing figures?
21. What was the subject of *Triumph of The Nerds?*
22. What was C4's series on addictive pleasures?
23. Who presented BBC2's *Vintner's Tales?*
24. Who presented *Quest For The Lost Civilisation?*
25. What was the subject of the documentary series *Absolute Truth?*
26. Who was the subject of the documentary *A Very Singular Man?*
27. Which Docu-soap featured yachtswoman Tracy Edwards?
28. Who circumnavigated the globe in 79 days and 7 hours?
29. What was the first global TV programme?
30. What was the first British fly on the wall documentary series?

ANSWERS

### Children's TV 1 (see Quiz 1)

**1.** Olive Oyl. **2.** Wimbledon Common. **3.** Fred Flintstone. **4.** A fox. **5.** *The Munsters.* **6.** Husband and wife. **7.** *Superted.* **8.** Booboo. **9.** *The Magic Roundabout.* **10.** *Thunderbirds.* **11.** The Browns. **12.** Yellow. **13.** A ship. **14.** A bear. **15.** Four. **16.** PAT1. **17.** Emu. **18.** Orville. **19.** *Crackerjack.* **20.** The Riddler. **21.** The Daily Planet. **22.** Silver. **23.** A saggy old cloth cat. **24.** Z. **25.** Dino. **26.** Bill and Ben. **27.** Sweep. **28.** Pigs. **29.** *The Addams Family.* **30.** A cartoon ghost.

## QUIZ 3 Pot Luck 1

**Answers: see Quiz 4, page 332**

LEVEL 1

1. In *Goodnight Sweetheart* where does Gary time travel to?
2. Who is agoraphobic in *Game On*?
3. What was Mavis Wilton's maiden name in *Coronation Street*?
4. Which Channel 4 sporting coverage is introduced by Derek Thompson?
5. Which series featured Tara King and Mother?
6. Which Australian series was subtitled *The McGregor Saga*?
7. Which soap featured the character Rick Alessi?
8. What is the name of Roy Clarke's sitcom about a snobbish woman and her embarrassing relations?
9. Who plays Foggy in *Last Of The Summer Wine*?
10. Who played a woodwork teacher in *The Beiderbeck Tapes*?
11. Who was the voice of cricket and did television commentaries?
12. What was the family business in *Nearest and Dearest*?
13. In which series did the characters David Addison and Maddie Hayes appear?
14. Who hosts *Watercolour Challenge*?
15. Which BBC2 chat show is hosted by Desmond Wilcox's wife?
16. Which series has been hosted by Eamonn Andrews and Michael Aspel?
17. On which series were Mark Lamarr and Ulrika Jonsson team captains?
18. Which S.F. series featured Martin Landau as John Koenig?
19. Which Williams hosts his own chat show?
20. Who presents *The Pepsi Chart Show* on Channel 5?
21. Who hosted the 1998 game show *The Moment of Truth*?
22. Which S.F. series features the character Jack Logan?
23. In which feelgood series did Victor French play Mark?
24. What is the children's Saturday morning programme featuring Otis?
25. Which action show had a super-helicopter hidden by its pilot, Stringfellow Hawke?
26. Which comedian succeeded Bruce Forsythe as host of *The Generation Game*?
27. Which channel shows *Xena: Warrior Princess* and *Hercules: The Legendary Journeys*?
28. Whose *Tales of The City* were a Channel 4 series?
29. Who presented *In Suspicious Circumstances*?
30. Which Knight presents his *Sunday Morning Breakfast Show*?

ANSWERS

**Music & Variety 1 (see Quiz 4)**

**1.** Domingo. **2.** Hughie Green. **3.** *Top of the Pops*. **4.** *Top Gun*. **5.** ITV. **6.** Donny and Marie. **7.** *Sunday Night At The Palladium*. **8.** *Come Dancing*. **9.** Rolf Harris. **10.** Australian. **11.** A magic act. **12.** Michael Aspel. **13.** *Game For A Laugh*. **14.** Summer Dance. **15.** Terry Wogan. **16.** Mike Yarwood. **17.** Chris Evans. **18.** Four. **19.** Sandie Shaw. **20.** Grey (it was old, too). **21.** Jimmy Nail. **22.** Davy Jones. **23.** Cliff Richards. **24.** Paula Yates. **25.** Matthew Kelly. **26.** Denis Norden. **27.** *Live Aid*. **28.** Robson and Jerome. **29.** Mr Blobby. **30.** Dana.

## QUIZ 4 Music & Variety 1

LEVEL 1

**Answers: see Quiz 3, page 331**

1. Which Placido is one of the *Three Tenors*?
2. Who presented the original *Opportunity Knocks*?
3. Which BBC programme presents the pop charts?
4. Chart toppers Berlin sang the theme music to which film starring Tom Cruise?
5. On which channel was the *Saturday Chart Show* broadcast?
6. Which two of the Osmonds hosted their own TV series?
7. On which night is *...Night At The Palladium* screened?
8. Former *Generation Game* hostess Rosemarie Ford introduced which evening dance series on BBC1?
9. Which TV entertainer sang *Tie Me Kangaroo Down* and *Two Little Boys*?
10. What nationality is TV entertainer Barry Humphries?
11. David Nixon was famed for what kind of TV act?
12. Who presents *This Is Your Life*?
13. Matthew Kelly, Sarah Kennedy, Henry Kelly and Jeremy Beadle formed the quartet which presented which madcap weekend show?
14. Which 1990s BBC2 series showcased famous ballets?
15. Which former DJ presented his chat show three times a week?
16. Which former BBC impressionist has the initials M.Y.?
17. Who hosts TFI Friday?
18. How many Monkees were there?
19. Which singer won the Eurovision Song Contest with *Puppet On A String*?
20. What colour was the *Whistle Test*?
21. In 1994 who sang the theme tune *Crocodile Shoes*?
22. Who was the British lead singer of *The Monkees*?
23. Which singer was televised singing in the Wimbledon rain in 1996?
24. Channel 4's *The Tube* was presented by which Paula?
25. Who hosts ITV's *Stars In Their Eyes*?
26. *It'll Be All Right On The Night* is hosted by who?
27. Which televised pop concert raised money for famine relief in Ethiopia?
28. Which TV duo topped the charts with *Unchained Melody*?
29. What was the title of Mr Blobby's first No 1 single?
30. Which Irish singer won the Eurovision Song Contest with *All Kinds Of Everything*?

ANSWERS

### Pot Luck 1 (see Quiz 3)

**1.** 1940's wartime London. **2.** Matthew. **3.** Riley. **4.** Horse Racing. **5.** *The Avengers*. **6.** Snowy River. **7.** *Neighbours*. **8.** *Keeping Up Appearances*. **9.** Brian Wilde. **10.** James Bolam. **11** John Arlott. **12.** A pickle factory. **13.** *Moonlighting*. **14.** Hannah Gordon. **15.** *Esther*. **16.** *This Is Your Life*. **17.** *Shooting Stars*. **18.** *Space 1999*. **19.** *Montel*. **20.** Dr. Fox. **21.** Cilla Black. **22.** Timecop. **23.** *Highway To Heaven*. **24.** *Saturday Aardvark*. **25.** *Airwolf*. **26.** Jim Davidson. **27.** Channel 5. **28.** Armistead Maupin. **29.** Edward Woodward. **30.** David Frost.

## QUIZ 5 Comedy 1

**Answers: see Quiz 6, page 334**

LEVEL 1

1. Who starred as Sid in *Bless This House*?
2. What is the first name of Mrs Bucket in *Keeping Up Appearances*?
3. Who is Gary's best friend in *Men Behaving Badly*?
4. Who is Wayne's wife in *Harry Enfield and Chums*?
5. Who is Gareth Hale's comedy partner?
6. Who was the comic with the "short fat hairy legs"?
7. Who are Monica, Rachel, Phoebe, Chandler, Joey and Ross?
8. What is *Frasier*'s surname?
9. Who was the cafe owner, played by Gordon Kaye, in *'Allo, 'Allo*?
10. What was Del Boy's surname in *Only Fools And Horses*?
11. Who was the star of *Sez Les*?
12. In which cartoon series do Itchy and Scratchy appear?
13. What is the English version of *All In The Family*?
14. Which comedy series is set in a Torquay hotel?
15. In which series is the character Sally Smedley?
16. Who is the star of *Spin City*?
17. Who was the last barman in *Cheers*?
18. Who was Ronnie Barker's comedy partner in *The Two Ronnies*?
19. In *Porridge* who was Lennie Godber's cellmate?
20. Which actor played Ernie Bilko?
21. Who played Eric Sykes' twin sister in *Sykes*?
22. Who was Stan's sister in *On The Buses*?
23. In *Absolutely Fabulous* who was Edina's best friend?
24. Who created Gizzard Puke?
25. Who played Barbara in *The Good Life*?
26. In which series was the character Frank Spencer?
27. Who portrays *Ellen*?
28. Who was Ritchie's flatmate in *Bottom*?
29. In *Goodnight Sweetheart* what is Nicholas Lyndhurst's character?
30. In which series is Dorian the next door neighbour?

ANSWERS

### Pot Luck 2 (see Quiz 5)

**1.** Lisa Riley. **2.** Raymond Cradock. **3.** *This Life*. **4.** Girl Friday. **5.** Bob Monkhouse. **6.** *Blue Peter*. **7.** Linda Carter. **8.** *Today's The Day*. **9.** Samantha Janus. **10.** Sally Jessy Raphael. **11.** Martin. **12.** *Goodnight Sweetheart*. **13.** *Neighbours*. **14.** *Birds Of A Feather*. **15.** *Love Thy Neighbour*. **16.** Helen. **17.** *Camberwick Green*. **18.** *Brookside*. **19.** *Hospital* . **20.** Swedish. **21.** *2 Point 4 Children*. **22.** Dervla Kirwan. **23.** *The Bill*. **24.** *Northern Exposure*. **25.** ITV. **26.** *Tomorrow's World*. **27.** Chris Packham. **28.** *Homicide*. **29.** *King Of The Hill*. **30.** Ruby Wax.

## QUIZ 6 Pot Luck 2

**Answers: see Quiz 5, page 333**

LEVEL 1

1. Who succeeded Jeremy Beadle as host of *You've Been Framed?*
2. Which character replaced Oscar Blaketon as the sergeant in *Heartbeat?*
3. What was the BBC2 drama series about young lawyers?
4. What was the title of Joanna Lumley's desert island documentary?
5. Who presented *Wipeout* after Paul Daniels?
6. Which children's programme features Katy Hall as one of three presenters?
7. Who plays Elizabeth in *Hawkeye?*
8. Which quiz about events on one particular day is presented by Martin Lewis?
9. Who plays DC Isobel de Pauli in the crime series *Liverpool One?*
10. Which chat show hostess has the christian name Sally?
11. Who had a girlfriend Clare in *Game On?*
12. In which series is Reg a 1940's policeman?
13. Which soap features the character Toadfish?
14. Which series features Darryl and Chris as convicted armed robbers?
15. Which series starred Rudolph Walker and Jack Smethhurst?
16. Which character was Gordon Brittas's wife in *The Brittas Empire?*
17. Which children's series had a postmistress named Mrs. Dingle?
18. Which soap has an omnibus edition on a Saturday Evening?
19. What does the H stand for in *M*A*S*H?*
20. What nationality is Ulrika Jonsson?
21. In which sitcom does Roger Lloyd Pack portray a plumber named Jake the Klingon?
22. Which star of *Ballykissangel* appeared in *Goodnight Sweetheart?*
23. Which series features DCI Jack Meadows?
24. Which series set in Alaska features the characters Holling, Maurice and Ed?
25. On which channel would you have found *He-Man and The Masters of the Universe?*
26. Which technology programme is presented by Peter Snow and Philippa Forrester?
27. Who presented *The X Creatures* on BBC1?
28. Which US crime series features detectives Pembleton and Bayliss?
29. Which animated series features Hank, Peggy and Bobby?
30. Who starred in *Ruby Does The Season?*

ANSWERS

**Comedy 1 (see Quiz 5)**

**1.** Sid James. **2.** Hyacinth. **3.** Tony. **4.** Waynetta. **5.** Norman Pace. **6.** Ernie Wise. **7.** The *Friends.* **8.** Crane. **9.** René. **10.** Trotter. **11.** Les Dawson. **12.** *The Simpsons* . **13.** *Till Death Us Do Part.* **14.** *Fawlty Towers.* **15.** *Drop The Dead Donkey.* **16.** Michael J. Fox. **17.** Woody Boyd. **18.** Ronnie Corbett. **19.** Fletch. **20.** Phil Silvers. **21.** Hattie Jacques. **22.** Olive. **23.** Patsy. **24.** Kenny Everett. **25.** Felicity Kendal. **26.** *Some Mothers Do 'Ave 'Em.* **27.** Ellen Degeneres. **28.** Eddie. **29.** Gary Sparrow. **30.** *Birds of A Feather.*

## QUIZ 7 Drama 1

**Answers: see Quiz 8, page 336**

LEVEL 1

1. Who did Mike Baldwin marry in 1986?
2. Which TV series starred Tyne Daly and Sharon Gless?
3. Where did the Robinson family become lost?
4. On which channel is *NYPD Blue* transmitted?
5. What rank is Mitch Buchanan in *Baywatch*?
6. Which series featured WDC Viv Martella?
7. Where was *Harry's Game* set?
8. Which Superhero is portrayed by Dean Cain?
9. What is the house in *The House of Cards*?
10. Which character was the butler in *Upstairs Downstairs*?
11. Which country was the location for *Jewel In The Crown*?
12. Who played Paris in *Mission Impossible*?
13. In which series does Robbie Coltrane portray Fitz?
14. Who plays the character of *Maisie Raine*?
15. Which 19th century hero does Sean Bean play?
16. What was the sequel to *Band of Gold*?
17. Who was Dr. Finlay's partner in practice?
18. Which character is played by George Clooney in *ER*?
19. What is Seigfried Farnon's occupation?
20. Which *Charlie's Angel* played Mrs. King?
21. Who was Dempsey's sidekick?
22. Which series featured the character Pug Henry?
23. Who played Jesus of Nazareth?
24. Who played Barlow?
25. Which western series featured Big John and Blue?
26. What was *Lou Grant's* occupation?
27. Which detective did Angie Dickenson portray?
28. Which of *Randall and Hopkirk* was not a ghost?
29. Who played Rowdy Yates in *Rawhide*?
30. Who presented *Tales of the Unexpected*?

ANSWERS

**Soaps 1 (see Quiz 8)**

**1.** The Queen Vic. **2.** Four times per week. **3.** A cat. **4.** The patio. **5.** A magazine. **6.** *Emmerdale Farm*. **7.** *Dynasty*. **8.** *Knott's Landing*. **9.** *Crossroads*. **10.** *Let The Blood Run Free*. **11.** Alf Roberts. **12.** *Crossroads*. **13.** *Soap*. **14.** Yorkshire. **15.** The Woolpack. **16.** Cindy Beale. **17.** Tinhead. **18.** He isn't married. **19.** *Brookside*. **20.** Kim. **21.** The Rover's Return. **22.** Dot Cotton. **23.** Mike Read. **24.** Mike Baldwin. **25.** Fred Elliott. **26.** Yorkshire TV. **27.** *Dynasty*. **28.** Jack Duckworth. **29.** *Dallas*. **30.** *Peyton Place*.

## QUIZ 8 Soaps 1

**Answers: see Quiz 7, page 335**

LEVEL 1

1. What is the name of the pub in Albert Square?
2. How many times each week is *Coronation Street* broadcast?
3. What animal appears on the opening credits of *Coronation Street*?
4. What was Trevor Jordache buried under in *Brookside*?
5. In the 1960s series *Compact*, what was Compact?
6. What was Emmerdale previously called?
7. In which US soap did Joan Collins star?
8. In which Landing did some of the Ewings settle after *Dallas*?
9. Which ITV soap featured actress Noelle Gordon and the character Amy Turtle?
10. Which is the Australian spoof medical soap?
11. Alf Roberts was mayor of Wetherfield in which ITV soap?
12. Which soap was set in a Birmingham motel?
13. Which comedy spoof series finished its weekly introductory plot summary with the words "Confused? You will be after the next exciting episode of ... "?
14. *Emmerdale* is set in which UK county?
15. What is the name of the pub in *Emmerdale*?
16. Who left *Eastenders* for France with two of her children?
17. Who is the metal-headed character in *Brookside*?
18. In *Coronation Street*, who is Ken Barlow married to?
19. Did the TV astrologer Russel Grant appear in *Brookside* or *Eastenders*?
20. Who was Frank Tate's murdered wife in *Emmerdale*?
21. Which pub sells Newton & Ridley beer?
22. June Brown plays which dotty character in *Eastenders*?
23. Which bespectacled comedian plays a major character in *Eastenders*?
24. Who owns the factory in *Coronation Street*?
25. Who is the Street's repetitive butcher?
26. Which TV company produces *Emmerdale*?
27. The Carringtons featured in which US soap?
28. Bill Tarmey plays which character in *Coronation Street*?
29. In which soap was JR shot?
30. Which Place was an early TV Soap?

ANSWERS

**Drama 1 (see Quiz 7)**

**1.** Susan Barlow. **2.** *Cagney and Lacey*. **3.** Space. **4.** Channel 4. **5.** Captain. **6.** *The Bill*. **7.** Northern Ireland. **8.** *Superman*. **9.** The Houses of Parliament. **10.** Hudson. **11.** India. **12.** Leonard Nimoy. **13.** *Cracker*. **14.** Pauline Quirke. **15.** Richard Sharpe. **16.** Gold. **17.** Dr. Cameron. **18.** Doug Ross. **19.** Vet. **20.** Kate Jackson. **21.** Makepiece. **22.** *The Winds Of War*. **23.** Robert Powell. **24.** Stratford Johns. **25.** *The High Chaparral*. **26.** Newspaper Editor. **27.** Pepper Anderson. **28.** Randall. **29.** Clint Eastwood. **30.** Roald Dahl.

## QUIZ 9 Pot Luck 3

**Answers: see Quiz 10, page 338**

LEVEL 1

1. Which series featured Dale Robertson as a railroad detective?
2. Who played Chicken George in *Roots*?
3. Who was the presenter of *Don't Forget Your Toothbrush*?
4. Which Clive chaired *Whose Line is it Anyway*?
5. In which US city did *Cheers* take place?
6. Which doctor set aside his Casebook in the 90s revival of the series?
7. Which character in *Absolutely Fabulous* was Edina's secretary?
8. Which American sitcom, set in Miami, was made into a British version *Brighton Belles*?
9. What was the sequel from *And Mother Makes Three*?
10. In which series were Gavin and Tim gay lovers?
11. Which series highlights technological milestones from *Tomorrow's World*?
12. Who was Henry's son in *Home To Roost*?
13. What was the computer game programme hosted by Dominic Diamond?
14. What was the name of the spoof TV station in the series starring Angus Deayton?
15. Which sport was featured in the sitcom *Outside Edge*?
16. In *Neighbours*, Erinsborough is a suburb of which city?
17. Who played Elizabeth Darcy in *Pride and Prejudice*?
18. Who starred as the host in *Knowing Me – Knowing You ....With Alan Partridge*?
19. What was the name of the series about dustmen starring Edward Woodward and Roy Hudd?
20. What is Commander Riker's christian name in *Star Trek: The Next Generation*?
21. Where is the drama series *Roughnecks* set?
22. In which series does Michael Culver play Prior Robert and Sean Pertwee play Hugh Beringer?
23. Which comedy series featured *The Veterinarians Hospital*, a place for old jokes?
24. On which night does *Noel's House Party* take place?
25. What was the full title of the comedy starring Rowan Atkinson set in Regency times?
26. Who played Barry The Brummie in *Auf Weidersehen Pet*?
27. Which medical series featured the characters Dr. Andrew Collin and Dr. Rajah?
28. What is the name of the hamlet near *Camberwick Green*?
29. In *Roughnecks* what is the nickname of the cook played by Ricky Tomlinson?
30. Which series featured Arkwright's corner shop?

ANSWERS

**Comedy 2 (see Quiz 10)**

**1.** Brooke Shields. **2.** *Taxi*. **3.** A Bigfoot. **4.** Frankie Howard. **5.** Vivian. **6.** *Duck Patrol*. **7.** Hancock. **8.** Lenny Henry. **9.** Robin Tripp. **10.** Debs. **11.** *Steptoe and Son*. **12.** Jerry. **13.** Rodney. **14.** John Goodman. **15.** Ross. **16.** Jerry. **17.** *Hi Di Hi!* **18.** Eric Morecambe. **19.** New York. **20.** Richard Wilson. **21.** In a bookstore. **22.** Garry Shandling. **23.** Cybil Shepherd. **24.** Stephen Fry. **25.** A stand up comedian. **26.** The Garnetts. **27.** *Have I Got News For You?* **28.** Mollie Sugden. **29.** J. **30.** Sybil.

## QUIZ 10 Comedy 2

**Answers: see Quiz 9, page 337**

LEVEL 1

1. Who is the star of *Suddenly Susan*?
2. Which series about New York cabbies starred Danny De Vito?
3. What was Harry in *Harry and the Hendersons*?
4. Who was Lurcio in *Up Pompeii!*?
5. Who was the punk in *The Young Ones*?
6. Which comedy series featured the *River Police*?
7. Which Nick is the chairman of *They Think It's All Over*?
8. Who is the star of *Chef*?
9. Which character was the *Man About The House*?
10. Who does Tony fancy in *Men Behaving Badly*?
11. Who are TV's rag and bone men?
12. In *The Good Life* who is Margo's husband?
13. In *Only Fools And Horses* who is Del's brother?
14. Who plays *Roseanne*'s husband?
15. In *Friends* who is Monica's brother?
16. What is *Seinfeld*'s christian name?
17. Which series featured Maplins Holiday Camp?
18. Who was 'The One With the Glasses'?
19. Where is *Spin City* set?
20. Who plays Victor Meldrew?
21. Where does *Ellen* work?
22. Who plays Larry Sanders?
23. Who was the female star of *Moonlighting*?
24. Who played Jeeves to Hugh Laurie's Bertie Wooster?
25. What is *Seinfeld*'s job?
26. Which family feature in *Til Death Us Do Part*?
27. Which comedy show is the TV version of radio's *News Quiz*?
28. Who plays Mrs Slocombe in *Are You Being Served*?
29. What is Homer Simpson's middle initial?
30. What is Basil Fawlty's wife's name?

ANSWERS

**Pot Luck 3 (see Quiz 9)**

**1.** Iron Horse. **2.** Ben Vereen. **3.** Chris Evans. **4.** Anderson. **5.** Boston. **6.** Finlay. **7.** Bubbles. **8.** *The Golden Girls*. **9.** *And Mother Makes Five*. **10.** *The Brittas Empire*. **11.** *TW Time Machine*. **12.** Matthew Willows. **13.** *Gamesmaster*. **14.** *KYTV*. **15.** Cricket. **16.** Melbourne. **17.** Jennifer Erle. **18.** Steve Coogan. **19.** *Common As Muck*. **20.** Will. **21.** On an Oil Rig. **22.** *Cadfael*. **23.** *The Muppet Show*. **24.** Saturday. **25.** *Blackadder The Third*. **26.** Tim Spall. **27.** *Cardiac Arrest*. **28.** Chigley. **29.** Cinders. **30.** *Open All Hours*.

## QUIZ 11 Sci-Fi 1

**Answers: see Quiz 12, page 340**

LEVEL 1

1. What position does Odo hold in *Deep Space 9*?
2. What relation to *Doctor Who* was his original travelling companion, Susan?
3. Who was the female communications officer aboard the first USS Enterprise?
4. What exalted position was attained by Sheridan on *Babylon 5*?
5. Which US official body do agents Scully and Mulder belong to?
6. Which series featured Moonbase Alpha?
7. What race is Lt. Worf in *Star Trek: The Next Generation*?
8. Who were *Captain Scarlet's* enemies?
9. Who is the captain of the USS *Voyager*?
10. Who was Sapphire's partner?
11. On which show did you find Lori Singer travelling in cyberspace?
12. "Only David Vincent knows" – about whom?
13. Who is "faster than a speeding bullet"?
14. Who is Batman's assistant?
15. Which Flash fought the evil Emperor Ming?
16. *The Hitch-Hiker's Guide* was a guide to what?
17. Who was assisted by robots called Tweaky and Theo?
18. According to the series title how many were in Blake's crew?
19. Who are flung from one dimension to the next at the end of each show?
20. Which spaceship did Lorne Green command?
21. Which space opera series was created by writers Morgan and Wong of X-files fame?
22. How many characters form the crew of *Red Dwarf*?
23. Which show about invading aliens had a one-letter title?
24. In which programme would you find an intelligent computer called KITT?
25. How was Number Six known?
26. Which alien plants invaded following a comet's blinding appearance?
27. "Anything can happen in the next half-hour" on which show?
28. What type of vehicle was *Streethawk*?
29. What colour was the *Incredible Hulk*?
30. Which lamborghini-driving crime-fighter was generated by a computer?

ANSWERS

### Pot Luck 4 (see Quiz 12)

**1.** *The Next Generation*. **2.** Magdalen College, Oxford. **3.** Clarissa Dickson Wright. **4.** *Roughnecks*. **5.** *Trumpton*. **6.** Sean Hughes. **7.** Leonard Rossiter. **8.** *Camberwick Green*. **9.** John Walton. **10.** *Heartbeat*. **11.** The DiMarco brothers. **12.** A hospital. **13.** Pipkins. **14.** Magpie. **15.** *Wednesday Night Out*. **16.** Circus Boy. **17.** Savile. **18.** Alf and Elsie. **19.** Pam Shriver. **20.** Williams. **21.** The Grundy Organisation. **22.** Athletics. **23.** *A Family At War*. **24.** *The Big Match*. **25.** *The Boys from the Blackstuff*. **26.** Dogs. **27.** Nurse. **28.** Helen. **29.** Butcher. **30.** *Six Five Special*.

## QUIZ 12 Pot Luck 4

**Answers: see Quiz 11, page 339**

LEVEL 1

1. In which Star Trek spinoff does 'Q' most frequently make an appearance?
2. Which team have won *University Challenge* two years running?
3. Who is Jennifer Paterson's colleague on *Two Fat Ladies*?
4. Which drama series was set on the oil rig Osprey Explorer?
5. Which series featured Mr. Clamp the greengrocer and Mr. Antonio the ice cream seller?
6. Who was the star of *Sean's Show*?
7. Who last role was as a supermarket manager in *Tripper's Day*?
8. In which children's series where the characters Mickey Murphy the Baker and PC McGary?
9. Which character did Ralph Waite portray in *The Waltons*?
10. Which drama features Claude Jeremiah Greengrass?
11. Who in *Eastenders* are Beppe, Bruno and Gianni?
12. What is *Jimmy's*?
13. On which children's programme did the characters Hartley Hare and Pig appear?
14. On which programme did Susan Stranks take-over from Jenny Handley?
15. On which variety show was *Name That Tune* a feature?
16. Who had an elephant called Bimbo?
17. Which Jimmy introduced the first *Top of The Pops*?
18. What were Rita Garnett's parents called?
19. Who is the American female commentator on BBC's coverage of Wimbledon?
20. Which showjumping commentator's first name was Dorien?
21. Which company produces *Neighbours*?
22. Which sport did Ron Pickering commentate on?
23. What was the drama series about a family in wartime Liverpool?
24. Which ITV sports programme featured Jimmy Hill?
25. Which 80s drama centered on Liverpudlian Yosser Hughes?
26. Which animals did Barbara Woodhouse usually appear with?
27. What is Charlie Fairhead's job at Holby City Hospital?
28. What was James' wife called in *All Creatures Great and Small*?
29. What is Lance Corporal Jones occupation in *Dads Army*?
30. Which was Britain's first pop TV show?

ANSWERS

### Sci-Fi 1 (see Quiz 11)

**1.** Security Chief. **2.** Grand-daughter. **3.** Lt. Uhura. **4.** President. **5.** FBI. **6.** *Space 1999*. **7.** Klingon. **8.** The Mysterons. **9.** Captain Janeway. **10.** Steel. **11.** *VR5*. **12.** *The Invaders*. **13.** *Superman*. **14.** Robin. **15.** *Flash Gordon*. **16.** The Galaxy. **17.** Buck Rogers. **18.** Seven. **19.** *The Sliders*. **20.** *Battlestar Galactica*. **21.** *Space – Above and Beyond*. **22.** Four. **23.** *V*. **24.** *Knight Rider*. **25.** *The Prisoner*. **26.** *The Triffids*. **27.** *Stingray*. **28.** A motorcycle. **29.** Green. **30.** *Automan*.

## QUIZ 13 Children's TV 2

**Answers: see Quiz 14, page 342** LEVEL 1

**1.** Which mouthy puppet rat first appeared on breakfast TV?
**2.** Who lived at Mockingbird Heights, 1313 Mockingbird Lane?
**3.** Kermit, Gonzo, Miss Piggy are all what?
**4.** Which country did *Paddington Bear* come from?
**5.** Which programme began with the words "Here is a house. Here is a door. Windows: one, two, three, four"?
**6.** In *Sesame Street*, what was the name of the grumpy creature who lived in a trash can?
**7.** What sort of animal was Skippy?
**8.** Who is Wile E Coyote always trying to catch?
**9.** Which Superhero does Princess Diana of Paradise Island become?
**10.** Which show featured the tallest, fastest, biggest and other outstanding achievements?
**11.** What did *Top Cat* sleep in?
**12.** Which program featured Parsley the Lion and Lady Rosemary?
**13.** Which Gerry and Sylvia pioneered Supermarionation?
**14.** What was the name of Mork's Earthling girlfriend?
**15.** What was the surname of *The Beverley Hillbillies*?
**16.** Who was the Caped Crusader?
**17.** *Animal Magic* was presented by who?
**18.** How was Granny Smith better known?
**19.** On *The Magic Roundabout*, what kind of creature is Brian?
**20.** What was *Worzel Gummidge*?
**21.** Which Mike drove the *Supercar*?
**22.** Which cartoon cat yells "I hate those meeces to pieces!"?
**23.** Which programme has been presented by John Noakes, Peter Purves, Janet Ellis, Simon Groom and Lesley Judd as well as many others?
**24.** *Pebbles And Bam Bam* was a spin-off from which other cartoon series?
**25.** Which former *Minder* played *Just William*?
**26.** The Fat Controller, Gordon, Bertie the Bus are all characters in which series?
**27.** Tucker, Zammo, Stu Pot and Roly all went to which school?
**28.** Musky and Vince were pals of which law-enforcing cartoon dog?
**29.** Who was Shari Lewis' famous puppet?
**30.** ITV's 80s kid's interest program was named after which acquisitive bird?

ANSWERS

**Drama 2 (see Quiz 14)**

**1.** Frank Marker. **2.** Terry McCann. **3.** Fred Dryer. **4.** *Elizabeth R*. **5.** *The Fall Guy*. **6.** Starsky. **7.** *Murder She Wrote*. **8.** Michael Elphick. **9.** Patrick McGoohan. **10.** Diana Rigg. **11.** *Tenko*. **12.** Barrister. **13.** Ian McShane. **14.** *Heartbeat*. **15.** Sarah Lancashire. **16.** *Prisoner Cell Block H*. **17.** Pauline Quirke. **18.** *The Untouchables*. **19.** *ER* . **20.** *Casualty*. **21.** *Upstairs and Downstairs*. **22.** Susannah Harker. **23.** *Soldier Soldier*. **24.** Alan Davies. **25.** Edward Woodward. **26.** Craig McClachlan. **27.** Robert Wagner. **28.** *The Professionals* . **29.** Don Johnson. **30.** Cagney.

## QUIZ 14 Drama 2

**Answers: see Quiz 13, page 341**

LEVEL 1

1. Which character was the *Public Eye*?
2. Who was Arthur Dailey's first minder?
3. Who was *Hunter*?
4. What was Glenda Jackson's royal role?
5. Which series featured Colt Seevers?
6. Which TV cop is played by Paul Michael Glaser?
7. Which mystery series stars Angela Lansbury?
8. Who played *Boon*?
9. Who was *The Prisoner*?
10. Who played Mrs Peel in *The Avengers*?
11. Which series featured women in a Japanese prison camp?
12. What was Horace Rumpole's profession?
13. Who plays *Lovejoy*?
14. Which series starred Nick Berry as a policeman?
15. Which ex-*Coronation Street* star appeared in *Where the Heart Is*?
16. What is the Australian series about a women's detention centre?
17. Who played *The Sculptress*?
18. In which series was the character Elliot Ness?
19. In which series are Peter Benton and Carol Hathaway?
20. Which series features Baz, Megan and Charlie?
21. Which drama series, set in the Edwardian era, featured the wealthy Bellamy family?
22. Which actress links *House of Cards* to *Ultraviolet*?
23. In which series did Robson and Jerome first appear together?
24. Who plays Jonathan Creek?
25. Who starred as *The Equaliser*?
26. Which ex-*Neighbours* actor starred in *Bugs*?
27. Who played Jonathan in *Hart To Hart*?
28. Who were Bodie and Doyle?
29. Who played Crockett in *Miami Vice*?
30. In *Cagney and Lacey* who was the sergeant?

ANSWERS

### Children's TV 2 (see Quiz 13)

**1.** Roland Rat. **2.** *The Munsters*. **3.** Muppets. **4.** Peru. **5.** *Play School*. **6.** Grover. **7.** A kangaroo. **8.** Roadrunner. **9.** *Wonder Woman*. **10.** *Record Breakers*. **11.** A trash can. **12.** *The Herbs*. **13.** Anderson. **14.** Mindy. **15.** The Clampetts. **16.** *Superman*. **17.** Johnny Morris. **18.** *Supergran*. **19.** A snail. **20.** A scarecrow. **21.** Mike Mercury. **22.** Mr Jinks. **23.** *Blue Peter*. **24.** *The Flintstones*. **25.** Dennis Waterman. **26.** *Thomas The Tank Engine*. **27.** *Grange Hill*. **28.** Deputy Dawg. **29.** Lamb Chop. **30.** *Magpie*.

## QUIZ 15 Comedy 3

LEVEL 1

**Answers: see Quiz 16, page 344**

1. Which series featured Blanche Deveraux?
2. In which series is the character Baldrick?
3. Who is Harry Enfield's writing partner on *Harry Enfield and Chums*?
4. In which series are Julia Sawalha and June Whitfield related?
5. Which characters were *Just Good Friends*?
6. What was Mrs Boswell's christian name in *Bread*?
7. Who played *The New Statesman*?
8. Which comedy series featured Ted Bovis?
9. Who played Sir Humphrey in *Yes, Minister*?
10. Where does BooBoo live?
11. Who is the female star of *Game On*?
12. What is Agent Smart's christian name in *Get Smart*?
13. Who plays Jeannie in *I Dream Of Jeannie*?
14. Who is Barbara's husband in *The Good Life*?
15. What is Tim Taylor's programme in *Home Improvements*?
16. Who was Lucy in *I Love Lucy*?
17. From which country does *Kids In The Hall* originate?
18. What was Alan Alda's role in *M*A*S*H*?
19. Which comedy series featured the Dead Parrot Sketch?
20. Which strange family had a niece named Marilyn?
21. To which family is Lurch the butler?
22. In which country is *'Allo, 'Allo* set?
23. Which sitcom features Bill and Ben Porter?
24. Who played Edmund Blackadder?
25. Who is *Caroline In The City*?
26. Who plays Sam Malone in *Cheers*?
27. Which sitcom is about catholic clergy on remote Craggy Island?
28. Which TV series was the forerunner of *The Naked Gun* films?
29. What is *Frasier*'s profession?
30. Who is the star of *The Fresh Prince Of Bel Air*?

ANSWERS

### Pot Luck 5 (see Quiz 16)

**1.** Joan Bakewell. **2.** They were both *Cheers* bartenders. **3.** Farmer Barleymo. **4.** He was run over by a tram. **5.** Jimmy Smits. **6.** Doctors. **7.** *Murder One*. **8.** Kathryn. **9.** James Martinez. **10.** BBC 2. **11.** Albert Hall. **12.** Woodentop. **13.** Roland Rat. **14.** *The Air Show*. **15.** *You've Been Framed*. **16.** Hawaii. **17.** Maureen Holdsworth. **18.** *Knight Rider*. **19.** *Murder She Wrote*. **20.** Ted Danson. **21.** James Garner. **22.** Hillsborough. **23.** Grizzley. **24.** Tony Stamp. **25.** John Le Carre. **26.** *Alias Smith and Jones*. **27.** Greengrass. **28.** Dervla Kirwan. **29.** Neely Capshaw. **30.** *L.A. Law*.

## QUIZ 16 Pot Luck 5

**Answers: see Quiz 15, page 343**

LEVEL 1

1. Who presented *Heart of The Matter* and *Late Night Line-up*?
2. What did Coach and Woody have in common?
3. What was the farmer's name in *Bod*?
4. How did Alan Bradley die in *Coronation Street*?
5. Who played Victor Sifuentes in *LA .Law*?
6. What profession do the characters Mark Greene and Kerry Weaver follow?
7. Which series featured the lawyer Theodore Hoffman?
8. What is Captain Janeway's christian name in *Voyager*?
9. Who is Greg Medavoy's partner in *NYPD Blue*?
10. Which channel shows *The Sky At Night*?
11. Where is *The Last Night Of The Proms* broadcast from?
12. What was the original title for *The Bill*?
13. Which rodent was the star of *Good Morning Britain*?
14. Which BBC2 series features aviation topics?
15. What is the series featuring viewers' amusing home video clips?
16. Where was *Magnum P. I.* set?
17. Who was Maude Grimes' daughter in *Coronation Street*?
18. Which series starred a black Pontiac TransAm as a hero?
19. Which series featured the character Jessica Fletcher?
20. Who was the star of *Gullivers Travels*?
21. Who played Woodrow in *Streets of Laredo*?
22. What was the name of the drama documentary about a football stadium disaster?
23. What was the nickname of mountain man James Adams?
24. Which character does Graham Cole portray in *The Bill*?
25. Who was the author of *Tinker Taylor Soldier Spy*?
26. Which series featured the character Hannibal Hayes?
27. Who in *Heartbeat* had a dog named Alfred?
28. Who played Assumpta Fitzgerald in *Ballykissangel*?
29. What is Geena Lee Nolin's character in *Baywatch*?
30. Which series starred Susan Dey as Grace Van Owen?

ANSWERS

**Comedy 3 (see Quiz 15)**

**1.** *The Golden Girls.* **2.** *Blackadder.* **3.** Paul Whitehouse. **4.** *Absolutely Fabulous.* **5.** Vince and Penny. **6.** Nellie. **7.** Rik Mayall. **8.** *Hi De Hi!* **9.** Nigel Hawthorne. **10.** Jellystone Park. **11.** Samantha Janus. **12.** Maxwell. **13.** Barbara Eden. **14.** Tom Good. **15.** *Tooltime.* **16.** Lucille Ball. **17.** Canada. **18.** Hawkeye Pierce. **19.** *Monty Python's Flying Circus.* **20.** *The Munsters.* **21.** *The Addams Family.* **22.** France. **23.** *2 Point 4 Children.* **24.** Rowan Atkinson. **25.** Lea Thompson. **26.** Ted Danson. **27.** *Father Ted.* **28.** *Police Squad.* **29.** A psychiatrist. **30.** Will Smith.

## QUIZ 17 Soaps 2

**Answers: see Quiz 18, page 346**

LEVEL 1

1. Who was Bobby Ewing's first wife in *Dallas?*
2. What was Tom Howard's business in *Howards Way?*
3. Who is Toyah's sister in *Coronation Street?*
4. Who is Ricky Butcher's wife in *Eastenders?*
5. In *Neighbours*, whose daughter was Julie Martin?
6. Who is Ailsa's husband in *Home And Away?*
7. Which pub did Alan Turner run in *Emmerdale?*
8. Which TV writer created *Brookside?*
9. In which Western state of the USA is *Knots Landing* set?
10. Which 60's US soap starred Mia Farrow and Ryan O'Neal?
11. Who was famed for his allotment in *Eastenders?*
12. Which character did Michelle Gayle portray in *Eastenders?*
13. Who was Bet Gilroy's estranged husband in *Coronation Street?*
14. What is Susan Kennedy's occupation in *Neighbours?*
15. Who was Bobby Ewing's mother in *Dallas?*
16. Who is Jacqui's dad in *Brookside?*
17. Which character in *Coronation Street* was married to Samir Rashid?
18. Who owned The Meal Machine in *Eastenders?*
19. Which character does John James portray in *The Colbys?*
20. In which establishment was the office of Ozcabs in *Eastenders?*
21. Who in *Coronation Street* was Gail Platt's late husband?
22. Who is Michael Ross's wife in *Home And Away?*
23. Name Debbie Martin's younger sister in *Neighbours*.
24. Who is Pete Beale's sister in *Eastenders?*
25. Which Hartman did Kimberley Davies portray in *Neighbours?*
26. Who sold her baby to the Mallets in *Coronation Street?*
27. Who is Max's wife in *Brookside?*
28. Which BBC1 soap was created by Tony Holland and Julia Smith?
29. Which Sean owned the Bookmakers in Rosamund Street around the corner from *Coronation Street?*
30. In *Coronation Street*, where did Rita find her dead husband, Ted Sullivan?

ANSWERS

**Sport 1 (see Quiz 18)**

**1.** Boxing. **2.** James Hunt. **3.** Denis Compton. **4.** *Superstars.* **5.** Snooker. **6.** Soccer. **7.** *World of Sport.* **8.** Ford. **9.** Italy. **10.** Darts. **11.** Statto. **12.** Keith Wolstenholme. **13.** Sue Barker. **14.** *Football Italia.* **15.** Snooker. **16.** A ski-jumper. **17.** *American Gladiators.* **18.** Greenwich. **19.** The University Boat Race. **20.** Aintree. **21.** ITV. **22.** Terry Wogan. **23.** Brut. **24.** The Summer Olympics. **25.** Bob Wilson. **26.** *Grandstand.* **27.** Emlyn Hughes. **28.** Ian St John and Jimmy Greaves. **29.** Football. **30.** Rory McGrath.

## QUIZ 18 Sport 1

**Answers: see Quiz 17, page 345**

LEVEL 1

1. On which sport was Reg Gutteridge a commentator?
2. Which late motor racing world champion commentated on Formula One?
3. Who was a footballer for Arsenal and a cricket player and commentator?
4. Which competition pitted champions of differing sports against each other?
5. For which sport is John Spencer a commentator?
6. For which sport is Barry Venison a pundit?
7. Which television sports programme was introduced by Dickie Davies?
8. Which company sponsored Monday Night Football on Sky TV in 1998?
9. From which country is Channel 4's Sunday football coverage?
10. For which sport is Eric Bristow renowned?
11. Who wears pyjamas on *Fantasy Football League*?
12. Who said, "They think it's all over – it is now" in 1966?
13. Who is the chairperson of *A Question Of Sport*?
14. On which sports programme does Joe Jordan appear?
15. What sport did Ted Lowe commentate on?
16. Who was Eddie The Eagle?
17. *Gladiators* was based on which US TV show?
18. In which park does the London Marathon start?
19. Which annual event features the crews of Oxford and Cambridge?
20. Where is The Grand National run?
21. Which channel took over Formula One coverage from BBC?
22. Who presents *Auntie's Sporting Bloomers*?
23. Henry Cooper advertised which aftershave?
24. Which multi-athletic event is screened in the summer every four years?
25. Which former Arsenal goalkeeper has presented football on both the BBC and ITV?
26. What is the name of the long running Saturday afternoon sports programme on BBC1?
27. Which former Liverpool football club captain was also captain on *Question of Sport*?
28. Who are *Saint and Greavsie*?
29. *The Manageress* was about a female manager in which sport?
30. Name Gary Lineker's hairy comic partner from *They Think It's All Over*.

ANSWERS

### Soaps 2 (see Quiz 17)

**1.** Pam. **2.** Boatbuilder. **3.** Leanne. **4.** Bianca. **5.** Jim Robinson. **6.** Alf. **7.** The Woolpack. **8.** Phil Redmond. **9.** California. **10.** *Peyton Place*. **11.** Arthur Fowler. **12.** Hattie Tavernier. **13.** Alec Gilroy. **14.** Head Teacher. **15.** Miss Ellie. **16.** Ron Dixon. **17.** Deirdre Raschid. **18.** Ian Beale. **19.** Jeff Colby. **20.** In the Cafe. **21.** Brian Tilsley. **22.** Pippa. **23.** Hannah. **24.** Pauline Fowler. **25.** Annelise Hartman. **26.** Zoe. **27.** Patricia Farnham. **28.** *Eastenders*. **29.** Sean Skinner. **30.** On a garden seat.

## QUIZ 19 Pot Luck 6

LEVEL 1

**Answers: see Quiz 20, page 348**

1. What was the theme tune of *Minder*?
2. Which series of interviews was conducted by John Freeman?
3. What is the name of the holographic doctor in *Voyager*?
4. Which of the lads in *Auf Weidersehen Pet* came from Bristol?
5. In which series was the character Mrs Miggins?
6. On which show did Caron Keating stand in for Judy Finnegan?
7. Which series featured Howard Cunningham?
8. Which program featured Neil the hippy?
9. Who shared a theatre box with Statler in *The Muppet Show*?
10. Who conceived and starred in *The Nanny*?
11. Who does Christopher Ellison portray in *The Bill*?
12. Which character was first played by Loretta Swit in a pilot episode?
13. Who portrays Dr. Mark Greene in *ER*?
14. What was the name of Bruce Willis's character in *Moonlighting*?
15. Which series starred Barry Evans as an English teacher?
16. In which series was The Master an enemy?
17. What was Jack Duckworth's first job at The Rovers Return?
18. In which other bar in Walford did Lofty work apart from the Queen Vic?
19. Who was Doug's wife in *Neighbours*?
20. Which soap featured a special video episode entitled *The Lost Weekend*?
21. Who was Peter Cook's partner in *Not Only But Also*?
22. Who presented the *Trouble-shooter* series on TV?
23. Which game show has been presented by both Lily Savage and Les Dawson?
24. Which *Mrs* presents her own chat show?
25. Which cop show featured an Arsenal footballer in a 1998 Christmas special?
26. What TV drama series was based on the novels set in Cornwall by Winston Graham?
27. John Archer was killed by what?
28. Which delivery man had a cat named Jess?
29. Which character does Michael Starke portray in *Brookside*?
30. Which TV detective was created by R.D. Wingfield?

ANSWERS

### Crime 1 (see Quiz 20)

**1.** George Carter. **2.** Hutch. **3.** Sun Hill. **4.** Morse. **5.** William Shatner. **6.** Miss Marple. **7.** John Watt. **8.** Cornwall. **9.** D.I. Frost. **10.** *Hill Street Blues*. **11.** *The Cops*. **12.** Raymond Burr. **13.** Chuck Norris. **14.** Mary Beth. **15.** A Mountie. **16.** Oscar Blaketon. **17.** *Between The Lines*. **18.** Andy. **19.** California. **20.** *Due South*. **21.** Tubbs. **22.** *Magnum P.I.* **23.** A Boxer. **24.** Adam Faith. **25.** Hercule. **26.** Wiggum. **27.** Amanda Burton. **28.** *Columbo*. **29.** *Kojak*. **30.** *Cracker*.

## QUIZ 20 Crime 1

**Answers: see Quiz 19, page 347**

LEVEL 1

1. Who is Regan's sergeant in *The Sweeney*?
2. Who is Starsky's partner?
3. What is *The Bill's* local nick?
4. Which detective's patch is Oxford?
5. Who played *TJ Hooker*?
6. Who is Agatha Christie's foremost lady sleuth?
7. Who was Charlie Barlow's sergeant in *Z Cars*?
8. Where is *Wycliffe* set?
9. Which cop does David Jason play?
10. Which police series was set on the Hill?
11. Name the BBC's gritty police drama, launched in 1998.
12. Who played Perry Mason?
13. Who plays *Walker – Texas Ranger*?
14. What are Lacey's christian names in Cagney and Lacey?
15. What is Constable Benton Fraser?
16. Which character was Nick Rowan's sergeant in *Heartbeat*?
17. Which series featured Tony Clark and Harry Taylor?
18. What is Sipowicz's first name in *NYPD Blue*?
19. In which American state was *LA. Law* located?
20. Which series featured Diefenbaker?
21. Who is Crockett's partner in *Miami Vice*?
22. Which series set in Hawaii stars Tom Selleck?
23. What was Terry's previous profession in *Minder*?
24. Who played *Budgie*?
25. What is Poirot's first name?
26. What is the name of the Police Chief in *The Simpsons*?
27. Who was the star of *Silent Witness*?
28. What was the name of Peter Falk's scruffy detective?
29. Whose first name was Theo?
30. In which series was there a female detective named Penhaligon?

ANSWERS

### Pot Luck 6 (see Quiz 19)

**1.** *I Could Be So Good For You.* **2.** *Face To Face.* **3.** Zimmerman. **4.** Bomber. **5.** *Blackadder.* **6.** *This Morning.* **7.** *Happy Days.* **8.** *The Young Ones.* **9.** Waldorf. **10.** Wendy Craig. **11** D.I. Burnside. **12.** Detective Chris Cagney. **13.** Anthony Edwards. **14.** David Addison. **15.** *Mind Your Language.* **16.** *Dr. Who.* **17.** Potman. **18.** The Dagmar. **19.** Pam Willis. **20.** *Brookside.* **21.** Dudley Moore. **22.** Sir John Harvey-Jones. **23.** *Blankety-Blank.* **24.** Merton. **25.** *The Bill.* **26.** *Poldark.* **27.** A tractor. **28.** *Postman Pat.* **29.** Sinbad. **30.** Inspector Frost.

## QUIZ 21 Comedy 4

LEVEL 1

**Answers: see Quiz 22, page 350**

1. Who is *Ellen*'s best friend?
2. Who did Shelley Long portray in *Cheers*?
3. Who played Brenda in *Baghdad Cafe*?
4. Whose daughters were Darlene and Becky?
5. Rose Marie and Morey Amsterdam starred in which comedy series?
6. What were the names of the two families in *Soap*?
7. Which character does Christopher Ryan play in *Bottom*?
8. Who is Connie Booth's character in *Fawlty Towers*?
9. What was Kim Hartman's character in *'Allo, 'Allo*?
10. By what name was Daisy Moses better known in *The Beverley Hillbillies*?
11. Who runs a catering business in *2 Point 4 Children*?
12. Who is Saffron's brother in *Absolutely Fabulous*?
13. Which hospital comedy starred Peter Bowles, James Bolam and Chrisopher Strauli?
14. What is *Chef* Lenny Henry's character first name?
15. Which sitcom was the song *My Little Horse* entered for a contest?
16. Who has a brother Niles?
17. Who plays Dave Lister in *Red Dwarf*?
18. In which show would you hear the catchphrase "suits you, sir"?
19. What rank is Ernie Bilko in *The Phil Silvers Show*?
20. Who was the star of *Police Squad*?
21. Who presents *Shooting Stars*?
22. *Threes Company* was the American version of which British sitcom?
23. Who plays Charlie in *Babes in The Wood*?
24. Who is Tim Taylor's assistant in *Tool Time*?
25. What is *Caroline in The City*'s occupation?
26. Which two of the *Friends* were an item?
27. Which series features Martin and Mandy as tenants?
28. Whose neighbours are the Leadbetters?
29. Which 1960s series featured Ricky Ricardo?
30. Which series starred Larry Hagman and Barbara Eden?

ANSWERS

### Pot Luck 7 (see Quiz 22)

**1.** *Something Outa Nothing*. **2.** Horse Racing. **3.** Jason King. **4.** Pop Music. **5.** Ayres. **6.** *Radio Times*. **7.** Alan Bleasdale. **8.** *Deals On Wheels*. **9.** Bobbie Charlton. **10.** Sergeant Wilson. **11.** Kenny Beale. **12.** Kenny. **13.** The Landlord of The Nags Head. **14.** *Ground Force*. **15.** The Golden Shot. **16.** Trevor MacDonald. **17.** Spain. **18.** Roy Dotrice. **19.** Itt. **20.** Nicole. **21** *Are You Being Served?* **22.** Dr. Peter Benton. **23.** *Pot Black*. **24.** Bobby Simone. **25.** *Bakersfield PD*. **26.** *Give us a Clue*. **27.** A dog and a cat. **28.** Don Estelle and Windsor Davies. **29.** Vulcan. **30.** *Desmond's*.

## QUIZ 22 Pot Luck 7

**Answers: see Quiz 21, see page 349**

LEVEL 1

1. Which song was a hit for Letitia Dean and Paul Medford?
2. On which sport was John Rickman a commentator?
3. Which screen hero was a thriller writer in *Department S*?
4. What was the subject of the children's programme *Lift-Off*?
5. Which Pam won *Opportunity Knocks* in the 1970s?
6. What is the name of BBC TV's listings magazine?
7. Who wrote the series *GBH*?
8. Which consumer programme was presented by Mike Brewer and Richard Sutton?
9. Who had a *Football Scrapbook* television programme?
10. Who was Uncle Arthur in *Dads Army*?
11. Which *Eastenders* character emigrated following an extra-marital affair?
12. Who gets killed in every *South Park* episode?
13. Who was Mike in *Only Fools And Horses*?
14. Which garden-revamping program stars Alan Titchmarsh?
15. On which game show did Anne Aston keep the scores?
16. Who do the magazine *Private Eye* refer to as Trevor Barbados?
17. In which country was *El Dorado* set?
18. Who played Vincent's father in *Beauty and The Beast*?
19. Who is Gomez & Morticia's super-hairy cousin in the *Addams Family*?
20. Which Renault advertising character frequently met her father in compromising situations?
21. Which series featured the character Young Mr. Grace?
22. Who is Eriq La Salle's character in *ER*?
23. Which game show is based on snooker?
24. Who is Andy's partner in *NYPD Blue*?
25. Which surreal US cop show only lasted one series in the early 1990s?
26. In which show were Una Stubbs and Lionel Blair team captains?
27. What animals are Ren and Stimpy?
28. Which actors had a hit with *Whispering Grass*?
29. What race is Dr Spock?
30. Which program is set in a Brixton barbers?

ANSWERS

### Comedy 4 (see Quiz 21)

**1.** Paige Clark. **2.** Diane Chambers. **3.** Whoopi Goldberg. **4.** *Roseanne*. **5.** *The Dick Van Dyke Show*. **6.** Tates & Campbells. **7.** Dave Hedgehog. **8.** Polly Sherman. **9.** Helga. **10.** Granny Clampett. **11.** Bill Porter and Rona. **12.** Serge. **13.** *Only When I Laugh*. **14.** Gareth. **15.** *Father Ted*. **16.** Frasier Crane. **17.** Craig Charles. **18.** *The Fast Show*. **19.** Master Sergeant. **20.** Leslie Neilson. **21** Vic Reeves & Bob Mortimer. **22.** *Man About The House*. **23.** Karl Howman. **24.** Al. **25.** Cartoonist. **26.** Ross and Rachel. **27.** *Game On*. **28.** Tom and Barbara Good. **29.** *I Love Lucy*. **30.** *I Dream of Jeannie*.

## QUIZ 23 News 2

**Answers: see Quiz 24, page 352**

LEVEL 1

1. Who presented *Models Close Up*?
2. Who presented *The Day The Universe Changed*?
3. Which programme was presented by Professor Robert Winston?
4. Who presented his *Postcard From Rio*?
5. Who presents *Countryfile*?
6. Which airline does Jeremy Spake work for in *Airport*?
7. On which channel was *Liberty! The American War Of Independence*?
8. Which documentary series starred Prince Edward?
9. Which hospital was featured in *Jimmy's*?
10. Which comedian completed a *World Tour Of Scotland*?
11. Who presented the opening programme on BBC Choice?
12. What is the first name of the presenter of *Portillo's Progress*?
13. What is the title of C4's Italian Football magazine?
14. What is Katie Derham's occupation?
15. Who presents *Cricket Monthly*?
16. Which sports show is presented by Danny Kelly?
17. Which C5 game show is hosted by Junior Simpson?
18. Who won the 1998 Eurovision Contest?
19. On which night is BBC2's *The Money Programme*?
20. On which programme is Oz Clarke a wine expert?
21. Which ex-England player presents *Football Focus*?
22. Who is Carol Barnes?
23. What does Sian Davies present?
24. *The People's Princess* was a tribute to whom?
25. Which current affairs programme is presented by Juliet Morris?
26. Which newsreader is Peter Snow's brother?
27. What is *Top Gear* presenter Willson's christian name?
28. On which day of the week was the World Cup Final 1998?
29. On which channel does Kirsty Young read the news?
30. Who co-presents *On The Ball* with Gabby Yorath?

ANSWERS

### Drama 3 (see Quiz 24)

**1.** *Boys From The Blackstuff.* **2.** Emma Thompson. **3.** America. **4.** A stunt man. **5.** The police force. **6.** Robbie Coltrane. **7.** *Millennium.* **8.** Lawyer. **9.** Richard Chamberlain. **10.** Larkin. **11.** Peter Bowles. **12.** *Reilly - Ace of Spies.* **13.** Nerys Hughes. **14.** John Thaw. **15.** A novelist. **16.** *The Singing Detective.* **17.** The fire service. **18.** A fashion house. **19.** Lady Chatterley. **20.** *Peak Practice.* **21.** *Sharpe.* **22.** Ben Elton. **23.** *A year In Provence.* **24.** *Cardiac Arrest.* **25.** Charles Dickens. **26.** George Eliot. **27.** McGann. **28.** Jane Austen. **29.** Elizabeth I. **30.** Shipping.

## QUIZ 24 Drama 3

**Answers: see Quiz 23, page 351**

LEVEL 1

1. Alan Bleasdale wrote the script for the 80's series *"Boys From The..."* what?
2. TV and film actor Kenneth Branagh was married to which actress?
3. *Bonanza* was set in which country?
4. What dangerous occupation did *The Fall Guy* have?
5. In which public service did *Juliet Bravo* serve?
6. Who stars as *Cracker* in the UK?
7. Which programme featured a man who could see into the minds of criminals?
8. What was the profession of most of the characters in *This Life*?
9. Who starred as *Doctor Kildare*?
10. Pam Ferris and David Jason played Ma and Pa who in *Darling Buds Of May*?
11. Which Peter starred in *The Irish RM* and with Penelope Keith in *To The Manor Born*?
12. In the series name, Reilly was Ace of what?
13. Which former *Liver Bird* played *The District Nurse*?
14. Which actor connects *The Sweeney, Morse* and *Kavanagh*?
15. What was the profession of Mary Fisher in *The Life and Loves Of A She Devil*?
16. The mystery drama written by Dennis Potter was called *The Singing...* what?
17. *London's Burning* follows the drama in which emergency service?
18. What kind of house was *The House Of Elliot*?
19. Which Lady, based on DH Lawrence's classic, was first televised in 1993?
20. What kind of Practice stars Kevin Whately as a rural GP?
21. Sean Bean stars as which 19th century British officer?
22. Which *Man From Auntie* comedian wrote *Stark*?
23. In the BBC series, John Thaw and Lindsay Duncan spent how long in Provence?
24. The BBC 2 medical drama was called *Cardiac* what?
25. Who wrote the classic *Martin Chuzzlewit*, dramatised by the BBC in 1994?
26. Which Victorian female author wrote *Middlemarch*?
27. Which family of four brothers starred in the historical drama, *The Hanging Gale*, set in 19th century Ireland?
28. The 1995 drama series *Pride And Prejudice*, was based on whose novel?
29. The MP Glenda Jackson starred on TV as which female British monarch?
30. What kind of transportation featured in *The Onedin Line*?

ANSWERS

**News 2 (see Quiz 23)**

**1.** David Bailey. **2.** James Burke. **3.** *The Human Body*. **4.** Clive James. **5.** John Craven. **6.** Aeroflot. **7.** Channel 4. **8.** Crown and Country. **9.** St. James, Leeds. **10.** Billy Connolly. **11.** Clive Anderson. **12.** Michael. **13.** *Gazzetta Football Italia*. **14.** Newsreader. **15.** David Gower. **16.** *Under The Moon*. **17.** *In The Dark*. **18.** Dana International (Israel). **19.** Sunday. **20.** Food And Drink. **21.** Gary Lineker. **22.** A Newsreader. **23.** Weather. **24.** Princess Diana. **25.** *Here And Now*. **26.** Jon. **27.** Quentin. **28.** Sunday. **29.** Channel 5. **30.** Barry Venison.

## QUIZ 25 Pot Luck 8

**Answers: see Quiz 26, page 354**

LEVEL 1

**1.** What was Frank Furillo's ex-wife's name in *Hill Street Blues?*
**2.** On which channel is *News at Ten?*
**3.** Which series features Denzil and Trigger?
**4.** Which title by Jules Verne was re-enacted by Michael Palin?
**5.** Which show featured Animal and Gonzo?
**6.** Who is in charge of the 15th squad of detectives in *NYPD Blue?*
**7.** Which programme featured the character Deep Throat?
**8.** What was Rebecca's surname in *Cheers?*
**9.** Which soap featured Malcolm McDowell in a guest role?
**10.** Who played Michael Murray in *GBH?*
**11.** Which Ray presents his World of Survival on BBC2?
**12.** Who played Laura in *The Dick Van Dyke Show?*
**13.** Who is Bart Simpson's oldest sister?
**14.** Which character did Joan Collins play in *Dynasty?*
**15.** Who first played *Robin of Sherwood?*
**16.** Who was Tom Howard's wife in *Howard's Way?*
**17.** Who was Barry Grant's mother in *Brookside?*
**18.** On which programme did Statto and Jeff Astle appear?
**19.** What was the name of the quiz where the guests sat in boxes?
**20.** Which Radio 4 'peoples' show does John Peel introduce?
**21.** In *Jonathon Creek* where does Jonathon live?
**22.** What are Lancelot, Guinevere and Arthur?
**23.** Who recorded *Anyone Can Fall In Love?*
**24.** Which show features video clips sent in by members of the public?
**25.** What is the pub in *Neighbours?*
**26.** Who wrote *Butterflies?*
**27.** What does Gary Imlach introduce?
**28.** Who was Callan's informer?
**29.** What was the policeman's name in *'Allo, 'Allo?*
**30.** Who presented *Stars on Sunday?*

ANSWERS

### Comedy 5 (see Quiz 26)

**1.** *MASH.* **2.** Martin Clunes. **3.** *The Odd Couple.* **4.** Derek Trotter. **5.** *Rhoda.* **6.** Sabrina. **7.** Barker and Corbett. **8.** Mildred. **9.** Maureen Lipman. **10.** *In Sickness and in Health.* **11.** The Meldrews. **12.** Edina. **13.** Colin Weatherby. **14.** Peter Cook. **15.** *Yes, Honestly.* **16.** Dibley. **17.** Brian Conley. **18.** Patrick Troughton. **19.** *Surgical Spirit.* **20.** Julian Clary. **21** Singles. **22.** Donald Sinden. **23.** *Up The Elephant And Round The Castle.* **24.** Ronnie Barker. **25.** Rosie. **26.** Shirley Maclaine. **27.** *Grace and Favour.* **28.** Harry H. Corbett. **29.** *Terry And June.* **30.** Holly.

## QUIZ 26 Comedy 5

**Answers: see Quiz 25, page 353**

LEVEL 1

1. Which series featured Col. Blake and Major Burns?
2. Who plays Gary in *Men Behaving Badly*?
3. In which series did Tony Randall play Felix Unger?
4. Who is David Jason's character in *Only Fools and Horses*?
5. Who had a sister named Brenda Morgenstern?
6. Who was the ...*Teenage Witch*?
7. Who were *The Two Ronnies*?
8. Who was George Roper's wife in *Man About The House*?
9. Who is playwright Jack Rosenthal's wife?
10. In which series did Eamonn Walker play Winston the home help?
11. Whose neighbours are Pippa and Patrick?
12. Which character in *Absolutely Fabulous* is a fashion magazine executive?
13. Who was the accident prone deputy manager of Whitbury Leisure Centre?
14. Who played the president of the U.S.A. in *Whoops Apocalypse*?
15. What was the sequel to *No Honestly* featuring Lisa Goddard?
16. Where was Dawn French the vicar of?
17. Which comedian and star of Jolson played an ex-con in *Time After Time*?
18. Which *Doctor Who* appeared in *The Two Of Us*?
19. Which sitcom starred Nicola MacAuliffe and Duncan Preston as surgeons?
20. Who was Julian in Terry and Julian?
21. What was the sitcom starring Judy Loe and Roger Rees set around a singles bar?
22. Who played the butler in *Two's Company*?
23. *Home James* was a spin off from which sitcom starring Jim Davidson?
24. Who played Clarence the short sighted removal man?
25. Which series was a sequel to *The Growing Pains of P.C. Penrose*?
26. Which American actress starred in *Shirley's World*?
27. Which sequel to *Are You Being Served* was set in a large country house?
28. Which *Steptoe and Son* actor's last series was *Grundy*?
29. What was the sequel to *Happy Ever After* starring June Whitfield and Terry Scott?
30. Which character in *Red Dwarf* was played by both Norman Lovett and Hattie Hayridge?

ANSWERS

### Pot Luck 8 (see Quiz 25)

**1.** Fay. **2.** ITV. **3.** *Only Fools And Horses*. **4.** *Around The World In 80 Days*. **5.** *The Muppet Show*. **6.** Lt. Fancy. **7.** *The X-Files*. **8.** Howe. **9.** *Crossroads*. **10.** Robert Lindsay. **11.** Mears. **12.** Mary Tyler Moore. **13.** Lisa. **14.** Alexis. **15.** Michael Praed. **16.** Jan. **17.** Sheila. **18.** *Fantasy Football League*. **19.** Celebrity Squares. **20.** *Home Truths*. **21.** In a windmill. **22.** Lottery draw machines. **23.** Anita Dobson. **24.** *You've Been Framed*. **25.** The Waterhole. **26.** Carla Lane. **27.** American Football. **28.** Lonely. **29.** Officer Crabtree. **30.** Jess Yates.

# QUIZ 27 Soaps 3

**Answers: see Quiz 28, page 356**

LEVEL 1

1. Which family live at No. 10 Brookside Close?
2. What was the surname of Alexis's third husband, Dex, in Dynasty?
3. Who was Pam and Bobby Ewing's son?
4. Who told her husband in *Eastenders* she was dying in an attempt to stop him from leaving her?
5. What had been the occupation of Betty Turpin's husband in *Coronation Street?*
6. In *Soap* who preceded Saunders as the Tate's butler?
7. Which character in *The Colbys* was played by Charlton Heston?
8. What was the name of Dot Cotton's husband?
9. Who is Ricky's boss at the Arches in *Eastenders?*
10. In *Neighbours* who was Daphne's husband?
11. Where in *Emmerdale* is The Woolpack located?
12. Who in *Eastenders* had two sons, David and Simon?
13. Who was Danni and Brett's mother in *Neighbours?*
14. In *Coronation Street* which of Liz McDonald's sons has been in prison?
15. Who owns a hairdressers in *Brookside?*
16. What was the name of Joe Mangel's son in *Neighbours?*
17. Who is Roy's son in *Eastenders?*
18. Which Channel 4 soap shows a map of Chester in its opening credits?
19. Who was Jim Robinson's entrepreneurial mother-in-law in *Neighbours?*
20. Which character in *Dallas* was portrayed by Priscilla Presley?
21. Which character did pop star Peter Noone play in *Coronation Street?*
22. What was Punk Mary's surname in *Eastenders?*
23. What was Don Brennan's trade in *Coronation Street?*
24. What was the name of Mavis Riley's budgie in *Coronation Street?*
25. Whose mother's name was Mo in *Eastenders?*
26. Which character does Brooke Satchwell play in *Neighbours?*
27. Who is Mark's wife in *Eastenders?*
28. Which character does Judy Nunn portray in *Home And Away?*
29. Who did Sarah Beaumont have an adulterous affair with in *Neighbours?*
30. Who is butcher Fred Elliot's nephew in *Coronation Street?*

ANSWERS

**Pot Luck 9 (see Quiz 29)**

**1.** Ena. **2.** Alan. **3.** The Sullivans. **4.** Paul Henry. **5.** Sylvia Costas. **6.** Anita Harris. **7.** *Bless This House.* **8.** *Local Heroes.* **9.** Michael Newman. **10.** Arnie Thomas. **11** Weather presenters. **12.** Camelot. **13.** 625. **14.** Astra. **15.** Esther Rantzen. **16.** Les Dawson. **17.** Kermit the Frog. **18.** Five **19.** A chat show host. **20.** Oprah. **21.** Basil Brush. **22.** *Magpie.* **23.** Derek Nimmo. **24.** Wilma. **25.** Gordon Kaye. **26.** Barcelona. **27.** Mel Smith. **28.** Mrs. Slocombe. **29.** Peter Sellers. **30.** Wilson.

## QUIZ 28 Pot Luck 9

LEVEL 1

**Answers: see Quiz 27, page 355**

1. What was Mrs Sharples' christian name in *Coronation Street*?
2. What was the first name of interviewer and presenter Whicker?
3. What was the first Australian soap shown in the U.K.?
4. Who recorded *Benny's Theme*?
5. Who is Andy Sipowicz married to in *NYPD Blue*?
6. Who starred in *Anita In Jumbleland*?
7. In which series did Robin Stewart play Sally Geeson's brother?
8. Which series is presented by Adam Hart-Davis?
9. Which character on *Baywatch* plays himself?
10. What was Tom Arnold's character in *Roseanne*?
11. What are Suzanne Charlton and John Kettley?
12. Who runs *The National Lottery*?
13. How many lines are transmitted in terrestrial television?
14. What satellites beam BSkyB programmes?
15. Who presented *That's Life*?
16. Who appeared with Roy Barraclough as Cissie and Ada?
17. Which Muppet is adored by Miss Piggy?
18. How many channels are available on analogue terrestrial television?
19. What is David Letterman?
20. What is chat show host Ms Winfrey's first name?
21. Which fox is a puppet?
22. Which programme did Mick Robertson and Douglas Rae present?
23. Who played Noote in *All Gas And Gaiters*?
24. Who is Fred Flintstone's wife?
25. Who plays Rene Artois in *'Allo, 'Allo*?
26. Where does Manuel come from in *Fawlty Towers*?
27. Who is Griff Rhys-Jones's comedy partner?
28. Who was worried about her pussy in *Are you Being Served*?
29. Which of *The Goons* was an international film star?
30. Which character is a sergeant in *Dad's Army*?

ANSWERS

### Soaps 3 (see Quiz 27)

**1.** The Corkhills. **2.** Dexter. **3.** Christopher. **4.** Angie Watts. **5.** A police sergeant. **6.** Benson. **7.** Jason Colby. **8.** Charlie. **9.** Phil Mitchell. **10.** Des Clarke. **11.** Beckindale. **12.** Pat Wicks. **13.** Cheryl Stark. **14.** Steve. **15.** Jacqui Dixon. **16.** Toby. **17.** Barry Evans. **18.** *Hollyoaks*. **19.** Helen Daniels. **20.** Jenna Wade. **21.** Stanley Fairclough. **22.** Smith. **23.** Taxi driver. **24.** Harriet. **25.** Frank Butcher. **26.** Anne Wilkinson. **27.** Ruth Fowler. **28.** Ailsa. **29.** Karl Kennedy. **30.** Ashley Peacock.

# QUIZ 29 Children's TV 3

**Answers: see Quiz 30, page 358**

LEVEL 1

1. Which series often featured Man At Arms and his daughter Teela?
2. Which *Dr Who* became *Worzel Gummidge*?
3. Former *Blue Peter* presenter Caron Keating is the daughter of which Irish-born female TV host?
4. How many days each week was *Play School* broadcast?
5. On which day did *Tiswas* appear?
6. On which channel was the *Multi-coloured Swap Shop*?
7. What colour was the *Pink Panther*'s sports car?
8. What colour are the *Smurfs*?
9. What was unusual about Clarence the lion in *Daktari*?
10. What kind of locomotive was Thomas?
11. How many *Teletubbies* are there?
12. Who played the *Knight Rider*?
13. Who is the female presenter of *The Gladiators*?
14. What was James T. Kirk?
15. In which series did the mute woman Marina appear?
16. Who said "time for bed"?
17. Which children's series featured Ant and Dec?
18. Who was *Grange Hill*'s headmistress?
19. Which cartoon series featured Fred and Barney?
20. Which series features a Christmas Appeal?
21. How was *Top Cat* known to his close friends?
22. Which cartoon series features a Great Dane?
23. Which Polish programme, shown on Channel 4, featured Toyah Wilcox and Nigel Kennedy narrating the English version, and a wooden main character?
24. What was *Ace Ventura*?
25. Who lives in Jellystone Park?
26. What was Flipper?
27. Who played *Batman* in the 1960s TV series?
28. Which postman had a black and white cat?
29. Who in *Thunderbirds* owned a pink Rolls Royce?
30. In *Grange Hill* what was Stebson's nickname?

ANSWERS

**Sport 2 (see Quiz 30)**

**1.** Saturday. **2.** True. **3.** David Baddiel and Frank Skinner. **4.** Saturday. **5.** Golf. **6.** *A Question Of Sport*. **7.** Damon Hill. **8.** Will Carling. **9.** 10pm. **10.** David Coleman. **11.** Nick Hancock. **12.** Sharon Davies. **13.** The javelin. **14.** Athletics. **15.** Desmond Lynam. **16.** Henry Cooper. **17.** Tennis. **18.** Monday. **19.** Steve Rider. **20.** *Match Of The Day*. **21.** *Nationwide Football League Extra*. **22.** Alistair McGowan. **23.** BBC1. **24.** *Fantasy Football League*. **25.** BBC2. **26.** Channel 4. **27.** Bicycles. **28.** Four. **29.** *Grandstand*. **30.** Gary Lineker.

## QUIZ 30 Sport 2

**Answers: see Quiz 29, page 357**

LEVEL 1

1. On which day is *Football Focus* broadcast?
2. Willy Carson was a *Question Of Sport* captain, true or false?
3. Which duo present *Fantasy Football League*?
4. On which night did Jimmy Hill first present *Match of the Day*?
5. Peter Aliss commentates on which sport?
6. Ian Botham was a captain on which TV sports quiz?
7. Which British motor racing champion was BBC Sports Personality of the Year in 1994?
8. Which former England captain presents rugby on ITV?
9. At what time is Sky's *Sports Centre* normally broadcast?
10. Who retired as host of *A Question Of Sport* in 1997?
11. *They Think It's All Over* is presented by who?
12. Which female champion swimmer was a Gladiator?
13. Fatima Whitbread was televised winning Olympic gold in which athletic discipline?
14. Which sport does Brendan Foster commentate on?
15. Desmond who presents sport on BBC?
16. Which boxer became BBC Sports Personality Of The Year in 1970?
17. Dan Maskell commentated on which sport?
18. On what day was *Match Of The Day Extra* broadcast?
19. Which Steve presents *Grandstand*?
20. Mark Lawrenson and Trevor Brooking are regulars on which football show?
21. Which late night series shows highlights of Nation-wide Football league matches?
22. On Channel 4 which impressionist, Alistair, hosted his *Football Backchat*?
23. Which channel hosts *Sports Review Of The Year*?
24. Ex-footballer Jeff Astle sings on which show hosted by Skinner and Baddiel?
25. Ski Sunday is broadcast on which channel?
26. Which channel broadcasts *Football Italia*?
27. With what form of transport is the Tour de France contested?
28. How many contestants are there in each episode of *Gladiators*?
29. Frank Bough hosted which Saturday afternoon sports programme?
30. Which BBC football presenter played for Leicester City and Tottenham Hotspur?

ANSWERS

### Children's TV 3 (see Quiz 29)

**1.** *He-Man and the Masters of the Universe.* **2.** John Pertwee. **3.** Gloria Hunniford. **4.** Five. **5.** Saturday. **6.** BBC1. **7.** Pink. **8.** Blue. **9.** He was cross-eyed and wore glasses. **10.** A tank engine. **11.** Four. **12.** David Hasselhoff. **13.** Ulrika Jonsson. **14.** Captain of the USS Enterprise. **15.** *Stingray.* **16.** Zebedee. **17.** *Byker Grove.* **18.** Mrs. McClusky. **19.** *The Flintstones.* **20.** *Blue Peter.* **21.** TC. **22.** *Scooby Doo.* **23.** *Pob.* **24.** The *Pet Detective.* **25.** Yogi Bear. **26.** A Dolphin. **27.** Adam West. **28.** *Postman Pat.* **29.** Lady Penelope. **30.** Gripper.

## QUIZ 31 Comedy 6

LEVEL 1

**Answers: see Quiz 32, page 360**

1. Who was the star of *Further Up Pompeii*?
2. Who is Rowan Atkinson's hapless silent character?
3. Which *Heartbeat* actor was *The Gaffer*?
4. Which spin off from *Man About The House* featured Brian Murphy and Yootha Joyce?
5. From which sitcom was *Going Straight* the sequel?
6. A sequel to *Last of The Summer Wine* featured the characters in their younger days. What was its title?
7. Who starred with Julia Mackenzie, as her husband, in *French Fields*?
8. In which county was Arkwright's corner shop?
9. Who played Tony Britton's son in *Don't Wait Up*?
10. What was the UK's first dedicated (non-terrestrial) comedy channel?
11. A pilot show entitled *Prisoner and Escort* became which sitcom?
12. The credits of which sitcom feature a tortoise?
13. Where did the Boswells live?
14. What was the series featuring Nicholas Lyndhurst and Clive Francis as inept spies?
15. Who wrote and sang the theme for *No Honestly*?
16. The nautical TV series *HMS Paradise* was based on which comedy radio show?
17. In which series did John Gordon Sinclair play a journalist?
18. Which sitcom featured Nellie and Eli Pledge?
19. What was the sequel to *The Likely Lads*?
20. What was the sitcom about servants and masters written by Jimmy Perry and David Croft?
21. Which Russ ran his *Madhouse* on TV?
22. Who starred as *Blackadder*'s sidekick Baldrick?
23. Which comic presents *In Bed With MeDinner*?
24. Who is Sid Little's comedy partner?
25. What are the first names of Fry and Laurie?
26. The painter and decorator Jacko appeared in which comedy series?
27. Which comedy's theme tune began with the words "I'm H-A-P-P-Y"?
28. In which town is *Fawlty Towers* set?
29. Which former Goon presented the religious programme *Highway*?
30. In *Only Fools And Horses* Del Boy's van had how many wheels?

ANSWERS

**Pot Luck 10 (see Quiz 32)**

**1.** Lilith. **2.** Jed Clampett. **3.** Jacko. **4.** Crusty. **5.** A cartoon. **6.** Donald Fisher. **7.** Harold Bishop. **8.** Orville. **9.** Clark Kent. **10.** Sue. **11.** Barnaby Jones. **12.** Ben Cartwright. **13.** William Hartnell. **14.** UK Gold. **15.** Doctor. **16.** Marshall Matt Dillon. **17.** Michael Landon. **18.** Richard Boone. **19.** He was the New York District Attorney. **20.** Jack Killian. **21.** Reg Watson. **22.** James Allen. **23.** Geoff Capes. **24.** An 11th Century Magician. **25.** Bob Grant. **26.** *Goodness Gracious Me.* **27.** *Bottom.* **28.** George Clooney. **29.** Sally Smedley. **30.** Bet Lynch.

## QUIZZ 32 Pot Luck 10

**Answers: see Quiz 31, page 359**

LEVEL 1

1. What was the name of *Frasier's* wife?
2. Who was Ellie Mae's pa in *The Beverley Hillbillies*?
3. Who did Karl Howman play in *Brushstrokes*?
4. What is the clown's name in *The Simpsons*?
5. What type of programme was *Dungeons & Dragons*?
6. Who is the headmaster in *Home and Away*?
7. Who is Madge's husband in *Neighbours*?
8. Which green duck is a puppet?
9. What is Superman's earthly name?
10. Who is Sooty's female friend?
11. Which private detective was portrayed by Buddy Ebsen?
12. Which character had three sons, Adam, Hoss and Little Joe?
13. Which *Doctor Who* starred in the very first *Carry On* film?
14. Which sattelite channel is famous for re-running old programmes?
15. What was *The Fugitive*'s profession?
16. Who did James Arness portray in *Gunsmoke*?
17. Who played Jonathan in *Highway To Heaven*?
18. Who played Paladin in *Have Gun Will Travel*?
19. Which post did Michael Hayes hold?
20. Which character was the D.J. in *Midnight Caller*?
21. Who created Neighbours?
22. Which James was 'in the pits' for ITV's Formula One coverage in 1998?
23. Who was the first British winner of *The World's Strongest Man*?
24. What was *Catweazle*?
25. Who played Jack in *On The Buses*?
26. On which show would you hear the catchphrase "Cheque, please"?
27. In which series is the character Dave Hedgehog?
28. Who played Booker in *Roseanne*?
29. Who in *Drop The Dead Donkey* is Henry's co-presenter?
30. Which landlady, in *Coronation Street*, was mugged on her way home from The Rovers Return?

ANSWERS

### Comedy 6 (see Quiz 31)

**1.** Frankie Howard. **2.** *Mr. Bean*. **3.** Bill Maynard. **4.** George & Mildred. **5.** *Porridge*. **6.** *First of The Summer Wine*. **7.** Anton Rodgers. **8.** Yorkshire. **9.** Nigel Havers. **10.** *Paramount Comedy*. **11** *Porridge*. **12.** *One Foot In The Grave*. **13.** Liverpool. **14.** *The Piglet Files*. **15.** Lyndsey De Paul. **16.** *The Navy Lark*. **17.** *Nelson's Column*. **18.** *Nearest & Dearest*. **19.** *Whatever Happened To The Likely Lads?* **20.** *You Rang M'Lord?* **21.** Russ Abbot. **22.** Tony Robinson. **23.** Bob Mills. **24.** Eddie Large. **25.** Stephen & Hugh. **26.** *Brush Strokes*. **27.** *Only When I Laugh*. **28.** Torquay. **29.** Harry Secombe. **30.** Three.

# QUIZ 33 Drama 4

LEVEL 1

**Answers: see Quiz 34, page 362**

1. In which south-western county was the 1970s series *Poldark* set?
2. What kind of bouquet featured Frank Finlay and Susan Penhaligon amidst family tensions in the 1970s?
3. Gemma Jones starred as *The Duchess* of which street on the BBC?
4. Richard O'Sullivan played which infamous 18th century highwayman in the 1980s ITV series?
5. Gordon Jackson was a butler in which 1970s series about an Edwardian family?
6. Robson and Jerome starred together in which ITV series about the army?
7. Pamela Anderson starred in which series about a beach lifeguard unit?
8. What does *ER* stand for?
9. In which drama series did Clive Russell play Archie, one of the rig crew?
10. Who played Dr. Claire Maitland in *Cardiac Arrest*?
11. Which medical emergency team were stationed at Cooper's Crossing, Australia?
12. Which star of *Tenko* appeared in *Waiting For God*?
13. In which series is the fictional village Aidensfield?
14. Which policeman in *The Bill* ran down and killed a pedestrian?
15. Which drama series featured the character Recall?
16. Anton Rodgers plays vet Noah Kirby in which series?
17. Who played Ma Larkin in *The Darling Buds Of May*?
18. What was the spin off series from *Beverley Hills 90210*?
19. In which country was the drama series *Amongst Women* set?
20. Which drama series features Glen Murphy as George?
21. Who played Cecil Rhodes in BBC's *Rhodes*?
22. Which actor was *The Chancer*?
23. In which series did Jack Davenport portray lawyer Miles?
24. In which series is Jake Henshaw a vet?
25. In which swashbuckling series did Pete Postlethwaite play Obadiah Hatesworth?
26. Who played Owen Springer in *Reckless*?
27. Which series features Dana and Fox?
28. Which Leslie Charteris character was portrayed by Ian Ogilvy?
29. Which spy series starred Ray Lonnen and Roy Marsden?
30. Which series starred Bill Cosby as a criminologist?

ANSWERS

### Soaps 4 (see Quiz 34)

**1.** Hilda Ogden. **2.** Diane. **3.** *Coronation Street.* **4.** di Marco. **5.** Ruth Wilkinson. **6.** Gail Platt. **7.** The Snug. **8.** Kenny. **9.** Fallon and Jeff. **10.** Ena Sharples. **11.** Spider. **12.** *The Waltons.* **13.** Sky. **14.** Oil. **15.** Chris Tate. **16.** Jimmy. **17.** Tiffany. **18.** Rita Sullivan. **19.** *The Blue Ridge Mountains of Virginia.* **20.** *Brookside* and *Family Affairs.* **21.** 1980s. **22.** Dot Cotton. **23.** Hazel Adair and Peter Ling. **24.** His girlfriend Jan. **25.** Jodie. **26.** Percy Sugden. **27.** Don Brennan. **28.** Leonard Swindley. **29.** *Brookside.* **30.** Percy Sugden.

## QUIZ 34 Soaps 4

**Answers: see Quiz 33, page 361**

LEVEL 1

1. Who had flying ducks on her wall in *Coronation Street*?
2. What was the name of Frank Butcher's eldest daughter in *Eastenders*?
3. In which soap did Joanna Lumley play Eileen Perkins?
4. Which family runs the Italian restaurant in *Eastenders*?
5. Who is Anne and Lance's mother in *Neighbours*?
6. Who is Sarah Louise's mother in *Coronation Street*?
7. In *Coronation Street* which bar did Minnie, Martha and Ena frequent in The Rovers Return?
8. Who was Pete Beale's brother in *Eastenders*?
9. Who in *Dynasty* had a son 'Little Blake'?
10. Which Ena was the caretaker at the Glad Tidings Mission in *Coronation Street*?
11. What is the name of Emily Nugent's nephew who stood for the Wetherfield council?
12. Which 1930's US family included Jim Bob and Olivia?
13. In *Neighbours*, what was the name of Kerry Bishop's daughter?
14. Which business was the main concern of the Ewings of *Dallas*?
15. Who is Zoe's brother in *Emmerdale*?
16. What is Jacqui Corkhill's husband's name in *Brookside*?
17. Who is Grant Mitchell's wife in *Eastenders*?
18. Which character does Barbara Knox portray in *Coronation Street*?
19. In which mountains of Virginia was Walton's Mountain?
20. In which two soaps has David Easter appeared?
21. In which decade was *Neighbours* first shown in the U.K.?
22. Which Dot was the laundrette manageress in *Eastenders*?
23. Which two writers, Hazel and Peter, created *Crossroads*?
24. In *Eastenders*, who did Den Watts meet while in Venice with Angie?
25. In *Soap* what was the name of Mary Campbell's gay son?
26. Percy who established a Neighbourhood Watch Scheme in *Coronation Street*?
27. Which *Coronation Street* taxi driver did Ivy Tilsley marry in 1988?
28. In *Coronation Street* who ran a haberdashery emporium in Rosamund Street?
29. In which Channel 4 soap did the Finnegans try to take over a night club?
30. Who owned a budgie called Randy in the *Coronation Street*?

ANSWERS

**Drama 4 (see Quiz 33)**

**1.** Cornwall. **2.** *A Bouquet Of Barbed Wire*. **3.** *The Duchess of Duke Street*. **4.** *Dick Turpin*. **5.** *Upstairs, Downstairs*. **6.** *Soldier, Soldier*. **7.** *Baywatch*. **8.** *Emergency Room*. **9.** *Roughnecks*. **10.** Helen Baxendale. **11.** *The Flying Doctors*. **12.** Stephanie Cole. **13.** *Heartbeat*. **14.** PC Tony Stamp. **15.** *London's Burning*. **16.** *Noah's Ark*. **17.** Pam Ferris. **18.** *Melrose Place*. **19.** Ireland. **20.** *London's Burning*. **21.** Martin Shaw. **22.** Clive Owen. **23.** *This Life*. **24.** *Noah's Ark*. **25.** *Sharpe*. **26.** Robson Green. **27.** *The X-Files*. **28.** *The Saint*. **29.** *The Sandbaggers*. **30.** *The Cosby Mysteries*.

## QUIZ 35 Pot Luck 11

**Answers: see Quiz 36, page 364**

LEVEL 1

1. Which S.F. series featured Sam Beckett?
2. Which series centred around the doctors of St. Elygius Hospital, Boston?
3. Who co-starred with Michael Douglas in *The Streets Of San Francisco*?
4. Which series starred Robert Carlyle as a Scottish policeman?
5. Which crime series of the sixties featured tales of the 65th Precinct of New York?
6. Who plays *Quincy*?
7. What kind of programme was *Mary Hartman, Mary Hartman*?
8. Who played Kid Curry in *Alias Smith and Jones*?
9. Which series featured the character Father Peter Clifford?
10. Who portrays Lois Lane in *The New Adventures of Superman*?
11. Which series featured the IMF team?
12. Which series centred around the inhabitants of Cicely, Alaska?
13. Which character did Judi Trott portray in *Robin Of Sherwood*?
14. Which ex-baseball star ran the *Cheers* bar?
15. Which series featured Tim Healy, Kevin Whately and Jimmy Nail as site workers in Germany?
16. Which series featured Rob and Laura Petrie?
17. Who was Samantha's husband in *Bewitched*?
18. Where is Frasier's radio station?
19. How many sons does Rab C Nesbit have?
20. Which of the *Golden Girls* was a southern belle?
21. Who is Dorothy's boyfriend in *Men Behaving Badly*?
22. Who is *Father Ted*'s housekeeper?
23. Who starred as *Murphy Brown*?
24. What was Ron Howard's character in *Happy Days*?
25. Who is the creator of *ER*?
26. Who lived at Nelson Mandela House, Peckham?
27. Who is Tony Hill's sister in *Eastenders*?
28. Which soap is set in Weatherfield?
29. In which series did Erika Eleniak play a lifeguard?
30. Which series of interviews was introduced by John Freeman?

ANSWERS

### Sport 3 (see Quiz 36)

**1.** West Ham United. **2.** Rugby Union. **3.** Horse Racing. **4.** Swimming. **5.** *Ski Sunday.* **6.** Sunday. **7.** Ryan Giggs. **8.** Boycott. **9.** ITV. **10.** Cricket. **11.** Scottish. **12.** The World Cup Finals. **13.** *Sick As A Parrot.* **14.** *Gladiators.* **15.** The Olympic Games. **16.** Ice Skating. **17.** Ski-jumping. **18.** The Oval. **19.** Rugby Union. **20.** Rupert Murdoch. **21.** Sky Sports. **22.** Andy Gray. **23.** Geoff Boycott. **24.** Yes. **25.** BBC2. **26.** Bob Wilson. **27.** Arsenal and Newcastle Utd. **28.** American Football. **29.** No. **30.** EuroSport.

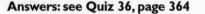

## QUIZ 36 Sport 3

**Answers: see Quiz 35, page 363**

LEVEL 1

1. Football commentator Trevor Brooking spent his playing career with which club?
2. Commentator Nigel Starmer-Smith is associated with which sport?
3. Julian Wilson, Richard Pitman, Peter Scudamore are associated with which sport?
4. Hamilton Bland commentates on which sport?
5. David Vine presented which Winter sports programme on BBC2?
6. *Football Italia* is broadcast on which afternoon?
7. Which Manchester United and Wales footballer provided tips on soccer skills on Channel 4?
8. Which Yorkshireman Geoff played and commentated on cricket?
9. On which channel is *The Big Match* broadcast?
10. Tony Lewis introduces coverage of what?
11. What nationality is sports presenter Hazel Irvine?
12. *My Granny Could've Done Better* documents the history of which football cup?
13. Which Channel 5 sports quiz, with a cliché for a title, is hosted by Jeremy Nicholas?
14. Rugby Union star Jeremy Guscott co-presents which ITV physical challenge series?
15. For what sporting event did the BBC use the theme *Tokyo Melody* in 1964?
16. What was Alan Weeks a specialist commentator on?
17. Which event did Eddie The Eagle compete in during the Winter Olympics?
18. In 1998, from where was the final test match for cricket televised?
19. What sport is Bill McLaren a commentator on?
20. Which Media Tycoon's company made a bid £635 million for Manchester United?
21. Which channel broadcasts Women's NBA?
22. Who introduces live Premiership football?
23. Which cricket commentator was sacked in 1998?
24. Does *No Balls Allowed* ever feature football?
25. Which is the only terrestrial channel *not* to broadcast live football?
26. Who introduces ITV's Champions League coverage?
27. Who contested the 1998 FA Cup final?
28. In which sport do teams contest the Superbowl?
29. Does Michael Owen host his own show?
30. Which channel broadcasts *Eurogoals*?

ANSWERS

### Pot Luck 11 (see Quiz 35)

**1.** *Quantum Leap.* **2.** *St. Elsewhere.* **3.** Karl Malden. **4.** *Hamish Macbeth.* **5.** *The Naked City.* **6.** Jack Klugman. **7.** A spoof soap. **8.** Ben Murphy. **9.** *Ballykissangel.* **10.** Teri Hatcher. **11.** *Mission Impossible.* **12.** *Northern Exposure.* **13.** Marian. **14.** Sam Malone. **15.** *Auf Wiedersehen Pet.* **16.** *The Dick Van Dyke Show.* **17.** Darren. **18.** Seattle. **19.** Two. **20.** Blanche Deveraux. **21.** Gary. **22.** Mrs. Doyle. **23.** Candice Bergen. **24.** Ritchie Cunningham. **25.** Michael Crichton. **26.** The Trotters. **27.** Sarah. **28.** *Coronation Street.* **29.** *Baywatch.* **30.** *Face To Face.*

## QUIZ 37 Comedy 7

LEVEL 1

**Answers: see Quiz 38, page 366**

1. What were the surnames of the famous comedy duo Eric and Ernie?
2. Frank Windsor starred as a sergeant in which army comedy series?
3. *The Fall And Rise...* of whom did we see on TV?
4. Which actress starred as the main character in *After Henry*?
5. The comedy *Bread* was set in which city?
6. Which Sid, of *Carry On* fame, starred in *Bless This House*?
7. What does Hank Hill sell in *King of the Hill*?
8. In *Fawlty Towers*, he was from Barcelona. Who was the character?
9. Maureen Lipman starred in which sitcom about an agony aunt?
10. Whose characters include an offensive drunk and a pathetic chat-show host?
11. Dudley Moore was one half of a famous comedy duo. Who was the other half?
12. Who starred in *Alas Smith And Jones*?
13. Richard Gordon wrote *Doctor In The* … what?
14. Whose catchphrase was "Oooh, no Mrs!"?
15. Which comedian and comic writer starred in Sykes alongside Hattie Jacques?
16. Which comedian sang about *Ernie, The Fastest Milkman In The West*?
17. *I Love Lucy* starred American comedienne Lucille who?
18. Warren Mitchell stars as which grumpy pensioner in *In Sickness And In Health*?
19. What do the following have in common: Jimmy Tarbuck, Lilly Savage, Ken Dodd and Stan Boardman?
20. Which 1980s BBC comedy was set in a holiday camp?
21. Granddad, Uncle Albert, Boysee and Trigger all appeared in which classic BBC series?
22. Which Paul is the creator of *The Fast Show*?
23. Who played Captain Mainwaring in *Dad's Army*?
24. Which of Fry and Laurie appeared as the Prince in *Blackadder the Third*?
25. Richard briers and Felicity Kendall lived what kind of life according to the title of their self-sufficient comedy?
26. Who hosts *Tibs And Fibs*?
27. In which comedy did the female agent warn Rene "I will say this only once"?
28. What are the Christian names of the comic duo *Wood and Walters*?
29. The comedy *Surgical Spirit* was set in what kind of building?
30. What is the setting for *Drop The Dead Donkey*?

ANSWERS

### Pot Luck 12 (see Quiz 38)

**1.** *Coronation Street.* **2.** Horse racing. **3.** Sooty. **4.** The Wedding of The Prince Of Wales and Lady Diana Spencer. **5.** *Blue Peter.* **6.** Bill Owen. **7.** Else. **8.** Paul Daniels. **9.** Norway. **10.** The Two Rons. **11.** *Supersonic.* **12.** Jane Tennison. **13.** Castor. **14.** Jim Henson. **15.** Barry Grant. **16.** *Bod.* **17.** John Major. **18.** Charades. **19.** Captain Mainwaring. **20.** *It Ain't Half Hot Mum.* **21.** David Jacobs. **22.** Lurcio. **23.** Athletics. **24.** Richard Cole. **25.** Blackstock. **26.** Mr. Burns. **27.** Mechanic. **28.** BBC1. **29.** Mr. Humphries. **30.** George Cole.

## QUIZ 38 Pot Luck 12

**Answers: see Quiz 37, page 365**

LEVEL 1

1. Which series was described as a story about six terraced houses, a shop and a pub?
2. On which sport was John Rickman a pundit?
3. Which puppet has been presented by father Harry and son Matthew?
4. Which Royal Event was televised on July 29th 1981?
5. Which children's programme featured Patch and Petra?
6. Who plays Compo in *Last of The Summer Wine*?
7. What was Alf's wife's name in *Til Death Us Do Part*?
8. Who was the host of *Odd One Out*?
9. Which country failed to score in the *Eurovision Song Contest*?
10. Who are referred to as 'The Management'?
11. What was Sid Little's nickname?
12. Which character does Helen Mirren play in *Prime Suspect*?
13. What is the name of Olive Oyl's brother?
14. Which puppeteer created a muppet for *Sam and Friends*?
15. Who is the last remaining original character in *Brookside*?
16. Which cartoon featured Mr. Copper?
17. Which character in *Spitting Image* commented on the peas?
18. Which party game was *Give us a Clue* based on?
19. Who called Pike 'You stupid boy' in *Dads Army*?
20. What was the comedy series about a concert party in India?
21. Who presented *Juke Box Jury*?
22. Who was Ludicrus Sextus's servant in *Up Pompeii*?
23. Which sport does Stuart Storey commentate on?
24. Who in *Eastenders* was known as Tricky Dicky?
25. In *Chef* what is Gareth's surname?
26. Who is Homer Simpson's boss?
27. What was Sid Hooper's occupation in *Crossroads*?
28. On which channel was *Mastermind* broadcast?
29. Whose catchphrase is 'I'm free' on *Are You Being Served*?
30. Who played Arthur Dailey in *Minder*?

ANSWERS

**Comedy 7 (see Quiz 37)**

**1.** Morecambe & Wise. **2.** *It Ain't Half Hot Mum.* **3.** Reginald Perrin. **4.** Prunella Scales. **5.** Liverpool. **6.** Sid James. **7.** Propane & propane accessories. **8.** Manuel the waiter. **9.** *Agony.* **10.** Steve Coogan. **11.** Peter Cook. **12.** Mel Smith and Griff Rhys Jones. **13.** *Doctor In The House.* **14.** Frankie Howerd. **15.** Eric Sykes. **16.** Benny Hill. **17.** Lucille Ball. **18.** Alf Garnett. **19.** All hail from Liverpool. **20.** *Hi-Di-Hi!* **21.** *Only Fools and Horses.* **22.** Whitehouse. **23.** Arthur Lowe. **24.** Hugh Laurie. **25.** *The Good Life.* **26.** Tony Slattery. **27.** *'Allo, 'Allo.* **28.** Victoria & Julie. **29.** A general hospital. **30.** A TV newsroom.

## QUIZ 39 Children's TV 4

**Answers: see Quiz 40, page 368**

LEVEL 1

**1.** In *Doctor Who*, who was K-9?
**2.** What was *Black Beauty*?
**3.** In *Happy Days* who was Ritchie's sister?
**4.** Who was the bird in cartoons with Sylvester?
**5.** Which series featured Miss Piggy?
**6.** Who were Herman and Lily?
**7.** On which programme was there a cat named Jason?
**8.** Which program featured Big Ted and Little Ted?
**9.** Who played *The Incredible Hulk*?
**10.** To which team did Face and Mad Murdock belong?
**11.** Who was the voice of *Mr. Magoo*?
**12.** Who is Huey, Dewey and Louie's uncle?
**13.** Which series about a secret helicopter starred Jan Michael Vincent?
**14.** Which sitcom featured Arnold and Willis Jackson?
**15.** Which US series featured Josh Saviano as Paul Pfeiffer?
**16.** Which colourful feline cartoon character has his own series?
**17.** In which series was Baron Silas Greenback the arch villain?
**18.** Which cartoon series featured Kanga and Piglet?
**19.** In which S.F. series does Maximillian Arturo appear?
**20.** Which character in *The Cosby Show* did Malcolm Jamal Warner portray?
**21.** Which pop music show featured *Legs and Co*?
**22.** What was the name of the boy doctor who had his own series?
**23.** Which popular children's soap is set in the North East?
**24.** The puppet Muffin was what kind of creature?
**25.** On *Watch With Mother*, who was the puppet baby clown?
**26.** *Sooty* is a puppet what?
**27.** What colour are Sweep's ears?
**28.** What are the twins called in *Rugrats*?
**29.** What was the surname of the famous Billy, a tubby schoolboy created by Frank Richards?
**30.** What did Bill and Ben live in?

ANSWERS

### Drama 5 (see Quiz 40)

**1.** *Ultraviolet.* **2.** *Supply And Demand.* **3.** Nadim Sawalha. **4.** Trinity. **5.** She was electrocuted. **6.** Harriet. **7.** Robert Pastorelli. **8.** *Dark Skies.* **9.** Lou Grant. **10.** Ricardo. **11.** *Rumpole of The Bailey.* **12.** Jonathan Brandis. **13.** Kyle McLachlan. **14.** *The Fugitive.* **15.** *Hamish Macbeth.* **16.** Los Angeles Tribune. **17.** *The Vanishing Man.* **18.** Adam Faith. **19.** *The Bill.* **20.** *Mission Impossible.* **21.** *Northern Exposure.* **22.** *ER.* **23.** Lotus Seven. **24.** Silent. **25.** Station Officer. **26.** *Crocodile Shoes.* **27.** *Hart To Hart.* **28.** Vegas. **29.** *All Creatures Great And Small.* **30.** Roger Moore.

## QUIZ 40 Drama 5

**Answers: see Quiz 39, page 367**

LEVEL 1

1. Which thriller series starred Jack Davenport as DS Michael Colefield?
2. In which Linda La Plante series did Larry Lamb play Simon Hughes?
3. In *Dangerfield* the father of actresses Nadia and Julia plays Dr. Shabaan Hamada. Who is he?
4. In which town is Lucas Buck the sheriff in *American Gothic*?
5. How did Assumpta die in *Ballykissangel*?
6. What was Makepiece's christian name in *Dempsey And Makepiece*?
7. Who plays Gerry Fitzgerald in *Fitz*?
8. In which drama S.F. series were the characters John Loengard and Kimberley Sayers?
9. Which spin off from *The Mary Tyler Moore Show* was a drama series?
10. What is Tubbs' first name in *Miami Vice*?
11. In which Drama series did Judge Guthrie Featherstone appear?
12. Who plays Lucas in *Seaquest DSV*?
13. Who played Special Agent Dale Cooper in *Twin Peaks*?
14. In which series did Lt. Gerard pursue a doctor?
15. Which drama series featured Wee Jock and The Clan McLopez?
16. Where did *Lou Grant* work in LA?
17. In which drama series does Neil Morrissey play Nick Cameron?
18. Which former pop singer starred in *Love Hurts*?
19. In which drama series does Colin Tarrant play Inspector Monroe?
20. Which series featured Barbara Bain as Cinnamon?
21. In which series was the character Marilyn Whirlwind a doctor's receptionist?
22. In which series was Anna Del Amico a hospital doctor?
23. What car did *The Prisoner* drive in the opening credits?
24. In the series starring Amanda Burton what kind of Witness were her cadavers?
25. In *London's Burning* what rank was Nick?
26. What was the title of a Jimmy Nail series and his hit record?
27. In which series were Jonathan and Jennifer crime fighters?
28. Where was Dan Tanna a private eye?
29. The characters Siegfried and Tristan Farnon appeared in which series?
30. Which suave UK actor links Simon Templar and Maverick?

ANSWERS

### Children's TV 4 (see Quiz 39)

**1.** A robot dog. **2.** A Horse. **3.** Joannie. **4.** Tweety Pie. **5.** *The Muppet Show.* **6.** *The Munsters.* **7.** *Blue Peter.* **8.** *Play School.* **9.** Lou Ferrigno. **10.** *The A Team.* **11.** Jim Backus. **12.** Donald Duck. **13.** *Airwolf.* **14.** *Diff'rent Strokes.* **12.** *The Wonder Years.* **16.** *The Pink Panther.* **17.** *Danger Mouse.* **18.** *Winnie The Pooh.* **19.** *Sliders.* **20.** Theo. **21.** *Top Of The Pops.* **22.** *Dougie Hauser M.D.* **23.** *Byker Grove.* **24.** A mule. **25.** *Andy Pandy.* **26.** A bear. **27.** Black. **28.** *Watch With Mother.* **29.** Billy Bunter. **30.** Flowerpots.

# QUIZ 41 Pot Luck 13

LEVEL 1

**Answers: see Quiz 42, page 370**

1. What was the name of the android in *Red Dwarf*?
2. Who replaced Nigel LeVaillant as *Dangerfield*?
3. Which comedy series featured the Clampetts?
4. Who presents *The Sky At Night*?
5. Who was Krystle Carrington's husband in *Dynasty*?
6. In *Steptoe And Son* what is the father's name?
7. What was *Quincy*?
8. Which series featured BA Baracus?
9. Who played the title role in *Faith in the Future*?
10. Which Irishman presents *The Eurovision Song Contest*?
11. Which TV comedy star recorded *Splish-Splash*?
12. To which singing group do Donny, Marie and Jimmy belong?
13. Who was Dick Grayson's alter-ego?
14. What is the name of *Rab C Nesbitt*'s youngest son?
15. What was the name of Granada's weekly review of the press?
16. What was the prequel of *The Fenn Street Gang*?
17. Which series starred Paula Wilcox and Richard Beckinsale?
18. Who was the quizmaster on *The Sky's The Limit*?
19. What was the name of ITV's Saturday sports programme?
20. Name the two high-voiced puppet pigs.
21. Where is *Coronation Street*?
22. In which city are the *Neighbours*?
23. Who presents *This Morning with Richard Madeley*?
24. What is the name of Hank Hill's wife?
25. What is the name of the 'big' kid in *South Park*?
26. Which soap is set in Summer Bay?
27. Who plays Guinan in *Star Trek: The Next Generation*?
28. What is *Dr. Who*'s time machine called?
29. What do Jeremy Clarkson and Quentin Willson present?
30. Who plays CJ in *Baywatch*?

ANSWERS

**Comedy 8 (see Quiz 42)**

**1.** *Keeping Up Appearances.* **2.** Victor Meldrew. **3.** *Agony Again.* **4.** *The Two Ronnies.* **5.** *An Actor's Life For Me.* **6.** *Brass Eye.* **7.** Husband and wife. **8.** *Terry and June.* **9.** *Porridge.* **10.** *Rising Damp.* **11.** A corner shop. **12.** *Citizen Smith.* **13.** Mel Smith. **14.** *The Golden Girls.* **15.** Eric Morecambe and Ernie Wise. **16.** Nora Batty. **17.** Jennifer Saunders. **18.** In prison. **19.** Glasgow. **20.** *Stressed Eric.* **21.** Les Dawson. **22.** Jessica. **23.** *Happy Days.* **24.** *Frasier.* **25.** Pamela Stephenson. **26.** A dog. **27.** Springfield. **28.** Three. **29.** *Monty Python.* **30.** Roman Empire.

## QUIZ 42 Comedy 8

**Answers: see Quiz 41, page 369**

LEVEL 1

1. Mrs Bucket, played by Patricia Routledge, appears in which BBC comedy?
2. Whose catchphrase is "I don't believe it!"?
3. What was the sequel to *Agony* starring Maureen Lipman, shown in 1995?
4. The opening credits to which duo's programmes featured two pairs of glasses?
5. Which 1990s BBC sitcom starred John Gordon Sinclair as an aspiring actor?
6. Chris Morris created and was the star of which Channel 4 comedy series that fooled celebrities with spoof news stories?
7. How were George and Mildred related in the ITV comedy?
8. Terry Scott and June Whitfield starred as which married couple?
9. Ronnie Barker played the lead role in which BBC comedy about prison inmates?
10. What was Rising in the ITV series starring Leonard Rossiter as a scheming landlord?
11. What kind of establishment did Arkwright run in *Open All Hours*?
12. Robert Lindsay played the role of which citizen?
13. Who plays *Mr Bean*?
14. *Brighton Belles* was the UK version of which hit US comedy?
15. Eric Bartholomew and Ernie Wiseman were better known as what?
16. Which Nora is renowned for her sharp tongue in *Last of the Summer Wine*?
17. Which comedienne wrote and starred in *Absolutely Fabulous*?
18. In *Birds Of A Feather*, where are Sharon and Tracy's husbands residing?
19. In which Scottish city does *Rab C Nesbitt* live?
20. Which adult cartoon character was stressed on BBC2?
21. Which late TV comedian was famed for playing the piano badly?
22. What was the name of Frank Spencer's daughter?
23. In which series did The Fonz appear?
24. Psychiatrists the Crane brothers feature in which Channel 4 Friday night comedy?
25. Billy Connolly is married to which *Not The Night O'clock News* comedienne?
26. Which programme features the bar "where everybody knows your name"?
27. In which town do *The Simpsons* live?
28. How many children did *Roseanne* have in her series?
29. According to the series title who had a *Flying Circus*?
30. *Up Pompeii* was set in the time of which empire?

ANSWERS

**Pot Luck 13 (see Quiz 41)**

**1.** Kryten. **2.** Nigel Havers. **3.** *The Beverley Hillbillies.* **4.** Patrick Moore. **5.** Blake. **6.** Albert. **7.** A pathologist. **8.** *The A Team.* **9.** Lynda Bellingham. **10.** Terry Wogan. **11.** Charlie Drake. **12.** The Osmonds. **13.** Robin. **14.** Gash. **15.** *What The Papers Say.* **16.** *Please Sir!* **17.** *The Lovers.* **18.** Hughie Green. **19.** *World of Sport.* **20.** *Pinky and Perky.* **21.** Weatherfield. **22.** Melbourne. **23.** Judy Finnegan. **24.** Peggy. **25.** Eric Cartman. **26.** *Home and Away.* **27.** Whoopi Goldberg. **28.** Tardis. **29.** *Top Gear.* **30.** Pamela Anderson Lee.

## QUIZ 43 Soaps 5

LEVEL 1

**Answers: see Quiz 44, page 372**

1. Which Rita owns The Kabin in *Coronation Street*?
2. In *Coronation Street* who was married to Derek Wilton?
3. What is Des Barnes' job in the Street?
4. Which landlady did Alec Gilroy marry in *Coronation Street*?
5. Who is Phil Mitchell's brother in *Eastenders*?
6. Who took over the fruit and veg stall from his uncle in *Eastenders*?
7. Who is the landlady of the Queen Vic?
8. In which city is Brookside Close?
9. Which Tate is in a wheelchair in *Emmerdale*?
10. In which US series were the characters Blake and Alexis?
11. What is Ricky Butcher's job in *Eastenders*?
12. Which of the Robinsons did Philip Martin marry in *Neighbours*?
13. Who was Vicky Fowler's publican father in *Eastenders*?
14. In *Crossroads* who did Benny call 'Miss Diane'?
15. In *Dynasty* who was Alexis's sister?
16. Which famed *Chariots Of Fire* composer recorded the *Brookside* theme?
17. In *Coronation Street* who was Des Barnes wife?
18. Which Beale had her husband shot in *Eastenders*?
19. Which *Neighbours* star sang *I Should be so Lucky*?
20. Who was Miss Bettabuy 1991 in *Coronation Street* and went on to marry Curly?
21. Which Karl is the G.P. in Ramsey Street?
22. Who was Terry Sullivan's best mate in *Brookside*?
23. Who was pub landlady Annie Walker's husband?
24. In *Dallas*, who was J.R.'s father?
25. In *Dynasty*, which actress Heather played Sammy Joe?
26. What is name of the headmaster in *Home And Away*?
27. In *Emmerdale*, who did Annie Sugden finally marry?
28. In *Eastenders*, which Frank had a car business called Deals on Wheels?
29. What is the name of Judy Malet's husband in the Street?
30. Who did Scott Robinson marry in *Neighbours*?

ANSWERS

### Pot Luck 14 (see Quiz 44)

**1.** Feltz. **2.** *The Big Breakfast.* **3.** The Worthington Cup. **4.** Astro. **5.** Miss Boathook. **6.** *Game For A Laugh.* **7.** The Great Sorprendo. **8.** Delia Smith. **9.** Heathrow. **10.** *Emmerdale.* **11.** Reverend Jim. **12.** Fred Savage. **13.** Channel 4. **14.** *Voyager.* **15.** Gary Coleman. **16.** *This Life.* **17.** 100 acre wood. **18.** 15. **19.** Liverpool Docks. **20.** Dennis Potter. **21.** Fly on the wall documentary. **22.** Denise Van Outen. **23.** David Attenborough. **24.** Jean-Paul Gaultier. **25.** Live TV. **26.** Swithinbank. **27.** Chris Tarrant. **28.** Geoff Hamilton. **29.** Ainsley Harriot. **30.** Jeremy Spake.

## QUIZ 44 Pot Luck 14

LEVEL 1

**Answers: see Quiz 43, page 371**

1. Which Vanessa had her own chat show?
2. Which morning programme was co-presented by Johnny Vaughn?
3. What did the Coca-cola Cup change its name to in 1998?
4. What was the name of The Jetsons' dog?
5. Who was Colonel K's secretary in *Dangermouse*?
6. Rusty Lee and Jeremy Beadle co-presented which programme?
7. Which magician is married to Victoria Wood?
8. Which TV cook's first series was *Family Fare*?
9. What was the setting for *Airport*?
10. In which series is the fictional village Beckingdale?
11. In *Taxi* what was Jim Ignatowski's nickname?
12. Who played Kevin Arnold in *The Wonder Years*?
13. Which channel broadcasts *Cutting Edge* documentaries?
14. Which S. F. series features the character Neelix?
15. Who played Arnold in *Diff'rent Strokes*?
16. In which programme would you find Milly and Egg?
17. Where do Winnie The Pooh and his friends live?
18. How many contestants start the quiz programme hosted by William G. Stewart?
19. From where was *This Morning* originally broadcast?
20. Which playwright created *Blackeyes*?
21. What type of programme was *Lakeside*?
22. Which breakfast time presenter appeared in *Babes In The Wood*?
23. Which presenter and programme maker has a brother Lord Dickie?
24. Which dress designer co-presented *Eurotrash*?
25. On which channel would you find *The Weather In Norwegian*?
26. Which Anne presented *Gardens of The Caribbean*?
27. Who presented *Man-O-Man*?
28. Which late TV personality had a garden at Barnsdale?
29. Which TV Chef presented *Party Of A Lifetime*?
30. Who was the Aeroflot customer care manager featured on *Airport*?

ANSWERS

### Soaps 5 (see Quiz 43)

**1.** Rita Sullivan. **2.** Mavis Wilton. **3.** Bookmaker. **4.** Bet Lynch. **5.** Grant. **6.** Mark Fowler. **7.** Peggy Mitchell. **8.** Liverpool. **9.** Chris. **10.** *Dynasty*. **11.** Car Mechanic. **12.** Julie Robinson. **13.** Den Watts. **14.** Diane Hunter. **15.** Caresse. **16.** Vangelis. **17.** Steph. **18.** Cindy Beale. **19.** Kylie Minogue. **20.** Racquel Worstenholme. **21.** Karl Kennedy. **22.** Barry Grant. **23.** Jack. **24.** Jock Ewing. **25.** Heather Locklear. **26.** Donald Fisher. **27.** Amos Brierley. **28.** Frank Butcher. **29.** Gary. **30.** Charlene Mitchell.

# QUIZ 45 Crime 2

**Answers: see Quiz 46, page 374**

LEVEL 1

1. In which series would you find the character Tosh Lines?
2. Which Victorian detective did Jeremy Brett portray?
3. Which series starred John Hannah as a pathologist?
4. Which TV detective was played by Mark McManus?
5. Which Chief of Detectives was in a wheelchair?
6. Which series featured Jack Lord as Steve McGarrett?
7. In which series did Jack Warner play a beat bobby?
8. Which detective was famous for sucking lollipops?
9. Which Jersey detective was played by John Nettles?
10. Who does Kevin Whately portray in *Inspector Morse*?
11. Paul Michael Glazier and David Soul starred as which crimefighting duo?
12. Who shot Mr Burns in *The Simpsons*?
13. Which Agatha Christie sleuth lives in St Mary's mead?
14. Which policeman worked in Dock Green?
15. What is TV detective Columbo's first name?
16. *Murder, She Wrote* stars which *Bedknobs and Broomsticks* actress?
17. Which crimefighter had a boss called Devon Miles, played by Edward Mulhare?
18. Which former Dr Who also played Sherlock Holmes?
19. Which Nick presents BBC's *Crime Watch*?
20. The original Saint was played by which Bond man?
21. Which BBC crime series featured the main character Inspector Jean Darblay?
22. Who starred in *Cracker*?
23. Which writer with the initials PD created Detective Chief Superintendent Dalgleish?
24. Who is Agatha Christie's Belgian sleuth?
25. Helen Mirren starred as Detective Chief Inspector Jane Tennison in which series?
26. In which city was *Thief Takers* set?
27. What was *In The Sky* according to the crime series starring Richard Griffiths?
28. Which ITV police detective is based in Cornwall?
29. Who stars as *Rumpole of the Bailey*?
30. Which Don plays *Nash Bridges*?

ANSWERS

**News 3 (see Quiz 46)**

**1.** Roger Cook. **2.** David Frost. **3.** CNN. **4.** ITV. **5.** The swingometer. **6.** The Queen's Coronation. **7.** BBC1. **8.** BBC. **9.** Nature. **10.** BBC2. **11.** *News At Ten*. **12.** Michael Parkinson. **13.** BBC1. **14.** Russell Harty. **15.** Melvyn Bragg. **16.** Jeremy Clarkson. **17.** Sir David Attenborough. **18.** BBC News 24. **19.** Sir Robin Day. **20.** *Tomorrow's World*. **21.** Tony Robinson. **22.** BBC1. **23.** Dr Miriam Stoppard. **24.** *Food And Drink*. **25.** BBC1. **26.** Lorraine Kelly. **27.** Alan Titchmarsh. **28.** The Duchess of York. **29.** *GMTV*. **30.** Sunday.

## QUIZ 46 News 3

**Answers: see Quiz 45, page 373**

LEVEL 1

1. Who risks life and limb in *The Cook Report*?
2. Who introduces programmes with the words "Hello, good evening and welcome"?
3. Which news service won awards for its coverage of the Gulf War?
4. ITN provides the news service for which channels?
5. What special device was used by John Snow during BBC television coverage of elections to show voting swings?
6. Which famous Royal event was screened around the world in 1953?
7. On which channel is the current affairs programme, *Panorama*?
8. Angela Rippon read the news for which TV company?
9. Sir David Attenborough is famed for presenting what type of documentary on TV?
10. The news and current affairs programme, *Newsnight*, is broadcast on which channel?
11. Which programme ends with 'And Finally'?
12. Which BBC interviewer is nicknamed Parkie?
13. John Craven presented news for children on which channel?
14. Which Harty presented chat shows on TV?
15. Who presents *The South Bank Show*?
16. Which Jeremy presents *Top Gear* on BBC2?
17. Which Knight presented *Life On Earth*?
18. What is the BBC's dedicated news channel called?
19. Which chairman of *Question Time* was famed for his bow ties?
20. Which BBC science series shows a baby swimming underwater in its opening credits?
21. Channel 4's archaeology series *Time Team* was presented by which comic actor?
22. Presenter Robert Kilroy-Silk appears on which channel?
23. Which Miriam is a TV doctor?
24. Jilly Goolden and Oz Clarke sample wine together on which BBC2 series?
25. Barry Norman presented profiles of films on which channel before moving to Sky?
26. Which Lorraine presented *GMTV*?
27. Who replaced the late Geoff Hamilton as presenter of *Gardener's World*?
28. Ruby Wax interviewed which Duchess on TV?
29. Eamonn Holmes presents which breakfast-time programme?
30. On which day does Sir David Frost present a breakfast programme?

ANSWERS

### Crime 2 (see Quiz 45)

**1.** *The Bill*. **2.** Sherlock Holmes. **3.** McCallum. **4.** Taggart. **5.** Ironside. **6.** *Hawaii Five-O*. **7.** *Dixon Of Dock Green*. **8.** Kojak. **9.** Bergerac. **10.** Sergeant Lewis. **11.** Starsky and Hutch. **12.** Maggie Simpson. **13.** Miss Marple. **14.** *Dixon of Dock Green*. **15.** Nobody knows – it has never been revealed. **16.** Angela Lansbury. **17.** *Knight Rider's* Michael Knight. **18.** Tom Baker. **19.** Nick Ross. **20.** Roger Moore. **21.** Juliet Bravo. **22.** Robbie Coltrane. **23.** P D James. **24.** Hercule Poirot. **25.** *Prime Suspect*. **26.** London. **27.** *Pie In The Sky*. **28.** Wycliffe. **29.** Leo McKern. **30.** Don Johnson.

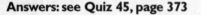

# QUIZ 47 Comedy 9

LEVEL 1

**Answers: see Quiz 48, page 376**

1. Which *Eastender* is now one of the *Hello Girls*?
2. According to the title of the comedy how many children does Belinda Lang have?
3. True or false: *The Good Life*'s Paul Eddington also played the Prime Minister?
4. Who is Stephanie Cole waiting for in the BBC comedy about a retirement home?
5. Which irreverent cartoon features Cartman and the ill-fated Kenny?
6. *Parker Lewis Can't...* do what, according to the title of the US high-school comedy?
7. What is the name of Hank Hill's son in *King Of The Hill*?
8. Which letter do the stars of *Absolutely Fabulous* all start their first names with?
9. Which sitcom was the song *My Little Horse* entered for a contest?
10. What is the name of the drunk in *The Simpsons*?
11. How many humans are there in *Red Dwarf*?
12. Who plays the husband in *Roseanne*?
13. What rank is Ernie Bilko in *The Phil Silvers Show*?
14. Who was the star of *Police Squad*?
15. What type of Product did Mark Thomas offer on Channel 4?
16. *Three's Company* was the American version of which British sitcom?
17. Who plays Charlie in *Babes in The Wood*?
18. Who is Tim Taylor's assistant in *Tool Time*?
19. What is *Caroline in The City*'s occupation?
20. Has Sylvester Stallone ever appeared on *Friends*?
21. Which series features Martin and Mandy as tenants?
22. Whose neighbours are the Leadbetters?
23. Which 1960s series featured Ricky Ricardo?
24. Which series starred Larry Hagman and Barbara Eden?
25. Which series featured Col Blake and Major Burns?
26. Who plays Gary in *Men Behaving Badly*?
27. In which series did Tony Randall play Felix Unger?
28. Who is David Jason's character in *Only Fools and Horses*?
29. Which character from *The Fast Show* said "This week, I have been mostly eating... "?
30. Which spoof news bulletin starred Steve Coogan and Chris Morris?

ANSWERS

**Pot Luck 15 (see Quiz 48)**

**1.** *Tomorrow's World.* **2.** Stephen Tompkinson. **3.** *Children's Hospital.* **4.** *Dangerfield* (Havers replaced Le Vaillant). **5.** *Light Lunch.* **6.** *Cider With Rosie.* **7.** Ray Mears. **8.** David Attenborough. **9.** Delia Smith. **10.** *This Morning.* **11** Danny de Vito. **12.** Oscar Blaketon. **13.** Alma Baldwin. **14.** Britton. **15.** Nigel. **16.** *London's Burning.* **17.** Deborah. **18.** David Hasselhoff. **19.** Alf Garnett. **20.** Cole. **21.** Sue Pollard. **22.** Sharon Watts. **23.** Kylie Minogue. **24.** *Holiday.* **25.** Parliamentary Channel. **26.** *Fitz.* **27.** 1986. **28.** Tennis. **29.** A Bicycle. **30.** Des Lynam.

## QUIZ 48 Pot Luck 15

**Answers: see Quiz 47, page 375**

LEVEL 1

1. Anya Sitaram, Jez Nelson and Craig Doyle are reporters on which technology programme?
2. Who starred in *Oktober* and *Ballykissangel*?
3. Which fly on the wall documentary comes from Alder Hay, Liverpool?
4. Where did one Nigel replace another?
5. Which daytime programme became *Late Lunch*?
6. Which Laurie Lee book has been made into an ITV film version?
7. Who presents *World of Survival* on BBC2?
8. Who presented *The Private Life Of Plants*?
9. Who presents *How To Cook* on BBC2?
10. Which daytime TV programme does Dr. Chris Steele appear on?
11. Which actor played Louie de Palma in *Taxi*?
12. Who runs the post office in *Heartbeat*?
13. Who did Don Brennan kidnap in his taxi in *Coronation Street*?
14. Which Fern presents *Ready Steady Cook*?
15. Who plays Dr. Jonathan Paige in *Dangerfield*?
16. In which drama series were Sicknote and Vaseline members of Blue Watch?
17. Who lives in the flat above Gary and Tony in *Men Behaving Badly*?
18. Which *Knight Rider* became a lifeguard?
19. Which bigoted character supported West Ham?
20. Which George portrayed Arthur Dailey in *Minder*?
21. Who played Peggy the chalet maid in *Hi De Hi*?
22. Which character in *Eastenders* was played by Letitia Dean?
23. Which former *Neighbours* actress had a hit with *The Locomotion*?
24. Which programme does Jill Dando present in the winter?
25. Which channel is dedicated to the House of Commons?
26. What is the U.S. version of *Cracker* called?
27. In which year was *Neighbours* first broadcast in Britain?
28. On which sport did Jack Kramer commentate?
29. What is the presenter of *Local Heroes* form of transport?
30. Who was the first male presenter of *How Do They Do That*?

ANSWERS

### Comedy 9 (see Quiz 47)

**1.** Letitia Dean. **2.** *2 Point 4 Children*. **3.** True – in *Yes, Prime Minister*. **4.** *Waiting For God*. **5.** *South Park*. **6.** Lose. **7.** Bobby. **8.** J (Joanna, Jennifer, Julia, June and Jane). **9.** *Father Ted*. **10.** Barney Gumble. **11.** One. **12.** John Goodman. **13.** Master Sergeant. **14.** Leslie Neilson **15.** Comedy. **16.** Man About The House. **17.** Karl Howman. **18.** Al. **19.** Cartoonist. **20.** No. **21.** *Game On*. **22.** Tom and Barbara Good. **23.** *I Love Lucy*. **24.** *I Dream of Jeannie*. **25** *MASH*. **26.** Martin Clunes. **27.** *The Odd Couple*. **28.** Derek Trotter. **29.** Jesse. **30.** *The Day Today*.

# QUIZ 49 Drama 6

**Answers: see Quiz 50, page 378**

LEVEL 1

**1.** What rank was Ted Roach in *The Bill*?
**2.** Which series featured reporters Joe Rossi and Billy Newman?
**3.** In which series were the characters Caleb and Merlyn Temple?
**4.** Which courtroom drama series featured Soapy Sam Ballard?
**5.** Who played Dr. Kristin Westphalen in *Seaquest DSV*?
**6.** Who is Zoe, a star of *Love Hurts*?
**7.** Who was Makepiece's American partner?
**8.** Who gave the last rites to Assumpta in *Ballykissangel*?
**9.** Which character does Edward James Olmos portray in *Miami Vice*?
**10.** Which acting Sutherland appeared in *Twin Peaks*?
**11.** Which TV Role has been played by both Julia Foster and Alex Kingston?
**12.** What was Taggart's invalid wife's name?
**13.** Which play about homelessness was made by Ken Loach?
**14.** Who played Lady Bellamy in *Upstairs Downstairs*?
**15.** Which TV Doctor played John Blackthorne?
**16.** What was Doyle's christian name in *The Professionals*?
**17.** Who played Anna Fairley in *Reckless*?
**18.** In which series set in Cumbria featured the character Danny Kavanagh?
**19.** Which drama series featured Miles and Ferdy?
**20.** In which series did David Bowie play a special agent?
**21.** Who created Adam Dalgliesh?
**22.** Who directed *Staggered* and starred in it as a toy salesman left on a remote island after his stag night?
**23.** Which Catherine Cookson drama starred Robson Green as Rory Connor?
**24.** Which series featured district nurses Ruth and Peggy?
**25.** In which series did Helen Baxendale portray Cordelia?
**26.** Who played DCI Nick Hall in *Thief Takers*?
**27.** In which series did Fitzpatrick and Drysdale appear as servicemen?
**28.** Whose ghost visited Mountie Fraser?
**29.** Which star of *If* appeared in *Our Friends In The North*?
**30.** Which character did John Nettles portray in *Midsomer Murders*?

ANSWERS

**Quiz & Games 1 (see Quiz 50)**

**1.** Bruce Forsyth. **2.** Melinda Messenger. **3.** Blind Date. **4.** Bullie. **5.** *Blockbusters*. **6.** Two. **7.** *Treasure Hunt*. **8.** Leslie Crowther. **9.** Black. **10.** Four. **11.** Lily Savage. **12.** *15 To 1*. **13.** Clive Anderson. **14.** Les Dennis. **15.** Pop music. **16.** Craig Charles. **17.** Challenge TV. **18.** Noel Edmonds. **19.** Cricketer. **20.** *The Century*. **21.** *Junkyard*. **22.** David Coleman. **23.** *Now Get Out Of That*. **24.** Paul Daniels. **25.** Angus Deayton. **26.** Gaby Roslin. **27.** *Ready Steady Cook*. **28.** Lloyd Grossman. **29.** Jilly Goolden. **30.** *Supermarket Sweep*.

## QUIZ 50 Quiz & Games 1

**Answers: see Quiz 49, page 377**

LEVEL 1

1. Which Bruce presented *The Generation Game*?
2. Who presents *Fort Bayard*?
3. Which programme does Cilla Black use for matchmaking?
4. Which cartoon character appeared in *Bullseye*?
5. Which show was famously hosted by Bob Holness?
6. How many contestants are there each day on *Countdown*?
7. Kenneth Kendall and Anneka Rice hosted which Channel 4 quiz in which contestants had to seek and answer clues?
8. Who first hosted *The Price Is Right*?
9. What colour was the famous contestant's chair on *Mastermind*?
10. How many contestants faced the challenge of the *Krypton Factor* in each episode?
11. Who hosts *Blankety Blank*?
12. What are the odds of winning the Channel 4 afternoon quiz hosted by William G Stewart?
13. Which barrister presents Channel 4's *Whose Line Is It Anyway*?
14. Who hosts *Family Fortunes*?
15. What is the subject of *Never Mind The Buzzcocks*?
16. Who hosts *Robot Wars*?
17. Which channel is dedicated to gameshows?
18. Who hosts *Telly Addicts*?
19. *They Think It's All Over* team captain David Gower was a captain in which sport?
20. Nicolas Parsons hosted an Anglia TV gameshow called *The Sale Of...* what?
21. In which show did Robert Llewellyn make teams build devices out of scrap?
22. Which chairman of *A Question Of Sport* retired in 1997?
23. Which program featured Bernard Falk putting contestants in sticky situations?
24. Who presents *Every Second Counts*?
25. Which movie quiz did Michael Aspell host in the 1970s?
26. Which Gaby presented *Whatever You Want*?
27. Which show features a 'trolly dolly?
28. Who nosed around stars homes in *Through The Keyhole*?
29. *The Great Antiques Hunt* is presented by which female wine connoisseur?
30. Dale Winton hosts what kind of Sweep?

ANSWERS

**Drama 6 (see Quiz 49)**

**1.** Detective Sergeant. **2.** *Lou Grant.* **3.** *American Gothic.* **4.** *Rumpole of The Bailey.* **5.** Stephanie Beacham. **6.** Wanamaker. **7.** Dempsey. **8.** Father Peter Clifford. **9.** Lt. Castillo. **10.** Kiefer. **11.** *Moll Flanders.* **12.** Jean. **13.** *Cathy Come Home.* **14.** Rachel Gurney. **15.** Richard Chamberlain. **16.** Ray. **17.** Francesca Annis. **18.** *The Lakes.* **19.** *This Life.* **20.** *Twin Peaks.* **21.** P.D. James. **22.** Martin Clunes. **23.** *The Gambling Man.* **24.** *Where The Heart Is.* **25.** *An Unsuitable Job For A Woman.* **26.** Nicholas Ball. **27.** *Soldier, Soldier.* **28.** His father. **29.** Malcolm McDowall. **30.** Detective Inspector Barnaby.

## QUIZ 51 Pot Luck 16

**Answers: see Quiz 52, page 380**

LEVEL 1

1. In which children's series were Mr. Carraway the fishmonger and Mr. Crockett the garage owner?
2. Which 60's series featured the refuse disposal crew of Thunderbird Three?
3. Which character did the late Gary Holton play in *Auf Weidersehen Pet*?
4. Who is Lesley Joseph's character in *Birds Of A Feather*?
5. Which comedy set in a newsroom featured Damien Day and George Dent?
6. Lieutenant B'Elanna Torres appears in which S.F. series?
7. Which actor played both Selwyn Froggitt and The Gaffer?
8. In which sitcom does Ryan Stiles play Lewis?
9. What is Dr. Maddox's christian name in *Casualty*?
10. What series was the prequel to *French Fields*?
11. Which programme has been presented by Mike Scott and Derek Grainger?
12. Which programme featured Dick Dastardly and Muttley?
13. What was Gladys Emmanuel in *Open All Hours*?
14. In which series are Sgt. Nick Schultz and Dash McKinlay?
15. Who was the star of *And Mother Makes Five*?
16. What was the comedy series set in a Tailors shop?
17. Whose body was discovered in the first episode of *Eastenders*?
18. Who worked in Miami Modes in *Coronation Street* with Dot Greenhalgh?
19. What is Mr. Rumbold's christian name in *Are You Being Served*?
20. Who was Richie Rich's minder?
21. What is the pub in *Heartbeat*?
22. What is the name of Patrick Moore's astronomy programme?
23. Which TV series featured the characters from radio's *Take It From Here*?
24. Who played Diana Weston's mother in *The Upper Hand*?
25. On which interior design programme does Andy Kane appear?
26. Which channel broadcast *The Phil Silvers Show*?
27. Who hosted *Never Mind The Buzzcocks*?
28. Which odd series featured celebs trying to complete various trials supposedly set by the Rangdo, leader of the planet Arg, who usually appeared as an Aspidestra?
29. Which character in *Dynasty* was played by both Pamela Sue Martin and Emma Sams?
30. Which *Dallas* character died in 1982?

ANSWERS

**Soaps 6 (see Quiz 52)**

**1.** *Coronation Street.* **2.** Three. **3.** Four. **4.** A wooly hat. **5.** *Take The High Road.* **6.** *Triangle.* **7.** Phil Redmond. **8.** Walford. **9.** *Heartbeat.* **10.** June Brown. **11.** The Kabin newsagent. **12.** *Crossroads.* **13.** Chester. **14.** Steve and Liz MacDonald. **15.** Grant Mitchell. **16.** Shortland Street. **17.** *Prisoner.* **18.** *Neighbours.* **19.** Ramsey Street. **20.** Sunday. **21.** Sunset. **22.** Shortland Street. **23.** *Emmerdale.* **24.** *Eastenders.* **25.** *Home And Away.* **26.** Platt. **27.** *Brookside.* **28.** Baldwin. **29.** Mike Reid. **30.** H.

## QUIZ 52 Soaps 6

**Answers: see Quiz 51, page 379**

LEVEL 1

1. Hilda Ogden was a major character in which series?
2. How many JRs were there in *Dallas*?
3. How many feet appeared in the closing credits of *The Bill*?
4. What was Benny's trademark item of clothing?
5. Complete the name of the Scottish TV soap set in the Highlands: *Take The...?*
6. Kate O'Mara featured in which short-lasting 1980s soap about a North Sea ferry company?
7. Which writer created both *Grange Hill* and *Brookside*?
8. *Eastenders* is set in which fictitious district of London?
9. Nick Berry went from *Eastenders* to a PC in which ITV Sunday evening series?
10. Who plays Dot Cotton in *Eastenders*?
11. Rita Sullivan runs which shop in *Coronation Street*?
12. Noelle Gordon was the manageress in which soap?
13. In which Cheshire city is Channel 4's *Hollyoaks* set?
14. Which couple in *Coronation Street* have sons named Andy and Steve?
15. Which character does Ross Kemp play in *Eastenders*?
16. Which New Zealand soap centres around a hospital?
17. Which Australian soap follows the trials and tribulations of a women's prison?
18. Which soap featured the Ramseys and the Robinsons?
19. In which street is *Neighbours* set?
20. On which day is the omnibus edition of *Brookside* aired?
21 What kind of Beach is broadcast on Channel 5?
22. The characters Rangi, Lionel and Nick appear in which street down under?
23. Seth Armstrong was the gamekeeper in which ITV series?
24. In which soap did Michelle Fowler gain a BA degree?
25. Shane and Angel were characters in which Aussie soap?
26. What is Gail and Martin's surname in *Coronation Street*?
27. Which soap is set in Liverpool?
28. The lingerie factory in *Coronation Street* is owned by Mike who?
29. Which comedian plays Frank Butcher in *Eastenders*?
30. In which cell block is *Prisoner* set?

ANSWERS

**Pot Luck 16 (see Quiz 51)**

**1.** *Camberwick Green.* **2.** *The Dustbinmen.* **3.** Wayne. **4.** Dorien. **5.** *Drop The Dead Donkey.* **6.** *Star Trek: Voyager.* **7.** Bill Maynard. **8.** *The Drew Carey Show.* **9.** Sean. **10.** *Fresh Fields.* **11.** Cinema. **12.** Wacky Races. **13.** A Nurse. **14.** *The Blue Heelers.* **15.** Wendy Craig. **16.** *Never Mind The Quality, Feel The Width.* **17.** Reg Cox. **18.** Elsie Tanner. **19.** Cuthbert. **20.** Eddie Catflap. **21.** The Aidensfield Arms. **22.** *The Sky At Night.* **23.** The Glums. **24.** Honor Blackman. **25.** *Changing Rooms.* **26.** BBC2. **27.** Mark Lamarr. **28.** *The Adventure Game.* **29.** Fallon. **30.** Jock Ewing.

## QUIZ 53 Comedy 10

LEVEL 1

**Answers: see Quiz 54, page 382**

1. Who was George Roper's wife in *Man About The House*?
2. Who is playwright Jack Rosenthal's wife?
3. In which series did Eamonn Walker play Winston the home help?
4. Which comedy features the occasionally self-styled El Barto?
5. Which character in *Absolutely Fabulous* is a fashion magazine executive?
6. Who was the accident prone deputy manager of Whitbury Leisure Centre?
7. Which show features Isaac Hayes as 'Chef'?
8. What was the sequel to *No Honestly* featuring Lisa Goddard?
9. Which channel produces *Beavis And Butthead*?
10. Which comedian and star of Jolson played an ex-con in *Time After Time*?
11. Which *Doctor Who* appeared in *The Two Of Us*?
12. Which sitcom starred Nicola MacAuliffe and Duncan Preston as surgeons?
13. Which sitcom was set in Maplin's Holiday Camp?
14. What was the sitcom starring Judy Loe and Roger Rees set around a singles bar?
15. Who played the butler in *Two's Company*?
16. *Home James* was a spin off from which sitcom starring Jim Davidson?
17. Who played Clarence the short sighted removal man?
18. Which series was a sequel to *The Growing Pains of P.C. Penrose*?
19. Which American actress starred in *Shirley's World*?
20. Did Gary get married in *Men Behaving Badly*?
21. What was Derek Fowlds recovering from in *Affairs of the Heart*?
22. What was the sequel to *Happy Ever After* starring June Whitfield and Terry Scott?
23. Which claymation featured cavemen?
24. Name the sequel to *In Bed With MeDinner*.
25. Which hapless, eccentric silent character always causes disaster?
26. Which *Heartbeat* actor was *The Gaffer*?
27. Which sitcom featured John Thaw and Reece Dinsdale?
28. From which sitcom was *Going Straight* the sequel?
29. Is Rab C Nesbit Irish or Scottish?
30. Who starred with Julia Mackenzie, as her husband, in *French Fields*?

ANSWERS

### Pot Luck 17 (see Quiz 54)

**1.** Ricky Tomlinson. **2.** Bianca Butcher. **3.** Pink Elephant. **4.** Suggs. **5.** *The Last Night Of The Proms.* **6.** Murray Walker and Martin Brundle. **7.** *Happy Days.* **8.** *Xena – Warrior Princess.* **9.** 4. **10.** Helicopter. **11.** Maggie Bolton. **12.** *Scrap Heap.* **13.** Julia Bradbury. **14.** Ian Wright. **15.** Jancis Robinson. **16.** Mick Johnson. **17.** Anthony Worrall Thompson. **18.** Jeremy Isaacs. **19.** Arthur C. Clarke. **20.** *Watching.* **21.** *Chef.* **22.** The Chuckle Brothers. **23.** *Daily Live.* **24.** *Upper Crust.* **25.** *Trauma.* **26.** *The Haunted Fishtank.* **27.** *In Your Dreams.* **28.** *Family Affairs.* **29.** Kermit The Frog. **30.** *Don't Wait Up.*

## QUIZ 54 Pot Luck 17

**Answers: see Quiz 53, page 381**

LEVEL 1

1. Who played Bobby Grant in *Brookside*?
2. What was Patsy Palmer's character in *Eastenders*?
3. In the children's series *Johnson and Friends* what animal is Johnson?
4. Who is the presenter of the Karaoke-style *Night Fever* on Channel 5?
5. Which annual event concludes with the playing of *Land of Hope And Glory*?
6. Who presents *Murray and Martin's F1 Special*?
7. Which U.S. series featured the character Potsie?
8. Which fantasy series stars Lucy Lawless?
9. How many zones are there in *The Crystal Maze*?
10. How did Anneka Rice fly in *Treasure Hunt*?
11. Which character does Kazia Pelka portray in *Heartbeat*?
12. Which Channel 4 series features two teams building a project from salvaged items?
13. Who presents Channel 5's *The Movie Chart Show*?
14. Who was the traveller in *Lonely Planet*?
15. Who presented her *Wine Course*?
16. Who has a son Leo in *Brookside*?
17. Who succeeded as chef on *Food And Drink*?
18. Who took over John Freeman's role in *Face To Face*?
19. Which S.F. novelist presented his *Mysterious World*?
20. Which comedy series featured the characters Brenda and boyfriend Malcolm?
21. What is Antonio Carluccio's occupation?
22. Who are the stars of *Chucklevision*?
23. Which lifestyle guide was presented by Paul Ross?
24. Which series featured the culinary arts of the nobility?
25. Which fly on the wall documentary followed the staff of Selly Oak Hospital, Birmingham?
26. Which programme presented by Ed Hall previewed the weeks television?
27. Which Channel 4 series was concerned with nightmares and dreams?
28. What is the twice-daily five times a week soap on Channel 5?
29. Which green creature was Frank Oz the voice of?
30. Which sitcom featured the Drs. Latimer?

ANSWERS

### Comedy 10 (see Quiz 53)

**1.** Mildred. **2.** Maureen Lipman. **3.** *In Sickness and in Health.* **4.** *The Simpsons.* **5.** Edina. **6.** *South Park.* **7.** Peter Cook. **8.** *Yes, Honestly.* **9.** Dibley. **10.** Brian Conley. **11.** Patrick Troughton. **12.** *Surgical Spirit.* **13.** *Hi-de-Hi!* **14.** *Singles.* **15.** Donald Sinden. **16.** *Up The Elephant And Round The Castle.* **17.** Ronnie Barker. **18.** Rosie. **19.** Shirley Maclaine. **20.** *Grace and Favour.* **21.** Heart attack. **22.** *Terry And June.* **23.** *Gogs.* **24.** *Still In Bed With MeDinner.* **25.** *Mr. Bean.* **26.** Bill Maynard. **27.** *Home To Roost.* **28.** *Porridge.* **29.** Scottish. **30.** Anton Rodgers.

## QUIZ 55 Children's TV 5

**Answers: see Quiz 56, page 384**

LEVEL 1

1. What was the name of the children's series about a seaside boarding house?
2. Which character aged 13 and three quarters was played by Gian Sammarco?
3. Which children's series featured Cut Throat Jake and Tom the Cabin Boy?
4. In which children's series was Mr. Cresswell the biscuit factory manager?
5. Which series featured Jim and Cindy Walsh and their two children?
6. In which children's series was Mr. Troop the Town Hall Clerk?
7. What was the name of Aaron Spelling's daughter who appeared in *Beverley Hills 90210*?
8. Which children's programme featured a canal boat owner?
9. In which children's cartoon series was the character Buggles Pigeon a flying ace?
10. What is the name of Wallace's dog?
11. Which character had Wish Wellingtons?
12. Which children's series features a boy genius who can make himself invisible?
13. Which S.F. series features Rembrandt Brown?
14. Which art show featured Morph?
15. Who presents *Fun House*?
16. What is the title of ITV's children's medieval comedy drama?
17. Whose *Excellent Adventures* are a cartoon series?
18. Who *Explains it All* on the children's series?
19. What is the children's series about a mystical board game?
20. Who is CITV's female witch?
21. Which children's programme featured Brian Cant and Humpty Dumpty?
22. Which animated character lived in a clock?
23. Who played Colin in the children's comedy drama *Microsoap*?
24. Which children's animated series features a polar bear and his chums?
25. Who presented *Live And Kicking* with Zoe Ball?
26. What was the name of the BBC's overnight service designed to be taped for children?
27. In which children's series did Richard Waites plays Cuthbert Lily?
28. If Bill was one, who was the other Flowerpot man?
29. Where did *The Borrowers* live?
30. Where would you find Florence and Dylan?

ANSWERS

### Drama 7 (see Quiz 56)

**1.** Berkeley Square. **2.** Colin Buchanan. **3.** A kidnapping. **4.** *Touch Of Evil.* **5.** John Alford. **6.** Cathy Tyson. **7.** *I, Claudius.* **8.** Roger Moore. **9.** Lynda La Plante. **10.** *A Year In Provence.* **11.** Charles Dance. **12.** Barbara Dickson. **13.** Both played by David Jason. **14.** *Dr. Finlay's Casebook.* **15.** Josh Griffiths. **16.** *Armchair Theatre.* **17.** Gillian Taylforth. **18.** Tom Georgeson. **19.** Columbo. **20.** *The Prisoner.* **21.** *Twin Peaks.* **22.** Dean Cain. **23.** *Hamish MacBeth.* **24.** *Reckless.* **25.** Tom Bosley. **26.** Charlie Fairhead. **27.** *Killer Net.* **28.** Amanda Burton. **29.** *Airwolf.* **30.** James Bowlam.

## QUIZ 56 Drama 7

**Answers: see Quiz 55, page 383**

LEVEL 1

1. Which BBC drama series was centred around the lives of three Edwardian nannies?
2. Who played Pascoe in *Dalziel and Pascoe*?
3. What was the subject of the two part drama *Seesaw*?
4. In which drama series did Robson Green portray Detective Dave Cregan?
5. Which Ex-*Grange Hill* actor appeared as Billy in *London's Burning*?
6. Who played Carol in *Band of Gold*?
7. Which series starred Derek Jacobi as a roman emperor?
8. Which future James Bond played Ivanhoe in the 1950s?
9. Who created *The Governor*?
10. Which story by Peter Mayle had John Thaw moving to France?
11. Which star of *The Golden Child* appeared in *Jewel In The Crown*?
12. Which Scottish singer appeared in *Band Of Gold*?
13. What have Blanco in *Porridge* and Scullion in *Porterhouse Blue* in common?
14. In which series was Janet McPherson a doctors housekeeper?
15. Which paramedic in *Casualty* lost his family in a house fire?
16. Which piece of furniture featured in the title of the Sunday night dramas of the sixties?
17. Which ex-*Eastender* appeared in the drama *Big Cat*?
18. Which actor appeared as a detective in both *Between The Lines* and *Liverpool One*?
19. What is the name of Peter Falk's rumpled detective?
20. In which series was No.2 played by Leo McKern?
21. Which series featured Special Agents Earle and Hardy?
22. Who played Rick in *Beverley Hills 90210*?
23. In which series is the character John McKeever?
24. In which series did Michael Kitchen play Richard Crane?
25. Who was the star of *Father Dowling Investigates*?
26. Who did Baz marry in *Casualty*?
27. Which Lynda la Plante series was set in the world of the Internet?
28. Who plays Sam Ryan in *Silent Witness*?
29. Which series featured the character Stringfellow Hawke?
30. Who starred in *The Beiderbecke Affair*?

ANSWERS

**Children's TV 5 (see Quiz 55)**

**1.** Seaview. **2.** Adrian Mole. **3.** *Captain Pugwash.* **4.** Chigley. **5.** *Beverley Hills 90210.* **6.** Trumpton. **7.** Tori. **8.** *Joshua Jones.* **9.** *Dangermouse.* **10.** Gromit. **11.** William. **12.** *Out Of Sight.* **13.** *Sliders.* **14.** *Take Hart.* **15.** Pat Sharp. **16.** *Knight School.* **17.** Bob And Ted. **18.** Clarissa. **19.** *Jumanji.* **20.** *Wizadora.* **21.** *Playschool.* **22.** Microscopic Milton. **23.** Jeff Rawle. **24.** *Noah's Island.* **25.** Jamie Theakston. **26.** Dynamo. **27.** *Zzzzzap.* **28.** Ben. **29.** Under the floorboards. **30.** *The Magic Roundabout.*

## QUIZ 57 Pot Luck 18

**Answers: see Quiz 58, page 386**

LEVEL 1

1. In which programme is Merlin a machine?
2. Who presents *Open House* on Channel 5?
3. Who presents *Strike It Rich?*
4. Which store was featured in *The Shop?*
5. Which adult animation series features Kyle, Kenny and Cartman?
6. What type of programme is Channel 5's *Sick as A Parrot?*
7. What nationality are comedians Roy and H.G.?
8. In which road do *The Simpsons* live?
9. Whose culinary series was *Far Eastern Cookery?*
10. What was the fly on the wall documentary about traffic wardens?
11. Which relation featured in the title of the commemoration of 75 years of the BBC?
12. Which black comedy series concerning gangland figures starred Mike Reid and James Fleet?
13. Who presents *X-Rated Ricki?*
14. Which chat show host was *All Talk?*
15. Which radio presenter hosted *Confessions?*
16. Who hosts *Masterchef?*
17. Which star of *Red Dwarf* was *A Prince Among Men?*
18. Which *Men Behaving Badly* actress appeared in *Kiss Me Kate?*
19. Which fly on the wall documentary featured Sunderland Football Club?
20. Who presented her Brunch on Channel 5?
21. Which behind the scenes documentary series featured a holiday centre?
22. Which ex-*Eastender* appeared in *Get Well Soon?*
23. Which comedian had a *Sunday Service?*
24. What was Wolfie's surname in the south London based sitcom?
25. From which country did *The Paul Hogan Show* originate?
26. In which series does Daphne Moon look after Martin Crane?
27. Which film actress went in search of orang-utans?
28. Which footballer's daughter presents *On The Ball?*
29. What was John Smith's nickname in *The A-Team?*
30. Where did Marshall Teller move to in Indiana?

ANSWERS

### Comedy 11 (see Quiz 58)

**1.** Yorkshire. **2.** Nigel Havers. **3.** *Have I Got News For You.* **4.** Alexi Sayle. **5.** Prison. **6.** Betty. **7.** Adam Faith. **8.** Lyndsey De Paul. **9.** *The Navy Lark.* **10.** The Dead Donkey. **11.** Arthur Dent. **12.** Spitting Image. **13.** *You Rang M'Lord.* **14.** Jimmy Mulville and Rory McGrath. **15.** Margaret. **16.** Major Charles Winchester. **17.** Kirstie Alley. **18.** Paul and Barry. **19.** Philadelphia. **20.** *The Vicar Of Dibley.* **21.** *Third Rock from The Sun.* **22.** Ben Porter. **23.** Joey Boswell. **24.** Yellow. **25.** Gordon Sinclair. **26.** Irish. **27.** Morecambe and Wise. **28.** The Liver Birds. **30.** *Soap.*

## QUIZ 58 Comedy 11

**Answers: see Quiz 57, page 385**

LEVEL 1

1. In which county was Arkwright's corner shop?
2. Who played Tony Britton's son in *Don't Wait Up*?
3. Which show once featured a tub of lard instead of a guest?
4. Who played Mr Bolovski in *The Young Ones*?
5. Where were the characters based in Porridge?
6. What was Frank Spencer's wife called?
7. Who played *Budgie* in the program of the same name?
8. Who wrote and sang the theme for *No Honestly*?
9. The nautical TV series *HMS Paradise* was based on which comedy radio show?
10. What do you drop in the newsroom comedy?
11. Who was the very English hero of *The Hitchhikers Guide To The Galaxy*?
12. Which programme was famous for its latex puppets?
13. What was the sitcom about servants and masters written by Jimmy Perry and David Croft?
14. Who wrote and starred in *Chelmsford 123*?
15. Which character is Victor Meldrew's wife in *One Foot In The Grave*?
16. Who replaced Major Frank Burns in *M*A*S*H*?
17. Who is the female star of *Veronica's Closet*?
18. What are the names of *The Chuckle Brothers*?
19. Where did the *Fresh Prince Of Bel Air* originate from?
20. Which sitcom features the character Geraldine Grainger?
21. In which comedy series are the characters Dick Solomon and Dr. Mary Albright?
22. Which plumber has an aggressive assistant Christine in *2 point 4 Children*?
23. Which character did Peter Howitt portray in *Bread*?
24. What colour were the taxis in the US sitcom *Taxi*?
25. Which Gordon stars in the ITV comedy *Loved By You*?
26. What nationality is TV comedian Frank Carson?
27. Whose Christmas special was watched by 28 million people in 1977?
28. Which Birds were Liverpudlian flatmates?
29. Tim Brooke-Taylor was one third of which comic trio?
30. In which show did the butler Benson originally appear?

ANSWERS

### Pot Luck 18 (see Quiz 57)

**1.** *The National Lottery Draw*. **2.** Gloria Hunniford. **3.** Michael Barrymore. **4.** Selfridges. **5.** *South Park*. **6.** A Comedy Sports Quiz. **7.** Australian. **8.** Evergreen Terrace. **9.** Madhur Jaffrey's. **10.** *Clampers*. **11.** Auntie. **12.** *Underworld*. **13.** Ricki Lake. **14.** Clive Anderson. **15.** Simon Mayo. **16.** Lloyd Grossman. **17.** Chris Barrie. **18.** Caroline Quentin. **19.** *Premier Passions*. **20.** Mariella Frostrup. **21.** *Seasiders*. **22.** Anita Dobson. **23.** Jack Dee. **24.** Smith. **25.** Australia. **26.** Frasier. **27.** Julia Roberts. **28.** Gabby Yorath (daughter of Terry). **29.** Hannibal. **30.** Eerie.

# QUIZ 59 News 4

**Answers: see Quiz 60, page 388**

LEVEL 1

1. Julia Somerville was newsreader with which news service?
2. Sue Cook and Jill Dando have presented which crimebusting series?
3. Which Sophie is a TV cook?
4. Michael Fish provided what type of news service?
5. Which Anne presented *Watchdog*?
6. Who presents the BBC's *999*?
7. What is the name of BBC's motoring programme presented by Jeremy Clarkson?
8. At what time is the BBC's late evening news programme?
9. Which brothers presented the 1997 General Election coverage on BBC and ITV?
10. How many guests form the panel on *Question Time*?
11. Big Ben appears at the start of which national news programme?
12. The late Gordon Honeycomb read the news on which channel?
13. Where was the marriage of Prince Charles and Lady Diana Spencer broadcast from?
14. Which Grade became head of Channel 4 in the 1980s?
15. Which Ms Ford was a BBC newsreader?
16. Who sang about John Kettley and Michael Fish?
17. Which BBC2 news programme is broadcast each weekday night?
18. Which Martin switched from news reporting to government in 1997?
19. The trial of which ex-American footballer was followed extensively on TV?
20. Anne Robinson presented which viewers reply series?
21. On which night is *Question Time* broadcast?
22. BBC1's *Country File* is presented by which children's newsreader?
23. The ITV wildlife series, *Birdwatch*, is hosted by naturalist Chris who?
24. *Animal Rescuers* follows the work of which Royal society?
25. On which channel is Montel William's chat show?
26. Which former Goodie presents the animal series *Animal House* on Channel 5?
27. British historian Richard Holmes takes us on what kind of walks on BBC2?
28. The garden challenge series, *Ground Force*, is presented by which TV gardener?
29. Which ITV series about real-life disasters was presented by Richard Madeley?
30. *Ricki Lake* hosts a chat show on which channel?

ANSWERS

**Crime 3 (see Quiz 60)**

**1.** *The Professionals*. **2.** *A Touch Of Frost*. **3.** Channel 4. **4.** *Columbo*. **5.** Jaguar. **6.** Haskins. **7.** *The New Avengers*. **8.** *Heartbeat*. **9.** New York Police Department. **10.** Inspector Morse's. **11.** *Prime Suspect*. **12.** *Quincy*. **13.** Kavanagh QC. **14.** *Heartbeat*. **15.** Dempsey. **16.** Edward Woodward. **17.** Both. **18.** Miami. **19.** *Porridge*. **20.** Agatha Christie. **21.** Helen Mirren. **22.** James Garner. **23.** Pierce Brosnan. **24.** Hoffman. **25.** *Magnum PI*. **26.** *Cracker*. **27.** Hill Street. **28.** Adam. **29.** A chef. **30.** Captain Haddock.

## QUIZ 60 Crime 3

**Answers: see Quiz 59, page 387**

LEVEL 1

1. Bodie and Doyle featured in which series?
2. David Jason stars as Jack Frost in which series?
3. Which channel featured an evening of cop shows called *The Blue Light Zone*?
4. Which American crime-fighter has a shabby raincoat and no known first name?
5. Which make of car did Inspector Morse drive?
6. Who was Regan's boss in *The Sweeney*?
7. Did Joanna Lumley play the role of Purdey in *The Avengers* or *The New Avengers*?
8. Nick Berry starred as PC and later Sergeant Nick Rowan in which series?
9. What does the NYPD in *NYPD Blue* stand for?
10. Kevin Whateley stars as whose police assistant?
11. Superintendent Jane Tennison is the lead character in which series?
12. Which medical examiner was played by Jack Klugman?
13. John Thaw plays which QC?
14. Which ITV police drama is set in 1960s Yorkshire?
15. Who was the male half of *Dempsey And Makepiece*?
16. Which Edward played *Callan*?
17. Which of the TV cops *Cagney and Lacey* was female?
18. Don Johnson starred in which Vice?
19. Who created Hercules Poirot?
20. The character Fletcher was a jailbird in which comedy series?
21. The star of *Prime Suspect* was Helen who?
22. Who plays Jim in *The Rockford Files*?
23. Who played *Remington Steele*?
24. Which character Theodore was played by Daniel Benzali in *Murder One*?
25. Tom Selleck played which Private Investigator?
26. The character Eddie Fitzgerald appears in which series?
27. Captain Furillo ran the blues in which street?
28. What is detective Commander Dalgleish's first name?
29. In *Pie In The Sky*, Henry combined policing with which other profession?
30. What is the name of Tin-Tin's fishy sailor friend?

ANSWERS

### News 4 (see Quiz 59)

**1.** ITN. **2.** *Crimewatch UK.* **3.** Sophie Grigson. **4.** The weather report. **5.** Anne Robinson. **6.** Michael Burke. **7.** *Top Gear.* **8.** 9 p.m. **9.** David and Jonathan Dimbleby. **10.** Four. **11.** *News At Ten.* **12.** ITV. **13.** St. Paul's Cathedral. **14.** Michael Grade. **15.** Anna Ford. **16.** Half Man, Half Biscuit. **17.** Newsnight. **18.** Martin Bell. **19.** OJ Simpson. **20.** *Points Of View.* **21.** Thursday. **22.** John Craven. **23.** Chris Packham. **24.** RSPCA. **25.** Channel 4. **26.** Bill Oddie. **27.** *War Walks.* **28.** Alan Titchmarsh. **29.** *Eye Of The Storm.* **30.** Channel 4.

## QUIZ 61 Pot Luck 19

LEVEL 1

**Answers: see Quiz 62, page 390**

1. Which Llewellyn presents his *Indoor Garden*?
2. What was the subject of *Several Careful Owners*?
3. Who is the bartender in *The Simpsons*?
4. Which children's detective was a Koala Bear?
5. Who is Dorothy's mother in *The Golden Girls*?
6. What is Sheriff Buck's first name in *American Gothic*?
7. Which series features twins Brittany and Cynthia Daniel?
8. In which series was Nathan Bridger the captain of a submersible?
9. Which fly on the wall documentary concerned cabin crew staff?
10. In which series was Troy the family pet?
11. What was *Robin's Nest*?
12. Which character played by Bill Maynard had the christian name Selwyn?
13. What was the occupation of the workers in *Common As Muck*?
14. Which angling programme was presented by Nick Fisher?
15. What was the BBC's longest running observational documentary series?
16. Whose comedy series was *As Seen On TV*?
17. Which summer 98 music festival event was hosted by John Peel?
18. Which S.F. drama series featured the invasion of Scotland by UFOs?
19. Whose series of sketches and stand up comedy was titled *Merry Go Round*?
20. Which sitcom starred Emma Wray as a nurse?
21. Which country did the game show *Endurance* come from?
22. Which quiz is presented by Bradley Walsh and Jenny Powell?
23. Who was the star of *Worzel Gummidge Down Under*?
24. What was *George and Mildred*'s surname?
25. Who hosted *That's Showbusiness*?
26. Who was Lenny in *Lenny's Big Amazon Adventure*?
27. What is *Donahue*'s first name?
28. Which Gaby was presenter of *The Real Holiday Show*?
29. Who was *The Man From Auntie*?
30. Which sitcom featured the characters Eric and Hattie?

ANSWERS

**Soaps 7 (see Quiz 62)**

**1.** Derek Wilton. **2.** *Eastenders*. **3.** Kathy Mitchell. **4.** *Prisoner Cell Block H*. **5.** Duffy. **6.** Jaqui Dixon. **7.** Toyah. **8.** Courtney. **9.** Steven Carrington. **10.** Louise Raymond. **11.** *Dynasty*. **12.** Janice. **13.** Max. **14.** Leanne Battersby. **15.** Viv. **16.** Ken Barlow. **17.** Sonia Jackson. **18.** Audrey Roberts. **19.** Bianca. **20.** Gary. **21.** Gail Tilsley. **22.** Don Brennan. **23.** *Prisoner*. **24.** Mandy (Lisa Riley). **25.** Samir Raschid. **26.** *Sweeney*. **27.** Daniel. **28.** Grant Mitchell. **29.** Firman's Freezers. **30.** Paul Usher.

## QUIZ 62 Soaps 7

**Answers: see Quiz 61, page 389**

LEVEL 1

1. Who had his gnome kidnapped in *Coronation Street*?
2. Which soap has a Sunday lunchtime omnibus edition?
3. Which character in *Eastenders* was played by Gillian Taylforth?
4. What was the original title of *Prisoner*?
5. Which character does Cathy Shipton portray in *Casualty*?
6. Which Jacqui in *Brookside* carried a child for Max and Susannah?
7. Which of the Battersbys was held hostage in a wood in *Coronation Street*?
8. What is the name of Grant Mitchell's daughter in *Eastenders*?
9. Who was Ted Dinard's gay lover in *Dynasty*?
10. Who is Grant Mitchell's mother-in-law in *Eastenders*?
11. Which soap starred John Forsythe and Linda Evans?
12. Which character in *Coronation Street* is married to Les Battersby?
13. Who is Susannah Farnham's husband in *Brookside*?
14. Who married Nick Tilsley in *Coronation Street*?
15. Who is Vic Windsor's wife in *Emmerdale*?
16. Who gave French lessons to Raquel in *Coronation Street*?
17. Who plays a trumpet in *Eastenders*?
18. Who in *Coronation Street* succeeded her husband as a Weatherfield councillor?
19. Who is Frank Butcher's daughter-in-law in *Eastenders*?
20. Who in *Brookside* is Lindsay Corkhill's husband?
21. Who bought a share in Alma's cafe in *Coronation Street* for £9,000?
22. Who burnt down Mike Baldwin's factory in *Coronation Street*?
23. In which series does Val Lehman play Bea Smith?
24. Which Dingle from *Emmerdale* presents *You've Been Framed*?
25. What was the name of Dierdre's late husband in *Coronation Street*?
26. What is Sinbad's surname in *Brookside*?
27. What is the name of Ken and Denise's son in *Coronation Street*?
28. Who had a relationship in *Eastenders* with his wife's mother Louise?
29. Where was Hayley Patterson an assistant manager in *Coronation Street*?
30. Which *Brookside* actor starred in *Liverpool One*?

ANSWERS

### Pot Luck 19 (see Quiz 61)

**1.** Roddy. **2.** One particular car's history. **3.** Moe. **4.** Archibald. **5.** Sophia. **6.** Lucas. **7.** *Sweet Valley High*. **8.** *Seaquest DSV*. **9.** *Airline*. **10.** *Dangerfield*. **11.** A restaurant. **12.** Froggitt. **13.** Dustbin men. **14.** *Screaming Reels*. **15.** *Doctors At Large*. **16.** Victoria Wood. **17.** Glastonbury. **18.** Invasion Earth. **19.** Alexei Sayle. **20.** *My Wonderful Life*. **21.** Japan. **22.** *Wheel Of Fortune*. **23.** Jon Pertwee. **24.** Roper. **25.** Mike Smith. **26.** Henry. **27.** Phil. **28.** Roslin. **29.** Ben Elton. **30.** Sykes.

## QUIZ 63 Comedy 12

LEVEL 1

**Answers: see Quiz 64, page 392**

1. Which US sitcom featured Zack and Screech?
2. Who is *Cybil's* best friend?
3. Who played Elaine Nardo in *Taxi*?
4. Which sitcom featured the Huxtable family?
5. Which character did Gary Coleman play in *Diff'rent Strokes*?
6. Who played Alex Keaton in *Family Ties*?
7. Which character did John Laurie portray in *Dad's Army*?
8. In which series do Sue Johnston and Ricky Tomlinson play Mam and Dad?
9. What was the title of Lenny Henry's Saturday night series?
10. In which sitcom did James Bolam play Terry Collier?
11. Which comedy series featured the character Samantha Stevens?
12. In which series did Norman Beaton play a hairdresser?
13. Who presented *Canned Carrot*?
14. Which comedy series was the forerunner to *Whoops Baghdad*?
15. In which series did Jim Hacker become Prime Minister?
16. In which sitcom did Elaine Stritch co-star with Donald Sinden?
17. Which UK sitcom featured Joe McGann as a housekeeper?
18. What was the setting for *Waiting For God*?
19. Who played Angela Thorne's working class downstairs neighbour in *Three Up Two Down*?
20. Which service was featured in *Get Some In*?
21. What is Cliff's surname in *Cheers*?
22. Which character is the producer of *The Larry Sanders Show*?
23. What are D.J.'s first names in *Roseanne*?
24. Which character does Michael Richards play in *Seinfeld*?
25. *In Drop The Dead Donkey* which character replaced Alex in the office?
26. What was Mike Berry's role in *Are You Being Served*?
27. In which sitcom does Tia Leone play Nora Wilde?
28. In which sitcom did Jeff Conway play Bobby Wheeler, a cab driver?
29. Which retired priest lives with *Father Ted*?
30. Which sitcom featured Janet Dibley and Nicholas Lyndhurst?

ANSWERS

### Pot Luck 20 (see Quiz 64)

**1.** Snooker. **2.** Rosie. **3.** *The Love Boat.* **4.** John Peel. **5.** Dave Benson Phillips. **6.** *Change That.* **7.** *Heartbeat.* **8.** Ron and Eth. **9.** Tom. **10.** David Frost. **11.** A Dolphin. **12.** *Space Precinct.* **13.** An Undertaker's. **14.** Hayley Patterson. **15.** Heathcliff. **16.** Indiana. **17.** Dave Allen. **18.** *Rawhide.* **19.** *Grandstand.* **20.** *The People's Century.* **21.** M6. **22.** Leo Firman. **23.** *Gaytime TV.* **24.** Cilla Black. **25.** London Weekend Television. **26.** Sunday. **27.** *The Great Antiques Hunt.* **28.** *Songs Of Praise.* **29.** Penn and Teller. **30.** *Style Challenge.*

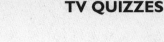

## QUIZ 64 Pot Luck 20

**Answers: see Quiz 63, page 391**

LEVEL 1

1. Which sport is the subject of *Big Break*?
2. What was PC Penrose's nickname?
3. Which US series featured the lives and relationships of people on a cruise ship?
4. Who narrated *Classic Homes* on Channel 4?
5. Who presents the children's show *Get Your Own Back*?
6. Which interior design programme is presented by Mark Curry?
7. In which series is The Aidensfield Arms?
8. What was the name of the lovers in *The Glums*?
9. Which Howard in *Howard's Way* was played by Maurice Colbourne?
10. Who presented *That Was The Week That Was*?
11. Who was Darwin in *Seaquest DSV*?
12. What was Gerry Anderson's 90's S.F. space series?
13. Where did *Billy Liar* work?
14. Who was the transsexual in *Coronation Street*?
15. What was Cliff Huxtable's full christian name in *The Cosby Show*?
16. In which state was *Eerie* a weird town?
17. Which Irish comedian was famous for his cigarette and bar stool?
18. Which western series was about a cattle drive?
19. Which Saturday sports programme is presented by Steve Rider?
20. Which series chronicled the 20th Century?
21. On which motorway is *Motorway Life* filmed?
22. Who was the boss of Firman's Freezers in *Coronation Street*?
23. Which series was presented by Rhona Cameron and Richard Fairbrass?
24. Who links *Blind Date* to *The Moment Of Truth*?
25. Which company celebrated *30 Years Of Laughter With Denis Norden*?
26. On which day is *Fully Booked* transmitted?
27. Which antiques show is presented by Jilly Goolden?
28. What is the Sunday evening hymns programme on BBC1?
29. Which magicians presented their *Unpleasant World*?
30. Which makeover programme was presented by John Leslie?

ANSWERS

**Comedy 12 (see Quiz 63)**

**1.** *Saved By The Bell.* **2.** Maryanne. **3.** Marilu Henner. **4.** *The Cosby Show.* **5.** Arnold. **6.** Michael J. Fox. **7.** Pte. Frazer. **8.** *The Royle Family.* **9.** *Lenny Goes To Town.* **10.** *Whatever Happened To The Likely Lads?* **11.** *Bewitched.* **12.** Norman's. **13.** Jasper Carrot. **14.** *Up Pompeii.* **15.** *Yes, Prime Minister.* **16.** *Two's Company.* **17.** *The Upper Hand.* **18.** An old people's home. **19.** Michael Elphick. **20.** Royal Air Force. **21.** Clavin. **22.** Arthur. **23.** David Jacob. **24.** Kramer. **25.** Helen. **26.** Bert Spooner. **27.** *The Naked Truth.* **28.** *Taxi.* **29.** Father Jack Hackett. **30.** *The Two Of Us.*

## QUIZ 65 Drama 8

**Answers: see Quiz 64, page 394**

LEVEL 1

1. What were the enemy in *Ultraviolet*?
2. In which fantasy series is MacLeod an immortal?
3. Which actor is newsreader John Suchet's brother?
4. Who wrote *Cold Lazarus*?
5. What was Nick Rowan's daughter's name in *Heartbeat*?
6. Which series starred Mr. T?
7. What was the name of the bar in *Ballykissangel*?
8. Which Scottish series featured Neil the Bus?
9. What is the christian name of Kavanagh QC?
10. Who did Eric Close play in *Dark Skies*?
11. Where was the wake for Assumpta in *Ballykissangel*?
12. In which series was Charlie Hume the Managing Editor of The Los Angeles Tribune?
13. Which series featured Detective Gina Calabrese?
14. In which series was there a Chief Superintendent Gordon Spikings?
15. What character in *The Waltons* was played by both Richard Thomas and Robert Wightman?
16. On which series was the writer of *Roughnecks* a presenter?
17. Which character is a barmaid at the Aidensfield Arms in *Heartbeat*?
18. Who recorded the music for *Robin Of Sherwood*?
19. Which Steven Poliakoff drama about a London cult starred Joely Richardson?
20. Who played Uncle Tom in *Rumpole Of The Bailey*?
21. Which ex-*Casualty* nurse plays a D.I. in *Dangerfield*?
22. In which series did David Duchovny play a special agent before *The X Files*?
23. In which series did Julia Sawalha play Lydia Bennett?
24. Which series about an antique dealer was set in East Anglia?
25. What was the subject of the drama *Threads*?
26. In which country was *Ballykissangel* set?
27. Which character is played by Jeff Stewart in *The Bill*?
28. In which series is Chris Stevens a DJ on KBHR?
29. Which series featured an angel named Jonathan?
30. Which Dennis Potter drama was recorded in 1976 but not broadcast until 1987?

ANSWERS

### Children's TV 6 (see Quiz 66)

**1.** Jimmy Savile. **2.** A London Comprehensive School. **3.** Ball. **4.** *Rainbow*. **5.** Adrian Mole's. **6.** Noel Edmonds. **7.** Dougal. **8.** Wales. **9.** John. **10.** Dave Prowse. **11.** *Worzel Gummidge*. **12.** Puppet pigs. **13.** *Rugrats*. **14.** *Blue Peter*. **15.** Ken Dodd. **16.** *Fraggle Rock*. **17.** Basil Brush. **18.** Record Breakers. **19.** *Peanuts*. **20.** *Rentaghost*. **21.** A cat and mouse. **22.** *The Wombles*. **23.** Radioactive blood. **24.** Black. **25.** Kryptonite. **26.** Baseball. **27.** Peter Duncan. **28.** Terry Nutkin. **29.** A lion. **30.** A bell.

## QUIZ 66 Children's TV 6

**Answers: see Quiz 65, page 393**

LEVEL 1

1. Which DJ and Mr Fixit ran charity marathons?
2. What is *Grange Hill?*
3. Which surname links TV presenters Johnny and Zoe?
4. Which show originally featured Rod, Jane and Freddy?
5. Whose mother was played by both Lulu and Julie Waltes?
6. Whose programme did Mr. Blobby first appear on?
7. Who was the dog in *The Magic Roundabout?*
8. Which country does Ivor The Engine come from?
9. Which character was the leader of *The Tomorrow People?*
10. Who links Darth Vader and The Green Cross Code Man?
11. Barbara Euphan Todd wrote about which scarecrow, the stories of whom were adapted for TV?
12. What were *Pinky and Perky?*
13. Which cartoon series is about talking babies?
14. Shep the dog originally appeared with John Noakes on which TV programme?
15. Which comedian created the Diddy Men?
16. On which Island did the Fraggles live?
17. Which puppet's catchphrase is "Boom, boom!"?
18. The knowledgeable twins Ross and Norris McWhirter helped present which TV series?
19. Charlie Brown and Snoopy appear in which cartoon series?
20. What was the children's comedy series featuring The Meakers and a group of ghosts?
21. What creatures are *Tom and Jerry?*
22. Which show featured Uncle Bulgaria?
23. *Spiderman* had what kind of special blood?
24. What colour is *Batman*'s cape?
25. Which substance makes *Superman* lose his special powers?
26. What is Charlie Brown's favourite sport?
27. Which former *Blue Peter* presenter went on to host Duncan Dares?
28. Which Terry hosted *The Really Wild Show?*
29. What creature was the puppet Lennie?
30. What does Noddy have on the end of his hat?

ANSWERS

**Drama 8 (see Quiz 65)**

**1.** Vampires. **2.** *Highlander.* **3.** David. **4.** Dennis Potter. **5.** Katie. **6.** *The A Team.* **7.** Fitzgerald's. **8.** *Hamish MacBeth.* **9.** James. **10.** John Loengard. **11.** On the hill above the lake where she and Peter walked. **12.** *Lou Grant.* **13.** *Miami Vice.* **14.** *Dempsey And Makepiece.* **15.** John Boy. **16.** *Tomorrow's World.* **17.** Gina Ward. **18.** Clannad. **19.** *The Tribe.* **20.** Richard Murdoch. **21.** Jane Gurnett. **22.** *Twin Peaks.* **23.** *Pride And Prejudice.* **24.** *Lovejoy.* **25.** Nuclear war. **26.** Ireland. **27.** PC Reg Hollis. **28.** *Northern Exposure.* **29.** *Highway To Heaven.* **30.** *Brimstone And Treacle.*

## QUIZ 67 Pot Luck 21

LEVEL 1

**Answers: see Quiz 68, page 396**

1. Who presented his C4 programme *Real Food*?
2. Which Weekend programme is presented by Anne Robinson?
3. On the quiz, whose *Price Is Right*?
4. Which science series was presented by Richard Vranch?
5. Of which football club is the subject of *The Alex Ferguson Story* the manager?
6. Which star of *The Color Purple* has her own talk show?
7. Who presented ITV's *What Will They Think Of Next*?
8. What was *Clothes Show* presenter Franklyn's christian name?
9. Who was Mandy to marry in *Game On*?
10. Who is Butch's father in *Emmerdale*?
11. What was the BBC's first digital channel?
12. Which channel broadcasts live League Cup football?
13. What is Pauline McLynn's character in *Father Ted*?
14. Who does Victoria Smurfit portray in *Ballykissangel*?
15. On which game show does Melanie Stace assist Jim Davidson?
16. What was Sanjay's surname in *Eastenders*?
17. From where were the 1998 Commonwealth Games televised?
18. Who was the presenter of *Still In Bed With MeDinner*?
19. Who is David Baddiel's co-presenter on *Fantasy Football League*?
20. What is Mr. Bing's first name in *Friends*?
21. Which children's TV presenter took over the stage role of Joseph?
22. What does Brendan Foster commentate on?
23. What was Jason Donavon's character in *Neighbours*?
24. Who is the northern motorbike fan who co-presents *Top Gear*?
25. In which fantasy series did Granny Weatherwax appear?
26. Who is Sally Webster's youngest daughter?
27. Who is magician Penn's partner?
28. On which channel is *DOSH*?
29. Who shares a show with Ren?
30. Who places the letters on *Countdown*?

ANSWERS

### Comedy 13 (see Quiz 68)

**1.** *Hogan's Heroes*. **2.** *Harry Enfield And Chums*. **3.** *Steptoe and Son*. **4.** Clair. **5.** Bob Ferris. **6.** Harry. **7.** BBC2. **8.** *The Vicar Of Dibley*. **9.** Ruby Wax. **10.** *Frasier*. **11.** Stan Butler. **12.** *Rab C. Nesbitt*. **13.** Lindsay Duncan. **14.** Antoine de Caulnes. **15.** Uncle. **16.** Ria. **17.** *Don't Wait Up*. **18.** *The Detectives*. **19.** Warren Mitchell. **20.** *Grace Under Fire*. **21.** Janice. **22.** *The Simpsons*. **23.** Mrs. Slocumbe. **24.** Edina's. **25.** Oil. **26.** *It Ain't Half Hot Mum*. **27.** Terry Gilliam. **28.** Rik Mayall. **29.** *Red Dwarf*. **30.** Car Dealer.

## QUIZ 68 Comedy 13

**Answers: see Quiz 67, page 395**

LEVEL 1

1. Which comedy series set in a POW camp starred Bob Crane?
2. In which series is the character Frank Doberman?
3. What was *Sanford and Son* an American version of?
4. What was Cliff's wife's name in *The Cosby Show*?
5. Who is Thelma's husband in *Whatever Happened to the Likely Lads*?
6. What is Bigfoot's name when he moves in with the Hendersons?
7. Which channel broadcasts *The Comedy Zone*?
8. In which sitcom do David and Hugo Horton appear?
9. Which comedienne *Does The Season*?
10. In which sitcom is the character Roz Doyle?
11. Who is Jack's driver in *On The Buses*?
12. Which comedy character has a son named Gash?
13. Who plays Louise in *Get Real*?
14. Who is the regular presenter of *Eurotrash*?
15. What relation is Arkwright to Granville in *Open All Hours*?
16. Who was Wendy Craig's character in *Butterflies*?
17. Which sitcom featured doctors Tom and Toby?
18. Which comedy series featured policemen Louie and Briggs?
19. Who starred in *The Thoughts Of Chairman Alf*?
20. What is the name of Brett Butler's sitcom?
21. What was that name of Gareth Blackstock's wife in *Chef*?
22. In which cartoon series is Principal Skinner a character?
23. Who was the senior saleslady of the ladies department of Grace Brothers?
24. Whose children were Serge and Saffron in *Absolutely Fabulous*?
25. What did *The Beverley Hillbillies* find on their land that made their fortune?
26. Which sitcom featured the character Gunner Lofty Sugden?
27. Which of the *Monty Python* team was an animator?
28. Who starred as *The New Statesman*?
29. Which S.F. series features Kochanski?
30. What was Boysie's occupation in *Only Fools And Horses*?

ANSWERS

**Pot Luck 21 (see Quiz 67)**

**1.** Nigel Slater. **2.** *Watchdog*. **3.** Bruce's. **4.** *Beat That Einstein*. **5.** Manchester United. **6.** Oprah Winfrey. **7.** Carol Vorderman. **8.** Caryn. **9.** Archie. **10.** Zak Dingle. **11.** BBC Choice. **12.** Sky Sports. **13.** Mrs. Doyle. **14.** Orla. **15.** *Jim Davidson's Generation Game*. **16.** Kapoor. **17.** Kuala Lumpur. **18.** Bob Mills. **19.** Frank Skinner. **20.** Chandler. **21.** Philip Schofield. **22.** Athletics. **23.** Scott Robinson. **24.** Steve Berry. **25.** *Discworld*. **26.** Sophie. **27.** Teller. **28.** Channel 4. **29.** Stimpy. **30.** Carol Vorderman.

# QUIZ 69 Quiz & Games 2

LEVEL 1

**Answers: see Quiz 70, page 398**

1. *Lucky Numbers* was hosted by which Shane?
2. Who presents *Play Your Cards Right* on ITV?
3. What was *Strike It Rich* previously called?
4. On which show did Bruce ask Anthea for a twirl?
5. *The Golden Shot* featured what kind of weapon?
6. What colour is the book on *This Is Your Life*?
7. Which former Dr Who presented the TV whodunnit game *Cluedo*?
8. *Celebrity Squares* was based on which game?
9. Which quiz game was based on darts?
10. How many contestants in total sit with Cilla at the end of each episode of *Blind Date*?
11. Which Terry presented *Blankety-Blank*?
12. Which TV magician hosted *Every Second Counts*?
13. *The Great Garden Game* is broadcast on which channel?
14. Who is the current presenter of *Call my Bluff*?
15. Which Michael has presented *Blockbusters*?
16. *Today's The Day* hosted by Martyn Lewis is broadcast on which channel?
17. What type of plant did the leader appear as on *The Adventure Game*?
18. On which evening of the week was *It's A Knockout* broadcast?
19. Which Lesley preceded Bruce Forsyth as host of *The Price Is Right*?
20. Sue Barker chairs *A Question of* … what?
21. Which show featured "the Phantom Raspberry Blower"?
22. How many male contestants are there in each episode of *Man-O-Man*?
23. What do the contestants do in *Stars In Their Eyes*?
24. What is the name of the show, hosted by Dale Winton, in which contestants guess the identity of other people's partners?
25. Which former *Krypton Factor* host presents *A Word In Your Ear*?
26. What percentage is the title of Channel 5's general knowledge quiz?
27. Chris Evans warned us *Don't Forget Your* … what in his Channel 4 game show?
28. Nicky Campbell and Carol Smillie asked contestants to spin which wheel?
29. What kind of maze did Richard O'Brien ask contestants to navigate?
30. Who does quizmaster Angus Deayton have news for on BBC2?

ANSWERS

**Pot Luck 22 (see Quiz 70)**

**1.** Sanjay. **2.** Antoine De Caulnes. **3.** Elephant. **4.** David Attenborough. **5.** Don Brennan. **6.** Nelson. **7.** Terry Pratchett. **8.** Esther Rantzen. **9.** Carol Smilie. **10.** Dale. **11.** Magenta. **12.** Consumer programme. **13.** Ulrika Jonsson. **14.** Farnham. **15.** Liza Tarbuck. **16.** Bob Langley. **17.** Ken Farrington. **18.** *10x10*. **19.** The Cafe. **20.** Beau Bridges. **21.** Kenneth Branagh. **22.** The Internet. **23.** Carlton Food Network. **24.** Barry Norman. **25.** Kieron Prendiville. **26.** *Blankety-Blank*. **27.** Kevin the Gerbil. **28.** *Lost In France*. **29.** BBC2. **30.** Quiz Show.

## QUIZ 70 Pot Luck 22

**Answers: see Quiz 69, page 397**

LEVEL 1

1. Who was Gita's husband in *Eastenders*?
2. Who presented *Euroballs*?
3. What kind of animal is *Babar*?
4. Who presented *The Private Life Of Plants*?
5. Which character in *Coronation Street* had only one leg?
6. What is HG of Roy And HG's surname?
7. Who wrote *Wyrd Sisters*?
8. Who presented *Hearts Of Gold*?
9. Who presented *Smillies' People*?
10. What is *Supermarket Sweep*'s Winton's first name?
11. What is the first name of presenter DeVine?
12. What type of programme is BBC2's *Just One Chance*?
13. Who hosted *The National Lottery Dreamworld*?
14. What is Max's surname in *Brookside*?
15. Who presented *She's Gotta Have It*?
16. Who presents *The Countryside Hour*?
17. Which ex-*Coronation Street* actor appears as Jack Gates in *Family Affairs*?
18. What is the name of BBC2's short series of 10 minute films by new directors?
19. What did Ivy run in *Last Of The Summer Wine*?
20. Who portrayed *Maximum Bob*?
21. Who narrated *Cold War*?
22. What was the subject of the documentary series *Glory of The Geeks*?
23. Which channel is dedicated to cookery?
24. Who is the father of presenter Samantha Norman?
25. Who created *Ballykissangel*?
26. Which game show is presented by Lily Savage?
27. Who was Roland Rat's sidekick?
28. Which series featured Gillian Taylforth as one of a family on their way to the 1998 World Cup?
29. Which terrestrial channel first broadcast *The X-Files*?
30. What kind of a programme is Channel 5's *100 Per cent*?

ANSWERS

**Quiz & Games 2 (see Quiz 69)**

**1.** Shane Richie. **2.** Bruce Forsyth. **3.** *Strike It lucky*. **4.** *The Generation Game*. **5.** A crossbow. **6.** Red. **7.** John Pertwee. **8.** Noughts and Crosses. **9.** *Bullseye*. **10.** Twelve. **11.** Terry Wogan. **12.** Paul Daniels. **13.** Channel 5. **14.** Bob Holmes. **15.** Michael Aspel. **16.** BBC2. **17.** Aspidestra. **18.** Friday. **19.** Lesley Crowther. **20.** Sport. **21.** *Tiswas*. **22.** Ten. **23.** Sing. **24.** *The Other Half*. **25.** George Burns. **26.** 100%. **27.** Toothbrush. **28.** *Wheel Of Fortune*. **29.** *The Crystal Maze*. **30.** *(Have I Got News For) You*.

## QUIZ 71 Soaps 8

LEVEL 1

**Answers: see Quiz 72, page 400**

1. Which *Brookside* ex-con became a teacher?
2. Which soap featured the characters Fin and Angel?
3. During a horse robbery, who was run over in *Emmerdale*?
4. Whose gaoling in *Coronation Street* even caused comment from Tony Blair?
5. Which medical series was set in St. Angela's Hospital?
6. Who was Simon Wicks' half brother?
7. In which soap were Todd and Katie Landers?
8. Which di Marco in *Eastenders* had an affair with Tiffany?
9. Which character in *Coronation Street* cheated on his girlfriend Fiona to sleep with her best friend Max?
10. In which soap was there a pizza parlour named Pizza Parade?
11. What was the name of the hotel in *Neighbours*?
12. Who does Belinda Emmett portray in *Home and Away*?
13. What substance is Lucy Benson hooked on in *Hollyoaks*?
14. Who is Lachie's brother in *Home and Away*?
15. What is the name of Fiona's son in *Coronation Street*?
16. What number in Ramsey Street do the Bishops live?
17. Who was Betty Williams' second husband in *Coronation Street*?
18. Whose mother had Alzheimer's disease in *Eastenders*?
19. Who is Ruth Benson's husband in *Hollyoaks*?
20. Who replaced Barbara Bel Geddes as Miss Ellie in *Dallas*?
21. In which series is PC Alf Ventress?
22. Which early soap was set in wartime Australia?
23. Which soap features Harchester United Football Club?
24. Who in *Eastenders* has twins named Lucy and Peter?
25. In *Neighbours* who did Des get engaged to after Daphne's death?
26. What is Eleanor Kitson's profession in *Brookside*?
27. In which soap did Bronwyn Davies marry Henry Ramsey?
28. Which actor played Lachie in Home and Away and Sam Kratz in *Neighbours*?
29. Who is Ollie Simpson's life partner in *Brookside*?
30. What did Norris Cole bury in the allotment in *Coronation Street*?

ANSWERS

### Drama 9 (see Quiz 72)

**1.** *The Bill.* **2.** Joel Fleishman. **3.** Steven Poliakoff. **4.** Dr. Mike Barrett. **5.** Lady Olivier (Joan Plowright). **6.** Emma. **7.** *London's Burning.* **8.** Tommy Lee Jones. **9.** Miriam Margolyes. **10.** Homicide. **11.** Inspector Pitt. **12.** Lawyer. **13.** Pauline Quirke. **14.** Duffy. **15.** Father Aiden O'Connell. **16.** *The Chief.* **17.** George Elliot. **18.** Ben Elton. **19.** Hilda Rumpole. **20.** Hamish Macbeth. **21.** Lawyer. **22.** Lisa Duffin. **23.** James Herriot. **24.** *The Onedin Line.* **25.** Quigley. **26.** Miss Ellie. **27.** Victorian. **28.** Stephen King. **29.** Dennis Potter. **30.** *The Governor.*

## QUIZ 72 Drama 9

LEVEL 1

**Answers: see Quiz 71, page 399**

1. Which series featured the character Chief Inspector Cato?
2. Who did Dr. Philip Capra replace in *Northern Exposure*?
3. Who wrote *The Tribe*?
4. Who did Rachel have an affair with in *Casualty*?
5. Which Lady was the star of the drama *This Could Be The Last Time*?
6. Who is Sean Dillon's teenage daughter in *Ballykissangel*?
7. In which series is the character Nick Georgiadis a station officer?
8. Who played the title role in *The Amazing Howard Hughes*?
9. Who plays Edna in *Supply and Demand*?
10. Which U.S. police series is set in Baltimore?
11. Which Victorian detective is played by Eoin McCarthy?
12. What is Ally McBeal's occupation?
13. Who played Olive Martin in *The Sculptress*?
14. Which former sister returned to *Casualty* as an agency nurse?
15. Which priest replaced Peter Clifford in *Ballykissangel*?
16. Which character was played by both Tim Piggott-Smith and Martin Shaw?
17. Who wrote *Middlemarch*?
18. Who wrote and starred in *Stark*?
19. Who in *Rumpole Of The Bailey* is 'She you must be obeyed'?
20. Which policeman's beat is Lochdubh?
21. What is *Petrocelli's* occupation?
22. What is Duffy's full name in *Casualty*?
23. Who created *All Creatures Great And Small*?
24. Which drama charted the fortunes of a Liverpool shipping family?
25. Who is Niamh's father in *Ballykissangel*?
26. Who was Jock Ewing's wife in *Dallas*?
27. In which era are the *Inspector Pitt Mysteries* set?
28. Who wrote *The Tommyknockers*?
29. Who wrote *Black Eyes*?
30. In which series did Janet McTeer play Helen Hewitt?

ANSWERS

### Soaps 8 (see Quiz 71)

**1.** Jimmy Corkhill. **2.** *Home And Away*. **3.** Kathy Tate. **4.** Deirdre Raschid. **5.** *Angels*. **6.** David. **7.** *Neighbours*. **8.** Beppe. **9.** Steve MacDonald. **10.** *Brookside*. **11.** Lassiters. **12.** Rebecca Nash. **13.** Heroin. **14.** James. **15.** Morgan. **16.** 24. **17.** Billy. **18.** Frank Butcher's. **19.** Kurt. **20.** Donna Reed. **21.** *Heartbeat*. **22.** *The Sullivans*. **23.** *Dream Team*. **24.** Ian Beale. **25.** Jane Harris. **26.** Solicitor. **27.** *Neighbours*. **28.** Richard Grieve. **29.** Eleanor Kitson. **30.** Angela's golf clubs.

## QUIZ 73 Pot Luck 23

LEVEL 1

**Answers: see Quiz 74, page 402**

1. Who's 'Angels' were undercover detectives?
2. Who was the streetwise informant in *Starsky And Hutch*?
3. Who did Biff Fowler sleep with on her wedding night?
4. What was BBC2's sheepdog trials programme called?
5. In which series is Jack Klugman a pathologist?
6. On which children's programme did Nigel Planer succeed Eric Thompson as narrator?
7. Which was the football highlights show, *Match Of The Day* or *The Big Match*?
8. Which sitcom was set behind the bars of H.M.P. Slade?
9. Who is the senior officer of Sun Hill in *The Bill*?
10. Who played Snudge in *The Army Game*?
11. Who is Tea Leone's husband?
12. In which series is Dr. Sean Maddox the senior house officer?
13. What was Wallace and Gromit's first adventure?
14. What sort of animal was *Mr Ed*?
15. What job did Beth Saunders do in *Dangerfield*?
16. Who was Alan Jackson's grandmother in *Eastenders*?
17. On which ship is Lt. Tom Paris an officer?
18. What was the full name of the satirical programme abbreviated to *TW3*?
19. Who narrated *Roobarb & Custard*?
20. Which entertainer's catch-phrase is "Awright!"?
21. Who starred with Peter Cook in *Not Only... But Also*?
22. Which ex-*Eastender* appeared in *Real Women*?
23. What was Roy Scheider's character in *Seaquest DSV*?
24. What is amateur detective Mrs Wainthropp's first name?
25. In 1963, which Fab Four pop group were panellists on *Juke Box Jury*?
26. Which BBC current affairs programme began broadcasting in 1953?
27. Who played Uncle in *Only Fools And Horses*?
28. Which S.F. show began by announcing "Do not adjust your set"?
29. Which ex-Tiswas host presents *Man-o-Man* on ITV?
30. Who presented *Tip Top Challenge*?

ANSWERS

**Comedy 14 (see Quiz 74)**

**1.** *The Simpsons*. **2.** Roy Clarke. **3.** Joey. **4.** Grace Bros. **5.** *To The Manor Born*. **6.** Cybill Shepherd. **7.** *The Vicar Of Dibley*. **8.** Lister. **9.** *Bottom*. **10.** Mark. **11.** Karl Howman. **12.** John Alderton. **13.** James Bolam. **14.** George Cole. **15.** Patricia Brake. **16.** Bruce Forsyth. **17.** Peter Jones. **18.** Patricia Hodge. **19.** Kathy Burke and Paul Whitehouse. **20.** *Chef*. **21.** Howard. **22.** Leonard. **23.** *Only When I Laugh*. **24.** Bouquet. **25.** Richard Briers. **26.** O'Reilly. **27.** *Oh Brother*. **28.** David Renwick. **29.** Principal Victoria. **30.** Ren.

## QUIZ 74 Comedy 14

**Answers: see Quiz 73, page 401**

LEVEL 1

1. Which cartoon series features Groundskeeper Willie?
2. Who wrote *Last of The Summer Wine?*
3. Whose surname in *Friends* is Tribiani? .
4. In which store was Mr. Rumbold the manager?
5. In which series did Richard de Vere buy Grantleigh Manor?
6. Who is *Cybill?*
7. Which sitcom featured Trevor Peacock as Jim Trott?
8. What is Dave's surname in *Red Dwarf?*
9. In which comedy series does the character Spudgun appear?
10. Which character was David's brother in *Roseanne?*
11. Who played *Mulberry* in the sitcom of that name?
12. Who played Hannah Gordon's husband in *My Wife Next Door?*
13. Which Likely Lad starred in *Second Thoughts?*
14. Who portrayed Henry Root in *Root Into Europe?*
15. Who played Ingrid in *Going Straight?*
16. Whose catchphrase was 'Nice to see you – to see you nice'?
17. Who played Mr. Fenner in *The Rag Trade?*
18. Which actress played an army officer in *Holding The Fort?*
19. Who were Harry Enfield's *Chums?*
20. What was Terry's job in *Fawlty Towers?*
21. Who was Marina courting in *Last Of The Summer Wine?*
22. Who was Ria's secret admirer in *Butterflies?*
23. Which sitcom featured Figgis, Glover and Norman?
24. How did Patricia Routledge pronounce her name in *Keeping Up Appearances?*
25. Who played Martin in *Ever Decreasing Circles?*
26. Which builder from Fawlty Towers appeared in *Ballykissangel?*
27. What was *Oh Father* starring Derek Nimmo a sequel to?
28. Who created Victor Meldrew?
29. What is the headmistress in *South Park* called?
30. What is the name of Stimpy's cartoon partner?

ANSWERS

### Pot Luck 23 (see Quiz 73)

**1.** Charlie's. **2.** Huggy Bear. **3.** Lady Tara Oakwell. **4.** *One Man And His Dog.* **5.** *Quincy.* **6.** *The Magic Roundabout.* **7.** *Match Of The Day.* **8.** *Porridge.* **9.** Chief Supt. Brownlow. **10.** Bill Fraser. **11.** David Duchovny. **12.** *Casualty.* **13.** *A Grand Day Out.* **14.** A (talking) horse. **15.** Journalist. **16.** *Blossom.* **17.** *U.S.S. Voyager.* **18.** *That Was The Week That Was.* **19.** Richard Briers. **20.** Michael Barrymore. **21.** Dudley Moore. **22.** Michelle Collins. **23.** Captain Nathan Bridger. **24.** Hetty. **25.** The Beatles. **26.** *Panorama.* **27.** Buster Merryfield. **28.** *The Outer Limits.* **29.** Chris Tarrant. **30.** Emma Forbes.

## QUIZ 75 Quiz & Games 3

LEVEL 1

**Answers: see Quiz 76, page 404**

1. *Blankety Blank* host Lily Savage hails from which northern city?
2. Which Bob chairs the comedy quiz *Not A Lot Of People Know That*?
3. How many celebrities contest the improvisation series *Whose Line Is It Anyway*?
4. What did *Strike It Lucky* change its name to?
5. Which *Watchdog* presenter, Alice, hosts the celebrity finance quiz, *Easy Money*?
6. Who is the presenter of *Countdown*?
7. Which boardgame inspired a whodunit show?
8. On which programme did Patrick Moore and Dominic Diamond both appear?
9. Which Bob is the comedy partner of Vic Reeves on *Shooting Stars*?
10. Which Derek Batey show tested how well couples knew each other?
11. On which game show is there a Yes/No interlude?
12. Which magician presented *Wipeout*?
13. Which Liverpudlian comedian hosted *Name That Tune*?
14. What is the first non-zero guaranteed minimum prize on *Who Wants To Be A Millionaire*?
15. Max Bygraves, Bob Monkhouse and Les Dennis all hosted which family game show?
16. Who presents both *Big Break* and *The Generation Game*?
17. Which former children's presenter hosts *Talking Telephone Numbers*?
18. What is the final event of *The Gladiators*?
19. What must you win to succeed at Richard O'Brien's Maze?
20. Which DJ Nicky is the presenter of *Wheel Of Fortune*?
21. Which quiz show featured opposing schools?
22. Which series trophy was won in 1998 by Magdalen College?
23. Which *Opportunity Knocks* host presented *Double Your Money*?
24. On which sports quiz show is Lee Hurst a panellist?
25. Which animal game show was presented by Dale Winton?
26. Which Shane hosts *Lucky Numbers*?
27. Who presented *Celebrity Ready Steady Cook*?
28. *Name That Tune* was originally part of which Wednesday Night variety show?
29. How many competitors were there in each episode of *Mastermind*?
30. BBC1's *Ask The Family* was hosted by which Robert?

ANSWERS

**Sport 4 (see Quiz 76)**

**1.** Eric Bristow. **2.** Snooker. **3.** Boxing. **4.** No. **5.** *Grandstand*. **6.** Three. **7.** USA. **8.** 1966 – England vs. West Germany. **9.** Paul Elliott. **10.** ITV. **11.** Herbie Hide. **12.** Royal Ascot. **13.** Tennis. **14.** Alan Shearer. **15.** Channel 4. **16.** Wembley. **17.** Liverpool. **18.** Ruud Gullit. **19.** Liverpool and Arsenal. **20.** *The Big Match*. **21.** 1980s. **22.** June. **23.** Chas and Dave. **24.** Brian Woolnough. **25.** David Vine. **26.** Freddie Mercury. **27.** Torville and Dean. **28.** Eurosport. **29.** Horse racing. **30.** *They Think It's All Over*.

## QUIZ 76 Sport 4

LEVEL 1

**Answers: see Quiz 75, page 403**

1. Who is darts' "Crafty Cockney"?
2. The Crucible hosts which sporting events?
3. Harry Carpenter is a commentator on which sport?
4. Did England win the Ashes in 1998?
5. *Football Focus* is part of which sports programme?
6. On *A Question Of Sport* how many members are there in each team?
7. From which country were the 1996 Summer Olympics broadcast?
8. In which year did England win the World Cup?
9. Which former Chelsea footballer helps present *Football Italia* on Channel 4?
10. On which channel is Formula 1 motor racing currently broadcast – BBC1 or ITV?
11. Which Herbie retained the WBO Heavyweight Championship in a fight against Willie Fischer televised live on Sky Sports?
12. Coverage of which annual Royal race meeting is broadcast by the BBC?
13. Former Great Britain international Mark Cox commentates on which racquet sport?
14. Who scored a first half penalty for England against Argentina in the 98 World Cup?
15. The sports magazine show *Transworld Sport* can be viewed on which channel?
16. From which stadium is the F.A. Cup Final televised each year?
17. With which football club did commentator Alan Hansen end his playing career?
18. Which former Chelsea manager helped present the 1988 World Cup Finals?
19. Who was playing when Brian Moore famously said "It's up for grabs now" in 1989?
20. Clive Tyldesley appears on which programme – *The Big Match* or *Match Of The Day*?
21. In which decade was the London Marathon first screened on TV?
22. Coverage of Wimbledon is traditionally broadcast in which month?
23. Which cockney duo composed and sang *Snooker Loopy*?
24. Who hosts *Hold The Back Page*?
25. Which David hosted *Super Stars*?
26. Who joined Montserrat Caballe on the BBC's theme for the Barcelona Olympics?
27. Name the British ice skating duo televised being awarded maximum marks in the World Championships.
28. Which satellite channel broadcasts ten-pin bowling?
29. With which sport is TV personality Willie Carson associated?
30. On which sports game show do the panellists have to 'feel the celebrity'?

ANSWERS

**Quiz & Games 3 (see Quiz 75)**

**1.** Liverpool. **2.** Bob Mills. **3.** Four. **4.** *Strike It Rich.* **5.** Alice Beer. **6.** Richard Whiteley. **7.** Cluedo. **8.** *Gamesmaster.* **9.** Mortimer. **10.** *Mr & Mrs.* **11.** *Take Your Pick.* **12.** Paul Daniels. **13.** Tom O'Connor. **14.** £1000. **15.** *Family Fortunes.* **16.** Jim Davidson. **17.** Philip Schofield. **18.** The Eliminator. **19.** Crystals. **20.** Campbell. **21.** *Top Of The Form.* **22.** *University Challenge.* **23.** Hughie Green. **24.** *They Think Its All Over.* **25.** *Pets Win Prizes.* **26.** Richie. **27.** Fern Britton. **28.** *Wednesday Night Out.* **29.** Four. **30.** Robert Robinson.

## QUIZ 77 Pot Luck 24

**Answers: see Quiz 78, page 406**

LEVEL 1

1. Which character was *Roseanne's* sister?
2. What was Norm's surname in *Cheers*?
3. Which Royal Prince appeared on *Des O'Connor Tonight* in 1998?
4. Who always told a long joke from a black chair on *The Two Ronnies*?
5. Who was "smarter than the average bear"?
6. What was Roobarb's feline companion called?
7. What kind of animated animal is Alvin?
8. What is the name of BBC1's early morning financial programme?
9. Which country's football league has a *Serie A*?
10. Which daytime show is presented by Richard Whiteley?
11. Which S.F. series featured the character Major Wilma Dearing?
12. In which series does Victor French play Mark?
13. Who were Brenda and Brandon Walsh's parents in *Beverley Hills 90210*?
14. What ex-Avenger appeared in *The Upper Hand*?
15. Which Bob assists Cilla Black in *Surprise, Surprise*?
16. Which programme became known as 'the antiques rogue show'?
17. Who presents *Through The Cake Hole*?
18. Which doctor in *Eastenders* had the christian name Harold?
19. What was the drama series set in Cornwall written by Winston Graham?
20. Which *Python* was a qualified doctor?
21. What is the christian name of the presenter of *Frostrup On Friday*?
22. Which series presented by Kate Sanderson features news items from the world of entertainment?
23. On which programme does Alice Beer appear?
24. On which series is Tiff Needell a presenter?
25. Which English actress played Dr. Tracey Clark in *Ally McBeal*?
26. In which U.S. series is there a policeman named Garner?
27. Which *Opportunity Knocks* presenter died in 1997?
28. What was Donna's surname in *The Jump*?
29. Who was *Desperately Seeking Something* on C4?
30. In which drama series were Milly and Anna lawyers?

ANSWERS

**Soaps 9 (see Quiz 78)**

**1.** Her brother in law. **2.** Brian Tilsley. **3.** Tiffany Mitchell. **4.** *Hollyoaks*. **5.** Jock Ewing. **6.** Rosie. **7.** Jeff and Fallon. **8.** Sam Mitchell. **9.** On a Sunliners special cruise. **10.** *Coronation Street*. **11.** *Family Affairs*. **12.** Joe Mangel. **13.** Ken Barlow. **14.** Mark Little. **15.** Woods. **16.** Vera Duckworth. **17.** Sue Jenkins. **18.** Cunningham. **19.** Anne Wilkinson. **20.** Fred Elliot. **21.** Grimes. **22.** Harry. **23.** *Brookside*. **24.** Nicholas Cochrane. **25.** Bet Gilroy. **26.** Susan Tully. **27.** Wendy Craig. **28.** Journalist. **29.** Alan Dale. **30.** Bouncer.

## QUIZ 78 Soaps 9

**Answers: see Quiz 77, page 405**

LEVEL 1

1. Which of her relations did Denise have an affair with in *Coronation Street*?
2. Who was murdered outside a nightclub in *Coronation Street* in 1989?
3. Which character in *Eastenders* is played by Martine McCutcheon?
4. Which soap features Sol and Kate Patrick?
5. Which *Dallas* character died in 1982?
6. Who is Sally Webster's eldest daughter in *Coronation Street*?
7. Who in *Dynasty* had a son named Little Blake?
8. Who is Grant and Phil's sister in *Eastenders*?
9. Where did Curly and Raquel spend their honeymoon in *Coronation Street*?
10. On which soap did Robbie Williams play an extra?
11. What was Channel 4's first major UK soap?
12. Who was Melanie's husband in *Neighbours*?
13. Which character has been in *Coronation Street* since its inception?
14. Which Big Breakfast presenter played Joe Mangel in *Neighbours*?
15. What is Terry's surname in *Emmerdale*?
16. What is Liz Dawn's character in *Coronation Street*?
17. Which Brookside actress was also Gloria in *Coronation Street*?
18. What is Judith's surname in *Hollyoaks*?
19. Who is Lance's sister in *Neighbours*?
20. Which butcher owns the corner shop in *Coronation Street*?
21. What is Maud's surname in *Coronation Street*?
22. What was Jacqui Dixon's baby's name in *Brookside*?
23. In which soap did Lily Savage appear?
24. Which ex-*Coronation Street* actor played Barry Scripps in *Heartbeat*?
25. What was Julie Goodyear's character in *Coronation Street*?
26. Who not only appeared in but directed *Eastenders*?
27. Which Eastender starred in *Hugh and I*?
28. What was Polly Becker's occupation in *Eastenders*?
29. Who played Dr. John Forrest in *The Young Doctors*?
30. What was the name of Mike's dog in *Neighbours*?

ANSWERS

### Pot Luck 24 (see Quiz 77)

**1.** Jackie Harris. **2.** Peterson. **3.** Edward. **4.** Ronny Corbett. **5.** Yogi Bear. **6.** Custard the cat. **7.** Chipmunk. **8.** *Business Breakfast*. **9.** Italy. **10.** *Countdown*. **11.** *Buck Rogers In The 25th Century*. **12.** *Highway To Heaven*. **13.** Jim and Cindy. **14.** Honor Blackman. **15.** Carolgees. **16.** *Lovejoy*. **17.** Jo Brand. **18.** Legg. **19.** Poldark. **20.** Graham Chapman. **21.** Mariella. **22.** *Electric Circus*. **23.** *Watchdog*. **24.** *Top Gear*. **25.** Tracey Ullman. **26.** *Baywatch*. **27.** Hughie Green. **28.** Brunos. **29.** Pete McCarthy. **30.** *This Life*.

## QUIZ 79 Comedy 15

LEVEL 1

**Answers: see Quiz 80, page 408**

1. What is comedian Sykes's first name?
2. Which Channel 4 comedy series is set in a TV Newsroom?
3. Who sang the theme song for the sitcom *On The Up*?
4. Which *Whose Line Is It Anyway* performer advertised a Canadian Airline?
5. Which actor appeared in both *One Foot In The Grave* and *KYTV*?
6. In which children's series did Tony Robinson play the Sheriff Of Nottingham?
7. Which company produced the *Tom and Jerry* cartoons?
8. Whose voice does Dan Castellaneta supply in *The Simpsons*?
9. What was the name of Dave Allen's first show?
10. What is the name of the pub in *Goodnight Sweetheart*?
11. Which US series featured the surgeons of the 4077th Mobile Army Surgical Hospital?
12. Which sitcom featured the workers of Fenner's Fashions?
13. What was Jessica's mum's name in *Some Mother's Do 'Ave 'Em*?
14. What was Saffy's proper name in *Absolutely Fabulous*?
15. Complete the comedy review title: *The Mary Whitehouse* ... ?
16. Who was Bertie Wooster if Dennis Price was Jeeves?
17. Which Street featured celebrity impressions by John Sessions?
18. Which class did Arthur Lowe try to keep under control as *AJ Wentworth B A*?
19. What was Bunter of Greyfriars first name?
20. What was the name of Eddie's wife in *Love Thy Neighbour*?
21. Who lived at Railway Cuttings, East Cheam?
22. Who was Miss Jones's landlord in *Rising Damp*?
23. Where did the *Happy Days* gang hang out?
24. What was Mr. Boswell's christian name in *Bread*?
25. Who played Timothy Lumsden in *Sorry*?
26. Who was 'The One with the Glasses' in the comedy duo Morecambe and Wise?
27. Alastair Sim played which litigious man in the sitcom about his ...*Misleading Cases*?
28. Who connects Purdy with Patsy?
29. Who played Penny in *Just Good Friends*?
30. Which cricketing sitcom starred Timothy Spall and Josie Lawrence?

ANSWERS

**Pot Luck 25 (see Quiz 80)**

**1.** *Ally McBeal*. **2.** Lowri Turner. **3.** Paul. **4.** Jean Alexander. **5.** Sophie Grigson. **6.** *The Creatives*. **7.** A Yorkshire Police station. **8.** Clive Anderson. **9.** Daniella Nardini. **10.** Kate Adie. **11.** *The A-Team*. **12.** Peter Davison. **13.** Wilkins. **14.** Ally. **15.** *A Question Of Sport*. **16.** Chris Hammond. **17.** Liam Cunningham. **18.** Clive James. **19.** John Humphries. **20.** Kim Basinger. **21.** Billy Cotton. **22.** Korea. **23.** Cliff Michelmore. **24.** Richard Dimbleby. **25.** *What's My Line*. **26.** Philip Schofield. **27.** Snoopy. **28.** DJ. **29.** The Rover's Return. **30.** *Grange Hill*.

# QUIZ 80 Pot Luck 25

**Answers: see Quiz 79, page 407**

LEVEL 1

1. Which US series featured the heroine seeing a dancing baby?
2. Who presented her chat show *Lowri*?
3. What was *Dangerfield*'s christian name?
4. Who played Auntie Wainwright in *Last Of The Summer Wine*?
5. Which cook presented a series on herbs?
6. Which sitcom starred and was written by Jack Docherty and Moray Hunter?
7. Where was the series *Out Of The Blue* located?
8. Which interviewing barrister was *All Talk*?
9. Which actress from *This Life* appeared in *Undercover Heart*?
10. Which journalist reported for the BBC from Tripoli in 1986 on the American bombing?
11. Which Team helped those in trouble in the 1980s?
12. Who played Tristan Farnon in *All Creatures Great And Small*?
13. What was the name of *The Family*?
14. What was the first name of McCoist in *McCoist And McCauley*?
15. Which sporting gameshow features a 'what happens next' board?
16. Who replaced Nick as Station Officer in *London's Burning*?
17. Who played Mossie Sheehan in *Falling For A Dancer*?
18. Which Australian presenter met *The Supermodels*?
19. Who presented *On The Record*?
20. Which American film actress appeared in Peugeot commercials?
21. Which bandleader had a son with the same name who became a BBC executive?
22. Where did *M*A*S*H* take place?
23. Who said 'And The Next Tonight Will Be Tomorrow Night'?
24. What was the name of broadcasters David and Jonathan's father?
25. Which quiz, hosted by Eamonn Andrews, featured Gilbert Harding as a panellist?
26. Which Joseph worked with a gopher?
27. Who is Spike's brother in *Peanuts*?
28. What was the name of *Roseanne*'s son?
29. Where did Vera and Jack Duckworth live in 1998?
30. In which children's series was there a rival school named Brookdale?

ANSWERS

**Comedy 15 (see Quiz 79)**

**1.** Eric. **2.** *Drop The Dead Donkey*. **3.** Dennis Waterman. **4.** Mike McShane. **5.** Angus Deayton. **6.** *Maid Marian and Her Merry Men*. **7.** MGM. **8.** Homer Simpson. **9.** *Dave Allen At Large*. **10.** The Royal Oak. **11.** *MASH*. **12.** *The Rag Trade*. **13.** Betty. **14.** Saffron. **15.** *Experience*. **16.** Ian Carmichael. **17.** *Stella Street*. **18.** Third Form. **19.** Billy. **20.** Joan. **21.** Hancock. **22.** Rigsby. **23.** Arnolds. **24.** Freddie. **25.** Ronnie Corbett. **26.** Eric Morecambe. **27.** AP Herbert. **28.** Joanna Lumley. **29.** Jan Francis. **30.** *Outside Edge*.

## QUIZ 81 Drama 10

**Answers: see Quiz 82, page 410**

LEVEL 1

1. Who was Lorcan Cranitch's character in *Ballykissangel*?
2. What was *The Jump* in the series of the same name?
3. Which drama series features the character Dr. Neil Bolton?
4. What is PC Quinnan's first name in *The Bill*?
5. Which Wonderwoman appeared in *Hawkeye*?
6. What was the name of Iain Banks's first drama series?
7. In which police series was John Kelly a detective?
8. Which adventure series starred Tony Curtis and Roger Moore?
9. What was Mrs. Peel's christian name in *The Avengers*?
10. Who played Charlie in *The Darling Buds Of May*?
11. Who created *Maximum Bob*?
12. Who played Caesar Augustus in *I, Claudius*?
13. Who portrayed Lillie in the story of *Lillie Langtrey*?
14. Who produced *Cathy Come Home*?
15. Who played Dr. Beth Glover in *Peak Practice*?
16. What was the name of ITV's children's drama showcase of the 1980s?
17. Which drama series featured Warren and Joe?
18. Draz and Kurt feature in which Australian series?
19. In which series does Ben Roberts play Chief Inspector Conway?
20. Who does Bill Cosby play in *The Cosby Mysteries*?
21. Which award winning film featured the life of Quentin Crisp?
22. How were Jimmy Nail's shoes described in his drama series title?
23. What was *Perry Mason*'s occupation?
24. Who played wheeler-dealer Frank Stubbs?
25. Who did Ruth Patchett become in Fay Weldon's novel and drama series?
26. Who was the Born Free actor who played John Ridd in *Lorna Doone*?
27. Which series was the sequel to *Public Eye*?
28. Which singer played Zoe Wanamaker's partner in *Love Hurts*?
29. Who was the Sheriff of Trinity in *American Gothic*?
30. In which surreal drama was Laura Palmer killed?

ANSWERS

**Children's TV 7 (see Quiz 82)**

**1.** *The Muppet Show.* **2.** A snail. **3.** Mungo. **4.** Batman. **5.** *Thunderbirds.* **6.** Grandpa Pickles. **7.** *Animaniacs.* **8.** Playschool. **9.** Red. **10.** *Rainbow.* **11.** Ball. **12.** Blue. **13.** Maggie Philbin. **14.** Pugwash. **15.** Linford Christie. **16.** Spinach. **17.** *Sesame Street.* **18.** *Animal Magic.* **19.** *Worzel Gummidge.* **20.** Saturday. **21.** *The Herbs.* **22.** Barbera. **23.** Robinson Crusoe. **24.** *The A-Team.* **25.** Pizza. **26.** *Bugs Bunny.* **27.** *Tin-Tin.* **28.** *Huckleberry Hound.* **29.** *Speedy Gonzales.* **30.** *Mr Magoo.*

## QUIZ 82 Children's TV 7

**Answers: see Quiz 81, page 409**

LEVEL 1

1. In which series did the wild and impetuous Animal play the drums?
2. What kind of creature was Brian in *The Magic Roundabout*?
3. In *Mary, Mungo and Midge*, which character was the dog?
4. What is Bruce Wayne's alter ego?
5. International Rescue featured in which puppet adventure series?
6. Which old man regularly looks after the *Rugrats*?
7. Which cartoon is set in the Warner Brothers' studio?
8. Which children's series showed a house in its opening credits?
9. What colour is *Postman Pat's* van?
10. Which series featured Zippy?
11. Which Johnny presented *Think Of A Number*?
12. What colour is *Thomas The Tank Engine*?
13. The *Multi-Coloured Swap Shop* was co-presented by which Maggie?
14. The cartoon pirate was Captain what?
15. Who took over *Record Breakers* and changed its name?
16. What was Popeye famous for eating?
17. Which show featured Big Bird and The Count?
18. Johnny Morris hosted which animal series?
19. Which Worzel was a scarecrow?
20. *Live And Kicking* is broadcast on which day?
21. Dill the Dog featured in which series?
22. Who partnered Hanna to produce TV cartoons?
23. Who was marooned on a desert island with Man Friday?
24. In which series did BA, Face and Hannibal appear?
25. What is the favourite food of the *Teenage Mutant Turtles*?
26. 'What's Up Doc?' is the catchphrase of which cartoon character?
27. Whose adventures did Hergé chronicle?
28. Which cartoon hound's favourite song was *My Darling Clementine*?
29. Who was the "fastest mouse in all Mexico"?
30. What was the short-sighted cartoon character whose voice was provided by Jim Backus?

ANSWERS

### Drama 10 (see Quiz 81)

**1.** Sean Dillon. **2.** An attempt to free a prisoner. **3.** *Heartbeat.* **4.** Dave. **5.** Linda Carter. **6.** *The Crow Road.* **7.** *NYPD Blue.* **8.** *The Persuaders.* **9.** Emma. **10.** Philip Franks. **11.** Elmore Leonard. **12.** Brian Blessed. **13.** Francesca Annis. **14.** Tony Garnett. **15.** Amanda Burton. **16.** *Dramarama.* **17.** *This Life.* **18.** *Heartbreak High.* **19.** *The Bill.* **20.** Guy Hanks. **21.** *The Naked Civil Servant.* **22.** Crocodile. **23.** Lawyer. **24.** Tim Spall. **25.** The She-Devil. **26.** Bill Travers. **27.** Marker. **28.** Adam Faith. **29.** Lucas Buck. **30.** *Twin Peaks.*

# QUIZ 83 Pot Luck 26

LEVEL 1

**Answers: see Quiz 84, page 412**

1. Which council workman was played by Bill Maynard?
2. Which star of Dallas appeared in *I Dream Of Jeannie*?
3. Which star of *The Rock Follies* had a No.1. hit with *Don't Cry For Me Argentina*?
4. Which Pamela appeared on *Not The Nine O' Clock News*?
5. Which demobbed RAF serviceman was played in a series by Kenneth Cranham?
6. Who was Christopher Timothy's character in *All Creatures Great And Small*?
7. Which northern lass famous for *She Knows You Know* starred in *Not On Your Nellie*?
8. In which series did Timothy West play Arkwright, a mill owner?
9. Who was Natasha's twin sister in *Grange Hill*?
10. Which TV cop recorded *Don't Give Up On Us Baby*?
11. Who was *Roseanne*'s real life husband who appeared in the series?
12. In *Home Improvements* what was Tim's job?
13. Which collie had her own TV series?
14. What was Lister's first name in *Red Dwarf*?
15. How many *Goodies* were there?
16. What was Dirty Den's surname in *Eastenders*?
17. Which weekly series was often televised from the Hammersmith Palais or The Lyceum?
18. Which talent show was presented by Hughie Green?
19. What was Jeff's surname in *Dynasty*?
20. Who is Cheggers?
21. What was Richard Beckinsale's character in *Rising Damp*?
22. Which programme linked Cyril Fletcher to Esther Rantzen?
23. Whose Half Hour featured 'the lad himself'?
24. What was chat show host Harty's first name?
25. Which Australian had a puppet named Kojee Bear?
26. Which Kennedy was *Game For A Laugh*?
27. Where does ITV get its revenue from?
28. What was the subject of the variety show *The Good Old Days*?
29. *Antiques Roadshow* is broadcast on which day of the week?
30. Whose boyfriend Liam was killed in *Grange Hill* while cycling to a school fight?

ANSWERS

**Comedy 16 (see Quiz 84)**

**1.** Alan B'Stard. **2.** Margaret Meldrew. **3.** *Dad's Army*. **4.** Derek Fowlds. **5.** Alec Callender. **6.** Tom And Barbara Good. **7.** The Yellowcoats. **8.** No. **9.** Norman Stanley Fletcher. **10.** Dawn French. **11.** *Absolutely Fabulous*. **12.** *Are You Being Served?* **13.** Laos. **14.** Nicholas Lyndhurst. **15.** *Birds Of A Feather*. **16.** The Fonz. **17.** Russ Abbot. **18.** Margaret. **19.** American. **20.** *It Ain't Half Hot Mum*. **21.** *Bread*. **22.** Ireland. **23.** The Boswells. **24.** Ian Lavender. **25.** Kenneth Williams. **26.** Chris Barrie. **27.** Dave Allen. **28.** Craig. **29.** Bob. **30.** The piano.

# QUIZ 84 Comedy 16

**Answers: see Quiz 83, page 411** LEVEL 1

1. Which MP was *The New Statesman*?
2. What is Annette Crosbie's character in *One Foot In The Grave*?
3. Which sitcom concerned the antics of a Home Guard platoon in the Second World War?
4. Who played Bernard in *Yes Minister*?
5. Who was Anton Rodgers' character in *May To December*?
6. Who practised self-sufficiency in Surbiton in a sitcom?
7. How were the camp entertainers known in *Hi De Hi*?
8. Does Maggie Simpson ever talk?
9. Which Ronnie Barker character was sent to Slade Prison?
10. Who is Lenny Henry's wife?
11. Edina, Saffron and Patsy appear in which comedy?
12. Mrs Slocombe and Captain Peacock featured in which series?
13. Where is Hank Hill's oriental neighour from?
14. Which actor stars in *Goodnight Sweetheart*?
15. Sharon and Tracy are the lead characters in which BBC comedy?
16. The actor Henry Winkler played which character in *Happy Days*?
17. Which TV comedian formerly led the pop group the Black Abbots?
18. What is the name of Victor Meldrew's wife in *One Foot In The Grave*?
19. Is *South Park* American or British?
20. Melvyn Hayes played Gloria in which series?
21. Nellie Boswell was the mother in which BBC sitcom?
22. *Ballykissangel* is set in which country?
23. Jean Boht starred as the mother of which TV family?
24. Who played Private Pike in *Dad's Army*?
25. Which Carry On star narrated *Will-O-The-Wisp*?
26. Which Chris starred in *The Brittas Empire* and *Red Dwarf*?
27. Which Irish comedian would say "may your God go with you"?
28. Which Wendy starred in *Butterflies*?
29. What is the first name of Mr. Fleming, the coughing 'country ways' presenter on the *Fast Show*?
30. With which musical instrument do you associate Dudley Moore?

ANSWERS

**Pot Luck 26 (see Quiz 83)**

**1.** Selwyn Froggitt. **2.** Larry Hagman. **3.** Julie Covington. **4.** Stephenson. **5.** Harvey Moon. **6.** James Herriot. **7.** Hylda Baker. **8.** Brass. **9.** Natalie. **10.** David Soul. **11.** Tom Arnold. **12.** TV Presenter of *Tooltime*. **13.** *Lassie*. **14.** Dave. **15.** Three. **16.** Watts. **17.** Come Dancing. **18.** Opportunity Knocks. **19.** Colby. **20.** Keith Chegwin. **21.** Alan Moore. **22.** *That's Life*. **23.** Tony Hancock's. **24.** Russell. **25.** Rolf Harris. **26.** Sarah. **27.** Advertising. **28.** *The Old Time Music Hall*. **29.** Sunday. **30.** Justine's.

## QUIZ 85 Crime 4

LEVEL 1

**Answers: see Quiz 86, page 414**

1. What was the name of Hercule Poirot's friend and assistant?
2. Which Lynda wrote *Prime Suspect*?
3. Which London policeman said "Good evening all"?
4. Which Conan Doyle detective fought the arch villain Moriarty?
5. Pierce Brosnan starred as Remington who?
6. Private detective Jim Rockford appeared in which popular series?
7. Did Regan and Carter both smoke in *The Sweeney*?
8. Which Hamish was the title character in a Scottish police drama?
9. Who had a sidekick called Tonto?
10. Jan Hammer wrote the theme music for which US police series?
11. Whose sidekick was called Rocky?
12. What was unusual about *Ironside*?
13. Who drives a red Jaguar?
14. Joan Hickson played which Agatha Christie sleuth?
15. Which TV company broadcast *Z Cars*?
16. Who starred as *Spender*?
17. What colour was Starsky And Hutch's car?
18. What does *Jonathan Creek* design for a living?
19. Which *A-Team* actor George played detective *Banacek*?
20. *Pacific* what was a US police series on Channel 5?
21. What was the name of Gordon Jackson's character in *The Professionals*?
22. Who is Dalziel's police partner?
23. Richard Wilson and Samantha Beckinsale star in which police series set on a river?
24. Which Raymond stars as Perry Mason?
25. Martyn Lewis presents which crime series on BBC1?
26. Which *Birds Of A Feather* star plays detective *Maisie Raine*?
27. What was Burnside's first name in *The Bill*?
28. Which Hetty, played by Patricia Routledge, Investigates?
29. In *The Wimbledon Poisoner*, which actor Robert attempted to kill his wife, played by Alison Steadman?
30. Was Kojak played by Raymond Burr?

ANSWERS

**Pot Luck 27 (see Quiz 86)**

**1.** Mr. Robson. **2.** Hanna-Barbera. **3.** Julie Kavner. **4.** *Fairly Secret Army*. **5.** William Hartnell. **6.** David Essex. **7.** The Gnomes Of Dulwich. **8.** *Man About The House*. **9.** Caresse. **10.** *The Rag Trade*. **11.** Bebe Daniels. **12.** Jeff Rawle. **13.** Judy Loe. **14.** Jaguar. **15.** *Auf Weidersehen Pet*. **16.** Priscilla White. **17.** Juke Box Jury. **18.** Liverpool. **19.** Roger Moore. **20.** Dudley Moore and Peter Cook. **21.** Fairclough. **22.** Amsterdam. **23.** Glenda Jackson. **24.** Farrah Fawcett. **25.** Jack Duckworth. **26.** Lady Jane Felsham. **27.** BBC 2. **28.** Titchmarsh. **29.** Charlie Dimmock. **30.** Wine.

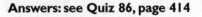

## QUIZ 86 Pot Luck 27

**Answers: see Quiz 85, page 413**

LEVEL 1

1. Which character did Stuart Organ play in *Grange Hill*?
2. Who directed *Tom and Jerry* cartoons?
3. Who is the voice of Marge Simpson?
4. In which series was Major Harry Truscott played by Geoffrey Palmer?
5. Who introduces *The Clothes Show*?
6. Which pop star starred in *The River*?
7. Where did Terry Scott and Hugh Lloyd portray garden ornaments?
8. Which series featured a trainee chef sharing a flat with two girls?
9. Who was writing a book about Alexis in *Dynasty*?
10. In which comedy series did Gillian Taylforth appear as a machinist before *Eastenders*?
11. Who was Ben Lyons's wife?
12. Which actor from *Drop The Dead Donkey* played *Billy Liar*?
13. Who was the late Richard Beckinsale's actress wife?
14. What car did Joey drive in *Bread*?
15. Which series about building workers in Germany was written by Dick Clement and Ian La Frenais?
16. What is Cilla Black's real name?
17. On which pop show did a 'Hooter' signify a miss?
18. With which English football team did Alan Hanson win cup honours?
19. Who first played Simon Templar on TV?
20. Who were Dud and Pete?
21. What was Rita Sullivan's former surname?
22. Where was *Van Der Valk* set?
23. Which MP played *Elizabeth R*?
24. Which Charlie's Angel married Lee Majors?
25. Who kept pigeons in *Coronation Street*?
26. What was Phyllis Logan's character in *Lovejoy*?
27. On which channel was *Not The Nine O'Clock News* shown?
28. Who is Alan presenter of *Gardeners World*?
29. Who is the redhead in *Ground Force*?
30. What is Jilly Goolden an expert on?

ANSWERS

**Crime 4 (see Quiz 85)**

**1.** Captain Hastings. **2.** Lynda La Plante. **3.** *Dixon Of Dock Green.* **4.** Sherlock Holmes. **5.** *Remington Steele.* **6.** *The Rockford Files.* **7.** Yes. **8.** *Hamish Macbeth.* **9.** The Lone Ranger. **10.** *Miami Vice.* **11.** *Boon.* **12.** He was confined to a wheelchair. **13.** *Inspector Morse.* **14.** *Miss Marple.* **15.** BBC. **16.** Jimmy Nail. **17.** Red. **18.** Magic tricks. **19.** George Peppard. **20.** *Pacific Blue.* **21.** Cowley. **22.** Pascoe. **23.** *Duck Patrol.* **24.** Raymond Burr. **25.** *Crime Beat.* **26.** Pauline Quirke. **27.** Frank. **28.** Wainthropp. **29.** Robert Lindsay. **30.** No (it was Telly Savalas).

# QUIZ 87 Drama 11

LEVEL 1

**Answers: see Quiz 88, page 416**

1. Steed and Gambit were the male stars in which TV adventure series?
2. In which BBC series did Tinker and Lady Jane appear?
3. Which Richardson starred in the Steven Poliakoff teleplay *The Tribe*?
4. What is the occupation of the lead character in *Bramwell*?
5. Who played *The Chancer*?
6. In *Silent Witness* what is Sam Ryan's profession?
7. In what type of building is *ER* set?
8. Which Sean stars as *Sharpe*?
9. Which Pam starred in *The Darling Buds Of May*?
10. In *Sapphire & Steel*, which title character did Joanna Lumley play?
11. *Poldark* was set in which century?
12. In which Western series did the Cartwrights reside at the Ponderosa?
13. In *A Family At War* in which northern city did the Ashtons live?
14. Which medical drama was set in Oxbridge General Hospital?
15. Which king was played by Keith Mitchell in 1970?
16. In which ITV series did the characters Dave Tucker and Paddy Garvey appear?
17. Amanda Burton appeared in which series about a doctors practice in Derbyshire?
18. The character Yosser Hughes featured in which drama series?
19. Which comedy duo played *Jeeves and Wooster*?
20. What was the name of James Herriott's wife in *All Creatures Great And Small*?
21. Which series is based at the fictitious Holby General Hospital?
22. Who was Reginald Perrin's boss?
23. Harry's Game was set in which part of the UK?
24. *The House Of Cards* was set in which governmental establishment?
25. The butler Hudson featured in which period drama?
26. In *This Life* was Ferdy or Miles gay?
27. Peter and Anna Mayle spent a year where?
28. *Tenko* was set during which war?
29. Which *Men Behaving Badly* star is also *The Vanishing Man*?
30. Which Royal was played by Amy Clare Seccombe in Channel 5's *The People's Princess: A Tribute*?

ANSWERS

**Soaps 10 (see Quiz 88)**

**1.** Paul Robinson. **2.** Betty Turpin. **3.** Bill Gregory. **4.** In a motorway crash. **5.** Alf Roberts. **6.** Todd. **7.** Harris. **8.** Annie Walker. **9.** Cousin. **10.** A lorry crashed into the Rovers Return near where Alf was sitting. **11.** Den and Angie Watts. **12.** Noele Gordon. **13.** *Emergency Ward.* **14.** Brookside Close. **15.** Angie. **16.** A rose. **17.** *The Colbys.* **18.** Australia. **19.** Ramsey Street. **20.** Mike Baldwin. **21.** The Kabin. **22.** Bet Gilroy. **23.** Bobby. **24.** Sugden. **25.** *Brookside.* **26.** The Snug. **27.** Katie. **28.** Jim Robinson. **29.** *Coronation Street.* **30.** Mavis Riley.

## QUIZ 88 Soaps10

LEVEL 1

**Answers: see Quiz 87, page 415**

1. Who did Gail Lewis marry in *Neighbours*?
2. Who was Gordon Clegg's real mother in *Coronation Street*?
3. Who did Elsie Tanner go to Portugal with in 1983?
4. How did Len Fairclough die in *Coronation Street*?
5. Who was the last Mayor of Weatherfield in *Coronation Street*?
6. Who was Katie Landers' brother in *Neighbours*?
7. What was Jane's surname in *Neighbours*?
8. Who was the last Mayoress of Weatherfield in *Coronation Street*?
9. What relation was Shane to Henry in *Neighbours*?
10. How did Alf Roberts end up in a coma in *Coronation Street*?
11. When *Eastenders* began who were in charge at The Queen Victoria?
12. Which *Crossroads* actress worked with John Logie Baird?
13. What was ITV's first hospital soap?
14. Where did Sinbad Sweeney live in 1998?
15. What was Sharon Watts mother's name in *Eastenders*?
16. What kind of flower is Ena Sharples?
17. In which series did Rock Hudson play Heather Locklear's father?
18. In which country is Cell block H in *Prisoner*?
19. Where do Susan and Karl Kennedy live?
20. Who fired Hayley in *Coronation Street* when he found out she was a transsexual?
21. Where do the *Coronation Street* characters buy their newspapers?
22. Who preceded The Duckworths as licensee of The Rovers Return?
23. Which Simpson was Sam's mother in *Home and Away*?
24. Which surname links Percy in one soap to Jack in another?
25. In which soap was Trevor Jordache buried under a patio?
26. Where in The Rovers Return would you have found Ena and Minnie having a drink?
27. Who was Todd Landers sister in *Neighbours*?
28. Who did Dr. Beverley Marshall marry in *Neighbours*?
29. Which soap moved from two to three transmissions a week in 1989?
30. Who did Victor Pendlebury go on a walking holiday with in *Coronation Street*?

ANSWERS

### Drama 11 (see Quiz 87)

**1.** *New Avengers.* **2.** *Lovejoy.* **3.** Joely. **4.** Doctor. **5.** Clive Owen. **6.** A pathologist. **7.** A hospital. **8.** Sean Bean. **9.** Pam Ferris. **10.** Sapphire. **11.** The 18th Century. **12.** *Bonanza.* **13.** Liverpool. **14.** *Emergency – Ward 10.* **15.** Henry VIII. **16.** *Soldier, Soldier.* **17.** *Peak Practice.* **18.** *Boys From The Blackstuff.* **19.** Fry and Laurie. **20.** Helen. **21.** *Casualty.* **22.** C.J. **23.** Northern Ireland. **24.** The House Of Commons. **25.** *Upstairs, Downstairs.* **26.** Ferdy. **27.** *A Year In Provence.* **28.** World War Two. **29.** Neil Morrissey. **30.** Princess Diana.

## QUIZ 89 Pot Luck 28

**Answers: see Quiz 90, page 418**

LEVEL 1

1. What is Mr Clarke from *Food And Drink's* christian name?
2. Which P.I. drove his employer's red Ferrari?
3. Where did a sum on a blackboard recurr often on television screens?
4. Which cookery competition is hosted by Lloyd Grossman?
5. On which talent show was Pam Ayres a winner?
6. In which series did Yosser Hughes first appear?
7. Which chat show host did The Bee Gees walk out on?
8. What liquid refreshment was advertised by Pete and Dud?
9. Who was Bernie Winters' brother?
10. Who plays Onslow in *Keeping Up Appearances?*
11. Who was the snail on *The Magic Roundabout?*
12. Who was the youngest Boswell boy in *Bread?*
13. In which series were Mrs Bridges and Mr Hudson?
14. What was featured in *Thank Your Lucky Stars?*
15. What is the christian name of actor McKern of *Rumpole* fame?
16. What is TV cook Grigson's first name?
17. In which comedy series was Penelope Wilton married to Richard Briers?
18. What was Hyacinth's husband's name in *Keeping Up Appearances?*
19. In which series was Geoffrey Palmer a collector of a variety of flying creature?
20. Who was Rita's father in *Till Death Do Us Part?*
21. Which saga was the last to be broadcast in black and white on the BBC?
22. Who created Hercule Poirot?
23. The Ministry of Funny Walks appeared in which series?
24. Which Ruth Rendell character is played by George Baker?
25. Which medieval monk is a crime solver?
26. Who ran the Neighbourhood Watch Scheme in *Coronation Street?*
27. Which 1960s western series was about a cattle drive and the drovers?
28. What is Rick Stein's gastronomic speciality?
29. Which actor in *Happy Days,* apart from Ron Howard, has directed feature films?
30. What was Bridget's surname in *Grange Hill?*

ANSWERS

**Comedy 17 (see Quiz 90)**

**1.** Clive Dunn. **2.** *Hi-Di-Hi!* **3.** *The Liver Birds.* **4.** Lenny Henry. **5.** *May To December.* **6.** *Please, Sir.* **7.** *The Tick.* **8.** *Terry And June.* **9.** Tony Hancock. **10.** Hattie Jacques. **11.** Three. **12.** Harry Enfield. **13.** No. **14.** Dorien. **15.** Chuckie. **16.** *The Fast Show.* **17.** A Giant Tortoise. **18.** Chris Morris. **19.** David Jason. **20.** Different. **21.** *The Young Ones.* **22.** *Viz.* **23.** Lulu. **24.** *'Allo, 'Allo.* **25.** *Bottom.* **26.** Michael Moore. **27.** Richard Briars. **28.** *Fawlty Towers.* **29.** Reginald Perrin. **30.** Wendy Richards.

## QUIZ 90 Comedy 17

**Answers: see Quiz 89, page 417**

LEVEL 1

1. Which Clive starred as Corporal Jones in *Dad's Army*?
2. In which BBC series did the Yellow Coats feature?
3. Nerys Hughes and Polly James starred together in which 1970s BBC comedy?
4. Who stars as the *Chef*?
5. Anton Rodgers starred in which series named after months of the year?
6. Fenn Street school featured in which comedy?
7. Which comedy cartoon superhero, named after an insect, often shouted "Spoon!"
8. What were the first names of the duo Scott and Whitfield?
9. Who presented his *Half Hour*?
10. Which Hattie starred opposite Eric Sykes?
11. How many seats did the Goodies' bike have?
12. Which Harry starred in *Men Behaving Badly*?
13. Does Bart visit the Moon in *The Simpsons*?
14. Lesley Joseph plays which character in *Birds Of A Feather*?
15. Which baby wore glasses in *Rugrats*?
16. On which show would you find the fictitious chaotic Spanish TV station Channel 9?
17. What creature appears in the opening and closing credits of *One Foot In The Grave*?
18. Who was the creator and presenter of Channel 4's irreverent satire *Brass Eye*?
19. Who played Granville in *Open All Hours*?
20. *Monty Python's Flying Circus* often changed sketch with the words "And now for something completely..." what?
21. Which comedy featured Vivien Bastard?
22. Which magazine created the Fat Slags?
23. Which Scottish singer portrayed Adrian Mole's mother?
24. Which spoof wartime series featured a painting by Van Clomp?
25. Which show features Eddie and Richie?
26. Who introduced *TV Nation*?
27. Who starred as Tom Good?
28. Miss Gatsby, Miss Tibbs and the Major were all guests at which hotel?
29. Who daydreamed of his mother-in-law as a hippo?
30. Which *Eastender* played Miss Brahms in *Are You Being Served?*

ANSWERS

### Pot Luck 28 (see Quiz 89)

**1.** Oz. **2.** Magnum. **3.** The Test Card. **4.** *Masterchef.* **5.** *Opportunity Knocks.* **6.** *Boys From The Blackstuff.* **7.** Clive Anderson. **8.** Guinness. **9.** Mike. **10.** Geoffrey Hughes. **11.** Brian. **12.** Billy. **13.** *Upstairs, Downstairs.* **14.** Pop Music. **15.** Leo. **16.** Sophie. **17.** *Ever Decreasing Circles.* **18.** Richard. **19.** *Butterflies.* **20.** Alf Garnett. **21.** *The Forsythe Saga.* **22.** Agatha Christie. **23.** *Monty Python's Flying Circus.* **24.** Wexford. **25.** Cadfael. **26.** Percy Sugden. **27.** *Rawhide.* **28.** Seafood. **29.** Henry Winkler. **30.** McClusky.

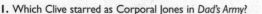

## QUIZ 91 News 5

LEVEL 1

**Answers: see Quiz 92, page 420**

1. On which channel is the science documentary series *Equinox* broadcast?
2. Which Jack hosts a late night chat show on Channel 5?
3. What is the name of ITV's breakfast channel?
4. *Watchdog: Value For Money* is presented by chatshow host Vanessa who?
5. What was the name of *Top Gear*'s boating series?
6. US presenter Jerry Springer hosts what kind of show?
7. Which British 1960s Supermodel hosts a chat show on ITV?
8. Which US comedienne presented the series *Ruby Does The Season*?
9. Which popular BBC1 science and technology programme first went on air in 1965?
10. Who was the regular astrologer on *Breakfast Time*?
11. The holiday programme *Wish You Were Here* was presented by which Judith?
12. Which *Mona Lisa* actor Bob rode an elephant in search of tigers?
13. Which university offers courses on BBC TV?
14. *What The Papers Say* is broadcast on which channel?
15. The viewers access programme on Channel 4 is called *Right To...* what?
16. BBC TV's book series *Bookworm* was introduced by which comedian, Griff?
17. What was the name of the BBC fashion show originally presented by Jeff Banks?
18. Patrick Moore hosts which long-running astronomy series?
19. Which Rat revived *TV-AM*'s ratings?
20. BBC2's *The Money Programme* was hosted by which ex-Blue Peter presenter Valerie?
21. Dr Ian Dunbar offers advice on training which animals?
22. Melvyn Bragg introduces which Sunday evening arts show?
23. Archaeology enthusiast Tony Robinson goes digging at sites with which Team?
24. Who presented *That's Life* in the 1970s?
25. Robert Kilroy-Silk hosts which talk show on BBC1?
26. Which series, started in 1956, looks at the week's newspapers?
27. Which John presented the talk show *The Time ... The Place* on ITV?
28. *Chrystal Rose* hosts what kind of show?
29. Is the science documentary series *Horizon* broadcast on BBC2 or Channel 4?
30. Which Angus presented *The Temptation Game*?

ANSWERS

**Sci-Fi 2 (see Quiz 92)**

**1.** *Quantum Leap*. **2.** *The 25th Century*. **3.** Anderson. **4.** Smith. **5.** A woman. **6.** *The Tomorrow People*. **7.** Superman. **8.** *The X Files*. **9.** Gabrielle. **10.** Mr. Croup. **11.** San Francisco. **12.** Red. **13.** Helicopter. **14.** Tanks. **15.** Magrathea. **16.** Adama. **17.** Decaptitation. **18.** *The Jetsons*. **19.** V. **20.** *Sapphire & Steel*. **21.** An amulet. **22.** *The Incredible Hulk*. **23.** *Babylon 5*. **24.** *Wonder Woman*. **25.** Six million. **26.** *Red Dwarf*. **27.** Harker. **28.** Simon McCorkindale. **29.** *Blake's 7*. **30.** *Flash Gordon*.

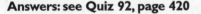

## QUIZ 92 Sci-Fi 2

**Answers: see Quiz 91, page 419**

LEVEL 1

1. What kind of Leap does actor Scott Bakula take in his time-travel drama?
2. To which century was *Buck Rogers* transported?
3. Which Gerry produced the Sci-Fi series *Space 1999*?
4. In *Dr. Who*, what was Sarah-Jane's surname?
5. In the comedy series *Weird Science* what do the two friends produce using their computer?
6. Who had a computer called TIM?
7. Lex Luther is the arch-enemy of which Superhero?
8. David Duchovny and Gillian Anderson play the lead characters in which US drama?
9. What is the name of *Xena: Warrior Princess*' scribely side-kick?
10. Who was Mr. Vandemar's murderous brother in *Neverwhere*?
11. In which city do the *Sliders* slide?
12. What colour is Beverley Crusher's hair in *Star Trek: Next Generation*?
13. What type of vehicle was *Blue Thunder*?
14. In *Space Above & Beyond*, what insulting term was used for clones?
15. Which planet in the *Hitch-Hiker's Guide to the Galaxy* was the home of Slartibartfast?
16. What was Lorne Greene's character in *Battlestar Galactica*?
17. How do you kill an immortal in *Highlander: The Gathering*?
18. Which cartoon series featured a space age family?
19. Which sci-fi series had one letter as its title?
20. Which time-fighting duo were assisted variously by Lead and Silver, amongst others?
21. From what did *Mandrake* draw his powers?
22. Lou Ferrigno played the part of which angry green transformation?
23. In which series did the characters G'kar, Morden and Delenn appear?
24. Which character was an Amazon princess turned superhero?
25. How many million dollars was the Bionic Man worth?
26. On which mining ship would you find robot janitors called Scutters?
27. Which Susannah helped Jack Davenport hunt vampires in *Ultraviolet*?
28. Who played the shape-shifting *Manimal*?
29. Avon and Gan were members of which sci-fi team?
30. Which character was a revolutionary on the planet Mongo?

ANSWERS

**News 5 (see Quiz 91)**

**1.** Channel 4. **2.** Jack Docherty. **3.** *GMTV*. **4.** Vanessa Feltz. **5.** *Top Gear Waterworld*. **6.** Chat show. **7.** Twiggy. **8.** Ruby Wax. **9.** *Tomorrow's World*. **10.** Russell Grant. **11.** Judith Chalmers. **12.** Bob Hoskins. **13.** *Open University*. **14.** BBC2. **15.** Reply. **16.** Griff Rhys-Jones. **17.** *The Clothes Show*. **18.** *The Sky At Night*. **19.** Roland. **20.** Valerie Singleton. **21.** Dogs. **22.** *The South Bank Show*. **23.** Esther Rantzen. **24.** Channel 4. **25.** *Kilroy*. **26.** *What The Papers Say*. **27.** John Stapleton. **28.** A talk show. **29.** BBC2. **30.** Angus Deayton.

# QUIZ 93 Pot Luck 29

**Answers: see Quiz 94, page 422**

LEVEL 1

1. Which Daily Mirror character was played on TV by James Bolam?
2. Whose *Audience With* ... featured singing with the *Spice Girls*?
3. Who plays a wobble board?
4. Who was Charlie Hungerford's son-in-law?
5. What are Cobra and Hunter?
6. What colour costumes do the lifeguards in *Baywatch* wear?
7. Who is John Mortimer's legal hero?
8. In which advert do Prunella Scales and Jane Horrocks appear?
9. Who played Endora in *Bewitched*?
10. Which member of Bucks Fizz became a TV presenter?
11. Which Simon left a 1960s pop group to present his own chat show?
12. Who presents *Surprise, Surprise*?
13. Which chocolate bar promised to help you "work, rest and play"?
14. What was Channel 4's film channel called, launched in November 1998?
15. Which Superheroic figure helped children to cross the road?
16. Which Meg appeared on *National Lottery Live*?
17. Who is credited with inventing TV?
18. Which independent TV company covers the London area?
19. Who is Sir David Attenborough's famous film director brother?
20. What kind of programmes did the late Geoff Hamilton present on BBC TV?
21. The TV fitness instructor Diana Moran is known as 'The Green...' what?
22. The Sunday evening programme *Highway* was hosted by which former Goon and singer?
23. Who hosted *Challenge Anneka*?
24. Who hosts *Blind Date*?
25. *The Big Breakfast* is broadcast on which channel?
26. Who presented *Film 97*?
27. What does BBC stand for?
28. Christopher Timothy starred in which acclaimed BBC vet drama?
29. Which BBC antiques series hosts weekly shows in venues around the country?
30. Is *Songs Of Praise* broadcast on BBC or ITV?

ANSWERS

## Children's TV 8 (see Quiz 94)

**1.** Fred Flintstone. **2.** A Killer Whale. **3.** BBC1. **4.** Bill and Ted. **5.** *Art Attack*. **6.** *Pet Detective*. **7.** Newcastle. **8.** Children's Independent Television. **9.** Zag. **10.** A dog. **11.** A penguin. **12.** Spiderman. **13.** Superman. **14.** Emma Forbes. **15.** *Power Rangers*. **16.** Yvette Fielding. **17.** BBC1. **18.** KITT. **19.** A cat. **20.** *Fingermouse*. **21.** Noddy. **22.** *Captain Scarlet*. **23.** Xena. **24.** Mars. **25.** Sooty. **26.** Four. **27.** A bear. **28.** A cat. **29.** *CHiPs*. **30.** *Live And Kicking*.

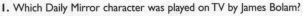

## QUIZ 94 Children's TV 8

**Answers: see Quiz 93, page 421**

LEVEL 1

1. Which stone-age cartoon character was played by John Goodman in the 1990s film?
2. What kind of creature features in the animated *Free Willy*?
3. The Saturday morning show *The Pop Zone* is broadcast on which channel?
4. Who have *Excellent Adventures* on Channel 4?
5. Neil Buchanan introduces which ITV children's art show?
6. What kind of detective is *Ace Ventura*?
7. In which north-eastern city is *Byker Grove* set?
8. What does CITV stand for?
9. Who is Zig the puppet's partner?
10. What kind of animal is *Lassie*?
11. *Pingu* is what type of creature?
12. Who was bitten by a radioactive spider and gained super powers?
13. Lois Laine is associated with which Superhero?
14. *Live and Kicking* was presented by Andi Peters and which Emma?
15. Which Rangers are teenage superheroes?
16. Which Yvette is a former *Blue Peter* presenter?
17. Andy Crane hosted children's evening TV with Ed The Duck on which channel?
18. What was the name of David Hasslehoff's talking car?
19. Heathcliff is what kind of cartoon animal?
20. Which children's series featured finger puppet animals?
21. Which Enid Blyton creation lives in toyland?
22. Which puppet Captain battles with the Mysterons?
23. Lucy Lawless stars as which Channel 5 Warrior Princess?
24. The *Biker Mice* are from which planet?
25. Which puppet bear celebrated his 50th birthday in 1998?
26. How many *Teletubbies* are there?
27. What kind of creature is *Paddington*?
28. *Garfield* is what kind of cartoon animal?
29. Which show was about US motorcycle cops?
30. Zoe Ball and Jamie Theakston present which Saturday morning show for children?

ANSWERS

### Pot Luck 29 (see Quiz 93)

**1.** *Andy Capp*. **2.** Elton John. **3.** Rolf Harris. **4.** Jim Bergerac. **5.** *Gladiators*. **6.** Red. **7.** *Rumpole of The Bailey*. **8.** Tesco. **9.** Agnes Moorehead. **10.** Cheryl Baker. **11.** Simon Dee. **12.** Cilla Black. **13.** Marts. **14.** FilmFour. **15.** The Green Cross Man. **16.** Mystic. **17.** John Logie Baird. **18.** Carlton TV. **19.** Sir Richard Attenborough. **20.** Gardening. **21.** The Green Goddess. **22.** Sir Harry Secombe. **23.** Anneka Rice. **24.** Cilla Black. **25.** Channel 4. **26.** Barry Norman. **27.** British Broadcasting Corporation. **28.** *All Creatures Great And Small*. **29.** *Antiques Roadshow*. **30.** BBC.

## QUIZ 95 Comedy 18

**Answers: see Quiz 96, page 424**

LEVEL 1

1. Jasper Carrott is Bob Louis in which BBC comedy?
2. In *Don't Wait Up* what did father and son, Tom and Toby, do for a living?
3. Dorothy, Blanche, Rose and Sophie were collectively known as what?
4. Does MTV make any comedy programmes?
5. Which blond actress plays Deborah in *Men Behaving Badly*?
6. Alec and Zoe Callender were the lead characters in which BBC1 sitcom?
7. What was the profession of *Steptoe And Son*?
8. In which comedy did Paul Shane appear as a holiday park comedian?
9. Michael Crawford played Frank Spencer in which sitcom?
10. Alan Alda was a US army surgeon in which long-running series?
11. Which comic cartoon series is set in the US town of Springfield?
12. Which Nigel starred in *Don't Wait Up*?
13. Audrey Fforbes-Hamilton was played by which Penelope?
14. Alf and Rita Garnett were leading characters in which comedy?
15. Complete the title: ... *Goes Forth*.
16. The character Charlie Burrows is a footballer-turned-housekeeper in which sitcom?
17. Which Jim was the lead character in *Yes, Prime Minister*?
18. Which former Minder was *On The Up*?
19. Rick, Neil, Vyvyan and Mike were known collectively as what?
20. Who played Patsy Stone in *Absolutely Fabulous*?
21. Terry who starred with June Whitfield in *Happy Ever After*?
22. Who played Alan B'Stard?
23. What is Rab Nesbitt's middle initial?
24. Oz, Neville and Denis were characters in which series set on building sites?
25. Where might you see Mariah Carey & Jim Carrey locked in a duel to the death?
26. Arnold Rimmer was a hologram on board which ship?
27. In which country was the sitcom *Duty Free* mostly set?
28. Which father and son lived in Oil Drum Lane, Shepherd's Bush?
29. Jerry, Elaine, Kramer and George are the four characters in which successful US sitcom?
30. The BBC comedy *Roger, Roger* concerns which public service?

ANSWERS

### Pot Luck 30 (see Quiz 96)

**1.** Hugh Scully. **2.** Husband and wife. **3.** Nick Owen. **4.** Craddock. **5.** Delia Smith. **6.** Rolf Harris. **7.** Alan Titchmarsh. **8.** Gary Lineker. **9.** John Logie Baird. **10.** Gaby Roslin. **11.** Carol Smillie. **12.** Access card. **13.** Westerns. **14.** *Songs Of Praise*. **15.** *Colditz*. **16.** Channel 4. **17.** *What's My Line?* **18.** Eamonn Andrews. **19.** Adam Faith. **20.** March 1997. **21.** Central. **22.** BBC2. **23.** *On The Night*. **24.** *Happy Days*. **25.** Mr Hooperman. **26.** Anneka Rice. **27.** *Minder*. **28.** Bruce Willis. **29.** A cigar. **30.** A hospital.

# QUIZ 96 Pot Luck 30

**Answers: see Quiz 95, page 423**

LEVEL 1

1. Which Hugh presents *Antiques Roadshow*?
2. How are ITV presenters Richard Madeley and Judy Finnigan related?
3. Who was Anne Diamond's co-presenter in the daytime show *Anne And Nick*?
4. What was the surname of the husband and wife TV cooks, Fanny and Johnny?
5. Which Delia is a TV cook?
6. Who presents *Animal Hospital* on BBC1?
7. Which Alan is a TV gardener?
8. Which former England football captain advertises crisps?
9. Which TV inventor had the middle name Logie?
10. Which Gaby presented *The Big Breakfast*?
11. *The Midweek Lottery* was first presented by which Carol?
12. What was advertised on TV as "your flexible friend"?
13. *Laramie* and *Maverick* were what sort of programmes?
14. What is the name of BBC1's Sunday evening religious service programme?
15. Which programme took place in a POW castle?
16. Which TV channel was involved in the making of the hit film *Four Weddings And A Funeral*?
17. In which show did people try to guess others' occupations?
18. Which Irish presenter hosted *This Is Your Life*?
19. Which pop singer starred as *Budgie*?
20. In which month of 1997 did Channel 5 start broadcasting?
21. Which TV company serves the Midlands?
22. Which channel was the UK's third terrestrial channel?
23. When will it be Alright with Dennis Norden?
24. Which show featured Richie Cunningham?
25. Who was Miles' boss in *This Life*?
26. The TV presenter Annie Rice is better known as who?
27. George Cole starred with Denis Waterman in which TV series?
28. Which Bruce starred in *Moonlighting*?
29. What did Jimmy Savile always hold in *Jim'll Fix It*?
30. The documentary Jimmy's was about what kind of establishment?

ANSWERS

**Comedy 18 (see Quiz 95)**

**1.** *The Detectives*. **2.** Doctors. **3.** *The Golden Girls*. **4.** Yes. **5.** Leslie Ash. **6.** *May To December*. **7.** Rag and bone men. **8.** *Some Mothers Do Ave Em*. **9.** *M*A*S*H*. **10.** *The Simpsons*. **11.** Nigel Havers. **12.** Penelope Keith. **13.** *Til Death Us Do Part*. **14.** Peter Bowles. **15.** *Blackadder*. **16.** *The Upper Hand*. **17.** Jim Hacker. **18.** Denis Waterman. **19.** *The Young Ones*. **20.** Joanna Lumley. **21.** Terry Scott. **22.** Rick Mayall. **23.** C. **24.** *Auf Wiedersehn Pet*. **25.** Celebrity Deathmatch. **26.** *Red Dwarf*. **27.** Spain. **28.** *Steptoe And Son*. **29.** *Seinfeld*. **30.** A Minicab service.

## QUIZ 97 Soaps 11

LEVEL 1

**Answers: see Quiz 98, page 426**

1. What was Kylie Minogue's character in *Neighbours*?
2. Which Liverpool Close is the title of a Soap?
3. What is "Curly" Watts' real name in *Coronation Street*?
4. Which soap character who was a Riley became a Wilton?
5. What colour is Bianca's hair in *Eastenders*?
6. Who is the mechanic who lives in *Coronation Street*?
7. What nationality is Ruth Fowler in *Eastenders*?
8. In which soap does Maud Grimes appear?
9. What was the name of Rita Sullivan's business in *Coronation Street*?
10. Where does Huw Edwards come from in *Eastenders*?
11. Cindy Beale appeared in which soap?
12. In *Coronation Street* who was Maureen's wheelchair-bound mother?
13. What was the scheming Fred Elliott's profession in *Coronation Street*?
14. Which of the MacDonald twins went to prison in *Coronation Street*?
15. How did Dave Glover die in *Emmerdale*?
16. The character Sinbad appears in which Channel 4 soap?
17. Tiffany and her daughter Courtney can be seen in which BBC series?
18. What was the profession of Ivy Brennan's husband in *Coronation Street*?
19. In 1997 for which national service did ex-*Eastenders* stars appear in a TV ad?
20. In *Neighbours* what did the following characters have in common – Scott, Lucy, Paul?
21. In *Coronation Street* which couple have a villainous son called Terry?
22. To which country did David Wicks move on leaving Albert Square?
23. What is the name of Bianca's mother in *Eastenders*?
24. In which soap does Barbara Windsor star?
25. Shane and Angel married in which Australian soap?
26. In *Coronation Street* who is Curly's estranged wife?
27. Near which Australian city is *Home and Away* set?
28. What is the name of Phil and Kathy Mitchell's son?
29. Tinhead appeared in which soap?
30. Betty Williams is a barmaid in which soap?

ANSWERS

**Pot Luck 31 (see Quiz 99)**

**1.** Swedish. **2.** Fish. **3.** Baron Greenback. **4.** BBC1. **5.** *Baywatch*. **6.** Paul Daniels. **7.** *Antiques Roadshow*. **8.** *The X-Files*. **9.** Judy Finnigan. **10.** Shane Richie. **11.** *The Cook Report*. **12.** *The Chancer*. **13.** *Tarrant On TV*. **14.** ITV. **15.** Magic shows. **16.** Cookery series. **17.** Gaby Roslin. **18.** Esther. **19.** Britain. **20.** Wensleydale. **21.** *The Learning Zone*. **22.** Phillip Schofield. **23.** Walton's Mountain. **24.** A TV doctor. **25.** *The Word*. **26.** *The Big Breakfast*. **27.** *Wildlife on One*. **28.** Gardening. **29.** *Youth TV*. **30.** *Changing Rooms*.

## QUIZ 98 Drama 12

**Answers: see Quiz 99, page 427**

LEVEL 1

1. Angel Jonathan and his companion Mark are travelling the Highway to where?
2. On Channel 4, Armistead Maupin offers More *Tales Of...* what?
3. Which mythical hero offered *The Legendary Journeys* on Channel 5?
4. What kind of princess is Xena according to the title of her series?
5. To which US family does Jim Bob belong?
6. The BBC1 medical drama is *Chicago* what?
7. Kevin Whateley plays what kind of investigator in *The Broker's Man*?
8. DJ Jack Killian answers what kind of caller?
9. Charisma, Sicknote, and Bayleaf have all been fire-fighters in which series?
10. Who wrote *Pennies From Heaven*?
11. Robson Green starred in which ITV army series?
12. Derek Thompson and Patrick Robinson played nurses in which BBC hospital drama?
13. According to the title of the spy series, who was from U.N.C.L.E.?
14. Vintage Western series, *Rawhide*, featured which Hollywood star?
15. In The BBC adaptation of Dickens's classic which Martin was portrayed by Paul Schofield?
16. Which actor/singer played Jed Sheppard in *Crocodile Shoes*?
17. *The Flying Doctors* was set in which country?
18. Which ITV series revolved around customs and excise?
19. Whose children included Primrose & Petunia?
20. *Maximum Bob* stars which US actor Beau as Judge Gibbs?
21. Who played Rocky in *Boone*?
22. Whose boss was Dr. Gillespie?
23. Where was *Poldark* set?
24. If Lord Bellamy was Upstairs, where were his servants?
25. What was *Revisited* in the classic series?
26. What was Rumpole's first name?
27. Which series was about a Yorkshire vet?
28. Who had an affair with Ken Masters in *Howards Way*?
29. Which series featured Mr. Shirovski as a music teacher?
30. What was detective Mrs. Wainthropp's first name?

ANSWERS

### Soaps 11 (see Quiz 97)

**1.** Charlene Robinson. **2.** *Brookside.* **3.** Norman. **4.** Mavis. **5.** Red. **6.** Kevin Webster. **7.** Scottish. **8.** *Coronation Street.* **9.** The Kabin. **10.** Wales. **11.** *Eastenders.* **12.** Maud Grimes. **13.** A butcher. **14.** Steve. **15.** In a fire. **16.** *Brookside.* **17.** *Eastenders.* **18.** A taxi driver. **19.** BT. **20.** All were members of the Robinson family. **21.** Jack and Vera Duckworth. **22.** Italy. **23.** Carol. **24.** *Eastenders.* **25.** *Home And Away.* **26.** Raquel. **27.** Sydney. **28.** Ben. **29.** *Brookside.* **30.** *Coronation Street.*

## QUIZ 99 Pot Luck 31

LEVEL 1

**Answers: see Quiz 97, page 425**

1. What nationality is Ulrika Jonsson?
2. Rick Stein presented programmes about which type of food?
3. What is *Dangermouse*'s nemesis called?
4. On which channel is the National Lottery televised live?
5. C J Parker was a character in which US series?
6. To which magician is Debbie McGee married?
7. Which BBC1 antiques show is broadcast on Sunday evenings?
8. In which series would you meet the Lone Gunmen?
9. Who is Richard Madeley's co-presenter on *This Morning*?
10. Which Shane advertises washing powder?
11. What is the name of the series presented by undercover reporter Roger Cook?
12. Clive Owen starred as which 1980s risk-taking businessman?
13. Which series showing compilations of TV clips is presented by Chris Tarrant?
14. *Morning Worship* is screened on which channel on Sunday Mornings?
15. What kind of shows do Penn and Teller present?
16. BBC1's *The Rankin Challenge* is what kind of series?
17. Who presents *Television's Greatest Hits* on BBC1?
18. What is the name of Esther Rantzen's chat show?
19. Dorinda Hafner presented *The Tastes of* which country on Channel 4?
20. Which cheese are Wallace and Gromit forever in search of?
21. Which Zone is BBC2's educational service?
22. Who hosted *Schofield's Quest* on ITV?
23. On what mountain do *The Waltons* live?
24. Hilary Jones has what role on TV?
25. Terry Christian co-presented which Channel 4 youth magazine programme?
26. Denise Van Outen and Johnny Vaughan co-presented which morning programme?
27. Name BBC1's long-running nature series, presented by Sir David Attenborough.
28. The BBC 2 series *The Beechgrove Garden* concerns which subject?
29. BBC2's *Watch This Or The Dog Dies* was subtitled *The History of...* what type of TV?
30. Handy Andy is the wizard with wood in which BBC interior design show?

ANSWERS

**Drama 12 (see Quiz 98)**

**1.** *Highway To Heaven*. **2.** The City. **3.** Hercules. **4.** *Xena: Warrior Princess*. **5.** *The Waltons*. **6.** *Chicago Hope*. **7.** An insurance investigator. **8.** *Midnight Caller*. **9.** *London's Burning*. **10.** Dennis Potter. **11.** *Soldier, Soldier*. **12.** *Casualty*. **13.** *The Man*. **14.** Clint Eastwood. **15.** *Martin Chuzzlewit*. **16.** Jimmy Nail. **17.** Australia. **18.** *The Knock*. **19.** Ma & Pa Larkin. **20.** Beau Bridges. **21.** Neil Morrissey. **22.** *Dr. Kildare* **23.** Cornwall. **24.** Downstairs. **25.** Brideshead. **26.** Horace. **27.** *All Creatures Great and Small*. **28.** Jan Howard. **29.** *Fame*. **30.** Hetty.

## LEVEL 2: THE MEDIUM QUESTIONS

For the majority of quiz situations, these questions are going to be your primary line of attack. They're tricky enough to make people think about the answer, but they're not so mind-straining that your audience is going to walk off feeling humiliated. And that's important. Where people fall down totally will be in program areas that they know nothing about. If you're setting a quiz for lone contestants, make good use of these questions.

If you're working with teams, you may find that this section is a little on the simple side. Pick any four or five people from the bar, and you'll find that between them, they watch quite a range of different shows, so they know most of the answers to this level of question. That means that scores for teams on this sort of material should be around the 75% mark, which leaves plenty of room for doing well or doing badly, but still lets everyone feel good about themselves.

So, either way, use these questions wisely. Rely on their power to help you out of a sticky situation (although that might just be beer on the pub carpet), and you won't go far wrong. They will provide the backbone of your quiz.

# QUIZ 1 Pot Luck 1

LEVEL 2

**Answers: see Quiz 2, page 430**

1. Which Anne presented *Watchdog*?
2. What type of programs does Sophie Grigson present?
3. What was the ocupaton of Dorothy McNabb in *Two's Company*?
4. Who punched her future husband in *Neighbours*, the first time they met?
5. Who went from *Doomwatch* to *The Detectives*?
6. What is the first name of *Kavanagh QC*?
7. What does *The Great Antiques Hunt* have as a mascot?
8. Which BBC TV commentator described the Queen's Coronation service?
9. What transport do the Two Fat Ladies favour?
10. In *Life And Loves Of a She Devil*, the cenral character Ruth was played by whom?
11. On top of what building was *Gardening Club* filmed?
12. What instrument does astronomer Patrick Moore play?
13. *Where The Heart Is* was set in which county?
14. What is the name of *Rab C Nesbitt's* wife?
15. In *Whoops Apocalypse* which comedian played Commissar Solzhenitsyn?
16. Jamiroquai's lead singer, Jay Kay, composed the theme for which sporting ITV feature?
17. Who played the leading female role in *Triangle*?
18. Which actor links *The A-Team* to *Battlestar Galactica*?
19. Which *Emmerdale* couple renewed their wedding vows in Ripon Cathedral?
20. In *Bramwell*, what is the name of the infirmary?
21. Which astrologer has worked on both the BBC's *Breakfast Time* and GMTV?
22. Who was the Radio Times' Sexiest Woman on TV in 1997?
23. Who starred as *Lovejoy*?
24. Which descendent of the Bounty mutineer Fletcher Christian appeared as the cook on *Breakfast-Time*?
25. Whose characters included Marcel Wave and Gizzard Puke?
26. In *Peak Practice*, which female doctor replaced Beth Glover?
27. Which role was played by Harry Enfield in *Men Behaving Badly*?
28. Who is the presenter of *Blind Date*?
29. In which English county was the soap *Howard's Way* set?
30. Which US actor accompanied Martin Bell on his election campaign?

ANSWERS

## Crime 1 (See Quiz 2)

**1.** Capt. Dobie. **2.** Fitz. **3.** Limehouse. **4.** *Callan.* **5.** An Astrologer. **6.** Alan Dobie. **7.** Nigel le Valliant. **8.** Forensic Pathologist. **9.** Radio West. **10.** The American legal system. **11.** *LA Law.* **12.** Jaguar. **13.** Stacey Keach. **14.** Frank Cannon. **15.** Leo McKern. **16.** Customs & Excise. **17.** Elliot Ness. **18.** Perry Mason. **19.** Martin Shaw. **20.** *The Sweeney* (Sweeney Todd) **21.** Lt. Burt Samuels. **22.** Frank Burnside. **23.** *Moonlighting.* **24.** Budapest. **25.** Maigret. **26.** *Murder One.* **27.** Det. Andy Sipowicz. **28.** Dr Watson. **29.** *Verdict.* **30.** *Crimewatch.*

## QUIZ 2 Crime 1

LEVEL 2

**Answers: see Quiz 1, page 429**

1. Who was Starsky and Hutch's Chief?
2. Which character does Robbie Coltrane play in *Cracker*?
3. In which district of London was *The Chinese Detective* set?
4. Who did Lonely pass information to?
5. What was the profession of David Gradley's partner in *Zodiac*?
6. Which actor played *Cribb*?
7. Which actor links *Dangerfield* to *Casualty*?
8. What was Dangerfield's occupation?
9. Who did Eddie Shoestring work for?
10. What was the subject of *The Defenders*?
11. Which American drama series starred, amongst others, Jimmy Smitz and Susan Dey?
12. Which make of car does Morse drive?
13. Micky Spillane's 'Mike Hammer' was played by which actor?
14. Which detective was played by William Conrad?
15. Who portrayed Rumpole of the Bailey?
16. What was the subject of *The Knock*?
17. Which agent did Robert Stack play in *The Untouchables*?
18. Who did Paul Drake work for?
19. Who preceded Tim Piggott-Smith as *The Chief*?
20. Which TV series took its title from the cockney rhyming slang for Flying Squad?
21. Al Waxman played which character in *Cagney and Lacey*?
22. Which Frank was a DI in *The Bill*?
23. Which series starred Cybil Shepherd and Bruce Willis?
24. In which European city is *Cadfael* filmed?
25. Rupert Davies and Richard Harris both played which TV character?
26. Which series starred Daniel Benzali as a defence lawyer?
27. In *NYPD Blue*, which character's son had joined the police before being killed in a bar?
28. Edward Hardwicke and David Burke have both played which character?
29. Which court drama is an updated version of *Crown Court*?
30. Nick Ross presents which real-life crime programme?

ANSWERS

**Pot Luck 1 (See Quiz 1)**

**1.** Robinson. **2.** Cookery. **3.** Thriller Writer. **4.** Charlene. **5.** Robert Powell. **6.** James. **7.** Bloodhound. **8.** Richard Dimbleby. **9.** Motorbike & sidecar. **10.** Julie T. Wallace. **11.** In the roof garden of the BBC's Lime Grove Studios, West London. **12.** Xylophone. **13.** Yorkshire. **14.** Mary. **15.** Alexei Sayle. **16.** *Formula One Grands Prix*. **17.** Kate O'Mara. **18.** Dirk Benedict. **19.** Frank and Kim Tate. **20.** The Thrift. **21.** Russell Grant. **22.** Helen Mirren. **23.** Ian McShane. **24.** Glynn Christian. **25.** Kenny Everett. **26.** Erica Matthews. **27.** Dermot **28.** Cilla Black. **29.** Hampshire. **30.** David Soul.

## QUIZ 3 Sci-Fi 1

LEVEL 2

**Answers: see Quiz 4, page 432**

1. What race does bar-owner Quark belong to?
2. Which spaceship was powered by the Infinite Improbability Drive?
3. Where was *Quatermass II* set?
4. Who was the creator of *TekWar*?
5. Which star of *The Color Purple* is a regular in *Star Trek-Next Generation*?
6. In The *X-Files* what is Mulder's first name?
7. In *Babylon 5*, Londo Molari is the Ambassador for which race?
8. Who played Frank Bach in *Dark Skies*?
9. What was the name of Michael Knight's robot car?
10. In which series did Lori Singer play an on-line crime-buster?
11. Who on Red Dwarf is Holly?
12. Which creature did Dr. David Banner become when stressed?
13. Who did Lorne Greene play in *Battlestar Galactica*?
14. Which series featured Tweaky?
15. Which series written by Ray Bradbury starred Rock Hudson?
16. Where do the *Sliders* slide to?
17. What was the sixties SF series starring James Darren?
18. What, speaking chemically, were *Sapphire and Steel* supposed to be?
19. Where would you have found Old Bailey selling Rook stew at the Floating Market?
20. Which futuristic organisation featured in the science fiction drama *UFO*?
21. Who created *Space Precinct*?
22. Which character did Sally Knyvette play in *Blake's Seven*?
23. Which hero was aided by the Destiny Angels?
24. In which series did you meet the character Duncan Macleod?
25. What number was Patrick McGoohan?
26. In which series did Roddy McDowall play a chimpanzee?
27. Which electronic hero was aided by Desi Arnaz Jr?
28. Which character did George Takei play in *Star Trek*?
29. How were Homo Superior more commonly known?
30. Who is Data's brother?

ANSWERS

### TV Comedy 1 (See Quiz 4)

**1.** *Max Headroom.* **2.** Baldrick. **3.** *A Fine Romance.* **4.** Felicity Kendall. **5.** Ada Crosswell & Walter Bingly. **6.**Colonel Hall. **7.** Samantha Janus, Denise Van Outen, Natalie Walter. **8.** $13\frac{3}{4}$. **9.** Brother and sister. **10.** Nicholas Lyndhurst. **11.** Judy Dench. **12.** The AA. **13.** Annie Briggs. **14.** A leisure centre. **15.** Will Smith. **16.** *The Goodies.* **17.** Julia Watson & Robert Kermode. **18.** Administrative Affairs. **19.** *The Howerd Crowd.* **20.** Jasper Carrott & Robert Powell. **21.** Vince & Penny. **22.** James Bolam. **23.** 1943. **24.** *Whoops Baghdad.* **25.** Paul Greenwood. **26.** Desi Arnaz. **27.** Windsor Davies. **28.** Leonard Rossiter. **29.**William G. Stewart. **30.** Dougal & Jack.

## QUIZ 4 TV Comedy 1

LEVEL 2

**Answers: see Quiz 3, page 431**

1. Who was the computer-created character who developed out of a science fiction TV film starring Matt Frewer?
2. What was the name of Tony Robinson's *Blackadder* character?
3. Which series starred Geoffrey Palmer and Dame Judy Dench as a middle-aged couple?
4. Who went from *Solo* to become *The Mistress?*
5. In *For the Love of Ada*, who were in love?
6. Who was Bilko's commanding officer, played by Paul Ford?
7. Who play the *Babes In The Wood?*
8. How old was Adrian Mole when he wrote his Secret Diary?
9. In *Sykes*, how were Eric and Hatty related?
10. Who plays a Trotter brother and Gary Sparrow?
11. Which Dame starred in *A Fine Romance?*
12. What national motoring organisation was portrayed in *The Last Salute?*
13. Who in the series *Sitting Pretty* was described as "the Jackie Onassis of Bethnal Green"?
14. What was the setting for *The Brittas Empire?*
15. Which rap singer plays the title role in *The Fresh Prince of Bel-Air?*
16. In which comedy series did a giant cat terrorise London?
17. Who played the respective children of the rivals in *Never The Twain?*
18. What ministry did Jim Hacker run before becoming PM?
19. What was the name of Franklin Howerd's first TV series in 1952?
20. Who are *The Detectives?*
21. Who were "Just Good Friends"?
22. Which Likely Lad ended up a patient in *Only When I Laugh?*
23. In *Goodnight Sweetheart* which year is the hero transported back to?
24. What was the sequel to *Up Pompeii!?*
25. In *The Growing Pains of PC Penrose*, which actor played the title role?
26. What was the name of Lucille Ball's husband who starred with her in *I Love Lucy?*
27. Which army sergeant turned antiques dealer?
28. Who starred as Reginald Perrin?
29. Which *Fifteen-to-One* presenter produced *Bless This House?*
30. What are Father Ted's equally odd colleagues called?

ANSWERS

### Sci-Fi 1 (See Quiz 3)

**1.** Ferengi. **2.** The Heart of Gold. **3.** In a chemical plant. **4.** William Shatner. **5.** Whoopi Goldberg. **6.** Fox. **7.**Centauri. **8.** J.T.Walsh. **9.** KITT. **10.** *VR5*. **11.** Ship's computer. **12.** The Incredible Hulk. **13.** Adama. **14.** Buck Rogers. **15.** *The Martian Chronicles.* **16.** Parallel Universes. **17.** *The Time Tunnel.* **18.** Elements. **19.** *Neverwhere.* **20.** SHADO. **21.** Gerry Anderson. **22.** Jenna. **23.** *Captain Scarlet.* **24.** *Highlander.* **25.** 6. **26.** *Planet of the Apes.* **27.** *Automan.* **28.** Sulu. **29.** *The Tomorrow People.* **30.** Lor.

## QUIZ 5 Quiz & Games Shows 1

**Answers: see Quiz 4, page 434**

LEVEL 2

1. Who first said 'Come on down' in the UK?
2. On what show would you find contestants playing with Lightning?
3. Who preceded Des O'Connor as host of *Take Your Pick*?
4. Who presented *Bullseye*?
5. Who hosted *The Krypton Factor*?
6. Who co-hosted the first season of *Robot Wars* with Phillippa Forrester?
7. Who hosted *Punchlines*?
8. Who was the host of *Going for Gold*?
9. What was the children's version of *Criss Cross Quiz*?
10. How many celebrity guests appear each week on *Blankety Blank*?
11. What was the top prize on *Turner Round The World*?
12. Who originally presented *Dotto*?
13. Name the quiz featured on *Sunday Night at the London Palladium*?
14. Who was Larry Grayson's co-host on *The Generation Game*?
15. Who presented *Family Fortunes* after Bob Monkhouse?
16. Which game show has been chaired by both Robert Robinson and Bob Holness?
17. Which programme has been chaired by Max Robertson and Michael Parkinson?
18. Which trophy has been won by both an underground train driver and a cabbie?
19. Which show hosted by Bob Monkhouse required phone contestants to direct the shooting of an arrow at a target?
20. Glyn Daniel chaired which popular quiz in which an expert panel had to identify unusual objects?
21. Who had charge of the gong in the yes/no interlude on *Take Your Pick*?
22. Who was the first woman to present *Busman's Holiday*?
23. Which Channel 4 show was both presented and devised by Tim Vine?
24. Name the team captains on *Shooting Stars*.
25. What is Channel 5's gardening quiz called?
26. Who resides over the Channel 4 quiz *Fifteen-to-One*?
27. On *Countdown*, how many points are awarded for correctly solving the conundrum?
28. Who hosted *Wheel of Fortune* after Nicky Campbell and before John Leslie?
29. Who hosted *The $64,000 Question*?
30. What shape are the cells that hold the letters on the *Blockbusters* board?

ANSWERS

**Current Affairs 1 (See Quiz 6)**

**1.** *This Week.* **2.** Jan Leeming. **3.** ITN. **4.** Russel Harty. **5.** Janet Street-Porter. **6.** Rory Bremner. **7.** Michael Wood. **8.** Alan Titchmarsh. **9.** Judy Finnegan. **10.** Nick Owen. **11.** Magnus Pike, David Bellamy, Miriam Stoppard. **12.** Adrian Childs. **13.** Lime Grove. **14.** John Freeman. **15.** Roger Bolton. **16.** *Childrens' Hospital.* **17.** John Nott. **18.** Richard Madeley. **19.** Patrick Moore. **20.** Michael Parkinson. **21.** Channel 4. **22.** Prince Charles. **23.** Jane MacDonald. **24.** Susanne Charlton. **25.** Oliver Sacks. **26.** Robert Kilroy-Silk. **27.** The Adelphi. **28.** Martin Bashir. **29.** Michael Nicholson. **30.** Michael Palin.

## QUIZ 6 Current Affairs 1

LEVEL 2

**Answers: see Quiz 5, page 433**

1. Which series boasted: 'A window on the world behind the headlines'?
2. Which female newscaster hosted *Pebble Mill*?
3. *Roving Report* was produced by which news team?
4. Which chat show host clashed with singer Grace Jones?
5. *DEF II* was produced by whom?
6. Which comic impersonates Trevor Macdonald's news reading on Channel 4?
7. Who presented *In The Footsteps of Alexander the Great*?
8. Who replaced the late Geoff Hamilton on *Gardener's World*?
9. Who is Richard Madeley's partner?
10. Who was Nick of Anne and Nick?
11. Who formed the original panel of experts on *Don't Ask Me*?
12. Who is the presenter of *Working Lunch*?
13. In which studios was *Tonight* produced?
14. Name the presenter of *Face to Face*.
15. Who presents *Right to Reply*?
16. Which award-winning television programme featured life on the paediatric wards?
17. Who walked out on Sir Robin Day during an interview in 1983?
18. Name the presenter of *Eye of the Storm*.
19. Who presents *The Sky at Night*?
20. Which chat show host recently returned after many years away?
21. Jon Snow presents which Channel's evening news service?
22. The documentary *A Prince For Our Time* was about which modern Royal?
23. Which singer found fame on *The Cruise*?
24. Which TV weathergirl is the daughter of a famous footballer?
25. Who presented *The Island of the Colour Blind*?
26. Which silver-haired presenter hosts a weekday morning debate show?
27. What was the name of the Liverpool Hotel in the fly-on-the-wall series of the same name?
28. Who interviewed Princess Diana on *Panorama* in 1995?
29. Who was ITN's Mike in the Falklands?
30. Who travelled from *Pole to Pole*?

ANSWERS

### Quiz & Games Shows 1 (See Quiz 5)

**1.** Leslie Crowther. **2.** *The Gladiators*. **3.** Michael Miles. **4.** Jim Bowen. **5.** Gordon Burns. **6.** Jeremy Clarkeson. **7.** Lenny Bennet. **8.** Henry Kelly. **9.** *Junior Criss-Cross Quiz*. **10.** Six. **11.** Two round the world air tickets. **12.** Robert Gladwell. **13.** *Beat the Clock*. **14.** Isla St.Clair. **15.** Les Dennis. **16.** *Call My Bluff*. **17.** *Going for a Song*. **18.** The Mastermind Trophy. **19.** *The Golden Shot*. **20.** *Animal, Vegetable, Mineral*. **21.** Alec Dane. **22.** Sarah Kennedy. **23.** *Fluke*. **24.** Mark Lamarr and Ulrika Johnson. **25.** *The Great Garden Game*. **26.** William G. Stewart. **27.** Ten points. **28.** Bradley Walsh. **29.** Bob Monkhouse. **30.** Hexagonal.

## QUIZ 7 Childrens' TV 1

LEVEL 2

**Answers: see Quiz 8, page 436**

1. Which superheroes had a robot janitor called Mo and a computer named Sentinel 1?
2. Who lives in Bedrock?
3. Who said 'Time for Bed' on *The Magic Roundabout*?
4. What tubby schoolboy was played by Gerald Campion?
5. Who grew between *The Flowerpot Men*?
6. What is the name of *Captain Simian*'s band?
7. What was Supergran's real name?
8. Which singer co-presented *Record Breakers* with both Roy Castle and Kris Akabusi?
9. What were Orinoco and Uncle Bulgaria?
10. Which magician did Basil Brush first appear with?
11. What were Flicka and Fury?
12. Which hero rode the mighty Battle Cat?
13. Who was the creator of *The Snowman*?
14. Who provided the voice for Father Christmas?
15. Who was the leader of the *Thundercats*?
16. Who did Ted Cassidy play in *The Addams Family*?
17. Which twins presented *Record Breakers*?
18. What colour was Lady Penelope's Rolls Royce?
19. Where was the Thunderbirds' base?
20. Which actor/singer played Teggs in *Grange Hill*?
21. Who played Grandpa in *The Munsters*?
22. Which entertainer made Gordon the Gopher a hit on childrens' television?
23. Jay North portrayed which trouble-making comic character?
24. Name the *Trumpton* firemen.
25. Who played Circus Boy?
26. In *Battle of the Planets*, 7-Zark-7 watched over G-Force from Center Neptune. What was the full name of his robot dog, Rover?
27. Who was the creator of *Morph*?
28. Which cowboy said, 'Hi ho Silver'?
29. Which substance is harmful to Superman's powers?
30. Who rode Trigger?

ANSWERS

### TV Comedy 2 (See Quiz 8)

**1.** *Hi-De-Hi!* **2.** Mrs. Miggins. **3.** A Fireman. **4.** Patricia Hayes. **5.** Judd Hirsh. **6.** Robbie Coltrane. **7.** *You'll Never Get Rich.* **8.** Dawn French & Jennifer Saunders. **9.** Caroline Wheatley's. **10.** *A Very Peculiar Practice.* **11.** Bayview Retirement Home. **12.** David Jason. **13.** Lulu. **14.** *Mapp & Lucia.* **15.** Three. **16.** Eddie. **17.** Peter Bowles. **18.** Fry & Laurie. **19.** Peckham. **20.** *Tool Time.* **21.** Conny Kujau. **22.** Molly Sugden. **23.** *Absolutely Fabulous.* **24.** Bill Oddie, Tim Brooke-Taylor, Graeme Gardener. **25.** Joey. **26.** Bryan Pringle. **27.** Fred & Ethel Mertz. **28.** Felicity Kendall. **29.** *House.* **30.** Timothy Spall.

## QUIZ 8 TV Comedy 2

LEVEL 2

**Answers: see Quiz 7, page 435**

1. *Russ Abbott's Madhouse* regular Jeffrey Holland also played the part of an entertainer in which comedy series?
2. Who ran the Tea Shop in *Blackadder The Third*?
3. What was *Boon* before he became a despatch rider?
4. Who starred as Edna the *Inebriate Woman*?
5. Who played the title role in *Dear John: USA*?
6. Which larger than life actor played Danny McGlone in *Tutti Frutti*?
7. Name the original title of *The Phil Silvers Show* starring the character Bilko?
8. Which female comic duo formed part of the *Comic Strip* team?
9. Honor Blackman plays whose passionate mother in *The Upper Hand*?
10. Which series told of the misadventures of young Dr Stephen Daker?
11. Which retirement home features in *Waiting For God*?
12. Who played the head porter, Scullion, in *Porterhouse Blue*?
13. Which singer/actress played Adrian Mole's mother in *The Growing Pains of Adrian Mole*?
14. Who are Elizabeth and Emmeline better known as?
15. How many arms did Zaphod Beeblebrox have in the *Hitchhiker's Guide to the Galaxy*?
16. What is the name of Martin Crane's dog in *Frasier*?
17. Which *To the Manor Born* actor starred in Lytton's Diary?
18. Which duo link *Blackadder* to *Jeeves and Wooster*?
19. In which district of South London was *Only Fools and Horses* set?
20. Name the DIY show in *Home Improvement.*
21. Alexei Sayle played which forger in *Selling Hitler*?
22. Which *Are you Being Served* actress played Nerys Hughes' mum in the *Liver Birds?*
23. In which comedy would you find the character Bubbles?
24. Name *The Goodies.*
25. Peter Howitt played which Boswell in *Bread*?
26. Sgt Flagg was played by which actor in *The Growing Pains of PC Penrose*?
27. What were the names of Lucille Ball's neighbours in *I Love Lucy*?
28. Which *Good Life* actress went it alone in *Solo*?
29. Complete the title of this series starring Sid James: *Bless This...*?
30. Who played Barry in *Auf Wiedersehen Pet*?

ANSWERS

### Childrens' TV 1 (See Quiz 7)

**1.** *The Space Sentinels.* **2.** *The Flintstones.* **3.** Zebedee. **4.** Billy Bunter. **5.** Little Weed. **6.** *The Space Monkeys.* **7.** Smith. **8.** Cheryl Baker. **9.** Wombles. **10.** David Nixon. **11.** *TV Horses.* **12.** He-Man. **13.** Raymond Briggs. **14.** Mel Smith. **15.** Lion-O. **16.** Lurch. **17.** The McWhirter Twins. **18.** Pink. **19.** Tracy Island. **20.** Sean McGuire. **21.** Al Lewis. **22.** Philip Schofield. **23.** Dennis the Menace. **24.** Pugh, Pugh, Barney McGrew, Cuthbert, Dibble & Grubb. **25.** Mickey Dolenz. **26.** 1-Rover-1. **27.** Tony Hart. **28.** The Lone Ranger. **29.** Kryptonite. **30.** Roy Rogers.

## QUIZ 9 Soaps 1

LEVEL 2

**Answers: see Quiz 10, page 438**

1. Who ran the Rovers Return before the Duckworths?
2. Which soap was made in Esholt until 1997?
3. In *Eastenders*, what was Carol Jackson's sister called?
4. In *Dallas* what relation was Cliff Barnes to Pamela Ewing?
5. Which *Coronation Street* actress achieved *Rapid Results* when she donned a leotard?
6. What kind of establishment was *Crossroads*?
7. Which *Brookside* baddie was buried under a patio?
8. How many episodes in total of *Albion Market* were recorded?
9. What is "Curly" Watts first name?
10. The soap opera *United!* was about what?
11. Which soap was a spin-off from *Dynasty*?
12. What was the first major UK soap on Channel 5?
13. Who left *Dallas* and became *The Man From Atlantis*?
14. Who had a brief affair with Ricky Butcher in *EastEnders*?
15. Who left *Eastenders* to become a policeman in *Heartbeat*?
16. Who shot J.R.?
17. Who is Sarah's brother in *EastEnders*?
18. Who was kidnapped by a UFO in the *Colbys*?
19. In *Brookside*, who did the Farnhams pay to act as a surrogate mother?
20. What was ITV's first long running twice-weekly soap?
21. What connects *Eastenders* and *Are You Being Served*?
22. Who in *Coronation Street* decided to have blue and white cladding on the front of their house?
23. Which English actress played Alexis in *Dynasty*?
24. What role did Bill Treacher play in *Eastenders*?
25. In which district of Melbourne is *Neighbours* set?
26. What kind of market stall did Pete Beale own in *Eastenders*?
27. *Home and Away* is set in which fictitious bay?
28. Who is the longest serving member of *Coronation Street*?
29. Where did Alexis marry Cecil Colby?
30. Which actress, better known for her comic roles, plays the Mitchell brothers' mum?

ANSWERS

### Drama 1 (See Quiz 10)

**1.** *Fantasy Island.* **2.** *Shane.* **3.** Mike Connors. **4.** His son. **5.** Robert Shaw. **6.** Beau. **7.** Bob Hoskins. **8.** Michael Gambon. **9.** *Dixon of Dock Green.* **10.** *Ultraviolet.* **11.** The Shiloh Ranch. **12.** Alex Hayley. **13.** Robert Louis Stevenson's *Treasure Island.* **14.** *The Prisoner.* **15.** Walnut Grove. **16.** The Bellamys. **17.** *The Chancer.* **18.** Hawaii. **19.** George Eliot. **20.** Wentworth Detention Centre. **21.** Sir Alec Guinness. **22.** Rory Calhoun. **23.** Margaret Kockwood. **24.** Stephanie Cole. **25.** Clive Mantle. **26.** Ferryfield Airport, Kent. **27.** Dame Peggy Ashcroft. **28.** His parents disappeared in the jungle. **29.** Roger Moore. **30.** Leslie Grantham.

# QUIZ 10 Drama 1

LEVEL 2

**Answers: see Quiz 9, page 437**

1. On which Island would you find Mr Rorke?
2. David Carradine starred in which Western series?
3. Who was *The Undercover Agent?*
4. Richard Rogers played which relation to William Tell in *The Adventures of William Tell?*
5. Who played Dan Tempest in *The Buccaneers?*
6. What was the name of Maverick's English cousin?
7. Which actor starred in the TV version of *Pennies from Heaven?*
8. Who starred as *The Singing Detective?*
9. What is the longest running police series on British TV?
10. Which 1998 vampire series starred Jack Davenport?
11. On which ranch was *The Virginian* set?
12. Who wrote the book on which the seventies mini series *Roots* was based?
13. The series *The Adventures of Long John Silver* was based on which book?
14. Which TV series contained the line, 'I am not a number, I am a free man'?
15. In which town is *The Little House on the Prairie?*
16. For whose household did Mr Hudson and Mrs Bridges work?
17. In which series did ex-investment banker Steven Crane help save a midlands car firm?
18. The 1979 mini-series *From Here to Eternity* was set in which US state at the time of Pearl Harbour?
19. Who wrote *Middlemarch?*
20. Which prison is *Prisoner Cell Block H* set in?
21. Who played the title role in *Smiley's People?*
22. Who was *The Texan?*
23. Who played the owner of *The Royalty Hotel*, Mrs Mollie Miller?
24. Which actress starred in *Tenko* and was later seen *Waiting for God?*
25. Who plays *Casualty*'s Little John?
26. At which real-life airport was the setting for *Garry Halliday?*
27. Which Dame starred in *Jewel in the Crown?*
28. How was *Jungle Boy* orphaned?
29. Who, early in his career, played Ivanhoe and Beau Maverick?
30. Which former publican ran *The Paradise Club?*

ANSWERS

**Soaps 1 (See Quiz 9)**

**1.** Bet Gilroy. **2.** *Emmerdale*. **3.** April. **4.** Brother. **5.** Beverly Callard. **6.** A motel. **7.** Trevor Jordache. **8.** 100. **9.** Norman. **10.** A football team. **11.** *The Colbys*. **12.** *Family Affairs*. **13.** Patrick Duffy. **14.** Nathalie. **15.** Nick Berry. **16.** Sue Ellen. **17.** Tony. **18.** Fallon. **19.** Jacqui Dixon. **20.** *Emergency-Ward* 10. **21.** Actress Wendy Richards. **22.** The Duckworths. **23.** Joan Collins. **24.** Arthur Fowler. **25.** Erinsborough. **26.** Fruit stall. **27.** Summer Bay. **28.** William Roache (Ken Barlow). **29.** In a hospital. **30.** Barbara Windsor.

## QUIZ 11 Pot Luck 2

LEVEL 2

**Answers: see Quiz 12, page 440**

1. Who presented *Son Of The Incredibly Strange Film Show*?
2. Peter Capaldi played The Angel Islington in which surreal BBC 2 series?
3. Who hosted drama workshops as the spoof "Professional Personality", Nicholas Craig?
4. Who or what was Orac?
5. In *Drop the Dead Donkey*, whose catchphrase was "I'm not here"?
6. What was Reggie Perrin's boss called?
7. Who plays *Dr. Quinn, Medicine Woman*?
8. Where did Paula Yates hold interviews on *The Big Breakfast*?
9. Which character's son had an affair with Sandy Merrick in *Emmerdale*?
10. Who was the presenter of the 1940's series *Television Garden*?
11. Which Geoff Hamilton series was first shown after his death?
12. The series *Lovejoy* was based on whose novels?
13. Where was Dot living before returning to Walford in 1997?
14. When did John Logie Baird first experiment in colour TV?
15. Who played the title role in the series *Kate*?
16. Which UK river featured in *Howard's Way*?
17. Where does *Master Chef* presenter Loyd Grossman originate from?
18. In *Brothers In Law*, Richard Briers played which up and coming barrister?
19. Who took a break from *Dr Finlay's Casebook* to be 'Mr Justice Duncannon'?
20. In *The Cheaters*, which insurance company did John Hunter work for?
21. Who first presented *Gardening Club* in 1955?
22. Who hosted *Jim'll Fix It*?
23. In what year was the first televised church service?
24. Which antiques expert starred in the original series of *Antiques Roadshow*?
25. In which program were three children sent through time hunting the Nidus, with which they could free the magician Rothgo from the trap of his evil enemy, Belor?
26. In which year was the *Radio Times* first published?
27. What was the name of the adult version of *Tiswas*?
28. Who presented *Saturday Stayback*?
29. In which series would you find Benton Frazer?
30. Who is Suzy Aitchison's comedienne mother?

ANSWERS

### TV Comedy 3 (See Quiz 12)

**1.** Ted Danson (*Cheers & Gulliver's Travels*). **2.** Bob was a girl. **3.** Rodney Trotter. **4.** Tom Selleck. **5.** Hywell Bennett. **6.** Dermot. **7.** Sir Harry Secombe. **8.** Army Motor Pool. **9.** A padlock. **10.** Dave Lister. **11.** Grace Brothers. **12.** A University Campus. **13.** Jacko. **14.** All starred Richard Beckinsale. **15.** Students. **16.** *Watching*. **17.** *All In Good Faith*. **18.** Alf Garnett. **19.** Depressed / Paranoid. **20.** The Nag's Head. **21.** Marty Feldman's. **22.** *The Two Ronnies*. **23.** Paul McCartney. **24.** 5, Sandra, Denise, Theo, Vanessa, Rudy. **25.** Catherine Zeta-Jones. **26.** Ben. **27.** New York. **28.** In a bank. **29.** Grace Allen. **30.** Cannon and Ball.

# QUIZ 12 TV Comedy 3

LEVEL 2

**Answers: see Quiz 11, page 439**

1. Which barman went on to become a Swift creation?
2. What was unusual about Bob in *Blackadder II*?
3. In *Only Fools and Horses*, who was studying computing?
4. Which former private investigator appeared as Monica's boyfriend in *Friends*?
5. Who starred as *Shelley*?
6. What was Harry Enfield's character called in *Men Behaving Badly*?
7. This Welsh singer and comedian provided voices for the telly Goons. Who is he?
8. What was the function of the army platoon to which Bilko was attached?
9. How did Mr Bean lock his car?
10. Who played the guitar on *Red Dwarf*?
11. What was the name of the store in *Are You Being Served?*
12. Where was the Practice based in the series *A Very Peculiar Practice*?
13. In *Brush Strokes*, what was the name of the lead character?
14. What is the connection between *Porridge, Bloomers* and *Rising Damp*?
15. What was the occupation of *The Young Ones*?
16. In which show did Brenda and Malcolm enjoy ornithology?
17. Which late '80s sitcom starred Richard Briers as a struggling inner-city vicar?
18. Whose son in law was a randy scouse git?
19. What was Marvin the Android's mental problem in the *Hitchihiker's Guide to the Galaxy*?
20. What is the name of the pub in *Only Fools and Horses*?
21. Whose first comedy series was called simply *Marty*?
22. If you heard, "So it's goodnight from me, and it's goodnight from him," which programme would you be watching?
23. Which former Beatles songwriter made a guest appearance in *Bread*?
24. How many children do Cliff and Claire Huxtable have in *The Cosby Show*?
25. Which actress played the role of Ma and Pa Larkin's eldest daughter, Marietta?
26. In *Two Point Four Children* what is the name of Bill's husband?
27. In which city is the sitcom *Spin City* set?
28. In *The Lucy Show*, Lucille Ball worked where?
29. George Burns appeared on TV with one of his wives. Whom?
30. Which duo starred in *Plaza Patrol*?

ANSWERS

## Pot Luck 2 (See Quiz 11)

**1.** Johnathan Ross. **2.** *Neverwhere*. **3.** Nigel Planer. **4.** A computer. **5.** Gus. **6.** CJ. **7.** Jane Seymour. **8.** On the bed in her 'Boudoir'. **9.** Alan Turner. **10.** Fred Streeter. **11.** *Paradise Gardens*. **12.** Johnathan Gash. **13.** Gravesend. **14.** 1927. **15.** Phyllis Calvert. **16.** The River Hamble, Hampshire. **17.** Boston, USA. **18.** Roger Thursby. **19.** Andrew Cruickshank. **20.** The Eastern Insurance Company. **21.** Percy Thrower. **22.** Jimmy Saville. **23.** 1946. **24.** Arthur Negis. **25.** *Into The Labyrinth*. **26.** 1923. **27.** OTT. **28.** Chris Tarrant. **29.** *Due South*. **30.** June Whitfeild.

## QUIZ 13 Crime 2

LEVEL 2

**Answers: see Quiz 14, page 442**

1. Who is the surrogate father in *NYPD Blue*?
2. What rank were Henry and Ray in *Hill Street Blues*?
3. Which role was played by both Loretta Swit and Sharon Gless?
4. Which police officer is central to the series *Heartbeat*?
5. What character did Robert Lee play in *The Chinese Detective*?
6. Which actor played Dodie and Boyle's boss?
7. In *Cribb*, name the famous elephant at London Zoo that was central to the plot in the episode called '*The Lost Trumpet*'.
8. Who played the title role in *Jemima Shore Investigates*?
9. What department did George Carter work for?
10. Which actor played Quincy?
11. What is Skinner's FBI title in the *X-Files*?
12. Who is the creator of *Cracker*?
13. Which orchestra played the theme from *Van Der Valk*?
14. Who does *Columbo* frequently cite as his inspiration?
15. Who played Dan Tanner?
16. Name the female detective in *Cracker*.
17. Where was the setting for *Bergerac*?
18. Which two actresses originally made up the team with Jill Gascoine in *C.A.T.S Eyes*?
19. In *Knight Rider*, Michael Knight worked for the Foundation for what?
20. What was the name of Kojak's brother?
21. Jeremy Brett played which detective?
22. Name the central character in the series *Juliet Bravo*.
23. What did TV detective Jim Rockford live in?
24. Who sang the theme song from *Moonlighting*?
25. Who frequently said the words, 'Evening all'?
26. Who played Elliot Ness in the TV version of *The Untouchables*?
27. Whose catchphrase was, 'Book him, Danno'?
28. Name the actress who plays Sgt. June Ackland in *The Bill*.
29. What was the name of the twisted tycoon played by Stanley Tucci in *Murder One*?
30. Name Perry Mason's female assistant.

ANSWERS

### Sci-Fi 2 (See Quiz 14)

**1.** Lead. **2.** Richard Anderson. **3.** *Seaquest DSV*. **4.** Jon Pertwee. **5.** Zen. **6.** Bernard. **7.** Manimal. **8.** B'Ellana Torres. **9.** A super-computer. **10.** Troy Tempest. **11.** Danny John-Jules. **12.** Dr. David Banner. **13.** Erin Grey. **14.** Odo. **15.** Radioactive. **16.** Gene Roddenberry. **17.** Peter Jones. **18.** *The Outer Limits*. **19.***Space 1999*. **20.** Cats. **21.** Stargate SG1. **22.** V. **23.** Leo McKern. **24.** The 1980s. **25.** Mr. X. **26.** Z'ha'dum. **27.** KARR. **28.** *The Invaders*. **29.** Project Blue Book. **30.** David McCallum.

## QUIZ 14 Sci-Fi 2

LEVEL 2

**Answers: see Quiz 13, page 441**

1. Which dark, shielding 'Element' assisted *Sapphire & Steel* in their first adventure?
2. Who played Oscar in *The Six Million Dollar Man*?
3. Which series features Roy Schneider in underwater adventures?
4. Who played the third incarnation of *Doctor Who*?
5. What was the Liberator's computer called?
6. What was Professor Quatermass' first name?
7. Simon McCorkindale starred as a shape-shifter in which series?
8. What is the name of *Voyager*'s half-Klingon crew-member?
9. In *A For Andromeda*, what did an alien radio signal instruct scientists to build?
10. Who was the captain of the *Stingray*?
11. Which actor played The Cat in *Red Dwarf*?
12. Who played Dr. David Banner in *The Incredible Hulk*?
13. Who played Buck Roger's partner Wilma Deering?
14. Which character does Rene Auberjonois play in *Star Trek: Deep Space Nine*?
15. What was special about the spider that bit Peter Parker and gave him special powers?
16. Who created *Star Trek*?
17. Who was the narrator of *The Hitchikers Guide to the Galaxy*?
18. Which programme starts with the words 'do not adjust your sets'?
19. In which series would you find Moonbase Apha?
20. What pet species did Alf most like eating?
21. Which series is a spinoff from a fim starring Kurt Russell and James Spader?
22. In which mini-series would you have seen Diana swallow a rat?
23. Who played the last Number 2?
24. In which future decade was *UFO* set?
25. In the *X-Files* who killed the Red-headed Man?
26. Which planet was the home of the Shadows in *Babylon 5*?
27. What was KITT's evil twin called?
28. Which 60s SF series did Roy Thinnes play David Vincent?
29. Which series was based on the US Air Force Project Blue Book UFO investigations?
30. Who was *The Invisible Man* in the 1970s?

ANSWERS

### Crime 2 (See Quiz 13)

**1.** Greg Medavoy. **2.** Lieutenant. **3.** Chris Cagney. **4.** PC Nick Rowan. **5.** Joe Ho, John's father. **6.** Gordon Jackson. **7.** Jumbo. **8.** Patricia Hodge. **9.** The Flying Squad. **10.** Jack Klugman. **11.** Assistant Director. **12.** Jimmy McGovern. **13.** The Simon May Orchestra. **14.** His wife. **15.** Robert Urich. **16.** Penhaligon. **17.** Jersey. **18.** Leslie Ash and Rosalyn Landor. **19.** Law & Government. **20.** Stavros. **21.** Sherlock Holmes. **22.** Insp. Jean Darblay. **23.** A Trailer. **24.** Al Jarreau. **25.** George Dixon (*Dixon of Dock Green*). **26.** Robert Stark. **27.** Steve McGarrett (*Hawaii Five-O*). **28.** Trudie Goodwin. **29.** Richard Cross. **30.** Della Street.

## QUIZ 15 Animals & Nature 1

LEVEL 2

**Answers: see Quiz 16, page 444**

1. Who plays Eddie in *Frasier*?
2. What was *The Littlest Hobo*?
3. What did the series of *Creature Comforts* animations advertise?
4. What product is associated with labrador puppies?
5. What was the name of the first award-winning documentary about Meercats?
6. Which childrens' show was presented by Terry Nutkin and Chris Packham?
7. Asta the dog featured in which series?
8. Who presented *Animal Magic*?
9. Vet David Grant appears in which RSPCA based series?
10. Who produced a television series named *Zoo Quest* in the 1950's?
11. In which series does Anton Rodgers play a vet?
12. Which breed of dog was Tricky Woo in *All Creatures Great and Small*?
13. Henry is a cartoon what?
14. What type of terrain is the land surround The Skeleton Coast?
15. What was the name of the Harts' dog in *Hart to Hart*?
16. Which city zoo sponsored the 1950's wildlife series *Zoo Quest*?
17. Which naturalist presented *Look* and *Faraway Look* in the 1950's and 1960's?
18. What is unusual about the Sundew?
19. Who was the posthumous presenter of *Paradise Gardens*?
20. What is the name of the cartoon dog in *Garfield & Friends*?
21. Where do you find the Giant Tortoise?
22. What type of creature does Rex Hunt work most closely with?
23. *Life in the Freezer* featured the natural history of which place?
24. Author and presenter Gerald Durrell had a zoo where?
25. In the title of the show, what was ... *Flicka*?
26. Who presented *Gardener's World* in 1998?
27. What was the name of David Bellamy's first TV series in1972?
28. Do penguins live at the North or South pole?
29. The naturalist Aubrey Buxton was the original presenter of which long-running ITV nature series?
30. What word commonly describes people who follow tornados?

ANSWERS

### TV Comedy 4 (See Quiz 16)

**1.** 12. **2.** Mrs Merton. **3.** John Lithgow. **4.** Miranda Richardson. **5.** Anthony Booth. **6.** Paul Eddington. **7.** He went to trek around the World. **8.** David and Clive Swift.. **9.** Master Sergeant. **10.** Phoebe. **11.** Sid James. **12.** Geraldine Granger. **13.** Pandora. **14.** Edina Monsoon. **15.** *You Rang, M'Lord?* **16.** Joanna Kanska. **17.** *Tutti Frutti.* **18.** Arnold Rimmer. **19.** *Hole in My Shoe.* **20.** Sunshine Cab Co. **21.** Jimmy Edwards. **22.** Mrs Overall. **23.** Liverpool. **24.** *Surgical Spirit.* **25.** Hercules. **26.** Bomber. **27.** David & Jenny. **28.** Excused-Boots Bisley. **29.** Nigel Hawthorn. **30.** Timothy Lumsden.

## QUIZ 16 TV Comedy 4

LEVEL 2

**Answers: see Quiz 15, page 443**

1. How many *Fawlty Towers* episodes were made?
2. Who is Caroline Aherne's alter-ego?
3. Who plays Dr Dick Solomon, the alien professor in *Third Rock from the Sun*?
4. Who played Queen Elizabeth I in the second series of *Blackadder*?
5. Who in real life is Cherie's dad and, on TV, was Alf's son-in-law?
6. Which *Prime Minister* appeared in *The Good Life*?
7. Why did Dermot leave *Men Behaving Badly*?
8. Which brothers link *Drop the Dead Donkey* and *Keeping up Appearances*?
9. What rank was Ernie Bilko in *The Phil Silvers Show*?
10. Who is Gary's wartime wife in *Goodnight Sweetheart*?
11. Who played Hancock's sidekick Sid?
12. What is *The Vicar of Dibley* called?
13. What was the name of Adrian Mole's girlfriend?
14. Who employed Bubbles as an incompetent PA?
15. Which sitcom was set in Lord Meldrum's stately home?
16. Which actress played Daker's Polish distraction Grete Grotowska in *A Very Peculiar Practice*?
17. Which comedy show in the 80s was named after a Little Richard hit?
18. Who was the main 'Smeg-Head'?
19. Neil from *The Young Ones* had a chart-topper with which song?
20. What was the cab firm called in *Taxi*?
21. The comedy *Whack-O!* starred who as the headmaster?
22. What was the name of the charlady in *Acorn Antiques*?
23. In which city did the Boswell family reside in *Bread*?
24. Which comedy featured Dr Sheila Sabatini?
25. What was the name of the horse owned by the Steptoes?
26. The ex-wrestler Pat Roach played which *Auf Wiedersehen Pet* character?
27. In *Two Point Four Children* what are the names of the children?
28. What was Private Bisley's nickname in *The Army Game*?
29. Who played Sir Humphrey Appleby in *Yes, Minister*?
30. What was the name of Ronnie Corbett's character in *Sorry!*?

ANSWERS

### Animals & Nature 1 (See Quiz 15)

**1.** Moose. **2.** A German Shepherd dog. **3.** Electricity. **4.** Andrex Toilet Tissue. **5.** *Meercats United.* **6.** *The Really Wild Show.* **7.** The Thin Man. **8.** Johnny Morris. **9.** *Animal Hospital.* **10.** David Attenborough. **11.** *Noah's Ark.* **12.** Pekinese. **13.** Cat. **14.** Desert. **15.** Freeway. **16.** London Zoo. **17.** Peter Scott. **18.** Carnivorous Plant. **19.** Geoff Hamilton. **20.** Odie. **21.** The Galapagos Islands. **22.** Fish. **23.** Antarctica. **24.** Isle of Wight. **25.** *My Friend...* **26.** Alan Titchmarsh. **27.** Bellamy on Botany. **28.** South. **29.** *Survival.* **30.** Chasers.

## QUIZ 17 Soaps 2

LEVEL 2

**Answers: see Quiz 18, page 446**

1. What was Ian Beale's catering business called?
2. Which Army captain played Mr Swindley in *Coronation Street*?
3. What did Raquel train to become?
4. In *Crossroads*, whose fiancee died on their wedding day?
5. Which tennis player's former father-in-law appeared in *Peyton Place*?
6. What was the name of the cook in *Dynasty*?
7. What was Tracy Corkhill's occupation in *Brookside*?
8. In *Crossroads*, who shot David Hunter?
9. Which actor played the market superintendent Derek in *Albion Market*?
10. Who are the feuding families in *Dallas*?
11. What is the name of the local football club in *EastEnders*?
12. What was Gail's maiden name in *Coronation Street*?
13. What was Lorna Cartwright's addiction in *EastEnders*?
14. Which soap role had Barbara Bel Geddes and Donna Reed shared?
15. Who was the Sheriff in *Flamingo Road*?
16. What domestic situation is Ken Barlow's claim to fame in *Coronation Street*?
17. After his character died in *Coronation Street*, actor Alan Rothwell appeared as a drug addict in which other soap?
18. Who played Constance McKenzie in *Peyton Place*?
19. What was the name of Jimmy Corkhill's son in *Brookside*?
20. Which Dallas star was in *I Dream of Jeannie* in the 1960s?
21. What was the name of the hospital that featured in *Emergency-Ward 10*?
22. How is Spider Nugent related to Emily Bishop in *Coronation Street*?
23. In *Coronation Street*, what does Mike Baldwin's company Underworld produce?
24. Which comedian lost his sense of humour as Frank in *EastEnders*?
25. What placed Kylie Corkhill's life in danger whilst she was in Sinbad's shop?
26. Which *Coronation Street* star went on to become a district nurse?
27. What role did Bill Treacher play in *EastEnders*?
28. Who ran The Kool for Kutz hairdressers in *EastEnders*?
29. What is the name of Grant and Tiffany's daughter in *EastEnders*?
30. In *Brookside*, whom did the Farnhams pay to act as a surrogate mother?

ANSWERS

### Childrens' TV 2 (See Quiz 18)

**1.** Oliver Tobias. **2.** Paddington. **3.** *Jackanory.* **4.** Snowy. **5.** The Teletubbies. **6.** Wimpey. **7.** Brown. **8.** Michael Rodd. **9.** Peter Glaze. **10.** Chihuahua. **11.** Woodstock. **12.** The Childrens' Television Workshop. **13.** Rag Dolly Anna. **14.** Huey, Louie & Dewey. **15.** Burt Ward. **16.** Basil Brush. **17.** Leila Williams. **18.** Anna Sewell. **19.** Daktari. **20.** Emma Forbes. **21.** Angelo. **22.** The Penguin. **23.** Mrs Goggins. **24.** Dave Prowse. **25.** Bamm-Bamm & Pebbles. **26.** Mr Benn. **27.** Bug Juice. **28.** Peter Sallis. **29.** Hanna-Barbara. **30.** John Gorman.

## QUIZ 18 Children's TV 2

LEVEL 2

**Answers: see Quiz 17, page 445**

1. Who played Arthur of the Britons?
2. Sir Michael Hordern was the voice of which popular bear?
3. Which storytelling programme had guest narrators?
4. What was the name of TinTin's dog?
5. Who lives in Home Hill?
6. Who was Popeye's hamburger-eating friend?
7. What was the surname of Just William?
8. Who presented *Screen Test*?
9. In *Crackerjack*, who played the comic stooge?
10. What type of dog is Ren?
11. What is the name of Snoopy's feathered friend?
12. Who produces *Sesame Street*?
13. Pat Coombs appeared with which doll?
14. Name Donald Duck's nephews.
15. Who played Robin in *Batman*?
16. With which puppet did Rodney Bewes appear?
17. Name the first female presenter of *Blue Peter*.
18. Who was the author of Black Beauty?
19. Which animal series starred Marshall Thompson?
20. Who co-presented the first series of *Live & Kicking* with Andi Peters?
21. What was the alien that Mike discovered in a wardrobe called?
22. Burgess Meredith played which character in *Batman*?
23. Who is the postmistress in Greendale?
24. Who was the Green Cross Code man?
25. Name the children in *The Flintstones*.
26. Who visited a costume shop before embarking on various adventures?
27. What is the daytime series about American children at summer camp called?
28. Who is the voice of Wallace from the duo Wallace and Gromit?
29. Which company produced *Huckleberry Hound* and *Yogi Bear*?
30. Which member of *Scaffold* appeared in *Tiswas*?

ANSWERS

### Soaps 2 (See Quiz 17)

**1.** The Meal Machine. **2.** Arthur Lowe. **3.** A Beautician. **4.** Benny. **5.** John McEnroe (Ryan O'Neal). **6.** Mrs Gunnerson. **7.** Hairdresser. **8.** Rosemary. **9.** David Hargreaves. **10.** The Ewings and the Barnes. **11.** Walford Town. **12.** Potter. **13.**Alcohol. **14.** Miss Ellie in *Dallas*. **15.** Titus Sample. **16.** He was the first to have an inside toilet. **17.** Brookside. **18.** Dorothy Malone. **19.** Jimmy Junior. **20.** Larry Hagman. **21.** Oxbridge General Hospital. **22.** Nephew. **23.** Underwear. **24.** Mike Reid. **25.** A gas-explosion. **26.** Sarah Lancashire. **27.**Arthur Fowler. **28.** Steve & Della. **29.** Courtney. **30.** Jacqui Dixon.

## QUIZ 19 Pot Luck 3

LEVEL 2

**Answers: see Quiz 20, page 448**

1. Who played John Wilder in *The Power Game*?
2. The original presenters of the BBC'S *Breakfast Time* were Frank Bough, Selena Scott, and one other. Who?
3. Who introduces *It'll be Alright on the Night*?
4. Which artist played a digeridoo?
5. *The Simpsons* became the longest-running cartoon family in 1997, replacing whom?
6. Who was the original weatherman on BBC's *Breakfast Time*?
7. Which character in *EastEnders* is Mark's wife?
8. In which year did the BBC TV schools service begin?
9. Which actress had to survive on her own on a desert isle?
10. Who is Jennifer Paterson's cooking partner?
11. What was the name of the first space ship used by *Blake's 7*?
12. Which fictional village is *Heartbeat* set in?
13. Which rodent starred on *TVAM*?
14. What was an Admag, banned by Parliament in 1963?
15. Who presented *The Human Body*?
16. What is the profession of the major characters in *This Life*?
17. What did the ARP Warden call Captain Mainwaring?
18. In which decade was *Hi-De-Hi!* first set?
19. Which early evening programme do Mel and Sue introduce?
20. Who is the current host of *Going for a Song*?
21. Which actress played *The Sculptress*?
22. Who was *Lovejoy*'s original love interest?
23. Which actor was Maxwell Smart?
24. Who played Tom Howard's wife in *Howard's Way*?
25. In which city was PI Daniel Pike based?
26. Who moved from *Blue Peter* in 1996 to *Songs of Praise*?
27. What TV first occurred during the 1953 Naval Review at Spithead?
28. Who played Adam Cartwright in *Bonanza*?
29. Which satellite was used for the first Transatlantic broadcast?
30. In what year did *The Sky at Night* begin?

ANSWERS

### TV Comedy 5 (See Quiz 20)

**1.** Tony Robinson. **2.** 'I only arsked'. **3.** Roseanne. **4.** *Porterhouse Blue*. **5.** Marcus. **6.** Globelink News. **7.** Bootsie. **8.** Neil Morrisey. **9.** Harry Lembeck & Allan Melvin. **10.** Gian Sammarco. **11.** Paul Nicholas. **12.** Joan Rivers. **13.** The 6th. **14.** Dr Bob Buzzard. **15.** Stonehenge. **16.** David Jason. **17.** Terry Gilliam. **18.** Edie. **19.** Desmond Morris. **20.** Frank Carson. **21.** Peggy Mount. **22.** Cannon & Ball. **23.** *Cheers*. **24.** Mrs Doyle. **25.** Gemma Palmer. **26.** Bernard. **27.** A parrot. **28.** *The Young Ones*. **29.** Kenneth Waller. **30.** Barbara Lott.

## QUIZ 20 TV Comedy 5

LEVEL 2

**Answers: see Quiz 19, page 447**

1. Name the actor who played Rowan Atkinson's *Blackadder* sidekick.
2. What was Bernard Breslaw's catchphrase in *The Army Game*?
3. Which US character has children called Becky, Darlene and DJ?
4. David Jason played Skullion in which series?
5. What is the name of Dorien's husband in *Birds of a Feather*?
6. What is the name of *Drop The Dead Donkey*'s TV news company?
7. When Granada revived *Bootsie and Snudge* in 1974, who had become a millionnaire?
8. Who plays Tony in *Men Behaving Badly*?
9. Who played Bilko's accomplices Corporals Barbarella and Henshaw?
10. Which actor played Adrian Mole?
11. In *The River*, the part played by David Essex was originally intended for which other well known singer?
12. Which comedienne presented *Can We Talk*?
13. At the end of which series of *Hancock's Half Hour* did Sid James leave the show?
14. In *A Very Peculiar Practice*, which doctor, played by David Troughton, didn't like his patients?
15. Which famous ancient site did Edina rearrange for a fashion show in *Ab Fab*?
16. Who played Blanco in *Porridge*?
17. Who was the American Python?
18. Which character does Thora Hird play in *Last of the Summer Wine*?
19. Who was the presenter of *Zoo Time*?
20. Whose catchphrase is "It's the way I tell 'em"?
21. Who played the 'dragon' in *George and The Dragon*?
22. Which comedy duo have the first names Tommy and Bobby?
23. Which Channel 4 sitcom led to the spin off *Frasier*?
24. What is the name of Father Ted's doting housekeeper?
25. What was the name of the central character in *Solo*?
26. What was the name of Sir Humphrey's over-zealous assistant in *Yes, Minister*?
27. What was Lady Lavender's pet, 'Captain', in *You Rang M'Lord*?
28. Who had a landlord called Jerzy Balowski?
29. In *Bread*, which actor played Grandad?
30. Which actress played the dreaded mother in *Sorry!*?

ANSWERS

### Pot Luck 3 (See Quiz 19)

**1.** Patrick Wymark. **2.** Nick Ross. **3.** Dennis Norden. **4.** Rolf Harris. **5.** *The Flintstones*. **6.** Francis Wilson. **7.** Ruth. **8.** September 1957. **9.** Joanna Lumley. **10.** Clarrisa Dickson Wright. **11.** The Liberator. **12.** Aidensfield. **13.** Roland Rat. **14.** An advertisement broadcast in the guise of a genuine programme. **15.** Sir Robert Winston. **16.** Lawyers. **17.** Napoleon. **18.** 1950s. **19.** *Late Lunch*. **20.** Michael Parkinson. **21.** Pauline Quirke. **22.** Lady Jane Felsham. **23.** Don Adams. **24.** Jan Harvey. **25.** Glasgow. **26.** Diane-Lousie Jordan. **27.** The first BBC TV broadcast from a ship at sea. **28.** Pernell Roberts. **29.** Telstar 1. **30.** 1957.

# QUIZ 21 Drama 2

LEVEL 2

**Answers: see Quiz 22, page 450**

1. Who played Lady Chatterley?
2. Who was the star of *Lou Grant* and *Rich Man, Poor Man*?
3. Who was the creator of *ER*?
4. In the 1950's, Conrad Philips was famous for playing which role?
5. Who played Bart in *Maverick*?
6. In which city was *Gunsmoke* set?
7. Keith Michell starred as which King Henry?
8. What was Zoë's job in *May to December*?
9. In *Blade on the Feather*, who starred as the retired Soviet spy?
10. Who sang the theme from *Rawhide*?
11. What was McCallum?
12. In which year was Dixon promoted from Police Constable to Sergeant in *Dixon of Dock Green*?
13. Jon Finch played which Australian outlaw?
14. In the serial *Cathy Come Home* which actor played Cathy's husband?
15. What was Tinker's surname in *Lovejoy*?
16. Who played the sheriff in *American Gothic*?
17. Which Canadian actor later seen in *Bonanza* starred in *Sailor of Fortune*?
18. What happens to the message tape in *Mission Impossible*?
19. Who took over from David Caruso in *NYPD Blue*?
20. What did Yozzer famously want?
21. What was the name of the evil organisation in *The Man From UNCLE*?
22. Which actress played the fiercely critical character Maud in *Flickers*?
23. Who was promoter Frank Stubbs?
24. What was the name of the cook in *Rawhide*?
25. Who played *The Virginian*?
26. What was the name of Big John's brother-in-law in *The High Chapparel*?
27. Margaret Lockwood played which character in *The Flying Swan*?
28. Hari Kumar in *Jewel In The Crown* was played by which actor?
29. In which city is *Hill Street Blues* set?
30. Who starred as an obnoxious gossip columnist named Lytton?

ANSWERS

**Crime 3 (See Quiz 22)**

**1.** Tim Vincent. **2.** 1937. **3.** Jaye Griffiths. **4.** *The Way Through the Woods*. **5.** Burke & Hare. **6.** Lady Antonia Fraser. **7.** CA Lejeune (The Observer). **8.** A restaurant. **9.** Los Angeles. **10.** Budapest. **11.** Inspector Alleyn. **12.** RD Wingfield. **13.** *The Detectives*. **14.** Judith. **15.** *Heartbeat*. **16.** Trevor Chapman. **17.** Charles Leno. **18.** Lewis Collins & Martin Shaw. **19.** Sun Hill. **20.** *Bewteen The Lines*. **21.** California. **22.** Columbo. **23.** *Spender*. **24.** Lynda la Plante. **25.** Anna Carteret. **26.** Jimmy Nail. **27.** James Hong. **28.** *Wycliffe & the Cycle of Death*. **29.** *Murder Most Horrid*. **30.** Robert Beatty.

## QUIZ 22 Crime 3

LEVEL 2

**Answers: see Quiz 21, page 449**

1. Which former *Blue Peter* presenter starred as *Dangerfield's* son?
2. In which year was the first TV broadcast of an Agatha Christie mystery?
3. Who played the female surveillance expert in the first series of *Bugs*?
4. What was the name of the feature-length one-off *Inspector Morse* film in 1995?
5. The 1939 dramatisation *The Anatomist* was about which pair of bodysnatchers?
6. The series *Jemima Shore Investigates* was based on whose novels?
7. Which newspaper critic adapted the stories for the first British Sherlock Holmes series in 1951?
8. What is 'Pie in the Sky' in the name of the series?
9. The crime series *Dragnet* was set in which US city?
10. In which European city was much of *Cadfael* filmed?
11. Which detective's 'love interest' was Agatha Troy?
12. *A Touch of Frost* is based on the books by which author?
13. Which series was a spin off from *Canned Carrott*?
14. What was Fitz's wife, played by Barbara Flynn, called in *Cracker*?
15. Which series was inspired by Nicholas Rhea's 'Constable' novels?
16. In *The Beiderbecke Affair*, what was the name of the amateur detective?
17. In *Boyd QC*, who played Boyd's clerk and narrator?
18. Who played Bodie and Doyle in *The Professionals*?
19. In which fictional area of London is *The Bill* set?
20. In which series did Neil Pearson star as ambitious Tony Clark?
21. Where was the police drama *Highway Patrol* set?
22. Which police detective is famous for his old mac?
23. In which series about a Geordie investigator did Denise Welch play Jimmy Nail's wife?
24. Which writer created *Prime Suspect*?
25. Which actress took over the role of Insp. Jean Darblay in *Juliet Bravo* in 1983?
26. Which Geordie actor plays Spender?
27. Which actor played Barry Chan in *The New Adventures of Charlie Chan*?
28. The character Wycliffe first appeared in which 1993 TV film?
29. Which comic crime show was Dawn French 's first major solo series?
30. *Dial 999* starred which Canadian as Det. Insp. Mike Maguire?

ANSWERS

### Drama 2 (See Quiz 21)

**1.** Joely Richardson. **2.** Ed Asner. **3.** Michael Crichton. **4.** William Tell. **5.** Jack Kelly. **6.** Dodge City. **7.** Henry VIII. **8.** PE Teacher. **9.** Donald Pleasance. **10.** Frankie Lane. **11.** Pathologist. **12.** 1964. **13.** Ben Hall. **14.** Ray Brooks. **15.** Moira Mannon. **16.** Cary Cole. **17.** Lorne Green. **18.** It self-destructs. **19.** Jimmy Smits. **20.** A job. **21.** THRUSH. **22.** Frances de la Tour. **23.** Timothy Spall. **24.** Wishbone. **25.** James Drury. **26.** Manolito. **27.** Ex-actress, Molly Manning. **28.** Art Malik. **29.** Chicago. **30.** Peter Bowles.

## QUIZ 23 Current Affairs 2

**Answers: see Quiz 24, page 452**

LEVEL 2

1. Name the presenter of *Cosmos.*
2. Who presented *Connections?*
3. Who interviewed J. Paul Getty and The Sultan of Brunei?
4. The ceiling of the Sistine Chapel features in which programme titles?
5. Who was the author and presenter of *Pebble Mill At One?*
6. From the top of which US building was *Roving Report* first broadcast?
7. Who famously "counted them all out, and counted them all back"?
8. What do Fyfe Robinson, Alan Wicker and Trevor Philpot have in common?
9. Who interviewed Prince Charles on the programme which marked the 25th anniversary of his investiture as Prince of Wales?
10. What was the name of the David Attenborough's series about Antarctica?
11. Which two Peters were among the first presenters of *Newsnight?*
12. Jeremy Spake found fame working for which airline?
13. What was Britain's first breakfast TV programme called?
14. What was the year in which *Picture Page* was finally broadcast?
15. Who hosted a satellite talk show called *Surviving Life?*
16. In which year was the BBC TV *Newsreel* introduced?
17. What does ITN stand for?
18. Which French explorer presented *Under The Sea?*
19. What is the longest running TV current affairs programme?
20. Who first presented *Panorama?*
21. Where was *Jimmy's* set?
22. Who was the BBC's royal correspondent at the time of Princess Diana's death?
23. In which year was *BBC TV News* first broadcast?
24. Which co founder of TV am was married to a future Leader of the House of Lords?
25. Whose reporting of the Ethiopian famine in 1984 inspired Bob Geldof's Band Aid?
26. Who launched a singing career after telling her story on *Lakesiders?*
27. Which science show was first transmitted six months before the first satellite launch?
28. What was the follow-up series to *Diving to Adventure?*
29. Who was the original producer of *Frontiers of Science?*
30. Who first introduced *This Week* in 1956?

ANSWERS

### TV Comedy 6 (See Quiz 24)

**1.** Wendy Richards. **2.** Edith. **3.** Alf Garnett. **4.** Les Dawson. **5.** Manchester City. **6.** Ronnie Barker. **7.** The Prince Regent. **8.** *Knowing Me Knowing You...with Alan Partridge.* **9.** Blue. **10.** *How's Your Father.* **11.** *Albert!* **12.** Paul Eddington. **13.** The Korean War. **14.** Michael Elphick and Angela Thorn. **15.** Deal. **16.** 2. **17.** Sally Geeson. **18.** *A Very Polish Practice.* **19.** Above the Cunningham's Garage. **20.** Scott Biao. **21.** Burt Reynolds. **22.** Christopher Lloyd. **23.** Ronnie Corbett. **24.** Rhoda's. **25.** American. **26.** Nurse Gladys Emmanuel. **27.** Mini. **28.** 13. **29.** Bebe Neuwirth. **30.** Fosters Lagers.

## QUIZ 24 TV Comedy 6

LEVEL 2

**Answers: see Quiz 23, page 451**

1. Who played Miss Brahms in *Are You Being Served?*
2. What is the name of Rene's wife in *'Allo 'Allo?*
3. Who first said "bloody" 78 times in half an hour in a sitcom?
4. Which comedian is quoted as saying, 'The mother in law thinks I'm effeminate; not that I mind that because beside her, I am'?
5. Which football team did Eddie Large play for before becoming a comedian?
6. Who played Fletcher in *Porridge?*
7. E. Blackadder Esq was butler to whom?
8. Which series had words from an Abba song in its title?
9. What was the colour of *Monty Python's* Big Red Book?
10. Harry Worth played the father in which comedy?
11. Which sitcom, starring Rodney Bewes, was the sequel to *Dear Mother... Love Albert?*
12. Who played Jim Hacker in *Yes Minister?*
13. In which war is *M*A*S*H* set?
14. Which actors played the bickering grandparents in *Three Up, Two Down?*
15. What was the name of Manuel's Andalucian hamster?
16. How many children does *Absolutely Fabulous* character Edina have?
17. Who played the daughter in *Bless This House?*
18. What was the name of the sequel to *A Very Peculiar Practice* which was set in Poland in 1992?
19. Where did Fonzie live?
20. Who played Chachie in *Joanie Loves Chachie?*
21. Who was the male star of *Evening Shade?*
22. Who played Rev. Jim in *Taxi?*
23. Who was the diminutive star of *Sorry!?*
24. Carleton was whose doorman?
25. What nationality were the men of *The Airbase?*
26. Who was the object of Ronnie Barker's affections in *Open All Hours?*
27. What kind of car did Mr Bean drive?
28. How many episodes were in the first series of *Auf Wiedersehen Pet?*
29. She played Frasier's wife in *Cheers.* Who is she?
30. Which brew did Paul Hogan advertise?

ANSWERS

### Current Affairs 2 (See Quiz 23)

**1.** Carl Sagan. **2.** James Burke. **3.** Alan Whicker. **4.** *The South Bank Show.* **5.** Bob Langley. **6.** The Empire State Building. **7.** Brian Hanrahan **8.** All were reporters on *Tonight.* **9.** Jonathan Dimbleby. **10.** *Life in the Freezer.* **11.** Snow & Hobday. **12.** Aerofloat. **13.** *Breakfast Time.* **14.** 1952. **15.** Sarah, Duchess of York. **16.** 1948. **17.** *Independent Television News.* **18.** Jacques Cousteau. **19.** *Panorama* (1953 -). **20.** Max Robertson. **21.** St. James Hospital, Leeds. **22.** Jennie Bond. **23.** 1954. **24.** Peter Jay. **25.** Michael Buerk. **26.** Emma Boundy. **27.** *The Sky At Night.* **28.** *Undersea World of Adventure.* **29.** James McCloy. **30.** Rene Catforth.

## QUIZ 25 Pot Luck 4

LEVEL 2

**Answers: see Quiz 26, page 454**

1. Who played the author Ian Fleming on televsion?
2. Which breakfast presenter hosted *Moviewatch*?
3. Which TV companies merged to form BSkyB?
4. Who played Jake Hanson in *Melrose Place*?
5. In 1957 how much did a colour TV cost?
6. What is *The X Files*' David Duchovny's masters degree in?
7. Who has produced *Kavanagh QC* and presented *Food & Drink*?
8. Who was the first male presenter of *Gladiators*?
9. Who was the first Director General of the BBC?
10. Which soap revolved around a West End department store?
11. Which pop star's production company launched *The Big Breakfast*?
12. Which company replaced Thames TV in the early 90s?
13. Which drink did Rutger Hauer advertise?
14. What does GMTV stand for?
15. How much did the first TV licence cost?
16. Which actor played Frank Marker?
17. Who played Hereward the Wake?
18. Which Kennedy was in love with Ann Wilkinson in *Neighbours*?
19. Who was the very first presenter of *This Is Your Life*?
20. Where was *Hadleigh* set?
21. Which role did Lane Smith play in *Superman*?
22. Which actor was *The Charmer*?
23. Who originally presented the sports summaries on *Breakfast Time*?
24. Which actress played Beryl in *The Loners*?
25. Who was the first Prime Minister to install a TV at home?
26. Roddy McMillan played which Scottish PI?
27. Which actor portrays Andy Dalziel?
28. Who presented *In Bed with MeDinner*?
29. Who gave the first direct TV broadcast by a Prime Minister in 1948?
30. Name the narrator of *The Valiant Years*.

ANSWERS

### Soaps 3 (See Quiz 26)

**1.** Geoffrey Hughes. **2.** Bobby. **3.** Bill Kenright. **4.** Oz-Cabs. **5.** Wellard. **6.** *Take The High Road.* **7.** *Brookside*. **8.** Linda. **9.** Sandra Gough. **10.** Frank. **11.** Manchester. **12.** Julia Smith. **13.** David Scarborough. **14.** Gary Ewing. **15.** Susannah. **16.** *Eldorado.* **17.** E20. **18.** In Kylie's Teddy-bear. **19.** She was pushed from some scaffolding. **20.** Danny. **21.** *Cracker*. **22.** Tessa Diamond. **23.** 10. **24.** *Dallas* (Priscilla Presley, Mary Crosby). **25.** Bevron. **26.** Pizza Parlour. **27.** Tin-Head. **28.** Thomas Edward Sweeney. **29.** Suffocated with a pillow. **30.** The Mobey.

## QUIZ 26 Soaps 3

**Answers: see Quiz 25, page 453**

LEVEL 2

1. Which *Coronation Street* former dustman is now *Keeping up Appearances*?
2. Who was Sam's mum in *Home and Away*?
3. Which impresario played Betty Turpin's Gordon in *Coronation Street*?
4. What was the name of the first minicab company in *EastEnders*?
5. What was the name of Robbie's dog in *EastEnders*?
6. Which soap was set on the Scottish Glendarroch Estate?
7. In which soap did Amanda Burton play Heather Huntington?
8. What was the name of Elsie Tanner's daughter?
9. Who played Hilda Ogden's daughter in *Coronation Street*?
10. What was the Christian name of Ken Barlow's father?
11. In which city was *Albion Market* set?
12. Which late producer was dubbed 'The Godmother of Soap'?
13. Who originally played Mark Fowler before Todd Carty?
14. Which Ewing moved to *Knotts Landing*?
15. What was the name of Max Farnham's first wife?
16. Which soap was launched in 1992 with the promise of 'sun, sand, sangria and sex'?
17. What is the postcode of the London Borough of Walford?
18. Where did Gary Stanlow hide drugs when Lindsey, Kylie and Mike left the country?
19. How did Sue, Terry Sullivan's wife, die?
20. What was the name of Sue and Terry's son?
21. What was the name of Jimmy Corkhill's dog?
22. Who was the creator of *Emergency-Ward 10*?
23. What number house did the Jordache family live at?
24. Which US soap starred the widow of a rock star and the daughter of an American singing and acting legend?
25. What was the name of Ron Dixon and Bev's house?
26. What was Mick Johnson's first shop in *Brookside* called?
27. What is the nickname of Carmel's son in *Brookside*?
28. What is Sinbad's real name?
29. How did Gladys Charlton die?
30. What was Ron Dixon's lorry called?

ANSWERS

### Pot Luck 4 (See Quiz 25)

**1.** Jason Connery. **2.** Johnny Vaughn. **3.** Sky Television and BSB. **4.** Grant Show. **5.** £175. **6.** English Literature. **7.** Chris Kelly. **8.** John Fashanu. **9.** Lord Reith. **10.** *Harper's, West One*. **11.** Bob Geldof. **12.** Carlton. **13.** Guinness. **14.** Good Morning Television. **15.** Ten shillings (50p). **16.** Alfred Burke. **17.** Alfred Lynch. **18.** Billy. **19.** Eamon Andrews. **20.** Yorkshire. **21.** Perry King. **22.** Nigel Havers. **23.** David Icke. **24.** Paula Wilcox. **25.** Ramsay MacDonald. **26.** Daniel Pike. **27.** Warren Clarke. **28.** Bob Mills. **29.** Clement Attlee. **30.** Richard Burton.

## QUIZ 27 Music & Variety 1

LEVEL 2

**Answers: see Quiz 28, page 456**

1. Who used to say, 'We thank you - we really do'?
2. The entrance to the studios of which TV company gave *The Tube* its name?
3. What is the connection between Peter Dimmock, Sylvia Peters, Brian Johnston, Terry Wogan, Angela Rippon and Rosemarie Ford?
4. Which song did the BBC release for *Children in Need* in 1997?
5. In which year was *The Good Old Days* first televised?
6. Which member of a famous singing family appeared in *Fame*?
7. Which pianist who had a hit with "*Side Saddle*" was a regular on *Billy Cotton's Band Show*?
8. Who were Legs and Co?
9. What was Britain's first *Eurovision Song Contest* entry?
10. This singer and one-time TV host changed his name from Nick Perido. Who was he?
11. Vince Hill presented which popular music series?
12. Which TV host sang 'Swinging in the Rain'?
13. Who starred in *Set 'Em Up Joe*?
14. Where is *TFI Friday* broadcast from?
15. Which large pink spotty character was introduced on *Noel's House Party*?
16. Whose name appeared 'Later' in the music shows of the early 1990s?
17. Which girlfriend of soccer's Ryan Giggs presented *The Word*?
18. Which *Men Behaving Badly* star briefly presented *The Tube*?
19. Which dancers appeared on *Sunday Night at The London Palladium*?
20. Whose catchphrase was 'You lucky people'?
21. In the first *Celebrity Stars in their Eyes*, who said "Tonight Matthew I'm going to be Cher"?
22. Which comedy duo's theme song, composed by one of them, was 'Goodbye-ee'?
23. Which opera star hosted a Saturday Night show in the autumn of 1998?
24. Which *Magpie* presenter was a regular *Juke Box Jury* panellist as "a typical teenager"?
25. What was the first full length musical play shown on TV in 1939?
26. Who replaced Richard Baker hosting the *Proms* on TV?
27. Which pop star hosted the 1998 *Miss World Contest* for Channel 5?
28. Which long-standing dance programme was first shown in 1949?
29. Which *Top of the Pops* presenter was voted Britain's best dressed man in 1998?
30. Where was the 1998 *Three Tenors Concert* televised from?

ANSWERS

### TV Comedy 7 (See Quiz 28)

**1.** Simon Callow. **2.** Rosie (PC Penrose). **3.** Sid. **4.** Lee Whitlock. **5.** Vienna. **6.** Gizzard Puke. **7.** Benny Hill. **8.** Anna Karen. **9.** Helen Atkinson Wood. **10.** Fred MacMurray. **11.** Hercules. **12.** Shelley Long. **13.** Hannah Gordon. **14.** *Whoops Baghdad.* **15.** *Saurday Night Armistice.* **16.** 3. **17.** TV repair man. **18.** Mathilda Ziegler. **19.** Valerie Harper. **20.** BJ Hunnicut. **21.** Nora Batty. **22.** Timothy Spall. **23.** Edina. **24.** 4. **25.** Hyacinth. **26.** *Ever Decreasing Circles.* **27.** *Outside Edge.* **28.** Sharon and Tracey. **29.** Dick Clement & Ian la Frenais. **30.** Lenny Godber.

## QUIZ 28 TV Comedy 7

LEVEL 2

**Answers: see Quiz 27, page 455**

1. Who played Tom Chance in *Chance in a Million?*
2. Paul Greenwood played which comic policeman?
3. What is the name of Ivy's husband in *Last Of The Summer Wine?*
4. Who played Harvey Moon's son?
5. In *Rising Damp*, Rigsby's cat shares its name with a capital city. What is it?
6. What was the name of Kenny Everett's punk caricature?
7. Fred Scuttle was an comic charcter created by which comedian?
8. Which actress played Reg Varney's sister, Olive, in *On The Buses?*
9. In *Blackadder The Third*, Mrs Miggins was played by which comic actress?
10. Who starred in *My Three Sons?*
11. What was the name of Steptoe and Son's horse?
12. Which *The Money Pit* actress played Diane Chambers in *Cheers?*
13. Who played *My Wife Next Door?*
14. What was the follow up to *Up Pompeii!?*
15. Which 1995 Saturday Night series was presented by Armando Iannucci?
16. How many sons does Tim have in *Home Improvement?*
17. What was Gary's job in the first series of *Goodnight Sweetheart?*
18. Who played Mr Bean's long suffering girlfriend?
19. Who starred as Rhoda?
20. Who was Trapper John's replacement in *M*A*S*H?*
21. Who was Wally's wife in *Last Of The Summer Wine?*
22. Who played Frank Stubbs?
23. Who is Saffron's mother in *Absolutely Fabulous?*
24. How many sons did Mrs Boswell have in *Bread?*
25. What was Mrs Bucket's first name in *Keeping Up Appearances?*
26. Penelope Wilton and Peter Egan appeared together as neighbours in which sitcom?
27. Which sitcom about a local cricket club starred Timothy Spall and Josie Lawrence as married couple?
28. Who were Dorien's neighbours in *Birds Of A Feather?*
29. Who wrote *Auf Wiedersehen Pet?*
30. Who was Fletcher's cellmate in *Porridge?*

ANSWERS

### Music & Variety 1 (See Quiz 27)

**1.** Hughie Green. **2.** 1983. **3.** All have presented *Come Dancing.* **4.** Perfect Day. **5.** 1953. **6.** Janet Jackson. **7.** Russ Conway. **8.** Dancers on *Top of the Pops.* **9.** 'All', sung by Patricia Brendin. **10.** Perry Como. **11.** *They Sold a Million.* **12.** Norman Vaughn. **13.** Joe Brown. **14.** The Riverside Studios, London. **15.** Mr Blobby. **16.** Jools Holland. **17.** Dani Behr. **18.** Leslie Ash. **19.** The Tiller Girls. **20.** Tommy Trinder. **21.** Carol Vorderman. **22.** Peter Cook and Dudley Moore. **23.** Leslie Garrett. **24.** Susan Stranks. **25.** Magyar Melody. **26.** James Naughtie. **27.** Ronan Keating. **28.** *Come Dancing.* **29.** Jamie Theakston. **30.** Paris.

## QUIZ 29 Children's TV 3

LEVEL 2

**Answers: see Quiz 30, page 458**

1. In which children's series did Sally James appear?
2. Where did Fred Flintstone work?
3. Who made *Worzel Gummidge*?
4. Geoffrey Bayldon played which children's character?
5. What is the number plate on the postman's van in Greendale?
6. Who was the first *Blue Peter* presenter to be sacked, for taking cocaine?
7. Name the snail in *The Magic Roundabout*.
8. Who was the star of *Dick Turpin*?
9. Which series was a role reversal version of Robin Hood?
10. Where do *the Munsters* live?
11. What colour are the Smurfs?
12. Who was Superted's friend?
13. Which series featured a pantomime horse?
14. Spike the Dog features in which cartoon?
15. Who first played Long John Silver in a television series?
16. What was the name of the lion in *The Lion, The Witch and The Wardrobe*?
17. Who hosted *Runaround*?
18. What is the name of Kermit the frog's nephew?
19. Which ventriloquist worked with Lenny the Lion?
20. Who was Ray Alan's inebriated dummy?
21. Which green duck wore a nappy?
22. Who 'rode' an ostrich?
23. What was the name of the cow in *The Magic Roundabout*?
24. Where was *Crackerjack* first produced?
25. Which E Nesbitt dramatisation featured a legendary bird?
26. What was Lamb Chop?
27. Where did the *Teenage Mutant Ninja Turtles* live?
28. From which century did *Catweazle* come?
29. For which character is Jay Silverheels remembered?
30. Whose language included the word "Flobalob"?

ANSWERS

**Crime 4 (See Quiz 30)**

**1.** William Gargan. **2.** Kate. **3.** Jane Tennison. **4.** Detective Sergeant. **5.** *The Chief.* **6.** Nigel le Valliant. **7.** Tuscon, Arizona. **8.** *NYPD Blue.* **9.** *The Chinese Detective.* **10.** *Dangermouse.* **11.** Tom Adams. **12.** He only has one eye. **13.** David Jason. **14.** Kevin Lloyd. **15.** Sue Cook. **16.** Monk. **17.** Covert Activities, Thames Section. **18.** Terry Venables. **19.** Chief Dan Matthews. **20.** Taggart **21.** Reg Wexford. **22.** Peter Davison. **23.** Hartley Section Police Station. **24.** Michael French. **25.** J. Carrol Naith. **26.** *City Central.* **27.** Robert Morley. **28.** Colin Dexter. **29.** Samantha Janus. **30.** Father-in-law.

## QUIZ 30 Crime 4

LEVEL 2

**Answers: see Quiz 29, page 457**

1. In *Martin Kane, Private Investigator*, which actor played the title role?
2. In *Heartbeat*, what was Nick's first wife called?
3. Which character does Helen Mirren play in *Prime Suspect*?
4. What rank was *Cribb* in the programme of the same name?
5. In which series did Alan Cade replace John Stafford in the top job?
6. Which actor plays the title role in *Dangerfield*?
7. Which city was *Petrocelli* set?
8. In which series did Jimmy Smits play Bobby Simone?
9. In which series did Det. Sgt. John Ho appear in the early 80s?
10. Which character had a partner called Penfold?
11. Who played Det. Chief Insp. Nick Lewis in *The Enigma Files*?
12. What disability is Columbo actor Peter Falk afflicted with?
13. Which actor plays D.I. Frost?
14. Which actor from *The Bill* died shortly after being sacked from the show because of his drinking?
15. Who did Jill Dando replace on *Crimewatch UK*?
16. What is *Cadfael's* profession?
17. What did C.A.T.S. stand for in the series *CATS Eyes*?
18. Who created *Hazell*?
19. Name the lead character in *Highway Patrol*.
20. Which Glasgow-based series developed from a three part thriller called *Killers*?
21. *Wolf to the Slaughter* was the first programme to feature which famous Ruth Rendell detective?
22. Which former Doctor Who played private detective Albert Campion?
23. In which police station was *Juliet Bravo* set?
24. Who partnered *Crime Traveller* Chloe Annett?
25. Which actor played Charlie Chan?
26. After leaving *EastEnders* which crime series did Paul Nicholls star in?
27. Who introduced the series *Lady Killers*?
28. Name the author of *Inspector Morse*.
29. Which Eurovision Song Contest entrant starred in *Liverpool One*?
30. What relation was Charlie Hungerford to Jim Bergerac?

ANSWERS

### Childrens' TV 3 (See Quiz 29)

**1.** *Tiswas.* **2.** Bedrock Quarry. **3.** The Crow Man. **4.** Catweazle. **5.** PAT I. **6.** Richard Bacon. **7.** Brian. **8.** Richard O'Sullivan. **9.** *Maid Marian and Her Merry Men.* **10.** Mockingbird Lane. **11.** Blue. **12.** Spottyman. **13.** *Rentaghost.* **14.** Tom & Jerry. **15.** Robert Newton. **16.** Aslan. **17.** Mike Read. **18.** Robin. **19.** Terry Hall. **20.** Lord Charles. **21.** Orville. **22.** Bernie Clifton. **23.** Ermintrude. **24.** Television Theatre, Shepherds Bush. **25.** *The Phoenix and The Carpet.* **26.** A puppet. **27.** In the sewers. **28.** 11th. **29.** Tonto. **30.** Bill & Ben (*The Flowerpot Men*).

# QUIZ 31 Drama 3

LEVEL 2

**Answers: see Quiz 32, page 460**

1. Who wrote *Widows*?
2. Who starred in the role of James Onedin?
3. Which Dennis Potter drama was banned in 1976 and shown in 1987?
4. She played *The Duchess of Duke Street.* Who was she?
5. Name the main protagonist in *The Adventures of William Tell.*
6. Who was the female star of *The Champions*?
7. What was the name of the series starring Jesse Birdsall and filmed on the Isle of Wight?
8. Which character did David Longton play in *Upstairs Downstairs*?
9. Where is the series that starred Kevin Whately and Sam Shepherd set?
10. In which steamy serial did Sean Bean star alongside Joely Richardson?
11. Which series used 'Cry Me a River' as the theme?
12. Which Estate was the subject for the filming of *Brideshead Revisited*?
13. Which son of a famous soap star starred in *Seaforth*?
14. Which Avenger appeared in *Upstairs Downstairs*?
15. What was Peter Graves' character called in *Mission Impossible*?
16. In which American State was *The Ponderosa*?
17. Who played the title role in *Hunter*?
18. What was the subject of the series *Flickers*?
19. Who was William Tell's enemy?
20. In which series did Geraldine James play Sarah Layton?
21. Who played Cpt. Grant Mitchell's shipmates Alfonso and Sean?
22. Who was Sarah in *Thomas and Sarah*?
23. Which rag-trade series featured Stephanie Beacham?
24. Which actor was Matt Houston?
25. Which drama series starred Bob Peck and Joe Don Baker?
26. In which century was *The Buccaneers* set?
27. Which actor pursued Dr Richard Kimble?
28. Who did Ed Byrnes play in 77 *Sunset Strip*?
29. Which company made *Cheyenne, Bronco* and *Tenderfoot*?
30. Who was the ramrod in *Rawhide*?

ANSWERS

## TV Comedy 8 (See Quiz 32)

**1.** *The Mary Whitehouse Experience.* **2.** Gregor Fisher. **3.** *Fawlty Towers.* **4.** Dustin Gee. **5.** Yetta Feldman. **6.** Betty Spencer. **7.** *Rising Damp.* **8.** Julia McKenzie. **9.** *Police Squad.* **10.** Paul Calf. **11.** *Rowan & Martins' Laugh-In.* **12.** *Magpie's* Jenny Handley is daughter to *Don't Wait Up's* Dinah Sheridan. **13.** Captain. **14.** Dervla Kirwan. **15.** Lance Percival. **16.** Dermot. **17.** Johnny Speight. **18.** Gunther. **19.** Latimer. **20.** *Dick & the Duchess.* **21.** Blamire. **22.** Reece Dinsdale. **23.** She has never been seen. **24.** Roadsweeper. **25.** Nick Frisbee. **26.** 'Radar' O'Reilly. **27.** F Troop. **28.** Sgt. Bilko. **29.** Lanford. **30.** Grace Brothers (*Are You Being Served?*).

## QUIZ 32 TV Comedy 8

LEVEL 2

**Answers: see Quiz 31, page 459**

1. Which Radio 1 comedy show spawned *Newman and Baddiel in Pieces*?
2. Who created the character Rab C Nesbit?
3. In classic comedy do Polly and the Major both appear?
4. Who was Les Dennis' late comedy partner?
5. Whose was the female ghost in *So Haunt Me*?
6. Who was married to Frank in *Some Mothers Do Ave Em*?
7. In which series did Richard Beckinsale and Frances de la Tour play harassed lodgers?
8. Who played Hester in *Fresh Fields*?
9. Which spoof cop series featured Leslie Neilson?
10. Which offensive drunk was created by Steve Coogan on Channel 4's *Saturday Zoo*?
11. Which comedy show did Dick and Dan compere?
12. What is the link between *Magpie* and the comedy *Don't Wait Up*?
13. In *Blackadder Goes Forth*, what rank was Blackadder?
14. Who was the star of both *Goodnight Sweetheart* and *Ballykissangel*?
15. Who created calypsos on *That Was The Week That Was*?
16. Which character was played by Harry Enfield in *Men Behaving Badly*?
17. Who wrote *'Til Us Do Part*?
18. In *Friends*, who in Central Perk is a secret admirer of Rachel?
19. What is the surname of father and son in *Don't Wait Up*?
20. The character Dick Starrett was a troubled American insurance investigator in which 50's comedy?
21. Who did Michael Bates play in *Last of the Summer Wine*?
22. Who played John Thaw's son in *Home to Roost*?
23. From the viewer's point of view, what is unusual about Niles' wife Maris in *Frasier*?
24. What was the occupation of Mr Boswell in *Bread*?
25. Which Brian Conley character has a puppet assistant called Larry the Loafer?
26. What was the nickname of Gary Burghoff's character in *MASH*?
27. What was the name of the US comedy about the cavalry?
28. Colonel Hall was which Master Sergeant's superior officer?
29. In which town does Roseanne live?
30. In which store did the actors Larry Martin and Arthur English appear?

ANSWERS

### Drama 3 (See Quiz 31)

**1.** Lynda la Plante. **2.** Peter Gilmore. **3.** *Brimstone and Treacle*. **4.** Gemma Jones. **5.** Landburgher Gessler. **6.** Alexandra Bastedo. **7.** Anneka. **8.** Lord Bellamy. **9.** The Peak District. **10.** Lady Chatterley. **11.** McCallum. **12.** Castle Howard. **13.** Linus Roach. **14.** Gareth Hunt. **15.** Jim Phelps. **16.** Nevada. **17.** Fred Dryer. **18.** Early British Cinema. **19.** Gessler. **20.** *The Jewel in the Crown*. **21.** Rupert Davies & Jack MacGowan. **22.** Pauline Collins. **23.** Connie. **24.** Lee Horsley. **25.** *Edge of Darkness*. **26.** 18th Century. **27.** Barry Morse. **28.** Kookie. **29.** Warner Brothers. **30.** Gill Favor.

## QUIZ 33 Pot Luck 5

**Answers: see Quiz 34, page 462**

LEVEL 2

1. Which sixties soap centred on the editorial office of a woman's magazine?
2. At the start of WWII how much notice did the government give the BBC to close their service?
3. Which form of art do you associate Nancy Kaminsky?
4. Which television region produced *Houseparty*?
5. Who is Emma Forbes' actress mother?
6. Who was the BBC's first director of TV?
7. Who is Mel Giedroyc's partner on *Late Lunch*?
8. What was the name of the head porter in *Porterhouse Blue* played by David Jason?
9. In *Tutti Frutti* how long had the rock band The Majestics been together?
10. Which firestation features in *London's Burning*?
11. *Soldier, Soldier* follows the activities of the fictitious "A" Company of which infantry regiment?
12. Which budding singer-songwriter did Jimmy Nail play in *Crocodile Shoes*?
13. Who was the host of *Lunchbox*?
14. Who supplied the BBC commentary for the Coronation of King George VI?
15. Which disc jockey married Anthea Turner?
16. Which gardener leads the *Ground Force* team?
17. What are the Christian names of the Hurt twins in *Family Affairs*?
18. What is the title of BBC 2's early morning educational programmes?
19. What forced daytime shutdown of TV transmissions in Feb-March 1947?
20. Which newsreader presents *I-Spy*?
21. How many lines are broadcast on UHF on British Television?
22. Which larger-than-life actor advertised sherry?
23. Which female television personality has a daughter named Trixie-Belle?
24. How long did the 1953 Coronation broadcast last?
25. Which impresario was the brother of Lou Grade?
26. Which channel broadcast *The Girlie Show*?
27. Who was the BBC's first DIY expert?
28. Which actor was 'Walker, Texas Ranger'?
29. *Sharpe* is set during which war?
30. Who does Roger Griffith play in *Pie In The Sky*?

ANSWERS

**Sport 1 (See Quiz 34)**

**1.** Gary Lineker. **2.** Putney. **3.** Kris Akabusi. **4.** David Coleman. **5.** Gabby Yorath. **6.** Ian St.John and Jimmy Greaves. **7.** *The Crucible*. **8.** Brian Johnson. **9.** David Gower & Gary Lineker. **10.** Gary Rhodes. **11.** 1936. **12.** John Inverdale. **13.** Rugby League. **14.** Greg Rusedski. **15.** Bob Wilson. **16.** London. **17.** *Auntie's Sporting Bloomers*. **18.** *Television Sports Magazine*. **19.** Snooker. **20.** Tennis. **21.** The Grand National. **22.** Angling. **23.** Channel 4. **24.** David Vine. **25.** Raymond Brookes-Ward. **26.** He was televised hitting 6 sixes off one over. **27.** Golf. **28.** James Hunt. **29.** Jimmy Hill. **30.** Brighton and Hove Albion.

## QUIZ 34 Sport 1

LEVEL 2

**Answers: see Quiz 33, page 461**

1. Which football presenter is a former Spurs and England captain?
2. Where is the starting point of the University Boat Race?
3. Which 400 metre runner presents *Record Breakers*?
4. Who was the first presenter of *Grandstand*?
5. Which female presenter joined Barry Venison presenting *On The Ball* in 1998?
6. Who are *Saint and Greavsie*?
7. Where is the 'hot' setting for snooker on television?
8. Who is cricket's 'Jonners'?
9. Who are captains of England and *They Think It's all Over*?
10. Which diminutive jockey was a team captain on *A Question of Sport*?
11. Which TV chef cooked on TV for his favourite team Manchester United?
12. Who first hosted the late evening sports chat show *On Side*?
13. Which sport were Eddie Waring and Ray French associated with?
14. Which tennis player was BBC Sports Personality of 1997?
15. Who presented *Football Focus* before leaving for ITV in 1994?
16. The first Olympics to be televised were held where?
17. Which BBC show transmits outtakes from sporting events gone wrong?
18. Which early 1950's sports programme was introduced by Max Robertson and screened on Wednesday evening?
19. With which TV sport do you associated Jimmy White?
20. Dan Maskell commentated on which sport?
21. Aintree is the location for which televised sporting event?
22. Footballer and manager Jack Charlton is often seen on TV in which other sport?
23. Which channel did cricket move to from the BBC in 1999?
24. Who presents *Ski Sunday*?
25. Which Raymond provides BBC's showjumping commentaries?
26. What was cricketer Gary Sobers TV claim to fame?
27. Which sport has been televised being played on the moon?
28. Which Formula One world champion commentated on Grand Prix races?
29. Which former Fulham player and Coventry chairman presented *MatchofThe Day*?
30. Which football team does Des Lynam support?

ANSWERS

### Pot Luck 5 (See Quiz 33)

**1.** Compact. **2.** 10 minutes. **3.** Painting. **4.** Southern. **5.** Nanette Newman. **6.** Gerald Cock. **7.** Sue Perkins. **8.** Skullion. **9.** 25 years. **10.** Blackwall. **11.** The King's Own Fusiliers. **12.** Jed Shepherd. **13.** Noele Gordon. **14.** Frederick Grisewood. **15.** Peter Powell. **16.** Alan Titchmarsh. **17.** Holly and Duncan. **18.** *The Learning Zone.* **19.** A fuel and power crisis. **20.** Julia Somerville. **21.** 625. **22.** Orson Welles. **23.** Paula Yates. **24.** Seven hours. **25.** Bernard Delfont. **26.** Channel 4. **27.** Barry Bucknall. **28.** Chuck Norris. **29.** The Napoleonic War. **30.** Inspector Henry Crabbe.

## QUIZ 35 Soaps 4

LEVEL 2

**Answers: see Quiz 36, page 464**

**1.** In *EastEnders* what are Ian Beale's twins called?
**2.** What did DD Dixon's shop sell?
**3.** Who was the best man at the marriage of Alf and Audrey Roberts?
**4.** Which *Brookside* character worked in a bar in order to buy a ticket to Rome?
**5.** What is Gerard Rebecchi's nickname in *Neighbours*?
**6.** What is the name of Kim Tate's son in *Emmerdale*?
**7.** Who was Annie Walker's husband in *Coronation Street*?
**8.** Who created *Brookside*?
**9.** In which country was *Eldorado* set?
**10.** Which soap was the first American one on British television?
**11.** In *Emmerdale*, who is the vet?
**12.** Name the three Kennedy children in *Neighbours*?
**13.** What is Curly Watt's Christian name?
**14.** Jason Donovan appeared as which character in *Neighbours*?
**15.** Which sixties soap was set in the offices of a magazine?
**16.** What is the name of the second pub in *Emmerdale*?
**17.** What was Pauline Fowler's mother's name?
**18.** In *Crossroads*, who did Paul Henry play?
**19.** Who played Blake Carrington in *Dynasty*?
**20.** Where is Ramsay Street?
**21.** Who played Joe Sugden in *Emmerdale*?
**22.** Which character left Albert Square for a job in the USA?
**23.** Which character in *Coronation Street* was played by Jean Alexander?
**24.** What job was Seth Armstrong offered by NY Estates?
**25.** Who was Dr Roger Moon in *Emergency-Ward 10*?
**26.** Who is Lachie's girlfriend in *Home and Away*?
**27.** What was the spin-off feature film made from *Emergency-Ward 10* in 1958?
**28.** Who opened "Deals on Wheels" in *EastEnders*?
**29.** What was the name of Derek Riley's wife in *Coronation Street*?
**30.** Which role did Clive Hornby play in *Emmerdale*?

ANSWERS

### TV Comedy 9 (SeeQuiz 36)

**1.** Tom Sharpe. **2.** *All At No 20.* **3.** Undertaker. **4.** The Hitler diaries hoax. **5.** *The Darling Buds of May.* **6.** Larry Grayson. **7.** Billy Connolly. **8.** Neil Simon. **9.** Sid Little. **10.** Graeme Garden. **11.** Dick Emery. **12.** Honor Blackman. **13.** Ellie May. **14.** Christopher Biggins. **15.** To make way for a Hyperspace By-Pass. **16.** Yootha Joyce. **17.** Jim Davidson. **18.** The Cat. **19.** His home-help, Winston. **20.** Tony Britton. **21.** Lynda Bellingham. **22.** *Happy Days.* **23.** Hazel Court. **24.** Luton Town. **25.** Alice Tinker. **26.** Pam Dawber. **27.** Jack Good. **28.** Eric Idle. **29.** Onslow. **30.** Roger Rees.

## QUIZ 36 TV Comedy 9

**Answers: see Quiz 35, page 463** LEVEL 2

1. Who wrote the original book upon which *Blott on the Landscape* was based?
2. In which series did Maureen Lipman take on student boarders, including Martin Clunes?
3. What was Private Fraser's occupation in *Dad's Army*?
4. *Selling Hitler* was a black comedy about what affair?
5. In which series did Philip Franks become David Jason's son in law?
6. Whose catchphrase was, 'Shut that door'?
7. Who is known as The Big Yin?
8. Who wrote *The Odd Couple*?
9. Who is Eddie Large's sidekick?
10. Which of the *Goodies* is a qualified doctor?
11. Which male comedian created the flirtatious character Mandy?
12. Which ex Bond girl played Caroline's mother in *The Upper Hand*?
13. What was the name of Jed Clampitt's daughter in the *Beverley Hillbillies*?
14. Who played Lukewarm in *Porridge*?
15. Why was the Earth destroyed in *A Hitchhiker's Guide to The Galaxy*?
16. Who played Mrs Roper in *George and Mildred*?
17. Which stand-up comedian starred in *Up The Elephant and Round The Castle*?
18. Who on *Red Dwarf* had the alter-ego Dwayne Dibley?
19. Who did Alf Garnett nickname Marigold?
20. Who plays Dr Toby Latimer?
21. Which *Faith* actress advertises stock cubes?
22. Which series was a spin-off from *American Graffiti*?
23. Who played the wife of Dick Starrett in *Dick And The Duchess*?
24. Of which football team was Eric Morecambe a director?
25. What was the name of the *Vicar of Dibley*'s curate?
26. Who played Mork's Mindy?
27. Who was the creator of the series *Oh Boy*?
28. Which ex Python wrote and performed the theme to *One Foot in the Grave*?
29. What was Hyacinth Bucket's brother in law called?
30. Which English actor appeared as Rebecca's boyfriend in *Cheers*?

ANSWERS

**Soaps 4 (See Quiz 35)**

**1.** Peter and Lucy. **2.** Flowers. **3.** Mike Baldwin. **4.** Sheila. **5.** Toadfish. **6.** James Francis. **7.** Jack. **8.** Phil Redmond. **9.** Spain. **10.** *Peyton Place*. **11.** Zoe Tate. **12.** Malcolm, Libby and Billy. **13.** Norman. **14.** Scott Robinson. **15.** *Compact*. **16.** The Malt Shovel. **17.** Lou Beale. **18.** Benny. **19.** John Forsythe. **20.** Erinsborough. **21.** Frazer Hines. **22.** Michelle Fowler. **23.** Hilda Ogden. **24.** Gamekeeper. **25.** John Alderton. **26.** Chloe. **27.** *Life in Emergency-Ward 10*. **28.** Frank Butcher. **29.** Mavis. **30.** Jack Sugden.

## QUIZ 37 Sci-Fi 3

**Answers: see Quiz 38, page 466**

LEVEL 2

1. Which TV playwright wrote the *Quatermass* serials?
2. Which sci-fi series began the day after President Kennedy's death?
3. Who starred as *Kolchak: The Nightstalker*?
4. What were the names of the computers in *Blake's Seven*?
5. Name the author of *The Hitch-Hiker's Guide to The Galaxy*.
6. What was the name of the first episode – and heroine – of *Neverwhere*?
7. Which comic hero was played by Dean Cain?
8. Which Edwardian adventurer had been trapped in ice and thawed out in the Sixties?
9. What kind of spacecraft was *Red Dwarf*?
10. Who was the star of *Darling* who appeared in *A For Andromeda*?
11. Who does Patrick Stewart play in *Star Trek: The Next Generation*?
12. In *The Avengers*, what was Peter Peel's widow called?
13. What was the revamped version of *Battlestar Galactica* called?
14. Which squad was Don Quick a member of in *The Adventures of Don Quick*?
15. How was Jaime Sommers better known?
16. In which BBC programme would you find the character of Dr Spencer Quist?
17. What name was given to the three superhumans whose job it was to maintain world peace, in the series first seen in the 60s and re-run in the 90s?
18. Which Rock featured in *The Martian Chronicles* mini-series?
19. Which programme starred Scott Bakula as Sam Beckett?
20. In *The X-Files* which character is a medic?
21. Dominick Hyde travelled into which 20th century decade?
22. How was David McCallum's character Daniel Westin also known?
23. In *UFO*, why had SHADO been set up?
24. Which star of *Baywatch* starred in *Knight Rider* in the 1980s?
25. In *The Stone Tapes*, what did the scientific team try to extract from the walls of a Victorian mansion?
26. Which 11th century wizard became trapped in the 20th century?
27. What was the profession of the *Six Million Dollar Man*?
28. *The Survivors* survived which global disaster?
29. In *Space: 1999*, part of which heavenly body is cast into space after a nuclear explosion?
30. Which character did Joanna Lumley play in *The New Avengers*?

ANSWERS

**Childrens' TV 4 (See Quiz 38)**

**1.** Actor Fulton Mackay. **2.** Popeye. **3.** Christopher Trace. **4.** Nick Park. **5.** Colonel White. **6.** Mike Nesmith. **7.** Parsley. **8.** Philip Schofield. **9.** The *Blue Peter* Badge. **10.** Mickey Dolenz. **11.** Muttley. **12.** Major Don West. **13.** *Playdays*. **14.** Ringo Starr. **15.** Lester Flat & Earl Scruggs. **16.** *The Wacky Races*. **17.** Worzel Gummidge. **18.** They both played Little John in TV versions of *Robin Hood*. **19.** Catwoman in *Batman*. **20.** Brains. **21.** Wombles. **22.** Yellow. **23.** *The Snowman*. **24.** *Rainbow*. **25.** *The Bigger Breakfast*. **26.** On a *Jim'll Fix It* medal. **27.** Charlie Brown. **28.** Cuddles. **29.** *Crackerjack!* **30.** Burt Ward.

## QUIZ 38 Childrens' TV 4

LEVEL 2

**Answers: see Quiz 37, page 465**

1. What is the link between *Fraggle Rock* and *Porridge*?
2. Which cartoon character has an anchor tattooed on his arm?
3. Who was the first male presenter of *Blue Peter*?
4. Name the creator of *Wallace and Gromit*.
5. Who was Captain Scarlet's superior?
6. Which member of *The Monkees* wore a woolly hat?
7. Name the lion in *The Herbs*.
8. Who preceded Andy Crane as presenter of *Children's BBC*?
9. Which badge features a sailing ship?
10. Which Monkee's father was The Count of Monte Cristo?
11. Who is Dick Dastardly's pet dog?
12. In *Lost in Space*, which character was played by Mark Goddard?
13. On which show might you visit the Roundabout Stop?
14. Who narrated the first series of *Thomas the Tank Engine and Friends*?
15. Which country recording artists appeared in *The Beverley Hillbillies*?
16. Which Hanna-Barbera cartoon featured Penelope Pitstop?
17. Which character lived in Scatterbrook?
18. What do Archie Duncan and Clive Mantle have in common?
19. Eartha Kitt and Julie Newmar both played which character?
20. Who wore glasses in *Thunderbirds*?
21. What sort of creatures were Tobermory and Orinoco?
22. What colour is Teletubby Laa Laa?
23. '*Walking in the Air*' was the theme for which cartoon film?
24. Rod, Jane and Freddy featured in which childrens' TV programme?
25. What is the name of the school holiday morning series for children on Channel 4?
26. On what would you find the words 'Jim Fixed It For Me'?
27. Who is Snoopy's owner?
28. What is the name of Keith Harris's talking monkey?
29. Complete the following, 'It's Friday, it's five o'clock, and it's...'
30. In the cartoon version of *Batman*, who provided the voice for Robin?

ANSWERS

### Sci-Fi 3 (See Quiz 37)

**1.** Nigel Kneale. **2.** *Doctor Who*. **3.** Darren McGavin. **4.** Orac, Zen and Slave. **5.** Douglas Adams. **6.** Door. **7.** *Superman*. **8.** Adam Adamant. **9.** A mining ship. **10.** Julie Christie. **11.** Capt. Jean-Luc Picard. **12.** Emma. **13.** *Galactica 1980*. **14.** The Intergalactic Maintenance Squad. **15.** *The Bionic Woman*. **16.** *Doomwatch*. **17.** *The Champions*. **18.** Rock Hudson. **19.** *Quantum Leap*. **20.** Dr Dana Scully. **21.** 1980s. **22.** *The Invisible Man*. **23.** To repel alien invaders. **24.** David Hasselhoff. **25.** Ancient traumatic memories. **26.** Catweazle. **27.** Astronaut. **28.** A pandemic disease. **29.** The Moon. **30.** Purdey.

## QUIZ 39 Food & Drink 1

LEVEL 2

**Answers: see Quiz 40, page 468**

1. Whose nickname is Woz?
2. Loyd Grossman presents which cookery programme?
3. Which cook's husband wore a monocle?
4. Which TV chef is a director of Norwich City football club?
5. Which Susan cooks on *This Morning*?
6. Who is chef Ross from *Light Lunch*?
7. Which form of transport is popular with the *Two Fat Ladies*?
8. Which chef also advertises Tate & Lyle and his own ready meals?
9. Name the former presenter of *Food and Drink*.
10. Which actress is host of the morning show *Good Living*?
11. What does the runner up receive on *Celebrity Ready Steady Cook*?
12. Who presented *Tastes of Britain*?
13. Which Indian actress is also a well-known food expert?
14. Which country does Glen Christian originate from?
15. Which chef uses a '*Hot Wok*'?
16. Which *Bird of a Feather* ran a café?
17. Name the larger than life West Indian lady TV cook.
18. What was the name of Keith Floyd's first TV series?
19. Who is Paul Rankin's Canadian wife who is also an expert chef?
20. In *Ready Steady Cook*, what are the symbols used to identify each team?
21. Who presents *Real Food* on Channel Four?
22. Who was *The Galloping Gourmet*?
23. Name Jilly Goolden's wine-tasting partner.
24. Philip Harben presented which type of programme on post-war TV?
25. Which TV cook is the daughter of late cookery expert Jane?
26. Valentina Harris specialises on food from which country?
27. In what did Rachel lose her engagement ring in *Friends*?
28. On which magazine programme did Keith Floyd show his skills in the early 1980s?
29. Name Keith Floyd's series which explored cooking in the Far East?
30. What would be the main ingredient if your meal was being prepared by Rick Stein?

ANSWERS

### TV Comedy 10 (See Quiz 40)

**1.** 1986. **2.** Shelley Winters. **3.** The Porters. **4.** Galton & Simpson. **5.** Grace (Under Fire). **6.** Buy the Book. **7.** Palaeontology. **8.** *Drop the Dead Donkey*. **9.** Peter McNicol. **10.** Miss Brahms. **11.** Simon Cadell. **12.** Ronnie Corbett. **13.** Foxie. **14.** Never the Twain. **15.** Fishing. **16.** Pamela Stephenson. **17.** *The Comedians*. **18.** *Whose Line is it Anyway?* **19.** *Monty Python*. **20.** Algernon. **21.** John le Mesurier. **22.** Renault Clio. **23.** Dawn French. **24.** Boysie. **25.** Dinah Sheridan. **26.** David Suchet. **27.** The Olympic Hotel. **28.** 4. **29.** Matthew and Henry Kelly. **30.** Stanley.

## QUIZ 40 TV Comedy 10

LEVEL 2

**Answers: see Quiz 39, page 467**

1. In which year was Jim Hacker elected Prime Minister?
2. Which actress played Roseanne's grandmother?
3. Which family had 'Two Point Four Children'?
4. Who wrote *Clochemerle*?
5. Which character does Brett Butler play in her TV series?
6. What is the name of the book shop in *Ellen*?
7. What is Ross's professional passion in *Friends*?
8. Which series took the viewer behind the scenes at Globelink News?
9. Who plays John in *Ally McBeal*?
10. Who did Wendy Richard play in *Are You Being Served*?
11. Who played Jeffrey Fairbrother, the original manager of the holiday camp in *Hi-De-Hi!*?
12. Who played Timothy Lumsden in *Sorry!*?
13. What did Citizen Smith's girlfriend's mother mistakenly call him?
14. Which 80's comedy series featured two feuding antiques dealers?
15. What is Sarge's hobby in *Duck Patrol*?
16. Who is Billy Connolly's wife?
17. On which show did Bernard Manning, Mike Reid and Jim Bowen come to prominence?
18. On which programme do Steven Frost, Greg Proops and Josie Lawrence regularly improvise?
19. Which show featured 'The Ministry For Silly Walks'?
20. What was the name of Lenny Henry's rastafarian character?
21. Who was Hattie Jacques husband?
22. Which car ad features Nicole running away from her marriage to Vic Reeves?
23. Which female comedian satirised Hannibal Lecter?
24. Who is the used car salesman in *Only Fools and Horses*?
25. Who plays Tom Latimer's mother in *Don't Wait Up*?
26. Which actor played Blott in *Blott on the Landscape*?
27. What is the name of the hotel in *Heartbreak Hotel*?
28. How many *Girls on Top* were there?
29. Which *Game For A Laugh* presenters shared a surname?
30. What was the name of Dorothy's ex-husband in *The Golden Girls*?

ANSWERS

### Food & Drink 1 (See Quiz 39)

**1.** Anthony Worrall Thompson. **2.** *Masterchef.* **3.** Fanny Craddock. **4.** Delia Smith. **5.** Susan Brooks. **6.** Burdon. **7.** Motorcycle & sidecar. **8.** Gary Rhodes. **9.** Michael Barry. **10.** Jane Asher. **11.** Wooden spoon. **12.** Dorinda Hafner. **13.** Madhur Jaffrey. **14.** New Zealand. **15.** Ken Hom. **16.** Sharon. **17.** Rusty Lee. **18.** *Floyd on Fish.* **19.** Jeanne **20.** Green Peppers & Red Tomatoes. **21.** Nigel Slater. **22.** Graham Kerr. **23.** Oz Clarke. **24.** A series on cuisine. **25.** Sophie Grigson. **26.** Italy. **27.** A lasagne. **28.** Here Today. **29.** *Far Flung Floyd.* **30.** Fish.

## QUIZ 41 Current Affairs 3

**Answers: see Quiz 42, page 470**

LEVEL 2

1. Which science programme have Maggie Philbin and William Woolhand presented?
2. Which *This Week* reporter reported on the Queen's 1977 visit to Northern Ireland which was banned from transmission?
3. What does Sister Wendy review?
4. Who founded *Roving Report*?
5. Trude Mostue found fame in a documentary training for which profession?
6. Jack Hargreaves presented which show?
7. Which presenter interviewed Charles and Diana two days before their wedding?
8. Which store featured in *The Shop*?
9. What was the name of the 1970 junior version of *The Sky at Night*?
10. Who was the first presenter of *Tonight*?
11. *City Hospital* with Gaby Roslin was broadcast live daily from where?
12. Which news magazine programme featured Magnus Magnusson as a reporter?
13. Name the presenter of the documentary series *This Wonderful World*.
14. Who was the Consultant Physician in the early programmes of *Your Life in Their Hands*?
15. Who was *Driving School's* most famous pupil?
16. Who founded CNN?
17. How did *Face to Face* open and close?
18. Who hosted the TV review programme *Did You See...?*
19. Which drama documentary caused a rift between Britain and Saudi Arabia?
20. Who took the first of the *Great Railway Journeys of the World*?
21. Who was the narrator of the series *Hollywood*?
22. Name the presenter and writer of the series *Ireland: A Television History*.
23. Which pun-like title was used for the docu soap about chalet girls in a ski resort?
24. When was *Newsnight* first aired?
25. Which women's prison featured in a four-night 1982 Granada TV documentary?
26. Who was the subject of the documentary *American Caesar*?
27. What was the follow up to David Attenborough's *Life on Earth* called?
28. Who was the first female presenter of the BBC's *Breakfast Time*?
29. What was the subject of the series *Crime Inc*?
30. In what year was *Crimewatch* UK first aired?

ANSWERS

### Drama 4 (See Quiz 42)

**1.** Doc. **2.** Chester. **3.** David Carradine. **4.** Kevin Whately. **5.** Holby General. **6.** The Welsh Mountains. **7.** Angela Baddeley. **8.** Blackwall. **9.** Robert Urich. **10.** Charlotte Rhodes. **11.** Eleanor Bramwell. **12.** *Shoulder to Shoulder.* **13.** Dennis Potter. **14.** *Rock Follies.* **15.** Myrtle Prout. **16.** *Poldark.* **17.** *The Girl From UNCLE.* **18.** Tara King. **19.** Lynda la Plante. **20.** The Travelling Bioscope Theatre. **21.** Mr Darcy (*Pride & Prejudice*). **22.** Michael Landon. **23.** Samantha Janus. **24.** *Warship.* **25.** Peter Mayle. **26.** Robson Greene. **27.** Trevor Howard & Celia Johnson. **28.** Dr Elizabeth Corday. **29.** *The Hanging Gale.* **30.** George Margo.

# QUIZ 42 Drama 4

**Answers: see Quiz 39, page 469**

LEVEL 2

**1.** Milburn Stone played which character in *Gunsmoke*?
**2.** Who had a limp in *Gun Law*?
**3.** Which actor was the star of *Kung Fu*?
**4.** Which *Morse* actor is also *The Broker's Man*?
**5.** In which hospital is *Casualty* based?
**6.** Where was *The Adventures of William Tell* filmed on location?
**7.** In *Upstairs, Downstairs*, Mrs Bridges was played by which actress?
**8.** Where is Blue Watch's fire station in *London's Burning*?
**9.** Who is the star of *Spencer: For Hire*?
**10.** What was the name of James Onedin's ship?
**11.** Which Victorian doctor does Jemma Redgrave play?
**12.** Name the series about the Suffragette movement.
**13.** Who was the writer of the series *Black Eyes*?
**14.** In which series about an all-girl group did Rula Lenska star?
**15.** Name the girl-next-door in *The Larkins*.
**16.** What's the name of the costume drama which featured the characters Ross and Demelza?
**17.** In which series did Noel Harrison partner Stephanie Powers?
**18.** Which character replaced Emma Peel in *The Avengers*?
**19.** Who created *Trial and Retribution*?
**20.** What was the name of Arnie Cole's theatre in *Flickers*?
**21.** Which literary hero has been played on TV by Peter Cushing, Alan Badel and Colin Firth?
**22.** Which late actor played an angel in *Highway to Heaven*?
**23.** In *Imogen's Face*, who played the title role?
**24.** Bryan Marshall starred as a naval captain in which series?
**25.** John Thaw portrayed this writer in *A Year in Provence*.
**26.** Which *Soldier, Soldier* actor also appeared in Touching Evil?
**27.** Who played the two lead roles in *Staying On*, set in India?
**28.** Which English doctor had an affair with Peter Benton in *ER*?
**29.** In which drama series did the McGann brothers play the Phelan brothers?
**30.** Who originally played Blackbeard in *The Buccaneers*?

ANSWERS

## Current Affairs 3 (See Quiz 41)

**1.** *Tomorrow's World.* **2.** Peter Taylor. **3.** Art. **4.** ITN Editor Geoffrey Cox. **5.** Vet. **6.** *Out of Town.* **7.** Angela Rippon. **8.** Selfridges. **9.** Seeing Stars. **10.** Cliff Mitchelmore. **11.** Southampton. **12.** *Tonight.* **13.** John Grierson. **14.** Dr Charles Fletcher. **15.** Maureen Rees. **16.** Ted Turner. **17.** Charcoal drawings of the week's subjects (by Feliks Topolsky). **18.** Ludovic Kennedy. **19.** *Death of a Princess.* **20.** Ludovic Kennedy. **21.** James Mason. **22.** Robert Kee. **23.** *War and Piste.* **24.** 1980. **25.** HM Prison Styal (*Living in Styal*). **26.** Gen. Douglas MacArthur. **27.** *The Living Planet.* **28.** Selina Scott. **29.** The *Mafia.* **30.** 1984.

## QUIZ 43 Pot Luck 6

LEVEL 2

**Answers: see Quiz 44, page 472**

1. Who was the last presenter of *Rugby Special* on BBC2?
2. Whose catchphrase was 'Walkies!'?
3. Where would you find Zippy, Bungle and George?
4. Which former Ulster TV presenter introduced the magazine programme *Sunday Sunday* for eight years?
5. Which keep fit expert was dubbed 'The Green Goddess'?
6. Who was the first female member of the *Ground Force* team?
7. Who journeyed *Around The Pacific Rim*?
8. Brian Glover played which private detective's man servant?
9. Which pop singer played a game show host in *Miami Vice*?
10. Who played Q in *Star Trek: The Next Generation*?
11. What was Peter Parker's alterego?
12. What was the subject of *Tour of Duty*?
13. In *Emmerdale*, what's the real life connection between Chris and Kim Tate?
14. Helen Baxendale played which character in *An Unsuitable Job for a Woman*?
15. What did the first televised Church service commemorate?
16. Name the presenter of *Through the Keyhole*.
17. Who played characters in *Fame* and *VR5*?
18. What was the estimated number of UK viewers of the 1953 Coronation?
19. Who was Marty Feldman's writing partner?
20. Jean Harvey, Nicholas Selby, and Gareth Davies played editors of which fictional magazine?
21. Who ended his programme with the words "The next *Tonight* is tomorrow night"?
22. On election nights who wields his Swingometer?
23. What was David Bellamy's chat show called?
24. Who presented *Mad Movies*?
25. Which actress played *The Very Merry Widow*?
26. Which cereal is advertised as the one that goes, 'Snap, Crackle and Pop'?
27. Which post did Alastair Milne hold finally at the BBC?
28. Who made the controversial *The War Game*?
29. Which organisation did Mary Whitehouse represent?
30. What is the BBC's house magazine?

ANSWERS

### TV Comedy 11 (See Quiz 44)

**1.** Sir Humphrey Appleby. **2.** Armed Robbery. **3.** Lisa Riley. **4.** *You Rang M'Lord?* **5.** Pvt. Godfrey. **6.** Jerzy Balowski. **7.** Liz Estensen. **8.** Lurcio. **9.** *The Bishop Rides Again.* **10.** Jaguar. **11.** Antiques. **12.** *Five Go Mad in Dorset.* **13.** Corky. **14.** Wendy Craig. **15.** Patsy Rowland. **16.** Sally Thomsett. **17.** Pearl. **18.** Artois. **19.** *Friends.* **20.** All-night bakery. **21.** *M*A*S*H.* **22.** Yellow. **23.** Paris. **24.** *After Henry.* **25.** *Alas Smith and Jones.* **26.** Roy Barraclough. **27.** Hot Gossip. **28.** Jerry. **29.** Steve Punt. **30.** *Last of the Summer Wine.*

## QUIZ 44 TV Comedy 11

LEVEL 2

**Answers: see Quiz 43, page 471**

1. Who was Jim Hacker's Cabinet Secretary?
2. What crime did Chris and Daryl commit in *Birds of a Feather*?
3. Who replaced Jeremy Beadle on *You've Been Framed*?
4. Which Croft & Perry sitcom was set in an Edwardian household?
5. Which character in *Dad's Army* had sisters named Dolly and Cissy?
6. What was the name of the landlord in *The Young Ones*?
7. Who, apart from Polly James, Pauline Collins and Nerys Hughes, has starred as a *Liver Bird*?
8. What was Frankie Howerd's character called in *Up Pompeii*?
9. Which late 60s sitcom starred Derek Nimmo as a bishop?
10. Which car did Joey drive in *Bread*?
11. In *Never The Twain* Windsor Davies and Donald Sinden were feuding member of which trade?
12. Which Enid Blyton spoof was made by the Comic Strip team in 1982?
13. Which policeman did Derek Guyler play in *Sykes*?
14. Who starred with Ronald Hines in *Not in Front of the Children*?
15. Who played Trevor's wife in *Bless This House*?
16. Who played Jo in *Man About the House*?
17. Who was Jethro's mother in *The Beverley Hillbillies*?
18. What was Rene's surname in *'Allo 'Allo*?
19. '*I'll Be There For You*,' was the theme music for which Channel 4 series?
20. What was the venue of the Keith Barron comedy *All Night Long*?
21. In which comedy series did David Ogden Stiers replace Larry Linville?
22. What colour was Del Boy's van?
23. In *Just Good Friends*, where did Vince and Penny finally marry?
24. In which comedy series did Joan Sanderson play the mother of Prunella Scales?
25. *Alas Sage and Onion* was a Christmas version of which comedy series?
26. Who partnered Les Dawson in the roles of Cissy and Ada?
27. Who were the dance troupe on *The Kenny Everett Video Show*?
28. What is Seinfeld's first name?
29. Who is Hugh Dennis' comic partner?
30. In which comedy series are Pearl and Marina rivals for the same man?

ANSWERS

**Pot Luck 6 (See Quiz 43)**

**1.** John Inverdale. **2.** Barbara Woodhouse. **3.** *Rainbow*. **4.** Gloria Hunniford. **5.** Diana Moran. **6.** Charlie Dimmock. **7.** Michael Palin. **8.** Campion. **9.** Phil Collins. **10.** John de Lancie. **11.** Spiderman. **12.** Vietnam. **13.** Husband and Wife. **14.** Cordelia. **15.** Battle of Britain Sunday. **16.** David Frost. **17.** Lori Singer. **18.** 20 Million. **19.** Barry Took. **20.** *Compact*. **21.** Cliff Mitchelmore. **22.** Peter Snow. **23.** *Bellamy's Bugle*. **24.** Bob Monkhouse. **25.** Moira Lister. **26.** Kelloggs Rice Krispies. **27.** Director General. **28.** Peter Watkins. **29.** The National Viewers and Listeners Association. **30.** *Ariel*.

## QUIZ 45 Soaps 5

LEVEL 2

**Answers: see Quiz 46, page 474**

1. What was Joan Collins character in *Dynasty*?
2. Where did Kathy Mitchell go when she left Albert Square?
3. Which star of *Goodnight Sweetheart* pulled the pints at the Woolpack?
4. Who was taken hostage in a Post Office raid in *Emmerdale*?
5. Which character was played by Leslie Grantham in *EastEnders*?
6. Who returned to *Neighbours* as a member of the Salvation Army?
7. Which character did Sarah Lancashire play in *Coronation Street*?
8. Who played Frank Tate in *Emmerdale*?
9. What was Anita Dobson's character in *EastEnders*?
10. Which real life father and son appeared in *Neighbours*?
11. Who did Victoria Principal play in *Dallas*?
12. What was the name of Minnie Caldwell's lodger in *Coronation Street*?
13. Who was Danni's mother in *Neighbours*?
14. Which character in *Crossroads* wore a woolly hat?
15. What was Dr Dawson's nickname in *Emergency Ward 10*?
16. Who has a husband in *EastEnders* named Ricki?
17. What was the name of the Ewing ranch?
18. Who did Nick Bates accidentally kill?
19. In which series did we meet the Tates and the Campbells?
20. Which of the *Neighbours* ran a chauffeuring service?
21. Who first ran the café in *EastEnders*?
22. Which company produces *Emmerdale*?
23. In which soap spoof would you find Mrs Overall?
24. In which hospital did Dr Baz Samuels work?
25. What was the name of Gita and Sanjay's daughter in *Eastenders*?
26. This character in *Neighbours* married Bronwen. Who is he?
27. Who was Caress's sister in *Dynasty*?
28. Which soap was originally to be called *The Midland Road*?
29. Which Mrs Frank Sinatra found fame in *Peyton Place*?
30. Who married Charlene in *Neighbours*?

ANSWERS

### Crime 5 (See Quiz 46)

**1.** Terence Alexander. **2.** Joe Ahearne. **3.** Daniela Nardini. **4.** Derek Martin. **5.** Miss Marple. **6.** Doctor. **7.** *The Cops*. **8.** PD James. **9.** Maria Aitken. **10.** Pathologist. **11.** *The Memoirs of Sherlock Holmes*. **12.** WPC Ackland. **13.** John Thaw. **14.** Mike Burden. **15.** Superintendant Mullett. **16.** Michael Denison. **17.** Gordon Jackson. **18.** *Dalziel & Pascoe*. **19.** Barbara Flynn. **20.** Robin Bailey and Michael Aldridge. **21.** Raffles. **22.** Britains largest anti-drug operation. **23.** Glen A Larson. **24.** Cagney. **25.** Hutch (Danid Soul). **26.** *Black Orchid*. **27.** Alligator. **28.** Shrewsbury. **29.** Hugh Williams. **30.** Carter.

## QUIZ 46 Crime 5

LEVEL 2

**Answers: see Quiz 45, page 473**

1. Who played Charlie Hungerford in *Bergerac*?
2. Who wrote *Ultraviolet*?
3. Who played Lois in *Undercover Heart*?
4. In *The Chinese Detective*, Ho's superior, Det. Chief Insp. Berwick, was played by which actor?
5. Joan Hickson played which Agatha Christie character?
6. What was the occupation of Nick Rowan's wife Kate in *Heartbeat*?
7. In which 1998 Tony Garnett series were officers Mel and Natalie?
8. Name the creator of Adam Dalgleish.
9. Jemima Shore had first appeared in *Quiet as A Nun*, in 1978. Who played Jemima?
10. What was Sam Ryan's occupation in *Silent Witness*?
11. Which was the last of the Jeremy Brett Sherlock Holmes productions in 1994?
12. In *The Bill*, which police officer was the target of an assassin?
13. Who played *Mitch* in the series of the same name?
14. Who is Inspector Wexford's DI assistant?
15. Who is Jack Frost's superior?
16. Which actor played Boyd QC?
17. Cowley in *The Professionals* was portrayed by which actor?
18. Warren Clarke and Colin Buchanan played which detective duo?
19. Which actress played Trevor's girlfriend Jill Swinburne in *The Beiderbecke Affair*?
20. In *Charters and Caldicott*, who played the two sleuths?
21. Who was EW Hornung's famous gentleman thief?
22. *Operation Julie* was based on facts about what?
23. Which TV impressarion created and produced *Knight Rider*?
24. Which of Cagney and Lacey was single?
25. Which 70s detective campaigned with Martin Bell in Tatton in 1997?
26. Name the first *Taggart* story shown without Mark McManus in 1995.
27. What was Crockett's pet in *Miami Vice*?
28. In which abbey is *Cadfael* based?
29. Inspector Marlowe was played by which actor in *The New Adventures of Charlie Chan*?
30. Which character did Dennis Waterman play to John Thaw's Regan?

ANSWERS

### Soaps 5 (See Quiz 45)

**1.** Alexis. **2.** South Africa. **3.** Michelle Holmes. **4.** Viv Windsor. **5.** Den Watts. **6.** Harold Bishop. **7.** Raquel Wolstenhume. **8.** Norman Bowler. **9.** Angie Watts. **10.** Jason & Terence Donovan. **11.** Pamela Ewing. **12.** Sonny Jim. **13.** Cheryl Stark. **14.** Benny. **15.** Digger. **16.** Bianca Butcher. **17.** Southfork. **18.** Jed Cornell. **19.** *Soap*. **20.** Helen Daniels. **21.** Sue Osman. **22.** Yorkshire Television. **23.** *Acorn Antiques*. **24.** Holby (*Casualty*). **25.** Shamilah. **26.** Henry Ramsay. **27.** Alexis. **28.** *Crossroads*. **29.** Mia Farrow. **30.** Scott Robinson.

## QUIZ 47 Quiz & Games Shows 2

LEVEL 2

**Answers: see Quiz 48, page 476**

1. Which newsreader presented *Treasure Hunt*?
2. How many 'lives' do *15 - 1* contestants start with?
3. Who was the first host of *University Challenge*?
4. In which show would you watch 'Mr Trick Shot'?
5. Which TV quiz had contestants bid for prizes, Nicholas Parsons presenting?
6. Who was Hughie Green's co-presenter on *Double Your Money*?
7. Who took over from Bob Monkhouse on *The Golden Shot*?
8. What was the booby prize on *3-2-1*?
9. What was ITV's mid-90s lunchtime culinary quiz?
10. Who replaced John Fashanu as a presenter on the *Gladiators*?
11. Who was replaced by Edward Tudor-Pole of Ten Pole Tudor fame on *The Crystal Maze*?
12. What was Britain's first daily game show, in which 16-18 year olds took part?
13. Who presented *Junior Criss Cross Quiz*?
14. Who was the host of *Play Your Cards Right*?
15. Which series required a panel to guess the profession of a contestant?
16. What is Channel 5's regular quiz for older contestants called?
17. On *The Sky's The Limit*, what could contestants win a voucher to do?
18. What was the very first Channel 4 programme to be televised?
19. How frequently was the quiz *Animal, Vegetable, Mineral* broadcast?
20. Who is the host of ITV's *Who Wants To Be A Millionaire*?
21. Which former radio programme moved to BBC TV in 1955?
22. Who was the original question master on *The Brains Trust*?
23. Who was the first blonde to present *Blankety Blank*?
24. How many *Celebrity Squares* were there?
25. Which winner of *New Faces* went on the present the show in the late 80s?
26. Who was the original question master of *Take Your Pick*?
27. Which show aimed to find the "Super-Person Of Great Britain"?
28. In *Treasure Hunt* how did Anneka Rice get from location to location?
29. Which Gaby Roslin show has its theme song sung by Status Quo?
30. Which Cilla Black show gave contestants a week to master a task with the hope of a £20,000 win?

ANSWERS

### TV Comedy 12 (See Quiz 48)

**1.** *Heartburn Hotel.* **2.** Dentist. **3.** Jennifer Saunders. **4.** Planet Ork. **5.** Edith Artois. **6.** In a hospital ward. **7.** Edina Monsoon. **8.** *Charge!* **9.** Harry Enfield & Paul Whitehouse. **10.** Rodney. **11.** Simon Callow. **12.** Monty Python. **13.** *Chalk.* **14.** *Ffizz.* **15.** *In Loving Memory.* **16.** Eddie Clocherty. **17.** Richard Gordon. **18.** James Hayter. **19.** Tabitha. **20.** Eric Sykes. **21.** *Before Your Very Eyes.* **22.** Arthur Askey. **23.** BBC TV. **24.** Benny Hill. **25.** MTV. **26.** The Abbotts. **27.** Chigwell, Essex. **28.** 'Rosie'. **29.** Gale Gordon. **30.** Charlie Higson.

## QUIZ 48 TV Comedy 12

LEVEL 2

**Answers: see Quiz 47, page 475**

1. Name John Sullivan's comedy with Tim Healy and Clive Russell as Falklands veterans.
2. What was Geoffrey Palmer's occupation in *Butterflies*?
3. Adrian Edmondson is the husband of one of his co-stars in *Comic Strip*. Who?
4. Where did Mork originate in *Mork and Mindy*?
5. Who sings in Bar Rene in *'Allo, 'Allo*?
6. Where was *Only When I Laugh* set?
7. Who did Bubbles work for in *Absolutely Fabulous*?
8. Robert Morley starred as an upper-class version of Alf Garnett in which comedy?
9. Who play the old gits?
10. In *Only Fools and Horses* who does Trigger refer to as Dave?
11. Who played Tom in Chance in a Million?
12. Who team sang 'I'm a Lumberjack'?
13. Which educational sitcom was set in Galfest High School?
14. Richard Griffiths was importing wine and skirting bankruptcy in which comedy?
15. Which sitcom featured Thord Hird running a funeral home?
16. Which Eddie was a character in *Tutti Frutti*?
17. Who wrote *Doctor In The House*?
18. Who starred as J Pinwright in the 1940's comedy series *Pinwright's Progress?*
19. In *Bewitched*, what was the name of Samantha's daughter?
20. Who wrote the scripts for the comedy series *The Howerd Crowd*?
21. Arthur Askey, Dickie Henderson and Diana Decker joined in which fortnightly BBC comedy series in the 1950s?
22. Who starred in the ITV sitcom *Love and Kisses*?
23. *The Benny Hill Show* first appeared in 1955 on which channel?
24. Which comedian wrote and starred in the silent TV film *Eddie In August*?
25. Which TV channel created *Celebrity Deathmatch*?
26. Which family featured in *Bless This House*?
27. Where do the *Birds of a Feather* live?
28. What was PC Penrose's nickname in *The Growing Pains of PC Penrose*?
29. Who played Lucille Ball's frustrated employer in *The Lucy Show*?
30. Who is Paul Whitehouse's writing partner for *The Fast Show*?

ANSWERS

### Quiz & Games Shows 2 (See Quiz 47)

**1.** Kenneth Kendall. **2.** Three. **3.** Bamber Gasgoyne. **4.** *Big Break.* **5.** *Sale of the Century.* **6.** Monica. **7.** Norman Vaughn and Charlie Williams. **8.** Dusty Bin. **9.** Quisine. **10.** Jeremy Guscott. **11.** Richard O'Brien. **12.** Blockbusters. **13.** Chris Kelly. **14.** Bruce Forsythe. **15.** *What's My Line?* **16.** 100 Per Cent Gold. **17.** Travel around the world. **18.** Countdown. **19.** Fortnightly. **20.** Chris Tarrant. **21.** *The Brains Trust.* **22.** Hugh Ross Williamson. **23.** Lily Savage. **24.** 9. **25.** Marti Caine. **26.** Michael Miles. **27.** *The Krypton Factor.* **28.** By helicopter. **29.** *Whatever You Want.* **30.** *The Moment of Truth.*

## QUIZ 49 Children's TV 5

LEVEL 2

**Answers: see Quiz 50, page 478**

1. What was the title of Roy Rogers' TV theme music?
2. Who loves Scooby snacks?
3. What nationality is Asterix?
4. Which series was translated into Irish and transmitted as *Tomas an Traien*?
5. Where does Yogi Bear live?
6. What instrument does Bart Simpson's sister, Lisa, play?
7. Which animated film from a Raymond Briggs story had Peter Auty singing to a famous flying sequence?
8. Who was Perky's partner?
9. Joe Inglis became resident vet on which show in 1998?
10. In which show might you meet Dump Pea?
11. How many windows featured in *Play School*?
12. Complete the following, taken from *Mr Ed*'s theme song, 'A horse is a horse...'
13. Who presented *Record Breakers* and got his name in the title?
14. Who might be accompanied by Snowy and Captain Haddock?
15. Which family lived under the floorboards?
16. What was the name of the dog in *The Woodentops*?
17. Who was the voice of the cartoon series *Willo the Wisp*?
18. What were *Roobarb and Custard*?
19. Where does *Paddington Bear* keep his marmalade sandwiches?
20. What was the name of *Captain Pugwash*'s ship?
21. Who narrated *Ivor the Engine* and *Noggin the Nog*?
22. What series featured Hammy the Hamster?
23. Jenny Hanley presented which ITV rival to *Blue Peter*?
24. What was the British name of *Top Cat*?
25. In which program would you have met Pootle, Posie and Perkin?
26. What is the name of the large yellow bird residing in *Sesame Street*?
27. Name the Teletubbies.
28. In which part of the country was *Byker Grove* set?
29. *Garfield* is what type of animal?
30. In which children's series could actress Sue Nicholls be seen playing Miss Popoff?

ANSWERS

### Pot Luck 7 (See Quiz 50)

**1.** Troy Kennedy Martin. **2.** The NEC, Birmingham. **3.** BBC TV. **4.** Andy Stewart. **5.** Vision Electronic Recording Apparatus (an early VCR). **6.** *Gamesmaster.* **7.** Peter O'Brien. **8.** Fairy Liquid **9.** JT Walsh. **10.** Maggie Fitzgibbon. **11.** *Twin Peaks.* **12.** North. **13.** The Beechgrove Garden. **14.** Rutland Weekend Television. **15.** Colin Baker. **16.** Danny Blanchflower. **17.** The Chelsea Flower Show. **18.** Kathleen Harrison. **19.** Ian Wright. **20.** Ainsley Harriott. **21.** 1932. **22.** In the Mood. **23.** David Dimbleby. **24.** Ray Mears. **25.** Prince Edward. **26.** Selina Scott. **27.** Jack Rosenthal. **28.** Gladioli. **29.** Leslie Welch. **30.** Bruce Johnson.

## QUIZ 50 Pot Luck 7

LEVEL 2

**Answers: see Quiz 49, page 477**

1. Who was the creator of *Edge of Darkness*?
2. Where was the location of the first live *Gardener's World* show?
3. *This Is Your Life* was first shown on which channel?
4. Who was the host of *The White Heather Club*?
5. What in TV production history was a VERA?
6. Dominic Diamond presented which computer programme?
7. Which Neighbour later appeared in *The Flying Doctors*?
8. Which product did Nanette Newman advertise?
9. Who played Frank Buck in *Dark Skies*?
10. Which star of *The Newcomers* appeared in *Manhunt*?
11. Kyle MacLachlan appeared in which unusual series?
12. Were Alexandra Palace TV studios in north or south London?
13. Which gardening programme came from Scotland?
14. Which fictitious TV station taught viewers to 'Ski in Your Home'?
15. Who was the sixth Dr Who?
16. Which footballer and Northern Ireland manager refused to be the subject of a *This Is Your Life* programme?
17. Name the annual gardening event screened from the Royal Hospital.
18. Who played 'Mrs Thursday'?
19. Which former Arsenal star hosted his own Friday Night chat show?
20. Which TV chef hosted *Party of a Lifetime*?
21. In which year were the first BBC TV studios formed?
22. What was Joe Loss's signature tune?
23. Which political commentator is brother of Jonathan and the son of Richard?
24. Who is the survival expert on *Wildtracks*?
25. Who was the Royal presenter of *Crown And Country*?
26. Which former newsreader hosted the *Clothes Show*?
27. Who is the screenwriting husband of Maureen Lipman?
28. What are Dame Edna Everage's favourite blooms?
29. In the post-war magazine programme *Kaleidoscope* who was the Memory Man?
30. What is Bruce Forsythe's real name?

ANSWERS

**Children's TV 5 (See Quiz 49)**

**1.** *Happy Trails to You.* **2.** Scooby Doo. **3.** Gaul. **4.** *Thomas the Tank Engine.* **5.** Jellystone Park. **6.** Saxophone. **7.** *The Snowman.* **8.** Pinky. **9.** *Blue Peter.* **10.** *Poddington Peas.* **11.** Three. **12.** '...of course, of course'. **13.** Linford Christie. **14.** Tintin. **15.** *The Borrowers.* **16.** Spotty Dog. **17.** Kenneth Williams. **18.** A dog and cat. **19.** Under his hat. **20.** The Black Pig. **21.** Oliver Postage. **22.** *Tales from the Riverbank.* **23.** Magpie. **24.** Boss Cat. **25.** *The Flumps.* **26.** Big Bird. **27.** Tinky-Winky, Dipsy, La-La, Po. **28.** North East. **29.** A Cat. **30.** *Rentaghost.*

## QUIZ 51 Crime 6

LEVEL 2

**Answers: see Quiz 52, page 480**

1. Who was Crockett's right hand man in *Miami Vice*?
2. Which newspaper crossword does Morse frequently complete?
3. Where was the setting for *Heartbeat*?
4. Who was the male star in *The Wasp's Nest*, the first Agatha Christie play to be televised in 1937?
5. Which 60 year old Lancashire detective has a sidekick called Geoffrey?
6. Which fictitious actor (played by Roy Clarke) is Pulaski?
7. Which sport did Lord Peter Wimsey play?
8. Who played 18 different roles in the first three series of *Murder Most Horrid*?
9. What was the name of the spin-off series from *Rockcliffe's Babies*?
10. What type of literature does Inspector Adam Dalgliesh write?
11. What was billed as 'The Ruth Rendell Christmas Mystery' in 1988?
12. Who plays Inspector Wexford?
13. Carl Galton (played by Iain Glen) led a violent north London gang in which serial?
14. Who played *Poirot* in the series of the same name?
15. What breed of dog did Columbo have?
16. What is the name of Sherlock Holmes' brother?
17. Who called people 'pussycat'?
18. Which actor played Campion's valet?
19. Who solved all his cases without even standing up?
20. Which legal champion frequently adjourned to Pomeroy's Wine Bar?
21. What was the 90s equivalent of the 60s series Crown Court called?
22. Which Government body did The Chief frequently clash with?
23. Where is *Cadfael* set?
24. Which series about a Highland policeman starred Robert Carlyle?
25. Where was *Waterfront Beat* based?
26. Who was Charlie Chan's 'Number One Son'?
27. Which supreme defence counsel was played for ten years by Raymond Burr?
28. In *The French Collection*, Spender went to which city?
29. What was the subject of *Between the Lines?*
30. Who left *EastEnders* to play D.I. Mick Raynor in 1994?

ANSWERS

### TV Comedy 13 (See Quiz 52)

**1.** Irene Handl & Warren Mitchel. **2.** Nicholas Parsons. **3.** *A Pinch of Snuff.* **4.** Camp Freemont, California. **5.** *'Allo, 'Allo.* **6.** Six. **7.** Ashley & Elaine. **8.** Mr Bean. **9.** 1956. **10.** Monsoon. **11.** 'Young' Mr Grace. **12.** Fluck & Law. **13.** Ruby Wax. **14.** *Auntie's Bloomers.* **15.** *Watching.* **16.** Agony Aunt. **17.** Nursie. **18.** Lulu. **19.** *Dinnerladies.* **20.** Blakey (*On the Buses*). **21.** Patrick O'Neal. **22.** *The New Statesman.* **23.** Laverne & Shirley. **24.** George Cole. **25.** Clive Swift. **26.** Ford Cortina. **27.** Paul Eddington. **28.** Rowan Atkinson. **29.** Alfie Bass. **30.** *Surgical Spirit.*

## QUIZ 52 TV Comedy 13

LEVEL 2

**Answers: see Quiz 51, page 479**

1. Who starred with Charlie Drake in *Drake's Progress*?
2. Which *Sale Of The Century Show* host first tasted fame in The Arthur Haynes Show?
3. In which crime drama did Hale and Pace make their straight acting debut in 1994?
4. To which army camp was Bilko transferred after leaving Fort Baxter?
5. Which sitcom was a spoof of *Secret Army*?
6. How many *Friends* are there?
7. Name the two lead characters in *The Two of Us*.
8. Which disaster-prone comedy character drove a mini?
9. In which year was *Hancock's Half Hour* first screened?
10. In *Absolutely Fabulous*, what is Edina's surname?
11. Who was the owner of the store in *Are You Being Served?*
12. Who made the puppets in *Spitting Image*?
13. Which of the *Girls on Top* was not British?
14. What is the BBC's outtakes show hosted by Terry Wogan called?
15. In which comedy series did sisters Brenda and Pamela live together?
16. Maureen Lipman played the part of what in *Agony*?
17. What was the name of Queen Elizabeth's female companion in *Blackadder*?
18. Who played Adrian's mother in *The Growing Pains of Adrian Mole*?
19. What a was Victoria Wood's first sitcom called?
20. Who used to say 'Get that bus out'?
21. Who played insurance investigator Dick Starrett?
22. Which show featured Alan Beresford B'Stard?
23. Which series featuring two girls was a spin-off from *Happy Days*?
24. In *Blott on the Landscape*, Sir Giles Lynchwood was played by which actor?
25. Who starred as Mr Nesbitt in *The Nesbitts Are Coming*?
26. What battered car does Mrs Bucket's son-in-law, Onslo, drive?
27. Minister James Hacker was played by which actor?
28. Who played Inspector Fowler in *The Thin Blue Line*?
29. Who played Private Bisley in *The Army Game*?
30. In which series did Nichola McAuliffe play the acerbic Sheila Sabatini?

ANSWERS

**Crime 6 (See Quiz 51)**

**1.** Tubbs. **2.** The Times. **3.** North Yorkshire. **4.** Francis L. Sullivan. **5.** Hetty Wainthropp. **6.** Larry Summers. **7.** Cricket. **8.** Dawn French. **9.** *Rockcliffe's Folly.* **10.** Poetry. **11.** *No Crying He Makes.* **12.** George Baker. **13.** *The Fear.* **14.** David Suchet. **15.** Bassett Hound. **16.** Mycroft. **17.** Kojak. **18.** Brian Glover. **19.** Ironside. **20.** Rumpole. **21.** *The Verdict.* **22.** The Home Office. **23.** Shrewsbury. **24.** *Hamish Macbeth.* **25.** London's Docklands. **26.** Barry Chan. **27.** Perry Mason. **28.** Marseilles. **29.** Police Internal Investigations. **30.** Leslie Grantham.

# QUIZ 53 Soaps 6

LEVEL 2

**Answers: see Quiz 53, page 482**

1. Who was the headmaster in *Home and Away*?
2. Who was Natalie Horrocks' son in *Coronation Street*?
3. Who was Walford's doctor in the early days of *EastEnders*?
4. Who links Bugs to *Neighbours*?
5. What happened to Emily Bishop's husband, Ernest?
6. Which *Neighbours* actor presented *The Big Breakfast*?
7. Who seduced Dave Glover in the stables in *Emmerdale*?
8. In *Brookside* where was Trevor Jordache buried?
9. Who played the part of Brad Willis in *Neighbours*?
10. How did Cindy leave the country when she left Ian in *EastEnders*?
11. Which soap had the working title *One Way Street*?
12. Who used to be a stripper in Ramsay Street?
13. Who played Sheila Grant in *Brookside*?
14. Who was Rod the Plod?
15. In *Emmerdale*, who was passed over in his father Jacob's will?
16. In *Dallas*, Lucy was the daughter of which of the Ewing clan?
17. At which number *Coronation Street* did the Ogdens live?
18. Which TV company was set up to make *Brookside*?
19. Which character did Sheila Mercier play in *Emmerdale*?
20. Which actress left Albert Square and returned to direct the soap?
21. In *Coronation Street* what was the job of the father of Fiona's baby?
22. Which soap had a restaurant called The Diner?
23. In 1980, who did Joe Sugden go to work for?
24. Which was the first soap to be shown on Channel 5?
25. Where did Liz move to when she left *Coronation Street* with Michael?
26. Which soap was set in Los Barcos?
27. How did Pat Sugden die?
28. Who left *EastEnders* and turned up in *The Hello Girls*?
29. In which US city was *The Colbys* set?
30. What is *Coronation Street's* newsagent's called?

ANSWERS

## Drama 5 (See Quiz 54)

**1.** Sir Francis Drake. **2.** Peter Strauss. **3.** Lily Langtree. **4.** The *Jewel in the Crown.* **5.** Algy Hernes. **6.** Marcia Blaines. **7.** Moll Flanders. **8.** *How Green Was My Valley.* **9.** Mrs Bridges. **10.** Children played by adults. **11.** Charles Ryder. **12.** Orson Welles. **13.** Alan Bennet. **14.** Prison Commandant. **15.** Chicken George. **16.** *Inn for Trouble.* **17.** *The Monocled Mutineer.* **18.** CS Lewis. **19.** A baby. **20.** John Duttine. **21.** Flint McCulloch. **22.** *Cardiac Arrest.* **23.** Ben Elton. **24.** Wellinton's. **25.** Dr Jack Kerruish. **26.** 1950s. **27.** *Pygmalion.* **28.** *Love Hurts.* **29.** *The Camomile Lawn* **30.** Imperial Crescent.

## QUIZ 54 Drama 5

**Answers: see Quiz 53, page 481**

LEVEL 2

1. Which Elizabethan seafarer and adventurer was played by Terence Morgan?
2. Which actor starred with Nick Nolte in *Rich Man, Poor Man*?
3. Francesca Annis played which actress acquaintance of Edward VII?
4. Which period drama set in India was based on *The Raj Quartet* novels?
5. Who played the headmaster in *To Serve Them All My Days*?
6. Miss Jean Brodie taught at which school for girls?
7. Julie Foster played which fun-seeking 17$^{th}$ century character?
8. Stanley Baker starred in which 1976 classic drama set in Wales and chronicled the lives of the Morgan family?
9. What was the name of the cook in *Upstairs, Downstairs*?
10. In what way was the TV play *Blue Remembered Hills* unusual?
11. Jeremy Irons played which character in *Brideshead Revisited*?
12. Which actor and director narrated *Shogun*?
13. *Fortunes of War* featured which Yorkshire playwright?
14. Bernard Hepton played which role in *Colditz*?
15. Complete the name of this character from *Roots*, 'Chicken ...' ?
16. What was the title of the feature film spin-off of *The Larkins*?
17. Paul McGann played Percy Topliss as what kind of mutineer?
18. *Shadowlands* was about which author?
19. In *Upstairs, Downstairs* Mrs Bridges appeared in court after stealing what?
20. *To Serve Them All My Days* starred actor John who?
21. What was the name of the trail scout, played by Robert Horton in *Wagon Train*?
22. In which series did Helen Baxendale star as Claire Maitland?
23. Who starred in his own TV adaptation of his novel *Stark*?
24. Sharpe was a cavalry officer in whose army in the first series of the drama?
25. In *Peak Practice* who joined the Cardale medics after working in Africa?
26. In which decade was Dennis Potter's *Lipstick on Your Collar* set?
27. Margaret Lockwood made her TV debut in which GB Shaw play in 1948?
28. In which series did Adam Faith play plumber Frank Carver?
29. Which adaptation of a Mary Wesley novel was Peter Hall's TV directorial debut?
30. Which London hotel featured in *The Inch Man*?

ANSWERS

**Soaps 6 (See Quiz 53)**

**1.** Mr Fisher. **2.** Tony. **3.** Dr Legg. **4.** Craig McLaughlin. **5.** He was killed in a bank raid. **6.** Mark Little. **7.** Kim Tate. **8.** Under the patio. **9.** Scott Michaelson. **10.** Eurostar. **11.** *Neighbours*. **12.** Daphne. **13.** Sue Johnstone. **14.** Rod Corkhill. **15.** Joe Sugden. **16.** Gary. **17.** 13 **18.** Mersey Television. **19.** Annie Sugden. **20.** Susan Tully. **21.** Policeman. **22.** *Home and Away*. **23.** NY Estates. **24.** *Family Affairs*. **25.** Milton Keynes. **26.** *Eldorado*. **27.** Car accident. **28.** Letitia Dean. **29.** Los Angeles **30.** The Kabin.

## QUIZ 55 Music & Variety 2

LEVEL 2

**Answers: see Quiz 56, page 484**

1. Which pop band helped to launch Channel 5?
2. When were the inter-regional competitions in *Come Dancing* introduced?
3. Who succeeded Bob Monkhouse as presenter of *Opportunity Knocks*?
4. Which presenter of *The Tube* was previously a member of the band *Squeeze*?
5. Where did The Three Tenors first perform together?
6. Who performed with Lord Lloyd Webber on *Top of the Pops* in 1998?
7. Which character in *The Young Ones* had a hit with 'Hole in My Shoe'?
8. Who sang "Life is the name of the game" in introducing his show?
9. What was the precursor of *The Good Old Days*?
10. What placing did the UK's first entry in the *Eurovision Song Contest* get?
11. In 1998 which Royal appeared on *Des O'Connor Tonight*?
12. Who played Marie Lloyd in *Our Marie*?
13. Which talent show had the theme song "You're A Star"?
14. Who was the illusionist who accompanied David Nixon on *It's Magic*?
15. Which 007 has presented Sunday Night at the London Palladium?
16. Who was the resident host of *Showtime*?
17. Which star of *Common as Muck* is President of the British Music Hall Society and a regular on radio?
18. Who first hosted *Whose Line Is It Anyway?*
19. Who first hosted *Sunday Night At The Palladium*?
20. Who added '*Who Else?*' to his show when he moved to Channel 4?
21. Who kicked her way through *Let's Face The Music and Dance* in '78?
22. Who produced *The Billy Cotton Band Show*?
23. On which show would you have seen Zoo and Ruby Flipper?
24. Whose music career took off after she appeared on *The Cruise*?
25. How many panellists were there on *Juke Box Jury*?
26. What days was *Cool For Cats* broadcast?
27. When was *Opportunity Knocks* first shown?
28. Which magician had a fan club called Secrets?
29. Who was in the first televised *Royal Variety Show* and celebrated 40 years in showbusiness in 1998?
30. 'Anyone Can Fall in Love' was a song from which soap's theme tune?

ANSWERS

### TV Comedy 14 (See Quiz 56)

**1.** Monica Geller. **2.** Vivien. **3.** Derek Fowlds. **4.** Tracey Ullman. **5.** Michael Williams. **6.** Dorien. **7.** Sarah Kennedy. **8.** Jeremy Beadle. **9.** Carmen Munroe. **10.** Edmund. **11.** A cat. **12.** David Griffin. **13.** Roy Clarke. **14.** Chef. **15.** Hale and Pace. **16.** Their children got married. **17.** Adrian Mole. **18.** Sarah, Duchess of York. **19.** Sheridan. **20.** *Norman*. **21.** *Grace and Favour*. **22.** Brenda Blethyn. **23.** David Jason was in *A Touch of Frost*. **24.** Spain. **25.** Graham Norton. **26.** Felicity Kendall. **27.** Jessica. **28.** Sermon from St Albions. **29.** 41. **30.** Cpl. Max Klinger.

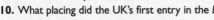

## QUIZ 56 TV Comedy 14

LEVEL 2

**Answers: see Quiz 55, page 483**

1. Which Friend is notoriously houseproud?
2. What was the name of the punk with studs in *The Young Ones*?
3. In *Yes, Prime Minister*, who played the Private Secretary Bernard Woolley?
4. Who was the female in *Three Of A Kind*?
5. Who is Judi Dench's real-life husband who starred with her in *A Fine Romance*?
6. Who is the man-hungry neighbour in *Birds of a Feather*?
7. Name the female presenter of *Game For A Laugh*.
8. Who hosted *You've Been Framed*?
9. Which former *PlaySchool* presenter played Shirley in *Desmond's*?
10. In *Blackadder II*, the Elizabethan period, what was Blackadder's first name?
11. What was Mrs Slocombe's pet?
12. Who replaced Simon Cadell as manager of the holiday camp in *Hi-De-Hi!*?
13. Who wrote *Last of the Summer Wine*?
14. What is Garth's occupation in *Birds of A Feather*?
15. Who created the villainous Two Rons?
16. In *Never The Twain*, what event brought together the lead characters?
17. Who kept a secret diary on ITV?
18. Who famously said "Nice hat" in a much hyped episode of *Friends*?
19. What is the name of Mrs Bucket's son?
20. What was Norman Wisdom's first TV sitcom?
21. What was the sequel to *Are You Being Served?* called?
22. Who starred in *All Good Things*?
23. Why were plans for a 1993 series of *Only Fools and Horses* put on hold?
24. In the second series of *Auf Wiedersehen Pet*, which country did they all travel to?
25. Which comic priest on *Father Ted* went on to host his own chat show?
26. Who played Gemma Palmer in *Solo*?
27. What was Frank and Betty Spencer's daughter called in *Some Mothers Do 'Ave 'Em*?
28. In which series did Harry Enfield play the Rev Tony Blair?
29. How old was Ronnie Corbett's character in *Sorry!*?
30. Name the character played by Jamie Farr in *M*A*S*H*.

ANSWERS

**Music & Variety 2 (See Quiz 55)**

**1.** The Spice Girls. **2.** 1953. **3.** Les Dawson. **4.** Jools Holland. **5.** *Italia 90*. **6.** Boyzone. **7.** Neil. **8.** Bruce Forsyth (*Generation Game*). **9.** *City Varieties*. **10.** 7th. **11.** Prince Edward. **12.** Pat Kirkwood. **13.** *New Faces*. **14.** Al Koran. **15.** Roger Moore. **16.** David Nixon. **17.** Roy Hudd. **18.** Cilve Anderson. **19.** Tommy Trinder. **20.** Rory Bremner. **21.** Angela Rippon. **22.** Billy Cotton Jnr. **23.** *Top of the Pops*. **24.** Jane McDonald. **25.** 4. **26.** Monday, Wednesday, Friday. **27.** 1956. **28.** Paul Daniels. **29.** Cliff Richard. **30.** *Eastenders*.

## QUIZ 57 Pot Luck 8

LEVEL 2

**Answers: see Quiz 58, page 486**

1. What is Mr Motivator's real name?
2. Whose wife, Debbie, was killed in an accident in *EastEnders*?
3. In which year did Granada TV start covering the North-West of England?
4. Which was the first truly local independent TV station?
5. On which UK TV programme did Clive James first appear?
6. Who presented the first *Gardener's World Live* show on BBC1 in 1993?
7. Which role did Robert play in *Two's Company*?
8. Which series of plays starred John Alderton and Pauline Collins in various guises?
9. Who played the lead role in *The Fall and Rise of Reginald Perrin*?
10. Name the Canadian born TV presenter and actor married to Barbara Kelly.
11. Who was the first Chief Executive of Channel 4?
12. On which show did Laurence Llewelyn find fame?
13. Which Python created *The Rutles*?
14. Who replaced Vanessa on ITV's daytime discussion show?
15. What is Roy Vasey's stage name?
16. When TV was interrupted in 1939 by WWII what programme was on?
17. How is Anthony Robert McMillan better known?
18. Whose catchphrase is 'I wanna tell you a story'?
19. Which of the *Two Fat Ladies* travels in the sidecar?
20. Who hosts a late night chat show on Channel 5?
21. Who first presented *Holiday*?
22. Who interviewed the male members of *Friends* on Channel 4?
23. Who played Marian to Michael Praed's Robin?
24. What was Joan Ferguson's nickname in *Prisoner Cell Block H*?
25. Who is Sting's actress wife?
26. The father is Johnny, the daughter is Zoe. What is their surname?
27. Which TV gardener wrote a steamy novel called Mr MacGregor?
28. Who was the star of *And Mother Makes Three*?
29. Name the presenter of *I, Camcorder*.
30. Who presents *The Antiques Roadshow*?

ANSWERS

**Current Affairs 4 (See Quiz 58)**

**1.** Nick Ross & Sue Cook. **2.** David Attenborough. **3.** Kate Adie. **4.** St.James Hospital, Leeds. **5.** *Panorama*. **6.** *Network* **7.** Magenta DeVine & Sankha Guha. **8.** Antoine de Caunes. **9.** Normski. **10.** 30 Degrees East. **11.** Electronic News Gathering **12.** Fiona Phillips. **13.** Mark Porter. **14.** David Attenborough. **15.** CIA. **16.** The Welsh Guards. **17.** Peter Sissons. **18.** The 25th anniversary of his Investiture. **19.** Terry Gilliam. **20.** Peter Frame. **21.** Nautilus. **22.** Peoples' Century. **23.** David Attenborough. **24.** Martin Bashir. **25.** Humphrey Burton. **26.** *The Diana Dors Show*. **27.** *The Tribe That Hides From Man*. **28.** Terry Thomas. **29.** *Now Showing*. **30.** John Craven.

## QUIZ 58 Current Affairs 4

**Answers: see Quiz 57, page 485** LEVEL 2

1. Who were the original presenters of *Crimewatch UK*?
2. Name the presenter of *The Living Planet*.
3. Who came prominence reporting the siege at the Iranian Embassy in 1980?
4. *Jimmy's* is a real life medical drama series set in which hospital?
5. Which programme featured a spoof spaghetti harvest?
6. Apart from *DEF II*, which C4 programme was produced by Janet Street-Porter?
7. Who were the presenters of *Rough Guide to Europe*?
8. Who presented *Rapido* on BBC 2?
9. Who presented *Dance Energy* on BBC 2?
10. At what longitude did Michael Palin trek from the North to the South Pole?
11. What does ENG stand for?
12. Who replaced Anthea Turner on the GMTV sofa?
13. Which doctor is a regular contributor to *Newsnight*?
14. Who presented *The Trials of Life*?
15. Which documentary examined America's Central Intelligence Agency?
16. *In The Company of Men* featured which army regiment?
17. Who did David Dimbleby replace on *Question Time*?
18. What was *Charles: Private Man, The Public Role* commemorating?
19. Which *Monty Python* member presented *The Last Machine*?
20. *Rock Family Trees* was based on the diagrams drawn by which music journalist?
21. Which 1995 documentary charted the development of the submarine?
22. Which BBC project aims to chronicle twentieth century historical events through the eyes of ordinary people who lived through them?
23. Who presented *The Private Life Of Plants*?
24. Who conducted the famous *Panorama* interview with Diana, Princess of Wales?
25. Who was the original presenter of the arts programme *Aquarius*?
26. What was the name of Diana Dors' afternoon talk show?
27. Which 1970 documentary searched for the Amazonian tribe, The Kreen-Akrore?
28. Who was Parkinson's very first guest on TV?
29. Which short-lasting film review series was presented by Michael Wood?
30. Who first presented *Newsround*?

ANSWERS

### Pot Luck 8 (See Quiz 57)

**1.** Derrick Evans. **2.** Nigel Bates. **3.** 1956. **4.** Southern Television, Southampton. **5.** *University Challenge*. **6.** Geoff Hamilton. **7.** Dorothy McNab's Butler. **8.** *Wodehouse Playhouse*. **9.** Leonard Rossiter. **10.** Bernard Bradan. **11.** Jeremy Isaacs. **12.** *Changing Rooms*. **13.** Eric Idle. **14.** *Trisha*. **15.** Roy 'Chubby' Brown. **16.** A Mickey Mouse cartoon. **17.** Robbie Coltrane. **18.** Max Bygraves. **19.** Clarissa Dickson Wright. **20.** Jack Docherty. **21.** Cliff Mitchelmore. **22.** Gaby Roslyn. **23.** Judi Trott. **24.** The Freak. **25.** Trudie Styler. **26.** Ball. **27.** Alan Titchmarsh. **28.** Wendy Craig. **29.** Robert Llewelyn. **30.** Hugh Scully.

## QUIZ 59 Children's TV 6

**Answers: see Quiz 60, page 488**

LEVEL 2

1. Name Dangermouse's sidekick.
2. Who was the original voice of the *Wombles*?
3. What animal was Flipper?
4. Who did Zoe Ball replace on *Live and Kicking*?
5. What type of bird was the Big Bird on *Sesame Street*?
6. How many *Monkees* were there?
7. What are the names of Fred and Barney's wives in *The Flintstones*?
8. Who was the TV artist in *Vision On*?
9. When *Bagpuss*' friend Professor Yaffle was asleep, what function did he serve?
10. One of the Addams Family's children is named after a day of the week. Which one?
11. What creature is Casper?
12. Which puppet was sad because it 'can't fly, right up to the sky'?
13. What was the name of Ken Dodd's puppet pals?
14. What was the name of Gloria Hunniford's daughter who was a *Blue Peter* presenter?
15. Which family lived at Mockingbird Heights, 1313 Mockingbird Lane?
16. In *The Flowerpot Men*, what was Slowcoach?
17. In which television series did Ray Winstone play Will Scarlett?
18. Who moved from Children's BBC front man to *Saturday Superstore* and *Going Live!*?
19. Who was television's first *Robin Hood*?
20. Whose catchphrase was 'Boom, Boom'?
21. What was the name of the Australian series about a kangaroo?
22. In which cartoon series would you find Muskie?
23. Who first hosted TV am's *Wide Awake Club*?
24. What was the nickname of Stebson in *Grange Hill*?
25. What type of creature is CBBC's Otis?
26. What is the name of the company which produces *Wallace and Gromit*?
27. Who presented *Zoo Time*?
28. Name Popeye's enemy.
29. Where did Wallace and Gromit go for *A Grand Day Out*?
30. Who sung '*Champion the Wonder Horse*'?

ANSWERS

**Comedy 15 (See Quiz 60)**

**1.** *Five Go Mad in Dorset.* **2.** Alexei Sayle. **3.** Albert & Victoria. **4.** Peter Bowles. **5.** Peter Sallis. **6.** Jennifer Aniston. **7.** Richard Briers. **8.** The washboard. **9.** Frank Skinner. **10.** *Desmond's.* **11.** Rebecca Howe. **12.** *Fresh Fields.* **13.** Caroline Aherne. **14.** *Jane in the Desert.* **15.** The Church Hall. **16.** Compo, Clegg & Blamire. **17.** *Father Ted.* **18.** *As Time Goes By.* **19.** 3. **20.** Michael Bentine. **21.** Angus Deayton. **22.** Nelson Mandela House. **23.** John Sullivan. **24.** Cissy and Ada. **25.** *All Quiet on the Preston Front.* **26.** *Bottoms Up.* **27.** Gary Holton. **28.** John Mahoney (Martin Crane). **29.** Bayview. **30.** Situation.

## QUIZ 60 TV Comedy 15

LEVEL 2

**Answers: see Quiz 59, page 487**

1. Which was the first *Comic Strip*?
2. Who played the landlord in *The Young Ones*?
3. What was the name of the comedy about a Victorian family starring Alfred Marks?
4. Who played *The Bounder*?
5. Which *Last of the Summer Wine* actor narrates *Wallace & Gromit*?
6. Which *Friends* star is the god daughter of the late Telly Savalas?
7. Which actor played Martin Bryce in *Ever Decreasing Circles*?
8. Which unusual instrument did Sykes' policeman friend, Derek Guyler play?
9. Which comedy performer was the male 'Rear of the Year' in 1998?
10. In which Channel 4 comedy did Porkpie appear?
11. What was the name of the bar manager played by Kirstie Alley in *Cheers*?
12. Anton Rodgers and Julia McKenzie played the primary roles in which comedy?
13. Who was the woman behind Mrs Merton?
14. What was the follow-up series to *Jane*?
15. In what building were *Dad's Army* based?
16. Who were the original three pals in *Last of the Summer Wine*?
17. Which series told the tale of three priests on an island?
18. Which sitcom used the music from Casablanca as its theme tune?
19. How many TV series did Norman Wisdom star in?
20. Which potty actor was the star of *All Square*?
21. Who asks the questions in *Have I Got News For You*?
22. In which building was the Trotter's flat in *Only Fools and Horses*?
23. Who wrote *Just Good Friends* and *Dear John*?
24. What were the gossipy women called played by Les Dawson and Roy Barraclough?
25. Paul Haigh and Colin Buchanan starred in which TA sitcom?
26. *Whack-O!* was turned into a feature film in 1960. What was the name of the film?
27. Which actor died before completion of the first series of *Auf Wiedersehen Pet*?
28. Who is the British-born male co-star of *Frasier*?
29. What was the name of the retirement home in *Waiting For God*?
30. What does the 'sit' of sitcom stand for?

ANSWERS

### Children's TV 6 (See Quiz 59)

**1.** Penfold. **2.** Bernard Cribbens. **3.** A dolphin. **4.** Emma Forbes. **5.** Canary. **6.** 3. **7.** Wilma & Betty. **8.** Tony Hart. **9.** Bookend. **10.** Wednesday. **11.** A ghost. **12.** Orville. **13.** The Diddy Men. **14.** Caron Keating. **15.** *The Munsters.* **16.** A tortoise. **17.** *Robin of Sherwood.* **18.** Phillip Schofield. **19.** Richard Greene. **20.** Basil Brush. **21.** Skippy. **22.** Deputy Dawg. **23.** Timmy Mallett. **24.** Gripper. **25.** Aardvark. **26.** Aardman Animations. **27.** Desmond Morris. **28.** Bluto. **29.** The Moon. **30.** Frankie Lane.

## QUIZ 61 Soaps 7

LEVEL 2

**Answers: see Quiz 62, page 490**

1. Who had an affair with Kim Tate in 1992?
2. Who took over Glendarroch estate after Elizabeth Cunningham was killed?
3. How did Leonard Kempinski die?
4. Who played Rodney Harrington in *Peyton Place*?
5. Who was Zoe Tate's girlfriend and moved into The Smithy with her?
6. What occupation was Mavis going to take up in the Lake District after she left *Coronation Street*?
7. What was the name of the hotel complex in *Neighbours*?
8. Who played the character Rachel Tate in *Emmerdale*?
9. Which actor played Dirty Den in *EastEnders*?
10. Who plays Butch Dingle?
11. Who owned a burger van in *Emmerdale*?
12. In *EastEnders* what was Phil and Kathy's son called?
13. Which soap mounted a 'Free George Jackson' campaign?
14. In *Dallas*, who did Miss Ellie marry after Jock died?
15. What major event occurred in *Emmerdale* on the 30th December, 1993?
16. Who went from *No Hiding Place* to *Coronation Street*?
17. Who plays Jack Sugden?
18. Which character does Alyson Spiro portray in *Emmerdale*?
19. How much did Frank offer Kim to move back to Home Farm?
20. Who was Zak Dingle's crooked brother?
21. Who is Tiffany's mother in *EastEnders*?
22. Who had dancing lessons with Terry Woods?
23. Who did Nick Bates kill?
24. Who did Sally Webster go into personal and business partnership with when she left Kevin?
25. How did Dave Glover die?
26. Why was *Emmerdale Farm* demolished?
27. Which soap was one of the BBC's first daytime scheduled serials?
28. Which two brothers did Cindy have affairs with in *EastEnders*?
29. What was Alma's surname before she married the Street's Mike Baldwin?
30. How did Shirley Turner die?

ANSWERS

### Pot Luck 9 (See Quiz 62)

**1.** *Grass Roots.* **2.** Judy Carne. **3.** Anthony Newly. **4.** *Floyd Uncorked.* **5.** Carroll O'Connor. **6.** Pauline Yates. **7.** Cot Death Syndrome. **8.** Antoine de Caunes. **9.** Clive Anderson. **10.** Barbara Feldon. **11.** Ray Walston. **12.** British Academy of Film and Televsion Arts. **13.** *Nighthawks.* **14.** Citroen. **15.** 30-line. **16.** Charles Hill. **17.** White City. **18.** Mack McKenzie. **19.** *The Real Life Holiday Show.* **20.** Monty Don. **21.** Angela Rippon. **22.** *World in Action.* **23.** Nixon. **24.** Gerald Seymour. **25.** The Earl of Listowel, Postmaster General. **26.** Dirk, Nasty, Stig & Barry. **27.** Rolf Harris (*Animlal Hospital*). **28.** Andy. **29.** David Frost. **30.** *Points of View* (Robinson).

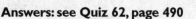

## QUIZ 62 Pot Luck 9

LEVEL 2

**Answers: see Quiz 61, page 489**

1. Richard Jackson presents which programme?
2. Which Judy was the *Laugh-In* girl?
3. Which actor played Gurney Slade?
4. What was Keith Floyd's series touring vineyards called?
5. Who played Archie Bunker?
6. Reggie Perrin's wife, Elizabeth was played by which actress?
7. Which cause does Ann Diamond campaign for?
8. Who introduces *Eurotrash*?
9. Who has a show called *All Talk*?
10. Who played 'Agent 99' in *Get Smart*?
11. Who was the star of *My Favourite Martian*?
12. What does BAFTA stand for?
13. Name the series which featured three nightwatchmen.
14. Which make of car did Bryan Brown advertise?
15. Was the original 1930's TV definition system 30-line, 50-line or 70-line?
16. Which TV doctor became chairman of the BBC?
17. Where is BBC TV Centre?
18. Which character did Kevin Dobson play in *Knotts Landing*?
19. Which holiday programme did Gaby Roslin introduce?
20. He presented *Real Gardens*. Who is he?
21. Which female newsreader danced with Morecambe and Wise?
22. What is the name of Granada TV's weekly current affairs programme?
23. Which president spoke live to the first man on the moon?
24. Name the writer of *Harry's Game*.
25. Who formally declared TV services open after its WWII closure?
26. Who were the 'pre-fab four' in *The Rutles*?
27. Which Australian presents programmes from the Harmsworth?
28. Which resident DIY expert on *Changing Rooms* is 'handy'?
29. Who created the company Paradine Productions?
30. Which programme has been presented by both Anne and Robert who share the same surname?

ANSWERS

### Soaps 7 (See Quiz 61)

**1.** Neil Kincaid. **2.** Lady Margaret & Sir John Ross-Gifford. **3.** A car struck him. **4.** Ryan O'Neal. **5.** Emma Nightingale. **6.** Running a guest house. **7.** Lassiters. **8.** Glenda McKay. **9.** Leslie Grantham. **10.** Paul Laughran. **11.** Mandy Dingle. **12.** Ben. **13.** *Brookside*. **14.** Clayton Barlow. **15.** The air disaster. **16.** Johnny Briggs. **17.** Clive Hornby. **18.** Sarah Sugden. **19.** £1 Million. **20.** Albert. **21.** Louise Raymond. **22.** Viv Windsor. **23.** Jed Cornell. **24.** Greg Kelly. **25.** Trying to save James Francis from a fire. **26.** To make way for Demdyke Quarry Access Road. **27.** *Neighbours*. **28.** Simon and David Wicks. **29.** Sedgewick. **30.** Shot in a Post-Office raid.

## QUIZ 63 Drama 6

LEVEL 2

**Answers: see Quiz 64, page 492**

1. The 1950's series *Fabian of Scotland Yard* was based whose career?
2. Who played Winston Smith in the 1954 adaptation of George Orwell's *1984*?
3. In the 1960s adaptation of *The Three Musketeers*, who played D'Artagnan?
4. In ITV's 1950's series, *The Adventures of Robin Hood*, who played the title role?
5. What was Robson Green's character called in *Soldier Soldier*?
6. *The Children of the New Forest* was serialised in three times. Who wrote the original?
7. Who was the lead in the detective series *Colonel March of Scotland Yard*?
8. In which series did Jimmy Nail play factory worker Jed Shepherd?
9. Which actress played Miss Kitty in *Gunsmoke*?
10. What were the first names of the two sisters in *The House of Eliott*?
11. Which drama series title meant 'roll call' in Japanese?
12. *Buccaneer* was concerned with which small air freight company?
13. As which character was Bernard Hill looking for a job?
14. *A Voyage Round My Father* was an autobiographical drama about which writer and barrister?
15. Which actress and model was CJ in *Baywatch*?
16. What have *Operation Diplomat* (1952), *Portrait of Alison* (1955), *The Scarf* (1959), *Paul Temple* (1970–1) in common?
17. *The Fall Guy* starred which actor?
18. Which traitor's meeting with Coral Browne was dramatised in *An Englishman Abroad*?
19. How long was each episode of *Sailor of Fortune*?
20. Which helicopter did Jan Michael Vincent pilot?
21. In which city is *ER* based?
22. What was the name of the cook in *Wagon Train*?
23. Who wrote *The Count of Monte Cristo*?
24. In *Widows*, what had been the women's husbands occupation before their deaths?
25. *The Buccaneers* was set in which Islands?
26. Who was the Range Rider?
27. Who replaced Michael Praed's *Robin of Sherwood* and became Robert of Huntingdon?
28. In which series did Ian Richardson first play MP Francis Urquhart?
29. In which series were the experiences of Major Pat Reid based?
30. Name *Jungle Boy*'s companion lion cub.

ANSWERS

**TV Comedy 16 (See Quiz 64)**

**1.** Dame Edna Everage. **2.** Michael Barrymore. **3.** *Birds of a Feather*. **4.** Belinda Lang. **5.** Bootsie & Snudge. **6.** Lord Percy. **7.** Tracey Ullman. **8.** Jo Brand. **9.** Bill Maynard. **10.** Leisure Centre. **11.** Marti Caine. **12.** Lollipop Man. **13.** Manchester. **14.** Le Chateau Anglais. **15.** Julian Clary. **16.** Keith Allen. **17.** Tim Brooke-Taylor. **18.** Inventing. **19.** Arthur Fonzarelli. **20.** Frogmella. **21.** Dr Tom Latimer. **22.** George Roper. **23.** *Atletico Partick*. **24.** Clive Swift. **25.** Marlene. **26.** Billy Connolly. **27.** Richard O'Sullivan. **28.** Paris. **29.** Paul and Pauline Calf. **30.** Johnny Speight.

## QUIZ 64 TV Comedy 16

LEVEL 2

**Answers: see Quiz 63, page 491**

1. The 'arts programme' *La Dame Axe Gladiolas* featured who?
2. Which comedy performer was managed by his wife Cheryl?
3. Which sitcom was set in a house called Dalentrace?
4. Who links *Dear John* to *2 Point 4 Children*?
5. What was the spin-off from *The Army Game*?
6. Tim McInnerny played which character in the second series of *Blackadder*?
7. In *Three of a Kind*, who was the female comedian?
8. Whose stand up comedy and sketch show was called *Through the Cakehole*?
9. Who played *The Gaffer*?
10. What was the setting for *The Brittas Empire*?
11. Which *New Faces* winner was born Lynne Shepherd in Sheffield?
12. In *Desmond's* what was Porkpie's former job?
13. Which city does Daphne Moon in *Frasier* originate from?
14. What was the name of the restaurant in *Chef!*?
15. Who performed as The Joan Collins Fan Club until Miss Collins' lawyers started to raise objections?
16. Who played the factory boss in *Making Out*?
17. Which one of the Goodies did NOT help write the sitcom *Astronauts*?
18. In *Last of the Summer Wine* what was Seymour's hobby, which often had disastrous results?
19. What was The Fonz's full name?
20. What's the name of Wayne and Waynetta Slob's daughter?
21. Which harassed young GP does Nigel Havers play in *Don't Wait Up*?
22. Who is the landlord in *Man About The House*?
23. Gordon Kennedy starred in which football-related sitcom?
24. Who plays Mrs Bucket's hen-pecked husband Richard?
25. What is the name of Boysie's wife in *Only Fools and Horses*?
26. Which Glaswegian was a member of the Humblebums?
27. Who starred as Robin Tripp?
28. In which capital city did Vince and Penny finally get married in *Just Good Friends?*
29. Which siblings appeared in Steve Coogan's *Three Fights, Two Weddings and a Funeral*?
30. Who specially wrote the script of *The Lady Is A Tramp* for Patricia Hayes?

ANSWERS

### Drama 6 (See Quiz 63)

**1.** Robert Fabian. **2.** Peter Cushing. **3.** Jeremy Brett. **4.** Richard Greene. **5.** Dave Tucker. **6.** Capt. Frederick Marryat. **7.** Boris Karloff. **8.** *Crocodile Shoes*. **9.** Amanda Blake. **10.** Beatrice and Evangeline. **11.** *Tenko*. **12.** Red Air. **13.** Yosser Hughes. **14.** John Mortimer. **15.** Pamela Anderson Lee. **16.** All were by Francis Durbridge. **17.** Lee Majors. **18.** Guy Burgess. **19.** 25 Minutes. **20.** *Airwolf*. **21.** Chicago. **22.** Charlie Wooster. **23.** Alexander Dumas. **24.** Crminals. **25.** The Bahamas. **26.** Jock Mahoney. **27.** Jason Connery. **28.** *House of Cards*. **29.** *Colditz*. **30.** Simba.

## QUIZ 65 Crime 7

LEVEL 2

**Answers: see Quiz 66, page 494**

1. Who played the ambitious detective Tony Clark in *Between the Lines*?
2. *Heartbeat* was set in the middle of which decade?
3. Which actor links *Rumpole* to *The Prisoner*?
4. Which 70s US detective was played by William Conrad?
5. Where did Nick Rowan originally arrive from in *Heartbeat*?
6. In the drama, *The Two Mrs Carrolls*, how did Geoffrey Carroll plan to murder his wife?
7. Which offbeat sleuth was played by Alan Davies opposite Caroline Quentin?
8. In which magazine did the *Addams Family* first appear?
9. Who partnered Det. Insp. Sam Sterne in *Sam Saturday*?
10. Whose refusal to make further series of *Shoestring* led to the creation of new sleuth Bergerac?
11. Which specialist squad featured in the first series of *Liverpool One*?
12. In *Dragnet*, who played officer Frank Smith?
13. Det. Chief Insp. Nick Lewis was consigned to the PPO in the *Enigma Files*. What was the PPO?
14. What award did David Jason win in 1993?
15. Who wrote *The Beiderbecke Affair*?
16. What is the name of Poirot's companion?
17. With which female detective did Fitz have a volatile relationship in *Cracker*?
18. Which drama, starting in 1984 was originally called *Woodentop*?
19. Who played Chief Inspector Roderick Alleyn in the 1993 BBC series?
20. *The Chief* was head of which fictitious constabulary?
21. Which New York duo did Victor Isbecki work with?
22. Which actor plays *Cadfael*?
23. Who wrote *Waterfront Beat*?
24. Who is the star of *Murder, She Wrote*?
25. Who was assisted by Magersfontein Lugg?
26. In *99-1*, what did DI Mick Raynor specialise in?
27. *Underworld* was a series about Britain's notorious criminals. Which actor narrated it?
28. Rupert Davies played which character in *The New Adventures of Charlie Chan*?
29. Who plays the title character in *Wycliffe*?
30. Who starred with Robert Powell in *The Detectives*?

ANSWERS

**Soaps 8 (See Quiz 66)**

**1.** Tiffany Mitchell. **2.** Brain Haemorrhage. **3.** Vicky. **4.** Sable. **5.** Wentworth. **6.** Sandra Gough. **7.** Pam. **8.** Mary Wilson. **9.** Tony and Sarah. **10.** Malandra Burrows. **11.** Queen Vic. **12.** Ethel Skinner. **13.** Fred Elliott. **14.** *Emmerdance.* **15.** Charlton Heston. **16.** Peggy Mitchell. **17.** *Casualty.* **18.** Beth Jordache. **19.** Trevor Jordache. **20.** Newton & Ridley. **21.** Den and Angie Watts. **22.** Heart attack. **23.** Tuesday & Friday. **24.** Jill Brown. **25.** *Angels.* **26.** *Call Oxbridge 2000.* **27.** Lucy. **28.** Judy Mallett. **29.** Vicar. **30.** Alec Monteath.

## QUIZ 66 Soaps 8

LEVEL 2

**Answers: see Quiz 65, page 493**

1. Which *EastEnders* character released her Secret Diary in 1999?
2. How did Peggy Skilbeck die?
3. In *Coronation Street* what was Alec Gilroy's grand daughter called?
4. Which character in *The Colbys* shared her name with a type of fur?
5. What was the name of the detention centre in *Prisoner Cell Block H*?
6. Who played Nellie Dingle?
7. Who was Bobby married to in *Dallas*?
8. Which Prime Minister's wife sent a letter of complaint when the London region decided not to transmit *Crossroads*?
9. In *EastEnders* what were Irene Hills' children called?
10. Which *Emmerdale* star had a hit with the song, 'Just This Side of Love'?
11. In which pub would you have bought Churchill Strong?
12. Which Albert Square character had a pug called Willie?
13. What is the name of *Coronation Street's* repetitive butcher?
14. What was the name of the 'Woolpacker's' album?
15. Which Hollywood superstar played Jason in The *Colbys*?
16. Who was Ricky Butcher's first mother in law in *EastEnders*?
17. Which medical series did Edwina Currie describe as left wing propaganda?
18. Which character did Anna Friel play in *Brookside*?
19. Who was buried under the patio in *Brookside*?
20. What is the name of the local brewery in *Coronation Street*?
21. Who were the original landlord and landlady of the Queen Vic?
22. How did Beth Jordache die?
23. On what days of the week was *Emergency-Ward 10* screened?
24. Who played Nurse Carole Young?
25. What was the BBC soap about student nurses called?
26. What was the 1961 spin-off from *Emergency-Ward 10*?
27. In *Neighbours*, what was the name of Jim Robinson's youngest daughter?
28. Which *Coronation Street* character had twins at Christmas 1998?
29. In *EastEnders* what was Alex Healy's profession?
30. Who played Dougal Lachlan in *Take the High Road*?

ANSWERS

### Crime 7 (See Quiz 65)

**1.** Neil Pearson. **2.** Mid-Sixties. **3.** Leo McKern. **4.** Cannon. **5.** London. **6.** Slow poisoning. **7.** *Jonathan Creek*. **8.** The New Yorker. **9.** Det. Sgt. Jim Butler. **10.** Trevor Eve. **11.** Drugs squad. **12.** Ben Alexander. **13.** The Prisoners' Property Office. **14.** Royal Television Society's Male Performer of the Year (*A Touch of Frost*). **15.** Alan Plater. **16.** Capt. Hastings. **17.** DS Jane Penhaligon. **18.** *The Bill*. **19.** Patrick Malahide. **20.** Eastland Constabulary. **21.** *Cagney and Lacey*. **22.** Derek Jacobi. **23.** Phil Redmond. **24.** Angela Lansbury. **25.** Campion. **26.** Undercover Operations. **27.** Bob Hoskins. **28.** Inspector Duff. **29.** Jack Shepherd. **30.** Jasper Carrott.

## QUIZ 67 Quiz & Games Shows 3

LEVEL 2

**Answers: see Quiz 68, page 496**

1. In the first series of *Blockbusters*, what was the maximum number of contestants competing at any one time?
2. Who was the first 'runner' in the helicopter in *Treasure Hunt*?
3. Who hosts *Have I Got News For You*?
4. What is the association between Ken Platt, Ted Ray and Jackie Rae?
5. On what fictional dragon planet was BBC 2's *The Adventure Game* set?
6. Who succeeded Tom O'Connor as host of *Name That Tune*?
7. In which quiz do contestants team up with a professional snooker player?
8. How many times per week was *Criss Cross Quiz* televised?
9. Name the host of *Supermarket Sweep*.
10. Which *Changing Rooms* presenter was voted '98 'Rear of the Year'?
11. Which show has a round called 'Feel the Sportsman'?
12. Name the host of *Blockbusters*.
13. Which crimebuster presented *Dotto*?
14. During *Sunday Night at the Palladium*, how much was the Beat the Clock jackpot prize?
15. How long after *Play Your Cards Right* was first transmitted was it renamed *Bruce Forsyth's Play Your Cards Right*?
16. Who presented the 90s version of *Going For A Song*?
17. *Bullseye* combined a quiz with which game?
18. Which former newsreader presented *What's My Line*?
19. Who is the presenter of *Countdown*?
20. Who asked *Who Wants To Be A Millionaire?* and offered the largest cash prize on TV?
21. The family game show *We Love TV* was presented by which TV personality?
22. Which TV company produced *Blockbusters*?
23. Who went from *Food and Drink* to *The Great Antiques Hunt*?
24. What was the fate of the famous black chair when *Mastermind* finished?
25. Who is Jim Davidson's longest serving *Generation Game* assistant?
26. How many clues how to be solved in 45 minutes in *Treasure Hunt*?
27. Who has presented *Blue Peter* and *Wheel of Fortune*?
28. Who was the announcer on *Take Your Pick*?
29. Name the original host of *Celebrity Squares*?
30. Which cult play was created by the first presenter of *The Crystal Maze*?

ANSWERS

### TV Comedy 17 (See Quiz 68)

**1.** Mel Smith & Griff Rhys Jones. **2.** *Secret Army*. **3.** Compo and Clegg. **4.** Alison Little. **5.** Tony Ferrino. **6.** Gwen Taylor. **7.** Frazer. **8.** *The Darling Buds of May*. **9.** Paul. **10.** The Guardian. **11.** Les Dawson. **12.** *Jane*. **13.** Ann Beach. **14.** Jack Dee. **15.** Eddie. **16.** Fascinating Aida. **17.** *The Fall and Rise of Reginald Perrin*. **18.** Delbert Wilkins. **19.** Seymour's. **20.** Alexei Sayle. **21.** Kenny Everett. **22.** *Ye Olde Spitting Image*. **23.** Swiss Tony. **24.** Ken Dodd. **25.** Rose & Daisy. **26.** John Sullivan. **27.** Handyman Hall. **28.** *Monty Python's Flying Circus*. **29.** Margaret. **30.** Ruby Wax.

# QUIZ 68 TV Comedy 17

**Answers: see Quiz 67, page 495**

LEVEL 2

1. Which comic duo present *Alas Smith And Jones*?
2. *'Allo, 'Allo* was a spoof of which drama series?
3. Which two of the three current old men were in the first *Last of the Summer Wine*?
4. What was the name of Tom Chance's partner in *Chance in a Million*?
5. Which Portuguese megastar did Steve Coogan create for *Comic Relief* 1997?
6. Who played Keith Barron's wife in *Duty Free*?
7. Which *Dad's Army* character often announced "We're doomed!"?
8. What was the first comedy serial to top the ratings with all six of its first series shows in 1991?
9. Peter Egan played the threat next door in *Ever Decreasing Circles*. What was his name?
10. *The Fainthearted Feminist* was based on the column in which newspaper?
11. Who created the character Cosmo Smallpiece?
12. Which cartoon character was dubbed "Darling of the Forces"?
13. Who played the busybody neighbour Sonia in *Fresh Fields*?
14. Which comedian made commercials for John Smith's beer in the early 90s?
15. What was the dog called in *Frasier*?
16. How were Dilly Keane, Adele Anderson and Denise Wharmby known collectively?
17. Which sitcom centred on life at Sunshine Desserts run by CJ?
18. Name the disc jockey portrayed by Lenny Henry.
19. Whose sister was played by Thora Hird in *Last of the Summer Wine*?
20. Who played the unscrupulous landlord in *The Young Ones*?
21. Which wacky DJ and comedy performer started out on *Nice Time* in 1968?
22. What was the name of the *Spitting Image* 1995 New Year special?
23. Which *Fast Show* character likens most things to "beautiful women"?
24. Which Liverpool comedian appeared in the *Dr Who* story *Delta And The Bannermen*?
25. What are the names of Hyacinth Bucket's two sisters?
26. Who wrote the script for *Only Fools and Horses*?
27. What was the name of the stately home in *Blott on the Landscape*?
28. Which show featured the celebrated Dead Parrot sketch?
29. What is the name of Victor Meldrew's long-suffering wife, played by Annette Crosby?
30. The *Girls on Top* were played by Dawn French, Jennifer Saunders, Tracey Ullman and who else?

ANSWERS

## Quiz & Games Shows 3 (See Quiz 67)

**1.** Three. **2.** Anneka Rice. **3.** Angus Deayton. **4.** All hosted *Spot the Tune*. **5.** Arg (Argond). **6.** Lionel Blair. **7.** *Big Break*. **8.** Three times per week. **9.** Dale Winton. **10.** Carol Smillie. **11.** *They Think It's All Over*. **12.** Bob Holness. **13.** Shaw Taylor. **14.** £1,000. **15.** 7 months. **16.** Michael Parkinson. **17.** Darts. **18.** Angela Rippon. **19.** Richard Whiteley. **20.** Chris Tarrant. **21.** Gloria Hunniford. **22.** Central TV. **23.** Jilly Golden. **24.** Magnus Magnusson took it home. **25.** Melanie Stace. **26.** 5. **27.** John Leslie. **28.** Bob Danvers-Walker. **29.** Lucille Ball. **30.** *The Rocky Horror Show*.

## QUIZ 69 Children's TV 7

LEVEL 2

**Answers: see Quiz 70, page 498**

1. Who presented *Live and Kicking* with Zoe Ball?
2. What were Ruff 'n' Ready?
3. In which year was *Rocket Robin Hood* set?
4. What kind of craft is Jimbo?
5. What did Rocky Jones do for a living?
6. What was the cartoon character *Dudley Do-Right*?
7. Dr Marsh Tracy was a leading character in which series set in Africa?
8. Who hosted the *Multi-Coloured Swap Shop*?
9. Who gave the voice to *Ollie Beak* the owl?
10. What was the school attended by Billy Bunter?
11. Which presenter of *Crackerjack* hosted a daily afternoon show on Radio 2?
12. What on *Teletubbies* is the Noo Noo?
13. Who was the voice of *Dangermouse*?
14. What was the canine cartoon version of the Three Musketeers called?
15. What was Fred and Wilma Flintstone's baby called?
16. Who alerted Bill and Ben to signs of danger?
17. *Follyfoot* was about what types of animals?
18. Who created *Magic Roundabout*?
19. In *Grange Hill* what was Samuel McGuire's nickname?
20. Bonnie Langford played whom in *Just William*?
21. In which series was the schoolteacher called Mr Onion?
22. Which Scottish actor was The Skunner Campbell, adversary of Supergran?
23. What does B.A. in BA Baracus stand for?
24. Who created *The Moomins*?
25. What was the name of the witch in the *Emu* children's series?
26. Who was the female presenter on *How 2*?
27. Who hosted *Fun House* on ITV?
28. Which locomotive was driven by Jones the Steam?
29. What was *Casey Jones*?
30. Who is the youngest of *The Simpsons*?

ANSWERS

### Soaps 9 (See Quiz 70)

**1.** 1987. **2.** Vic & Viv Windsor. **3.** *High Road.* **4.** Liverpool. **5.** *Brookside.* **6.** Manchester. **7.** Maxine. **8.** Edna. **9.** Gardener. **10.** Peggy and Louise **11.** E20. **12.** The Beales & the Fowlers. **13.** Kylie Minogue. **14.** The Queen Vic. **15.** *Civvy Street.* **16.** Emily and Matthew. **17.** Los Barcos. **18.** *Eldorado.* **19.** Beckindale. **20.** Max Wall. **21.** St. Angela's. **22.** Annie. **23.** Thirteen. **24.** Hotten. **25.** His garden gnome. **26.** The Kabin. **27.** Wicksy. **28.** *Eastenders.* **29.** Ashley. **30.** *Eastenders.*

## QUIZ 70 Soaps 9

LEVEL 2

**Answers: see Quiz 69, page 497**

1. In which year was Elizabeth Cunningham killed in *Take the High Road*?
2. Who took over Emmerdale's local Post Office in 1993?
3. In 1994, *Take the High Road*'s name was shortened to what?
4. *Brookside* is located in which city?
5. *Damon and Debbie* was a spin-off from which soap?
6. *Albion Market* was a covered market set in which city?
7. What was Fiona's assistant called at *Coronation Street*'s hair salon?
8. What was Harry Cross's wife's name in *Brookside*?
9. In *Crossroads*, what did Carney do for a living?
10. What are Courtney Mitchell's grannies called in *EastEnders*?
11. What is the postal code for *EastEnders*?
12. Who were the two central families featured in *EastEnders*?
13. Who played Charlene in *Neighbours*?
14. What is the name of the local pub in *EastEnders*?
15. What was the name of the 1988 *EastEnders* special, set in Christmas 1942?
16. What were the name's of Max and Susannah Farnham's children?
17. *Eldorado* was set in which fictitious village in Spain?
18. Patricia Brake and Jesse Birdsall appeared together in which soap?
19. Which fictitious village features in *Emmerdale*?
20. Which comedian in 1979 appeared as the grumpy Arthur Braithwaite?
21. Which hospital featured in *Angels*?
22. In *EastEnders* what was George Palmer's club owning daughter called?
23. How many episodes of *Coronation Street* were originally made?
24. What is the nearest market town to *Emmerdale*?
25. In *Coronation Street*, who did Derek suddenly lose and then start to receive holiday postcards from?
26. What's the name of Rita Sullivan's newsagents?
27. Which part was played by Nick Berry?
28. Before presenting *Daytime Live*, Ross Davidson could be seen in which soap?
29. In *Coronation Street* what was the name of Fred Elliott's nephew?
30. Which soap is associated with a laundrette owned by Mr Papadopoulos?

ANSWERS

### Children's TV 7 (See Quiz 69)

**1.** Jamie Theakston. **2.** A cat and dog. **3.** 2000A.D. **4.** An aeroplane. **5.** Space Ranger. **6.** A Mountie. **7.** *Daktari.* **8.** Noel Edmunds. **9.** Wally Whyton. **10.** Greyfriars. **11.** Ed Stewart. **12.** A vacuum cleaner. **13.** David Jason. **14.** *Dogtanian and the Three Muskhounds.* **15.** Pebbles. **16.** Weed. **17.** Horses. **18.** Serge Danot. **19.** Zammo. **20.** Violet Elizabeth. **21.** *The Herbs.* **22.** Iain Cuthbertson. **23.** Bad Attitude. **24.** Tove Jansson. **25.** Grotbags. **26.** Carol Vorderman. **27.** Pat Sharpe. **28.** *Ivor the Engine.* **29.** A train driver. **30.** Maggie.

## QUIZ 71 Sport 2

LEVEL 2

**Answers: see Quiz 72, page 500**

1. Barry Davies commentates on which sport?
2. Superstars champion Brian Hooper participated in which athletic sport?
3. In which year was a football home international first televised?
4. Who presented *Superstars*?
5. Football from which country is broadcast on Channel 4 on Sundays?
6. Other than football *Match of the Day* has been regularly used as a programme title for which sport?
7. On BBC's *Sportsnight*, which presenter succeeded David Coleman?
8. *The Superbowl* is screened on which TV channel?
9. Which cricketer has been a team captain on *A Question of Sport*?
10. Who was the ITV wrestling commentator?
11. Before becoming a sports presenter, Sue Barker was a player of which sport?
12. Who was the first woman presenter of *Grandstand*?
13. In which year was *Match of the Day* first televised?
14. Former *Grandstand* presenter Frank Bough joined who after leaving the BBC?
15. Murray Walker is associated with which sport?
16. Which former Blue Peter star presented darts?
17. Who was the presenter of *Sportsview*?
18. Which newspaper reporter presented *Star Spangled Soccer*, about football in the US?
19. Murphy's Mob featured which sport?
20. *Holiday Show* presenter Kathy Taylor competed in which athletic discipline?
21. On the BBC, it's *Match of the Day*. What is it's equivalent on ITV?
22. *It's a Knockout* star Eddy Waring was the regular BBC commentator on which sport?
23. TV presenter Suzanne Dando was captain of which British Olympics team?
24. Which sport is featured in *Playing for Real*?
25. On *A Question of Sport*, how many points are awarded for a home question?
26. Saint and who are TV sports pundits?
27. Cricket presenter Richie Benaud was captain of which nation's cricket side?
28. Who was the first host of the ITV outtakes show *Oddballs*?
29. Which racing commentator recently retired after commentating on The Grand National in 1998?
30. Whose last commentary before retiring was the 1998 World Cup Final?

ANSWERS

### TV Comedy 18 (See Quiz 72)

**1.** Sergeant. **2.** Jasper Carrott. **3.** Peter Wagg. **4.** *Naked Video.* **5.** Luke (Jack Galloway). **6.** Alice. **7.** 1966. **8.** Joanna & Tom. **9.** *Girls on Top*. **10.** Roseville, Kansas. **11.** *The Golden Girls*. **12.** Stephen Moore. **13.** On a bicycle. **14.** Plastic toys for cereal packets. **15.** Larry Grayson. **16.** Tony Hancock. **17.** Plumber. **18.** Lenny Henry. **19.** Benny Hill. **20.** Hinge & Bracket. **21.** Miss Babs (Celia Imrie). **22.** Gloria. **23.** Pettigrew. **24.** Clipboard. **25.** A Bakery. **26.** Jim Davidson. **27.** A Rolling Stones concert. **28.** Vicky, Robin's Girlfriend. **29.** *Never Say Never Again*. **30.** Mrs Worboys.

## QUIZ 72 TV Comedy 18

LEVEL 2

**Answers: see Quiz 71, page 499**

1. In *Dad's Army*, what rank was Wilson played by John le Mesurier?
2. Who made a banned spoof record about *The Magic Roundabout*?
3. Who produced *The Max Headroom Show*?
4. In which comedy series was Rab C Nesbitt first seen?
5. Who was Felicity Kendall the mistress to?
6. Who was Geraldine's verger in *The Vicar of Dibley*?
7. Which year did Fitz have a one night stand with his son's mother in *Relative Strangers*?
8. What are the names of the two children in *The Upper Hand*?
9. Which sitcom featured 'Spare Cheeks' magazine?
10. Which town lay near the camp at which Bilko and his platoon were based?
11. *The Brighton Belles* was an adaptation of which US sitcom?
12. Who played Adrian Mole's slobbish father?
13. How did Scullion in *Porterhouse Blue* travel around the college?
14. In *The Good Life* what did Jerry Leadbetter's company make?
15. Whose fictional characters included Slack Alice and Apricot Lil?
16. Whose middle names were Aloysius St John?
17. What was Vince Tulley's trade in *Side by Side*?
18. Which 16 year old winner of *New Faces* starred in *The Fosters*?
19. Which comedian famous for his sitcoms and sketches starred with Michael Caine in *The Italian Job*?
20. On TV, how were George Logan and Patrick Fyffe better known?
21. Who owned Acorn Antiques?
22. What was Bombardier Beaumont's nickname in *It Ain't Half Hot Mum*?
23. Who was Jimmy Edward's assistant headmaster in *Whack-O!*?
24. What does Denis Norden always hold in *It'll Be Alright on the Night*?
25. Where did Bill Porter work in *Two Point four Children*?
26. Whose catchphrase was 'nick nick'?
27. Where did Vince and Penny first meet in *Just Good Friends*?
28. Tessa Wyatt played whom in *Robin's Nest*?
29. TV's funnyman Rowan Atkinson appeared in which Bond film?
30. Who is the Meldrew's naïve female friend?

ANSWERS

**Sport 2 (See Quiz 71)**

**1.** Soccer. **2.** Pole-vault. **3.** 1947. **4.** David Vine & Ron Pickering. **5.** Italy (Serie A). **6.** Tennis at Wimbledon. **7.** Harry Carpenter. **8.** Channel 4. **9.** Ian Botham. **10.** Kent Walton. **11.** Tennis. **12.** Helen Rollason. **13.** 1964. **14.** Sky. **15.** Motor Racing. **16.** Peter Purvis. **17.** Peter Dimmock. **18.** Ian Woolridge. **19.** Football. **20.** Pentathlon. **21.** *The Big Match.* **22.** Rugby League. **23.** The British Olympic Gymnastics Team. **24.** Subuteo Table Soccer. **25.** 1 Point. **26.** Greavsie. **27.** Australia. **28.** Eamonn Holmes. **29.** Peter O'Sullivan. **30.** Brian Moore.

# QUIZ 73 Pot Luck 10

**Answers: see Quiz 74, page 502**

LEVEL 2

1. Who was the creator of *Star Trek*?
2. Who played the Bionic Man?
3. Who was Richard and Judy's first guest when their programme moved to London?
4. Which arts show replaced *Aquarius* in 1977?
5. For what were Mary Malcolm and Sylvia Peters known?
6. On which show do you hear advice from Bunny Campione and Henry Sandon?
7. Who plays Michael Hayes?
8. Which actor has actress daughters named Michelle and Karen?
9. Who left *The Big Breakfast* on New Year's Day 1999?
10. Who played Samuel and Pearl Foster in the comedy *The Fosters*?
11. Which film buff left the BBC for Sky in 1998?
12. Which celebrity chased around in a beach buggy answering challenges?
13. Which spin-off from *Holiday* features celebrities working in holiday resorts?
14. What was the first British TV soap?
15. Where did The Robinsons get lost?
16. From where on the moon did Neil Armstrong broadcast?
17. What is the name of Magnus's presenter daughter?
18. Which fictitious group sang '*All You Need is Lunch*' and '*WC Fields Forever*'?
19. Who starred in *My Three Sons*?
20. Who was the opposing team captain to John Parrott on *A Question of Sport*?
21. *Every Loser Wins* was a hit sung by which former soap star?
22. Who played the Professor in *Sliders*?
23. Who was *Man-O-Man*'s first presenter?
24. Who played Ben Casey?
25. *The Squirrels* was set in an accounts department of what kind of business?
26. Whose nickname is "Parky"?
27. Who presented *Motorworld*?
28. Who was *Our man In Goa*?
29. Who presented *The Good Sex Guide*?
30. Name the original host of *Going for a Song*.

ANSWERS

**Drama 7 (See Quiz 74)**

**1.** Terence Cooper. **2.** Lucy Gannon. **3.** Lieutenant Beamish. **4.** *The House of Elliott.* **5.** *The Chancer.* **6.** Robert Hardy. **7.** *London's Burning.* **8.** Miss Kitty. **9.** *I, Claudius.* **10.** A football club. **11.** Builders. **12.** Cardinal Wolsey. **13.** Faye Weldon. **14.** Vanity Fair. **15.** Francesca Annis. **16.** Thora Hird. **17.** Charlie Chaplin. **18.** Brian Blessed. **19.** Father Aiden. **20.** James Herriot. **21.** Ron Randell. **22.** *Love Hurts.* **23.** They are real members of the public. **24.** Joan Hickson. **25.** Miriam. **26.** *The Monocled Mutineer.* **27.** Jodie Foster. **28.** Air Hostess. **29.** Quentin Crisp. **30.** Clint Walker.

## QUIZ 74 Drama 7

**Answers: see Quiz 73, page 501**

LEVEL 2

**1.** Who succeeded George Margo as Blackbeard?
**2.** Which writer created *Soldier, Soldier?*
**3.** Peter Hammond played which character in *The Buccaneers?*
**4.** Which drama series about a fashion house was written by actresses Eileen Atkins and Jean Marsh?
**5.** In which series did the hero's girlfriend, Jo Franklin, run off with his enemy, Piers?
**6.** Which troubleshooter later played Churchill?
**7.** Which show would feature Blue Watch B25 Blackwall?
**8.** In *Gunsmoke*, what was the name of the Long Branch saloon keeper?
**9.** Derek Jacobi played the title role in which series about a Roman Emperor?
**10.** What did *The Manageress* manage?
**11.** *Grafters* was about brothers in which trade?
**12.** Patrick Troughton played which character in *The White Falcon?*
**13.** Who wrote *Big Women*, about a feminist publishing house, shown on Channel 4?
**14.** Rachel from *This Life* went on to star as the heroine of which Andrew Davis adaptation of a classic novel?
**15.** Who played the 'older woman' opposite Robson Green in *Reckless?*
**16.** Who was *Waiting For the Telegram* in *Talking Heads 2?*
**17.** Which bowler hatted comic was portrayed on TV by Joe Geary?
**18.** Who played the title role in *John Silver's Return to Treasure Island*, screened in 1986?
**19.** Who replaced Father Peter in *Ballykissangel?*
**20.** Who wrote about life at *Skeldale House?*
**21.** Which actor played *O.S.S.* Agent, Major Frank Hawthorne?
**22.** Which drama series told of forty something single girl Tessa Piggott?
**23.** What is unusual about the members of the jury in the courtroom drama *Verdict?*
**24.** Which actress played the receptionist in *The Royalty?*
**25.** What was Lovejoy's car called?
**26.** In which controversial WWI drama did Paul McGann play Percy Toplis?
**27.** Who played Tatum O'Neil's film role in the TV version of *Paper Moon?*
**28.** What was the occupation of Molly Manning's daughter in *The Flying Swan?*
**29.** Who was the subject of *The Naked Civil Servant?*
**30.** Which actor played Cheyenne Bodie?

ANSWERS

### Pot Luck 10 (See Quiz 73)

**1.** Gene Rodenberry. **2.** Lee Majors. **3.** OJ Simpson. **4.** *The South Bank Show.* **5.** As TV Announcers. **6.** *The Antiques Roadshow.* **7.** David Caruso. **8.** Roy Dotrice. **9.** Denise Van Outen. **10.** Norman Beeton & Isabel Lucas. **11.** Barry Norman. **12.** Anneka Rice (*Challenge Anneka*). **13.** *Holiday: Fasten Your Seatbelt.* **14.** The Grove Family. **15.** *Lost in Space.* **16.** Tranquillity Base. **17.** Sally Magnusson. **18.** The Rutles. **19.** Fred MacMurray. **20.** Ally McCoist. **21.** Nick Berry. **22.** John Rhys Davies. **23.** Chris Tarrant. **24.** Vince Edwards. **25.** TV Hire firm. **26.** Michael Parkinson. **27.** Jeremy Clarkson. **28.** Clive Anderson. **29.** Margi Clarke. **30.** Max Robertson.

## QUIZ 75 Crime 8

LEVEL 2

**Answers: see Quiz 76, page 504**

1. Who was obsessed with his 'little grey cells'?
2. Which comedy duo first played Reginald Hill's detectives *Dalziel and Pascoe* on TV?
3. What was the nationality of the creator of French detective *Maigret*?
4. In which drama was there a global crime syndicate called THRUSH?
5. What is *Dangerfield*'s occupation?
6. Eric Richards plays which character in *The Bill*?
7. Which actor plays *Kavanagh QC*?
8. Which 1995 drama set in South Yorkshire followed the hectic duties of a CID unit headed by DI Eric Temple?
9. Which pop star played Crockett's girl friend in *Miami Vice*?
10. What was the name of the novelist in *Murder She Wrote*?
11. The President of the Court was played by which actor in *Crime of Passion*?
12. *Rumpole of the Bailey* made it's first appearance in which 1970's BBC series?
13. Which 60s classic was about Chief Supt Lockhart and also starred Johnny Briggs?
14. Who played Hugh Ryan in *Ryan International*?
15. Which nephew joined Arthur Daley in later series of *Minder*?
16. Which actor played *Shoestring*?
17. *Barlow at Large* was a spin-off from which police drama series?
18. Which lady barrister featured in the series *Justice*?
19. Which crime writer created Paul Temple?
20. Who portrayed Lord Peter Wimsey in the 1970's series?
21. Which comedy by Ben Elton was set in Gasforth police station?
22. Which actor played *Maigret*?
23. Name the creator of *Van Der Valk*.
24. Which lawyer's secretary was Della Street?
25. Who conducted an investigation of the facts regarding Jack the Ripper?
26. *Hunter's Walk* was set in which fictitious Midland's town?
27. Who was the parking lot attendant in *77 Sunset Strip*?
28. What was the occupation of John Sutherland in *Sutherland's Law*?
29. Which women's prison featured in *Within These Walls*?
30. Which police drama had a recipe or cookery tip in every episode?

ANSWERS

### TV Comedy 19 (See Quiz 76)

**1.** Painter & Decorator. **2.** Frankie Howerd. **3.** Daphne and Norman. **4.** Paul McCartney. **5.** Deborah. **6.** In a bedsit. **7.** Sebastopol Terrace. **8.** Hyacinth Bucket. **9.** Janet Dibley. **10.** Michael Palin. **11.** *The Krankies*. **12.** Kathy Burke. **13.** *Radio Active*. **14.** Thelma. **15.** Wendy Craig. **16.** A night-club in 'Swinging London'. **17.** Lowlands University. **18.** Spike Milligan. **19.** Flat Feet **20.** Piers Fletcher-Dervish. **21.** Mollie Sugden. **22.** John Bird and John Fortune. **23.** Klinger. **24.** Patricia Drake. **25.** 6. **26.** *May to December*. **27.** Mel Smith. **28.** *Mork and Mindy*. **29.** Morecambe and Wise. **30.** Bouncers ('The Man-age-ment').

## QUIZ 76 TV Comedy 19

LEVEL 2

**Answers: see Quiz 75, page 503**

1. What was Jacko's occupation in *Brush Strokes*?
2. Whose catchphrases included "Titter ye not!"?
3. In *Just Good Friends* what were Penny's parents called?
4. Kate Robbins is a cousin of which ex Beatle?
5. What is the name of the character played by Leslie Ash in *Men Behaving Badly*?
6. Where did John live after his divorce in *Dear John*?
7. Which road did Sykes live in?
8. Who had neighbours called Elizabeth and Emmet?
9. Who played Elaine in *The Two of Us*?
10. Which comic actor wrote *East of Ipswich* which was adapted for television?
11. How were Ian and Janette Tough better known?
12. Who plays Waynetta Slob?
13. KYTV developed from which anarchic radio show?
14. In *The Likely Lads*, who did Bob eventually marry?
15. Which star of *Butterflies* and *And Mother Makes Five* wrote scripts as Jonathan Marr?
16. In *Hancock's*, Tony Hancock was the owner of what kind of establishment?
17. What was the name of the university in *A Very Peculiar Practice*?
18. Who provided the voice of Eccles in *The Tele Goons*?
19. At the end of *The Likely Lads* both Bob and Terry enlisted for the army but why was Bob rejected?
20. Michael Troughton played Alan B'Stard's assistant. What was his name?
21. Who played Sandra's over-bearing mother in *The Liver Birds*?
22. Who were the two main members of the cast of *The Long Johns*?
23. Which male character in *M*A*S*H* dressed in women's clothing?
24. Fletcher's daughter Ingrid in *Porridge* was played by which actress?
25. How many episodes of *Andy Capp* were shown on television?
26. In which series did Anton Rogers play solicitor Alec Callender?
27. Which comic played Colin in *Colin's Sandwich*?
28. Which comedy series shot Robin Williams to superstardom?
29. Which duo were originally formed with the encouragement of one of their mothers, Sadie Bartholomew?
30. What was the primary occupation of the villainous Two Rons in *Hale and Pace*?

ANSWERS

### Crime 8 (See Quiz 75)

**1.** Hercule Poirot. **2.** Hale and Pace. **3.** Belgian. **4.** *The Man from U.N.C.L.E.* **5.** Forensic Medical Examiner. **6.** Sgt. Bob Cryer. **7.** John Thaw. **8.** *Out of the Blue*. **9.** Sheena Easton. **10.** Jessica Fletcher. **11.** Anthony Newlands. **12.** *Play for Today*. **13.** *No Hiding Place*. **14.** Kieran Moore. **15.** Ray. **16.** Trevor Eve. **17.** *Softly, Softly*. **18.** Harriet Peterson. **19.** Francis Durbridge. **20.** Ian Carmichael. **21.** *The Thin Blue Line*. **22.** Rupert Davies. **23.** Nicolas Freeling. **24.** Perry Mason. **25.** Stratford Johns & Frank Windsor. **26.** Broadstone. **27.** Kookie. **28.** Procurator Fiscal. **29.** HMP Stone Park. **30.** *Pie in the Sky*.

# QUIZ 77 Current Affairs 5

**Answers: see Quiz 78, page 506**

LEVEL 2

1. Who led the BBC's news programme when Princess Diana's death was announced?
2. Who presented *The Human Zoo*?
3. Who left *Newsnight* for *Tomorrow's World* in 1997?
4. What is the subject of *One Foot in The Past*?
5. Where did Harty Go To in 1984?
6. The documentary *The Ascent of Man* was presented by whom?
7. *The World At War* documented which war?
8. Who has presented *Newsround* and *Here and Now*?
9. Where did Michael Palin travel after *Around the World in 80 Days*?
10. Which satellite channel had the slogan 'Make the voyage'?
11. Who hosted *Police Five* for nearly 30 years?
12. What was the sequel to the series *Don't Ask Me*?
13. Who added her name to the *Mysteries* series?
14. Where did the Wilkins, the subject of the documentary *The Family*, live?
15. What was the follow-up to *The Family*, 10 years after the original?
16. Which BBC 2 programme won a series of BAFTA awards for "Best Programme Without a Category"?
17. What 1975 documentary was about two runaway children in London?
18. Which news programme launched the two-presenter format in the UK?
19. What has ITN traditionally called its newsreaders?
20. The *HMS Brilliant* patrolled waters off the coast of where in 1995?
21. The history of what subject was explored in *All You Need Is Love*?
22. Which 1978 documentary saw the British Colonial Force policing Hong Kong?
23. *A Detective's Tale*; *A Villain's Tale*; *A Brief's Tale*; and *A Prisoner's Tale* were the four plays in which 1978 series?
24. Which newsreader was an original presenter of *Top Gear*?
25. Which two women have presented main news bulletins for BBC and ITV?
26. Which steeplejack appeared in his own show?
27. *Life On Earth* was presented by which naturalist?
28. Who chaired *Question Time* for the first ten years of its existence?
29. Who took over the chair of *Question Time* in 1989?
30. Which Newmarket trainer featured in the 1992 documentary *The Racing Game*?

ANSWERS

**Music & Variety 3 (See Quiz 78)**

**1.** Englebert Humperdinck. **2.** Val Doonican. **3.** Keith Fordyce. **4.** Alma Cogan. **5.** The Grenadiers. **6.** Ray Alan. **7.** *The Pepsi Show*. **8.** Frank Sinatra. **9.** Jarvis Cocker. **10.** Derek Guyler. **11.** Katie Boyle. **12.** Don Lang's Frantic Five. **13.** Harry Secombe. **14.** A London airport restaurant. **15.** Dave Allen. **16.** Jack Good. **17.** *The Old Grey Whistle Test.* **18.** Leonard Sachs. **19.** Michael Barrymore. **20.** Gus Goodwin. **21.** Comic Relief. **22.** Brian Conley. **23.** All debuted in *New Faces*. **24.** *Starlight* (1937). **25.** *The Goodies*. **26.** *Praise Be!* **27.** Bruce Forsyth. **28.** Noel Edmunds. **29.** *Sunday, Sunday*. **30.** Zoe Ball.

## QUIZ 78 Music & Variety 3

**Answers: see Quiz 77, page 505** LEVEL 2

1. Who failed an audition for *Opportunity Knocks* as Gerry Dorsey but found superstardom later on?
2. Who would have asked you to "name that tune in one"?
3. Who was the male compere of *Ready Steady Go?*
4. Who was called British TV's first lady of popular music in the late 1950s/early 60s?
5. In *Chelsea At Nine* who were the resident song and dance troupe?
6. Which ventriloquist had a dummy called Lord Charles?
7. Which Channel 5 show highlighted the best hit singles?
8. The 1998 *Royal Variety Show* was a tribute to which singer who died that year?
9. Who interrupted Michael Jackson's stage performance at the *Brit Awards?*
10. Who presented *The City Varieties?*
11. Which British lady presented the *Eurovision Song Contest* for many years?
12. Which resident band backed solo artists on *Six-Five Special?*
13. Who has presented *Highway* and *Songs of Praise?*
14. A special New Year's Eve show called *Twelve-Five Special* was presented from where?
15. *The Val Doonican Show* provided a regular comedy spot for which Irish comedian?
16. Who was the creator and producer of *Oh Boy!?*
17. Bob Harris introduced which weekly Rock programme from 1972?
18. Who was the compere of *The Good Old Days?*
19. Whose *Saturday Night Out* was followed by a series with only his surname in the title?
20. Who was the first presenter of *Drumbeat?*
21. 'Living Doll' by Cliff Richard and the Young Ones raised money for which charity?
22. Which entertainer's Saturday night show included his 'Car Boot Quiz'?
23. What connects Victoria Wood, Marti Caine, Lenny Henry and Jim Davidson?
24. In which variety programme did Gracie Fields make her first TV appearance?
25. In which show was 'The Funky Gibbon' first heard?
26. What was the compilation of *Songs of Praise* clips presented by Thora Hird called?
27. A special variety show from the London Palladium was screened in 1998 to celebrate whose 70th birthday?
28. Who hosted the 1979 version of *Juke Box Jury?*
29. Name the 80's daytime magazine show about the London entertainment scene.
30. Who hosted *Hit, Miss or Maybe* in 1998?

ANSWERS

**Current Affairs 5 (See Quiz 77)**

**1.** Martyn Lewis. **2.** Desmond Morris. **3.** Peter Snow. **4.** The history of old property. **5.** *Hollywood.* **6.** Dr Jacob Bronowski. **7.** WW II. **8.** Juliet Morris. **9.** *Pole to Pole.* **10.** Discovery Channel. **11.** Shaw Taylor. **12.** *Don't Just Sit There.* **13.** Carol Vorderman. **14.** Reading. **15.** *The Family: The After Years.* **16.** *Arena.* **17.** *Johnny Go Home.* **18.** *News at Ten.* **19.** Newscasters. **20.** Bosnia. **21.** The History of Pop. **22.** *Hong Kong Beat.* **23.** *Law & Order.* **24.** Angela Rippon. **25.** Weather Forecasting. **26.** Fred Dibnah. **27.** David Attenborough. **28.** Julia Somerville and Anna Ford. **29.** Peter Sissons. **30.** Luca Cumani.

## QUIZ 79 Soaps 10

LEVEL 2

**Answers: see Quiz 80, page 508**

1. A novel by Grace Metalious was the basis for which sixties US soap?
2. Which *Eastenders* actor played Graham Lodsworth in *Emmerdale*?
3. What is unusual about Hayley Patterson in *Coronation Street*?
4. In which soap did comedian Larry Grayson once appear?
5. Australian soap, *Sons and Daughters*, featured which two families?
6. Which *Coronation Street* actor could be seen stripping off in *The Full Monty*?
7. Who did Deirdre have an affair with while still married to Ken Barlow?
8. Who played the Geordie porter Jimmy Powell in *Casualty*?
9. Which character does Chris Chittell play?
10. In *Home and Away* Craig McLachlan played a character with which name also famous for a character in a British soap?
11. Which soap featured the fictional Moldavia in one of its plots?
12. In which valley is *A Country Practice* set?
13. Who played Carol in *The Rag Trade*?
14. Which character in *Coronation Street* was fatally injured in a dispute outside a nightclub?
15. Which newspaper did Tony work for in *Eastenders*?
16. Who was Lorraine's son in *Eastenders*?
17. What was the name of Jason Donovan's character in *Neighbours*?
18. In *Dallas* where was JR when he was shot?
19. Who is Claire's guardian in *Eastenders*?
20. Which star of *Kiss Me Kate* moved to *Dallas*?
21. Who played Meg Mortimer in *Crossroads*?
22. Who played Krystal Carrington in *Dynasty*?
23. Which 60s pop star played hairdresser Viv in *Albion Market*?
24. Which 80s soap was popular in its home country France but failed over here?
25. Curly Watts is the manager of which supermarket?
26. What is the name of Mark Fowler's younger brother?
27. Which *Dynasty* star's autobiography was called *Past Imperfect*?
28. In which soap did President Reagan's ex wife star?
29. What was Rita's maiden name in *Coronation Street*?
30. What is the name of Grant and Phil Mitchell's mother in *Eastenders*?

ANSWERS

### TV Comedy 20 (See Quiz 80)

**1.** Nurse. **2.** The Management. **3.** Fort Baxter, Kansas. **4.** Pauline Quirke & Linda Robson. **5.** Judi Dench. **6.** Susan Penhaligon. **7.** Peckham. **8.** Mr Bean. **9.** Karl Howman. **10.** Inspector 'Blakey' Blake. **11.** Las Vegas. **12.** Rizzo. **13.** Scotland. **14.** Alan B'Stard. **15.** Margi Clarke. **16.** Teacher. **17.** Libby. **18.** A General Hospital. **19.** Nicola McAuliffe. **20.** Georgie Fame. **21.** Ronnie Barker. **22.** Roy Clarke. **23.** Glasgowe. **24.** His ex-wife, Helen. **25.** His girlfriend Vicky. **26.** *Oh! Doctor Beeching*. **27.** Derek Nimmo. **28.** A Security Guard. **29.** Joan Greenwood. **30.** Four.

## QUIZ 80 TV Comedy 20

LEVEL 2

**Answers: see Quiz 79, page 507**

1. What is Dorothy's profession in *Men Behaving Badly*?
2. The Two Rons featured in their own series. What was it called?
3. Name the original army camp at which Sgt. Bilko was stationed?
4. Name the actresses who are *Birds of a Feather*.
5. Who stars with Geoffrey Palmer in *As Time Goes By*?
6. Who played Mike and Laura's daughter in *A Fine Romance*?
7. In which London borough was *Desmond's* barber shop?
8. Which star of the small screen went on to make *The Ultimate Disaster Movie*?
9. Which actor was frequently to be seen with *The Babes In The Wood*?
10. In *On the Buses* whose catchphrase was "I 'ate you Butler"?
11. Where abroad were a trio of Mrs Merton shows screened from in 1997?
12. What was the rat called on the *Muppet Show*?
13. Where was the series *Naked Video* first made?
14. Which fictional MP was treasurer of the 'Keep Britain Nuclear' pressure group?
15. Who played Queenie in *Making Out*?
16. What was Tom O'Connor's profession before he found fame on *The Comedians*?
17. Name Grace's daughter in *Grace Under Fire*.
18. *Surgical Spirit* was set in what kind of establishment?
19. The role of female surgeon Sheila Sabatini was played by which actress?
20. Who wrote the theme music to the comedy *Yes-Honestly*?
21. Which comedian played Fletcher in *Porridge*?
22. *Keeping Up Appearances* was written by whom?
23. Where was cockney wide boy stranded in *Bad Boys*?
24. In *Don't Wait Up*, who does Tom have to pay rent to for his doctor's surgery?
25. Who did Robin Tripp live with in *Robin's Nest*?
26. Which 90s sitcom created highlighted the decline of the railways in the 60s?
27. Whose comic roles included Brother Dominic in *Oh Brother* and Noote in *All Gas and Gaiters*?
28. What was Victor Meldrew before retiring?
29. Name the oddball landlady in *Girls on Top*.
30. How many sons did Nellie Boswell have in *Bread*?

ANSWERS

**Soaps 10 (See Quiz 79)**

**1.** *Peyton Place*. **2.** Ross Kemp. **3.** She was born Harold Patterson. **4.** *Crossroads*. **5.** The Palmers and the Hamiltons. **6.** Bruce Jones. **7.** Mike Baldwin. **8.** Robson Green. **9.** Eric Pollard. **10.** Grant Mitchell. **11.** *Dynasty*. **12.** Wandin Valley. **13.** Sheila Hancock. **14.** Brian Tilsley. **15.** The Walford Gazette. **16.** Joe Wicks. **17.** Scott Robinson. **18.** In his office. **19.** Nigel. **20.** Howard Keel. **21.** Noel Gordon. **22.** Linda Evans. **23.** Helen Shapiro. **24.** *Chateauvallon*. **25.** Firmans' Freezers. **26.** Martin. **27.** Joan Collins. **28.** *Falcon Crest*. **29.** Littlewood. **30.** Peggy.

## QUIZ 81 Children's TV 8

LEVEL 2

**Answers: see Quiz 82, page 500**

1. Timmy Mallett, Michaela Strachan and Tommy Boyd presented which TV-AM children's programme?
2. What was Keith Chegwin's pop music programme?
3. *Saturday Superstore* was presented by which DJ?
4. Where do the Ewoks live?
5. What was Dougal's favourite food on the *Magic Roundabout*?
6. What was it that Tweety Pie "taut" he "taw"?
7. Fraser Hines wore a kilt in *Dr Who*. True or False?
8. In which geological feature were *The Space Sentinels* based?
9. Richard O'Sullivan played which highwayman in the 1980s?
10. On which channel did Pob appear?
11. Who is Bod's aunt?
12. Who hosted *The Quack Chat Show*?
13. On which afternoon in the week was *Playaway* shown on TV?
14. In *The Flintstones*, what was the Rubble baby called?
15. Who presented *Jim'll Fix It*?
16. Diana Dors played which character in the 1976 adaptation of *Just William*?
17. In Britain it was called *Just Dennis*. How was it known in the USA?
18. The fifties series *Whirlybirds* was about what?
19. Who played the little girl in *Skippy The Bush Kangaroo*?
20. Which alien organisation were G-Force opposing in *Battle of the Planets*?
21. Who played Maid Marion in the 1977 BBC version of *Robin Hood*?
22. How many times a week was *Magpie* screened on children's TV?
23. On what days is *Blue Peter* screened?
24. Which redhead played Violet Elizabeth Bott in the 70s series of *Just William*?
25. What was *Mandrake*?
26. Who was the talkative woodpecker in *Bagpuss*?
27. Who was *Muffin The Mule*'s human companion?
28. Who was Mr Pastry?
29. What was the name of Larry The Lamb's canine chum?
30. Who were *Andy Pandy*'s two friends?

ANSWERS

**Pot Luck 11 (See Quiz 82)**

**1.** Saint and Greavsie. **2.** Dave. **3.** Geoff Hamilton. **4.** *Radiolympia Radio Show.* **5.** *News 24.* **6.** Verity Lambert. **7.** Roseanne. **8.** The Interlude. **9.** Richard Chamberlain. **10.** Malaya. **11.** Jess Yates. **12.** Johnny Carson. **13.** Nell Dunn. **14.** *Cardiac Arrest.* **15.** Gallifrey. **16.** Tony Robinson. **17.** Jeremy Irons. **18.** Michael Aspel. **19.** Carmen Munroe. **20.** Arkwright. **21.** Eric Sykes and Hattie Jacques. **22.** 1954. **23.** Dennis Waterman. **24.** Val Doonican. **25.** Sheila Steafel. **26.** Shauna Lowry. **27.** Antonio Carlucci. **28.** Des O'Connor. **29.** *The A-Team.* **30.** Millicent Martin.

## QUIZ 82 Pot Luck 11

**Answers: see Quiz 81, page 509**

LEVEL 2

1. Which soccer pundits' show was started with a spot on *World of Sport*?
2. In *Only Fools and Horses* what does Trigger always call Del Boy?
3. Name the late presenter of *Gardener's World*.
4. During the BBCs experimental period in 1936 live transmissions were sent to which show at Olympia?
5. What is the BBC's rolling news service called?
6. Who founded Verity Productions?
7. Which US comedienne bought the US rights to *Absolutely Fabulous*?
8. Where were kittens playing with wool and the potter's wheel featured?
9. Which former Dr Kildare played John Blackthorne in the 80s *Shogun*?
10. Where was *Tenko* set?
11. Who first introduced *Stars on Sunday*?
12. Name the long-time host of *The Tonite Show*.
13. Who wrote *Up the Junction*?
14. In which series did Helen Baxendale play doctor?
15. Which planet does *Dr Who* come from?
16. Who is the presenter of *Time Team*?
17. Who was the Oscar-winning actor who appeared in *Playaway*?
18. Name the *This is Your Life* former newsreader?
19. In *The Fosters*, who played their busybody neighbour, Vilma?
20. In *Open All Hours*, what was the name of the corner-shop keeper?
21. Which 'brother and sister' lived at 28 Sebastopol Terrace during the 70s sitcom?
22. In which year was the soap *The Grove Family* first transmitted?
23. Who sang the theme from *Minder*?
24. Which singer do you associate with sweaters and a rocking chair?
25. Who was the regular female performer on *The Frost Report*?
26. Which Irish redhead co presents *Animal Hospital*?
27. Who presented his *Italian Feast*?
28. Which chat show host has interviewed Tony Blair and William Hague on his TV show?
29. Which group of renegades were played by George Peppard, Dirk Benedict, Dwight Schultz and Mr T?
30. Who sang the theme to *That was the Week that Was*?

ANSWERS

### Children's TV 8 (See Quiz 81)

**1.** *Wideawake*. **2.** *Cheggers Plays Pop*. **3.** Mike Reid. **4.** Endor. **5.** Sugar lumps. **6.** 'A Puddy Tat'. **7.** True. **8.** A volcano (extinct). **9.** Dick Turpin. **10.** Channel 4. **11.** Aunt Flo. **12.** Keith Harris & Orville. **13.** Saturday. **14.** Bamm-Bamm. **15.** Jimmy Saville. **16.** Mrs Bott (Violet Elizabeth's mother). **17.** Dennis the Menace. **18.** Two helicopter pilots. **19.** Liza Goddard. **20.** Spectra. **21.** Diana Keen. **22.** Twice per week. **23.** Monday & Thursday. **24.** Bonnie Langford. **25.** A Magician. **26.** Professor Yaffle. **27.** Annette Mills. **28.** Richard Herne. **29.** Dennis the Dachshund. **30.** Teddy & Looby-Loo.

## QUIZ 83 Animals & Nature 2

LEVEL 2

**Answers: see Quiz 84, page 512**

1. What kind of dog does Hamish Macbeth own?
2. What animal appears in the opening sequences of *Northern Exposure*?
3. What non-human primate formed part of the experiment in *First Born*?
4. What was the name of Bernie Winter's St Bernard?
5. Cheetah was the chimpanzee companion of which jungle dweller?
6. Which animal is seen on the opening sequence of *Coronation Street*?
7. *One By One* featured which zoo vet?
8. Wally Whyton, the voice of *Ollie Beak* the owl, sang of Willum. Who was Willum?
9. Who was the pupeteer behind Basil Brush?
10. What was the name of *Blue Peter*'s first pet dog?
11. Which horse created by Mary O'Hara featured in a fifties children's saga?
12. What kind of cartoon animal is *Snagglepuss*?
13. Which naturalist was made controller of BBC 2 in 1965?
14. Who was Roland Rat's sidekick?
15. Which husband and wife team presented *The Amateur Naturalist*?
16. Which Australian celebrity presented *Animal Hospital*?
17. Which comic pretended to kill himself in despair over global warming before going looking for lemurs in Madagascar?
18. Which famous animal impersonator appeared with Morecambe and Wise?
19. Which brand of dog food claimed it "prolongs active life" according to its TV commercial?
20. A series of adverts links Billy Connolly to which type of fish?
21. What was the name of Jed Clampett's pet dog in the *Beverly Hillbillies*?
22. Which well-known environmentalist and botanist is impersonated by Lenny Henry?
23. Who is the vet in *Emmerdale*?
24. Which BBC comedy series character mistook a Dachshund for a telephone?
25. Whose veterinary surgery was located in the fictional town of Darrowby?
26. In which series do we meet real-life vet Trude Mostue?
27. Which canine hero's home was Fort Apache?
28. On whose programme did the Cookie Bear appear?
29. Who are *Chip 'n' Dale*?
30. What kind of animal was Fury?

ANSWERS

### TV Comedy 21 (See Quiz 84)

**1.** It burns down. **2.** Reg Varney. **3.** Dennis Waterman. **4.** *Cheers.* **5.** Marlene. **6.** NHS Hospital. **7.** Milkwoman. **8.** Michael J. Fox. **9.** Paul Hogan. **10.** Tony Danza. **11.** Tom Sharpe. **12.** Ernest. **13.** Privet. **14.** Five years. **15.** Actress Janine Duvitski. **16.** Vic Reeves. **17.** *Murder Most Horrid II.* **18.** Roseanne. **19.** Lily Pond. **20.** Judy Carne. **21.** Lofty. **22.** Alison Steadman. **23.** Andrew Marshall. **24.** Seinfeld. **25.** Mrs Overall. **26.** Montgomery. **27.** *The Army Game.* **28.** Lily Savage. **29.** *Rutland Weekend Television.* **30.** Paul Merton.

## QUIZ 84 TV Comedy 21

LEVEL 2

**Answers: see Quiz 83, page 511**

1. In *One Foot In The Grave*, what happens to Victor Meldrew's house while he is on holiday in Spain?
2. Who was the driver in *On The Buses*?
3. Who played Tony Carpenter in *On the Up*?
4. Which bar does Sam Malone run?
5. In *Only Fools and Horses* what is Boycie's wife called?
6. What was the setting of *Only When I Laugh*?
7. What is the occupation of the object of Granville's affections in *Open All Hours*?
8. Which *Back To The Future* star is deputy mayor in Channel 4's *Spin City*?
9. Which Australian comedian played Pat Cleary in *Anzacs*?
10. Who played Joe McGann's equivalent in the US version of The *Upper Hand*?
11. Who wrote the book on which the TV series, *Porterhouse Blue* was based?
12. What was Sgt. Bilko's first name?
13. In *Please Sir* what was Bernard Hedges' nickname?
14. What sentence was given to Norman Stanley Fletcher at the beginning of *Porridge*?
15. Who links *One Foot In The Grave* and *Waiting For God*?
16. Which comic's real name is Jim Moir?
17. What was the follow-up to comedy series *Murder Most Horrid*?
18. Who changed her surname from Barr to Arnold and then dropped her surname?
19. Liza Goddard played Matt's secretary in *Yes Honestly*. What was her character's name?
20. Who was the British female on Rowan and Martin's *Laugh In*?
21. What was Gunner Sugden's nickname in *It Ain't Half Hot Mum*?
22. In *Selling Hitler* who played the role of Goering's daughter, Edda?
23. Which half of the Marshall-Renwick writing team created *Two Point Four Children*?
24. Which sitcom had a Manhattan deli called Monk's?
25. What was the name of Julie Walter's character in *Acorn Antiques*?
26. What was Ma and Pa Larkin's eldest son called?
27. Which comedy series was based at Hut 29 the surplus ordnance depot at Nether Hopping?
28. How is Paul O'Grady better known?
29. Which show was about 'Britain's smallest TV network'?
30. Who revived Galton and Simpson scripts for a rerun of Hancock sketches in the 90s?

ANSWERS

### Animals & Nature 2 (See Quiz 83)

**1.** A West Highland Terrier. **2.** An Elk. **3.** A gorilla. **4.** Schnorbitz. **5.** Tarzan. **6.** Cat. **7.** Donald Turner. **8.** A pussycat. **9.** Ivan Owen. **10.** Petra. **11.** Flicka. **12.** A lion. **13.** David Attenborough. **14.** Kevin the Gerbil. **15.** Gerald & Lee Durrel. **16.** Rolf Harris. **17.** John Cleese. **18.** Percy Edwards. **19.** Pal. **20.** Goldfish. **21.** Duke. **22.** David Bellamy. **23.** Zoe Tate. **24.** Victor Meldrew. **25.** The Farnons' (*All Creatures Great and Small*). **26.** *Vets in Practice*. **27.** Rin-Tin-Tin. **28.** Andy Williams. **29.** Cartoon chipmunks. **30.** A stallion.

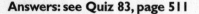

## QUIZ 85 Drama 8

LEVEL 2

**Answers: see Quiz 86, page 514**

1. In *Bronco*, which actor played the title role?
2. Who played the title role in *The Adventures of William Tell*?
3. Who played Anna in *This Life*?
4. Which daughter of Rosemary Harris starred in the 1995 *Pride and Prejudice*?
5. In which steamy series did Harriet Walter play Charity Walton?
6. Who played Dr Kildare's mentor?
7. Which seedy dance hall did Danny and Frank Kane run, played by Leslie Grantham and Don Henderson?
8. In which drama did Dennis Potter create Arthur Parker?
9. Which playwright is married to actress Maureen Lipman?
10. What does Rumpole always call the judges?
11. Where was *St Elsewhere* based?
12. Squire Gurth, companion of *Ivanhoe* was played by which actor?
13. Who played henpecked husband, Alf, in *The Larkins*?
14. Which DJ wrote the theme song for *Trainer*, sung by Cliff Richard?
15. Tim Piggott-Smith played which character in *Jewel in the Crown*?
16. Which actor was the Japanese POW Commandant in *Tenko*?
17. Which actress, famous as a wife in a 90s sitcom, played Henry's first wife in *The Six Wives of Henry VIII*?
18. What was the occupation of Mike Nelson in *Sea Hunt*?
19. Which regiment featured in *Soldier Soldier*?
20. Which spy drama with Alec Guinness focused on the agency known as 'the circus'?
21. Robert Mitchum played which character in the WWII drama *The Winds Of War*?
22. Between which years did *Sunday Night Theatre* run on BBC TV?
23. Which famous cowboy guest starred in '*The Colter Craven Story*' taken from *Wagon Train*?
24. Which Philadelphia based drama featured the Westons and Steadmans?
25. Who played the title role in *Garry Halliday*?
26. Richard Chamberlain was the star of which drama set in mediaeval Japan?
27. Which actor played the *Jungle Boy*?
28. Which *ER* actor appeared in *Roseanne*?
29. Which saga about a black American family starred OJ Simpson?
30. Which brothers were Bo and Luke?

ANSWERS

### Crime 9 (See Quiz 86)

**1.** Helen Forrester. **2.** Horace Rumpole. **3.** GK Chesterton. **4.** Crockett (*Miami Vice*). **5.** Kate Jackson. **6.** Anouska Hempel. **7.** Safe Deposit Boxes. **8.** Alan Wheatley. **9.** MG. **10.** Stacey Keach. **11.** Garfield Morgan. **12.** Miss Marple. **13.** Stratford Johns & Frank Windsor. **14.** Dave. **15.** Tony Curtis. **16.** *Magnum PI*. **17.** James Bolam. **18.** Jack Roffey. **19.** Hercule Poirot. **20.** Policeman. **21.** Into those who played cricket and those who did not. **22.** *Thames Valley*. **23.** Colin Blakely. **24.** Christopher Strauli. **25.** Det. Supt. Steve Hackett. **26.** Pepper. **27.** Leslie Nielsen. **28.** Terry Venables. **29.** A Bank Robber. **30.** Jane Tennison.

## QUIZ 86 Crime 9

**Answers: see Quiz 85, page 513**

LEVEL 2

1. Who replaced the actress Googie Withers in the prison series *Within These Walls*?
2. Leo McKern played which well-known Old Bailey lawyer?
3. *Father Brown* was based on which author's famous amateur detective?
4. Which US cop lived on a boat called St Vitus Dance?
5. Who played Mrs King in *The Scarecrow and Mrs King*?
6. Which actress played the astrologer Esther Jones in *Zodiac*?
7. What did the two small-time crooks steal in the series *Turtle's Progress*?
8. Who played the first TV Sherlock Holmes in 1951?
9. What car did Nick restore in *Heartbeat*?
10. Who played detective Mike Hammer but spent time in Reading jail for real life drug offences?
11. Who played the Flying Squad boss, Det. Chief Insp. Haskins in *The Sweeney*?
12. Who always got the better of Inspector Slack?
13. Which two actors appeared in the lead roles in *Second Verdict*?
14. In *Minder*, who owned the Winchester club?
15. Who played the US half of the duo in *The Persuaders*?
16. Which PI was bossed around by Higgins, his employer's representative?
17. Which actor played Trevor Chapman in *The Beiderbecke Affair*?
18. Who was the main author in *Boyd QC*?
19. Which detective lived at Whitehaven Mansions?
20. What was Doyle's occupation before joining *The Professionals*?
21. How did Charters and Caldicott divide the world?
22. The 1982 controversial fly on the wall police documentary filmed which police force?
23. Who played Det. Insp. Richard Lee in *Operation Julie*?
24. Which actor played Bunny Manners in the series *Raffles - The Amateur Cracksman*?
25. Which police detective played by Patrick Mower was featured in the series *Target*?
26. In *Police Woman* what was Sgt. Suzanne Anderson known as?
27. Which star of the *Naked Gun* films starred in the zany *Police Squad* in the 80s?
28. *Hazell* was based on the crime novels by Gordon Williams and who else?
29. What was Frank Ross in *Out*?
30. Who did Helen Mirren play in *Prime Suspect*?

ANSWERS

### Drama 8 (See Quiz 85)

**1.** Ty Hardin. **2.** Conrad Phillips. **3.** Daniela Nardini. **4.** Jennifer Ehle. **5.** *The Men's Room.* **6.** Raymond Massey. **7.** *The Paradise Club.* **8.** *Pennies From Heaven.* **9.** Jack Rosenthal. **10.** Old darling. **11.** Boston. **12.** Robert Brown. **13.** David Kossoff. **14.** Mike Read. **15.** Ronald Merrick. **16.** Burt Kwouk. **17.** Annete Crosby **18.** Freelance Aquanaut. **19.** King's Fusiliers Infantry Regiment. **20.** *Tinker, Tailor, Soldier, Spy.* **21.** 'Pug' Henry. **22.** 1955-59. **23.** John Wayne. **24.** *Thirtysomething.* **25.** Terence Longdon. **26.** *Shogun.* **27.** Michael Carr-Hartley. **28.** George Clooney. **29.** *Roots.* **30.** *The Dukes of Hazard.*

## QUIZ 87 Pot Luck 12

LEVEL 2

**Answers: see Quiz 88, page 516**

1. The coronation of which monarch was the first to be broadcast?
2. The Director General, Hugh Carleton Greene, was the brother of which novelist?
3. What is the spending limit for each team on *Changing Rooms*?
4. In *To the Manor Born*, what was the name of the Manor?
5. What was Dudley Moore always searching for in the series of Tesco ads?
6. How were PJ and Duncan also known?
7. What was the name of the company in *The Squirrels*?
8. Which gardening programme developed from *Gardening Club* in 1968?
9. In which show would you meet Ludicrus Sextus and Stovus Primus?
10. Why does Carol Hershey hold the record as the most seen face on British TV?
11. What was the name of the character played by David Jason in *Open All Hours*?
12. Which Esther Rantzen series was a follow up to *Braden's Week*?
13. What are the first names of scriptwriters Galton and Simpson?
14. Who asked, 'so who would live in a house like this...'?
15. Which royal relative was the subject of *This Is Your Life* in jubilee year, 1977?
16. Which *Top Gear* presenter was given his own chat show in 1998?
17. Who hosted the pop programme *America's Top Ten*?
18. Who played Mr Grove in *The Grove Family*?
19. What is the name of the spiky-haired TV chef?
20. Queen Elizabeth II is the only British sovereign to have ever visited a TV studio. True or false?
21. What do The Osmonds, The Jackson Five and The Beatles have in common?
22. Dickens and Fenster had the same trade. What was it?
23. What was Boon before he was forced into retirement?
24. Name the original presenter of *Gardening Club*.
25. Which tennis star took over from Anneka Rice in *Treasure Hunt*?
26. Which series asked the question "Who killed Laura Palmer?"
27. Who wrote *Barmitzvah Boy*?
28. In *Dr Who*, who played Romana and was also married to Tom Baker?
29. Which sister channel to UK Gold used the slogan 'You can't help getting involved'?
30. Whose TV career took off after the highly publicised breakdown of her marriage to a rugby player?

ANSWERS

### TV Comedy 22 (See Quiz 88)

**1.** John Sessions. **2.** June Whitfield. **3.** William Hartnell. **4.** Linda Robson. **5.** *Coast-to-Coast.* **6.** Joan Simms. **7.** Ian Carmichael. **8.** The man from the Pools Company. **9.** Mel Smith and Griff Rhys Jones. **10.** Gary. **11.** Michael Crawford. **12.** Ticket Tout. **13.** Milkman. **14.** Norman Tebbit. **15.** Harold and Albert Steptoe. **16.** Annie Briggs. **17.** Jimmy Tarbuck. **18.** Composer. **19.** *Canned Carrot.* **20.** A building site. **21.** Leslie Crowther. **22.** Shirley Temple. **23.** Bella Emberg. **24.** Audrey Fforbes-Hamilton. **25.** TV repair man. **26.** Steve Punt. **27.** Tutti Frutti. **28.** Ronnie Barker. **29.** Miriam Karlin. **30.** The *Paul Calf Video Diary.*

## QUIZ 88 TV Comedy 22

**Answers: see Quiz 87, page 515**

LEVEL 2

1. Which Scottish comedian and actor was born John Marshall in 1953?
2. Who played Arthur's wife in *The Arthur Askey Show*?
3. Who played Sgt Major Bullimore in *The Army Game*?
4. Which Bird of a Feather played Maggie in *Shine On Harvey Moon*?
5. In which comedy did Lenny Henry play a DJ on the run?
6. In *On the Up*, starring Dennis Waterman, which Joan played his cook?
7. Who was the *Batchelor Father*?
8. What was Snudge in the second series of *Bootsie and Snudge*?
9. Which duo from *Not The Nine O'Clock News* formed their own company Talk Back Productions?
10. Martin Clunes plays which character in *Men Behaving Badly*?
11. Which sitcom star was famous for doing his own stunts including roller skating under a lorry?
12. What does Frank Stubbs do for a living?
13. In *Beryl's Lot*, what did Beryl's husband do for a living?
14. In *Spitting Image* which of Thatcher's cabinet was portrayed as a skinhead bully?
15. Who lived at Mews Cottage, Oil Drum Lane?
16. Whose catchline was "Phenomenal" in *Sitting Pretty*?
17. Which comic became resident compere on *Sunday Night at the London Palladium*?
18. In *Yes Honestly*, what was Matt's occupation?
19. In which Jasper Carrott series did *The Detectives* make their debut?
20. What was the setting for the action in *Big Jim and the Figaro Club*?
21. Who was a *Big Boy Now!*?
22. What nickname did Alf Garnett give his son in law?
23. In *Russ Abbot's Madhouse*, who was Russ's female sidekick?
24. What was Penelope Keith's character in *To The Manor Born*?
25. What is Gary Sparrow's job in *Goodnight Sweetheart*?
26. Newman, Baddiel, Dennis and who else formed *The Mary Whitehouse Experience*?
27. Which comedy featured the Scottish kings of rock *The Majestics*?
28. How was Gerald Wiley, who wrote scripts for The Two Ronnies, otherwise known?
29. In The Rag Trade which actress's catchphrase was "Everybody out"?
30. What was the name of Paul Calf's own show?

ANSWERS

### Pot Luck 12 (See Quiz 87)

**1.** George VI (1937). **2.** Graham Greene. **3.** £500. **4.** Grantleigh. **5.** Chickens. **6.** Ant and Dec. **7.** International Rentals. **8.** *Gardeners' World*. **9.** *Up Pompeii!* **10.** She appeared on the test card. **11.** Granville. **12.** *That's Life*. **13.** Ray & Allen. **14.** Loyd Grossman. **15.** Lord Mountbatten. **16.** Jeremy Clarkson. **17.** Casey Kasem. **18.** Edward Evans. **19.** Gary Rhodes. **20.** True. **21.** All have been portrayed in cartoons. **22.** Carpentry. **23.** A Fireman. **24.** Percy Thrower. **25.** Annabel Croft. **26.** *Twin Peaks*. **27.** Jack Rosenthal. **28.** Lalla Ward. **29.** UK Living. **30.** Julia Carling.

## QUIZ 89 Soaps 11

LEVEL 2

**Answers: see Quiz 90, page 518**

1. In *Eastenders*, who is Beppe's brother?
2. Who was Hattie's granddad in *Eastenders*?
3. Who is the landlady of the Rovers Return?
4. Which soap pub sells a pint of Churchills?
5. Where did Caress appear?
6. Who did Peter Dean play in *EastEnders*?
7. Who went from *Emergency-Ward 10* to the Woolpack?
8. How many actresses have played Lucy in *Neighbours*?
9. Who was Des's first wife in *Neighbours*?
10. What is the name of the local newspaper in *Emmerdale*?
11. What was the business of *Falcon Crest*?
12. What is the family link between *Eastenders* and *Faith in the Future*?
13. Which *Last of the Summer Wine* actress played Doris Luke in *Crossroads*?
14. What is Betty Turpin's famous dish?
15. Which actor played Sir Lancelot before moving into *Coronation Street*?
16. Who in *Emmerdale* does Billy Hartman portray?
17. Which actress star of *The Bitch* ran the *Crossroads* motel?
18. Who was Ivy Brennan's son?
19. Who was confined to a wheelchair in *Crossroads*?
20. Who created *Emmerdale*?
21. In what year was *Emmerdale Farm* first broadcast?
22. Which character in *Knotts Landing* did Ted Shackleford play?
23. In *EastEnders*, which of the Jackson family witnessed a bank robbery causing them to leave the Square?
24. Who was the creator of *Coronation Street*?
25. In *Coronation Street* what was Des Barnes brother called?
26. Who appeared in the very first scene in *Emmerdale Farm*?
27. Which *EastEnders* star is a regular panellist on radio's *Just A Minute*?
28. Who plays Kathy Glover?
29. Which celebrity opened the refurbished Woolpack in *Emmerdale*?
30. Who recorded *Hillbilly Rock, Hillbilly Roll*?

ANSWERS

### Sci-Fi 4 (See Quiz 90)

**1.** Martin Landau. **2.** *Red Dwarf*. **3.** *Lost in Space*. **4.** Tracy. **5.** Gerry and Sylvia Anderson. **6.** Gareth Thomas. **7.** The Moon. **8.** Astronomer Fred Hoyle. **9.** Gary. **10.** Time travel project. **11.** Three. **12.** An earthquake. **13.** Mr Spock. **14.** James Garner. **15.** Submarine. **16.** *Supercar*. **17.** Gor. **18.** Environmental Harm. **19.** Nathan Spring. **20.** *Survivors*. **21.** Windsor Davies. **22.** Lou Ferigno. **23.** Lorne Green. **24.** *The Outer Limits*. **25.** Boris Karloff. **26.** Roddy McDowell. **27.** *The Six Million Dollar Man*. **28.** Jellybabies. **29.** *Doomwatch*. **30.** Mayhew.

## QUIZ 90 Sci-Fi 4

LEVEL 2

**Answers: see Quiz 89, page 517**

**1.** Who played the Moonbase Commander in *Space: 1999?*
**2.** Which series was originally called *Dave Hollins-Space Cadet?*
**3.** In which TV series was the character Dr. Zachary Smith?
**4.** Which family feature in *Thunderbirds?*
**5.** Whose first attempt at real life Sci-Fi was in *UFO?*
**6.** In *Blake's Seven,* who played Blake?
**7.** *Target Luna* featured a trip around what?
**8.** Who created *A For Andromeda?*
**9.** Which Ewing starred in *Space Precinct?*
**10.** What was the *Quantum Leap* in the sci show of the same name?
**11.** Of the first four Quatermass series how many were released on the cinema circuit?
**12.** In '*The Stranger*' episode from the series *One Step Beyond,* Harold Kaskett saved three children from what natural disaster?
**13.** In *Star Trek* who relaxes by playing 3-D chess?
**14.** Who, famous as Jim Rockford, starred in the mini series *Space?*
**15.** What sort of vehicle was Stingray?
**16.** Which children's series had Mike Mercury and Professor Popkiss?
**17.** What was the nickname of the baby in *First Born?*
**18.** What did the *Doomwatch* team investigate?
**19.** Who was *Starcop?*
**20.** Which 70s series, rerun on satellite, told of people who remained after a killer plague struck the world?
**21.** Which star of *It Ain't Half Hot Mum* provided the voice of Major Zero in *Terrahawks?*
**22.** Who played the *Incredible Hulk?*
**23.** Which Western star captained the *Battlestar Gallactica?*
**24.** Which 60s series was an anthology of frightening Sci-Fi stories?
**25.** Which actor famous for his horror roles narrated *Out of This World?*
**26.** Which Hollywood actor played Galen in *The Planet of the Apes?*
**27.** Which Man was bionic?
**28.** Which type of sweet did Tom Baker's *Dr Who* enjoy?
**29.** Which 70s series starred Robert Powell as Toby Wren?
**30.** What was Richard's surname in *Neverwhere?*

ANSWERS

**Soaps 11 (See Quiz 89)**

**1.** Gianni. **2.** Jules. **3.** Vera Duckworth. **4.** The Queen Vic. **5.** *The Colbys.* **6.** Pete Beale. **7.** Richard Thorpe. **8.** 3. **9.** Daphne. **10.** Hotten Courier. **11.** Vineyard. **12.** Sisters Julia & Nadia Sawalha. **13.** Kathy Staff. **14.** Hotpot. **15.** William Russell. **16.** Terry Wood. **17.** Sue Lloyd. **18.** Brian Tilsley. **19.** Sandy. **20.** Kevin Laffam. **21.** 1972. **22.** Gary Ewing. **23.** Billy. **24.** Tony Warren. **25.** Colin. **26.** Joe Kendall & Peggy Skilbeck. **27.** Wendy Richards. **28.** Malandra Burrows. **29.** Ian Botham. **30.** The Woolpackers.

# QUIZ 91 Children's TV 9

LEVEL 2

**Answers: see Quiz 92, page 520**

1. On which programme would you find Humpty and Jemima?
2. Harry Corbett is associated with which puppet?
3. Where did *Larry The Lamb* live?
4. Which fox have both David Nixon and Roy North worked with?
5. Which school did Billy Bunter attend?
6. What did Bill and Ben live in?
7. What animals were Rag, Tag and Bobtail respectively?
8. What did prizewinners on *Crackerjack* receive?
9. Who was *He-Man's* arch-enemy?
10. Who was the "Wonder Horse"?
11. Who cried "Hi, Ho, Silver, and away!" at the end of each episode of his show?
12. What was the name of *Blue Peter* presenter John Noakes' dog?
13. What was Archie Andrews in *Educating Archie*?
14. What was *Metal Mickey*?
15. Who played the Sheriff of Nottingham in *Maid Marian and Her Merry Men*?
16. What did Mr. Benn's shopkeeper wear on his head?
17. What was the name of the punk dog on *Tiswas*?
18. In *Teletubbies* the baby's face is in the middle of what?
19. What was the name of *Rainbow's* pink hippo?
20. In which town does Postman Pat do his rounds?
21. On which day does *The Snowman* come alive?
22. Who was the voice of Toad in the 1983 animated serialisation of *Wind In The Willows*?
23. What was Aunt Sally in *Worzel Gummidge*?
24. Who narrated the 1980's animated series *Thomas The Tank Engine*?
25. Name the 4 children who feature in *The Chronicles Of Narnia*?
26. Who played *The Storyteller* on Channel 4?
27. Who played the editor, schoolgirl Lynda Day, in *Press Gang*?
28. Who led *The Smurfs*?
29. Who played the gawky schoolboy Peter Payne in *Teenage Health Freak*?
30. Which comedy series featured an intergalactic TV station and earthbound reporters?

ANSWERS

## TV Comedy 23 (See Quiz 92)

**1.** Roger Dervish. **2.** Caroline Aherne. **3.** Boswell. **4.** Oscar Wilde and Aubrey Beardsley. **5.** Sisters. **6.** Alfred. **7.** He buried her late husband. **8.** *It Ain't Half Hot Mum*. **9.** Ruby Wax. **10.** Denise Coffey & Julie Stevens. **11.** Bernie Winters. **12.** Captain Kremmen. **13.** Victoria Wood. **14.** John Alderton & Pauline Collins. **15.** Industrial dispute. **16.** Mike Yarwood. **17.** Malaya. **18.** Tony Selby. **19.** *Yes Minister*. **20.** Russ Abbot. **21.** Agony. **22.** Van Clomp. **23.** *The Two Ronnies*. **24.** Geraldine. **25.** Ali Oopla. **26.** Steve Coogan. **27.** Mrs Slocombe. **28.** Sid James. **29.** *Auntie's Natural Bloomers*. **30.** The Big One.

## QUIZ 92 TV Comedy 23

LEVEL 2

**Answers: see Quiz 91, page 519**

1. In *Outside Edge*, who was the captain of the village cricket team?
2. How is Caroline Hook now known once again?
3. What is the surname of the family in *Bread*?
4. In *Albert and Victoria*, what were the names of the two gentlemen who Albert Hackett would not have mentioned in his home?
5. What tie linked rich June Whitfield and poor Pat Coombs in *Beggar My Neighbour*?
6. What was the name of Harry Corbett's character in *The Best Things In Life*?
7. How did Ada and Walter meet in *For The Love of Ada*?
8. Which sitcom featured The Royal Artillery Concert Party?
9. Which of the *Girls on Top* spent five years with the RSC?
10. Who played the female lead roles in *Girls About Town*?
11. Which half of a comedy duo had a St Bernard called Schnorbitz?
12. What was the name of Kenny Everett's whacky space captain?
13. Who wrote the Screen One TV film *Pat and Margaret*?
14. Which husband and wife team starred in *No-Honestly*?
15. Why was there a seven month delay before the last episode of *Fawlty Towers*?
16. Whose career blossomed with his impersonations of Harold Wilson and Ted Heath?
17. *The Misfit* had returned to London after having lived the good life for many years where?
18. Who played the barking-dog Corporal in *Get Some In!*?
19. Which programme was the first to win the BAFTA Best Comedy series three years in succession, in the 1980s?
20. Which *Madhouse* host has also played Fagin in *Oliver!* at the Palladium?
21. Which Maureen Lipman series did Anna Raeburn advise on?
22. In *'Allo, 'Allo* who painted 'The Fallen Madonna with the Big Boobies'?
23. Which duo played the detectives Charley Farley and Piggy Malone?
24. What was the name of the Goods' goat in *The Good Life*?
25. Which character did Frankie Howerd play in *Whoops Baghdad!*?
26. Who played the title role in *I'm Alan Partridge*?
27. In *Are You Being Served?* who showed a constant concern for her pussy?
28. Who was head of the Abbott household?
29. Which *Auntie's Bloomers* show showed outtakes from wildlife programmes?
30. Mike McShane was Sandi Toksvig's large lodger in which series?

ANSWERS

**Children's TV 9 (See Quiz 91)**

**1.** *Playschool.* **2.** Sooty. **3.** Toytown. **4.** Basil Brush. **5.** Greyfriars. **6.** Flowerpots. **7.** Hedgehog, fieldmouse, rabbit. **8.** *Crackerjack* Pencil. **9.** Skeletor. **10.** Champion. **11.** The Lone Ranger. **12.** Shep. **13.** A dummy. **14.** A talking robot. **15.** Tony Robinson. **16.** A fez. **17.** Spit. **18.** Sun. **19.** George. **20.** Greendale. **21.** Christmas Eve. **22.** David Jason. **23.** A fairground dummy. **24.** Ringo Starr. **25.** Peter, Susan, Edmund, Lucy. **26.** John Hurt. **27.** Julia Sawalha. **28.** Papa Smurf. **29.** Alex Langdon. **30.** *Wysiwig.*

# QUIZ 93 Pot Luck 13

LEVEL 2

**Answers: see Quiz 94, page 522**

1. Who succeeded Farrah Fawcett-Majors in *Charlie's Angels*?
2. Name the presenter of *Changing Rooms*.
3. Which comedian's father appears on *WatchDog*?
4. Who founded Verity Productions?
5. Who presented *The Great Egg Race*?
6. Name the female presenter of *Robot Wars*.
7. Which Knight advertised eggs?
8. Who played Charlie Endell in *Budgie*?
9. On what days of the week was the soap *Triangle* broadcast?
10. Which five times Wimbledon doubles title winner with Martina Navratilova commentates for the BBC at the championships?
11. Who played Elizabeth in *Blackadder II*?
12. Which Channel 4 artistic competition is associated with Hannah Gordon?
13. What is the name of Oprah Winfrey's production company?
14. Who is the actor father of Emily Lloyd?
15. What was the occupation of Bradley Walsh before he became a TV star?
16. Who undertook the task to circumnavigate the world 115 years after Phileas Fogg?
17. Which duo present *Late Lunch* on Channel Four?
18. Which Pan's People dancer married Robert Powell?
19. Which late night Channel 4 chat show was hosted by Jonathan Ross?
20. What ingredient did Gary Rhodes advertise on TV?
21. What was the name of the regular band on *The Last Resort*?
22. Which two actors played the lead roles in *Two's Company*?
23. Which person on TV was famous for his Odd odes?
24. Which show first screened in 1963 featured resident singer Kathy Kirby?
25. Where did *Billy Liar* work?
26. Which actor played *The History Man*?
27. What company featured in the BBC soap, *Triangle*?
28. Who was Cilla Black's male accomplice in the early episodes of *Surprise, Surprise*?
29. In which year did John Logie Baird commence experiments in TV?
30. Which film and TV star was born Daniel Kaminski?

ANSWERS

## Current Affairs 6 (See Quiz 94)

**1.** Rampton. **2.** Sally Magnusson. **3.** Robin Day. **4.** £19 Million. **5.** Laurence Olivier. **6.** John Craven. **7.** Bernard Braden. **8.** Anne Lawson & John Bonney. **9.** Robert Robinson. **10.** Tempo. **11.** Winston Churchill's. **12.** Alistair Cook's. **13.** Newsweek. **14.** *News at Ten*. **15.** *Newsnight*. **16.** The General Strike. **17.** *Carrot Confidential*. **18.** Angela Rippon. **19.** Trevor McDoughnut. **20.** Reginald Bosenquet. **21.** Sue Lawley. **22.** BBC 1. **23.** Sandy Gall. **24.** Angola. **25.** 1981-2. **26.** Michael Parkinson. **27.** Desmond Wilcox. **28.** Heathrow. **29.** Kilroy. **30.** Kenneth Clarke.

## QUIZ 94 Current Affairs 6

LEVEL 2

**Answers: see Quiz 93, page 521**

1. Which top security hospital was featured in *The Secret Hospital*?
2. Who was given a major TV interview with Earl Spencer after Diana's death?
3. Who was the first presenter of *Question Time*?
4. How much money was raised in relief funds in response to the documentary *Year Zero - The Silent Death Of Cambodia*?
5. Which actor narrated *The World At War*?
6. Who presented News Swap on *Multi Coloured Swap Shop*?
7. Who presented *All Our Yesterdays* between 1987 and 1989?
8. Which couple had a *Journey Of A Lifetime* through the Holy Land in the 1960s?
9. Who was the first host of *Points Of View*?
10. Which arts programme was hosted by Lord Harewood?
11. *The Valiant Years* was based on which Prime Minister's memoirs?
12. *America* was whose personal history of the USA?
13. David Jessel presented which news programme?
14. Sir Alistair Burnett read which news?
15. Presenter Kirsty Wark appears on which BBC2 daily news series?
16. In 1976 Robert Kee read news commemorating the $50^{th}$ anniversary of what?
17. Jasper Carrott's satirical news series was "*Carrot...*" what?
18. Who was the first female newsreader on British TV?
19. What is the name of Lenny Henry's comic newsreader?
20. Which late newsreader's autobiography was *Let's Get Through Wednesday*?
21. Which former newsreader hosts *Desert Island Discs*?
22. Nicholas Witchell read the news on which channel?
23. Which ITN newscaster reported back from the Afghanistan war?
24. Which African country did Diana visit in the landmines documentary?
25. Jan Leeming was "Newsreader of the Year" in which two consecutive years?
26. Who first interviewed George Michael about his arrest in the USA?
27. Who presented the 1978 BBC documentary *Americans*?
28. Which UK airport was featured in the 1978 BBC documentary *Airport*?
29. Which former MP has a morning talk show?
30. Who presented the documentary series *Civilisation*?

ANSWERS

### Pot Luck 13 (See Quiz 93)

**1.** Cheryl Ladd. **2.** Carol Smillie. **3.** Harry Enfield's. **4.** Verity Lambert. **5.** Prof. Heinz Wolff. **6.** Phillipa Forrester. **7.** Sir Bernard Miles. **8.** Iain Cuthbertson. **9.** Monday & Wednesday. **10.** Pam Shriver. **11.** Miranda Richardson. **12.** *Watercolour Challenge*. **13.** Harpo. **14.** Roger Lloyd Pack. **15.** Soccer player. **16.** Michael Palin. **17.** Mel and Sue. **18.** Babs. **19.** *The Last Resort*. **20.** Sugar. **21.** Steve Naïve and the Playboys. **22.** Elaine Stritch & Donald Sinden. **23.** Cyril Fletcher. **24.** Stars & Garters. **25.** Undertaker's. **26.** Anthony Sher. **27.** Triangle Line Ferry Co. **28.** Christopher Biggins. **29.** 1924. **30.** Danny Kaye.

# QUIZ 95 Drama 9

LEVEL 2

**Answers: see Quiz 96, page 524**

1. What was *Jungle Boy*'s zebra companion called?
2. Which handy US action man has been described as 'the ultimate boy scout'?
3. What is the real-life name of *The Prisoner*'s Village?
4. What are the names of the Maverick brothers?
5. Which actor played Danger Man?
6. Who played Edward in *Edward and Mrs Simpson*?
7. Who played Beau in *Maverick*?
8. Name the two Stephanies who co-starred in *Tenko*.
9. Which film star appeared in the lead role in *The Winds of War*?
10. In which children's drama did Ant and Dec find fame?
11. In *Blade on the Feather*, who played the mysterious visitor sent to kill the old man?
12. What was the name of the Russian-speaking male celebrity in *Airport*?
13. Which Beethoven Symphony was the haunting theme music to the 70s drama *Manhunt*?
14. Who played Tony Blair in Buccaneer?
15. What name was given to the mini series of half hour plays for TV in early 70s?
16. Who played the title role in *Drake's Venture*?
17. *The Chancer*'s greatest enemy, Jimmy Blake, was played by whom?
18. Which actor played Remington Steele?
19. Who played Casanova in the series scripted by Dennis Potter?
20. In which production did Kenneth Branagh play *Guy Pringle*?
21. In *Flickers*, what was Arnie Cole's personal ambition?
22. Who played the Sherrif of Nottingham in *Robin of Sherwood*?
23. What was the sequel series to *Hammer House of Horror* in 1984/85?
24. Who proved to be a traitor in *Neverwhere*?
25. In which fictitious town was *The Spoils Of War* Set?
26. In *Staying On* which two characters remained in India after the British Raj?
27. What is the occupation which Neeley, Cody and Donna have in common?
28. Who wrote *Brideshead Revisited*?
29. Which 1981 drama was the first to be set in a psychiatric unit?
30. Who was the writer and star of *Nanny*?

ANSWERS

## TV Comedy 24 (See Quiz 96)

**1.** Brabinger. **2.** Ronnie Barker. **3.** *The Wrong Trousers*. **4.** Nicholas Parsons. **5.** Peter Ustinov. **6.** *Love Thy Neighbour*. **7.** *My Wife Next Door*. **8.** Lewis Collins. **9.** The Soothsayer. **10.** Coupland. **11.** Bob Dylan & Levon Helm. **12.** *The Comedians*. **13.** Jimmy Perry & David Croft. **14.** Freddie Starr. **15.** *Birds of a Feather*. **16.** Cliff Richard. **17.** Blamire. **18.** Both were doctors. **19.** Blooming Marvellous. **20.** Arabella Weir. **21.** Jesse Birdsall. **22.** Helen. **23.** George & Mildred. **24.** Robert Lindsay. **25.** South Worfordshire. **26.** Tony Britton. **27.** Paul Nicholas & Jan Francis. **28.** Next Door. **29.** Michael Crawford. **30.** Michael Palin and Terry Jones.

## QUIZ 96 TV Comedy 24

LEVEL 2

**Answers: see Quiz 95, page 523**

1. In *To The Manor Born* what was Audrey's butler called?
2. Which Ronnie was famous for spoonerisms?
3. Which TV film won an Oscar in 1994 for best animation?
4. Which *Sale of the Century* presenter was Arthur Haines' straight man?
5. Who provided the voice-overs for the comedy *Clochemerle*?
6. Eddie and Joan Booth lived next door to Gill and Barabara Reynolds in which comedy?
7. George and Suzy Bassett were a couple getting divorced in which comedy?
8. Who played the irritatingly well-off friend Gavin in *The Cuckoo Waltz*?
9. Who said, 'Woe, woe and thrice woe' in *Up Pompeii!*?
10. Which Diana starred with Sid James in *Bless This House*?
11. Who wrote the song used as the theme music for *Absolutely Fabulous*?
12. Which stand up series from 1971 introduced Mike Reid, Bernard Manning and Frank Carson to our screens?
13. *Hi-De-Hi!* was created by which famous writing partnership?
14. Who with Peter Goodwright was the resident impressionist on *Who Do You Do?*
15. Which sitcom centred on Mrs Stubbs and her sister?
16. Rick in *The Young Ones* was a fan of which pop star?
17. Which character did Micheal Bates play in *Last of the Summer Wine*?
18. What profession do father and son share in *Don't Wait Up*?
19. In which series were Clive Mantle and Sarah Lancashire expecting a baby?
20. Who is worried about the size of her bum in the fast show?
21. Which *Eldorado* actor was also in the sitcom *Blind Men*?
22. What is the name of Dr Tom Latimer's ex-wife?
23. Which couple were played by Brian Murphy and Yootha Joyce?
24. Who played the self styled leader of the Tooting Popular Front in *Citizen Smith*?
25. Sir Giles Lynchwood was MP for which area in *Blott on the Landscape*?
26. In *Robin's Nest* who played the father of Robin's girlfriend, Vicky?
27. Which two actors are *Just Good Friends*?
28. Where did the Grandad Boswell live in *Bread*?
29. Which two ex Pythons starred in *Ripping Yarns*?
30. Which actress played the long-suffering Betty in *Some Mother's Do 'Ave 'Em*?

ANSWERS

### Drama 9 (See Quiz 95)

**1.** Quaggo. **2.** McGyver. **3.** Portmeirion. **4.** Bart & Brett. **5.** Patrick McGoohan. **6.** Edward Fox. **7.** Roger Moore. **8.** Stephanies Beacham & Cole. **9.** Robert Mitchum. **10.** *Byker Grove*. **11.** Tom Conti. **12.** Jeremy. **13.** Fifth. **14.** Bryan Marshall. **15.** *Thirteen Minute Theatre*. **16.** John Thaw. **17.** Leslie Phillips. **18.** Pierce Brosnan. **19.** Frank Finlay. **20.** *Fortunes of War*. **21.** To make Comedy Films. **22.** Nickolas Grace. **23.** *Hammer House of Mystery and Suspense*. **24.** Hunter. **25.** Whitstanton. **26.** Tusker & Lucy Smalley. **27.** Lifeguards in *Baywatch*. **28.** Evelyn Waugh. **29.** *Maybury*. **30.** Wendy Craig.

## QUIZ 97 Soaps 12

**Answers: see Quiz 99, page 527**

LEVEL 2

1. Which comedian played Zak Dingle's brother?
2. Which 60s soap centred on the activities within a struggling soccer club?
3. Which 70s medical saga began in a twice weekly afternoon slot?
4. What was the title of *Coronation Street* creator Tony Warren's autobiography?
5. In which soap was the Cattleman's Club?
6. What is Vera Duckworth's son called?
7. Which character did Mia Farrow play in *Peyton Place*?
8. Which actors, later chart-topping singers, played Scott and Charlene in *Neighbours*?
9. Which Corkhill became a policeman in *Brookside*?
10. Where did Jonathan Gordon-Davis's girlfriend Cherie live before she came to England?
11. Who did Val Lehman play in *Prisoner Cell Block H*?
12. Which singer/actress played Ros Thorne in *Eastenders*?
13. Ken Barlow was a reporter with which newspaper?
14. Who plays Jude Cunningham in *Hollyoaks*?
15. Who does Diane Burke play in *Brookside*?
16. What was Anne Malone's job in *Coronation Street*?
17. Which character does Anna Brecon play in *Emmerdale*?
18. Who was the loving foster mum in *Home and Away*?
19. Which couple have a daughters named Leanne and Toyah in *Coronation Street*?
20. Who is Lady Tara Oakwell's chauffeur?
21. What was Mandy's burger van called in *Emmerdale*?
22. Who plays Kevin Webster in *Coronation Street*?
23. Which nasty character is played by Chris Chittell in *Emmerdale*?
24. Who is Lindsay Corkhill's husband?
25. Who played Sam in *Neighbours* and Dr Lachlan Fraser in *Home and Away*?
26. Where did the Carrington's live in *Dynasty*?
27. What is Chloe's daughter's name in *Home and Away*?
28. Which soap was a spin off of *Dallas*?
29. Who eloped to Gretna Green to get married in *Coronation Street*?
30. Who lied to Deirdre about being an airline pilot?

ANSWERS

### Crime 10 (See Quiz 98)

**1.** The informer who turned him in. **2.** Kenneth Moore. **3.** John Mortimer. **4.** *The Sweeney.* **5.** Hartley. **6.** A clockmender's. **7.** *Bergerac.* **8.** Theodore Hoffman. **9.** *Cadfael.* **10.** *Cracker.* **11.** Jack Frost. **12.** Det. Chief Superintendents Barlow & Watt. **13.** Patrick Malahide. **14.** CI5. **15.** Det. Inspector Waugh. **16.** Stratford Johns. **17.** Nick Berry. **18.** Pathologist. **19.** Michael Medwin. **20.** Ken Franklin. **21.** Lovejoy. **22.** Barry Foster. **23.** Lucas. **24.** Neil Morrissey. **25.** Andrew Faulds. **26.** Ngaio Marsh. **27.** Iain Cuthbertson. **28.** Edd Byrnes. **29.** Det. Insp. Steve Bollinger. **30.** Richard Briers.

## QUIZ 98 Crime 10

LEVEL 2

**Answers: see Quiz 97, page 525**

1. In *Out*, what was Frank Ross obsessed with discovering after being released from prison?
2. In *Father Brown*, who played the sleuth?
3. Who was the barrister-playwright creator of *Rumpole*?
4. Which series began as an *Armchair Theatre* one off called Regan?
5. In which fictitious town was Juliet Bravo set?
6. Freelance detective Bulman also ran what kind of shop?
7. Which detective was the son in law of Charlie Hungerford?
8. What was the name of Daniel Benzali's character in *Murder One*?
9. Which famous sleuth did Ellis Peters create?
10. In which crime drama series created by Jimmy McGovern did DS Jane Penhaligon appear?
11. Who is the town of Denton's most famous offbeat detective?
12. In *Second Verdict*, who investigated famous crimes from the past?
13. Which actor played the character Det. Sgt Chisholm in *Minder*?
14. *The Professionals* worked for which organisation?
15. Which Inspector appeared in *Something to Hide* in 1968?
16. In *Barlow at Large*, which actor played Det. Chief Supt. Barlow?
17. Who sang the theme music to early editions of *Heartbeat?*
18. In *Inspector Morse* what was the profession of Max?
19. Who played *Shoestring*'s radio station boss?
20. *International Detective* was which PI?
21. Who was assisted by Eric and Tinker?
22. Which actor portrayed *Van Der Valk*?
23. What was the name of Maigret's assistant?
24. Which 'man behaving badly' became *Boon*'s sidekick Rocky?
25. Who narrated *On Trial?*
26. Whose novels were adapted for *The Inspector Alleyn Mysteries*?
27. In *Sutherland's Law*, which actor played John Sutherland?
28. In *77 Sunset Strip*, which actor played Kookie?
29. Who walked "the lonely streets of London with his police dog, 'Ivan'"?
30. Who played his first leading role in the series *Brothers In Law*?

ANSWERS

### Quiz & Game Shows 4 (See Quiz 99)

**1.** *The Crystal Maze*. **2.** Ian Hislop and Paul Merton. **3.** *Small Talk*. **4.** *Big Break*. **5.** Bob Monkhouse. **6.** Sandi Toksvig. **7.** Jeremy Hawk. **8.** Jenny Powell. **9.** Tom O'Connor. **10.** Jilly Goolden. **11.** *Strike It Rich* and *Strike It Lucky*. **12.** George Daws. **13.** Loyd Grossman. **14.** Fred Dineage. **15.** *100 Per Cent*. **16.** Monica Rose. **17.** David Jacobs. **18.** Magnus Magnusson. **19.** *Mr and Mrs*. **20.** Nicholas Parsons. **21.** Hamper. **22.** *The Krypton Factor*. **23.** Cilla Black. **24.** £1,000. **25.** Each correct answer. **26.** Kenny Everett. **27.** Contestants had to answer questions without saying 'yes' or 'no'. **28.** *Can't Cook, Won't Cook*. **29.** *Fifteen to One*. **30.** 3.

## QUIZ 99 Quiz & Games Shows 4

LEVEL 2

**Answers: see Quiz 98, page 526**

1. In which show did contestants have to collect time crystals?
2. Name the two team captains on *Have I Got News For You*?
3. Ronnie Corbett presented which quiz show based on children's perceptions?
4. In which quiz show did Jim Davidson make his BBC TV debut?
5. Who replaced Paul Daniels as questioner on *Wipeout*?
6. Who was the first female team captain on *Call My Bluff*?
7. Name the original quiz master of *Criss Cross Quiz*?
8. Nicky Campbell and who host *Wheel of Fortune*?
9. Who presented the crossword based quiz *Crosswits*?
10. Who presents *The Great Antiques Hunt*?
11. Which two successful quiz shows were hosted by Michael Barrymore?
12. Name the big baby who keeps the score in *Shooting Stars*?
13. Who is the American presenter of *Through the Keyhole*?
14. Who hosted the weekday elimination quiz *Pass The Buck*?
15. On the first anniversary of her death which quiz show's questions were all on the subject of the late Princess of Wales?
16. Who was the female assistant on *The Sky's The Limit*?
17. Who succeeded Eamonn Andrews as chair of *What's My Line* in the 1970's?
18. Who was the question master on *Mastermind*?
19. Alan Taylor was the original quizmaster on which quiz in which couples answered questions about each other?
20. *Sale of the Century* was hosted by whom?
21. What does the runner up receive on *Ready Steady Cook*?
22. Which game show aimed to find 'the Super Person of Great Britain'?
23. Who hosted the first series of *The Moment of Truth*?
24. In *Double Your Money*, how much was the treasure trail prize?
25. *I Love Lucy* starred which comedienne?
26. Which comic and former DJ provided the voice over for *Celebrity Squares*?
27. What happened during the sixty second spot in *Take Your Pick*?
28. What was the name of the daytime culinary game show for reluctant chefs?
29. Which general knowledge quiz is a regular show before Countdown?
30. On *The Krypton Factor*, how many contestants were there each week?

ANSWERS

**Soaps 12 (See Quiz 97)**

**1.** Bobby Knutt. **2.** *United!* **3.** *General Hospital.* **4.** *I Was Ena Sharples' Father.* **5.** *Dallas.* **6.** Terry. **7.** Alison. **8.** Jason Donovan, Kylie Minogue. **9.** Rob. **10.** Canada. **11.** Bea Smith. **12.** Clare Grogan. **13.** The Weatherfield Recorder. **14.** Davinia Taylor. **15.** Kate Rogers. **16.** Supermarket Manager. **17.** Lady Tara Oakwell. **18.** Pippa Ross. **19.** The Battersbys. **20.** Biff. **21.** Mandy's Munchbox. **22.** Michael le Vell. **23.** Eric Pollard. **24.** Gary. **25.** Richard Greive. **26.** Denver. **27.** Olivia. **28.** *Knotts Landing.* **29.** Nick & Leanne Tilsley. **30.** John Lindsay.

## LEVEL 3: THE HARD QUESTIONS

Ah yes, the hard questions. Cackle fiendishly, and take just a moment to stroke your white, diamond-collared cat before rubbing your hands together gleefully, because these questions are the real McCoy. The posers in this selection will sort the men out from the boys, and no mistake. If you do find any boys in the public bar by the way, be sure to let the landlord know, so he can give them a packet of crisps and a bottle of coke and send them outside. The quizzes in this section will make even the most dedicated TV addict or couch potato quake with fear. No-one is going to get loads of them correct, so if someone turns out an incredible score on these questions, search their coat for a copy of this book.

When you're setting a quiz, use these questions sparingly, like hot chilli powder. Even for teams, they're going to be tricky. You'll need to allow some time for people to think about each question, too. What you don't want to do is make an entire night's TV quizzing out of these, because you'll only make people feel stupid, and everyone hates a smart alec who makes them look dumb. A few of these questions, strategically placed, can go a long way.

## QUIZ 1 Music & Variety 1

LEVEL 3

**Answers: see Quiz 2, page 530**

1. Which pop show was the title of a Squeeze hit?
2. Who had success with the song *Hi-Fidelity*?
3. Who was the entertainment committee chairman at *The Wheeltappers and Shunters Social Club*?
4. What was Clannad's first TV theme hit?
5. Who sang *Nappy Love*?
6. On which show did the Rolling Stones make their national TV debut?
7. Which TV group sang the song *OK*?
8. With which all-female group did *Hi-De-Hi!*'s Su Pollard start her entertainment career?
9. Who sang the theme song of the comedy *Going Straight*?
10. Jackie Lee sang the theme tune for which children's favourite?
11. *The Maigret Theme* brought success for which band leader?
12. Which duo were the stars of the musical drama *Ain't Misbehavin'*?
13. The BBC record charts are compiled by who?
14. In *Tutti Frutti*, who was bass player with The Majestics?
15. On which show did pianist Bobby Crush make his TV debut?
16. *Thank You For Being A Friend* was whose theme?
17. Who was the choreographer of Pan's People?
18. How were the singing brothers Tony, Mike and Denis better known?
19. Who accompanied Lesley Garret in a memorable 'Three Little Maids form School' in her 1998 TV show?
20. Who sang the *Auf Wiedersehn Pet* theme song?
21. What was the name of the Salvation Army group which regularly sang on TV?
22. Which record producer changed his name from Michael Haues?
23. Why was the Byrds song *Eight Miles High* banned by BBC TV?
24. Which soap theme was composed by Eric Spear?
25. Why did *Rock Follies*' Charlotte Cornwell sue the Sunday People?
26. The series *Off The Record* concerned what?
27. Which type of instruments did Bruno play in *Fame*?
28. What type of music was played on *Honky Tonk Heroes*?
29. Name the *Opportunity Knocks* winner who went on to star in *Gypsy on Broadway*.
30. What was the name of the 60's heavy rock programme broadcast on BBC1?

ANSWERS

### Sci Fi 1 (see quiz 2)

**1.** Cranially-implanted limiter. **2.** "Oh no, not again." **3.** The Angel Islington. **4.** A 5 million year old Martian spacecraft. **5.** Chakram. **6.** Transuranic. **7.** Bruce Campbell. **8.** Dean Stockwell. **9.** Knight Automated Roving Robot. **10.** Santini Air. **11.** *Batman and Robin*. **12.** Cursor. **13.** Black Panther. **15.** Greg Evigan. **16.** Major. **17.** Sydney Bloom. **18.** Demeter City. **19.** The Friends. **20.** Ferengi. **21.** Purple. **22.** Autons. **23.** The Neutral Zone. **24.** Jaunting. **25.** Rover. **26.** Scutters. **27.** Harry Dean Stanton. **28.** Marcus Cole. **29.** Harlan Ellison. **30.** The Free Men.

## QUIZ 2 Sci Fi 1

LEVEL 3

**Answers: see Quiz 1, page 529**

1. In *Blake's 7*, Gan could not commit violent acts. Why?
2. What were the last words of the bowl of petunias in *Hitch-Hiker's Guide to the Galaxy*?
3. Who organised the murder of Door's family in *Neverwhere*?
4. What alien discovery was made in *Quatermass And The Pit*?
5. What is the correct name of *Xena: Warrior Princess*'s 'round killing thing'?
6. According to Sapphire & Steel, which "Heavy Elements may not be used where there is life"?
7. Who plays Autolycus, King of Thieves, in *Hercules: The Legendary Journeys*?
8. Which actor accompanies Sam Beckett on his *Quantum Leaps*?
9. The Knight Industries Two Thousand had an evil counterpart. What was its full name?
10. What firm did Ernest Borgnine run in *Airwolf*?
11. Who was the Sandman an evil enemy of?
12. *Automan* created solid objects out of thin air with the aid of what/who?
13. *Manimal* had two preferred non-human shapes, a hawk and which other?
14. Which race is Lt. Tuvak a representative of in *Star Trek: Voyager*?
15. Who played Jake Cardigan in *TekWar*?
16. What rank was Don West in *Lost In Space*?
17. In VR5, Lori Singer starred as which computer expert?
18. In which city was *Space Precinct* set?
19. Which group opposed the Fathers in *Wild Palms*?
20. Which race is led by The Great Nagus in *Deep Space Nine*?
21. What colour is Klingon blood?
22. Which of *Dr. Who*'s enemies posed as shop dummies, sofas and other artificial items?
23. After the Treaty of Algeron which zone was created in *Star Trek: Next Generation*?
24. How did *The Tomorrow People* refer to teleportation?
25. What was the name of the device looking like a weather baloon that guarded The Village?
26. What are the janitorial robot 'helping hands' on the *Red Dwarf* called?
27. Which star of *Alien* played a trailer park owner in *Twin Peaks*?
28. In *Babylon 5*, who gave up his life so that Ivanova could live?
29. Which Sci-fi writer served as creative consultant to the 80s *Twilight Zone*?
30. Which Switzerland-based group was the goal of the young heroes fighting *The Tripods*?

ANSWERS

### Music & Variety 1 (see Quiz 1)

**1.** *Cool For Cats.* **2.** The Kids From Fame. **3.** Colin Crompton. **4.** *Harry's Game.* **5.** The Goodies. **6.** *Thank Your Lucky Stars.* **7.** The Little Ladies. **8.** *Midnight News.* **9.** Ronnie Barker. **10.** *Rupert Bear.* **11.** Joe Loss. **12.** Robson Green & Jerome Flynn. **13.** Gallup. **14.** Fud O'Donnell. **15.** *Opportunity Knocks.* **16.** *The Golden Girls.* **17.** Flick Colby. **18.** The King Brothers. **19.** Patricia Hodge & Lily Savage. **20.** Joe Fagin. **21.** Joy Strings. **22.** Mickey Most. **23.** It was though to be about drugs. **24.** *Coronation Street's.* **25.** The paper accused her of having a big bottom. **26.** The recording industry. **27.** Keyboards. **28.** Country & Western. **29.** Bonnie Langford. **30.** *Colour Me Pop.*

## QUIZ 3 Sport 1

LEVEL 3

**Answers: see Quiz 4, page 532**

**1.** What was the first sport shown on ITV, in 1955?
**2.** Which sports event had the most viewers in 1994?
**3.** Who replaced Peter Dimmock as presenter of the pioneering *Sportsview*?
**4.** Which boxing commentator won the American Sportscasters' Association International Award in 1989?
**5.** Who was the first BBC Sports Personality of the Year of the 1990s?
**6.** Which two sports presenters have separately hosted *How Do They Do That?*
**7.** Who became LWT's Deputy Controller after a career in football management?
**8.** On which channel is *Sunday Grandstand* broadcast?
**9.** Jack Solomon's *Scrapbook* concerned which sport?
**10.** Who aspires to become a professional boxer in the comedy *Taxi*?
**11.** Which programme covered the International Sheepdog Trials?
**12.** What BBC sport competition was first won by Ray Reardon?
**13.** Which sportsman recorded *We Shall Not Be Moved*?
**14.** On which sport does Dorian Williams commentate?
**15.** Which sport was featured in *Cudmore's Call*?
**16.** Which Royal organised the *Grand Knockout Tournament*?
**17.** Who was the UK's very first American football commentator?
**18.** Who replaced Bob Wilson as presenter of *Football Focus*?
**19.** Which pop star featured in the closing ceremony of the 1984 Summer Olympics?
**20.** Who went from editor of the Cheshire County Press to TV sports reporter?
**21.** Who did Stuart Hall replace as host of *It's A Knockout*?
**22.** *The Sporting Triangles* teams wore what colours?
**23.** Who presented *Pro Celebrity Golf*?
**24.** For how many years did Dickie Davis present *World of Sport*?
**25.** The theme from *Chariots Of Fire* was used by the BBC for which Olympics?
**26.** Why in 1975 did Michael Angelow receive big publicity after visiting Lords?
**27.** For the coverage of which sporting event did the BBC launch its colour service?
**28.** What sport featured in *The Winning Streak*?
**29.** Who refereed the TV football match between the Rovers Return and Maurice Jones Building on *Coronation Street*?
**30.** Which breakfast food was advertised by Ian Botham and Henry and George Cooper?

ANSWERS

### TV History (see Quiz 4)

**1.** Lord Reith. **2.** 1955. **3.** 1964. **4.** 1923. **5.** 1955. **6.** 1936. **7.** Alexandra Palace. **8.** Philip Harben. **9.** Calais. **10.** Ramsay MacDonald. **11.** 1932. **12.** Eamonn Andrews. **13.** Gerald Cock. **14.** Jasmin Bligh. **15.** Don Gemmell. **16.** 11,000. **17.** Patrick Troughton. **18.** Inspector Fabian. **19.** Frederick Grisewood. **20.** *Double or Drop*. **21.** *Treasure Trail*. **22.** Billie Whitelaw. **23.** Lucille Ball. **24.** Battle of Britain Sunday. **25.** Fred Streeter. **26.** A national fuel and power crisis. **27.** Marriage of Princess Elizabeth to Lt Philip Mountbatten. **28.** Clement Atlee. **29.** Leslie Welch. **30.** 1957 (September).

## QUIZ 4 TV History

LEVEL 3

**Answers: see Quiz 3, page 531**

1. Who was the very first Director General of The BBC?
2. In which year did Independent Television first hit the screens?
3. In which year did BBC2 commence broadcasting?
4. In which year was the *Radio Times* first published?
5. In which year was the *TV Times* first published?
6. In which year was the first BBC TV broadcast service commenced?
7. From where did the BBC TV service transmit?
8. Who was famous for his 50s cookery shows, *Cookery Lesson* and *What's Cooking?*
9. The first programme broadcast from France featured which town?
10. Who was the first Prime Minister to install TV in his home in the 1930s?
11. In which year were the first BBC TV studios founded?
12. Who chaired the first broadcasts of *What's My Line*?
13. Who was the BBC's first Director of TV?
14. Who was the BBC's first TV announcer?
15. Who presented *The Good Old Days* before Leonard Sachs?
16. In 1939 an estimated how many TV's were in regular use – 15,000, 13,000 or 11,000?
17. Which Dr Who was the first TV Robin Hood for children?
18. Which character played by Bruce Seton was one of the first TV detectives?
19. Who supplied the BBC commentary for the Coronation of King George VI?
20. What was the name of the quiz show on *Crackerjack*?
21. On which part of *Double Your Money* could you win the £1,000?
22. Who played George Dixon's daughter in the early years of *Dixon of Dock Green*?
23. Which comedienne was the neighbour of Fred and Ethel Mertz in a popular 50s sitcom?
24. What did the first ever TV church service celebrate?
25. Who was the presenter of the 1940's series Television Garden?
26. What forced the daytime shutdown of transmissions in Feb-March 1947?
27. Which Royal wedding was televised during November 1947?
28. Who gave the first direct TV broadcast by a Prime Minister?
29. In the post-war magazine programme *Kaleidoscope*, who was the "Memory Man"?
30. In which year did the BBC TV schools service begin?

ANSWERS

### Sport 1 (see Quiz 3)

**1.** Boxing. **2.** Torvill and Dean's Olympic Dance. **3.** Brian Johnston. **4.** Harry Carpenter. **5.** Liz McColgan. **6.** Desmond Lynam and Eamonn Homes. **7.** Jimmy Hill. **8.** BBC2. **9.** Boxing. **10.** Tony. **11.** *One Man And His Dog.* **12.** *Pot Black.* **13.** Big Daddy. **14.** Showjumping. **15.** Sailing. **16.** Prince Edward. **17.** Nicky Horne. **18.** Sam Leitch. **19.** Lionel Richie. **20.** David Coleman. **21.** David Vine. **22.** Yellow, green, red. **23.** Peter Allis. **24.** 16 years. **25.** The 1984 Olympics. **26.** He streaked on the pitch. **27.** Wimbledon. **28.** Rally driving. **29.** Derek Wilton. **30.** Shredded Wheat.

## QUIZ 5 Comedy 1

LEVEL 3

**Answers: see Quiz 6, page 534**

1. Which character did Brigit Forsyth portray in *Whatever Happened To The Likely Lads?*
2. In *M*A*S*H* what number was the medical unit?
3. Which composer conducted Eric Morecambe on the piano?
4. Which comedian played Al Johnson?
5. Who owned a dog called Fanny?
6. Who was the animator in the *Monty Python* team?
7. Who played a female driver in *Taxi?*
8. What are Lily Savage's 'children' called?
9. Which star of *Seinfeld* was the voice of Hugo in Disney's *The Hunchback of Notre Dame?*
10. What is Cliff's job in *Cheers?*
11. Which sport did Sam Malone play as a professional?
12. What was the nickname of the Inspector in *On The Buses?*
13. Which Carla created the *Liver Birds?*
14. Who created *Curry And Chips?*
15. Who was the star of *Ripping Yarns?*
16. In *No Place Like Home*, who starred as Arthur Crabtree?
17. Which actress appeared as Sid's wife in *Bless This House?*
18. What was Arthur Askey's catchphrase?
19. Where was *Get Well Soon* set?
20. Who used to say "She knows you know"?
21. Who played Bill in *Love Thy Neighbour?*
22. Who created the show *The Comedians?*
23. Patrick Cargill played the father in which family sitcom?
24. What was Arkwright's affliction?
25. Which comic trio dodged the traffic on a three-seater bike?
26. Who played Mrs Cravat opposite Tony Hancock?
27. What was Joe McGann's character in *The Upper Hand?*
28. Which comedian appeared in the TV play *An Evening With Gary Lineker?*
29. Who played Thora Hird's husband in *Meet The Wife?*
30. Which actor played Spike in *Hi-De-Hi!?*

ANSWERS

### Drama 1 (see Quiz 6)

**1.** Greer Garson. **2.** Michelle Collins. **3.** Slavery. **4.** Whitstanton Iron Works. **5.** Luberon. **7.** Barbara Gray. **8.** Jenny Seagrove and Deborah Kerr. **9.** HMP Stone Park. **10.** Jack Ford. **11.** PC David Graham. **12.** Billie Whitelaw. **13.** Mrs Murray. **14.** *Tenko Reunion.* **15.** Nigel Havers. **16.** On the Titanic. **17.** London. **18.** Toy Marsden. **19.** In a disused sandpit near Wareham, Dorset. **20.** Dale Cooper. **21.** *The Troubleshooters.* **22.** Michael Angelis. **23.** Nigel Davenport (father of Jack). **24.** Denholm Elliot. **25.** Editor of a newspaper. **26.** Three. **27.** Ray Lonnen. **28.** David Addison. **29.** Jack Frost. **30.** Original broadcast date was also the start of the Falklands Crisis.

## QUIZ 6 Drama 1

LEVEL 3

**Answers: see Quiz 5, page 533**

1. Which *Mrs Minerva* film star featured in *How He Lied To Her Husband* on TV?
2. Which ex EastEnder starred in the raunchy drama *Real Women*?
3. What was the trade in the drama series *A Respectable Trade*?
4. What was the name of the iron works which featured in *The Spoils Of War*?
5. Where in Provence did Peter Mayle recount his Year?
6. Who played Dr Edward Roebuck, head of a psychiatric unit, in the 80's drama *Maybury*?
7. What was the name of the lead character in *Nanny*, played by Wendy Craig?
8. Which two actresses played Emma Harte in Barbara Taylor Bradford's mini series *A Woman of Substance*?
9. Which prison featured in *Within These Walls*?
10. Which character was the hero of *When the Boat Comes In*?
11. Which role did Oscar winner Colin Welland play in *Z Cars*?
12. Who played the Dietrich-like character Bertha Freyer in the comic drama, *Private Schulz*?
13. What was the name of Robert Lindsay's pensioner mum in *GBH*?
14. What was the title of the 110-minute conclusion of the series *Tenko*?
15. Which actor played Randolph Churchill in *Winston Churchill – The Wilderness Years*?
16. In *Upstairs Downstairs* how did Lady Marjorie die?
17. In which city was the serial *World's End* set?
18. Which Roy played Jack Ruskin in the drama *Airline*?
19. Where was the BBC1 drama *Beau Geste* actually shot?
20. Who tried to solve the Laura Palmer mystery in *Twin Peaks*?
21. What were subsequent series of *Mogul* called?
22. Who played Chrissy in *Boys From The Blackstuff*?
23. Which father of a *This Life* star played James Brant in Trainer?
24. Who played the Smiley role in the ITV's *A Murder of Quality* in 1991?
25. In *Foxy Lady*, what was Daisy Jackson's job?
26. How many singles were there in the first series of *Thirtysomething*?
27. Who played the character Brown in the political thriller *Harry's Game*?
28. Who did Bruce Willis play on TV opposite Cybill Shepherd?
29. Which TV detective was a reluctant George Cross recipient?
30. Why was the final episode of *I Remember Nelson* held over for six months before being broadcast?

ANSWERS

### Comedy 1 (see Quiz 5)

**1.** Thelma. **2.** The 4077th. **3.** Andre Previn. **4.** Brian Conley. **5.** Julian Clary. **6.** Terry Gilliam. **7.** Marilu Henner. **8.** Bunty and Jason. **9.** Jason Alexander. **10.** Postman. **11.** Baseball. **12.** Blakey. **13.** Carla Lane. **14.** Johnny Speight. **15.** Michael Palin. **16.** William Gaunt. **17.** Diana Coupland. **18.** "Hello Playmates". **19.** 1940s TB sanatorium. **20.** Hylda Baker. **21.** Rudolf Walker. **22.** Jonny Hamp. **23.** *Father, Dear Father.* **24.** A stammer. **25.** *The Goodies.* **26.** Patricia Hayes. **27.** Charlie. **28.** Paul Merton. **29.** Freddie Finton. **30.** Jeffrey Holland.

## QUIZ 7 Soaps 1

LEVEL 3

**Answers: see Quiz 8, page 536**

1. Which ex soap star played Roy Osborne's mother in the sitcom *Get Well Soon*?
2. What was ITV's first 'soap' in 1955 called?
3. Which breakfast TV presenter starred as himself on *Brookside*?
4. Which three North Sea ports were visited by the ferry in *Triangle*?
5. What was the name of the ferry company in *Triangle*?
6. Which soccer expert was a consultant on the 60s soap *United!*?
7. Whose sister did Paula Wilcox play in *Coronation Street*?
8. Who was the narrator in *The Waltons*?
9. Which 60s soap followed the goings on at a large West End department store?
10. Jean Harvey, Nicholas Selby and Gareth Davies were editors of which fictional magazine?
11. Which soap shared its theme music with *The Upper Hand*?
12. Who played Gregory Sumner in *Knot's Landing*?
13. Which former soap star hosted *The Saturday Banana* in her teens?
14. Who as well as Grant claimed to be Courtney's father in *EastEnders*?
15. Who in *Home and Away* owned a car called 'The Bambino'?
16. Which *Coronation Street* actor's real name is William Piddington?
17. In *Heartbeat*, what is Sergeant Blaketon's first name?
18. Which twins from *Neighbours* were Des O'Connor's assistants on *Take Your Pick*?
19. In which year did the story of *The Sullivans* begin?
20. Which musical star appeared as a dodgy car dealer in *EastEnders* in 1998?
21. Luke Perry portrayed which character in *Beverley Hills 90210*?
22. In *Home and Away*, where did Joey live before moving in with Irene?
23. Which former *Coronation Street* actor played Jack Gates in *Family Affairs*?
24. Who has starred in *Emmerdale Farm*, *Coronation Street* and *Crossroads* but is most famous for her role in a long running sitcom?
25. What was the subtitle of the 1998 Albert Square video The Mitchells?
26. How were Justine and Aaron related in *Home and Away*?
27. In *The Bill* what was Tosh Lines' real first name?
28. In which Valley was *Falcon Crest* first filmed?
29. Which EastEnders star was Mrs Dale's milkman in the days of the classic radio soap?
30. With which family did *Home and Away*'s Aaron live?

ANSWERS

### Quiz & Game Shows 1 (see Quiz 8)

**1.** *The Gong Show.* **2.** *Ice Warriors.* **3.** *Tell The Truth.* **4.** *Connoisseur.* **5.** Gordon Burns. **6.** In a safe. **7.** *Pass The Buck.* **8.** *Lingo.* **9.** A gold key. **10.** Jeremy Beadle. **11.** *Bob's Full House.* **12.** Larry Grayson. **13.** Channel 4. **14.** *University Challenge.* **15.** A giant typewriter. **16.** David Jacobs. **17.** *What's My Line.* **18.** 100. **19.** *Masterteam.* **20.** Arthur Fowler in *Eastenders.* **21.** Bernie Winters. **22.** *The Newly Wed Game.* **23.** Four. **24.** Penelope Keith. **25.** *Connections.* **26.** Anthea Redfern. **27.** Henry Cooper and Cliff Morgan. **28.** Bob Danvers Walker. **29.** *Clapperboard.* **30.** *A Question Of Sport.*

## QUIZ 8 Quiz & Game Shows 1

LEVEL 3

**Answers: see Quiz 7, page 535**

1. Frankie Howerd hosted which game show?
2. Which Dani Behr show was fast action, laser lit and on skates?
3. Which game show started with the words "My name is..."?
4. Which 80s arts quiz was hosted by Bamber Gascoigne?
5. Who originally hosted *Password*?
6. In *The $64,000 Question*, how were the questions secured?
7. George Layton hosted which game show?
8. Which quiz was hosted by Paul Daniel's son?
9. What object was given to winning guests on *Through The Keyhole*?
10. Who was the original host of *Chain Letters*?
11. Which Bob Monkhouse game show was based on bingo?
12. Who hosted *The Man Who Got Away*?
13. On which channel was *Cyberzone* broadcast?
14. What is British TV's longest running quiz show?
15. What giant object featured on *All Clued Up*?
16. Who replaced Eamonn Andrews as chairman of *What's My Line?* in 1970?
17. Which show required guests to sign in?
18. On *Bullseye* what score was required to win the star prize?
19. Angela Rippon hosted which master quiz?
20. Which soap character appeared in the fictional quiz show *Cat And Mouse*?
21. Which comic hosted *Whose Baby*?
22. What couples game show was presented by Gloria Hunniford?
23. How many children appeared in each episode of *Ask The Family*?
24. Which *Good Life* star presented *What's My Line*?
25. On which show were questions asked by Sue Robbie?
26. Which game show assistant won a Miss Longest Legs contest judged by her future husband?
27. Who were the original captains on *A Question Of Sport*?
28. Who announced the prizes in the early years of *Take Your Pick*?
29. Chris Kelly chaired which kids TV quiz?
30. Princess Anne was a contestant in which TV quiz?

ANSWERS

### Soaps 1 (see Quiz 7)

**1.** Anita Dobson. **2.** *Sixpenny Corner.* **3.** Eamonn Holmes. **4.** Felixstowe, Gothenburg and Amsterdam. **5.** Triangle Line. **6.** Jimmy Hill. **7.** Ray Langton's. **8.** John Boy. **9.** *Harpers West One.* **10.** *Compact.* **11.** *Knot's Landing.* **12.** William Devane. **13.** Susan Tully. **14.** Tony Hills. **15.** Angel. **16.** William Tarmey (Jack Duckworth). **17.** Oscar. **18.** Gayle and Gillian Blakeney. **19.** 1939. **20.** Anthony Newley. **21.** Dylan McKay. **22.** The commune. **23.** Ken Farrington. **24.** Kathy Staff. **25.** *Naked Truths.* **26.** Sister and brother. **27.** Alfred. **28.** Napa Valley, California. **29.** Bill Treacher (Arthur Fowler). **30.** With the Stewarts.

## QUIZ 9 Pot Luck 2

LEVEL 3

**Answers: see Quiz 10, page 538**

**1.** What was Britain's first half hour animation series?
**2.** Who was resident chef on *Good Morning* With Anne & Nick?
**3.** Who investigates *The Big Story*?
**4.** What is Caprice's surname?
**5.** Who was the manager who caused a stir in the doc soap *Hotel*?
**6.** What are the surnames of Mel & Sue?
**7.** In 1957 how much did a colour TV cost?
**8.** What was Channel 4's series of animations and animation-related programmes?
**9.** Sophie Anderton hosted which fashion magazine show?
**10.** The results of which General Election were the first to be televised?
**11.** Who was *The Mind Traveller*?
**12.** Which was the first British channel transmitted exclusively on the 625 line system?
**13.** Who spoke the first words on GMTV?
**14.** Which TV presenter was Bob Geldof's father in law?
**15.** Which gardening programme developed from *Gardening Club* in 1968?
**16.** Which conqueror of Everest has presented *Tomorrow's World*?
**17.** Which husband and wife team have presented *Watchdog*?
**18.** Who was the first woman weather presenter on BBC TV?
**19.** Who is *Top Gear's* primary motorbike correspondent?
**20.** Which husband and wife team went *On Safari*?
**21.** Alexei Sayle played the part of Commissar Solzhenitsyn in which 1982 series?
**22.** Which doctors hosted *Where There's Life*?
**23.** Which musical star played Berel Jastrow in *The Winds of War*?
**24.** What was Francis William's role on *Breakfast Time*?
**25.** On which show do Anna Ryder Richardson, Graham Wynn and Carol Smillie appear?
**26.** Which programme has Alan Hanson and Mark Laurenson as football analysts?
**27.** Who organised the annual *Miss World* event?
**28.** In *Coronation Street* what was Annie Walker's daughter's name?
**29.** Who was the female in *Three of a Kind* when Mike Yarwood was one of the three?
**30.** What was the film programme presented by Dave Lee Travis?

ANSWERS

**Children's TV 1 (see Quiz 10)**

**1.** Tony Hart. **2.** *Play School.* **3.** Billy Wright & Danny Blanchflower. **4.** 'Ah do declare'. **5.** Lorraine Chase. **6.** Jenny and Willy. **7.** Jon Pertwee. **8.** David Jason. **9.** 1947. **10.** Aquamarina. **11.** *Wallace and Gromit.* **12.** 50p. **13.** Poetry for children. **14.** Diane Youdale. **15.** Huw Wheldon. **16.** *The Adventures of Mick and Montmorency.* **17.** Kenneth Williams. **18.** Sylvester McCoy. **19.** Patricia Driscoll. **20.** Fred Quimby. **21.** Percy Thrower. **22.** Michael Angelis. **23.** Inventor Black. **24.** Mitch. **25.** *Christmas With The Appleyards.* **26.** Mr Quelch. **27.** *Andy Pandy.* **28** Peter Hawkins. **29.** Sama and Elizabeth Williams. **30.** Richard Scarry.

## QUIZ 10 Children's TV 1

LEVEL 3

**Answers: see Quiz 9, page 537**

1. Who designed the *Blue Peter* badge?
2. Which children's show was BBC2's first transmission?
3. Which two footballers presented *Junior Sportsview*?
4. What was the catchphrase of Yogi Bear's girlfriend?
5. Who played Dolly Clothes-Peg to Jon Pertwee's Worzel Gummidge?
6. What were the Woodentop twins called?
7. Which *Dr Who* played the Judge in the 1946 adaptation of *Toad Of Toad Hall*?
8. Who was Toad in the 80s animation *The Wind in the Willows*?
9. *Larry The Lamb* first appeared on TV in which year?
10. Which song was the closing theme to *Stingray*?
11. Which animated characters have a family TV guide in Radio Times?
12. Which coin had magical powers in *The Queen's Nose*?
13. What was the subject of *Wham Bam Strawberry Jam!*?
14. Which former Gladiator presented *Finders Keepers*?
15. Who hosted *All Your Own*, a series of children's interests demonstrated by children?
16. Charlie Drake and Jack Edwards appeared as which children's TV duo in the 1950s?
17. Who was the voice of the computer SID in *Galloping Galaxies*?
18. Which Doctor Who was a presenter of *Vision On*?
19. Which Maid Marion presented the children's TV's *Picture Book*?
20. The name of which producer appeared at the end of the early *Tom and Jerry* cartoons?
21. Who designed *Blue Peter's* Italian sunken garden?
22. Who replaced Ringo Starr narrating *Thomas the Tank Engine and Friends*?
23. Whose magic ray had transformed Granny Smith into Supergran?
24. In *Supercar*, what was Jimmy's talking monkey called?
25. What was the name of the special Christmas reunion episode of *The Appleyards* in1960?
26. What was the name of Billy Bunter's frustrated school master?
27. Which came first – *Andy Pandy* or *The Flowerpot Men*?
28. Who provided the voices for *Bill and Ben*?
29. *Rag, Tag and Bobtail* were glove puppets operated by which duo?
30. Whose Busy World has featured on BBC?

ANSWERS

### Pot Luck 2 (see Quiz 9)

**1.** *Stressed Eric.* **2.** Ainsley Harriott. **3.** Dermot Murnaghan. **4.** Bourret. **5.** Eileen Downey. **6.** Giedroyc & Perkins. **7.** £175. **8.** *Four-mations.* **9.** *Desire.* **10.** 1950s. **11.** Oliver Sacks. **12.** BBC2. **13.** Eamonn Holmes. **14.** Jess Yates. **15.** *Gardener's World.* **16.** Rebecca Stephens. **17.** John Stapleton & Lynne Faulds Wood. **18.** Barbara Edwards. **19.** Steve Berry. **20.** Armand & Michaela Denis. **21.** *Whoops Apocalypse.* **22.** Miriam Stoppard & Rob Buckman. **23.** *Topol.* **24.** Weatherman. **25.***Changing Rooms.* **26.** *Match Of The Day.* **27.** Eric Morley. **28.** Joan **29.** Lulu. **30.** *The Golden Oldie Picture Show.*

## QUIZ 11 Comedy 2

LEVEL 3

**Answers: see Quiz 12, page 540**

**1.** Which comedy double act appeared with Jasper Carrott?
**2.** What business did Nellie Pledge run?
**3.** Who wrote *An Evening With Gary Lineker*?
**4.** Which important character does Barry Bostwick play in *Spin City*?
**5.** For which role is Ardal O'Hanlon best known?
**6.** What was the first comedy shown on Channel 4?
**7.** Who links Rhoda with *The Simpsons*?
**8.** What was the name of Robert Guillame's butler?
**9.** Who kidnapped Burt Campbell in *Soap*?
**10.** Name Jimmy Nail's character in *Auf Weidersehn Pet*?
**11.** Who married Alice Tinker in the *Vicar Of Dibley*?
**12.** Who appeared in *Men Behaving Badly* but was not recognised by Gary and Tony?
**13.** Who starred in *Stand Up for Nigel Barton*?
**14.** In 1979, the last episode of which sitcom netted 24 million viewers, the highest of that year?
**15.** What was the BBC equivalent of *You've Been Framed,* hosted by Shane Richie?
**16.** Who had a pet hamster called SPG?
**17.** How is the sometime comic actor Michael Smith better known?
**18.** Which magician married comedienne Victoria Wood?
**19.** In which comic series did Joe Lynch play a tailor?
**20.** Which David starred in *A Sharp Intake Of Breath*?
**21.** Which Goodie turned Twitcher?
**22.** Who starred in the title role in *I Dream Of Jeannie*?
**23.** Which former PM's secretary was a consultant on the first two series of *Yes Minister*?
**24.** In which series did Harry Worth play himself as a brass band conductor?
**25.** Who was played by Jamie Farr in *M*A*S*H*?
**26.** In which comedy did Ted Bovis appear as an entertainer?
**27.** Whose son was called Spud-U-Like?
**28.** Which part did Liza Tarbuck play in *Watching*?
**29.** What career did Jo Brand follow before being a successful comedy performer?
**30.** What is Ben's trade in *Two Point Four Children*?

ANSWERS

### Drama 2 (see Quiz 12)

**1.** Joanne Whalley. **2.** Mel Smith. **3.** James Fox. **4.** John Mortimer. **5.** Eric Porter. **6.** *Washington – Behind Closed Doors*. **7.** John Thaw. **8.** WWII. **9.** *St Elsewhere*. **10.** Laura and Kate. **11.** David Hemmings. **12.** David Soul. **13.** Thamesford. **14.** Alan Bates. **15.** The Sherpa Tensing Ward. **16.** Jane Seymour. **17.** *Give Us A Break*. **18.** Julia Sawalha. **19.** The British Army. **20.** Martin Shaw. **21.** Jeremy Sandford. **22.** Russia. **23.** John Gielgud and Laurence Olivier. **24.** Their deceased husbands. **25.** *Big Deal*. **26.** Bounty Hunter. **27.** White Ghost. **28.** Gestapo. **29.** Richard Belzer. **30.** Maurice.

# QUIZ 12 Drama 2

LEVEL 3

**Answers: see Quiz 11, page 539**

1. Who appeared in her first major role in *A Kind Of Loving*?
2. Which comedian played the straight part of Tom Craig in BBC1's *Muck And Brass*?
3. Who played Nancy Astor's husband, Waldorf, in the drama *Nancy Astor*?
4. *A Voyage Round My Father* was the story of which writer?
5. Who played Chamberlain in *Winston Churchill, The Wilderness Years*?
6. Which 70s drama was based on the novel *The Company* by John Ehrlichman?
7. Who played Bomber Harris in the controversial drama?
8. *We'll Meet Again* was set during which war?
9. Which 80s medical drama was produced by the same company as *Hill Street Blues*?
10. In *Spender*, what were Spender's daughters called?
11. Who played secret agent *Charlie Muffin*?
12. Who played Rick Blaine in the 1980s TV remake of *Casablanca*?
13. Which Constabulary did Barlow and Watt work for in *Softly Softly Task Force*?
14. In the 1980s which actor played the traitor Guy Burgess?
15. In *The Singing Detective*, Philip E Marlow was confined to which hospital ward?
16. Which Bond girl played Mrs Simpson in *The Woman He Loved*?
17. Which 1983 drama showed actors Paul McGann and Robert Lindsay taking on the best in the snooker halls of London?
18. Which sitcom star took on a classic role as Mercy Pecksniff in *Martin Chuzzlewit*?
19. *The Irish RM*, played by Peter Bowles, had previously retired from which army?
20. Which US actor portrayed JFK in the TV drama *Kennedy*?
21. Who scripted the controversial *Cathy Come Home* in the mid 60s?
22. Where had *Reilly-Ace Of Spies* been born?
23. In *Brideshead Revisited* Jeremy Irons and Anthony Andrews played the central characters but who played their fathers?
24. In *Widows* the four women stage a robbery based on the previous plans of whom?
25. Ray Brooks played the habitual gambler Robby Box in which BBC drama?
26. What did *The Fall Guy* do to earn money in addition to being a stunt man?
27. In which episode of *Cracker* did Fitz travel to Hong Kong?
28. Which organisation did Helene Moskiewicz infiltrate, as shown in *A Woman At War*?
29. Who plays John Munch in *Homicide: Life On The Streets*?
30. Who does Barry Corbin play in *Northern Exposure*?

ANSWERS

## Comedy 2 (see Quiz 11)

**1.** Punt & Dennis. **2.** A pickle factory. **3.** Arthur Smith. **4.** The mayor. **5.** Father Dougal McGuire. **6.** *The Comic Strip Presents: Five Go To Dorset.* **7.** Julie Kavner (played Brenda opposite Rhoda & was the voice of Marge Simpson). **8.** *Benson.* **9.** Aliens. **10.** Oz. **11.** Hugo. **12.** Kylie Minogue. **13.** Keith Barron. **14.** *To The Manor Born.* **15.** *Caught In The Act.* **16.** Rick (*The Young Ones*). **17.** Michael Crawford. **18.** The Great Surprendo. **19.** *Never Mind The Quality, Feel The Width.* **20.** David Jason. **21.** Bill Oddie. **22.** Barbara Eden. **23.** Lady Falkender. **24.** *Oh Happy Band.* **25.** Cpl. Klinger. **26.** *Hi-De-Hi!* **27.** Wayne and Waynetta Slob's. **28.** Brenda. **29.** Psychiatric Nurse. **30.** A plumber.

# QUIZ 13 Pot Luck 3

LEVEL 3

**Answers: see Quiz 14, page 542**

1. What were the christian names of The Smother Brothers?
2. What was the name of the BBC's 60s forerunner of *Whose Line Is It Anyway?*
3. What was the hit record in 1956 recorded by Eamonn Andrews?
4. Which JB was allegedly called 'The Thinking Man's Crumpet'?
5. Who co-presented *Notes and Queries* With Clive Anderson?
6. Who should have been *This Is Your Life's* first victim, but he found out?
7. Which award did *That's Life* bestow on shoddy goods?
8. Which afternoon series was presented by Mrs. Leigh Lawson?
9. On which television programme did Victoria Wood make her debut?
10. What dance series was presented by Wayne Sleep?
11. Which song did Marti Webb record to help a child shown on *That's Life* with liver disease?
12. Which two companies merged to create Thames TV?
13. Charles, the score reader in *Telly Addicts,* is a regular in which radio programme?
14. Which former Butlin's redcoat was born Michael Parker?
15. Which programme was presented by Peter McCann and Kate Bellingham?
16. Who kept the scores on *Bullseye?*
17. Who played Laura la Plaz, a trick shot artiste, in *Dad's Army?*
18. Who did Renee Bradshaw marry in *Coronation Street?*
19. Which Australian was 'Late' and is now *On TV?*
20. Which variety show was hosted by Kenneth Williams?
21. In which year did *Eastenders* begin on British Television?
22. Which satirist and broadcaster was co-founder of *TV-AM?*
23. Which former Ambassador to Washington presented *A Week In Politics?*
24. What did Teletext Ltd replace in 1993?
25. What was the name of the clothes shop that Emily Nugent ran in *Coronation Street?*
26. Where was Ricardo Montalban the host?
27. Which crime solving show presenter hosted the quiz show *Dotto* in the 50s?
28. In 1979, who performed St. Mark's Gospel on TV?
29. Which former presenter of *World In Action* was made a lord in 1998?
30. Which actor links *M*A*S*H* to House Calls?

ANSWERS

**Soaps 2 (see Quiz 14)**

**1.** Rebecca Fisher. **2.** Nurse. **3.** *Heartbreak High.* **4.** Lili Mae. **5.** Denise Welch. **6.** Procter and Gamble. **7.** *Crossroads.* **8.** *Emergency Ward 10.* **9.** Carmen Silvera (Edith). **10.** Joel. **11.** Brett Starke. **12.** Duncan Acres. **13.** Angleton. **14.** Rod Corkhill. **15.** Rio. **16.** Pat Wicks. **17.** Cathy Beale. **18.** Rodney Harrington (Ryan O'Neal). **19.** Hardware shop. **20.** Terry Raymond. **21.** Polly Becker. **22.** Greg Kelly. **23.** Sweeney. **24.** *Sweet Valley High.* **25.** A roadie. **26.** Ken Barlow. **27.** *The Parade.* **28.** Eric Pollard. **29.** *The Practice.* **30.** Deals On Wheels.

## QUIZ 14 Soaps 2

LEVEL 3

**Answers: see Quiz 13, page 541**

1. Which member of the Fisher family did Travis marry in *Home and Away*?
2. What is Maggie Bolton's profession in *Heartbeat*?
3. Alex Dimitriades played Nick in which soap?
4. In *Knot's Landing* which character had the surname Clements?
5. Which *Coronation Street* actress played Marsha Stubbs in *Soldier, Soldier*?
6. Which soap manufacturer set up their own studio in the US to produce their own soaps?
7. Which was the first UK soap to be seen five days a week?
8. Which soap had the original title *Calling Nurse Roberts*?
9. Which comedy actress played Camilla Hope in the 60s soap *Compact*?
10. Which brother of Travis moved back to *Summer Bay*?
11. Who in *Neighbours* had a sister named Danni?
12. What is the real name of the ranch called South Fork in *Dallas*?
13. Where was *The Newcomers* set?
14. Who in *Brookside* was beaten up on his wedding day?
15. In *Dynasty* what was Alexis's dog called?
16. Who married Roy Evans in *Eastenders*?
17. Who in *Eastenders* was reunited with her daughter Donna after many years apart?
18. Which role did the one time father in law of John McEnroe play in *Peyton Place*?
19. Which short lived soap was set in in the inner suburb of Castlehulme?
20. Who is Simon and Tiffany's father in *Eastenders*?
21. Which Polly was a Walford Gazette reporter?
22. Who has had affairs with both Maxine and Sally in the Street?
23. What is Sinbad's surname in *Brookside*?
24. Name the teen soap which feature twin sisters.
25. What was Rod's profession in *Eastenders*?
26. Which character was once editor of the Weatherfield Gazette?
27. What was the area of *Brookside* destroyed in an explosion?
28. Who was forced to sell his wine bar to Cathy Glover in *Emmerdale*?
29. When *Coronation Street* went on air four times per week, on which extra day was it broadcast?
30. What was the name of the used car lot in *Eastenders*?

ANSWERS

### Pot Luck 3 (see Quiz 13)

**1.** Dick and Tom. **2.** *Impromptu.* **3.** *Shifting Whispering Sands.* **4.** Joan Bakewell. **5.** Carol Vorderman. **6.** Stanley Matthews. **7.** Heap of the Week. **8.** *Twiggy's People.* **9.** *That's Life.* **10.** *The Hot Shoe Shuffle.* **11.** *Ben.* **12.** ABC and Associated Rediffusion. **13.** *The Archers.* **14.** Michael Barrymore. **15.** *Tomorrow's World.* **16.** Tony Green. **17.** Barbara Windsor. **18.** Alf Roberts. **19.** Clive James. **20.** *International Cabaret* **21.** 1985. **22.** David Frost. **23.** Peter Jay. **24.** Oracle. **25.** Gamma Garments. **26.** *Fantasy Island.* **27.** Shaw Taylor. **28.** Alec McCowen. **29.** Gus McDonald. **30.** Wayne Rogers.

## QUIZ 15 News 1

LEVEL 3

**Answers: see Quiz 16, page 544**

1. The launch of which evening programme in 1980 was the first time the BBC had combined news and current affairs at a regular time?
2. Which fellow GMTV reporter is Fiona Phillips married to?
3. Who in 1982 took over the reins of *Omnibus* for a short time?
4. Michael Woods went in search of which wars?
5. Who was the first face of Channel 5 News?
6. Which presenter has the middle name Paradine?
7. Who replaced Brian Walden on LWT's *Weekend World*?
8. In which year did Gordon Honeycombe retire from news-reading?
9. Which John grilled his guests on *Face To face*?
10. What nationality was explorer Hans Hass?
11. How did Wogan embarrass himself during the very first episode of his chat show?
12. Which Royal was the very first to be interviewed on TV?
13. Which late night current affairs series replacing *Tonight*?
14. Who hosted the Daybreak section in the first days of TV am?
15. Which award winning current affairs series began with the slogan 'A window on the world behind the headlines'?
16. Who was the first presenter of *Cinema*?
17. What is the most expensive war documentary ever made?
18. Who continued to read the news while Nicholas Witchell sat on a demonstrator?
19. Who presented *One To One*?
20. How many years had *The Sky At Night* been televised in 1998?
21. Cliff Richard, Cilla Black and Lulu accompanied which ITV broadcast in July 1969?
22. Which two of the first *News At Ten* presenters had first names beginning with A?
23. Who took over presentation of *Panorama* in 1967?
24. A documentary about which prison was hosted by Jimmy Saville?
25. Who was the first sports presenter on *Newsnight*?
26. What nationality was political commentator Robert McKenzie?
27. For which event were satellite pictures used for news broadcasts in Britain?
28. Who finished shows with the words "Goodnight and sleep well"?
29. Which documentary series examined the life of astronaut Buzz Aldrin?
30. Which BBC newsreader was the first actually to be seen?

ANSWERS

### Comedy 3 (see Quiz 16)

**1.** *The Wonder Years.* **2.** *Doogie Hauser MD.* **3.** A lager mitt. **4.** *Wayne's World.* **5.** Rory and H.G **6.** Brian Wilde. **7.** Richard Vranche. **8.** Lowlands. **9.** Edina. **10.** Robin Bailey. **11.** *A Funny Thing Happened On The Way To The Forum.* **12.** Joe Baker. **13.** Joan Sanderson. **14.** *Marriage Lines.* **15.** Christopher Ryan. **16.** *A Fine Romance.* **17.** Leah Thompson. **18.** Phil Silvers'. **19.** The Clampetts (*The Beverley Hillbillies*). **20.** Woody Harrelson. **21.** Eric Chappell. **22.** Barry Took. **23.** *Sorry.* **24.** Maureen Lipman's mother. **25.** *Please Sir.* **26.** Mrs Polouvicka. **27.** *OTT.* **28.** Roz Doyle. **29.** Peter Cook and Dudley Moore. **30.** Benny Hill.

## QUIZ 16 Comedy 3

LEVEL 3

**Answers: see Quiz 15, page 543**

1. Which programme featured Fred Savage as a boy growing up?
2. Name the teenage doctor?
3. What unusual present did Tony bring back from holiday for Gary in *Men Behaving Badly*?
4. Dana Garvey co-starred in whose World?
5. Which Australian duo hosted the show *The Big House*?
6. Who played Bloody Delilah in *The Dustbinmen*?
7. Who was the pianist in the first series of *Whose Line Is It Anyway?*
8. In which university was *A Very Peculiar Practice* set?
9. In *Absolutely Fabulous* who has a son called Serge?
10. Who played Uncle Mort in *I Didn't Know You Cared*?
11. Which stage show was *Up Pompeii!* based on?
12. Name Jack Douglas' comedy partner.
13. Who played Eleanor in *After Henry*?
14. Which 60s series starred Richard Briers and Prunella Scales?
15. Who played Mike in *The Young Ones*?
16. In which series do Judi Dench and Geoffrey Palmer play a married couple?
17. Who stars as *Caroline In The City*?
18. In whose show would you have met Private Paparrelli?
19. Which family were neighbours to the stuffy Drysdales?
20. Who starred as the dim-witted bartender in *Cheers*?
21. Who created *Rising Damp*?
22. Which comedy writer was a presenter of *Points of View* for many years?
23. Barbara Lott starred as an overbearing mother in which BBC comedy?
24. Which character did Maria Charles play in *Agony*?
25. Peter Denyer appeared as Dennis in which 60s/70s comedy?
26. Who became Audrey's mother in law in *To the Manor Born*?
27. What was the late night adult version of *Tiswas* called?
28. Peri Gilpin plays which radio producer?
29. Which duo starred in the series *Not Only ... But Also*?
30. Name the comedian who played Bottom in the 1964 TV adaptation of *A Midsummer Night's Dream*?

ANSWERS

### News 1 (see Quiz 15)

**1.** *Newsnight.* **2.** Martin Frizzell. **3.** Barry Norman. **4.** The Trojan Wars. **5.** Kirsty Young. **6.** David Frost. **7.** Matthew Parris. **8.** 1976. **9.** John Freeman. **10.** German. **11.** He fell over. **12.** Prince Philip. **13.** *24 Hours.* **14.** Robert Kee. **15.** *This Week.* **16.** Bamber Gascoigne. **17.** *World At War.* **18.** Sue Lawley. **19.** Michael Parkinson. **20.** 41 years. **21.** Televising of the first moon landing. **22.** Alistair Burnet & Andrew Gardner. **23.** Sir Robin Day. **24.** Broadmoor. **25.** David Davies. **26.** Canadian. **27.** John F Kennedy's funeral. **28.** Sir Robin Day. **29.** *Return To Earth* **30.** Kenneth Kendall.

## QUIZ 17 Music & Variety 2

LEVEL 3

**Answers: see Quiz 18, page 546**

1. Who composed the theme music for the documentary series *The Cosmos*?
2. On which Saturday night show were the Television Toppers a regular feature?
3. Which holiday company used *Step Into A Dream* to help promote its business?
4. Was *Hold Me Now* Johnny Logan's first or second Eurovision winning song?
5. What was highly unusual about the group The Archies who reached No 1 with *Sugar Sugar*?
6. As a boy *Duran Duran's* Simon le Bon made his TV debut in an ad for what product?
7. Who sang about a funky gibbon?
8. Which TV presenter was part of the girl band Faith, Hope and Charity?
9. Which pop star appeared in *How to be Cool*?
10. Which TV dance group released the song *Lover Please*?
11. *The Monkees* TV show was produced by which US television company?
12. Who won *The Eurovision Song Contest* when it was held in Brighton?
13. What was *Six-Five Special* presenter Don Lang's real name?
14. How was chart topper Ivor Biggun known to watchers of *That's Life*?
15. Who presented *No Limits* on BBC2?
16. Which song did Gloria Hunniford release with little success in the charts?
17. Which Hollywood dancer starred in the BBC's *Carissima* in the late 50's?
18. Which pop show has been hosted by Stevi Merike, David Jensen and Mike Reid?
19. Which *Clash* song was used to advertise jeans?
20. Who hosted the children's pop show *Razzamatazz*?
21. Who hosted a TV *Sketch Pad*?
22. Soap star Sophie Lawrence released *Love's Unkind* in 1991. Who had originally sung it in the 1970's?
23. Who sang *Something Tells Me* as a theme song to a Saturday night show?
24. Anne Nightingale presented which BBC2 pop show?
25. On whose show did Tom Jones make a comeback in the 1980s?
26. What was the *Van Der Valk* theme music called?
27. Which Sex Pistols song was banned by the BBC because of its anti-Royal theme?
28. Which comic released the song *Didn't You Kill my Brother?*
29. TV scientist Magnus Pike featured in which Thomas Dolby song?
30. About what did Patrick MacNee and Honor Blackman sing together?

ANSWERS

### Pot Luck 4 (see Quiz 18)

**1.** *Six-Five Special.* **2.** 1988. **3.** *All You Need Is Love.* **4.** Brian Connell. **5.** Steve Race. **6.** *Bygones.* **7.** *Freud on Food.* **8.** David Nixon. **9.** Peter Baldwin. **10.** Mike Smith. **11.** Noele Gordon. **12.** *Queenie's Castle.* **13.** Sammy Joe's. **14.** *The Rag Trade.* **15.** Jaclyn Smith. **16.** Derek Guyler. **17.** *Family Fortunes.* **18.** Reggie Perrin. **19.** Isla Blair. **20.** JVC. **21.** Baker-Donaher. **22.** *The Price Is Right.* **23.** Gordon Burns. **24.** Lt. Commander LaForge. **25.** Bartender. **26.** Paul and Barry Elliot. **27.** No (he was in *Brass*, though). **28.** Eddie. **29.** Paula Wilcox. **30.** *Man In A Suitcase.*

## QUIZ 18 Pot Luck 4

LEVEL 3

**Answers: see Quiz 17, page 545**

1. Which pop show was *Dig This* a successor to?
2. In what year was *Neighbours* first shown twice a day?
3. What was Tony Palmer's series on pop music called?
4. Which bearded interviewer had his own series of programmes in the 1970s?
5. Who was the chairman of *My Music*?
6. What was the Anglian series on Victoriana?
7. What was Clement's cookery series called?
8. Which entertainer had a 'Magic Box'?
9. Which *Coronation Street* star starred in the sitcom *Girls About Town*?
10. Who presented *Toolbox*?
11. Which soap actress presented *Songs That Matter*?
12. In which series did Roy from *Eastenders* appear with Diana Dors?
13. Which character's father did Rock Hudson play in *Dynasty*?
14. In which comedy series revival did Gillian Taylforth appear before *Eastenders*?
15. Who played Kelly in *Charlie's Angels*?
16. Whose role was Corkie in *Sykes*?
17. Max Bygraves, Bob Monkhouse and Les Dennis all hosted which game show?
18. Which character's middle name was Iolanthe?
19. Who played the widow next door in *The Bounder*?
20. Which company in Japan established the VHS video format?
21. Which family appeared in the fly-on-the-wall *Sylvania Waters*?
22. On which game show did Bruce Forsyth succeed Leslie Crowther?
23. Who hosted Searchline on *Surprise Surprise* for five years?
24. Which SF character has the first name Geordi?
25. What is Moe's occupation in *The Simpsons*?
26. What are the real names of the stars of *Chucklevision*?
27. Was Timothy West in *Bread*?
28. What was the name of Chandler's annoying roommate in *Friends*?
29. Who had to look on *The Bright Side*?
30. Which series featured the Ex-agent McGill?

ANSWERS

### Music & Variety 2 (see Quiz 17)

**1.** Vangelis. **2.** *The Black and White Minstrel Show.* **3.** Butlins. **4.** Second. **5.** They were a cartoon band and didn't exist in real life. **6.** Pepsi. **7.** *The Goodies.* **8.** Dani Behr. **9.** Roger Daltry. **10.** The Vernons Girls. **11.** NBC. **12.** Abba. **13.** Gordon Langhorn. **14.** Doc Cox. **15.** Jonathan King. **16.** A cover version of *True Love.* **17.** Ginger Rogers. **18.** *Pop Quest.* **19.** *Should I Stay Or Should I Go.* **20.** Alistair Pirie. **21.** Bobby Davro. **22.** Donna Summer. **23.** Cilla Black. **24.** *The Old Grey Whistle Test.* **25.** Jonathan Ross'. **26.** *Eye Level.* **27.** *God Save The Queen.* **28.** Alexei Sayle. **29.** *She Blinded Me With Science.* **30.** *Kinky Boots.*

## QUIZ 19 Children's TV 2

LEVEL 3

**Answers: see Quiz 20, page 548**

**1.** Who wrote the scripts for *Rag, Tag and Bobtail*?
**2.** Who was the original compere of *Crackerjack*?
**3.** Which children's programme did Emma Thompson's mother present?
**4.** The 1950s comedy *Mick and Montmorency* was originally called what?
**5.** Which soccer side does Children's TV's Zoe Ball support?
**6.** What was the name of the junior version of *The Sky At Night* first screened in 1970?
**7.** Which former *Blue Peter* presenters hosted the programme *Next* in 1994?
**8.** Which non profit making organisation funded the early programmes of *Sesame Street*?
**9.** Eileen Brown, Josephina Ray and Peter Hawkins provided the voices for which children's puppet family?
**10.** Who created Morph?
**11.** Who retired as series editor of *Blue Peter* in 1988?
**12.** Who narrated *Roobarb and Custard*?
**13.** Which book was read on *Jackanory* to celebrate the programme's 3000th edition?
**14.** Which US president's son has co-presented *Record Breakers*?
**15.** Who was the female vocalist on *Rainbow*?
**16.** What was Sooty's friend the snake called?
**17.** Who sang the theme tune of *The Adventures Of Champion*?
**18.** Which ventriloquist operated *Lenny The Lion*?
**19.** What was *Noggin the Nog*'s son called?
**20.** When was *Play Away* screened?
**21.** Which programme has been sponsored by a company which makes a glue stick?
**22.** Who wrote the *Pink Panther* theme?
**23.** Who wrote the original *Lone Ranger* stories for radio?
**24.** Jan and Vlasta Dalibor were the operators of which famous puppet duo?
**25.** Which role did future pop star Michelle Gayle play in *Grange Hill*?
**26.** Who was the voice of Basil Brush?
**27.** Which puppet dog appeared with Wally Whyton on *Tuesday Rendezvous*?
**28.** Who replaced Phillip Schofield as CBBC presenter?
**29.** Who presented the rough travel guide on *DEF II*?
**30.** Who replaced Christopher Trace as presenter of *Blue Peter* in 1967?

ANSWERS

### Drama 3 (see Quiz 20)

**1.** *Upstairs, Downstairs.* **2.** A Lotus Elan. **3.** The poet John Milton. **4.** *The Power Game.* **5.** *Electra.* **6.** Alan Bennett. **7.** David Jason. **8.** *Virgin Of The Secret Service.* **9.** *The Ten Commandments.* **10.** Dr Gillespie. **11.** *Hawkeye and the Last Of The Mohicans.* **12.** Lloyd Bridges. **13.** Ray Brooks. **14.** Katrina. **15.** *Upstairs Downstairs.* **16.** 52. **17.** Martha Plimpton. **18.** *The Virginian.* **19.** *Secret Army.* **20.** Gary Cole. **21.** *The Hard Man.* **22.** Scotland. **23.** Goldberg. **24.** *Alias Smith and Jones.* **25.** Herself. **26.** Uganda. **27.** The Vietnam War. **28.** Angel's actress Fiona Fullerton was married to Simon. **29.** *Elizabeth. R* **30.** Taffy.

## QUIZ 20 Drama 3

LEVEL 3

**Answers: see Quiz 19, page 547**

1. Which drama was set at 165 Eaton Place?
2. What car did Emma Peel drive in *The Avengers*?
3. Who was the subject of *Paradise Restored*?
4. Sir John Wilder was a character in which drama?
5. Which 60's ITV play was spoken entirely in Greek?
6. *Selling Hitler* featured which playwright in an acting role?
7. Which comic went straight in *Amongst Barbarians*?
8. The spy character Captain Robert Virgin featured in which 60's series?
9. Which 1971 drama series appropriately had ten episodes?
10. What was the name of *Dr Kildare*'s boss?
11. John Hart and Lon Chanry Jnr starred together in which Western series?
12. Who starred in *Sea Hunt*?
13. *The Big Deal* starred who?
14. Which character was played by Joan Collins in *Monte Carlo*?
15. The US series *Beacon Hill* was based on which successful British drama?
16. *A Family At War* consisted of how many episodes?
17. Who played Helene Moskiewitz in *A Woman At War*?
18. Who was the foreman at the Shiloh Ranch?
19. Kessler was a spin-off of which series?
20. Who stars in *Midnight Caller*?
21. Novelist Edna O'Brien guested in which drama?
22. *The Houseman's Tales* was set in which country?
23. Which part was played by Harold Pinter himself in the 1987 adaptation of his play *The Birthday Party*?
24. The character Hannibal Hayes had an alias in which Western series?
25. Coral Browne played who in Alan Bennett's *An Englishman Abroad*?
26. Where was *Raid On Entebbe* set?
27. *The Quiet Man* was set during which war?
28. What is the link between *Angels* and Simon MacCorkingdale?
29. Which 70's series had episodes entitled *Lion's Club* and *Sweet England's Pride*?
30. Who was the Welsh pirate in *The Buccaneers*?

ANSWERS

**Children's TV 2 (see Quiz 19)**

**1.** Louise Cochrane. **2.** Eamonn Andrews. **3.** *Play School.* **4.** *Jobstoppers.* **5.** Manchester United. **6.** *Seeing Stars.* **7.** Valerie Singleton and John Noakes. **8.** Children's Television Workshop. **9.** *The Woodentops.* **10.** Nick Park. **11.** Biddy Baxter. **12.** Richard Briers. **13.** *The Hobbit.* **14.** Ron Reagan Jr. **15.** Jane Tucker. **16.** Ramsbottom. **17.** Frankie Laine. **18.** Terry Hall. **19.** Prince Knut. **20.** Saturday afternoons. **21.** *Art Attack.* **22.** Henry Mancini. **23.** Fran Striker. **24.** *Pinky and Perky.* **25.** Fiona Wilson. **26.** Ivan Owen. **27.** Fred Barker. **28.** Andy Crane. **29.** Magenta de Vine. **30.** Peter Purves.

## QUIZ 21 Soaps 3

LEVEL 3

**Answers: see Quiz 22, page 550**

1. Who owned the Dagmar pub in *Eastenders*?
2. Who was the mysterious head of the sect which Zoe joined in *Coronation Street*?
3. What was BBC Wales' soap, seen on BBC2 as *People of the Valley*?
4. How were Carol and April related in *Eastenders*?
5. Which three surnames did Jane Rossington have in *Crossroads*?
6. What was the job of *Home and Away's* Grant Mitchell?
7. Who had a pizza round in *Eastenders*?
8. In *Coronation Street* how did Ken's first wife die?
9. What character did Rebecca Ritters play in *Neighbours*?
10. Anne Charleston portrayed which *Neighbour*?
11. What was the first name of Jack Duckworth's mother in law?
12. Who wrote the lyrics of the theme for *Neighbours*?
13. Which soap star's mother starred in South Pacific at Drury Lane in the 1950s?
14. Who was the first husband in real life of the actress who played Allison Mackenzie in a US soap?
15. Which beer is the Woolpack famous for serving?
16. Which actor played Len Fairclough's partner in a *Coronation Street* building business?
17. How did Cheryl Starke die in *Neighbours*?
18. What was the name of Jim Robinson's youngest daughter?
19. What do Benny in *Crossroads* and Compo in *Last Of The Summer* Wine have in common?
20. Where did *Howard's Way* take place?
21. Which soap did Ronald Allan appear in before *Crossroads*?
22. Who were the original owners of the café in *Eastenders*?
23. What was the first US daytime series to be shown in the UK?
24. What nationality was Elsie Tanner's son-in-law?
25. Which Aussie soap featured the Palmers and Hamiltons?
26. What was Karl Kennedy's profession in *Neighbours*?
27. Which soap had a cafe called the Hot Biscuit?
28. Which actor links *Bugs* and *Neighbours*?
29. Which female *On The Buses* star joined *Eastenders*?
30. To which south coast city did Bill Webster move to the first time he left *Coronation Street*?

ANSWERS

**Comedy 4 (see Quiz 22)**

**1.** Barry Cryer. **2.** George Layton. **3.** Yootha Joyce. **4.** Billy Connelly. **5.** Alf Ramsey. **6.** Wilf. **7.** A bottling plant. **8.** Audrey Fforbes Hamilton. **9.** Thora Hird. **10.** Ivy. **11.** Miriam Karlin. **12.** Sunshine. **13.** He was his brother. **14.** Emma Thompson. **15.** Coach. **16.** Connie Booth. **17.** David Kelly. **18.** Mechanic. **19.** Sausage Factory. **20.** Healy. **21.** Stackton Tressle. **22.** *The Offer.* **23.** Richard Griffith and Frances de la Tour. **24.** John Alderton. **25.** Roger Thursby. **26.** David Nobbs. **27.** Medford. **28.** Eric Duffy. **29.** *Para Handy.* **30.** Charlie Higson.

## QUIZ 22 Comedy 4

LEVEL 3

**Answers: see Quiz 21, page 549**

1. Who was the Chairman of *Jokers Wild*?
2. Which George wrote the scripts for *Don't Wait Up*?
3. Who played Mildred in *George and Mildred*?
4. Name the husband of Pamela Stephenson.
5. What was Alf Garnett originally to have been called?
6. What was the name of the zoo keeper in *Three Up Two Down*?
7. Where did Laverne and Shirley work?
8. Penelope Keith played which character in *To the Manor Born*?
9. Who was the female star of *Hallelujah*?
10. Name the character who runs the café in *Last of the Summer Wine*.
11. In *The Rag Trade*, whose catchphrase was, 'Everybody out'?
12. Name the cab company in *Taxi*.
13. Richard Pearson played Victor Meldrew's relation in *One Foot in the Grave*. How were they related?
14. Which Oscar winner's first TV comedy series was called *Alfresco*?
15. In *Cheers*, Woody replaced which character behind the bar?
16. Who played Polly Sherman in *Fawlty Towers*?
17. Who played the one-armed help in *Robin's Nest*?
18. What was the Fonz's trade in *Happy Days*?
19. Where was *Both Ends Meet* set?
20. Which Tim was one of *The Boys From The Bush*?
21. Where did Hinge and Bracket live?
22. What was the original *Comedy Playhouse* called that became the series *Steptoe & Son*?
23. Which actor and actress played husband and wife in *A Kind of Living*?
24. Which John played the star of *Father's Day*?
25. Which character was just starting his legal career in *Brothers In Law*?
26. Name the author of *A Bit of a Do*.
27. Who was Terry and June's surname in *Terry and June*?
28. Who played Sharon's boyfriend in *Please Sir*?
29. What was the name of the Scottish series following the comic adventures of a fishing boat crew?
30. Who was the co-writer of *The Fast Show* with Paul Whitehouse?

ANSWERS

### Soaps 3 (see Quiz 21)

**1.** Wilmot-Brown. **2.** Nirab. **3.** *Pobol Y Cym.* **4.** Sisters. **5.** Richardson, Harvey, Chance. **6.** Teacher. **7.** Robbie. **8.** Electrocuted with a hairdryer. **9.** Hannah Martin. **10.** Madge Bishop. **11.** Amy. **12.** Jackie Trent. **13.** Larry Hagman. **14.** Frank Sinatra (Mia Farrow). **15.** Efram Monks. **16.** Jerry Booth. **17.** She was killed in a car accident. **18.** Lucy. **19.** A woolly hat. **20.** Tarrant. **21.** Compact. **22.** Ali and Sue. **23.** Santa Babara. **24.** Polish. **25.** *Sons and Daughters.* **26.** A doctor. **27.** *Dallas.* **28.** Craig McClaughlin. **29.** Anna Karen. **30.** Southampton.

## QUIZ 23 Pot Luck 5

LEVEL 3

**Answers: see Quiz 24, page 552**

1. Which star of *Ben Hur* guested on *Friends*?
2. Which 'Mrs Thatcher' plays Valerie in *Noah's Ark*?
3. In which sitcom is Miss Wilkins a lodger?
4. Which presenter of *Gardeners World* died in 1996?
5. What was the name of Brian Benben's character in *Dream On*?
6. What was the name of Larry Sanders' wife?
7. Who alternated with Lecy Goranson the role of Becky in *Roseanne*?
8. Who was the first person to win the BBC *Sports Personality of the Year* twice?
9. Which actor links Jed Stone to Marty Hopkirk?
10. In 1998 what rank had Jacqui Reed achieved in *Taggart*?
11. Jonathan Maitland is an investigator on which Weekend programme?
12. Who played Miss Fozzard in *Talking Heads II*?
13. Who is the mother of actresses Vanessa and Lynn Redgrave?
14. In which series did Alan Davies travel Europe with a video camera?
15. Who became the caretaker of the community centre in *Coronation Street* in 1983?
16. Who played Mr. Peabody in *The Jewel In The Crown*?
17. On *Spitting Image* who was portrayed as a slug?
18. Which quiz show were Paddy Feeny and Geoffrey Wheeeler question masters on?
19. Euston Films was an offshoot of which TV company?
20. Who hosted *Trick or Treat* with Mike Smith?
21. What type of correspondent for the BBC was Michael Cole before he went to work for Mohammed Al-Fayed?
22. What was the first theme music to *The Sky at Night* called?
23. Which ITV region is the largest in terms of area?
24. Which actor appeared in *Dixon of Dock Green* and *Grange Hill*?
25. Which part did Mrs Gene Roddenberry play in *Star Trek:The Next Generation*?
26. What was Anne Robinson's job on *Breakfast Time*?
27. Which former *Coronation Street* star played Liz in *Bloomin' Marvellous*?
28. What was the name of Brenda's daughter in *Bagdad Cafe*?
29. Which show was originally called *These Friends of Mine* before taking on its star's name?
30. In *All In The Family* what was Archie's daughter's name?

ANSWERS

### Who's Who 1 (see Quiz 24)

**1.** Jennifer Sauders. **2.** Willie Rushton. **3.** Robert Robinson. **4.** George Clooney. **5.** Lord Lichfield. **6.** Train Driver. **7.** Anthony Andrews. **8.** Vanessa Feltz. **9.** Nanette Newman. **10.** Clergyman. **11.** Tatton. **12.** Newcastle. **13.** Miner. **14.** Joanne Whalley. **15.** Jane Seymour. **16.** Left Foot. **17.** Millicent. **18.** Kidney. **19.** Stephen Fry. **20.** Tony Slattery. **21.** Badminton. **22.** David Coleman. **23.** Mr Motivator. **24.** Madame Tussaud's. **25.** St Andrews. **26.** Catherine Zeta Jones. **27.** Twiggy. **28.** Tracey Ullman. **29.** Peter Ustinov. **30.** Arsenal.

## QUIZ 24 Who's Who 1

LEVEL 3

**Answers: see Quiz 23, page 551**

1. Who is Mrs Adrian Edmondson?
2. Who played Plautus in *Up Pompeii!* and co-founded *Private Eye*?
3. Who was interviewing Kenneth Tynam when he famously used the 'F' word for the first time on British TV?
4. Which actor links the 80s sitcom E/R and the 90s medical drama ER?
5. Which Earl has presented *Miss World*?
6. What was the occupation of *Mastermind* champion Christopher Hughes?
7. Which star of *Brideshead Revisitied* shares a birth date with sports commentator Brendan Foster?
8. Which talk show hostess has a daughter called Allegra?
9. Which actress is the mother of presenter Emma Forbes?
10. What was the profession of Sir David Frost's father?
11. Ex-BBC man Martin Bell became MP for which constituency in 1998?
12. Rowan Atkinson is former student of which University?
13. What occupation did *Hi De Hi!'s* Paul Shane have on leaving school?
14. Which future Hollywood star played Angela Reid in *Emmerdale*?
15. How is TV actress Joyce Frankenberg better known?
16. Where does Roseanne have a tattoo of a pink rose?
17. What is Anthea Tuner's middle name?
18. Bruce Forsyth has only one of which organ?
19. Which TV star fled from the play *Cell Mates* because of stage fright?
20. Which *Whose Line Is It Anyway?* star is a black belt at judo?
21. Gary Webster of *Minder* was a county player in which sport?
22. Which sports commentator won the Manchester Mile in 1949?
23. Who produced a fitness video called BLT Workout?
24. Anneka Rice was removed from which famous London venue in 1997?
25. Frank Muir was Rector of which university from 1976 to 1979?
26. Which TV star duetted with David Essex on *True Love Ways* in 1994?
27. Who was the first woman on *This Is Your Life* when it transferred to ITV in 1969?
28. Which British comedienne played Emily Winthrop in *The Simpsons*?
29. Which writer and actor was David Niven's batman in WWII?
30. Which soccer side does Clive Anderson support?

ANSWERS

**Pot Luck 5 (see Quiz 23)**
**1.** Charlton Heston. **2.** Angela Thorne. **3.** *Game On.* **4.** Geoff Hamilton. **5.** Martin Tupper. **6.** Jeannie. **7.** Sarah Chalke. **8.** Henry Cooper. **9.** Kenneth Cope. **10.** Detective sergeant. **11.** *Watchdog.* **12.** Patricia Routledge. **13.** Rachel Kempson. **14.** *One For The Road.* **15.** Percy Sugden. **16.** Peter Jeffrey. **17.** Kenneth Baker. **18.** *Top Of The Form.* **19.** Thames TV. **20.** Julian Clary. **21.** Royal correspondent. **22.** *At The Castle Gate* by Sibelius. **23.** Grampian. **24.** Nicholas Donnelly. **25.** Nurse Christine Chapel. **26.** TV critic. **27.** Sarah Lancashire (Raquel). **28.** Debbie. **29.** *Ellen.* **30.** Gloria.

## QUIZ 25 Quiz & Game Shows 2

LEVEL 3

**Answers: see Quiz 26, page 554**

**1.** Which show hosted by Cheryl baker and Rose King helped people to realise their fantasies?
**2.** Who was the original host of *The Golden Shot*?
**3.** *You Bet!* was based on a game show from which country?
**4.** Who replaced Michael Aspel as presenter of *Child's Play*?
**5.** Who originally shared the chair of *What's My Line* with Eamonn Andrews?
**6.** Who hosted the 70s quiz game *Whodunnit?*
**7.** What were the two colours on the basic *Blockbusters* answer board?
**8.** *The Pyramid Game* was presented by who?
**9.** Who chaired *Ask Me Another*?
**10.** How many times a week is *Supermarket Sweep* shown on ITV?
**11.** What did Michael Miles ask contestants to do in his TV quiz?
**12.** How many contestants start in *Pass The Buck*?
**13.** Who was the train-driving *Mastermind* champ?
**14.** How many homes were featured on each episode of *Through The Keyhole*?
**15.** Which ITV game show consisted of teams of people with the same occupation?
**16.** Which two Michaels have chaired *Give Us A Clue*?
**17.** Who asked the questions unseen in the first series of *Winner Takes All*?
**18.** Which Joe hosted *Face The Music*?
**19.** Cleo Rocos was the assistant on which game show?
**20.** Who was the original host of *Stars In Their Eyes*?
**21.** Which quiz required contestants to pick odds when answering questions?
**22.** Max Bygraves preceded whom as presenter of *Family Fortunes*?
**23.** Who was Richard Wilson in *Cluedo*?
**24.** What question – the title of the game show – did Noel Edmonds ask?
**25.** Who was the most northerly team on the very first *University Challenge*?
**26.** What had to be linked on *Connections*?
**27.** Which quiz show was presented by Loyd Grossman?
**28.** Which game show did Annabel Croft star in after *Treasure Hunt*?
**29.** What was the prize to avoid on *3-2-1*?
**30.** In which show do the contestants compete in four zones?

ANSWERS

### Children's TV 3 (see Quiz 26)

**1.** *Go With Noakes*. **2.** John and Sue Peters. **3.** Sam. **4.** Nigel Planer. **5.** Ken Wilberforce. **6.** Posh Paws. **7.** Mike Read. **8.** Jonathon Morris. **9.** Only 13. **10.** *Yellow Submarine*. **11.** Murgatroyd. **12.** Quincy. **13.** Guy Henry. **14.** Sir Michael Hordern. **15.** John Masefield's. **16.** *The A-Team*'s. **17.** Jefferson Davies. **18.** *Deputy Dawg*. **19.** Sam. **20.** Frances Hodgson-Burnett. **21.** Ron Perlman. **22.** A telephone. **23.** Mearth. **24.** *Thomas The Tank Engine*. **25.** 52, Festive Road. **26.** Leo Carillo. **27.** 12 years. **28.** One. **29.** *Marine Boy*. **30.** Archie Andrews.

## QUIZ 26 Children's TV 3

LEVEL 3

**Answers: see Quiz 25, page 553**

1. What was the name of the late 70's *Blue Peter* series featuring John Noakes?
2. Who discovered Worzel Gummidge at Scatterbrook Farm?
3. Who helped Daddy Woodentop in his garden?
4. Who narrated *The Magic Roundabout* when it was revived by Channel 4 in the 90s?
5. In the children's comedy *Metal Mickey* which character built Mickey the robot?
6. On *Swap Shop* what was the pet dinosaur called?
7. Who was 'General Manager' of the *Saturday Superstore*?
8. Which ex *Bread* star presented *The Movie Game for children*?
9. How many episodes of *Postman Pat* were originally made?
10. The company that produced *The Snowman* also created a *Beatles* cartoon. Which one?
11. What was the *Magpie* mascot called on the show of the same name?
12. What was Mr Magoo's first name?
13. Which young actor starred as *Young Sherlock* in the 1982 Granada series?
14. Who provided the voice of Badger in the 1983 animated version of *The Wind In The Willows*?
15. The fantasy adventure serial, *The Box Of Delights*, was based on whose original stories?
16. Whose regular adversary was Lieutenant Decker?
17. What were Boss Hogg's christian names in *Dukes Of Hazzard*?
18. Which Deputy kept law and order in Mississippi?
19. What was the name of the eagle in the *Muppet Show*?
20. Who wrote *The Little Princess* which was serialised on TV?
21. Who played the beast in the 1988 TV adaptation of *Beauty And The Beast*?
22. What do *the Munsters* keep in the coffin near their front door?
23. Who was Mork's son?
24. Whose friends are Annie and Clarabel?
25. Where did Mr Benn live?
26. Who played the side-kick Pancho on TV?
27. For how many years was *Magpie* broadcast on TV?
28. How many series of *The Flowerpot Men* were made?
29. In which series did the dolphin, Splasher, appear?
30. What was the name of the first dummy to have its own TV show?

ANSWERS

### Quiz & Game Shows 2 (see Quiz 25)

**1.** *My Secret Desire.* **2.** Jackie Rae. **3.** Holland. **4.** Ronnie Corbett. **5.** Gilbert Harding. **6.** Edward Woodward. **7.** Blue and white. **8.** Steve Jones. **9.** Franklyn Engleman. **10.** Three. **11.** *Take Your Pick.* **12.** Twelve. **13.** Christopher Hughes. **14.** Two. **15.** *Busman's Holiday.* **16.** Michael Aspel and Michael Parkinson. **17.** Geoffrey Wheeler. **18.** Joe Cooper. **19.** *Brainstorm.* **20.** Leslie Crowther. **21.** *Winner Takes All.* **22.** Les Dennis. **23.** Rev Green. **24.** *Whatever Next?* **25.** Leeds (v Reading). **26.** Letters. **27.** *Relative Knowledge.* **28.** *Interceptor.* **29.** Dusty Bin. **30.** *The Crystal Maze.*

## QUIZ 27 Pot Luck 6

LEVEL 3

**Answers: see Quiz 28, page 556**

1. In which 60's comedy series were the characters Buddy Sorrell and Sally Rogers?
2. Who succeeded Mr. Grainger as senior salesman, Gentlemen's Department, Grace Brothers?
3. In *GBH* which character played by Michael Palin was headmaster of a school?
4. Who played Marjory in *Talking Heads II*?
5. Which children's series featured Mr. Zed and starred Garry Miller?
6. Who succeeded Anneka Rice on *Treasure Hunt*?
7. What was the last round on *The Krypton Factor*?
8. What kind of dealers were on *Play Your Cards Right*?
9. In which children's series did Ant McPartin appear?
10. What surname do the Chuckle Brothers share in real life?
11. What rank is Worf in *Deep Space Nine*?
12. In which sitcom do Sally and Tommy Solomon appear?
13. Who were the resident band on *Six Five Special* in the late 50s?
14. Who was Ray's brother in *Grange Hill*?
15. Who was the housekeeper in *Father Ted*?
16. *Men Behaving Badly* star Leslie Ash was born on the same day as which royal?
17. Radio and TV actress Lucy Davis is the daughter of which comedian?
18. What university studies do David Baddiel and Vanessa Feltz have in common?
19. What colour are Jane Seymour's eyes?
20. Who was described as 'A bowling alley reject' in the 1989 Blackwell's Worst Dressed Women List?
21. How is TV funny man Robert Nankeville better known?
22. Paul Shane was junior champion in which sport?
23. Which soccer side does Danny Baker support?
24. Where did Hughie Green serve in WWII?
25. Which actor released a solo album *Heart and Soul* in 1990?
26. Which knight has appeared on *Baywatch*?
27. Which astronomer appeared on the BBC coverage of the first moon landing?
28. Which profession did Janet Street-Porter train for before embarking on a TV career?
29. What was the western Hero Cheyenne's surname?
30. In *Z Cars* who was Fancy Smith's partner?

ANSWERS

### Comedy 5 (see Quiz 28)

**1.** Harry Enfield. **2.** Foggy. **3.** Gillies Hospital. **4.** Hannibal Lecter. **5.** Mr Lewis. **6.** Jean Claude Van Damm. **7.** Lili Tomlin. **8.** They were all spin-offs of the *Mary Tyler Moore Show.* **9.** Choked on a chicken bone. **10.** A hardware store. **11.** Dick Clement and Ian La Frenais. **12.** Mike Flaherty. **13.** "Just the one!" **14.** Dyan Cannon. **15.** Pauline. **16.** Sharon's. **17.** Cornie Wagstaffe. **18.** *Preston Front.* **19.** William Moore. **20.** Patricia Brake. **21.** Max Wall. **22.** Stephanie Cole. **23.** The Rutles. **24.** A pirate. **25.** David Kelly. **26.** David O'Mahoney. **27.** Jimmy Tarbuck's (Liza). **28.** Vivian. **29.** Germaine Greer. **30.** Frank Skinner.

## QUIZ 28 Comedy 5

LEVEL 3

**Answers: see Quiz 27, page 555**

1. Which comedian created Frank Doberman?
2. Which character does Brian Wilde play in *Last Of The Summer Wine*?
3. Which hospital featured in *Surgical Spirit*?
4. Gerald Kaufman was portrayed as which film character on *Spitting Image*?
5. What was the name of Frank Spencer's neighbour played by Glynn Edwards in *Some Mother Do 'Ave 'Em*?
6. Which martial arts expert made a guest appearance on *Friends*?
7. The telephone girl on *Laugh In* was played by which actress?
8. What do Rhoda, Phylis and Lou Grant all have in common?
9. How had the ghost Yetta died, in *So Haunt Me*?
10. What business did the Cunninghams run in *Happy Days*?
11. Name the two writers of *Porridge*?
12. What is the name of Michael J Fox's character in *Spin City*?
13. In *On the Up* what was Mrs Wembley's usual response when offered a drink?
14. Who played Whipper Cone in *Ally McBeal*?
15. What was the name of Rachel Davies' character in *Making Out*?
16. Whose husband was played by Alun Lewis in *Birds Of A Feather*?
17. Clare Kelly played which part in ITV's *The Cuckoo Waltz*?
18. What was the name of the BBC comedy about the trials and tribulations of the ATS?
19. Who starred as Mollie Sugden's other half in *My Husband And I*?
20. Which actress played Ingrid in *Porridge* and *Going Straight*?
21. Whose alias was Professor Wallofsky?
22. Which *Waiting For God* star could be seen as Betty Sillito in *A Bit Of A Do*?
23. On RWT who were Dirk, Ron, Stig and Barry collectively?
24. What was *Captain Butler*?
25. Who played the one-armed odd-job man, Albert Riddle, in *Robin's Nest*?
26. What is Dave Allen's real name?
27. Which comedian's daughter appeared in *Watching*?
28. Which of the *Young Ones* was played by Adrian Edmondson?
29. Who was the female presenter of *Nice Time* with Kenny Everett and Jonathan Routh?
30. Chris Collins took his stage name from which member of his dad's pub dominoes team?

ANSWERS

### Pot Luck 6 (see Quiz 27)

**1.** *The Dick Van Dyke Show.* **2.** Mr. Goldberg. **3.** Jim Nelson. **4.** Julie Walters. **5.** *Jamie.* **6.** Annabel Croft. **7.** General Knowledge. **8.** Dolly. **9.** *Byker Grove.* **10.** Elliot. **11.** Lt. Commander. **12.** *Third Rock From The Sun.* **13.** Don Lang and His Frantic Five. **14.** Kenny. **15.** Mrs Doyle. **16.** Prince Andrew. **17.** Jasper Carrott. **18.** Both read English at Cambridge. **19.** One's green, one's brown. **20.** Roseanne. **21.** Bobby Davro. **22.** Table Tennis. **23.** Millwall. **24.** Royal Canadian Airforce. **25.** Bruce Willis. **26.** Sir Paul McCartney. **27.** Patrick Moore. **28.** Architect. **29.** Bodie. **30.** Jock Weir.

## QUIZ 29 Soaps 4

LEVEL 3

**Answers: see Quiz 30, page 558**

1. What was Kylie Minogue's character's job in *Neighbours*?
2. Which long standing *Coronation Street* actor was a skilled stuntman?
3. Who was Cliff Barnes sister in *Dallas*?
4. Which actor played Sarah's father in *Eastenders* and Travis in *Blake's Seven*?
5. Who was Jack Ewing's old business partner in *Dallas*?
6. Which two series did Kylie Minogue appear in before *Neighbours*?
7. In which city did the Carringtons live?
8. At which studios is the *Eastenders* set sited?
9. In *Coronation Street* what was Jack Walker's hobby?
10. What were the names of the two families which featured in *Soap*?
11. What was Dave Crosby's nickname in *Brookside*?
12. What was Des Clark's occupation in *Neighbours*?
13. In *Neighbours*, how was Des' wife Daphne killed?
14. Which *Coronation Street* actress is a patron of the Manchester Taxi Drivers Association?
15. Dorothy Burke was the headmistress in which Australian soap?
16. Which soap star produced a fitness video called *Secrets of Fitness and Beauty*?
17. How was *Neighbour* Kerry Bishop killed?
18. Which Robinson was manager of Lassiters?
19. Who in *Coronation Street* met her death after being hit by a bus?
20. Who played Clayton Fallone in *Dallas*?
21. Which actor John plays the evil Nick Cotton?
22. Who were Cheryl Starke's twins in *Neighbours*?
23. Which *Hollyoaks* star recorded *When I Need You*?
24. Actor Guy Pearce played which *Neighbours* character?
25. In *Hollyoaks* what was the name of Mandy Richardson's brother?
26. Which character was played by Linda Gray in *Dallas*?
27. Which *Spice Girl* appeared in *Emmerdale* as an extra?
28. In which soap did Demi Moore find fame?
29. Who was the second actress to play Fallon in *Dynasty*?
30. What was the name of Jacqui's club in *Brookside*?

ANSWERS

### Drama 4 (see Quiz 30)

**1.** Liverpool. **2.** Fort Courage. **3.** Eric. **4.** A radio station. **5.** Magnus Pym. **6.** *Tutti Frutti.* **7.** *Tenko.* **8.** Master Po. **9.** The Hapsburgs. **10.** Lucy Briers. **11.** The Marchmains. **12.** Robert Wagner. **13.** *Lou Grant.* **14.** New York. **15.** Anthony Hopkins. **16.** Belgium. **17.** *Brass.* **18.** *Scoop.* **19.** Howard Rollins. **20.** Nigel Havers. **21.** *A Very British Coup.* **22.** Tennessee Williams. **23.** John Thaw. **24.** Flying pioneer Amy Johnson. **25.** Arthur Hailey. **26.** *Rebecca.* **27.** Michael Palin. **28.** Doug McClure. **29.** *Shady Tales.* **30.** Jenny Seagrove.

## QUIZ 30 Drama 4

LEVEL 3

**Answers: see Quiz 29, page 557**

**1.** Where was the play *No Trams To Lime Street* set?
**2.** F-Troop was based at which fort?
**3.** Who was *Lovejoy*'s motorbiking sidekick?
**4.** The drama *Thin Air* concerned the running of what?
**5.** Who was *A Perfect Spy*?
**6.** In which series did Suzi Kettles appear?
**7.** Which drama series was inspired by the life of Margo Turner whose story had been researched for *This Is Your Life*?
**8.** Who was the blind mentor in *Kung Fu*?
**9.** *The Fall Of Eagles* was the story of which European Royal family?
**10.** Which daughter of a star of *The Good Life* played Mary Bennet in the 1995 *Pride and Prejudice*?
**11.** Whose family seat was Brideshead Castle?
**12.** Who was the only American actor in the *Colditz* cast?
**13.** Which newspaper editor was played by Ed Asner?
**14.** In which city was *Family Affair* set?
**15.** In *The Bunker* who played Adolf Hitler?
**16.** *The Secret Army* was set in which country?
**17.** In which series featured Bradley Hardacre?
**18.** Donald Pleasance and Denholm Elliott starred in which drama about a newspaper?
**19.** Who played Virgil Tibbs on TV?
**20.** Who played Gorse in *The Charmer*?
**21.** In which series did a steel-worker, Harry Perkins, rise to become Prime Minister?
**22.** Who wrote *The Glass Menagerie*, adapted for TV in 1974?
**23.** Who starred as journalist Mitch?
**24.** The television play *Amy* concerned which famous female?
**25.** Which US writer created *The Moneychangers*?
**26.** Joanna David featured in the title role of which adaptation of a du Maurier novel?
**27.** Which Python starred in *GBH*?
**28.** Who played Trampas in *The Virginian*?
**29.** In which series did we meet the character Gordon Shade?
**30.** Who did Deborah Kerr succeed as *A Woman Of Substance*?

ANSWERS

**Soaps 4 (see Quiz 29)**
**1.** Car mechanic. **2.** Bryan Mosley (Alf Roberts). **3.** Pam Ewing. **4.** Brian Croucher. **5.** Digger Barnes. **6.** *The Henderson Kids, The Sullivans.* **7.** Denver. **8** . Elstree. **9.** Bowls. **10.** The Campbells and the Tates. **11.** Bing. **12.** Bank manager. **13.** In a car accident. **14.** Liz Dawn (Vera Duckworth). **15.** *Neighbours.* **16.** Joan Collins. **17.** She was shot while trying to save some chicks. **18.** Paul. **19.** Ida Barlow. **20.** Howard Keel. **21.** John Altman. **22.** Brett and Danni. **23.** Will Mellor (Jambo). **24.** Mike. **25.** Lewis. **26.** Sue Ellen. **27.** Mel B. **28.** *General Hospital.* **29.** Emma Samms. **30.** Bar Brookie.

## QUIZ 31 News 2

LEVEL 3

**Answers: see Quiz 32, page 560**

1. Which naturalist presented *The First Eden*?
2. What did Bette Midler try to get Parkie to do live on TV?
3. GP Barry Brewster was the subject of which series on BBC1?
4. About which islands did Prince Philip present a documentary in the 60s?
5. Who presented *An Englishman's Home*?
6. Which TV celebrity explored *Castles Abroad*?
7. On which mountain did Mick Burke, a BBC cameraman, meet his death?
8. The funeral of which statesperson was the subject of *The Valiant Man*?
9. What is *News At Ten*'s claim to fame?
10. Which Labour Shadow Cabinet minister moved to Sky?
11. What was the title of the very first documentary about custom and excise officers?
12. Who introduced *Living With Waltzing Matilda*?
13. Why did ITV fail to show coverage of the Queen's Silver Jubilee?
14. *The Most Dangerous Man In The World* highlighted the events of the assassination attempt on which public figure in 1981?
15. *This Year's Blonde* was about whom?
16. Who was seen on TV making a public speech during a Wembley pop concert in 1990?
17. Which TV presenter sang the hit song *Shifting Whispering Sands*?
18. *Global Village* was presented by who?
19. Muriel Gray hosted which show about fashion?
20. In which year did Judith Chalmers start presenting *Wish You Were Here*?
21. Who presented a series about wine on Channel 4?
22. Who made the mistake of trying to sing an Elvis hit at the end of *Viva Elvis*?
23. Who did Anna Ford replace as a BBC newsreader?
24. Which documentary was about the writer Georges Simenon?
25. Name the sixties early evening programme presented by Simon Dee.
26. Where were cameras allowed for the first time during the Coronation?
27. Which ship featured in *Sailor*?
28. What did celebrity Fred Dibnah do for a living?
29. Which news programme was the first to announce the appointment of Margaret Thatcher as leader of the Conservative Party?
30. On which consumer programme did Esther Rantzen make her TV debut?

ANSWERS

### Pot Luck 7 (see Quiz 32)

**1.** Harry Secombe. **2.** *Never The Twain.* **3.** Chris Kelly. **4.** Jessica. **5.** *Hinge and Bracket.* **6.** *Nationwide.* **7.** Ernest. **8.** Orbit City Earth. **9.** *This Morning.* **10.** *Tarby's Fame Game.* **11.** Gregory Sumner. **12.** Esther. **13.** Terry Wogan. **14.** Tracy Ullman. **15.** *Give Us A Clue.* **16.** *The Flintstones.* **17.** *Points Of View.* **18.** *Voyage To The Bottom Of The Sea.* **19.** Magnus. **20.** Gymnastics. **21.** Yates. **22.** Television Studio. **23.** Edna Everage. **24.** Parkinson. **25.** Chester. **26.** Peter Cook. **27.** Anthony Newley – he appeared in *The Upper Hand* and was married to Joan Collins. **28.** Richard Wilson. **29.** *Softly, Softly.* **30.** *Z Cars.*

## QUIZ 32 Pot Luck 7

LEVEL 3

**Answers: see Quiz 31, page 559**

1. Which Goon presented *Highway*?
2. In which series were Oliver and Simon antique dealers?
3. Who presented *Clapperboard*?
4. Who was Chester Tate's wife in *Soap*?
5. How are George Logan and Patrick Fyffe better known?
6. Which early evening programme was presented by Michael Barrett?
7. In *Dangermouse*, what was Penfold's first name?
8. Where do *The Jetsons* live?
9. Which daytime show moved from Liverpool docks to London?
10. Which game show did Jimmy Tarbuck go on to present when he left *Winner Takes All*?
11. Who was William Devane's character in *Knots Landing*?
12. What was Grandma Walton's first name?
13. Who named Lucy Ewing 'The Poison Dwarf'?
14. Which of the cast of *Three Of A Kind* had her own U.S. series?
15. In which series did Liza Goddard take over a captain's role from Una Stubbs?
16. In which series was the local newspaper 'The Daily Slate'?
17. Which series has had three Robinsons as presenters?
18. In which futuristic series was the character Admiral Nelson?
19. What was TV presenter and scientist Dr Pike's christian name?
20. At which sport did presenter Suzanne Dando represent Britain?
21. What was the surname of TV presenters Jess and Paula?
22. Where would you find Dollies and Cue Cards?
23. Which Australian character had a husband Norm?
24. On whose chat show was Harry Stoneham musical director?
25. What was the name of the deputy in *Gun Law*?
26. Which satirist had a hit with *The Ballad Of Spotty Muldoon*?
27. Which actor/singer connects *The Upper Hand* to *Dynasty*?
28. Who played Dr Thorpe in *Only When I Laugh*?
29. In which series was there a detective named Harry Hawkins?
30. Leonard Rossiter played a detective sergeant in which series?

ANSWERS

### News 2 (see Quiz 31)

**1.** Sir David Attenborough. **2.** Take his clothes off. **3.** *The Doctor.* **4.** The Galapagos Islands. **5.** John Betjeman. **6.** Roy Castle. **7.** Everest. **8.** Winston Churchill. **9.** It was TV's first regular news bulletin. **10.** Austin Mitchell. **11.** *The Duty Men.* **12.** Alan Whicker. **13.** They were on strike. **14.** The Pope. **15.** Marilyn Monroe. **16.** Nelson Mandela. **17.** Eamonn Andrews. **18.** David Frost. **19.** *Frocks on The Box.* **20.** 1973. **21.** Jancis Robinson. **22.** Jonathan Ross. **3.** Angela Rippon. **24.** *Mirror Of Maigret.* **25.** Dee Time. **26.** Inside Westminster Abbey. **27.** HMS *Ark Royal.* **28.** Steeplejack. **29.** *John Craven's Newsround.* **30.** *The Braden Beat.*

## QUIZ 33 Comedy 6

LEVEL 3

**Answers: see Quiz 34, page 562**

1. How was William White better known?
2. What is Rebecca's surname in *Cheers*?
3. What was Vivian studying in the *Young Ones*?
4. What was 'Robin's Nest' in the sitcom of the same name?
5. Who created The Baldy Man?
6. Which actress appeared in *Bread* and *A Taste Of Honey*?
7. Who starred as entrepreneur Richard De Vere?
8. Which *Laugh In* star had a UK hit in 1968 with *Here Comes the Judge*?
9. Who played Bishop Len in *Father Ted*?
10. What was the name of Dorien's husband in *Birds Of A Feather*?
11. Which long running comedy series came to an end with the episode *Goodbye, Farewell And Amen*?
12. Which Australian stand up comedian styles himself as the Beige Sensation?
13. In which series did we meet The Phantom Raspberry Blower Of Old London Town?
14. Which comedian opened a folk club called The Boggery in Solihull?
15. Which actor links *It Ain't Half Hot Mum* and *Last Of The Summer Wine*?
16. Who plays Norm in *Cheers*?
17. Noel Dyson appeared as which character in *Father, Dear Father*?
18. Who provided the music on Kenny Everett's *Making Whoopee*?
19. Which pseudonym did Reginald Perrin assume when he attended his own funeral?
20. Where is Frasier's apartment in *Frasier*?
21. What type of car did Joey drive in *Bread*?
22. When *Fawlty Towers* was shown in Spain, what nationality did Manuel become in order not to cause offence?
23. What was Judi Dench's first TV comedy series?
24. Ashley and Elaine were the main characters in which ITV sitcom?
25. Who presented his *Laughter Show*?
26. For whom did the Fonz stand in during the phone marriage to Lori Beth?
27. In total, how many TV series of *Monty Python* were transmitted?
28. In *A Kind Of Living*, The Beasleys came from which town?
29. Johnathan Ross, Mel Smith and Griff Rhys Jones hosted which 1989 telethon?
30. In which US comedy did Corporal Henshaw appear?

ANSWERS

### Music & Variety 3 (see Quiz 34)

**1.** *Love and Fury* (The Tornadoes). **2.** 1987. **3.** *It's Now Or Never.* **4.** Arlene Phillips. **5.** *The Hot Shoe Show.* **6.** Tom O'Connor. **7.** Roy Walker. **8.** Middlemiss. **9.** *Kiss Me Kate.* **10.** Gerorge Chisholm. **11.** *Kiss Me Quick.* **12.** Benny Hill. **13.** Johnny Todd. **14.** ATV. **15.** Billy Crystal. **16.** Doug Ross. **17.** Andre Previn. **18.** *All Creatures Great And Small.* **19.** Andy Williams. **20.** Janice Nicholls. **21.** Madge. **22.** *The Generation Game.* **23.** Bob Monkhouse. **24.** *Strike It Lucky.* **25.** Paul Shane and Bob Monkhouse. **26.** Peter Cushing. **27.** Paul Daniels. **28.** David Copperfield. **29.** Billy Smart's. **30.** Gheorghe Zamfir.

## QUIZ 34 Music & Variety 3

LEVEL 3

**Answers: see Quiz 33, page 561**

1. What was the original theme tune of *Juke Box Jury*?
2. In which year did the BBC remove *Whistle Test* from their schedule?
3. The tune of which Elvis song was used to sell ice cream?
4. Who founded the dance group, *Hot Gossip*?
5. Bonnie Langford was the lead female dancer in which TV show?
6. Who presented *Wednesday Night At Eight*?
7. Which of The Comedians hosted a quiz show featuring popular sayings?
8. Which Jayne presents the *O-Zone*?
9. What was the first musical film shown on BBC2?
10. Which trombonist featured in a comedy spot on *The Black And White Minstrel Show*?
11. Which Elvis record did The Beatles predict a hit when they appeared on *Juke Box Jury* in 1963?
12. Whose creation was Fred Scuttle?
13. Which folk song was the basis for the famous theme tune to *Z Cars*?
14. Which ITV company presented *Saturday Spectacular*?
15. Who hosted the 1998 Academy Award Show from Hollywood?
16. Who was judged by Radio Times as the sexiest male TV doctor?
17. Which composer appeared with Morecambe and Wise on Christmas Day 1971?
18. Which series was voted by Radio Times readers The Best TV Drama Of All Time in 1998?
19. Whose popular shows introduced British audiences to *The Osmonds*?
20. Whose catchphrase on *Thank Your Lucky Stars* was "Oi'll give it foive"?
21. Which *Neighbours* character appeared with Dame Edna Everage?
22. Which show features a conveyor belt of prizes?
23. Which game show host did we have *An Audience with..?*
24. 'Hot Spots' are a feature on which game show?
25. Who sang the theme music for *You Rang M'Lord*?
26. Which horror actor worried about being paid as a guest on Morecambe and Wise?
27. Whose magic show featured 'The Bunko Booth'?
28. Which comic has the same name as a Dickens character?
29. Which circus was a television holiday favourite?
30. Who recorded Doina De Jale, the theme song for *Light of Experience*?

ANSWERS

### Comedy 6 (see Quiz 33)

**1.** Larry Grayson. **2.** Howe. **3.** Medicine. **4.** Fulham restaurant. **5.** Gregor Fisher. **6.** Rita Tushingham. **7.** Peter Bowles.**8.** Pigmeat Markham. **9.** Jim Norton. **10.** Marcus. **11.** *M*A*S*H*. **12.** Bob Downe. **13.** Two Ronnies. **14.** Jasper Carrott. **15.** Michael Bates. **16.** George Wendt. **17.** Nanny. **18.** Bob Kerr's Whoopee Band. **19.** Martin Wellbourne. **20.** Elliott Bay Towers. **21.** A Jaguar. **22.** Italian. **23.** *A Fine Romance*. **24.** *The Two Of Us*. **25.** Les Dennis. **26.** Richie Cunningham. **27.** Four. **28.** Bolton. **29.** *Comic Relief*. **30.** *Bilko*.

## QUIZ 35 Soaps 5

LEVEL 3

**Answers: see Quiz 36, page 564**

1. Which female character was shot in the Queen Vic but survived?
2. In *Eastenders*, who was imprisoned for embezzlement?
3. Which former *Coronation Street* actress was mayoress of her home town Blackburn?
4. Who owns the video shop in *Hollyoaks*?
5. Who was cast as Amanda Woodward in *Melrose Place*?
6. Name the former *Eastenders* female star who also appeared in *Get Well Soon*.
7. Which actor played Jim Robinson in *Neighbours*?
8. Which soap star produced a fitness video called *Rapid Results*?
9. Todd Carty plays which soap character?
10. Which former *Emmerdale* star has also been *Doctor Who*'s assistant?
11. Name the author of *The Thorn Birds*.
12. What was the nickname of Dirty Den's cellmate?
13. Which soap based in a fashion house has a valuable sounding title?
14. Which *Last Of The Summer Wine* actress appeared as Doris Luke in *Crossroads*?
15. What was Ian Bleasdale's character in *Take The High Road*?
16. In *Angels*, who starred as Nurse Jo Longhurst?
17. Which *EastEnders* star recorded *Subterranean Homesick Blues*?
18. Which Avenger appeared in *Coronation Street*?
19. Exactly how many episodes of the short-lived BBC soap, *Eldorado*, were broadcast?
20. Which BBC soap commenced in 1985?
21. What is the marital connection between Pat Wicks and Cathy Mitchell?
22. In which soap did Alec Baldwin find fame?
23. Which Queen did the Street's Alma Baldwin portray on film?
24. Who was Sue Ellen's sister in *Dallas*?
25. Who had an affair with both David and Simon Wicks?
26. Sophia Loren was reputedly the first choice for which role in *Dynasty*?
27. Who in *Coronation Street* had a star named after his wife?
28. Which former star of *Brookside* played Poppy Bruce in Emmerdale?
29. Which Albert was Valerie Barlow's uncle in *Coronation Street*?
30. Which *Dynasty* star duetted with Bing Crosby on *Let's Not Be Sensible* in 1962?

ANSWERS

### Pot Luck 8 (see Quiz 36)

**1.** Varley. **2.** Maddie. **3.** Michael Grade. **4.** The Academy Awards. **5.** Bessie. **6.** Niece. **7.** Psychiatrist. **8.** Diane Keen. **9.** The High Street. **10.** Paul Merton. **11.** Newcastle. **12.** Chief O'Brien. **13.** Jaye Griffiths. **14.** Les Dennis. **15.** Miranda. **16.** *The Dick Van Dyke Show.* **17.** *Local Heroes.* **18.** Nancy Bartlett. **19.** Harriet Thorpe. **20.** *The Simpsons.* **21.** *Kiss Kiss Bang Bang.* **22.** Channel 4. **23.** Sebastian. **24.** American Football. **25.** *A Grand Day Out.* **26.** Wishbone. **27.** *King Of The Hill.* **28.** Antiques, including toys and teddy bears. **29.** Anthony Newley. **30.** Peter Dimmock.

## QUIZ 36 Pot Luck 8

LEVEL 3

**Answers: see Quiz 35, page 563**

1. What was the chimney sweep's name in *Camberwick Green*?
2. Who was Alex and Virginia Hayes' daughter?
3. Which former Head of Channel 4 was born on the same day as Lynn Redgrave?
4. Billy Crystal won an Emmy in 1998 for hosting which annual event?
5. What was the name of Lord Belborough's steam engine in Chigley?
6. What relation, if any, is *Bramwell* star Jemma Redgrave to actress Vanessa Redgrave?
7. What was Lilith Crane's profession in *Cheers*?
8. Who was the *Foxy Lady* played by?
9. Where did Helen give birth in *The Brittas Empire*?
10. Whose show had a regular sketch set in a newsagent and tobacconist's kiosk in an Underground station?
11. Kate Adie is a former student of which university?
12. Who was the Head Engineer on *Star Trek: Next Generation*?
13. Which star of *Bugs* played D.I. Sally Johnson in *The Bill*?
14. How is TV presenter Leslie Heseltine better known?
15. What is the name of Hollin and Shelly's baby in *Northern Exposure*?
16. In which 60's sitcom did Richard Deacon play Mel Cooley?
17. Which series featured Adam Hart Davis seeking out inventors and inventions?
18. What was Sandra Bernhardt's character in *Roseanne*?
19. Who played Fleur in *Absolutely Fabulous*?
20. Side Show Bob featured in which cartoon series?
21. Which cinema magazine programme was presented by Charlie Higson?
22. On which channel was the motoring series *Driven* transmitted?
23. What is Rowan Atkinson's middle name?
24. Bill Cosby was offered a professional trial in which sport?
25. In which episode did Wallace and Grommit go to the moon?
26. Who was Paul Brinegar's character in *Rawhide*?
27. In which cartoon series are the neighbours called 'Khan'?
28. What kind of expert is Bunny Campione?
29. Which actor, singer, songwriter made a guest appearance in *Eastenders* as a used car dealer?
30. Who was the original presenter of *Sportsview*?

ANSWERS

### Soaps 5 (see Quiz 35)

**1.** Michelle Fowler. **2.** Arthur Fowler. **3.** Madge Indle (Renee Roberts). **4.** Tony. **5.** Heather Locklear. **6.** Anita Dobson. **7.** Alan Dale. **8.** Beverley Callard. **9.** Mark Fowler in *Eastenders*. **10.** Fraser Hines. **11.** Colleen McCullough. **12.** Barnsey. **13.** *Gems.* **14.** Kathy Staff. **15.** Joe Reilly. **16.** Julie Dawn Cole. **17.** Tom Watt (Lofty Holloway). **18.** Joanna Lumley. **19.** 158. **20.** *Eastenders.* **21.** They were both married to Pete Beale. **22.** *The Doctors.* **23.** Cleopatra (in *Carry On Cleo*). **24.** Kristen. **25.** Cindy Beale. **26.** Alexis Carrington. **27.** Curly Watts. **28.** Anna Friel. **29.** Albert Tatlock. **30.** Joan Collins.

## QUIZ 37 Drama 5

LEVEL 3

**Answers: see Quiz 38, page 566**

1. Where was *Tumbledown* set?
2. In *Bonanza* what was the name of Adam's horse?
3. What was the name of the TV series of the works of Jean-Paul Sartre?
4. In which city was *St Elsewhere* set?
5. In country was *The Regiment* set?
6. *The Fugitive* was inspired by which Victor Hugo novel?
7. What was Dame Peggy Ashcroft's character in *The Far Pavilions*?
8. Name the first Western series to be transmitted in full colour.
9. In which series about gambling did the Dragon Club feature?
10. Who wrote the novel *Anna Karenina*, adapted for TV in 1961?
11. Who played Chrissie's wife in *Boys From The Blackstuff*?
12. What was the first name of the butler in *Upstairs, Downstairs*?
13. Which town was featured in *Sunset Strip*?
14. Who wrote *Lace*?
15. Who starred in *Luke's Kingdom*?
16. What is the character Harry Lime better known as?
17. Robert Powell played which John Buchan creation on TV?
18. Which role did David Suchet play in Reilly Ace of Spies?
19. What was the name of the chimp on *Fantasy Island*?
20. Who starred as the *Mayor of Casterbridge*?
21. Who had *Have Gun Will Travel* printed on business cards?
22. Which 70's drama showed a Russian doll in its opening credits?
23. *The Onedin Line* was set in which city?
24. Who starred opposite Timothy Dalton in *Sins*?
25. How much money did Ken Masters win in a power boat race in *Howard's Way*?
26. What royal adornment featured at the start of each episode of *An Age Of Kings*?
27. What was the title of the BBC series dramatising the life of Lewis Carroll?
28. Who in *The Winds of War* was nicknamed 'Pug'?
29. The play series *Armchair Theatre* began life on BBC. With which TV company did its existence end in 1974?
30. Who starred as Sarah in *Upstairs, Downstairs*?

ANSWERS

**Children's TV 4 (see Quiz 38)**

**1.** David Icke. **2.** Red. **3.** *Whirligig.* **4.** Snowdonia. **5.** Snagglepuss. **6.** Fred. **7.** Emu's. **8.** John Hurt. **9.** The sound of a cockerel's crow. **10.** Paul Daniels. **11.** Reuben Kincaid. **12.** *Thomas The Tank Engine.* **13.** 1952. **14.** Frank Oz. **15.** "Nanu Nanu". **16.** Mr Rusty's. **17.** Tennessee. **18.** *Huckleberry Hound.* **19.** Sylvester McCoy. **20.** *William Tell.* **21.** Pebbles and Bamm-Bamm. **22.** The Zee Zone. **23.** Jai. **24.** Oink. **25.** They both had the same theme music. **26.** Planet Guk. **27.** Bill Hayes. **28.** Gary Miller. **29.** *The Little House On The Prairie.* **30.** A pig.

## QUIZ 38 Children's TV 4

LEVEL 3

**Answers: see Quiz 37, page 565**

1. Who was responsible for sport on *Saturday Superstore*?
2. What is the main colour of the Dukes' car, the General Lee?
3. In which series did Mr Turnip appear?
4. On which mountains was the 1950s series *William Tell* made?
5. Which cartoon character says "Heavens to Murgatroyd"?
6. What was the name of the pet tortoise on *Blue Peter*?
7. Whose arch enemy is Grotbags?
8. Who starred in *The Storyteller*?
9. In *Fun House* how was the discovery of a star prize announced?
10. Which TV celebrity hosted *Wizbit*?
11. Who managed the *Partridge Family*?
12. Whose friends are Henry and Gordon?
13. In which year did *Sooty* first appear on TV?
14. In *The Muppets* who was the original voice of Miss Piggy?
15. In *Mork and Mindy*, what was the Orkan expression for 'Goodbye'?
16. Whose barrel organ provided the theme music for *The Magic Roundabout*?
17. According to the theme music, Davy Crockett was born a mountain in which state?
18. Which cartoon character is "the biggest clown in town"?
19. Who was the seventh Dr Who?
20. Which TV hero had a friend called Bear?
21. Which two cartoon characters attended Bedrock High School?
22. Where does Captain Ze live?
23. What was the name of *Tarzan*'s orphan friend?
24. What was the name of the seal in *Stingray*?
25. What musically links *William Tell* and the *Lone Ranger*?
26. In *Terrahawks*, of which planet was Zelda the Imperial Queen?
27. Who sang the theme for *Davy Crockett*?
28. Who sang the theme song for *Robin Hood* in the 1950s?
29. Which house was located in Minnesota?
30. Ace reporter Huxley was what animal?

ANSWERS

### Drama 5 (see Quiz 37)

**1.** The Falkland Islands. **2.** Beauty. **3.** *Roads To Freedom.* **4.** Boston. **5.** India. **6.** Victor Hugo's *Les Miserables.* **7.** Barbie Batchelor. **8.** *Bonanza.* **9.** *Big Deal.* **10.** Leo Tolstoy. **11.** Julie Walters. **12.** Angus. **13.** Hollywood. **14.** Shirley Conran. **15.** Oliver Tobias. **16.** *The Third Man.* **17.** Richard Hannay. **18.** Inspector Tsientsin. **19.** Chester. **20.** Alan Bates. **21.** *Paladin.* **22.** *Tinker, Tailor, Soldier, Spy.* **23.** Liverpool. **24.** Joan Collins. **25.** £10 000. **26.** A crown. **27.** Alice. **28.** Commander Henry. **29.** Thames. **30.** Pauline Collins.

## QUIZ 39 Comedy 7

LEVEL 3

**Answers: see Quiz 40, page 568**

1. *Car 54* was based at which New York precinct police station?
2. Who grasped his ears before transmitting back to his planet?
3. The US comedy, *Tabatha*, was a short-lived spin-off of which other series?
4. Which actress connects *Man About The House* with the game show *Crazy Companions*?
5. What is Bill and Ben's surname in *Two Point Four Children*?
6. Which actor connects *Poldark* and the comedy *Dear John*?
7. Which ostentatious character did Peter Blake play in *Dear John*?
8. Robert Llewellyn played the part of a robot with a conscience in which series?
9. Who made a guest appearance as the Duke of Wellington in *Blackadder The Third*?
10. In which sitcom would you find the Cafe Nervosa?
11. Which house did Hester and William rent in *French Fields*?
12. Within which show did *The Fresh Prince of Bel Air* appear in the UK?
13. Who played Phoebe's twin sister Ursula in *Friends*?
14. What was Bernard Hedges' nickname in *Please Sir*?
15. Who was Jethro's sister in *The Beverley Hillbillies*?
16. Name Bilko's camp commandant at Fort Baxter.
17. Who was the pianist in *It Ain't Half Hot Mum*?
18. What were the names of the female characters played by Les Dawson and Roy Barraclough?
19. Who played the harrassed mother in *The Cabbage Patch*?
20. What was the name of the doctor played by Robin Nedwell In *Doctors In The House*?
21. Which of the *Golden Girls* played Sly Stallone's mother?
22. The *Three Of A Kind* trio consisted of Lenny Henry, Tracy Ullman and who else?
23. Who links *Do Not Adjust Your Set* with *Open All Hours*?
24. Who appeared in both *Porridge* and *Fraggle Rock*?
25. Fred Gwynne starred in which police comedy?
26. Who starred in the comedy *Atmosphere*?
27. In *Happy Days* who belonged to the Leopards Lodge?
28. Which TV comic politician had a wife called Sarah?
29. George Logan is better known as which female comic?
30. Who was the comedienne behind Gayle Tuesday?

ANSWERS

**Sci - Fi 2 (see Quiz 40)**

**1.** Magicthighs. **2.** Scorpio. **3.** He got a second Rimmer. **4.** Sigma 957. **5.** Macqui. **6.** Langly. **7.** Ed Bishop. **8.** Silver. **9.** David Vincent. **10.** Changeling. **11.** Erin Grey. **12.** Phone off the hook. **13.** Dirk Benedict. **14.** *Quatermass and The Pit.* **15.** Warrior. **16.** McGee. **17.** Galaxy class. **18.** *The Adventures of Superman.* **19.** 900 years old. **20.** Kirsty. **21.** Chipper. **22.** White. **23.** A comet. **24.** W.I.N. **25.** St. John. **26.** *The Prisoner* himself, Number Six. **27.** Hera. **28.** An addictive form of Virtual Reality. **29.** Venus. **30.** Garth Knight.

## QUIZ 40 Sci - Fi 2

LEVEL 3

**Answers: see Quiz 39, page 567**

1. Who was Broomfondle's colleague in *The Hitchhiker's Guide to the Galaxy*?
2. Which ship had a subservient computer called Slave?
3. When Lister tried to install Kochanski's holodisc in *Red Dwarf*, what happened?
4. Which system in *Babylon 5* was known for being a place where First Ones lurked?
5. What terrorist organisation did *Voyager*'s Commander Chakotay belong to?
6. Along with Frohike and Byers, who completes the Lone Gunmen?
7. Who was the American star of *UFO*?
8. Who was the technician who aided *Sapphire & Steel* in two adventures?
9. Who did Roy Thinnes play?
10. What race was Odo in *Star Trek: Deep Space Nine*?
11. Who played Wilma Deering?
12. What needed to be special about Sydney's computer in *VR5* to let her enter her dreamlike virtual worlds?
13. Who played Starbuck in *Battlestar Galactica*?
14. In which series were alien bodies found during the excavation for an Underground extension?
15. What designation did Richard Mayhew eventually earn in *Neverwhere*?
16. What was the name of the reporter investigating *The Incredible Hulk*?
17. The Enterprise is which class of starship?
18. *Lois and Clark* is the sequel to which series?
19. How old was *Doctor Who* supposed to be?
20. What was the name of Jack's jilted wife-to-be in *Ultraviolet*?
21. In *Land Of The Giants*, what was the name of the dog?
22. What colour was also the name of Captain Scarlett's boss?
23. In *The Day of the Triffids*, what blinded most of the population?
24. Who did *Joe 90* work for?
25. What was Stringfellow Hawke's brother called?
26. Who was finally revealed to be *The Prisoner*'s Number One?
27. Which goddess is Hercules' most dedicated enemy?
28. In *TekWar*, what is Tek?
29. Who was Steve Zodiac's girlfriend?
30. Like KITT, *Knight Rider* Michael Knight had an evil double. What was his name?

ANSWERS

**Comedy 7 (see Quiz 39)**

**1.** 53rd Precinct. **2.** Mork. **3.** *Bewitched.* **4.** Paula Wilcox. **5.** Porter. **6.** Ralph Bates. **7.** Kirk St Moritz. **8.** *Red Dwarf.* **9.** Stephen Fry. **10.** *Frasier.* **11.** Les Hirondelles. **12.** *Def II.* **13.** Lisa Kudrow (who also plays Phoebe). **14.** Privet. **15.** Ellie-May. **16.** Colonel John Hall. **17.** Gunner Graham. **18.** Cissie and Ada. **19.** Julia Foster. **20.** Dr Duncan Waring. **21.** Estelle Getty. **22.** David Copperfield. **23.** David Jason. **24.** Fulton Mackay. **25.** *Car 54 Where Are You.* **26.** Russ Abbot. **27.** Howard Cunningham. **28.** Alan B'Stard. **29.** Evadne Hinge. **30.** Brenda Gilhooly.

# QUIZ 41 Pot Luck 9

LEVEL 3

**Answers: see Quiz 42, page 570**

1. Which ex-PM was born on the same day as Python Eric Idle?
2. Richard Wilson aka Victor Meldrew was awarded an honorary doctorate by which university?
3. What is the theme for *Blue Peter* called?
4. Who did Griff Rhys Jones replace in the *Not The Nine O'clock News* team?
5. What was the name of Brian Wilde's character in *Porridge*?
6. Which 'Man Behaving Badly' narrated *Red-Handed*?
7. Who links *Scrapheap* to *Red Dwarf*?
8. Who presented the quiz show *Pass The Buck*?
9. What does Mark Freden talk about on *GMTV*?
10. Which US comedienne has her own C5 chat show?
11. Who on Channel 5 is *The Antique Hunter*?
12. How is Ray Burns better known?
13. Who said 'What a beautiful pair of knockers' on *Blue Peter*?
14. Who presented *Bookworm*?
15. Melanie and Martina Grant assist Pat Sharp on which game show?
16. Mike Yarwood had soccer trials with which clubs?
17. Which former page 3 girl presented the game show *Fort Boyard*?
18. Which Gladiator produced a fitness video called *Summer Circuit*?
19. Joanna Lumley and Jennifer Saunders were asked to edit which UK magazine?
20. Which medal did commentator Kenneth Wolstenhulme win in WWII?
21. What was the subject of the *Grange Hill* song *Just Say No*?
22. Who played a womanising PR man in the 70s sitcom *Casanova*?
23. What was Miriam Stoppard's profession?
24. Who originally was the voice of Mr. Kipling in the cake ads?
25. What was the name of the series where Robbie Coltrane was a Majestic?
26. Which TV star duetted with Barbra Streisand on *Till I Loved You* in 1988?
27. Which actor has played Captain Hillio, Butler and The Governor in Doctor Who?
28. Which financial programme was presented by Maya Even?
29. Who had a ventriloquist's dummy named Chuck?
30. What kind of food was advertised by Alf Roberts?

ANSWERS

**Soaps 6 (see Quiz 42)**

**1.** Rural Garage. **2.** Victoria Principal. **3.** Jackie Ingram. **4.** Dannii Minogue (Emma). **5.** *The Doctors*. **6.** Pam St Clement (Pat Evans). **7.** David Barlow. **8.** Ron Jenkins. **9.** Patsy Palmer. **10.** Jean Alexander. **11.** To stay with grandfather Alec after the accidental death of her parents. **12.** Norman Bowler (Frank Tate). **13.** Gwen Lockhead. **14.** Malandra Burrows. **15.** GPO. **16.** Aveline. **17.** Water polo. **18.** Anita Dobson. **19.** Hilda and Stan Ogden. **20.** Amanda Barrie. **21.** Terence Donovan. **22.** Gibbons. **23.** Patrick Duffy. **24.** Vin and Denise Welch. **25.** Toy theatres. **26.** Darius Perkins. **27.** Louise Jameson). **28.** Sue Johnston. **29.** Bill Maynard. **30.** Gail.

## QUIZ 42 Soaps 6

LEVEL 3

**Answers: see Quiz 41, page 569**

1. Where was ITV's first soap *Sixpenny Corner* set?
2. Which *Dallas* star was born the same day as musician Stephen Stills?
3. Who married Mike Baldwin in 1990 in *Coronation Street?*
4. Which *Home and Away* star recorded *Love and Kisses?*
5. In which soap did Ellen Burstyn find fame?
6. Which EastEnder once played Mrs Eckersley in *Emmerdale?*
7. Who did Irma Ogden marry in *Coronation Street?*
8. Which part did Gandhi star Ben Kingsley play in *Coronation Street?*
9. Which *Eastenders* actress became Mrs Nick Love in 1998?
10. Which ex-soap star played Christine Keeler's mother in the movie *Scandal?*
11. Why did Victoria move to the Rovers Return in *Coronation Street?*
12. Which former *Emmerdale* star played Harry Hawkins in *Softly Softly?*
13. Which character did Patricia Brake play in *Eldorado?*
14. Which future soap star became the youngest winner of *New Faces* when she won in the mid 70s?
15. Who did Frank Barlow work for?
16. 'Sugar La Marr' in *Coronation Street* went on to play whom in *Bread?*
17. Ross Davidson alias Andy in *EastEnders* was an international in which sport?
18. Which ex-Albert Square favourite wrote a book *My East End?*
19. With whom did Eddie Yeats lodge in *Coronation Street?*
20. Which Street actress's real name is Shirley Ann Broadbent?
21. Who has played Al Simpson in *Home & Away*, and Doug Willis in *Neighbours?*
22. What was surname of *Neighbours* doctor Clive?
23. Which star of *Dallas* was a singer with the Seattle Opera?
24. Which father and daughter appeared in *Coronation Street* in 1998 as father in law and daughter in law?
25. What sort of toys does Peter Baldwin, once Derek Wilton, collect?
26. In *Neighbours* who originally played Scott Robinson?
27. Which Dr Who assistant turned up in an Italian restaurant in Walford?
28. Which ex *Brookside* actress's autobiography was called *Hold on to the Messy Times?*
29. Which *Heartbeat* star played Mickey Malone in *Coronation Street?*
30. Who was Paul Robinson's second wife in *Neighbours?*

ANSWERS

### Pot Luck 9 (see Quiz 41)

**1.** John Major. **2.** Glasgow. **3.** *Barnacle Bill.* **4.** Chris Langham. **5.** Mr. Barrowclough. **6.** Neil Morrissey. **7.** Robert Llewellyn. **8.** Fred Dineage. **9.** Hollywood Gossip. **10.** Roseanne. **11.** David Dickinson. **12.** Captain Sensible. **13.** Simon Groom. **14.** Griff Rhys Jones. **15.** *Fun House.* **16.** Stockport Count and Oldham Athletic. **17.** Melinda Messenger. **18.** Jet (Diane Youdale). **19.** Marie Claire. **20.** DFC. **21.** Drug abuse. **22.** Leslie Philips. **23.** Doctor. **24.** James Hayter. **25.** *Tutti Frutti.* **26.** Don Johnson. **27.** Martin Jarvis. **28.** *The Money Programme.* **29.** Jodie in *Soap.* **30.** Crisps (Alberts).

## QUIZ 43 Drama 6

LEVEL 3

**Answers: see Quiz 44, page 572**

1. *Hadleigh* was set in which county?
2. What was Anthony Quayle's character in *The Strange Report*?
3. Which character's residence was Melford Park?
4. Why was the *Big Breadwinner Hog* removed from the screens in 1969?
5. Which character did Nyree Dawn Porter play in *The Forsythe Saga*?
6. What was *The Prisoner's* number?
7. Which secret agent featured in *Wet Job* in 1981?
8. Who starred as Napoleon Solo?
9. In which drama did an antiques dealer lead a double life as a secret agent?
10. Who wrote the pilot for *London's Burning* but not the series which followed?
11. Name the BBC's twice weekly drama which was the first made by them in colour.
12. How many of Rockcliffe's Babies were female?
13. Which *Upstairs, Downstairs* star was the real life wife of Dr Who Jon Pertwee?
14. Which actor, famous as Fagin in *Oliver!* has starred in *The Avengers*?
15. Who played Lola Lasagne in the *Batman* TV series?
16. Which actress who played *Moll Flanders* in the 90s once starred in *Grange Hill*?
17. Which series was based on *Butch Cassidy and the Sundance Kid*?
18. Which comic went straight in *One Fine Day*?
19. Which Dame starred as Queen Mary in *Edward And Mrs Simpson*?
20. What was the follow-up series to *Bouquet Of Barbed Wire*?
21. Which TV doctor lived in Tannochbrae?
22. What did Hine do for a living?
23. What Fleet Street first was played by Francesca Annis in *Inside Story*?
24. What did Glenda Jackson have done to her hair in order to play Queen Elizabeth I?
25. *Wagontrain* was a spin-off of which film?
26. Who helped save Douglas Motors in the 80s?
27. *Lou Grant* was Editor of which newspaper?
28. Who did Peter Egan play in *Lillie*?
29. Which group of soldiers was imprisoned in Stalag 13?
30. Which drama commemorated the 20th anniversary of JFK's death?

ANSWERS

### Comedy 8 (see Quiz 44)

**1.** *Laverne and Shirley* **2.** Buddy Boy. **3.** George Burns. **4.** Richard Briers. **5.** Bill Oddie. **6.** *The Comic Strip*. **7.** Mr Cromwell. **8.** *Chitty Chitty Bang Bang*. **9.** Sarah's. **10.** Charlie Drake. **11.** Ernest. **12.** Devereaux. **13.** St Andrews. **14.** *A Bit Of A Do*. **15.** Anita Dobson. **16.** Norman. **17.** 1989. **18.** *The Falcons*. **19.** Bill Oddie. **20.** Musky and Vince. **21.** Dinsdale. **22.** Anthony Booth. **23.** Jasper Carrott. **24.** Kathy Staff. **25.** Tony Robinson. **26.** *Spitting Image*. **27.** The RAF. **28.** *The Good Companions*. **29.** Julian Clary. **30.** 1988.

## QUIZ 44 Comedy 8

LEVEL 3

**Answers: see Quiz 43, page 571**

1. In which US comedy did the characters Lenny and Squiggy appear?
2. In *Mr Ed*, what did the horse always call Wilbur?
3. Whose catchphrase was 'Say goodnight Gracie'?
4. Who played the lodger in *Goodbye Mr Kent*?
5. Which ex Goodie was born on the same day as Michael Howard?
6. Who presented the comic play *The Fly*, in which the genes of a hooligan were mixed with those of a video director?
7. In *Please Sir* what was the name of the headmaster?
8. Benny Hill made an appearance in which comic musical film about a car?
9. Whose daughter was Clare in *After Henry*?
10. Which comic starred in *Bingo Madness*?
11. Sergeant Bilko's first name was what?
12. What was Blanche's surname in *The Golden Girls*?
13. John Cleese was awarded an honorary doctorate of which university?
14. David Jason married Gwen Taylor in which comedy?
15. Who starred in *Split Ends*?
16. What is the name of Dame Edna's husband?
17. *Comic Relief* was first televised in which year?
18. Which gang did the Fonz belong to?
19. Which of the *Goodies* had a starring role in *The Bubblegum Brigade*?
20. Name *Deputy Dawg*'s two sidekicks.
21. What was the name of *Monty Python*'s giant hedgehog?
22. Who played Alf's son-in-law?
23. Which comedian wrote the autobiography *Sweet And Sour Labrador*?
24. Which *Last Of The Summer Wine* star appeared in *No Frills*?
25. Which comic/writer/presenter appeared naked in *Who Dares Win*?
26. Which comic series was banned from caricaturing Mickey Mouse?
27. From which service had Harvey been demobbed at the start of *Shine On Harvey Moon*?
28. In which 1980s comedy did the Dinky Doos feature?
29. Which comedian has four initials, J.P.M.S?
30. In which year did Ronnie Barker retire from TV?

ANSWERS

**Drama 6 (see Quiz 43)**

**1.** Yorkshire. **2.** Adam Strange. **3.** Haleigh's. **4.** Due to complaints of excessive violence. **5.** Irene. **6.** Six. **7.** Callan. **8.** Robert Vaughan. **9.** *The Baron.* **10.** Jack Rosenthal. **11.** *The Doctors.* **12.** Two. **13.** Jean Marsh. **14.** Ron Moody. **15.** Ethel Merman. **16.** Alex Kingston. **17.** *Alias Smith And Jones.* **18.** Dave Allen. **19.** Dame Peggy Ashcroft. **20.** *Another Bouquet.* **21.** Dr Finlay. **22.** Arms salesman. **23.** Fleet Street's first female editor. **24.** It was shaved. **25.** *Wagonmaster.* **26.** *The Chancer* (Steven Crane). **27.** The Los Angeles Tribune. **28.** Oscar Wilde. **29.** *Hogan's Heroes.* **30.** *Kennedy.*

## QUIZ 45 News 3

LEVEL 3

**Answers: see Quiz 46, page 574**

1. Who walked out on an interview with David Dimbleby when asked about royalties from an autobiography?
2. Robin Hall and Jimmie MacGregor were singers on which current affairs programme?
3. Cliff Michelmore first presented *Holiday* in which year?
4. Shortly after commentating on which state occasion did Richard Dimbleby die?
5. Who travelled around the world to present the documentary series *Civilisation*?
6. What was newsreader Anna Ford's claim to fame?
7. Which two newsreaders presented the very first *News At Ten*?
8. What did *Omnibus* replace as BBC's arts programme?
9. How did Frank Muir describe Joan Bakewell?
10. Which Scottish pop star had his own chat show in the early 1980s?
11. What did Reginald Bosanquet's father invent in the sporting world?
12. What was *News Review*'s claim to fame when it was introduced in the mid-60s?
13. Which crimestopper is known as *Whispering Grass*?
14. Which BBC news programme was first broadcast in 1953?
15. What did Grace Jones hit Russell Harty with on his show?
16. Who succeeded Brian Walden as presenter of *Weekend World*?
17. Name the documentary made by Granada about the Beatles' visit to New York.
18. *Fame Is The Spur* featured which political party?
19. From which hospital was *Hospital* broadcast?
20. What was *This Week* renamed for one year in its 30+ year run?
21. What kind of shop did newsreader Kenneth Kendall open on retiring from TV?
22. What was Robert McKenzie's very last political documentary before he died?
23. Which presenter was a co-founder of *TV-AM*?
24. What was the name of the mini-series about Martin Luther King?
25. *The Rough Guide* travel series formed part of which BBC2 programme?
26. *The Stars* was the sequel to which series?
27. Trevor McDonald was awarded an honorary doctorate of which university?
28. To whom did Prince Charles admit he spoke to plants?
29. Who won an award for her reports from Libya?
30. Why was Prince Edward in the headlines in 1987?

ANSWERS

### Pot Luck 10 (see Quiz 46)

**1.** Charles Dance. **2.** Kathy Kirby. **3.** Crystal Palace. **4.** John Pertwee. **5.** *Riverboat.* **6.** Jed Stone. **7.** Maggie FitzGibbon. **8.** Flint McCullough. **9.** Christopher Hughes. **10.** Tuesday. **11.** Christopher Connelly. **12.** Rory McGrath & Jimmy Mulville. **13.** Lucy And Ricky Ricardo. **14.** Claire Rayner. **15.** Jimmy Tarbuck. **16.** Guy Pierce. **17.** Ryan O'Neal. **18.** Bath salts. **19.** M. **20.** Katie Boyle. **21.** *Scene and Hird.* **22.** *Eastenders.* **23.** Frank Muir. **24.** Bronco. **25.** Richard Rogers. **26.** A street market. **27.** Dresses. **28.** Tenderfoot. **29.** Derby County. **30.** Bernard Bresslaw.

## QUIZ 46 Pot Luck 10

LEVEL 3

**Answers: see Quiz 45, page 573**

1. Chris Tarrant was born on the same day as which star of *The Jewel in the Crown*?
2. *Stars and Garters* featured which female singing star?
3. Angus Deayton had a soccer trial with which club?
4. Which Dr Who served on HMS Hood in WWII?
5. Which 1960s western series featured a stern wheel paddle steamer?
6. What was Sonny Jim's real name in *Coronation Street*?
7. Which Australian singer appeared in *The Newcomers*?
8. Who was the scout in *Wagon Train*?
9. Which *Mastermind* drove a train for the London Underground?
10. On which day did *Watch with Mother* feature *Andy Pandy*?
11. Who played Jodie Foster's father in *Paper Moon*?
12. Which duo co-wrote and starred in *Chelmsford 123*?
13. Whose neighbours were Fred and Ethel?
14. Who is taller – Jill Dando or Claire Rayner?
15. Which TV comedian had the number plate COM IC?
16. Which *Neighbours* actor appeared in the film *L.A. Confidential*?
17. If Christopher Connelly was Norman who played Rodney?
18. Which luxury did Esther Rantzen choose on *Desert Island Discs*?
19. Actor Robert Brown appeared as which spymaster on film?
20. Which Italian Countess hosted the Eurovision Song Contest?
21. What was Thora Hird's autobiography called?
22. In which soap was there a character named George Holloway?
23. Who wore pink bow ties on *Call My Bluff*?
24. Which cowboy had the surname Layne?
25. Who composed the music for *Victory At Sea*?
26. What was *Honey Lane*?
27. Which of her possessions did Janet Street Porter sell at auction in 1997?
28. What was the alternative name of the television western series *Sugarfoot*?
29. Which soccer side does actor Robert Lindsay support?
30. Which giant actor appeared in *The Army Game*?

ANSWERS

**News 3 (see Quiz 45)**

**1.** Harold Wilson. **2.** *Tonight.* **3.** 1969. **4.** The Coronation. **5.** Lord Kenneth Clark. **6.** She was ITN's first female newsreader. **7.** Alastair Burnett and Andrew Gardner. **8.** *Monitor.* **9.** The thinking man's crumpet. **10.** B A Robertson. **11.** The googly in cricket. **12.** It was the world's first news programme for the deaf. **13.** Shaw Taylor. **14.** *Panorama.* **15.** Her handbag. **16.** Matthew Parris. **17.** *Yeah!, Yeah!, Yeah!* **18.** Labour. **19.** Bolton Hospital, Lancashire. **20.** *TV Eye.* **21.** An antiques shop. **22.** *Pursuit Of Power.* **23.** David Frost. **24.** *King.* **25.** *DEF II.* **26.** *The Planets.* **27.** Plymouth. **28.** Alastair Burnett. **29.** Kate Adie. **30.** He had resigned from the marines.

# QUIZ 47 Children's TV 5

LEVEL 3

**Answers: see Quiz 48, page 576**

**1.** What was the name of *Rupert Bear*'s elephant friend?
**2.** What was the first children's programme on BBC2?
**3.** In which city did *Ollie Beak* live?
**4.** Which Western star always wore a black hat?
**5.** Which ranch did Gene Autry own?
**6.** On which river did the town of Tickle lie?
**7.** Who always ended shows with the words "Bye, bye, everyone. Bye, bye"?
**8.** In which country was *Elephant Boy* set?
**9.** Who commanded *Stingray*?
**10.** Why breed of dog was *Scooby Doo*?
**11.** Who created the *Cisco Kid*?
**12.** Which legendary pirate's girlfriend was called Peggetty?
**13.** Who spoke the language Oddle Poddle?
**14.** Which adversaries of the Suntots cause pollution?
**15.** In which comedy were the Kravitzes the next door neighbours?
**16.** On which island did the Doozers reside?
**17.** Kissyfur was what kind of animal?
**18.** What was the name of Gomez Addam's pet octopus?
**19.** Which superheroine "makes them look like a bunch of fairies"?
**20.** Which ex-pop singer presented *Puddle Lane*?
**21.** What does Fred Flintstone wear on his feet?
**22.** Which London tourist attraction did a *Blue Peter* presenter once climb on TV?
**23.** Which rap artist was the first to have a cartoon series?
**24.** What did Davy Crockett call his rifle?
**25.** Who did the Soup Dragon live with?
**26.** In the *A-Team,* what was Face's real name?
**27.** Who wrote about *Eric the Viking*?
**28.** Which children's TV presenter was lead singer with Kenny?
**29.** Which soccer side does Timmy Mallett support?
**30.** Who made up the *Space Sentinels* with Mercury and Astria?

ANSWERS

**Soaps 7 (see Quiz 48)**

**1.** Slim Jim. **2.** The Albert Memorial Hospital. **3.** Leeds United. **4.** The Wandin Valley. **5.** Anne Haddy. **6.** Leslie. **7.** Jill Richardson. **8.** Bank Manager. **9.** Kevin Webster. **10.** Daphne **11.** As a Gorilla. **12.** EWING. 3 **13.** Dickie Fleming. **14.** Betty Turpin. **15.** Connie Hall. **16.** Kominsky. **17.** Etta. **18.** Irma Ogden. **19.** Damon Grant. **20.** Sharon Watts. **21.** Mr. Papadopolous. **22.** Gloria Todd. **23.** Jack Duckworth. **24.** Florists. **25.** Punk Mary. **26.** Des Clarke. **27.** Debbie Wilkins. **28.** Larry Hagman. **29.** Ted Shackleford. **30.** Boxing Day 1991.

## QUIZ 48 Soaps 7

LEVEL 3

**Answers: see Quiz 47, page 575**

1. In *Coronation Street* what was Eddie Yeats' C.B. handle?
2. In which hospital is *The Young Doctors* set?
3. Which soccer side does Liz Dawn – alias Vera Duckworth – support?
4. Where is *A Country Practice* located?
5. Which *Neighbours* actress played Rosie in *Sons And Daughters*?
6. What was Maggie Clegg's husband's name in *Coronation Street*?
7. Who did Stan Harvey marry in *Crossroads*?
8. What did Philip Martin do for a living when he first appeared in *Neighbours*?
9. In *Coronation Street* who had a sister Debbie who moved to Southampton?
10. Which *Neighbours* character was engaged to Shane Ramsey?
11. How was Clive dressed when he almost sabotaged Des and Daphne's wedding in *Neighbours*?
12. What was J.R. Ewing's number plate on his car?
13. Who divorced Audrey in *Coronation Street* because of her affair with Ray Langton?
14. Who had a sister Maggie in *Coronation Street*?
15. Who stabbed Ray Krebbs in *Dallas* in 1988?
16. What was Rachel's surname in *Eastenders*?
17. What was Hattie Tavernier's mother's name in *Eastenders*?
18. Who ran the grocery side of the post office & corner shop in *Coronation Street*?
19. Who sent a rude valentine card to a teacher in *Brookside*?
20. Who in *Eastenders* visited Jan to persuade her not to see Dennis Watts again?
21. Who in *Eastenders* inherited the laundrette in 1992?
22. Who occupied a flat in the same premises as Alan & Jenny Bradley in *Coronation Street*?
23. Who did the electrical wiring that caused the fire at *Coronation Street's* Rovers Return?
24. In *Coronation Street* what business did Maggie Dunlop own?
25. In *Eastenders* who tried to sabotage Ozcabs?
26. In *Neighbours* who was Joan Langdon's fiancee?
27. Who did Saheed make obscene phone calls to in *Eastenders*?
28. Which star of *Dallas* appeared in *The Eagle Has Landed*?
29. Who links *Space Precinct* to *Knot's Landing*?
30. On which day did Mark Fowler in *Eastenders* tell his parents that he was HIV positive?

ANSWERS

**Children's TV 5 (see Quiz 47)**

**1.** Edward Trunk. **2.** *Playschool.* **3.** Liverpool. **4.** Hopalong Cassidy. **5.** Melody Ranch. **6.** The River Tum. **7.** Harry Corbett on the *Sooty Show.* **8.** Sri Lanka. **9.** Troy Tempest. **10.** A Great Dane. **11.** Writer O'Henry. **12.** Long John Silver's. **13.** Bill and Ben. **14.** The Smoggies. **15.** *Bewitched.* **16.** *Fraggle Rock.* **17.** A bear. **18.** Aristotle. **19.** *Supergran.* **20.** Neil Innes. **21.** Nothing - his feet are bare. **22.** Nelson's Column. **23.** M C Hammer. **24.** Old Betsy. **25.** *The Clangers.* **26.** Templeton Peck. **27.** Terry Jones. **28.** Keith Chegwin. **29.** Wycombe Wanderers. **30.** Hercules.

## QUIZ 49 Comedy 9

LEVEL 3

**Answers: see Quiz 50, page 578**

1. Of which Gang Show was Jim Davidson formerly a member?
2. Which actress starred in *Piggy In The Middle*?
3. *Let's Be Frank* starred who in the title role?
4. Which comic actress had an imaginary friend called Marlene?
5. Harry H Corbett owned a corner shop in which TV series?
6. Who plays the word-confounding policeman in *'Allo, 'Allo?*
7. *Please Sir* was set in which area of London?
8. Which patriot had pictures of the Queen and Winston Churchill hanging on his wall?
9. Which soccer side does comedian Bernard Manning support?
10. Which star of *Yes, Minister* was a conscientious objector in WWII?
11. Which actor, famous for a successful sitcom, released a solo album *What Is Going to Become of Us All* in1976?
12. Which part of his body has Dave Allen lost part of?
13. Who played Milo O'Shea's mother in *Me Mammy*?
14. Who played Alf Garnett's wife?
15. Jane Asher competed for the same man with Felicity Kendal in which series?
16. On whose show did Susie Butcher play the muddled anchor woman?
17. What number was Bilko's Formula to remove wrinkles?
18. In the 1970s remake of the *Rag Trade* who took Reg Varney's original part?
19. In *Watching* which male character's surname was Stoneway?
20. Bob Buzzard was a doctor in which BBC comic series?
21. What kind of restaurant was above the *Cheers* bar?
22. Who played Fletcher's wife?
23. What colour was Adrian Edmondson's hair in the *Young Ones*?
24. What is the name of *Monty Python*'s theme music?
25. Who did the *Auf Wiedersehn Pet* gang call Erics?
26. Which male comic starred in *Going Gently*?
27. Who were the first two *Ab Fab* stars to appear on *Friends*?
28. Carol Royle and Simon Cadell starred together in which comedy?
29. In which US comedy did Potsie feature?
30. Which actress did Anton Rodgers marry in *Fresh Fields*?

ANSWERS

### Pot Luck 11 (see Quiz 50)

**1.** *Cyborg.* **2.** Martin Bell. **3.** Dutch. **4.** Gibbons. **5.** Martin Clunes. **6.** *We Can Work It Out.* **7.** Bernadette O'Farrell. **8.** Brenda Blethyn. **9.** Aviation. **10.** *Dempsey and Makepiece.* **11.** Jimmy Tarbuck. **12.** Robert Wightman. **13.** *Lou Grant.* **14.** The Brick. **15.** Oasis Publishing. **16.** Leonard Nimoy. **17.** Gloria Hunniford. **18.** Wolverhampton. **19.** Alessi. **20.** Joan Greenwood. **21.** Jerry Stevens. **22.** Penelope Keith. **23.** Jonathan Dimbleby. **24.** Mike Smith. **25.** Commander Chakotay. **26.** *Brookside.* **27.** Squadron Leader Rex. **28.** Luton Town. **29.** World Illustrated. **30.** Beavis and Butthead.

## QUIZ 50 Pot Luck 11

LEVEL 3

**Answers: see Quiz 49, page 577**

1. Which book was the basis for *The Six Million Dollar Man*?
2. Which former BBC war correspondent became an MP?
3. What nationality was Carla, played by Kylie Minogue, in *The Sullivans*?
4. What is chat show host Leeza's surname?
5. Which star narrated the *Rottentrolls*?
6. Which consumer programme was presented by Judy Finnegan?
7. Who was the first actress to play Maid Marian in *The Adventures Of Robin Hood*?
8. Who starred in *The Labours Of Erica*?
9. What was the subject of the 1980 series *Diamonds In The Sky*?
10. In which series did Tony Osoba play Det. Sgt. Chas Jarvis?
11. Who presented *Winner Takes All*?
12. Who succeeded Richard Thomas as John Boy in *The Waltons*?
13. In which 80's US series was there a photographer named Dennis 'The Animal' Price?
14. What is the name of Holling's bar in *Northern Exposure*?
15. What was the name of the publishing company in *Executive Stress*?
16. Who played The Great Paris in *Mission Impossible*?
17. Which Irish presenter shares a birth date with Bobby Hatfield of *The Righteous Brothers*?
18. Sue Lawley was awarded an honorary doctorate by which university?
19. Gayle and Gillian Blakeney played which twins in *Neighbours*?
20. Who played the landlady in *Girls On Top*?
21. Who was the host of *TV Quiz*?
22. Who played a lady MP in *No Job For A Lady*?
23. Which Dimbleby presented *First Tuesday*?
24. Who hosted *The Funny Side*?
25. Who is second in command of the Voyager in *Star Trek: Voyager*?
26. Presenter Paula Yates made a guest appearance in which soap?
27. Who did Tim Woodward play in *A Piece Of Cake*?
28. Which soccer side does Nick Owen, formerly of Good Morning With Anne and Nick, support?
29. Which fictional magazine featured in *Shirley's World*?
30. Who duetted with Cher on *I Got You Babe* in 1994?

ANSWERS

**Comedy 9 (see Quiz 49)**

**1.** *Ralph Reader's Gang Show.* **2.** Liza Goddard. **3.** Frankie Howerd. **4.** Beryl Reid. **5.** Grundy. **6.** Arthur Bostram. **7.** The East End. **8.** Alf Garnett. **9.** Manchester City. **10.** Paul Eddington. **11.** Jon Le Mesurier. **12.** Finger. **13.** Anna Manahan. **14.** Dandy Nicholls. **15.** *The Mistress.* **16.** Victoria Wood's. **17.** Formula 7. **18.** Christopher Beeny. **19.** Malcolm's. **20.** *A Very Peculiar Practice.* **21.** A seafood restaurant. **22.** Patricia Brake. **23.** Orange. **24.** Liberty Bell. **25.** Germans. **26.** Norman Wisdom. **27.** Jennifer Saunders and June Whitfield. **28.** *Living Without George.* **29.** *Happy Days.* **30.** Julia McKenzie.

## QUIZ 51 Drama 7

LEVEL 3

**Answers: see Quiz 52, page 580**

1. In *King's Royal,* what was the company producing?
2. In *The Rockford Files* how much did Jim Rockford charge per day?
3. What was the name of James Bolam's character in *When The Boat Comes In*?
4. Which actor portrayed Disraeli in *Edward The Seventh?*
5. Which series based on Arnold Bennett's work was ITV's longest-running drama in 1976?
6. What sort of journalist was Lytton in *Lytton's Diary*?
7. Which part did John Hurt take in *I, Claudius*?
8. In *Roots,* which part was played by John Amos?
9. *Spend, Spend, Spend* told the story of which football pools winner?
10. What happened to *The Professionals* in the very last episode?
11. Who starred as Moses in the 1970's?
12. Jeremy Irons, Christopher Blake and Peter Davison vied for the attentions of Mel Martin in which 70s adaptation of an H E Bates novel?
13. Who requested changes to the script of *Tumbledown*?
14. In which state was *Laramie* set?
15. What was the Manageress's name as played by Cherie Lunghi?
16. Where did Frank and Tessa marry in *Love Hurts*?
17. In which women's prison was *Within These Walls* set?
18. Who published *Nanny* under a male pseudonym?
19. In *First Among Equals* which political party were elected to power?
20. Which character did Francesca Annis play in *Edward VII* and another 70s series with her name in the title?
21. Which moviestar of the late 90s played Pte. Mick Hopper in *Lipstick on Your Collar*?
22. In which country was *Fields of Fire* set?
23. Who played Anthony Blunt on TV?
24. What was the name of Leslie Grantham's character in *The Paradise Club*?
25. Who portrayed Donald Campbell in *Across The Lake*?
26. Which actress found a cream cracker under her settee in *Talking Heads*?
27. Which family did Mrs Bridges cook for?
28. Which political figure was played on TV by Faye Dunaway?
29. Which *Blue Peter* presenter appeared in *Fallen Hero*?
30. How long was Marlon Brando's appearance in *Roots, The Next Generation*?

ANSWERS

### Crime 1 (see Quiz 52)

**1.** Galloway. **2.** Darren McGavin. **3.** Chief Superintendent. **4.** Dave Creegan. **5.** Superintendent Albert Tyburn. **6.** Amanda Donohoe. **7.** Sparta. **8.** Chicago. **9.** Amanda Redman. **10.** *Miami Vice*. **11.** Cousin Tel. **12.** Iolani Palace. **13.** David Lynch. **14.** *Highway Patrol.* **15.** Kevin McNally. **16.** *Cracker.* **17.** Noel Harrison. **18.** Sylvia Costas **19.** John Creasey. **20.** A blue lamp. **21.** Paul Moriarty (George Palmer). **22.** Det. Insp. Purbright. **23.** *Hill Street Blues.* **24.** Harry Morgan. **25.** Hartley. **26.** Maverick. **27.** Michael Medwin. **28.** Leslie Ash. **29.** Reece Dinsdale. **30.** He was a lawyer.

## QUIZ 52 Crime 1

LEVEL 3

**Answers: see Quiz 51, page 579**

**1.** Who did Burnside replace in the CID?
**2.** Who played Carl Kochak in *The Night Stalker*?
**3.** What rank was Spikings in *Dempsey and Makepiece*?
**4.** Which character did Robson Green play in *Touching Evil*?
**5.** Which character did Trevor Eve play in *Heat of the Sun*?
**6.** Who played the bisexual British attorney in *LA Law*?
**7.** Which Mississippi town was In the *Heat of the Night* set?
**8.** Where were the outdoor scenes of *Hill Street Blues* filmed?
**9.** Who is Beck?
**10.** In which U.S. crime series did Phil Collins make a guest appearance as a criminal?
**11.** Who was Hazell's sidekick?
**12.** In *Hawaii Five O* where was the seat of the Hawaiian government?
**13.** Who starred as Gordon Cole in *Twin Peaks*?
**14.** Broderick Crawford appeared in which 1960s crime series?
**15.** Who played Jack Taylor in *Chiller*?
**16.** Judith Fitzgerald was a character in which crime series?
**17.** Which English actor was *The Girl From UNCLE*'s sidekick?
**18.** Who was the public defender in *NYPD Blue* before she married Andy Sipowics?
**19.** Whose novels were *Gideon's Way* based on?
**20.** What was above George Dixon's head outside the station?
**21.** Which 90s EastEnders star played Jake Barratt in *The Gentle Touch*?
**22.** Which detective did Anton Rodgers play in *Murder Most English*?
**23.** In which series did Pizza Man appear?
**24.** Which *Dragnet* actor appeared in *M*A*S*H*?
**25.** In *Juliet Bravo*, where was the police station?
**26.** Which western spoof did James Garner star in before he became investigator Jim Rockford?
**27.** Who played *Shoestring*'s boss?
**28.** In *Cat's Eyes*, who starred as Fred?
**29.** Who plays Charlie Scott in *Thief Takers*?
**30.** What did *Matlock* do for a living?

ANSWERS

### Drama 7 (see Quiz 51)

**1.** Whisky. **2.** $200 plus expenses. **3.** Ford Seaton. **4.** Sir John Gielgud. **5.** *Clayhanger.* **6.** Gossip columnist. **7.** Caligula. **8.** Kunte Kinte. **9.** Viv Nicholson. **10.** They crashed their dinghy into the boat they were pursuing. **11.** Burt Lancaster. **12.** *Love for Lydia.* **13.** Defence Secretary George Younger. **14.** Wyoming. **15.** Gabriella Benson. **16.** Russia. **17.** Stone Park Women's Prison. **18.** Wendy Craig. **19.** Labour. **20.** Lille Langtry. **21.** Ewan McGregor. **22.** Australia. **23.** Ian Richardson. **24.** Danny Kane. **25.** Anthony Hopkins. **26.** Thora Hird. **27.** The Bellamys. **28.** Eva Peron. **29.** Peter Duncan. **30.** Nine minutes.

## QUIZ 53 Who's Who 2

LEVEL 3

**Answers: see Quiz 54, page 582**

1. What relation is ER's George Clooney to 50s songstress Rosemary Clooney?
2. Simon Mayo and Timmy Mallet both attended which university?
3. How is TV funny lady Joan Molinsky better known?
4. What is Robson Green's middle name?
5. Which political interviewer was South of England show jumping champion in 1964?
6. IWhich TV presenter produced a fitness video called *Fit For Life*?
7. Which soccer side does sports presenter Jim Rosenthal support?
8. Which TV presenter used to be in a group called Memphis 5?
9. Which husband and wife TV stars had the number plate 8 DEB?
10. What was Dawn French's profession before becoming famous?
11. Which TV presenter once held the title Miss Parallel Bars?
12. Which job did Jeremy Beadle once have in a circus?
13. Which pianist and sometime Countdown 'expert' was born the same day Rachmaninov died?
14. What is Clive Anderson's profession?
15. Who scripted the first series of *Blackadder* with Rowan Atkinson?
16. Which Australian hosted *The Big Breakfast* with Zoe Ball?
17. Who played keyboards with a rock band called Fine China?
18. Who played the Emperor Nero in the acclaimed *I Claudius*?
19. Who famously ditched her ring and fur coat but kept her VW Golf?
20. Which actress is president of the Dyslexia Institute?
21. Which TV presenter is Lord Puttnam's son in law?
22. Who made her TV debut in 1989 in *The Big World Cafe*?
23. About whom did Kitty Muggeridge say "he rose without trace"?
24. Who shot to fame as Polly in *The Camomile Lawn*?
25. Who became the BBC's youngest ever scriptwriter aged 21 in 1980?
26. Who wrote the theme song for *Hearts of Gold*?
27. Who played Max de Winter opposite Emilia Fox in *Rebecca*?
28. Who played Rhett Butler in the TV sequel to *Gone With the Wind*?
29. On which show did Julia Carling parody Princess Diana in the operating theatre?
30. Which interviewer was described by an interviewee as 'the thinking woman's crumpet gone stale'?

ANSWERS

**Music & Variety 4 (see Quiz 54)**

**1.** Vanessa Mae **2.** David Soul **3.** Topo Gigio **4.** Phil Collins **5.** Parkinson **6.** Jack Jones **7.** 'Everyone we meet' **8.** The Brit Pop Awards **9.** Julie Felix **10.** *The Ed Sullivan Show.* **11.** Raw Sex **12.** The *Andy Williams Show* **13.** Rock Follies **14.** Whispering **15.** *Six Five Special!* **16.** The 80's hit was released by Kim Wilde whose father, Marti, co-presented *Oh Boy!* **17.** *The Hot Shoe Show* **18.** *My Kind of People.* **19.** The theme to *Hazell* **20.** 1990 **21.** *My Music* **22.** *Song By Song* **23.** Harry Secombe **24.** Petula Clark **25.** At The Palace **26.** Roy Hudd **27.** *Hotel Babylon.* **28.** Andrew and Julian Lloyd Webber **29.** Roger Daltry **30.** Apple Films.

## QUIZ 54 Music & Variety 4

LEVEL 3

**Answers: see Quiz 53, page 581**

1. Which young female violinist featured on *Top Of The Pops?*
2. Which U.S. TV cop sung on *Top Of The Pops* apart from Kojak?
3. What was the mouse puppet on *Sunday Night at the London Palladium* called?
4. Which singer hosted a show where fans could ring and request songs to be sung?
5. On whose chat show did Sammy Cahn accompany the host?
6. Who sang the theme to *Love Boat?*
7. Who did the Monkees get the funniest looks from?
8. Which music awards were co-hosted in 1989 by Sam Fox?
9. Name the female folk singer on *The Frost Report.*
10. Which US variety show was originally called *The Toast of the Town?*
11. Roland Rivron was one half of which comic musical duo?
12. Donny Osmond made his first regular TV appearances on which show?
13. In which series did we first meet *The Little Ladies?*
14. What is the nickname of the former *Whistle Test* presenter, Bob Harris?
15. On which show did Adam Faith make his TV debut?
16. What is the connection between the 80s hit *Kids In America* and the 50s show *Oh Boy!?*
17. Wayne Sleep starred opposite Bonnie Langford in which TV dance show?
18. Which talent spotting show was hosted by Michael Barrymore?
19. Maggie Bell hit the charts with which detective theme?
20. Pavarotti sang the theme for the World Cup Finals in which year?
21. Steve Race hosted which music programme?
22. Julia McKenzie starred as a singer in which musical programme?
23. Which musical Mr Pickwick went on to receive a Knighthood?
24. Who was the star of the 50's series Pet's Parlour?
25. TV comics Harry H Corbett and Wilfrid Brambell met royalty where according to their chart hit?
26. Who explored *Halls of Fame?*
27. Which music show did Dani Behr present after *The Word?*
28. Who composed the music for the *South Bank Show?*
29. Which pop star took the role of McHeath in *The Beggar's Opera* on TV?
30. The Beatles TV film *Magical Mystery Tour* was made by which film company?

ANSWERS

### Who's Who 2 (see Quiz 53)

**1.** Nephew. **2.** Warwick. **3.** Joan Rivers. **4.** Golightly. **5.** Jonathan Dimbleby. **6.** Gloria Hunniford. **7.** Oxford United. **8.** Melvyn Bragg. **9.** Paul Daniels and Debbie McGee. **10.** Teacher. **11.** Carol Smillie. **12.** Ringmaster. **13.** Richard Stilgoe. **14.** Barrister. **15.** Richard Curtis. **16.** Mark Little. **17.** Michael Barrymore. **18.** Christopher Biggins. **19.** Paula Hamilton. **20.** Susan Hampshire. **21.** Loyd Grossman. **22.** Mariella Frostrup. **23.** David Frost. **24.** Tara Fitzgerald. **25.** Ben Elton. **26.** Lynsey de Paul. **27.** Charles Dance. **28.** Timothy Dalton. **29.** *The Big Breakfast.* **30.** Melvyn Bragg.

## QUIZ 55 Pot Luck 12

LEVEL 3

**Answers: see Quiz 56, page 584**

1. Joanna Lumley was awarded an honorary doctorate of which university?
2. Where did the live, real-time Christine Kochanski join the *Red Dwarf* team from?
3. What is John Cleese's real name?
4. Which ex *Gladiators* presenter is a karate black belt?
5. Which soccer side does actor John Alderton support?
6. Which luxury did Helen Mirren choose on *Desert Island Discs*?
7. What was the name of William Shatner's Doberman Pinscher dog?
8. What was the female resistance worker's name in *'Allo 'Allo*?
9. Who played the female bank manager in *Joint Account*?
10. What was the TV version of *The Clitheroe Kid* called?
11. Who was Gail Emory's cousin in *American Gothic*?
12. In which series is the local paper *The Lochdubh Listener*?
13. Which service did Anthea Turner work for before she found media fame?
14. Who presented the new *Candid Camera*?
15. Which character in *Reckless* used a dog sled team in his attempt to return to his ex-wife to tell her she was making a mistake about remarrying?
16. Which star of a 70s adventure Sci-Fi series was a former Miss America?
17. In which year was TV naturalist Sir David Attenborough awarded his knighthood?
18. On *That's Life*, what was the name of the little old lady who became an overnight star after being interviewed in the street?
19. What was the name of the office boy in *The Slap Maxwell Story*?
20. Who played George Drummond in *The Drummonds*?
21. Who kept the score on *Bullseye*?
22. Which entertainer died on the same day in 1990 as Muppet creator Jim Henson?
23. Harry Mudd was a character in which sci-fi series?
24. In *This Is David Lauder*, what was Lauder's job?
25. What was the name of the series in which Tony Wilkinson experienced living rough?
26. Sally Jones was the sports presenter on which breakfast programme?
27. Who welcomed viewers on the opening night of BBC 2?
28. What was *Hooperman's* first name?
29. What did Rollo and Bedrock do for a living?
30. Sheila Gish played which characters in *Small World*?

ANSWERS

**Comedy 10 (see Quiz 56)**

**1.** Leonard Rossiter. **2.** She plays the piano. **3.** The second series. **4.** An eye doctor. **5.** Galton and Simpson. **6.** Sue Pollard. **7.** A poet. **8.** Cannon and Ball. **9.** A chauffeur. **10.** Sgt Bilko. **11.** *'Allo, 'Allo.* **12.** Dubois (Benson was his first name). **13.** Paul Shane. **14.** Leslie Ash. **15.** *Cuckoo Waltz.* **16.** Warden Hedges. **17.** Marigold. **18.** Lenny Henry. **19.** Harrap. **20.** Dudley Moore. **21.** *Chalk and Cheese.* **22.** Carla's. **23.** Selling used cars. **24.** *M*A*S*H.* **25.** Stan Butler. **26.** Harry H Corbett. **27.** Bernard Hedges. **28.** Malcolm. **29.** Eli. **30.** *Take Three Girls.*

## QUIZ 56 Comedy 10

LEVEL 3

**Answers: see Quiz 55, page 583**

1. Who played the title role in *Tripper's Day*?
2. What does Victoria Wood have in common with Les Dawson apart from being a comic?
3. For which series of *Blackadder* did Ben Elton first become a co-writer?
4. What was Ralph Malph studying to be in *Happy Days*?
5. Which duo wrote the scripts for *Steptoe and Son*?
6. Which *Hi De Hi!* star used to be in a group called Midnight News?
7. What was Jonathan Morris's character in *Bread* aspiring to be?
8. Who were originally called the Harper Brothers?
9. What did Jim Davidson play in *Home James*?
10. The character Joan Hogan was whose girlfriend?
11. In which comedy did Colonel von Klinkerhoffen appear?
12. What was the surname of the Tate's butler in *Soap*?
13. Which singing comedy star appeared as an impresario in *Very Big Very Soon*?
14. Which star of a sitcom quartet was a backing singer for Smiley & Co?
15. In which ITV comedy did the married characters Chris and Fliss Hawthorne feature?
16. Who nicknamed Captain Mainwaring Napoleon?
17. What was Winston's nickname in *In Sickness And In Health*?
18. Who created the DJ Delbert Wilkins?
19. What is the surname of dad and daughter Simon and Samantha, in *Me and My Girl*?
20. Who is taller Ronnie Corbett or Dudley Moore?
21. In which ITV comedy did Michael Crawford play a cockney in a gentrified street?
22. Whose ex-husband is called Nick Tortelli in *Cheers*?
23. To what end did Roy Kinnear use his power in *The Clairvoyant*?
24. This classic comedy was based on the novel by Dr Richard Hornberger. What is it?
25. What was the name of Reg Varney's character in *On The Buses*?
26. Who starred in *Mr 'Aitch*?
27. What was the name of John Alderton's teacher character in *Please Sir*?
28. What is Mrs Merton's 'son' called?
29. What was the name of Jimmy Jewel's character opposite Hilda Baker's Nellie Pledge?
30. In 1969 actresses Liza, Angela and Susan were the trio of stars in which series?

ANSWERS

### Pot Luck 12 (see Quiz 55)

**1.** Kent. **2.** Parallel dimension. **3.** John Cleese. **4.** John Fashanu. **5.** Hull City. **6.** Silk Underwear. **7.** Kirk. **8.** Michelle. **9.** Hannah Gordon. **10.** *Just Jimmy*. **11.** Caleb Temple. **12.** *Hamish MacBeth*. **13.** AA. **14.** Bob Monkhouse. **15.** Richard Crane. **16.** Lynda Carter (*Wonder Woman*). **17.** 1985. **18.** Annie. **19.** Charlie. **20.** Richard Pasco. **21.** Tony Green. **22.** Sammy Davis Jr. **23.** *Star Trek*. **24.** Investigative reporter. **25.** *Down And Out*. **26.** *BBC Breakfast Time*. **27.** Denis Touhy. **28.** Harry. **29.** They were truckers. **30.** Fulvia and Desiree Zapp.

## QUIZ 57 Soaps 8

LEVEL 3

**Answers: see Quiz 58, page 586**

1. What relation in *Neighbours* was Harold Bishop to Joe Mangel?
2. Who was Joe Mangel's niece, a secretary, in *Neighbours*?
3. Who did Den catch with Angie in their sitting room in *Eastenders*?
4. Who did Percy Sugden lock in Hilda Ogden's shed in *Coronation Street*?
5. Which *Coronation Street* star recorded Where Will You Be?
6. Who left Brookside Close for a job in Wolverhampton?
7. In *Eastenders* while working at The Meal Machine who did Hattie fall in love with?
8. Which luxury did Leslie Grantham, formerly Dirty Den, choose on *Desert Island Discs*?
9. Who opened a hair salon in Rosamund Street and employed Elsie Tanner?
10. Which two different characters has Beverley Callard played in *Coronation Street*?
11. In *Emmerdale* which Esholt inn was originally used as *The Woolpack*?
12. Which councillor stopped the tarmacking of *Coronation Street*?
13. Which happened first, JR's shooting or Meg Richardson leaving *Crossroads*?
14. Who helped the Street's Emily in Gamma Garments to take care of the Gamma Man?
15. Who was the first soap star to receive an honour from the Queen?
16. In which series was soap's first test tube baby?
17. Who took Deirdre in with Tracy after she was made homeless?
18. Which BBC boss was responsible for introducing *Eastenders*?
19. Which famous soap actress was Cherie Booth's step mother?
20. How is actress Sylvia Butterfield better known?
21. What was the name of the dog saved by the Robinson's after an accident in *Neighbours*?
22. Who first persuaded Helen in *Neighbours* to exhibit her paintings?
23. In *Dynasty* who kidnapped Fallon's child?
24. In *Coronation Street* who punched Billy Walker on the nose when he was fired?
25. In *Dallas* what was Stephen Farlowe's nickname?
26. Who died from a fall from Alexis's balcony in *Dynasty*?
27. What was the name of Den Watt's girlfriend in *Eastenders* played by Jane How?
28. Which ex-*Eastender* was lead singer with Milan?
29. In *Brookside* who lived with the Jackson's before moving in with Pat and Sandra?
30. Who was Blake Carrington's half sister in The Colbys?

ANSWERS

### Children's TV 6 (see Quiz 58)

**1.** Billy Bean. **2.** Janet Waldo. **3.** A sheep. **4.** Barney. **5.** "King of the wild frontier". **6.** *The Partridge Family*. **7.** His brother's waistcoat. **8.** Tony Robinson. **9.** Leonard Rossiter. **10.** Roger de Courcey (of Nooky Bear fame). **11.** Keith Harris. **12.** John and Sue. **13.** *The O Zone*. **14.** Geri Halliwell. **15.** *The Flintstones*. **16.** Morocco Mole. **17.** Go-karts. **18.** Motley Hall. **19.** *Grizly Adams*. **20.** *Today Is Saurday Wear A Smile*. **21.** Jim Henson and Frank Oz. **22.** Pink. **23.** 1976. **24.** A flower. **25.** Cookery. **26.** *Crackerjack*. **27.** Eric Thompson. **28.** Frank Gorshin. **29.** Basil Brush. **30.** *Do Not Adjust Your Set*.

## QUIZ 58 Children's TV 6

LEVEL 3

**Answers: see Quiz 57, page 585**

1. Which fictional character invented the "cartoonerator"?
2. Who provides the voice for Penelope Pitstop?
3. What kind of animal was Nobby who introduced *Ghost Train*?
4. Which boy found *Stig of the Dump*?
5. Of what was Davy Crockett the king, according to his theme song?
6. Which family had a dog called Simon?
7. What did the *Lone Ranger* make his mask from?
8. Who presented *Stay Tooned*?
9. Who narrated *The Perishers*?
10. Who owned a racehorse called Nooky?
11. Who hosted *Cuddles and Co*?
12. Who were the two young friends of *Worzel Gummidge*?
13. What was the first children's show Zoe Ball presented on terrestrial TV?
14. Which Spice Girl turned down the offer of hosting a cable children's show before finding fame with the band?
15. In which series did Ed Sullystone make appearances?
16. What was the name of *Secret Squirrel*'s partner?
17. Which means of transport featured in the children's game show, *Fun House*?
18. As a ghost where did Arthur English live?
19. Whose friends were Mad Jack and Nakuma?
20. What did *Tiswas* stand for?
21. Who were the two creators of the *Muppets*?
22. What colour was *Rainbow*'s George?
23. In which year was the *Multi-coloured Swap Shop* first broadcast?
24. What does Ermintrude have in her mouth?
25. What type of spot did Emma Forbes first present on *Going Live!*?
26. Pip Hinton could be seen singing on which Friday children's show?
27. Who first narrated *The Magic Roundabout*?
28. Who played The Riddler in *Batman*?
29. Which puppet was said to be modelled on comic actor Terry-Thomas?
30. David Jason helped present which 1960s children's show?

ANSWERS

**Soaps 8 (see Quiz 57)**

**1.** Father in law. **2.** Jane Harris. **3.** Andy O'Brien. **4.** The men from the water board. **5.** Sue Nicholls (Audrey Roberts). **6.** Barry Grant. **7.** Steve Elliot. **8.** Metal detecter. **9.** Alan Howard. **10.** Liz McDonald and June Dewhurst. **11.** The Commercial Inn. **12.** Len Fairclough. **13.** JR's shooting. **14.** Dennis Tanner. **15.** Violet Carson OBE. **16.** *Crossroads*. **17.** Emily Bishop. **18.** Michael Grade. **19.** Pat Phoenix. **20.** Liz Dawn (Vera in *Coronation Street*). **21.** Patch. **22.** Des Clarke. **23.** Alfred Grimes. **24.** Fred Gee. **25.** Dusty. **26.** Mark Jennings. **27.** Jan. **28.** Martine McCutcheon. **29.** Terry Sullivan. **30.** Dominique Devereaux.

## QUIZ 59 Pot Luck 13

LEVEL 3

**Answers: see Quiz 60, page 588**

1. Which programme would you connect with Jonathan Routh?
2. How is TV actor Donald Wayne better known?
3. Which horror actor's voice is heard on Michael Jackson's *Thriller*?
4. How many words were there according to the name of the game show hosted by Ray Allan?
5. Who briefly replaced Paul Merton on *Have I Got News For You*?
6. How is Geoffrey David Nugent better known?
7. Who played Matlock?
8. Hugh Laurie of Jeeves and Wooster fame won an Oxbridge blue for which sport?
9. Name the two stars of *Executive Stress*?
10. Where in France did Penny reunite with Vince in *Just Good Friends*?
11. Which luxury did Bob Monkhouse choose on Desert Island Discs?
12. What does 'breaking the fourth wall' mean in TV terms?
13. In which series did Richard Eden play a unconventional lawman?
14. Which soap powder did the star of *Cracker* advertise?
15. Which spoof police series features a Captain Trunk?
16. Which show featured the Whirly Wheeler with tragic consequences?
17. Where is Chris Evans' home town?
18. Who did *The Equalizer* work for?
19. Who shot to fame after the 1994 Eurovision Song Contest?
20. What is the first round on *A Question Of Sport*?
21. Who tried to teach Pauline Quirke and Linda Robson to sing in *Jobs For the Girls*?
22. What breed of dog was companion to the detective Cluff?
23. Which TV company produced *First Tuesday*?
24. Which was the first production company to produce *The Big Breakfast*?
25. Who presented Channel 4's religious series *Canterbury Tales*?
26. Who is the doctor in *Hamish MacBeth*?
27. Which humorist's autobiography was called *Unreliable Memoirs*?
28. Who played Solly in *It Ain't Half Hot Mum*?
29. In *GBH*, what did GBH stand for?
30. Which soccer side does Nigel Havers of *Dangerfield* support?

ANSWERS

### Drama 8 (see Quiz 60)

**1.** M M Kayes. **2.** *The Onedin Line.* **3.** Blair Brown. **4.** *The Jewel In The Crown.* **5.** *The Love Boat.* **6.** Robert Shaw. **7.** *Shadowlands.* **8.** Kizzy. **9.** Texas. **10.** Toranaga and Ishido. **11.** Omar Sharif. **12.** How *Green Was My Valley.* **13.** Ian Richardson. **14.** A psychiatrist. **15.** *Gunsmoke.* **16.** Dr. John McUre. **17.** *Cat On A Hot Tin Roof.* **18.** Anthony Valentine. **19.** Alan Bates. **20.** Dennis Potter. **21.** *The Country Diary of an Edwardian Lady.* **22.** Willy. **23.** *Z-Cars.* **24.** Francesca Annis. **25.** *Blind Justice.* **26.** *Gunsmoke.* **27.** A tennis coach. **28.** Sean Bean. **29.** Ossie Whitworth. **30.** *War And Remembrance.*

# QUIZ 60 Drama 8

LEVEL 3

**Answers: see Quiz 59, page 587**

1. *The Far Pavilions* was based on whose novel?
2. In which series did the ship *Charlotte Rhodes* feature?
3. Who played Jacqueline Kennedy opposite Martin Sheen's JFK?
4. In which series did the policeman Merrick appear?
5. How was the Pacific Princess otherwise known?
6. Which Jaws star appeared in *Buccaneers*?
7. In which drama did Joss Ackland portray C S Lewis?
8. Who was Chicken George's mother in *Roots*?
9. In which state did *Rawhide* commence the trail?
10. Who were the two Japanese rivals in *Shogun*?
11. In *Harem*, who starred as a Sultan?
12. Stanley Baker and Sian Phillips starred together in which Welsh drama?
13. Who played Nehru in *Mountbatten, The Last Viceroy*?
14. What was Herbert Lom's profession in *The Human Jungle*?
15. The Longbranch Saloon featured in which Western?
16. Who created *Cardiac Arrest*?
17. Which television version of a Tennessee Williams play did Robert Wagner and Natalie Wood appear in?
18. Which star of Callan appeared in *Colditz* as a German officer?
19. Which actor won a BAFTA for *An Englishman Abroad* in 1982?
20. Who wrote *Lipstick On Your Collar*?
21. What was the series based on the life of Edith Holden?
22. Which character did Peter Lupus play in *Mission Impossible*?
23. In which 60s police series was there a sergeant named Twentyman?
24. Who played Madame Bovary in the 70s drama series?
25. In which drama series did Jane Lapoitaire portray a barrister?
26. In which Western did the feisty Kitty Russell appear?
27. What did Bill Cosby pretend to be in *I Spy*?
28. Who played Mellors to Joely Richardson's *Lady Chatterley*?
29. What was the name of the vicar played by Christopher Biggins play in *Poldark*?
30. What was the sequel to *Winds Of War*?

ANSWERS

## Pot Luck 13 (see Quiz 59)

**1.** *Candid Camera.* **2.** Don Johnson. **3.** Vincent Price. **4.** *Three Little Words.* **5.** Eddie Izzard. **6.** Spider. **7.** Andy Griffith. **8.** Rowing. **9.** Peter Bowles and Penelope Keith. **10.** At the top of the Eiffel Tower. **11.** Picture of Marilyn Monroe. **12.** Character talking to viewers in an aside. **13.** *Robocop.* **14.** Persil. **15.** *Sledgehammer.* **16.** *The Late Late Breakfast Show.* **17.** Warrington. **18.** The Organised Task Force. **19.** Michael Flatley (Riverdance). **20.** The picture board. **21.** Lesley Garrett. **22.** A collie. **23.** Yorkshire TV. **24.** Planet 24. **25.** Ian Hislop. **26.** Dr Brown. **27.** Clive James. **28.** George Layton. **29.** Great British Holiday. **30.** Ipswich Town.

## QUIZ 61 Comedy 11

LEVEL 3

**Answers: see Quiz 62, page 590**

1. In which comedy would you hear the words "I hate you Butler!"?
2. Who presented *Q5* on the BBC?
3. On which series did the *Monty Python* team first appear together?
4. Which *Likely Lad* starred in *Dear Mother... Love Albert*?
5. Who played Jeeves opposite Ian Carmichael's Wooster in 1985?
6. Which *Eastender* played the original old moo in *Till Death Us Do Part*?
7. Which sitcom star wrote a biography of John LeMesurier?
8. On which show did Caroline Aherne develop her Mrs Merton character on TV?
9. The comedy *Please Sir* was inspired by which 60's British film?
10. Which comic starred in *No, That's Me Over Here*?
11. In which series did Donald Sinden and Leslie Phillips play vicars?
12. Who was Thora Hird's husband in *Meet The Wife*?
13. What were the full names of *The Likely Lads*?
14. Which film was based on *The Army Game*?
15. What did Richard Branson do to show his displeasure when interviewed by Clive Anderson?
16. Who starred in Up the Elephant and Round the Castle?
17. Bernard Manning hosted which social club on TV?
18. Who played Mike Channel on KYTV?
19. Who created Captain Kremmen?
20. In *Last Of The Summer Wine* which character claimed to have been a corporal in the army?
21. Who went from *Are You Being Served* to *Take A Letter Mr Jones*?
22. Which show featured Down Your Doorstep?
23. Where was Ain't Misbehavin' set?
24. What occupation did Anton Rodgers have in *May To December*?
25. Who played Mavis to Les Dennis' Vera?
26. What was the name of the heavy metal band created by *The Comic Strip*?
27. What did Ralph Bates' character do for a living in *Dear John*?
28. Who played *The Climber*, the bakery worker with a high IQ?
29. Which play did *The Dustbinmen* develop from?
30. What did Liza Goddard's character do for a living in *Roll Over Beethoven*?

ANSWERS

### News 4 (see Quiz 62)

**1.** Magnus Magnusson. **2.** The Queen Mother. **3.** Prince Edward. **4.** Birth control. **5.** Powergen. **6.** 1989. **7.** Aall presented *Weekend World.* **8.** A Victorian kitchen garden **9.** Norman Tebbit. **10.** Raising of Henry VIII's flagship, The Mary Rose. **11.** Malcolm Muggeridge. **12.** Sir David Attenborough. **13.** A reporter. **14.** Clive James. **15.** Barnsley. **16.** James Callaghan. **17.** Alastair Burnett. **18.** Sibelius' Karelia Suite. **19.** Harold Wilson. **20.** Panorama. **21.** Elton John. **22.** *Kilroy.* **23.** Vincent Hanna. **24.** *Down Your Way.* **25.** Russell Harty. **26.** Mike Barratt. **27.** Desmond Morris and Sarah Kennedy. **28.** *Up A Gum Tree.* **29.** Buckingham Palace. **30.** *Just A Nimmo.*

## QUIZ 62 News 4

LEVEL 3

**Answers: see Quiz 61, page 589**

1. Who charted the history of *The Viking*?
2. The horse racing documentary *Royal Champion* featured which royal?
3. Who presented *The Duke's Award*?
4. What was the subject of the programme *In The Club*?
5. Who sponsors the ITV Weather nationally?
6. In which year was Prime Minister's Question Time first televised?
7. What have Peter Jay, Brian Walden and Matthew Parris got in common as far as television is concerned?
8. What did gardener Harry Dodson restore on TV?
9. Which other politician joined Austin Mitchell in the presentation of a Sky chat show?
10. Why was there much TV attention in the Solent in October 1982?
11. Who was known as St. Mugg?
12. *Lost Worlds, Vanished Lives* was presented by who for the BBC?
13. What did *Man Of The World* do for a living?
14. Who sent postcards from Rio and Chicago?
15. From which town does Michael Parkinson originate?
16. Political interviewer Peter Jay is the son-in-law of which former PM?
17. Who retired from reading the *News At Ten* in 1991?
18. Which music accompanied This Week?
19. Who presented *A Prime Minister On Prime Ministers*?
20. Which current affairs programme was described as The Window On The World?
21. Who was the very first guest on *Wogan*?
22. What did *Day To Day* change its name to?
23. Which political reporter guested in *Blackadder*?
24. How was *Home Town* known on the radio?
25. Who took in a *Grand Tour* for his last TV series?
26. Who was the first presenter of *Nationwide*?
27. Who were the presenters of ITV's *Animal Roadshow*?
28. What kind of tree did David Bellamy go up?
29. The interior of which London building was first televised in 1969?
30. What was the name of Derek Nimmo's chat show?

ANSWERS

**Comedy 11 (see Quiz 61)**

**1.** *On The Buses* **2.** Spike Milligan. **3.** *The Frost Report.* **4.** Rodney Bewes. **5.** Dennis Price. **6.** Gretchen Franklin. **7.** Derek Nimmo. **8.** *The Dead Good Show.* **9.** *To Sir With Love.* **10.** Ronnie Corbett. **11.** *Our Man At St Mark's.* **12.** Freddie Frinton. **13.** Terry Collier and Bob Ferris. **14.** *I Only Arsked.* **15.** Threw water over him. **16.** Jim Davidson. **17.** *The Wheeltappers And Shunters Social Club.* **18.** Angus Deayton. **19.** Kenny Everett. **20.** Foggie. **21.** John Inman. **22.** *The Big Breakfast.* **23.** Harrogate. **24.** A solicitor. **25.** Dustin Gee. **26.** Bad News. **27.** A teacher. **28.** Robin Nedwell. **29.** There's a hole in your dustbin Delilah. **30.** Music teacher.

## QUIZ 63 Soaps 9

LEVEL 3

**Answers: see Quiz 64, page 592**

1. Where did Tracy Hobbs work at *Crossroads*?
2. Who abducted Vicky Fowler in *Eastenders*?
3. In *Peyton Place* who died of a cerebral haemorrhage after a fight with Rodney Harrington?
4. Which Neighbours star recorded Don't It Make You Feel Good?
5. Who gave Derek Wilton a lift back from a coach trip to London in *Coronation Street*?
6. Which soap star advertised Cinzano with Leonard Rossiter?
7. Which character appeared in the first scene of the first episode of *Coronation Street*?
8. What was Ethel's middle name in *Eastenders*?
9. What was the name of the nightclub where Alan McKenna saw Fiona sing?
10. Who died in *Crossroads* just before she was due to marry Benny?
11. Who shared a flat above the corner shop with Doreen Lostock in *Coronation Street*?
12. Who was Todd Fisher's mother in *Sons and Daughters*?
13. Who was Blake's best man at his wedding to Alexis in *Dynasty*?
14. In *Eastenders* what was Debbie Bates' former husband's name?
15. In *Neighbours* whose part has been played by three different actresses, including Sasha Close?
16. Who was Rita Sullivan's first husband in *Coronation Street*?
17. Who in *Dallas* left South Fork when Julie Grey died?
18. What was the date of the *Crosssroads* fire?
19. What is Tracy Barlow's middle name?
20. Who was Dot Cotton's grandson in *Eastenders*?
21. Which festival was Emmerdale Farm part of in 1979?
22. What was the name of Ian Beale's loan business in *Eastenders*?
23. In whose house was Lynne Johnston found murdered in *Coronation Street*?
24. Who in the *Colbys* married Prince Michael of Moldavia?
25. Which doctor fell in love with Krystle Carrington in *Dynasty*?
26. Who in *Coronation Street* moved into Len Fairclough's house?
27. Who was Debbie Wilkins' partner in *Eastenders*?
28. Who was shot at Ewing Oil in 1984 by Katherine Wentworth?
29. Which ex-Eastender began her career as a backing singer with Mari Wilson?
30. In *Crossroads* who ran a travel agents after their marriage?

ANSWERS

### Pot Luck 14 (see Quiz 64)

**1.** Barnet. **2.** Beer and cigarette machine. **3.** Anthea Turner **4.** Richard Jordan. **5.** Gloria Hunniford. **6.** Liz Hurley. **7.** Delta City. **8.** John Hurt. **9.** John Hurt. **10.** P.D.James. **11.** Maurice. **12.** Ernestine and Gwendolyn. **13.** *The Hitch Hiker's Guide To The Galaxy.* **14.** Adam Dalgleish. **15.** Lisa Bonet. **16.** Noel Dyson. **17.** Barry Bostwick. **18.** Ray MacAnally. **19.** Colin Welland. **20.** Ivy Unsworth. **21.** Alice. **22.** Pat Coombs. **23.** Colonel Marea. **24.** *Favourite Things.* **25.** The Gestapo. **26.** Betty. **27.** John Slater. **28.** *The Defenders.* **29.** *City Lights.* **30.** Colin Baker.

## QUIZ 64 Pot Luck 14

LEVEL 3

**Answers: see Quiz 63, page 591**

1. Which soccer side does John Motson support?
2. Which luxury did Harry Enfield choose on *Desert Island Discs*?
3. Who did Eamonn Holmes nickname Miss Tippy Toes?
4. Who played Harley Gage in *The Equalizer*?
5. Which TV presenter married hairdresser Stephen Way in 1998?
6. Who made her TV debut as Dennis Potter's Christabel?
7. In which city is *Robocop* set?
8. Which 'Caligula' was also 'Quentin Crisp'?
9. Which male has worn the most make up on *They Think It's All Over*?
10. Which former BBC Governor received a peerage in 1991 and writes detective novels?
11. Who owns KBHR , the radio station, in *Northern Exposure*?
12. What were the first names of The Snoop Sisters?
13. Magrathea featured in which series?
14. Who investigated in the TV series *Cover Her Face*?
15. Who plays Denise in *The Cosby Show*?
16. Who played the wife of Potter?
17. In *George Washington*, who played the title role?
18. Who played chief suspect Sir William Gull in *Jack The Ripper*?
19. Who played table top games in *Late Night Line Up*?
20. Who was Thora Hird's character in *In Loving Memory*?
21. Who worked as a waitress at Mel's Diner?
22. Who starred with Peggy Mount in *You're Only Young Twice*?
23. Which Scotland Yard cop was played by Boris Karloff?
24. What was the title of the TV equivalent of *Desert Island Discs*?
25. Robert Hardy played a member of what in *Jenny's War*?
26. Who served the tea at Emu's Broadcasting Company?
27. Which John assisted Pinky and Perky?
28. E.G. Marshall was a regular in which 60's American courtroom series?
29. The character Willie Melvin featured in which comedy?
30. Which Dr. Who appeared in *War and Peace*?

ANSWERS

**Soaps 9 (see Quiz 63)**

**1.** The Leisure Centre. **2.** Audrey Whittingham. **3.** Joe Chernak. **4.** Stefan dennis (Paul Robinson). **5.** Norris Cole. **6.** Joan Collins. **7.** Florrie Lindley. **8.** Mae. **9.** Shirelle's. **10.** Maureen Flynn. **11.** Sheila Birtles. **12.** Irene. **13.** Cecil Colby. **14.** Liam Tyler. **15.** Lucy Robinson. **16.** Harry Bates. **17.** Pam Ewing. **18.** November 5th. **19.** Lynette. **20.** Ashley. **21.** Ilkley Literature Festival. **22.** Flying Saucer. **23.** Len Fairclough's. **24.** Amanda. **25.** Nick Toscanni. **26.** Chalkey Whiteley. **27.** Andy O'Brien. **28.** Michelle Collins. **29.** Celestine. **30.** Andy and Ruth.

## QUIZ 65 Sci - Fi 3

LEVEL 3

**Answers: see Quiz 66, page 594**

**1.** What was the name of Spock's father?
**2.** Which actress starred as *Alice In Wonderland* and also played a *Dr Who* companion?
**3.** Who plays Jadsir Dax?
**4.** Who created – and wrote much of – *Babylon 5*?
**5.** Who was the Bionic Man's boss?
**6.** Name the first actress to play Catwoman on TV?
**7.** Which sixties sci-fi series featured Dr Peter Brady?
**8.** Which celebrated *X-Files* episode portrayed Mulder and Scully as Men In Black?
**9.** What is the name of William Shatner's character in *TekWar*?
**10.** Which actor plays *Voyager*'s hologrammatic doctor?
**11.** What stigma does *Space: Above and Beyond*'s Commander McQueen labour under?
**12.** Who plays the professor in *Sliders*?
**13.** What is *Robocop*'s name?
**14.** What was Dayna's speciality in *Blake's 7*?
**15.** Where did Marshall Teller live?
**16.** What is required to regenerate otherwise dead vampires in *Ultraviolet*?
**17.** Who played Toby in *Doomwatch*?
**18.** Where was the first Floating Market held in *Neverwhere*?
**19.** Which actor led the fight against the invaders in *The War of the Worlds* TV series?
**20.** In which season did Kryten join the regulars on *Red Dwarf*?
**21.** In *The Tripods*, how was the practice of implanting mind control devices known?
**22.** What make of car did *Automan* drive?
**23.** What type of bomb was at the center of the crisis in *Whoops! Apocalypse*?
**24.** How many adventures did *Sapphire & Steel* have?
**25.** Who was the creator of *The Incredible Hulk*?
**26.** Who was the producer of *Buck Rogers in the 25th Century*?
**27.** Who played Tasha Yar?
**28.** What was the weak spot in KITT's protective bodywork?
**29.** When was *1990*, starring Edward Woodward, broadcast?
**30.** Who played *Max Headroom*?

ANSWERS

### Comedy 12 (see Quiz 66)

**1.** Skullion. **2.** Jan Francis. **3.** Chris Langham. **4.** The Queen Mother. **5.** Gowan. **6.** Alan B'Stard. **7.** George Layton. **8.** Liza Goddard. **9.** Sherman **10.** Margaret Thatcher. **11.** Christopher Beeny. **12.** Arthur Lowe. **13.** *Citizen Smith.* **14.** Alan Alda. **15.** Roper. **16.** Arthur Mullard and Queenie Watts. **17.** Selwyn Froggitt. **18.** Frances de la Tour. **19.** Ellie May. **20** Tony Hancock. **21.** *Rhoda.* **22.** Alexei Sayle. **23.** Tommy Cooper. **24.** *Taxi.* **25.** Colonel Hall. **26.** Freddie Davis. **27.** Sonny, Shirley & Benjamin. **28.** *All In Good Faith.* **29.** Larry Grayson. **30.** Jenny.

## QUIZ 66 Comedy 12

LEVEL 3

**Answers: see Quiz 65, page 593**

1. Who tried to remove inflated condoms from the college courtyard in *Porterhouse Blue*?
2. Denis Waterman starred opposite who in *Stay Lucky*?
3. In the *Not The Nine O'Clock News* team who did Griff Rhys Jones replace?
4. Which royal did Beryl Reid provide the voice for on *Spitting Image*?
5. What was the surname of the Major in *Fawlty Towers*?
6. Which MP represented the fictitious constituency of Haltenprice?
7. Which *That's Life* contributor wrote Executive Stress?
8. Who played Dinsdale Landen's mistress in *Piggy In The Middle*?
9. In Fawlty Towers, what was Polly's surname?
10. Which real life PM made a guest appearance in a special edition of *Yes, Minister*?
11. Who played Thora Hird's nephew in *In Loving Memory*?
12. Who starred as *Potter*?
13. Who led the Tooting Popular Front?
14. Who won awards with *M*A*S*H* in the roles of director, writer and cast member?
15. What was *George and Mildred*'s surname?
16. Which Arthur and Queenie took the lead roles in *Yus My Dear*?
17. What was the surname of the character, Selwyn, played by Bill Maynard?
18. Who connects *Rising Damp* and *A Kind Of Living*?
19. Who was Grandma trying to find a mate for in the *Beverley Hillbillies*?
20. Who was *The Lad Himself*?
21. Which US female title character told us she was born in December of 1941 at the beginning of her show?
22. Who the sang the song *'Ello John, Got A New Motor*?
23. Who was Spike Milligan talking about when he described him as 'One of the greatest clowns the world has ever seen'?
24. In which BBC series did the character Elaine Nardo appear?
25. Who was the commander of Bilko's Fort Baxter?
26. Who was known as Mr Parrot Face?
27. What were the three children called in The Fosters?
28. In which series did Richard Briers play a vicar?
29. Who created Slack Alice?
30. Who was suffering *Life Without George*?

ANSWERS

**Sci-Fi 3 (see Quiz 65)**

**1.** Sarek. **2.** Deborah Watling. **3.** Terry Farrell. **4.** J Michael Straczynski. **5.** Oscar. **6.** Julie Newmar. **7.** *The Invisible Man.* **8.** Jose Chung's From Outer Space. **9.** Bascom. **10.** Robert Picardo. **11.** He was biogenetically engineered and tank-bred. **12.** John Rhys-Davies. **13.** Alex Murphy. **14.** Making and using weapons. **15.** *Eerie, Indiana.* **16.** The blood of a 'live' vampire. **17.** Robert Powell. **18.** Battersea Power Station. **19.** Jared Martin. **20.** 3. **21.** Capping. **22.** Lamborghini Countach. **23.** Quark bomb. **24.** Six. **25.** Stan Lee. **26.** Glen A Larson. **27.** Denise Crosby. **28.** There wasn't one. **29.** 1977-78. **30.** Matt Frewer.

## QUIZ 67 Drama 9

LEVEL 3

**Answers: see Quiz 68, page 596**

**1.** Who portrayed Rupert Murdoch in *Selling Hitler*?
**2.** *Connie* was set in which city?
**3.** In which Western did actor Raymond St Jacques appear?
**4.** Who wrote the Channel 4 series Melissa?
**5.** The controversial series *A Time to Dance* was written by whom?
**6.** What was Robson Greene's profession in *Reckless*?
**7.** Which Woman's Own fashion editor's first novel eventually became a Channel 4 blockbuster mini series?
**8.** Which character did Joss Ackland portray in *Shadowlands*?
**9.** Who played Albert Campion?
**10.** Which Eastender starred in *Winners and Losers*?
**11.** Which Swedish actress played Hedda Gabler in 1963 on TV?
**12.** For which production in 1976 did Mick Jackson win the BAFTA for direction?
**13.** In which drama series was there a nuclear plant named Northmoor?
**14.** Which part did John Cleese play in BBC TV's production of *Taming Of The Shrew*?
**15.** In which 1990s series is *Danse Macabre* the theme music?
**16.** Which John Osborne play did Jack Lemmon star in as Archie Rice?
**17.** What was Rosemary Leach's character in *Jewel In The Crown*?
**18.** Who played Campion's manservant?
**19.** Which crime series featured George Sewell and Deren Nesbitt?
**20.** Which series first starred Alfred Burke as a private detective?
**21.** Which series starred Kenneth Haigh as Joe Lampton?
**22.** Which 1971 series of plays featured greed, jealousy, and other sins?
**23.** Which family featured in *A Family At War*?
**24.** In which Jane Austen story did Ann Firbank play Ann Elliot?
**25.** Which American tough guy actor appeared with Liz Fraser in *Man And Boy*?
**26.** What was the 1970s political thriller series set in the future?
**27.** Name the 60s crime series featuring the Royal Canadian Mounted Police.
**28.** In *I, Claudius*, who starred as Caligula?
**29.** Where is the base of *The Flying Doctors*?
**30.** In which character Harold Pinter play, adapted for TV in 1987, did the character Godberg feature?

ANSWERS

### Children's TV 7 (see Quiz 68)

**1.** 'Turn off your television set and go do something more interesting instead'. **2.** Johnny Ball. **3.** *Billy Bunter.* **4.** Gaby Roslin. **5.** Anthea Turner. **6.** Rowlf the dog. **7.** *The Wombles.* **8.** Terry Wogan. **9.** *Andy Pandy* **10.** Four. **11.** *Rainbow.* **12.** *Billy Bunter.* **13.** Huw Wheldon. **14.** Ian Holm & Penelope Wilton. **15.** Susan Dey. **16.** John McGeorge and Larry Harmon. **17.** *Supergran.* **18.** Wrexham. **19.** Mickey Dolenz. **20.** Patricia Driscoll. **21.** *Hong Kong Phooey.* **22.** *The Fairly Pointless Show.* **23.** Moosylvania. **24.** Yellow & green. **25.** Robin Hood. **26.** Tomato ketchup. **27.** Dr Tiger Ninestein. **28.** With the Horn Resounding. **29.** Nero **30.** On the ceiling.

## QUIZ 68 Children's TV 7

LEVEL 3

**Answers: see Quiz 67, page 595**

**1.** What did the *Why Don't You?* team oddly ask you to do during their theme tune?
**2.** Who presented *Think of a Number?*
**3.** Which 50s show was shown twice daily – for children and later for adults?
**4.** Whose first TV job was presenting *Hippo* on Sky's Superchannel?
**5.** Who has hosted *Up2U, Blue Peter* and *Going Live?*
**6.** Who played piano on the *Muppet Show?*
**7.** With which children's characters is Mike Batt associated?
**8.** Who narrated *Stoppit and Tidyup?*
**9.** Which programme was the vety first on *Watch With Mother?*
**10.** How many Z's are there in *Sooty's* magic spell?
**11.** Which show did the actor who played Detective Constable Scatliff in *Z Cars* go on to present?
**12.** Who did Mr Quelch try to keep under control?
**13.** Who hosted the children's talent show, *All Your Own?*
**14.** Which husband and wife team played Pod and Homily in *The Borrowers?*
**15.** Which member of the *Partridge Family* appeared in *L.A. Law?*
**16.** Who provided the voices of the cartoon *Laurel and Hardy?*
**17.** Which heroine wore a Tam-O-Shanter?
**18.** Which soccer side did *Blue Peter's* Tim Vincent support?
**19.** Which former pop star produced *Metal Mickey?*
**20.** Which Patricia read the *Picture Book?*
**21.** Which super-sleuth masqueraded as a "mild-mannered janitor"?
**22.** What was the subtitle of the show *Do Not Adjust Your Set?*
**23.** Where did Bullwinkle live?
**24.** What colour are Big Ears' trousers?
**25.** Archie Duncan and Alexander Gauge played the friends of which 50s hero?
**26.** Which food accompaniment brought *Count Duckula* back to life?
**27.** Who was the leader of the *Terrahawks?*
**28.** How did *Eric The Viking* wake up the Gods?
**29.** What was the name of the caterpillar in *Dangermouse?*
**30.** In which unusual place did Jumblie sleep?

ANSWERS

### Drama 9 (see Quiz 67)

**1.** Barry Humphries. **2.** Nottingham. **3.** *Rawhide.* **4.** Alan Bleasdale. **5.** Melvyn Bragg. **6.** A surgeon. **7.** Barbara Taylor Bradford (A Woman of Substance). **8.** C. S. Lewis. **9.** Peter Davidson. **10.** Leslie Grantham. **11.** Ingrid Bergman. **12.** *Threads.* **13.** *Edge of Darkness.* **14.** Petruchio. **15.** *Jonathan Creek.* **16.** *The Entertainer.* **17.** Aunt Fenny. **18.** Brian Glover. **19.** *Special Branch.* **20.** *Public Eye.* **21.** *Life At The Top.* **22.** *The Ten Commandments.* **23.** The Ashtons. **24.** *Persuasion.* **25.** Telly Savalas. **26.** *The Guardians.* **27.** *R.C.M.P.* **28.** John Hurt. **29.** Coopers Crossing. **30.** *The Birthday Party.*

## QUIZ 69 Pot Luck 15

LEVEL 3

**Answers: see Quiz 70, page 598**

**1.** In *City Lights*, what did the lead character aspire to be?
**2.** Who starred opposite Ian Hendry in *The Lotus Eaters*?
**3.** Who wrote and directed *Jessie*?
**4.** Who made an *Enquiry into the Unknown*?
**5.** Which sci-fi series features Jump Gates?
**6.** What was Howard Rollins character in In *The Heat Of The Night*?
**7.** Where did Maddie Hayes meet her future husband?
**8.** Who was known as Soapy in *Rumpole of The Bailey*?
**9.** In whose show did PC Monkhouse appear?
**10.** Who did *Banacek* work for as a detective?
**11.** Who played the lead in *Testament of Youth*?
**12.** What was the name of the series featuring the female private eye, Claire McGarron?
**13.** Which soccer side does Michael Palin support?
**14.** On *The Fame Game*, who introduced new comedians?
**15.** Which TV personality started her career on Hong Kong radio?
**16.** Who was the central figure in *The Power Game*?
**17.** In which series did Gary Coleman play Arnold?
**18.** Who hosted *Here to Stay*?
**19.** What was the name of the dog in *The Thin Man*?
**20.** Who links *Angels One Five* and *The Importance of Being Earnest*?
**21.** In *The Mogul*, who played Driscoll?
**22.** Who starred in the comedy, *The Melting Pot*?
**23.** *Laverne and Shirley* were played by which actors?
**24.** Whose sister was Ophelia Frump?
**25.** Name the duo who presented *Something to Treasure*, a series about collecting?
**26.** What was Carlos first job in *Crossroads*?
**27.** Which bookmakers featured in the TV drama *Big Deal*?
**28.** Sue Ingle presented which wildlife series?
**29.** Who played Ali in *EastEnders*?
**30.** In *A Sharp Intake of Breath*, who starred opposite David Jason?

ANSWERS

### Soaps 10 (see Quiz 70)

**1.** Alan Partridge. **2.** Mrs. Bates. **3.** Joseph. **4.** Dany McCall (Owen). **5.** No. 23. **6.** Bill Kenwright. **7.** Lucy Ewing. **8.** Annie. **9.** Wendy Richard. **10.** Jenna. **11.** Paula Wilcox. **12.** Barry Grant. **13.** David Hunter. **14.** Kelvin Carpenter. **15.** Christopher. **16.** He was a diver. **17.** Sally Whittaker (Sally Webster). **18.** Ben Carrington. **19.** Gary Webster. **20.** Bill Waddington (Percy Sugden). **21.** Susan Tully. **22.** *Crossroads King's Oak.* **23.** Ray Krebbs. **24.** Billy. **25.** Albert Tatlock. **26.** Bobby Ewing. **27.** Sharon Watts. **28.** By decorating his office with toxic paint. **29.** X-23. **30.** Sonny.

## QUIZ 70 Soaps 10

LEVEL 3

**Answers: see Quiz 69, page 597**

1. Who first lived in the bungalow in *Brookside*?
2. Who did Ken Barlow have an affair with in 1972 in *Coronation Street*?
3. Who was Blake Carrington's manservant in *Dynasty*?
4. Which *Brookside* star recorded *Whose Love Is It Anyway*?
5. At what address was Reg Cox's body found in Albert Square in *Eastenders*?
6. Which ex *Coronation Street* actor turned impresario is a director of Everton FC?
7. Who modelled for Alex Ward in *Dallas*?
8. What was the name of Punk Mary's daughter in *Eastenders*?
9. Which EastEnder appeared on a Sammy Davis Jr Special with Mandy Rice-Davies?
10. In *Dallas* who was Lucas Wade's daughter?
11. Which star of *The Lovers* played Janice Langton in the Street?
12. In *Brookside* who lived in France with Lucy Collins?
13. In *Crossroads* who was Adam Chance's best man?
14. Who was Ian and Lofty's partner in their knitwear business in *Eastenders*?
15. What was the name of Harry and Concepta Hewitt's son in *Coronation Street*?
16. What did Shane Ramsey do in *Neighbours* before his accident?
17. Which soap actress who shares her first name with her character has a husband who wrote scripts for *Emmerdale*?
18. Who in *The Colbys* was Alexis' partner in South China Sea Oil?
19. Which star of *Minder* played Graham in *Eastenders*?
20. Which Street star made his first TV appearance from Olympia in 1946?
21. Which former soap star presented *The Saturday Banana* with Bill Oddie?
22. What did *Crossroads* change its name to in 1987?
23. Who did Paul Morgan defend in a manslaughter case in *Dallas*?
24. Which one of the Corkhills in *Brookside* was an electrician?
25. Who in *Coronation Street* had been awarded the Military Medal?
26. Whose attempted murder was Cliff Barnes arrested for in 1984 in *Dallas*?
27. Who ran a Kissogram business from the Queen Victoria in *Eastenders*?
28. How did Adam try to kill Jeff in *Dynasty*?
29. What was Burt's alien substitute's name in *Soap*?
30. Angie left Albert Square for Majorca with whom?

ANSWERS

### Pot Luck 15 (see Quiz 69)

**1.** A writer. **2.** Wanda Ventham. **3.** Bryan Forbes. **4.** Dr Jacob Bronowski. **5.** *Babylon 5*. **6.** Virgil Tibbs. **7.** On a train. **8.** Sam Ballard. **9.** *The Lenny Henry Show*. **10.** An insurance company. **11.** Cheryl Campbell. **12.** *Legwork*. **13.** Sheffield United. **14.** Stan Boardman. **15.** Anneka Rice. **16.** Sir John Wilder. **17.** *Diff'rent Strokes*. **18.** Robert Kilroy-Silk. **19.** Asta. **20.** Actor Michael Denison. **21.** Barry Foster. **22.** Frank Carson. **23.** Cindy Williams and Penny Marshall. **24.** Morticia Addams'. **25.** Su Evans and Geoffrey Bond. **26.** A chef. **27.** Gills. **28.** *Wildtrack*. **29.** Nejdet Salih. **30.** Jacqueline Clarke.

## QUIZ 71 Music & Variety 5

LEVEL 3

**Answers: see Quiz 72, page 600**

1. What is Johnny Logan's *Eurovision* claim to fame?
2. Which comic was the manager at Revolver?
3. Where was *Fame* set?
4. What was *Russ Abbot's Madhouse* previously called?
5. Which weatherman was a hit on *Top Of The Pops*?
6. Which song did French and Saunders sing with Bananarama?
7. Who presented *The Roxy*?
8. Paul McCartney recorded which soap theme?
9. According to the theme song what could you have a fish in *When The Boat Comes In*?
10. Which Jane portrayed Edith Piaf on TV?
11. Which pop show moved from Manchester to London?
12. Peter Cook sang a ballad about whom?
13. Who plays the piano on *Whose Line Is It Anyway*?
14. Ron Grainger composed the music for which popular BBC Sci-Fi series?
15. Who was the voice of Robin in the Muppet's hit song *Half Way Down The Stairs*?
16. In which decade did the *Grand Ole Oprey* first reach UK screens?
17. Who had a recording label called Rodent?
18. Which TV personalities/DJ's released their version of *It Takes Two, Baby*?
19. Who sang the *Postman Pat* theme song?
20. Which band first released *All Right Now*, used to sell chewing gum?
21. Whose daughter is Julie, formerly in the pop group Guys And Dolls?
22. How many adjudicators were on the talent show, *New Faces*, each week?
23. Waylon Jennings sang the theme for who?
24. Who starred in *No Excuses* as a rock singer?
25. On which show did the Beatles make their TV debut?
26. Which UK conductor was the subject of a 1980s drama?
27. Musician Richard Stilgoe first appeared on TV in which current affairs programme?
28. On *Ready, Steady Go* what was singer Millie dubbed?
29. Who sang *Back Home* on *Top Of The Pops* in 1970?
30. Which TV personality was called Mr Guitar?

ANSWERS

### Comedy 13 (see Quiz 72)

**1** Assumpta (*Ballykissangel*), Phoebe (*Goodnight Sweetheart*). **2.** Clive Dunn. **3.** Shirley. **4.** Carla Lane. **5.** Holmfirth. **6.** *Alas Smith And Jones.* **7.** *Girls On Top.* **8.** Freddie Boswell. **9.** Dr Thorpe. **10.** Derek. **11.** *The Fame Game.* **12.** *Laugh-In.* **13.** Sophia. **14.** David Copperfield. **15.** *Dad's Army's* John Le Mesurier was married to Hattie. **16.** *The Morecambe and Wise Show.* **17.** Zoe in *May To December.* **18.** Ernie Wise. **19.** Phil Cool. **20.** He became a factory foreman. **21.** Ian Lavender. **22.** *Hallelujah.* **23.** Vet. **24.** *Les Girls.* **25.** Nurse. **26.** Perry Mason. **27.** *Pop-It-In Pete.* **28.** Corky. **29.** The RAF. **30.** It went missing.

## QUIZ 72 Comedy 13

LEVEL 3

**Answers: see Quiz 71, page 599**

1. Which two pub landladies have been played by Dervla Kirwan?
2. Who connects *The Army Game* with *Dad's Army*?
3. Who was Laverne's comedy partner?
4. Which sitcom writer was born Romana Barrack?
5. *Last Of The Summer Wine* is set in which real life Yorkshire town?
6. In which series did Griff Rhys Jones and Mel Smith first team up after leaving *Not The Nine O'Clock News*?
7. Dawn, Jennifer, Ruby and Tracey were collectively what?
8. What is the first name of the father in *Bread*?
9. Which doctor was played by Richard Wilson in *Only When I Laugh*?
10. Tim Brooke-Taylor played which character in *Me And My Girl*?
11. On which show did Harry Enfield make his TV debut?
12. The catchphrase "Very interesting – but stupid" is associated with which series?
13. Which of *The Golden Girls* was born in Sicily?
14. Who created the character Old Scrunge?
15. What connects *Dad's Army* to Hattie Jacques?
16. At the end of whose show did Janet Webb usually steal the thunder by singing?
17. Who did Alec meet and marry after acting as her divorce lawyer?
18. Which comedian's 1991 autobiography was called *Still On My Way to Hollywood*?
19. Who was the star of *Cool It*?
20. What did Bilko do for a living after leaving the army?
21. Who played in *The Glums* on TV?
22. Name the comedy centred on the goings on in the Salvation Army?
23. What was Paul Nicholas' job in *Close To Home*?
24. In which comedy did the agency Maggie's Models feature?
25. What did Julie Walters train to be before her show business career?
26. In *May To December* which TV lawyer does Alec wish he could emulate?
27. What was the name of Larry Grayson's fictitious postman?
28. What was the nickname of the amiable police officer in *Sykes*?
29. Which armed service featured in the 1970s series *Get Some In*?
30. What happened to the President's brain on *Spitting Image*?

ANSWERS

### Music & Variety 5 (see Quiz 71)

**1.** The first entrant to win Eurovision twice. **2.** Peter Cook. **3.** New York. **4.** *Variety Madhouse.* **5.** John Kettley. **6.** *Help.* **7.** David Jensen. **8.** *Crossroads.* **9.** A little dishy. **10.** Jane Lapotaire. **11.** *Top Of The Pops.* **12.** *The Ballad Of Spotty Muldoon.* **13.** Richard Vranch. **14.** *Dr Who.* **15.** Jerry Nelson. **16.** 1950's. **17.** Roland Rat. **18.** Bruno Brookes and Liz Kershaw. **19.** Ken Barrie. **20.** Free. **21.** Bruce Forsyth's. **22.** Four. **23.** *Dukes of Hazzard.* **24.** Charlotte Cornwell. **25.** *People & Places.* **26.** Sir Thomas Beecham. **27.** *Tonight.* **28.** Queen Of Bluebeat. **29.** The England World Cup squad. **30.** Bert Weedon.

## QUIZ 73 Pot Luck 16

LEVEL 3

**Answers: see Quiz 74, page 602**

1. What was the name of Penny's boss in *Just Good Friends*?
2. Who starred as the doctor in *Enemy at the Door*?
3. Who was the star of *Colin's Sandwich*?
4. Where did the characters of *The Glittering Prize* meet?
5. What four letters did *TJ Hooker* have on his uniform?
6. In *Mork and Mindy*, Mindy's father owned what kind of shop?
7. What was the name of Ronnie Corbett's wife in *Now Look Here*?
8. What was Max in *The Bionic Woman*?
9. In *The Water Margin*, how many knights were reborn to fight tyranny?
10. Who held two nurses hostage in *Brookside*?
11. Which 1969 comedy paired John Fortune and Eleanor Bron?
12. In *Moonlighting*, what was Bert Viola's middle name?
13. On which talent show did singer/impressionist Joe Longthorne make his TV debut?
14. Which *Carry On* regular appeared in *Shillingbury Blowers*?
15. Who played the neighbour in *George and Mildred*?
16. Which actor played Kuba in *Casualty*?
17. In *Crossroads*, which comedian drove Meg Mortimar to her wedding?
18. Who owned the circus in the 1950s series *Circus Boy*?
19. In *Auf Wiedersehen Pet*, who played Wayne's German girlfriend?
20. In *Quincy*, who owned the bar Danny's Place?
21. Which New Zealand-born actress starred in *Zodiac*?
22. What is the name of Bob and Terry's local pub in *The Likely Lads*?
23. In which country was Joanna Lumley born?
24. What was the registration number of *The Saint*'s car?
25. Who played the title role in *Ellery Queen – Whodunnit*?
26. Who succeeded Jeremy Beadle as presenter of *Chain Letters*?
27. Name the writer of *Open All Hours*.
28. What did Peter Davidson run in *Holding The Fort*?
29. In which year was the *Grand National* first televised?
30. Who ran *The New Globe* in *Falcon Crest*?

ANSWERS

### Drama 10 (see Quiz 74)

**1.** Raina. **2.** Frederick Raphael. **3.** Lynn. **4.** *Hine.* **5.** *Justice.* **6.** *The Rivals Of Sherlock Holmes.* **7.** John Gielguid. **8.** The Mayor. **9.** Sian Phillips. **10.** *The Mind of Mr. J. G. Reader.* **11.** Cribb. **12.** *Kate.* **13.** *The Main Chance.* **14.** *The Misfit.* **15.** *Murder One.* **16.** Ray Brooks. **17.** The North Sea. **18.** *Between The Lines.* **19.** Victor. **20.** *The Blackstuff.* **21.** Zebulin. **22.** *Cardiac Arrest.* **23.** *I Spy.* **24.** Lonely. **25.** *Shogun.* **26.** *Minder.* **27.** Jill Gascoigne. **28.** *The Planemakers.* **29.** *War and Remembrance.* **30.** Douglas Wilmer.

## QUIZ 74 Drama 10

LEVEL 3

**Answers: see Quiz 73, page 601**

1. Which character did Helena Bonham Carter portray in *Arms And The Man*?
2. Who wrote *The Glittering Prizes*?
3. Who is Vanessa Redgrave's acting sister?
4. What was the 1970s series about an arms salesman starring Barrie Ingram?
5. In which series did Margaret Lockwood play a barrister?
6. Which 1970s series featured crime stories by late Victorian writers?
7. Who performed excerpts from Shakespeare named collectively *The Ages Of Man*?
8. Which part did Alan Bates play in *The Mayor Of Casterbridge*?
9. Who starred with Stanley Baker in *How Green Was My Valley*?
10. What was the series about a crime-detecting clerk created by Edgar Wallace?
11. Who was the Victorian detective played by Alan Dobie?
12. Which series starred Phyllis Calvert as a journalist?
13. What was the name of the series starring John Stride as a solicitor?
14. Which series starred Ronald Fraser as an ex-colonial returning to Britain?
15. In which series did Stanley Tucci play Richard Cross?
16. Who played Carol White's husband in *Cathy Come Home*?
17. In *Roughnecks* where is the rig Osprey Explorer?
18. In which series did Siobhan Redmond portray Det. Maureen Connell?
19. What was Det. Isbecki's first name in *Cagney and Lacey*?
20. What was the original play that the series *Boys From The Blackstuff* was based on?
21. What was Grandpa Walton's first name?
22. In which drama series was there a Dr. Monica Broome?
23. In which series did Robert Culp and Bill Cosby play Government agents?
24. Who did *Callan* befriend in Wormwood Scrubs?
25. Which mini-series featured Lord Toranaga?
26. Which series featured a special with Terry aboard the Orient Express?
27. Which Gentle Touch actress appeared in *CATS Eyes*?
28. Which series was the forerunner of *The Power Game*?
29. What was the sequel to *The Winds Of War*?
30. Who starred on ITV as Sherlock Holmes in 1975?

ANSWERS

### Pot Luck 16 (see Quiz 73)

**1.** C.J. Styles. **2.** Bernard Horsfall. **3.** Mel Smith. **4.** At Cambridge University. **5.** LCPD. **6.** A music shop. **7.** Laura. **8.** A bionic dog. **9.** 108. **10.** John Clarke. **11.** *Where Was Spring*. **12.** Quentin. **13.** *Search for a Star*. **14.** Jack Douglas. **15.** Norman Eshley. **16.** Christopher Rozycki. **17.** Larry Grayson. **18.** Big Tim Champion. **19.** Lysette Anthony. **20.** Danny Tarvo. **21.** Anouska Hempel. **22.** The Wheatsheaf. **23.** India. **24.** STI. **25.** Jim Hutton. **26.** Andrew O Connor. **27** Roy Clark. **28.** His own brewery. **29.** 1960. **30.** Richard Channing.

## QUIZ 75 Children's TV 8

LEVEL 3

**Answers: see Quiz 76, page 604**

1. *Ruff 'n' Reddy* were what types of animals?
2. Which 80s series was based on the Alan Parker film of the same name?
3. After eating a particular fruit, what alter ego did Eric become?
4. Which satellite channel was established in the USA in 1977 as CBN Satellite Service?
5. What was James Adams better known as?
6. What was the name of the spacecraft on *Get Fresh*?
7. In *Lost In Space*, how many children were there?
8. What did Evil Edna look like in *Will O'The Wisp*?
9. In *Voyage To The Bottom Of The Sea*, what was the name of the Admiral?
10. Whose invincible friend was called Moggie?
11. Who had a computer called TIM?
12. The cartoon series *Droids* was the spin-off of which film?
13. What is *The Flintstones'* daily newspaper?
14. What was the full name of *Top Cat*'s sidekick Benny?
15. Who played the title role in *John Silver's Return To Treasure Island*?
16. What kind of animal is children's TV presenter Scally?
17. In which year was the cartoon *Rocket Robin Hood* set?
18. What was the name of the *Beverley Hillbillies*' bloodhound?
19. Which children's favourite hosted *The Joke Machine*?
20. Name the oldest Womble.
21. Who presented the game show *Finders Keepers*?
22. How much did Matthew Corbett pay his father, Harry, to secure full ownership of *Sooty*?
23. Who was the storyteller in *The Hot Chestnut Man*?
24. Which star of Kula Shaker is the great nephew of the lady who appeared with *Muffin the Mule*?
25. What was the subject of the 1950s children's series *Rex and Rinty*?
26. Who replaced Michael Rodd as presenter of *Screen Test*?
27. Which children's series was inspired by Monica Dickens and featured Arthur English?
28. What was Southern TV's adventure series starring Wendy Padbury?
29. Who was the sheriff of *Four Feather Falls*?
30. What was Madeleine from *Bagpuss*?

ANSWERS

### Soaps 11 (see Quiz 76)

**1.** Shirley Cheriton. **2.** Michelle. **3.** Jed Stone. **4.** Burnley. **5.** Jennings. **6.** Linda Welch. **7.** Malandra Burrows (Kathy). **8.** Envirosphere. **9.** Heliopolis. **10.** Derek Thompson (Charlie Fairhead). **11.** Max. **12.** Jamie Clarke. **13.** The Collins Family. **14.** Lofty. **15.** Scottish. **16.** Roger Larson. **17.** Crossgill Cottage. **18.** Mark Fowler. **19.** Maureen Flynn. **20.** Phyllis Pearce. **21.** Terry. **22.** Elsie Tanner. **23.** Meg and Hugh Mortimer. **24.** No.11. **25.** Brentwich. **26.** Taff Acre. **27.** 35, Mafeking Terrace, London, W14. **28.** Newcastle. **29.** Hassan Osman. **30.** John Alderton and Jill Browne.

## QUIZ 76 Soaps 11

LEVEL 3

**Answers: see Quiz 75, page 603**

1. Who played Debbie Wilks in *Eastenders*?
2. Who dyed Lofty's hair in *Eastenders* causing it to turn green?
3. Who did Eddie Yeats meet from *Coronation Street* in prison?
4. Which soccer side does Johnny Briggs alias Mike Baldwin support?
5. What was Krystle Carrington's former surname?
6. Whose death in *Crossroads* was Benny suspected of?
7. Which *Emmerdale* star recorded *Just This Side of Love*?
8. What as the name of the pyramid selling scheme that Derek Wilton was involved in?
9. In *Emmerdale* what was the name of the Greek restaurant in Hotten?
10. Which *Casualty* star played Will Thurley in *Brookside*?
11. Who in *Neighbours* was Madge's youngest brother?
12. What was the name of Des' son in *Neighbours*?
13. Who moved into Brookside Close in the first episode?
14. In *Eastenders* who acted as midwife when Sue Osman gave birth to Ali Jr?
15. What nationality was Andy O'Brien in *Eastenders*?
16. Who in *Dallas* raped Lucy Ewing?
17. In Emmerdale where was Annie Sugden when she was trapped by fire?
18. Which *Eastenders* character was played by David Scarboro until the actor's suicide?
19. Who died in *Crossroads* just before her marriage to Benny?
20. Who became Des Barnes' housekeeper when she lost her job at the cafe in *Coronation Street*?
21. What was the name of Renee Bradshaw's brother, who was in the army?
22. The deaths of Albert Tatlock and Stan Ogden occurred the same year as which *Coronation Street* star's departure?
23. Which *Crossroads* wedding took place the same year as Ray and Deirdre Langton's?
24. What number did Elsie Tanner live at?
25. Which football club was the subject of *United!*?
26. What was the first English language serial to come from Wales?
27. What was the setting for the 70s series *Rooms*?
28. Where did Mark first meet Gill in *Eastenders*?
29. Which baby died in his cot in *Eastenders* in 1985?
30. In *Emergency Ward 10* which doctor and nurse were real-life husband and wife?

ANSWERS

### Children's TV 8 (see Quiz 75)

**1.** Cat and dog. **2.** *Fame.* **3.** *Bananaman.* **4.** Family Channel. **5.** *Grizzly Adams.* **6.** The Millennium Dustbin. **7.** Three. **8.** A TV set. **9.** Nelson. **10.** Alfie Atkins. **11.** *The Tomorrow People.* **12.** *Star Wars.* **13.** The Daily Slate. **14.** Benny The Ball. **15.** Brian Blessed. **16.** A dog. **17.** Year 2000. **18.** Duke. **19.** Basil Brush. **20.** Great Uncle Bulgaria. **21.** Neil Buchanan. **22.** £30,000. **23.** Johnny Morris. **24.** Crispian Mills (great nephew of Annette Mills). **25.** A Mountie, his dog and his horse. **26.** Brian Trueman. **27.** *Follyfoot.* **28.** *Freewheelers.* **29.** Tex Tucker. **30.** A doll.

## QUIZ 77 Comedy 14

LEVEL 3

**Answers: see Quiz 78, page 606**

1. In *Sorry,* what did Ronnie Corbett's character do for a living?
2. Name the husband and wife who worked together in *Forever Green.*
3. Whose sidekick is Madge Allsop?
4. When *Spitting Image* was repeated in 1991, what was the series called?
5. Who played Dermot in *Men Behaving Badly*?
6. Who did Cliff live with in *Cheers*?
7. Who wrote *It's Ulrika* for Ulrika Jonsson?
8. Who played the eponymous space-bound housewife in *Come Back Mrs Noah*?
9. Who played the hard up landlady in *All at No 20*?
10. Which German officer was keen on Rene in *'Allo, 'Allo*?
11. Which *On The Buses* actor appeared in *Beggar My Neighbour*?
12. In which LWT series did James Beck play the title role?
13. What was Col. Blake's christian name in *M*A*S*H*?
14. Which sitcom featured Louie, Alex and Latka?
15. Pat Phoenix and Prunella Gee were feuding landladies in which sitcom?
16. Which sitcom star was married to *Are You Being Served?* writer Jeremy Lloyd for just four months?
17. Who played Nellie Pledge's brother in *Nearest and Dearest*?
18. Which actor was *Comrade Dad*?
19. In which series did Jennifer Saunders play multiple roles?
20. Which sitcom starred Simon Cadell and Carol Royle?
21. In which series did Maria Charles play Maureen Lipman's mother?
22. In which series were Beryl and Geoffrey courting?
23. Who was the banker in *The Beverley Hillbillies*?
24. Where did Herman Munster work?
25. Which character did Hylda Baker play in *Nearest and Dearest*?
26. Who in *Please Sir* was his 'Mother's Little Soldier'?
27. Who links the *Professionals* to *The Cuckoo Waltz*?
28. In *May to December* what was Miss Flood's married name?
29. In *Dad's Army* who was in charge of the Eastgate platoon?
30. Who played the title characters in *Pat and Margaret*?

ANSWERS

### Pot Luck 17 (see Quiz 78)

**1** Liberace. **2.** Robin Bailey. **3.** Susan Gilmore. **4.** Blair General. **5.** Kaz Gara. **6.** Inspector Abberline. **7.** Clive James. **8.** *Budgie*. **9.** Thora Hird. **10.** Tessa Sanderson. **11.** Mary Malcolm. **12.** Gay Byrne. **13.** James Farenton. **14.** Julia Hills. **15.** The Ant Hill Mob. **16.** Barbara Murray. **17.** *Battlestar Galactica*. **18.** Grey Kettle. **19.** *The Tellygoons*. **20.** Manchester. **21.** Boston. **22.** *Rowan and Martin's Laugh-In*. **23.** Eyecatchers. **24** The Corner Family. **25.** George Inn. **26.** Floella Benjamin. **27.** Geraldine James. **28.** A fashion boutique. **29** Clarence E. Mulford. **30.** Peter Barkworth.

## QUIZ 78 Pot Luck 17

LEVEL 3

**Answers: see Quiz 77, page 605**

1. How was performer Wladzir Valentino better known?
2. Who links *Potter* and *I Didn't Know You Cared*?
3. Who played a mad furniture designer in *Maelstrom*?
4. What was the name of the hospital in *Dr Kildare*?
5. In *The Strange Report*, who played Adam Strange's American assistant?
6. What was the name of Michael Caine's character in *Jack The Ripper*?
7. Who was the TV critic on *Saturday Night People*?
8. How was the character Ronald Bird better known?
9. Who played Bill Fraser's mother in *Flesh and Blood*?
10. Which Olympic medalist was a team captain on *Sporting Triangles*?
11. Which TV announcer was described as having 'a bubbling voice of captivating quality'?
12. Who presented *The Late Late Show*?
13. Which actor played the pilot of *Blue Thunder* in the TV series?
14. Who links *Who Dares Wins* to *The Refuge*?
15. Who helped protect Penelope Pitstop from The Hooded Claw?
16. Who played John Wilder's wife in *The Power Game*?
17. In which series might you meet Captain Apollo?
18. In *Hot Metal*, who used the phrase, 'Her Majesty's Press…'?
19. In which madcap series did Eccles and Bluebottle feature?
20. From which city was *Open Air* broadcast?
21. Where was *Banacek* set?
22. In which show might you have heard all about beautiful downtown Burbank?
23. What was the name of the agency in *Me And My Girl*?
24. What was the name of the family in *Not in Front of the Children*?
25. Who created *The Black and White Minstrel Show*?
26. Who was the presenter of *Tree House*?
27. Which actress was George Cole's wife in *Blott on the Landscape*?
28. What kind of shop did Jan Howard run in *Howard's Way*?
29. Who was the creator of *Hopalong Cassidy*?
30. Name the star of *Later Starter*?

ANSWERS

### Comedy 14 (see Quiz 77)

**1.** Librarian. **2.** John Alderton and Pauline Collins. **3.** Dame Edna's. **4.** *Spitting Back.* **5.** Harry Enfield. **6.** His Ma. **7.** Vic Reeves. **8.** Molly Sugden. **9.** Maureen Lipman. **10.** Lt. Gruber. **11.** Reg Varney. **12.** *Romany Jones.* **13.** Henry. **14.** *Taxi.* **15.** *Constant Hot Water.* **16.** Joanna Lumley. **17.** Jimmy Jewell. **18.** George Cole. **19.** *Happy Families.* **20.** *Life Without George.* **21.** *Agony.* **22.** *The Lovers.* **23.** Mr. Drysdale. **24.** At a funeral home. **25.** Nellie Pledge. **26.** Frankie Abbott. **27.** Lewis Collins. **28.** Tipple. **29.** Captain Square. **30.** Victoria Wood and Julie Walters.

## QUIZ 79 News 5

LEVEL 3

**Answers: see Quiz 80, page 608**

**1.** Who was known as 'The Voice Of America'?
**2.** Who wrote *Jacob's Ladder*?
**3.** Brian is actually Brian Walden's middle name. What is his first name?
**4.** Who held a TV interview with Prince Andrew and Lady Sarah Ferguson prior to their marriage?
**5.** Which newsreader appeared in *Doctor Who* as himself in 1966?
**6.** Who presented *Chronicle* for the BBC?
**7.** Which newsreader helped us trace family trees in a series on the subject?
**8.** What is TV's longest running wildlife series?
**9.** What would a TV journalist mean if he mentioned the acronym ENG?
**10.** Who presented *All Our Yesterdays*?
**11.** Who presented *Monitor*?
**12.** What was the Queen's youngest son's programme about the Duke of Windsor called?
**13.** What was the subject of *The Epic That Never Was*?
**14.** From where in Hampshire is there televised an annual Air Show?
**15.** Name the ITV 1970s series on the plight of the South American Indians?
**16.** Which subject was featured in the documentary *The Hardest Way Up*?
**17.** Who took part in the BBC documentary *Girl Friday*?
**18.** Who presented *Pioneers Of Modern Painting*?
**19.** Who UK news presenter interviewed Saddam Hussein just before the Gulf War in 1990?
**20.** Which country was the subject for the documentary *Edge Of Blue Heaven*?
**21.** Who narrated the fly on the wall series *Love And Marriage*?
**22.** Who presented the daytime *City Hospital*?
**23.** Which newsreader has written a book called The Loch Ness Story?
**24.** Which late pop singer named 'The British Elvis' featured in an *Omnibus* documentary?
**25.** Who accompanied Rory McGrath on a *Holiday to California*?
**26.** Who presented *The Car's The Star*?
**27.** Who narrated *Fraud Squad*?
**28.** Which newsreader advertised Cow & Gate baby food as a child?
**29.** What was the rock in *Death On the Rock*?
**30.** In which city is the Adelphi Hotel featured in the BBC documentary *Hotel*?

ANSWERS

### Sport 2 (see Quiz 80)

**1.** Steven Carrington. **2.** Eric Sykes. **3.** *Gone With The Wind.* **4.** Wrestling. **5.** Shaw Taylor. **6.** Ron Pickering. **7.** *TV-AM.* **8.** Michael Owen. **9.** Kathy Taylor. **10.** Swedish. **11.** Pole Vault. **12.** Faure's Pavane. **13.** Manchester United. **14.** Silverstone. **15.** Ruud Gullit. **16.** Bob Wilson. **17.** Norris. **18.** Leonard Martin. **19.** Willie Carson. **20.** Golf. **21.** Rome. **22.** Steve Ovett. **23.** Chris Brasher. **24.** Frank Bruno. **25.** Rock-climbing. **26.** Brian Blessed. **27.** Dennis Waterman. **28.** Alan Weeks. **29.** Boxing. **30.** The Final of the World Snooker Championship between Denis Taylor and Steve Davis.

## QUIZ 80 Sport 2

LEVEL 3

**Answers: see Quiz 79, page 607**

1. Who was the manager of a football team in the soap *Dynasty*?
2. Which comic wrote the golfing comedy, *The 19th Hole*?
3. Which film theme was used by the BBC for the 1996 Olympics?
4. What did Kent Walton commentate on on *World of Sport*?
5. Which crimestopper presented a TV series about the card game bridge?
6. Which BBC sports commentator was married to an Olympic long jump champion?
7. Jimmy Greaves previewed films on which breakfast programme?
8. Who was only the third soccer player to win the BBC *Sports Personality of the Year* after more than 40 years of the award?
9. Which former pentathlete is now known for her holiday trips on TV?
10. What nationality was the first winner of *European Superstars*?
11. Which was *World Superstar* competitor Bob Seaman's event in the Olympics?
12. Which music was used by the BBC for the 1998 World Cup?
13. Which football team did BskyB bid £635 million for in 1998?
14. Where is the British Grand Prix now televised from?
15. Which former Chelsea manager commentated for the BBC in 1997?
16. Which former Goalkeeper is a football presenter for ITV?
17. Who was former sports reporter Ross McWhirter's twin brother?
18. Who first read the football results on *Grandstand*?
19. Which jockey was a team captain on *Question Of Sport*?
20. Henry Longhurst was the BBC commentator on which sport?
21. Where were the Summer Olympic Games of 1960 televised from?
22. Which 1500 metres champion is a commentator for ITV?
23. Which former Olympian organises the London Marathon?
24. Which boxer appeared as a damsel in a Shakespearean sketch?
25. Joe Brown was often featured in televised outside broadcasts. What is his activity?
26. Which actor attempted Everest in a television film?
27. Who presented *Match of the Seventies* in 1995?
28. Who was the BBC ice hockey reporter?
29. What sport did Jim Neilly commentate on?
30. What event was watched at midnight by 18.5 million people – the largest ever audience at this time of day?

ANSWERS

### News 5 (see Quiz 79)

**1.** Ed Murrow. **2.** David Jacobs. **3.** Alastair. **4.** Sue Lawley. **5.** Kenneth Kendall. **6.** David Dimbleby. **7.** Gordon Honeycombe. **8.** *Survival.* **9.** Electronic News Gathering. **10.** Brian Inglis. **11.** Huw Wheldon. **12.** *Edward on Edward.* **13.** Alexander Korda's unfinished *I, Claudius.* **14.** Farnborough. **15.** *Disappearing World.* **16.** Mountaineering. **17.** Joanna Lumley. **18.** Sir Kenneth Clarke. **19.** Trevor McDonald. **20.** Mongolia. **21.** Joanna Lumley. **22.** Gaby Roslin. **23.** Nicholas Witchell. **24.** Billy Fury. **25.** David Gower. **26.** Quentin Willson. **27.** John Nettles. **28.** Martyn Lewis. **29.** Gibraltar. **30.** Liverpool.

## QUIZ 81 Drama 11

LEVEL 3

**Answers: see Quiz 82, page 610**

1. Who was Lockhart in three police drama series?
2. Which soap actor played a Det. Sergeant in *No Hiding Place?*
3. Who played Telford in *Telford's Change?*
4. Which actor first shared a *Z Car* with James Ellis?
5. Which future Hollywood star played Nancy Astor's playboy husband in the 1982 BBC2 series?
6. In which 1993 TV adaptation of a Jilly Cooper novel did Patrick Ryecart star?
7. Which James Bond starred opposite Stefanie Powers in *Mistral's Daughter?*
8. Who played Mrs Bennet in *Pride and Prejudice?*
9. Which ITV comedy drama set in London spanned 15 years between 1979 and 1994?
10. Which mother and daughter have played Max de Winter's second wife in separate productions of Rebecca?
11. Whose dramatised Jane Austen's *Persuasion* for TV and changed the ending?
12. Who was the lesbian in *Drop The Dead Donkey?*
13. What was the name of Robert Lindsay's political character in *GBH?*
14. Which LA Law actor starred in *The Tommyknockers?*
15. Who was seen in silhouette in the introduction of his television plays?
16. Which Hollywood star played Trevor Eve's mistress in *The Politician's Wife?*
17. What was the name of the Falklands veteran in *Tumbledown?*
18. Which character did Allyce Beasley play in *Moonlighting?*
19. Sir Guy Of Gisburne featured in which TV series?
20. Which English actress appeared in L.A. Law as C.J Lamb?
21. In which Bronte drama did Tara Fitzgerald play Helen?
22. Which wife of impresario Eddie Kulukundis starred in *The Grand?*
23. Which actress's real name is Ilynea Lydia Mironoff?
24. Who said, "you might very well think that, but I couldn't possibly comment"?
25. In which series was Ron Smollet a bobby?
26. Willy Armitage was a character in which action series?
27. In '92 which drama had the highest ratings then for a costume drama?
28. Which Lady Nunn played TV detective Anna Lee?
29. Who is the doctor in *Ballykissangel?*
30. Which Oscar winner played Woodrow F. Coll in *Lonesome Dove?*

ANSWERS

**Pot Luck 18 (see Quiz 82)**

**1.** Barry Norman. **2.** Door knobs. **3.** Eddie Albert. **4.** Lady Lucinda Lambton. **5.** The attempts to free American hostages imprisoned in Iran. **6.** *It's Gary Shandling's Show.* **7.** Two. **8.** *Now.* **9.** James Garner. **10.** Blake Edwards. **11.** *Space Patrol.* **12.** Tristram Coffin. **13.** Football. **14.** *Beat The Teacher.* **15.** Buffy and Jody. **16.** Flower shop. **17.** Helen Walker. **18.** *The Phil Silvers Show.* **19.** Glynis Barber (of Dempsey & Makepeice). **20.** Heather Cooper. **21.** Subbuteo table football. **22.** *Secret Agent* **23.** Christopher Biggins. **24.** Rabies. **25.** Fairchild. **26.** *Little House – A New Beginning.* **27.** Frank Finlay. **28.** She was a milk lady. **29.** David Kossoff. **30.** Dale Robertson.

## QUIZ 82 Pot Luck 18

LEVEL 3

**Answers: see Quiz 81, page 609**

1. Who wrote the documentary *Talking Pictures*?
2. In *Bewitched*, what objects did Aunt Clara like to collect?
3. Who played Oliver Douglas in *Green Acres*?
4. Who explored public toilets on *Forty Minutes*?
5. What was the subject of the documentary *444 Days … And Counting*?
6. In which show did the main character use a flashback machine?
7. How many series of *Fawlty Towers* were made and broadcast?
8. Which show had the slogan, 'Sit tight in your chair, and we'll take you there!'?
9. In *Space*, who played Norman Grant?
10. Which director created the TV series *Peter Gunn*?
11. In which series did the puppet Larry Dart appear?
12. Who played the professor in TV's *King of the Rocket Men*?
13. In *The Lovers*, what was it that Richard Beckinsale loved but his girlfriend hated?
14. In which BBC show, hosted by Bruno Brookes, did children compete against their teachers?
15. What were the names of the orphaned twins in *The Family Affair*?
16. In *The Mistress*, what kind of shop was owned by the lead character?
17. What was the name of the character played by Penelope Keith in *Sweet Sixteen*?
18. In which show did Dick Van Dyke make his TV debut?
19. Which TV cop was in the crew of *Blake's Seven*?
20. Who presented the documentary *The Planets*?
21. Name the sport which featured in *Playing For Real*?
22. What was the title of *Danger Man* changed to in America?
23. Who links *Poldark* to *Surprise, Surprise*?
24. An outbreak of which disease was the subject of the drama *The Mad Death*?
25. In *Executive Stress* what was the surname of Caroline and Donald?
26. What was the sequel to *The Little House on the Prairie*?
27. Who in 1971 played the role of Casanova on TV?
28. What did Barbara Flynn's character do for a living in *Open All Hours*?
29. Who starred opposite Peggy Mount in *The Larkins*?
30. Which actor was Dale Winton named after?

ANSWERS

### Drama 11 (see Quiz 81)

**1.** Raymond Francis. **2.** Johnny Briggs. **3.** Peter Barkworth. **4.** Jeremy Kemp. **5.** Pierce Brosnan. **6.** *Riders*. **7.** Timothy Dalton. **8.** Alison Steadman. **9.** *Minder*. **10.** Joanna David, Emilia Fox. **11.** Andrew Davies. **12.** Helen. **13.** Michael Murray. **14.** Jimmy Smits. **15.** Alfred Hitchcock. **16.** Minnie Driver. **17.** Robert Lawrence. **18.** Agnes DiPesto. **19.** *Robin Of Sherwood*. **20.** *The Tenant of Wildfell Hall*. **21.** Father MacAnally. **22.** Susan Hampshire. **23.** Helen Mirren. **24.** Francis Urquhart (*House of Cards*). **25.** *The Bill*. **26.** *Mission Impossible*. **27.** *Lady Chatterley's Lover*. **28.** Imogen Stubbs. **29.** Michael Ryan. **30.** Tommy Lee Jones.

## QUIZ 83 Comedy 15

LEVEL 3

**Answers: see Quiz 84, page 612**

1. What is the acting connection between Gilly Coman and Melanie Hill?
2. In which comedy series did Natasha Pyne and Ann Holloway appear as sisters?
3. Which series starred Irene Handl and Wilfred Pickles?
4. What was the title of the programme about a joke-telling contest between comedians?
5. Which soccer side does Jo Brand support?
6. Who played Albert in *Albert and Victoria*?
7. What was the title of the ATV show starring Marty Feldman?
8. Who scripted his Channel 4 sitcom *Blue Heaven*?
9. Which comedian played Johnny McKenna in *The Detectives*?
10. What was Jean Stapleton's role in *Bagdad Cafe*?
11. What are Mr. Humphries forenames in *Are You Being Served*?
12. Which henpecked husband in a sitcom is in real life a former husband of writer Margaret Drabble?
13. What was Lilith's maiden name in *Cheers*?
14. What was *Ellen*'s character's surname?
15. In *'Allo, 'Allo* what was Herr Flick's first name?
16. Whose parents were Rita and Les in *Just Good Friends*?
17. What was the title of entertainer Paul O' Grady's TV series?
18. Which sitcom features Majors Healy and Nelson?
19. Which actor from *Casualty* was Dawn French smitten by in *The Vicar Of Dibley*?
20. What is Dec of the duo *Ant and Dec* surname?
21. In *Dead Ernest*, what was Ernest's profession before he died?
22. Who played the large lodger in *The Big One*?
23. Who played Beryl in *Beryl's Lot*?
24. Which BAFTA award winning actress starred in *The Labours Of Erica*?
25. Which of The Three Degrees starred in *The Land Of Hope And Gloria*?
26. Who was the star of *Dora*, a 1970s sitcom?
27. Where was the sitcom *Down The Gate* set?
28. Who replaced Cicely Courtneidge as Stan Butler's mother in *On The Buses*?
29. Who played Pippa in *One Foot In The Grave*?
30. Who starred as photographer *The Magnificent Evans*?

ANSWERS

**Soaps 12 (see Quiz 84)**

**1.** William Tarmey (Jack Duckworth). **2.** Dean Sullivan (Jimmy Corkhill). **3.** Vodka and Tonic. **4.** Black Forest Clinic. **5.** Richard and Esther Shapiro. **6.** Tony Warren. **7.** Helicopter accident. **8.** Monday **9.** Larry Grayson. **10.** *The Mikado.* **11.** Grant Mitchell. **12.** Mike Baldwin. **13.** Poodle. **14.** Lowestoft. **15.** Clive Gibbons. **16.** Gill. **17.** Elaine Paige. **18.** Maggie Clegg. **19.** Mark Jennings. **20.** Sickle Cell. **21.** Braddock County. **22.** The Weatherfield Gazette. **23.** Adam Chance. **24.** The police suspected her of stealing a car. **25.** John James and Emma Samms. **26.** Ralph Hardwick. **27.** *The Practice.* **28.** *Emergency Ward 10.* **29.** Christopher Beeny. **30.** Raul.

## QUIZ 84 Soaps 12

LEVEL 3

**Answers: see Quiz 83, page 611**

1. Which soap actor conducted the Halle Orchestra in 1989?
2. Which Brookside actor played Sam Jackson in Radio Merseyside's *The Merseysiders*?
3. What is Rita Sullivan's favourite tipple?
4. Which German soap was first shown on Channel 4 in 1988?
5. Which husband and wife were co producers of *Dynasty*?
6. Whose autobiography was called *I Was Ena Sharples' Father*?
7. How did Jock perish in *Dallas*?
8. *Coronation Street* is broadcast on which days?
9. Who appeared as Meg and Hugh's chauffeur on their wedding day?
10. Which Gilbert & Sullivan opera was playing on Derek's car radio as he died in *Coronation Street*?
11. In *Eastenders* who had an affair with his mother-in-law?
12. Who is Amanda Barrie's character in *Coronation Street* married to?
13. What breed of dog was Rowley in *Eastenders*?
14. Reg Holdsworth left for a supermarket where when he left the Street's corner shop?
15. Who almost sabotaged Des and Daphne's wedding in *Neighbours*?
16. Who did Mark Fowler marry in 1992 just before she died in *Eastenders*?
17. Which musical star played Caroline Winthrop in *Crossroads*?
18. Who was Betty Turpin's sister in *Coronation Street*?
19. What was the name of Krystle's former husband in *Dynasty* whom Alexis was accused of killing?
20. From which disease did Lloyd Tavernier suffer in *Eastenders*?
21. In which county was Southfork ranch?
22. Which newspaper did Ken Barlow purchase and then resell?
23. Who was manager of the *Crossroads* health centre?
24. Why was the Street's Sally stopped by the police during her driving test?
25. Who were the two actors who returned to *Dynasty* after *The Colbys* ended?
26. In *Brookside*, who met Madge through a lonely hearts ad after his wife died?
27. In which soap did the Castlehulme Health Centre feature?
28. What was the first soap to be transmitted twice a week on ITV?
29. Which *Upstairs Downstairs* actor appeared as the youngest son in The Grove Family?
30. What was the name of The Ewing's butler?

ANSWERS

### Comedy 15 (see Quiz 83)

**1.** They both played Aveline in *Bread.* **2.** *Father, Dear Father.* **3.** *For The Love Of Ada.* **4.** *Jokers Wild.* **5.** Crystal Palace. **6.** Alfred Marks. **7.** *The Marty Feldman Comedy Machine.* **8.** Frank Skinner. **9.** Jimmy Tarbuck. **10.** Jasmine Zweibel. **11.** Wilberforce Clayborne. **12.** Clive Swift (Richard Bucket). **13.** Sternin. **14.** Morgan. **15.** Otto. **16.** Vince's. **17.** *The Lily Savage Show.* **18.** *I Dream Of Jeannie.* **19.** Clive Mantle. **20.** Donnelly. **21.** Teacher. **22.** Mike McShane. **23.** Carmel McSharry. **24.** Brenda Blethyn. **25.** Sheila Ferguson. **26.** Dora Bryan. **27.** Billingsgate Fishmarket. **28.** Doris Hare. **29.** Janine Duvitski. **30.** Ronnie Barker.

## QUIZ 85 Who's Who 3

LEVEL 3

**Answers: see Quiz 86, page 614**

**1.** What relation was ex Channel 4 Head Michael Grade to the late Lord Lew Grade?
**2.** What is sports presenter Bob Wilson's middle name?
**3.** Who was the only woman in the 1980s to win the BBC *Sports Personality of the Year* on her own?
**4.** Which soccer side does Roy Walker support?
**5.** Which presenter used to be in the group Jet Bronx and the Forbidden?
**6.** Who married Peter Hook in Las Vegas in 1994
**7.** Who was the first co presenter of *Surprise Surprise* with Cilla Black?
**8.** Which actor is the son of Margaret Thatcher's Attorney General?
**9.** What was the name of David Furnish's TV profile of Elton John?
**10.** Which star of sitcom and theatre made her TV debut opposite John Gielgud in *The Mayfly and the Frog*?
**11.** Which TV couple met on the set of *Ballykissangel*?
**12.** In 1990 who founded Animal Line with TV writer Carla Lane?
**13.** Whose memoirs were called *Stare Back and Smile*?
**14.** What was the only part of Nicholas Lyndhurst visible in his first TV appearance?
**15.** Who famously appeared in ads for Tesco chasing chickens in France?
**16.** Who played *Globelink's* Dave Charnley?
**17.** Which presenter is the daughter of a veteran radio newsreader Clive?
**18.** Who hosted the quiz *Gagtag*?
**19.** Who launched the cable TV station L!VE TV?
**20.** Which was the first show hosted by Anthea Turner to have her name in the title?
**21.** Which magician's wife wrote songs for *That's Life*?
**22.** Which journalist and TV personality is Lady Nicholas Lloyd?
**23.** Which actress is the mother of Sam West?
**24.** Which TV presenter wrote a book called *Rock Stars in their Underpants*?
**25.** Who first hosted the quiz show *Home Truths*?
**26.** What is Yorkshireman Timothy West's middle name?
**27.** Who's autobiography was called *Dear Me*?
**28.** Which Suchet brother is older?
**29.** Which actress is the wife of writer-director Mike Leigh?
**30.** Which TV personality has children called Betty Kitten and Honey Kinny?

ANSWERS

### Children's TV 9 (see Quiz 86)

**1.** Peter Wheeler. **2.** *Get This*. **3.** *Timeslip*. **4.** Paddy and Mary. **5.** A baby elephant on roller skates. **6.** Pippin Fort. **7.** Gareth 'Gaz Top' Jones. **8.** *HR Pufnstuf*. **9.** Ding a Ling. **10.** Llaniog. **11.** Smallfilms. **12.** Bernard Cribbins. **13.** Denise Coffey. **14.** *Blue Peter*. **15.** Bengy. **16.** *Children of The New Forest*. **17.** *Live and Kicking*. **18.** *It'll Never Work*. **19.** Mildred Hubble. **20.** Spacely Space Sprockets. **21.** *Wham, Bam, Strawberry Jam*. **22.** *Sooty*. **23.** *Art Attack*. **24.** The Osmonds. **25.** Joe 90. **26.** Helen Rollason. **27.** Dennis Waterman. **28.** Ross King. **29.** Verity Lambert. **30.** *Lassie's Rescue Rangers*.

# QUIZ 86 Children's TV 9

LEVEL 3

**Answers: see Quiz 85, page 613**

1. Who presented *Full House*?
2. Which children's information show was presented by Harry Fowler and Kenny Lynch?
3. What was the children's S.F. series starring Spencer Banks?
4. What were the names of Mickey Murphy's children in *Camberwick Green*?
5. In *The Flintstones* what was Wilma's vacuum cleaner made from?
6. Who devised and hosted the first *Children's Royal Variety Show*?
7. Which male presenter first joined Fred Dinenage for *How 2*?
8. In which children's comedy did Witchiepoo feature?
9. What was Hokey Wolf's fox friend called?
10. In *Ivor the Engine*, which station did Dai look after?
11. Which company did Oliver Postgate and Peter Firmin set up?
12. Who held the record for reading most stories on *Jackanory*?
13. Who was the female regular on *Do Not Adjust Your Set*?
14. Which children's TV series celebrated its 40th birthday in 1998?
15. What was the name of the cartoon puppy created by William Timyn?
16. Which Captain Marryat story was a 1998 Sunday evening serial?
17. Where can you see *The Rugrats* on a Saturday morning?
18. What is BBC's award-winning children's series featuring crazy inventions?
19. What was the name of *The Worst Witch*?
20. In *The Jetsons*, where did George Jetson work?
21. What was the name of BBC2's children's poetry series?
22. Which well known puppet character was purchased on Blackpool Pier in 1948?
23. Which children's art and craft programme was presented by Neil Buchanan?
24. Which US group were the first major guests on Jim'll Fix It?
25. Who was the Most Special Agent for World Intelligence Network?
26. Who was the first female presenter of *Newsround*?
27. Who played William when Richmal Crompton's stories were first adapted for the small screen?
28. Who hosted *Young Krypton* in 1988?
29. Who was the first producer of Dr Who?
30. What was the animated series of *Lassie* called?

ANSWERS

## Who's Who 3 (see Quiz 85)

**1.** Nephew. **2.** Primrose. **3.** Fatima Whitbread. **4.** Blackpool. **5.** Loyd Grossman. **6.** Caroline Aherne. **7.** Christopher Biggins. **8.** Nigel Havers. **9.** Tantrums and Tiaras. **10.** Felicity Kendal. **11.** Stephen Tomkinson and Dervla Kirwen. **12.** Linda McCartney and Rita Tushingham. **13.** Joanna Lumley. **14.** Hands. **15.** Dudley Moore. **16.** Neil Pearson. **17.** Gaby Roslin. **18.** Bob Monkhouse. **19.** Janet Street-Porter. **20.** *Turner Round the World.* **21.** Victoria Wood. **22.** Eve Pollard. **23.** Prunella Scales. **24.** Paula Yates. **25.** Steve Wright. **26.** Lancaster. **27.** Peter Ustinov. **28.** John. **29.** Alison Steadman. **30.** Jonathan Ross.

## QUIZ 89 Comedy 16

LEVEL 3

**Answers: see Quiz 90, page 618**

**1.** In which sitcom did Ian Carmichael play a single foster-father?
**2.** Who played the landlady in *All At Number 20*?
**3.** Which title did William Melvyn have in *All Gas And Gaiters*?
**4.** Who played Bev Harris in *Roseanne*?
**5.** In which programme did Philip Drummond adopt two brothers?
**6.** In which sitcom did Meredith Baxter Birney play Elyse Keaton?
**7.** Who links *Duck Patrol* to *One Foot In The Grave*?
**8.** Which actress from *You Rang M'lord* had dated Prince Andrew?
**9.** Which distinguished film actor appeared in the sitcom *Young At Heart*?
**10.** Which company produced *Drop The Dead Donkey*?
**11.** Which star of *Mona Lisa* appeared in *Thick as Thieves*?
**12.** In which series did Claire Buckfield succeed Claire Woodgate as Jen?
**13.** Which *Saint* appeared in the sitcom *Tom, Dick and Harriet*?
**14.** Who appeared in *Family Ties* as Laura Miller?
**15.** Which *Dad's Army* actor was the star of *My Old Man*?
**16.** What was the name of Nicholas Lyndhurst's character in *The Two Of Us*?
**17.** Who was Corporal Henshaw's sergeant?
**18.** In which series was there a butler named Dubois?
**19.** Which female film star's name was adopted by Alf Garnett for his son-in-law?
**20.** What was the name of Terry's sister in *The Likely Lads*?
**21.** What was the name of the cowboy builder in *Fawlty Towers*?
**22.** Where did E.L. Wisty sit in his sketches?
**23.** Who played Maureen Lipman's secretary in *Agony*?
**24.** Who played Laura Petrie in a U.S. comedy series?
**25.** What was the comedy series starring Robin Askwith and Brian Glover?
**26.** Who was Ronald Forfar's character in *Bread*?
**27.** What was the 1950s series starring Bebe Daniels and Ben Lyons?
**28.** Who played Hans in *'Allo, 'Allo*?
**29.** Which football team does Frank Skinner support?
**30.** In which series did Fletch attain his freedom?

ANSWERS

**News 6 (see Quiz 90)**

**1.** *News 24.* **2.** Spain. **3.** *Tomorrow's World.* **4.** The used car market. **5.** Alexei Sayle. **6.** BBC1. **7.** *Meet The Ancestors.* **8.** Gardening. **9.** Egypt. **10.** In *The Footsteps Of Alexander The Great.* **11.** Irish. **12.** Ally McCoist. **13.** Clive Anderson. **14.** The M6. **15.** Joan Bakewell. **16.** Edward Heath. **17.** David Dimbleby. **18.** Llew Gardner. **19.** Selina Scott. **20.** Bernard Falk. **21.** Julian Pettifer. **22.** John Pilger. **23.** Svetlana Stalin. **24.** Phillip Tiberman. **25.** *News At Ten.* **26.** *The Time - The Place.* **27.** Henry Kelly. **28.** Ludovic Kennedy. **29.** *Nationwide.* **30.** David Dimbleby.

## QUIZ 90 News 6

LEVEL 3

**Answers: see Quiz 89, page 617**

**1.** What is the name of the BBC's 24-hour television news service?
**2.** In which country is the ITV magazine show *Lunch In The Sun* based?
**3.** Philippa Forrester introduces which BBC1 science and technology series?
**4.** The Channel 4 series *Deals On Wheels* dealt with which type of car market?
**5.** Who was the comedian who explored *Great Railway Journeys* with the BBC?
**6.** On which channel did we meet *Vets In Practice*?
**7.** Archaeologist and historian Julian Richards asked us to meet whom on BBC2?
**8.** With which subject is the BBC series *Ground Force* concerned?
**9.** In which country was TV traveller and reporter Alan Whicker born?
**10.** Michael Wood led us in the footsteps of which ancient Emperor on BBC2?
**11.** What nationality is presenter Eamonn Holmes?
**12.** Which Scottish soccer star hosts a BBC chat show with Fred MacAulay?
**13.** Which barrister hosts a talk show?
**14.** What UK motorway was featured in ITV's *Motorway Life*?
**15.** The Sunday evening topical discussion show *Heart Of The Matter* is hosted by who?
**16.** Which former Tory Prime Minister was profiled in BBC2's *A Very Singular Man*?
**17.** Who made the controversial 70s documentary *Yesterday's Men*?
**18.** Which former *News at Ten* presenter hosted CBS's *West 57th Show*?
**19.** Who was the presenter of *Person To Person* in the late 1970s?
**20.** Name the former Nationwide reporter who presented *Sin On Sunday*?
**21.** Who won a BAFTA award in 1969 for his coverage of the Vietnam War?
**22.** Who examined the consumer battle between Pepsi and Coca Cola?
**23.** Which Russian did Malcolm Muggeridge spend *A Week With..* in 1982?
**24.** Who narrated the documentary *Nagasaki – The Return Journey*?
**25.** Which news programme was the first to have two newsreaders?
**26.** Mike Scott was the original host of which ITV talk show?
**27.** Which of the *Game For A Laugh* team presented *Good Morning Britain*?
**28.** Who presented *Midweek*?
**29.** What replaced *Tonight* on BBC1 as the evening news and current affairs programme?
**30.** *An Ocean Apart* was presented by who?

ANSWERS

### Comedy 16 (see Quiz 89)

**1.** *Bachelor Father.* **2.** Maureen Lipman. **3.** Bishop. **4.** Estelle Parsons. **5.** *Diff'rent Strokes.* **6.** *Family Ties.* **7.** Richard Wilson. **8.** Catherine Rabett. **9.** John Mills. **10.** Hat Trick. **11.** Bob Hoskins. **12.** *2 Point 4 Children.* **13.** Ian Ogilvy. **14.** Courtney Cox. **15.** Clive Dunn. **16.** Ashley. **17.** Bilko. **18.** *Soap.* **19.** Shirley Temple. **20.** Audrey. **21.** O'Reilly. **22.** On a park bench. **23.** Diana Weston. **24.** Mary Tyler Moore. **25.** *The Bottle Boys.* **26.** Freddie Boswell. **27.** *Life With The Lyons.* **28.** West Bromwich Albion. **29.** *Fairly Secret Army.* **30.** *Going Straight.*

## QUIZ 91 Soaps 13

LEVEL 3

**Answers: see Quiz 92, page 620**

1. Whose wedding did Walter Lankersham interrupt in *Dynasty*?
2. Which early *Eastender* was diagnosed as having Multiple Sclerosis?
3. *Crossroads* actors Terence Rigsby and Norman Bowler had previously appeared together in which police series?
4. What did Alf Roberts help to conceal in the cellar at The Rovers Return?
5. When Rita originally appeared in *Coronation Street*, what assumed name did she use?
6. Who played Annie Walker's son in the Street?
7. Which soap actor sang with a group called *Take Ten*?
8. How much money did Ivy Brennan give to Mike Baldwin to help settle the gambling debts of her husband, Don?
9. What were the first three surnames Valene had in *Knot's Landing*?
10. In which soap did Kylie Minogue play the part of Char?
11. Which Carrington was named after her wonderfully blue eyes?
12. In *Dallas* who married the same man on two separate occasions?
13. Jeff and Doreen Horton are which *Coronation Street* child's grandparents?
14. In *Coronation Street*, who won a night out with Mike Baldwin in a raffle?
15. Which newspaper was owned by Alexis in *Dynasty*?
16. Who first sang the *Neighbours* theme song?
17. Who did *Lovejoy* play in *Dallas*?
18. Who owned The Diner with Ailsa in the early showings of *Home and Away*?
19. In *The Colbys* whose baby was adopted at birth?
20. Who was the Baldwins cleaning lady in *Coronation Street*?
21. At which soccer side's ground was action filmed for *United!*?
22. Who played neighbour Joyce Harker in *The Newcomers*?
23. In which soap did Sly and Serena appear?
24. In *The Colbys* how did Jeff almost meet his death?
25. Which former President's wife had a role in *Falcon Crest*?
26. Who did Stan Richards play in *Emmerdale*?
27. Who was referred to as Queen of the Soaps?
28. Who owned The Southern Cross Ranch?
29. Who gave Frank and Pat Butcher fluffy dice as a wedding present?
30. Who spoke the first and last ever words in *Crossroads*?

ANSWERS

### Pot Luck 20 (see Quiz 92)

**1.** Bamber Gascoigne. **2.** Sheila Gish. **3.** Constance. **4.** A fertility symbol. **5.** Captain Martin Block. **6.** *The Crucible*. **7.** Bill Kerr. **8.** David Rasche. **9.** A brothel. **10.** Alison Steadman. **11.** *Falcon Crest*. **12.** Mick Miller. **13.** *Father Matthew's Daughter*. **14.** Mel Blanc. **15.** Soccer. **16.** They were both divorced. **17.** *A Country Practice*. **18.** Anna Raeburn. **19.** Rita Penner. **20.** Ellis Ward. **21.** Marion. **22.** Tim Piggot-Smith. **23.** $10,000. **24.** Cheyenne. **25.** *Young Doctors*. **26.** David Threlfall. **27.** *Follyfoot*. **28.** Michael Barrymore. **29.** Persse McGarrigle. **30.** Red Rock.

## QUIZ 92 Pot Luck 20

LEVEL 3

**Answers: see Quiz 91, page 619**

1. *Victorian Values* was written and presented by who?
2. Who starred opposite Denis Lawson in *That Uncertain Feeling*?
3. In *Peyton Place*, who owned a bookshop?
4. What did Nicky Henson wear around his neck in *Fawlty Towers*?
5. What was the name of the harassed Captain in *Car 54, Where Are You*?
6. What was the name of the newspaper in *Hot Metal*?
7. In *The Heroes*, who played Paddy McDowell?
8. Who starred in *Sledge Hammer*?
9. What did Luke Mae run in *Flamingo Road*?
10. Who played the school teacher in *P'tang Yang Kipperbang*?
11. Dan Fixx was a character in which soap?
12. Name the regular comedian in *The Funny Side*.
13. In which series did James Bolam play a priest?
14. Who was the voice of *Bugs Bunny*?
15. Frank Bough of *Breakfast Time* fame won an Oxbridge blue for which sport?
16. What did Kate and Allie have in common?
17. In which soap was Councillor Muldoon a character?
18. Which real-life agony aunt assisted in the creation of the comedy *Agony*?
19. What was the name of Vince's mother in *Just Good Friends*?
20. Who assisted Bruce Forsyth on *You Bet*?
21. Barry Ryan's mother appeared on *Spot The Tune* – what was her name?
22. Who links *Fame is the Spur* and *Jewel in the Crown*?
23. How much did it cost to stay for a weekend on *Fantasy Island*?
24. The western *Bronco* was a spin-off of which other western series?
25. Sister Jefferies was a character in which soap?
26. Who starred as *The Marksman*?
27. Desmond Llewellyn appeared on TV as the owner of which farm?
28. Name the host of the quiz *Get Set, Go*.
29. In *Small World*, who wrote poetry?
30. What was the name of the Indian character in *Casey Jones*?

ANSWERS

### Soaps 13 (see Quiz 91)

**1.** Blake and Krystle Carrington's. **2.** Colin Russel. **3.** *Softly, Softly.* **4.** A greyhound. **5.** Mrs Bates. **6.** Kenneth Farringdon. **7.** William Tarmey (Jack Duckworth). **8.** One thousand pounds. **9.** Ewing, Gibson, Waleska. **10.** *The Henderson Kids.* **11.** Krystle. **12.** Su Ellen. **13.** Tommy Duckworth. **14.** Hilda Ogden. **15.** The Denver Mirror. **16.** Barry Crocker. **17.** Don Lockwood. **18.** Bobby Simpson. **19.** Monica Colby's. **20.** Hilda Ogden. **21.** Stoke City. **22.** Wendy Richard. **23.** *Dallas.* **24.** By inhaling paint fumes. **25.** Ronald Reagan's ex-wife Jane Wyman. **26.** Seth Armstrong. **27.** Noele Gordon. **28.** Clayton Farlow. **29.** Charlie Cotton. **30.** Jill.

## QUIZ 93 Music & Variety 6

LEVEL 3

**Answers: see Quiz 94, page 622**

1. Which songstress recorded the theme to *Howard's Way*?
2. Arthur Daley featured in which single by the Firm?
3. Which group recorded the single *TV*?
4. Which former Playboy centrefold presented *The Word* aged 17?
5. What was Chris Evans first pop series, on Sky?
6. Who composed Cilla's 1960s theme song *Step Inside Love*?
7. How are Charles Hodge and David Peacock otherwise known?
8. Which famed pop 1950s pop show was broadcast for only one year?
9. Freddie Davies won *Opportunity Knocks* – what was his nickname?
10. What was the subject of the series *Applause, Applause*?
11. Who appeared as Hylda Baker's brother in a sitcom and was partnered on stage by Ben Warris?
12. How many Royal Variety performances did Morecambe and Wise appear in together?
13. Singer and actress Debbie Allen appeared in which series set in a stage school?
14. The GoJos featured in which Irishman's variety show?
15. On which show was there a feature called *Sofa Soccer*?
16. Who hosted the BBC New Comedy Awards for 1998?
17. Who recorded the theme for *Linford's Record Breakers*?
18. Which solo entertainer ended his shows by singing *May Each Day*?
19. In which year did Brotherhood Of Man win *The Eurovision Song Contest*?
20. *Elgar* and *Debussy* were films made for *Omnibus* by whom?
21. Which TV and musical star is the son of the lead singer with 50s band *The Southlanders*?
22. Which actor recorded an album called *Down Wind with Angels*?
23. Boxer Freddie Mills appeared on which ground-breaking music programme?
24. Which music show is sponsored by a soft drinks company?
25. *The Flower Duet* from Lakme by Delibes was used by which arline in an ad?
26. Where did the first *Songs of Praise* come from?
27. On which show did the host have a built in ashtray in his armchair?
28. Which former Bonzo Dog Doo Dah Band member hosted a comedy music show?
29. What was Leonard Sach's title on *The Good Old Days*?
30. Which Italian-American singer had his show on the BBC preceding *Sportsview*?

ANSWERS

**Comedy 17 (see Quiz 94)**

**1.** Tony Banta. **2.** Alfie Bass. **3.** Radio 4. **4.** Joan Sanderson. **5.** Anna Raeburn. **6.** Robin Tripp. **7.** *Marriage Lines.* **8.** Eve Matheson. **9.** Ireland. **10.** Jethrene Bodene. **11.** Roger. **12.** Nick Hancock. **13.** *Mind Your Language.* **14.** Jones. **15.** Laura. **16.** Talbot Rothwell. **17.** Rob Buckman. **18.** Headmaster. **19.** *Porridge.* **20.** Angela Thorne. **21.** St. Bernard. **22.** Norman Beaton. **23.** Shot apprehending a suspect during a robbery. **24.** Andrew Sachs. **25.** *Caroline In The City.* **26.** *Dream On.* **27.** Coach. **28.** *Ellen.* **29.** Sykes. **30.** They are the writers.

## QUIZ 94 Comedy 17

LEVEL 3

**Answers: see Quiz 93, page 621**

**1.** Who was the boxer in *Taxi*?
**2.** Who played 'Excused-Boots' Bisley in *The Army Game*?
**3.** From which medium did the sitcom *An Actor's Life For Me* originate?
**4.** Who played Prunella Scales' mother in *After Henry*?
**5.** Which agony aunt co-wrote *Agony*?
**6.** Which man lived in the flat above the Ropers?
**7.** What was the name of the series featuring Richard Briars and Prunella Scales?
**8.** Who did Lesley Dunlop replace as Zoe in *May To December*?
**9.** In which country was *Me Mammy* set?
**10.** Which other character did Max Baer Jr. portray apart from Jethro in *The Beverley Hillbillies*?
**11.** What was Monsieur LeClerc's first name in *'Allo, 'Allo*?
**12.** Who joined Punt and Dennis in *Me, You and Him*?
**13.** In which series was Francois Pascal an English student?
**14.** What was Paula Wilcox's surname in her series playing a single mum?
**15.** What was Miss Lancing's first name in *The Brittas Empire*?
**16.** Who wrote the *Carry On Laughing* Christmas Specials?
**17.** Which doctor presented *The Pink Medicine Show*?
**18.** What was Noel Howlett's position in *Please Sir*?
**19.** *Prisoner and Escort* was the pilot for which sitcom?
**20.** Who played *Farrington of the FO*?
**21.** Which breed of dog was the family pet in *Father, Dear Father*?
**22.** Who played Lenny Henry's dad in *The Fosters*?
**23.** In *Frasier*, how did Martin Crane become an invalid?
**24.** Who played Frances De La Tour's husband in *Every Silver Lining*?
**25.** The actress who played Michael J. Fox's mother in *Back To The Future* plays a cartoonist in which sitcom?
**26.** Which surreal series featured a book editor named Martin Tupper?
**27.** What was Ernie Pantuso's nickname in *Cheers*?
**28.** Which sitcom character once owned 'Buy The Book'?
**29.** Which comedian Eric was the oldest – Idle, Morecambe or Sykes?
**30.** What do Jerry and Phil do in *The Larry Sanders Show*?

ANSWERS

### Music & Variety 6 (see Quiz 93)

**1.** Marti Webb. **2.** *He's Alright.* **3.** The Flying Lizards. **4.** Amanda de Cadenet. **5.** *The Power Station.* **6.** Paul McCartney. **7.** Chas and Dave. **8.** *Oh Boy!* **9.** Parrot Face. **10.** The Music Hall. **11.** Jimmy Jewel. **12.** Five. **13.** *Fame.* **14.** Val Doonican. **15.** *Noel's Houseparty.* **16.** Phil Jupitus. **17.** 911. **18.** Andy Williams. **19.** 1976. **20.** Ken Russell. **21.** Gary Wilot. **22.** Dennis Waterman. **23.** *Six Five Special.* **24.** *The Pepsi Chart Show.* **25.** British Airways. **26.** Tabernacle Baptist Church, Cardiff. **27.** *Jim'll Fix It.* **28.** Neil Innes (*The Innes Book of Records*). **29.** Chairman. **30.** Perry Como.

## QUIZ 95 Children's TV 10

LEVEL 3

**Answers: see Quiz 96, page 624**

**1.** Which children's channel did Warner Amex found in the US in 1979?
**2.** Who designed the *Blue Peter* logo?
**3.** Who created *Ollie Beak*?
**4.** What was the last word of the Pink Panther song?
**5.** Which character from *Noel's Houseparty* had a No.1 Hit in 1993?
**6.** What is *Buffy*'s predestined role?
**7.** What was the name of Ivan Owen's vulpine puppet character?
**8.** What creature was Musky in *Deputy Dawg*?
**9.** Which former Olympic Champion hosts *Record Breakers*?
**10.** Who ran the TV station PPC TV?
**11.** Who was the pianist on *Play Away*?
**12.** Which school featured in *Press Gang*?
**13.** In which cartoon series did an elephant called Shep appear?
**14.** Which character did Alexander Gauge portray in *The Adventures of Robin Hood*?
**15.** Ant Jones featured in which children's series?
**16.** Which BBC children's series lead to the biggest toy success of 1997?
**17.** Who are Bart Simpson's favourite cartoon characters?
**18.** Which female puppet appeared on the *Rainbow* after Geoffrey left?
**19.** The producer of *Roobarb and Custard* likened the cat and dog relationship as that between which two comedians?
**20.** Who played the headmaster in *Teenage Health Freak*?
**21.** Who was Dr. Bunsen Honeydew's assistant?
**22.** Which future soap star played Gerry in *Going Out*?
**23.** What type of creature was Colonel K in *Dangermouse*?
**24.** Where in *Camberwick Green* would you meet Captain Snort?
**25.** Which spaceship crew did Miss Piggy belong to?
**26.** On which channel was *Pob* broadcast?
**27.** Tim Brooke-Taylor, Harry Enfield and Enn Reitel were the voices for which children's series?
**28.** Who were the stars of *The Quack Chat Show*?
**29.** Who created Henry the cat?
**30.** How is Theodore Geisel better known?

ANSWERS

### Pot Luck 21 (see Quiz 96)

**1.** Stringfellow. **2.** Black. **3.** 1930's. **4.** *Rising Stars.* **5.** *The Banana Splits.* **6.** The Haddons. **7.** A boat. **8.** Abbott. **9.** Jack Rosenthal. **10.** *Howard's Way.* **11.** Terry Wogan. **12.** Neville. **13.** Zaphod Beeblebrox. **14.** Grot. **15.** Her hand. **16.** Denis Quilley. **17.** *Blake's Seven.* **18.** Connie Hines. **19.** Billy Burke **20.** *Family Feud.* **21.** Faith Ashley. **22.** *Ask Pickles.* **23.** Theresa. **24.** Henry Willows. **25.** It had no presenter. **26.** 'Mother'. **27.** *Masterteam.* **28.** *God's Gift.* **29.** Brian Inglis. **30.** Bob Hope.

## QUIZ 96 Pot Luck 21

LEVEL 3

**Answers: see Quiz 95, page 623**

1. In *Airwolf*, what was Hawke's first name?
2. What colour did western character Adam Cartright always dress in?
3. In which decade was the series *South Riding* set?
4. Which talent show was hosted by Arthur Askey?
5. Snarky and Friegle were members of which gang?
6. Which family featured in *All at Number 20*?
7. In *Return of the Antelope*, what was The Antelope?
8. What was Sid's surname in *Bless this House*?
9. Who created *The Dustbinmen*?
10. Abby Urquhart appeared in which soap?
11. Who presented a *Guide to the BBC*?
12. In *Auf Wiedersehen Pet*, who got tattooed?
13. Who had two heads in *The Hitchhiker's Guide To The Galaxy*?
14. What did Reginald Perrin call his shop?
15. Where does Helen Mirren have a tattoo of a pair of crosses?
16. Who was the star of *Murder of a Moderate Man*?
17. In which sci-fi series was Roj the leader?
18. Who played Carol in *Mister Ed*?
19. Who did Samantha Egger Portray in *Ziegfeld: The Man and His Women*?
20. *Family Fortunes* was based on which US quiz?
21. Who was called 'The Snow Queen' in *Wish Me Luck*?
22. Wilfred and Mabel presented which *Jim'll Fix It* forerunner?
23. In *Dallas*, what was the name of Southfork's maid?
24. What was the name of John Thaw's character in *Home To Roost*?
25. Who was the presenter of *The Rock and Roll Years*?
26. What did *The Avengers* call their boss?
27. Which quiz was hosted by Angela Rippon?
28. What is the name of the dating game show hosted by Claudia Winkleman?
29. *All Our Yesterdays* was originally presented by who?
30. For which comic actor did Bob Monkhouse write gags?

ANSWERS

### Children's TV 10 (see Quiz 95)

**1.** Nickelodeon. **2.** Tony Hart. **3.** Wally Whyton. **4.** Toe. **5.** Mr. Blobby. **6.** Vampire Slayer. **7.** *Basil Brush*. **8.** Muskrat. **9.** Lynford Christie. **10.** *Pinky and Perky*. **11.** Jonathan Cohen. **12.** Norbridge High. **13.** *George Of The Jungle*. **14.** Friar Tuck. **15.** *Grange Hill*. **16.** *Teletubbies*. **17.** *Itchy and Scratchy*. **18.** Cleo. **19.** Tony Hancock and Sid James. **20.** Tony Robinson. **21.** Beaker. **22.** Linda Robson. **23.** Walrus. **24.** Pippin Fort. **25.** *Pigs In Space*. **26.** Channel 4. **27.** *Barney*. **28.** Keith Harris and Orville. **29.** Bob Godfrey and Stan Hayward. **30.** Dr Seuss.

## QUIZ 97 Drama 13

LEVEL 3

**Answers: see Quiz 98, page 626**

1. Which series starred Kate O'Mara on a North Sea ferry?
2. In which series was there a detective named Pepper?
3. Who played Professor Quatermass in the 1950s on television?
4. Which mini series had 130 million viewers on its first transmission?
5. Who played Ted Danson's wife in *Gullivers Travels*?
6. Who created *The Baron*?
7. Whose first stage play *Talent* was adapted for TV in 1979?
8. Who played the governor in *Within These Walls*?
9. What was Susan Hampshire's role in *The Pallisers*?
10. What was the sequel to *Bouquet of Barbed Wire*?
11. What did Kathleen Harrison's Mrs Thursday do for a living?
12. Which star of *The Bill* since its 1983 pilot is a qualified scuba diving instructor?
13. Who was Roger Smith's character in 77 *Sunset Strip*?
14. In which film did PC George Dixon first appear?
15. Who created the police series *87th Precinct*?
16. In which series did John Hillerman play Higgins?
17. Which member of Spandau Ballet appeared in *Supply And Demand*?
18. Walter Winchell narrated which crime series?
19. Which adventure featured characters Wilde and Sinclair?
20. Who was Roddy McMillan's character in *Hazell*?
21. In which country was Ben Hall an outlaw?
22. What was the name of the Yorkshire detective played by Leslie Sands?
23. Who starred in both *The Protectors* and *Howards Way*?
24. Who played *Big Breadwinner Hog*?
25. Which area of London was featured in a Neil Dunn Wednesday Play?
26. Which Avenger played a footman in *Upstairs Downstairs*?
27. What was Alan Wheatley's character in *The Adventures of Robin Hood*?
28. What nationality is Leo McKern?
29. Which Oscar winner played a PC in *Z-Cars*?
30. I which series did Lynn Darby play the girlfriend of a petty criminal?

ANSWERS

**Soaps 14 (see Quiz 306)**

**1.** Ali's Café. **2.** Sandra Stubbs. **3.** Juan Martin. **4.** *Kathy and Me*. **5.** Arncliffe and Esholt. **6.** *Dallas*. **7.** Sheila Mercier (Annie Sugden) in *Emmerdale* is Brian Rix's sister. **8.** The Alps. **9.** *General Hospital*. **10.** Earl Hammer Jnr. **11.** London. **12.** Hairdresser. **13.** Jane Wyman. **14.** *Peyton Place*. **15.** *The Newcomers*. **16.** Darius Perkins. **17.** The Cooper family. **18.** Flamingo Road. **19.** She was shot dead. **20.** *The Flying Doctors*. **21.** Blake Carrington. **22.** A ventriloquist's dummy. **23.** The QE2. **24.** Morgan Fairchild. **25.** Two. **26.** Portugal. **27.** Lucy, John Ross and Christopher. **28.** Ross Kemp. **29.** A motor mechanic. **30.** Alec Gilroy.

## QUIZ 98 Soaps 14

LEVEL 3

**Answers: see Quiz 97, page 625**

1. In *Eastenders*, how was Café Osman previously known?
2. Who replaced Hilda Ogden as cleaner at the Rover's Return?
3. Which guitarist played the theme music to *The Thornbirds*?
4. What was Gillian Taylforth's autobiography called?
5. Which two villages have been used for Beckindale?
6. In which soap did the town of Braddock appear?
7. What is the connection between Brian Rix and *Emmerdale*?
8. Which mountains were on Hilda Ogden's wall?
9. The character Dr Bywaters featured in which soap?
10. Who narrated *The Waltons*?
11. *Market In Honey Lane* was set in which UK city?
12. In *Albion Market* what was singer/actress Helen Shapiro's occupation?
13. Who won a Golden Globe in 1984 for playing Angela Channing?
14. Name the first US soap to appear on British TV.
15. What soap would you be watching if the cast were Angleton New Town?
16. Who played Scott Robinson before Jason Donovan?
17. What was the surname of the family which featured in *Newcomers*?
18. Which soap was based on a novel by Robert Wilder?
19. In *Dallas*, what happened to April while on honeymoon with Bobby Ewing?
20. Which Doctors were based in Coopers Crossing?
21. The Denver-Carrington Corporation belonged to who in *Dynasty*?
22. In *Soap* what was Chuck?
23. When Meg Mortimar sailed away from *Crossroads* on route to New York, which ship did she sail on?
24. Which soap actress's real name is Patsy McClenny?
25. In the *Brookside* siege how many people lost their lives?
26. To which country did Elsie Tanner move to from *Coronation Street*?
27. Who were Miss Ellie's grandchildren in *Dallas*?
28. Which soap star played D.I. Monk in the first series of *Birds of a Feather*?
29. What was Charlene's occupation in *Neighbours*?
30. When Bet Lynch wanted to go to Spain to work who lent her the airfare?

ANSWERS

### Drama 13 (see Quiz 97)

**1.** *Triangle.* **2.** *Policewoman.* **3.** Andre Morell. **4.** *Roots.* **5.** Mary Steenbergen. **6.** John Creasey. **7.** Victoria Wood. **8.** Googie Withers. **9.** Lady Glencora. **10.** *Another Bouquet.* **11.** Charlady. **12.** Mark Wingett (Jim Carver). **13.** Jeff Spencer. **14.** *The Blue Lamp.* **15.** Ed McBain. **16.** *Magnum.* **17.** Martin Kemp. **18.** *The Untouchables.* **19.** *The Persuaders.* **20.** Choc Minty. **21.** Australia. **22.** Cluff. **23.** Tony Anholt. **24.** Peter Egan. **25.** Clapham Junction. **26.** Gareth Hunt. **27.** The Sheriff of Nottingham. **28.** Australian. **29.** Colin Welland. **30.** *Budgie.*

## QUIZ 99 News 7

LEVEL 3

**Answers: see Quiz 100, page 628**

1. The long running programme about TV, *Did You See...?*, was hosted by whom?
2. Which founder member of BBC's *Breakfast Time* team left the weather spot to go to *Sky News*?
3. Which BBC reporter was at the scene of the Iranian Embassy Siege?
4. Who introduced *Just Another Day*?
5. Marion Foster was a presenter on which BBC lunchtime programme?
6. Who had to cut his news bulletin short because he was unwell?
7. How are Moira Armstrong and Pamela Armstrong related?
8. Which twice weekly Thames show was presented by Mavis Nicholson?
9. Which Bob co-hosted *Open Air*?
10. Which soccer side does GMTV's John Stapleton support?
11. Who presented *Newsround Weekly* when it was introduced in 1977?
12. Trevor McDonald wrote biographies of which two cricketers?
13. What were the interviewers in the series *We Want An Answer*?
14. Which weekly programme reviewed the outpourings of Fleet Street?
15. *A Week In Politics* was broadcast by which channel?
16. Tom Mangold specialised in reporting on what?
17. On which Scottish news programme did the *Tube*'s Muriel Gray make appearances?
18. Which newsreader wrote the novel *Chasing The Dragon*?
19. Which newscaster was the first to present a programme for the retired on Channel 4?
20. *Now Get Out Of That* was hosted by which former *Nationwide* reporter?
21. Whose books include *Cats in the News* and *Dogs in the News*?
22. On which channel could *News View* be watched?
23. Who links *Crimewatch UK* to *Daytime Live*?
24. Which Natalie appeared on *Open Air*?
25. *Split Screen* was presented by who?
26. *Taking Liberties* was introduced by who?
27. According to the title of the series, David Lomax reported on what kind of matters?
28. Susan Rae went from Radio 4 to which BBC morning programme?
29. Helen Rollason presented which evening news programme?
30. Who did Gillian Reynolds replace as presenter of *Face The Press* on ITV?

ANSWERS

### Comedy 18 (see Quiz 100)

**1.** Mollie Sugden. **2.** Shirley Stelfox. **3.** Jim Hacker. **4.** *Yus My Dear.* **5.** Morecambe and Wise. **6.** Shaun. **7.** Dawn French. **8.** *Plaza Patrol.* **9.** *In For A Penny.* **10.** *M*A*S*H.* **11.** Lisa. **12.** *Odd Man Out.* **13.** Experimental psychology. **14.** Harry Secombe. **15.** *Fawlty Towers.* **16.** Chumley on the Water. **17.** Chandler. **18.** *Spin City.* **19.** The Ramsden Reminder. **20.** Jebediah Springfield. **21.** *Third Rock From The Sun.* **22.** Pennsylvania. **23.** Gym Teacher. **24.** Brian Blessed. **25.** Gemma. **26.** Eric Idle. **27.** Corporal Springer. **28.** Jimmy Mulville. **29.** A Bike Shop. **30.** Catherine Bach.

## QUIZ 100 Comedy 18

LEVEL 3

**Answers: see Quiz 99, page 627**

1. Which actress famous for sitcoms played Nellie Harvey in *Coronation Street*?
2. Who first played Rose in *Keeping Up Appearances*?
3. Who was Bernard Woolley Private Secretary to?
4. In which 1970s sitcom did Wally and Lily move from a gypsy caravan to a housing estate?
5. Which comedy partnership appeared in *Running Wild*?
6. What is the sheep's name in *A Close Shave*?
7. Which comedienne starred in *Murder Most Horrid*?
8. In which sitcom did Cannon and Ball appear as security officers?
9. What was the ITV sitcom set in a public convenience?
10. In which U.S. sitcom is there a Father Mulcahy?
11. Who was created by two school friends in *Weird Science*?
12. John Inman starred in which comedy set in a seaside rock factory?
13. What did Mel Smith study at Oxford University?
14. Whose autobiography was called *Arias and Raspberries*?
15. *Basil The Rat* was an episode in which comedy series?
16. Where was *The River* set?
17. Which of the *Friends* had a girlfriend called Janice?
18. In which series are Carter and Stewart city employees?
19. What was the name of the newspaper in *Foxy Lady*?
20. Who was the founder of *The Simpsons'* home town?
21. In which sitcom did Wayne Knight play Officer Don?
22. Which state did *The Fresh Prince Of Bel Air* come from originally?
23. What is Zoe's occupation in *May To December*?
24. Who played the Duke of Edinburgh's father in *Blackadder*?
25. What was the name of Felicity Kendal's character in *Solo*?
26. Who created *Rutland Weekend Television*?
27. Who was Michael Medwin's character in *The Army Game*?
28. Who played Aulus Paulinus in the Roman spoof *Chelmsford 123*?
29. What was Dan Conner's hobby that became his business in *Roseanne*?
30. Who played Daisy in *The Dukes Of Hazzard*?

ANSWERS

### News 7 (see Quiz 99)

**1.** Ludovic Kennedy. **2.** Francis Wilson. **3.** Kate Adie. **4.** John Pitman. **5.** *Pebble Mill At One.* **6.** Peter Woods. **7.** They are not related at all. **8.** *Afternoon Plus.* **9.** Bob Wellings. **10.** Manchester City. **11.** Lucy Mathen. **12.** Clive Lloyd and Viv Richards. **13.** Children. **14.** *What The Papers Say.* **15.** Channel 4. **16.** Crime. **17.** *Scotland Today.* **18.** Sandy Gall. **19.** Robert Dougall. **20.** Bernard Falk. **21.** Martyn Lewis. **22.** BBC2. **23.** Sue Cook – who presented both. **24.** Natalie Anglesey. **25.** Margo McDonald. **26.** David Jessel. **27.** *Business Matters.* **28.** *Open Air.* **29.** *Newsround.* **30.** Anthony Howard.

## QUIZ 101 Pot Luck 22

LEVEL 3

**Answers: see Quiz 102, page 630**

1. What was the name of the dog-like character in the cartoon *Will O'The Wisp*?
2. Where did Sharon and Elsie work?
3. Who presented the children's show *Going a Bundle*?
4. Angela Down played which character in *Take Three Girls*?
5. Who chaired *Ask Me Another*?
6. *The Day The Universe Changed* was presented by which BBC science expert?
7. Which reporter met a lost tribe in Brazil in 1970?
8. What was Cash's surname in *Cash and Cable*?
9. Alf Garnett's son-in-law lived in which city?
10. Who hosted the show *Running Late*?
11. Which impressionist starred in the 1960s show *Three of a Kind*?
12. What did Geoffrey do for a living in *The Lovers*?
13. Who links *The A-Team* and *Chopper One*?
14. Hayley Mills played Tilly Grant in which series?
15. What kind of hat did the detective Mr Rose wear?
16. In which series did Professor Popkiss appear?
17. What was the name of the playwright in *An Englishman's Castle*?
18. Which pop singer starred in the TV mini-series *Blood And Orchids*?
19. Who played the title role in *The Travels of Jaimie McPheeters*?
20. Sharon Duce played a gambling addict's girlfriend in which 1980's series?
21. Bill Conte wrote the theme tune for which soap?
22. Which character did Tony Selby play in *Get Some In*?
23. What was Chris's job in *The Cuckoo Waltz*?
24. Who starred as The Snoop Sisters?
25. In which city was the World War II drama *And a Nightingale Sang* set?
26. Who links *Wings* to *Piece of Cake*?
27. Who did Rosie Tindall meet at the start of *No Strings*?
28. What was the full name of the character played by Windsor Davies in *Never The Twain*?
29. The drama, *Shalom Salaam* was set in which city?
30. Which game show was co-hosted by Wie Wie Wong?

ANSWERS

### Children's TV 11 (see Quiz 102)

**1.** Julia Sawalha. **2.** Una Stubbs. **3.** *Rupert Bear.* **4.** Patricia Hayes. **5.** *Stopit And Tidyup.* **6.** Dedication. **7.** Richard the Lionheart. **8.** *The Hobbit.* **9.** A doctor. **10.** *Josie And The Pussycats.* **11.** Tom of T.H.U.M.B. **12.** Mike Reid. **13.** Rolf Harris. **14.** Marshall Thompson. **15.** Sir Basil and Lady Rosemary. **16.** A bow tie. **17.** Connie Booth. **18.** Shari Lewis. **19.** Vicky Licorish. **20.** Mark Curry. **21.** Four. **22.** Red and yellow. **23.** *SuperTed.* **24.** Alberto Frog. **25.** Bella and Ursula. **26.** Simon Groom. **27.** *Follyfoot.* **28.** *The Adventures of Twizzle and Torchy.* **29.** Michael Bentine. **30.** Knightmare.

## QUIZ 102 Children's TV 11

LEVEL 3

**Answers: see Quiz 101, page 629**

1. Which future sitcom star played Lynda Day in *Press Gang*?
2. Who played Mrs Plugg in *Morris Minor's Marvellous Motors*?
3. Ray Brooks narrated the stories of which character?
4. Who narrated *Gran*?
5. Which children's series was narrated by Terry Wogan?
6. According to the first *Record Breakers* theme song what did you need to be a record breaker?
7. Name the future king played by Dermot Walsh.
8. *The Return Of The King* was based on which book?
9. What was the profession of *Ramar Of The Jungle*?
10. Hanna-Barbera created which cartoon all-girl band?
11. What was the name of the tiny spy in the cartoon *King Kong*?
12. Which future soap star presided over *Runaround*?
13. Who was Koojee Bear's human companion?
14. Which actor starred as *Daktari*?
15. Who owned the garden in *The Herbs*?
16. What does BooBoo wear around his neck?
17. Who in 1980 played *Little Lord Fauntleroy*'s mother?
18. Who had a puppet called Charlie Horse?
19. Which female presenter was in the coffee shop in *Saturday Superstore*?
20. Who presented *Blue Peter* and *Screen Test*?
21. How many daughters were there in *The Little House On The Prairie*?
22. What were the colours of the two teams in *Cheggers Plays Pop*?
23. Victor Spinetti provided voices for which superhero cartoon?
24. Who was conductor of the band in *Bod*?
25. What were the names of *George Of The Jungle*'s two girlfriends?
26. Which *Blue Peter* presenter was once arrested on assignment in Japan?
27. On which farm did Christina Rodska appear?
28. What was Gerry Anderson's first TV series called?
29. Who created *The Bumblies*?
30. In which show would Treguard warn contests "Temporal Disruption occurring!"

ANSWERS

### Pot Luck 22 (see Quiz 101)

**1.** The Moog. **2.** In a printing factory. **3.** Harry Fowler. **4.** Avril. **5.** Franklin Engelmann. **6.** James Burke. **7.** Adrian Cowell. **8.** Canover. **9.** Liverpool. **10.** Donald Trelford. **11.** Mike Yarwood. **12.** Bank Clerk. **13.** Dirk Benedict. **14.** *The Flame Trees of Thika.* **15.** A bowler. **16.** *Supercar.* **17.** Peter Ingrim. **18.** Kris Kristofferson. **19.** Kurt Russell. **20.** *Big Deal.* **21.** *Falcon Crest.* **22.** Corporal Marsh. **23.** Newspaper reporter. **24.** Helen Haynes and Mildred Natwick. **25.** Newcastle. **26.** Tim Woodward. **27.** Sam. **28.** Oliver Smallbridge. **29.** Leicester. **30.** *The Golden Shot.*

## QUIZ 103 Drama 14

LEVEL 3

**Answers: see Quiz 104, page 632**

1. What is the family link between *Up The Junction* and *Cathy Come Home?*
2. Who parked the cars in *77 Sunset Strip?*
3. Which lawyer's christian name is Horace?
4. What was Patrick Duffy's name in *The Man From Atlantis?*
5. Who played No. 1 in *The Prisoner?*
6. In which county was Paul Dangerfield a GP?
7. Which German series featured the story of a U-boat and its crew?
8. Carol Drinkwater and Lynda Bellingham both played which role?
9. Which late private detective was played by Ken Cope?
10. In which series is there a pub named Fitzgerald's?
11. Who played Captain Pellow in ITV's *Hornblower?*
12. In *The Man From UNCLE*, who wore the number 11 on his badge?
13. What was Eric Porter's character in *The Forsythe Saga?*
14. On whose book was *The History Man* based?
15. Who played Inspector Alleyn in the pilot for the subsequent series with Patrick Malahide?
16. Who played Sgt Fletcher in the Miss Marple series before becoming another detective's sidekick?
17. In which town was *Capstick's Law* set?
18. Which Douglas sister did Steven Crane have an affair with in *The Chancer?*
19. In *Kennedy*, who portrayed Bobby Kennedy?
20. *Gentlemen And Players* was set in which business world?
21. Which star of *The Men's Room* is the niece of actor Christopher Lee?
22. Which actor in a long running drama series wrote a book called *Vet Behind the Ears?*
23. Caine was what type of priest in *Kung Fu?*
24. What or who was Fred in *The Duchess Of Duke Street?*
25. Which drama used 1,000 Yugoslavian Territorial Army members as extras?
26. In which drama did The Rana of Blithar appear?
27. Who starred as Richard Gaunt in *The Regiment?*
28. Who played Danny in *Fame?*
29. In *Marcus Welby MD*, who played the doctor's assistant?
30. *A Piece Of Cake* featured which of the armed forces?

ANSWERS

### Soaps 15 (see Quiz 104)

**1.** Angie Watts. **2.** Stan Ogden. **3.** *Falcon Crest.* **4.** Victoria Principal. **5.** *On The Inside.* **6.** Beckindale (in *Emmerdale*). **7.** Howard Duff. **8.** Sharon Watts, his daughter. **9.** *Santa Barbara.* **10.** Harmon Springs. **11.** Laura in *Brookside.* **12.** Father Ralph de Bricassar. **13.** *Compact.* **14.** Richard Channing. **15.** Kelvin. **16.** David Jacobs. **17.** Pat. **18.** *Brookside.* **19.** *The Waltons.* **20.** Painting. **21.** Roy Evans. **22.** Amanda Burton. **23.** Elizabeth Dawn. **24.** Darren Day. **25.** Linda Evans. **26.** Leo and Lynne. **27.** Cecile died before the ceremony was completed. **28.** A greyhound. **29.** Christmas. **30.** None.

## QUIZ 104 Soaps 15

LEVEL 3

**Answers: see Quiz 103, page 631**

1. Which early *Eastender* tried to commit suicide by takin an overdose of pills?
2. Who did Vera Duckworth buy the *Coronation Street* window cleaning round from?
3. In which soap did the newspaper the New Globe appear?
4. Which Dallas star duetted with Andy Gibb on *All I Have to Do Is Dream* in 1981?
5. What was the name of the *Prisoner: Cell Block H* theme tune?
6. In which village might you have found Sergeant McArthur keeping law and order?
7. Who played Titus Semple in *Flamingo Road*?
8. Who did Dirty Den call Princess?
9. In which soap did the Carnation Killer leave a white carnation at the scenes of his crimes?
10. In which fictitious town was *Dynasty* set?
11. Who was the second soap victim (after Valerie Barlow) to die from electrocution?
12. Who did Richard Chamberlain play in *The Thorn Birds*?
13. Which 1960s soap did the *'Allo, 'Allo* actress Carmen Silvera appear in?
14. What was the name of the racecourse owner in *Falcon Crest*?
15. Which character left Albert Square to go to university in East Anglia?
16. Which creator of *Knot's Landing* shares his name with a UK radio and TV personality?
17. In *Eastenders*, who was Pete Beale's first wife?
18. The Green Lantern takeaway featured in which soap?
19. The TV tales of whom are based on the novel Spender's Mountain?
20. What was Helen's hobby in *Neighbours*?
21. Which *Eastenders* character shares his name with a football manger sacked in favour of a Frenchman?
22. Which former *Brookside* star married photographer Sven Arnstein?
23. Which actress was spotted by Larry Grayson who cast her as Dot on his TV show?
24. Who in real life has dated 'Beth' and 'Maxine' from two different soaps?
25. Which *Dynasty* star released a single *Don't You Need* in 1979?
26. What were the names of Tom's two children in *Howard's Way*?
27. What occurred during the wedding ceremony of Cecile Colby and Alexis Carrington?
28. In *Coronation Street* what kind of animal was Lucky?
29. In *Eastenders* Dot Cotton only drinks alcohol at what time of the year?
30. How many people were killed in the Rovers Return fire?

ANSWERS

### Drama 14 (see Quiz 103)

**1.** Author of *Junction* Nell Dunn married *Cathy* author Jeremy Sandford. **2.** Kookie. **3.** Rumpole. **4.** Mark Harris. **5.** Patrick McGoohan. **6.** Warwickshire. **7.** *Das Boot.* **8.** Helen Herriot. **9.** Marty Hopkirk. **10.** *Ballykisangel.* **11.** Robert Lindsay. **12.** Napoleon Solo. **13.** Soames. **14.** Malcolm Bradbury's. **15.** Simon Williams. **16.** Kevin Whately. **17.** Bowdale. **18.** Victoria. **19.** John Shea. **20.** City finance. **21.** Harriet Walter. **22.** Christopher Timothy. **23.** A Shaolin (Buddhist) Priest. **24.** The porter's dog **25.** *War and Peace.* **26.** *The Far Pavillions.* **27.** Christopher Cazenove. **28.** Carlo Imperato. **29.** Charles Brolen. **30.** The RAF.

## QUIZ 105 Comedy 19

LEVEL 3

**Answers: see Quiz 106, page 634**

1. Which painter advertised Flash?
2. Who played Dr Jake Ramorey in *Friends*?
3. What was Paul's occupation in *Ever Decreasing Circles*?
4. Which stand-up comic wears large collars and carries many pens in his top pocket?
5. Who links *Second Thoughts* to *Faith In The Future*?
6. What was Derek Nimmo's character in *Oh Brother*?
7. Which sitcom star produced a fitness video called *Let's Dance*?
8. The character Kirk St Moritz appeared in which comedy series?
9. Which football team does June Whitfield support?
10. To whom did Clive Anderson say "there's no beginning to your talents"?
11. Who wrote and sang the theme song for the 70s sitcom *No Honestly*?
12. What was Alec Callander's young wife's name in *May to December*?
13. Which character was the bigoted American *Archie Bunker* based on?
14. Which character's girlfriend was played by Donna from *Eastenders*?
15. In which series did Uncle Mort appear?
16. Who played Mr Big?
17. Dermot Kelly was which comic's sidekick?
18. In *Beggar My Neighbour*, who played the well-off couple?
19. In which series did R. S. M. Brittain appear?
20. Who was the star of *Idiots Weekly, Price 2d*?
21. The Cemetery Gates were on which bus driver's route?
22. What was the first name of Keith Barron's character in *Duty Free*?
23. Who starred in *L For Lester*?
24. Who was the star of *Now – Something Else*?
25. What was Harry McGhee's character in *The Worker*?
26. Sheila Burnett could be seen on which stunt series?
27. What was the name of the cousins in *Perfect Strangers*?
28. How many sons did David Jason have in *A Bit Of A Do*?
29. Steve Nallon provided the voice of which Prime Minister on *Spitting Image*?
30. In *Only Fools And Horses* what had been Uncle Albert's rank in the merchant navy?

ANSWERS

**Pot Luck 23 (see Quiz 106)**

**1.** *The Black and White Minstrel Show.* **2.** Arnold Swain. **3.** 1985. **4.** *Young Musician of the Year.* **5.** Beresford. **6.** *Farrington of the F.O.* **7.** *Nancy Drew.* **8.** Maurice Roeves. **9.** Nemesis. **10.** The Blue Moon Detective Agency. **11.** D.I. Halero. **12.** Gene Barry. **13.** Peter Barkworth. **14.** Sean Bean. **15.** Tim. **16.** Norwich. **17.** A bear. **18.** Gordon. **19.** Peter Purves. **20.** Grantleigh Manor. **21.** Miriam Karlin. **22.** Robin Bailey. **23.** Alvin Childers and Spencer Williams. **24.** Photographer. **25.** Howard Hesseman (as Dr Johnny Fever). **26.** Holby City Hospital. **27.** Honor Blackman. **28.** Hywel Bennett. **29.** Gerald Harper. **30.** Boulder City.

## QUIZ 106 Pot Luck 23

LEVEL 3

**Answers: see Quiz 105, page 633**

1. Margaret Savage was a principal dancer on which show?
2. Who bigamously married Emily in *Coronation Street*?
3. In which year was the House of Lords first televised live?
4. Humphrey Burton introduced which annual youth competition?
5. What was the middle name of MP Alan B'Stard?
6. In which series did Angela Thorne play an overseas diplomat?
7. Pamela Sue Martin played which youthful detective on TV?
8. Who links *Danger UXB* and *Tutti-Frutti*?
9. Who did *The Champions* work for?
10. Which agency did Maddie and David run?
11. What was the name of the Detective Inspector in *The Men from Room Thirteen*?
12. Who played Bat Masterton in *The Adventurer*?
13. In *The Price*, who starred as the husband of Harriet Walter?
14. Which actor has '100% Blade' tattooed on his arm?
15. Who created the *Blue Peter* cartoon, *Bleep and Booster*?
16. In which city is Anglia TV based?
17. What was *Gentle Ben*?
18. Angus is Angus Deayton's middle name, what is his first name?
19. Who hosted *Babble*?
20. Old Ned was the gardener at which manor?
21. Who played Paddy in *The Rag Trade*?
22. Who narrated *The Poudles*?
23. What were the real names of Amos and Andy?
24. How did *The Magnificent Evans* make a living?
25. In *WKRP In Cincinnati*, who starred as a Doctor?
26. Where did Ewart Plimmer work?
27. Which star of *The Upper Hand* has a brown belt at judo?
28. Who starred in *The Consultant*?
29. Who played a caped crusader in *Adam Adamant*?
30. In which city did *Mork and Mindy* live?

ANSWERS

### Comedy 19 (see Quiz 105)

**1.** Karl Howman (Jacko). **2.** Joey. **3.** Hairdresser. **4.** Harry Hill. **5.** Lynda Bellingham. **6.** Dominic. **7.** Richard Wilson. **8.** *Dear John.* **9.** Wimbledon. **10.** Jeffrey Archer. **11.** Lynsey de Paul. **12.** Zoe. **13.** Alf Garnett. **14.** *Mr. Bean.* **15.** *I Didn't Know You Cared.* **16.** Peter Jones. **17.** Arthur Hayes. **18.** Reg Varney and Pat Coombs. **19.** *Alfred Marks Time.* **20.** Peter Sellers. **21.** Stan Butler's. **22.** David. **23.** Brian Murphy. **24.** Rory Bremner. **25.** Mr Pugh. **26.** *Candid Camera.* **27.** Larry and Balki. **28.** Two. **29.** Margaret Thatcher. **30.** Stoker.

## HOW TO SET UP YOUR OWN

# PUB QUIZ

It isn't easy, get that right from the start. This isn't going to be easy. Think instead of words like; 'difficult', 'taxing', 'infuriating' consider yourself with damp palms and a dry throat and then, when you have concentrated on that, put it out of your mind and think of the recognition you will receive down the local, imagine all the regulars lifting you high upon their shoulders dancing and weaving their way around the pub. It won't help but it's good to dream every once in a while.

## What you will need:

- A good selection of biros (never be tempted to give your own pen up, not even to family members)
- A copy of this book
- A set of answer sheets photocopied from the back of the book
- A good speaking voice and possibly a microphone and an amp
- A pub
- At least one pint inside you
- At least one more on your table
- A table

## What to do:

Choose your local to start with, there is no need to get halfway through your first quiz and decide you weren't cut out for all this and then find yourself in the roughest pub in Christendom 30 miles and a long run from home.

Chat it through with the landlord and agree on whether you will be charging or not, if you don't then there is little chance of a prize for the winners other than a free pint each and this is obviously at the landlord's discretion – if you pack his pub to bursting then five free pints won't worry him, but if it's only you and a two others then he may be less than unwilling, as publicans tend to be.

If you decide on a payment entry keep it reasonable, you don't want to take the fun out of the quiz; some people will be well aware that they have very little hope of winning and will be reluctant to celebrate the fact by mortgaging their house.

Once location and prize are all sorted then advertising the event is paramount, get people's attention, sell sell, sell or, alternatively, stick up a gaudy looking poster on the door of the bogs. Be sure to specify all the details, time, prize and so on – remember you are selling to people whose tiny attention span is being whittled down to nothing by alcohol.

After this it is time for the big night, if you are holding the event in the 'snug' which seats ten or so you can rely on your voice, if not you should get hold of a good microphone and an amplifier so that you can boom out your questions and enunciate the length and breadth of the pub (once again, clear this with the landlord and don't let liquid anywhere near the electrical equipment). Make sure to practice, and get comfortable with the sound of your own voice and relax as much as possible, try not to rely on alcohol too much or "round one" will be followed by "rown' too" which will eventually give way to "runfree". Relax with your voice so that you can handle any queries from the teams, and any venomous abuse from the 'lively' bar area.

When you enter the pub make sure you take everything listed above. Also, make sure you have a set of tie-break questions and that you instruct everybody who is taking part of the rules – and be firm. It will only upset people if you start handing out impromptu solutions and let's face it the wisdom of Solomon is not needed when you are talking pub quiz rules; 'no cheating' is a perfectly healthy stance to start with.

Finally, keep the teams to a maximum of five members, hand out your answer papers and pens and, when everybody is good and settled, start the quiz. It might not be easy and it might not propel you to international stardom or pay for a life of luxury but you will enjoy yourself. No, really.

**ANSWERS** **Part One**

| | |
|---|---|
| 1 ______ | 16 ______ |
| 2 ______ | 17 ______ |
| 3 ______ | 18 ______ |
| 4 ______ | 19 ______ |
| 5 ______ | 20 ______ |
| 6 ______ | 21 ______ |
| 7 ______ | 22 ______ |
| 8 ______ | 23 ______ |
| 9 ______ | 24 ______ |
| 10 ______ | 25 ______ |
| 11 ______ | 26 ______ |
| 12 ______ | 27 ______ |
| 13 ______ | 28 ______ |
| 14 ______ | 29 ______ |
| 15 ______ | 30 ______ |

## ANSWERS Part Two

1 ______

2 ______

3 ______

4 ______

5 ______

6 ______

7 ______

8 ______

9 ______

10 ______

11 ______

12 ______

13 ______

14 ______

15 ______

16 ______

17 ______

18 ______

19 ______

20 ______

21 ______

22 ______

23 ______

24 ______

25 ______

26 ______

27 ______

28 ______

29 ______

30 ______

**ANSWERS** **Part Three**

1 ________________

2 ________________

3 ________________

4 ________________

5 ________________

6 ________________

7 ________________

8 ________________

9 ________________

10 ________________

11 ________________

12 ________________

13 ________________

14 ________________

15 ________________

16 ________________

17 ________________

18 ________________

19 ________________

20 ________________

21 ________________

22 ________________

23 ________________

24 ________________

25 ________________

26 ________________

27 ________________

28 ________________

29 ________________

30 ________________

## *QUIZ 51* FRED ASTAIRE ........ LEVEL 1

*Answers – see page 61*

1 What was Fred Astaire's full real first name?
2 Who was Astaire's most famous dancing partner?
3 What relation to Fred was Adele Astaire?
4 Which item of formal dress was the name of a famous Astaire movie?
5 With which co-star Judy did he appear in *Easter Parade*?
6 For which 70s disaster film set in a skyscraper was Astaire Oscar-nominated?
7 Which rainbow was the title of a 1968 movie with Fred Astaire?
8 What completes the quote about an Astaire screen test, 'Can't sing, can't act, can ____ a little'?
9 In the 'Cheek to Cheek' number in *Top Hat* which part of Ginger Rogers's dress kept blowing up Astaire's nose?
10 In their first movie together Astaire and Rogers were 'Flying Down to' where?
11 Which Rita starred with Astaire in *You'll Never Get Rich*?
12 How many times did he receive an Oscar for a specific role?
13 *On the Beach* was what type of 'first' for Astaire in 1959?
14 In which decade of the 19th century was Astaire born?
15 Which classic Beatles album features Fred Astaire – among many others – on the cover?
16 What parts of Fred Astaire were heavily insured?
17 In which decade of the 20th century did Astaire die, aged 88?
18 Which Kelly did he replace in *Easter Parade*?
19 What comes after 'Top hat, white tie' in the song from *Top Hat*?
20 Who was his male co-star in *Holiday Inn* – which introduced 'White Christmas' to audiences?
21 In 1936 Astaire and Rogers starred in 'Follow the' what?
22 In the 1930s Astaire starred in 'The Gay' what?
23 Which 'Swing' film featured 'The Way You Look Tonight'?
24 In which decade did Astaire and Rogers star in their first movie together?
25 Which Hepburn was his co-star in *Funny Face*?

**Answers Living Legends** (see Quiz 49)
**1** Hepburn. **2** Redford. **3** *Forrest Gump*. **4** Kerr. **5** 1930s. **6** The Bee Gees. **7** Roger Moore. **8** Elizabeth Taylor. **9** Reeve. **10** O'Toole. **11** Barbra Streisand. **12** Paul Newman. **13** Sean Connery. **14** Van Gogh. **15** Doris Day. **16** Michael Caine. **17** Hepburn. **18** *Funny Girl*. **19** Caine. **20** *Mary Poppins*. **21** Doris Day. **22** England. **23** Popeye. **24** Barbra Streisand. **25** Charles Bronson.

## *QUIZ 52* POT LUCK 21 ........ LEVEL 1

*Answers – see page 62*

1 What type of 'Storm' starred Sigourney Weaver and Kevin Kline in 1997?
2 Does *Pulp Fiction* last 50, 150 or 250 minutes?
3 Which famous Claudette tested for the role of Scarlett O'Hara?
4 In which decade of the 20th century was Laura Dern born?
5 Which Billy starred in *When Harry Met Sally*?
6 On what vehicle did Steve McQueen try to flee in *The Great Escape*?
7 Which actress links *Basic Instinct* and *Last Action Hero*?
8 Which water-linked film took over from *Waterworld* as the most costly to make?
9 *Yankee Doodle Dandy* starred which James?
10 Kathleen Turner was concerned with Prizzi's what?
11 Which Susan starred in *The Client*?
12 Brigitte Bardot had a theatre named after her in which French city?
13 Who created Tom and Jerry at MGM in the 40s?
14 *The Music Lovers* was about which Russian composer?
15 Which son of a *M*A*S*H* star starred in *Young Guns II*?
16 Which Richard replaced John Travolta in *American Gigolo*?
17 Where is 'The Sword', according to the Disney film title?
18 Which TV cartoon character did John Goodman play in a movie?
19 Who sang 'The Shoop Shoop Song' in *Mermaids*?
20 Which word follows 'The Fisher' in a Robin Williams movie title?
21 Which star actor was in *Top Gun, Jerry Maguire* and *Born on the Fourth of July*?
22 Who played the lead role in *The Wizard of Oz*?
23 In which decade of the 20th century was Dame Judi Dench born?
24 Whose real name is James Baumgarner?
25 What was the Bond theme for *From Russia with Love* called?

**Answers Pot Luck 20** (see Quiz 50)
**1** Hooch. **2** Carrey. **3** Once a year. **4** Michelle Pfeiffer. **5** *Away*. **6** Murray. **7** Nicholas. **8** Blondes. **9** Irons. **10** 1990s. **11** Cruise. **12** Flash. **13** He sneezed. **14** Winger. **15** 1930s. **16** Batman. **17** Johnny Depp. **18** Seven. **19** Annette Bening. **20** *Show*. **21** *A Star Is Born*. **22** Hanks. **23** 1970s. **24** Alan Parker. **25** Bowler.

## *QUIZ 53* FILM COMPANIES ........ LEVEL 1

*Answers – see page 67*

1 Which Sam was the G in MGM?
2 Which company, famous for animation, bought Miramax in 1993?
3 What did R stand for in RKO?
4 What was the amalgamation of the Fox Film Corporation and 20th Century Pictures called?
5 Which Harry founded Columbia?
6 Which Mary was the only female founder member of United Artists in 1919?
7 Whose first classic comedies were put out by Essanay?
8 Which blockbuster from Steven Spielberg revived the fortunes of Universal Pictures in the 80s?
9 Which company merged with Time Inc. in 1989?
10 Which British company had a wild cat in its name?
11 Which Australian-born publishing tycoon bought 20th Century Fox in 1985?
12 Which actor was the Lancaster in the Hecht–Lancaster company?
13 Which former Beatle set up HandMade Films?
14 Which Steven set up Dreamworks?
15 Which Brothers bought out First National in 1929?
16 What sort of movies were Hammer famous for?
17 What did the first M stand for in MGM?
18 Which animal was the symbol of MGM?
19 Which computer-generated 'Story' was created by Pixar?
20 Which Japanese company paid $3.4 billion for Columbia in 1990?
21 Which Howard bought a large share of RKO in 1948?
22 What was the first name of Mayer of MGM fame?
23 Which borough of west London gave its name to comedies in the 40s and 50s made in its studios?
24 What was the surname of father and son Darryl F. and Richard of 20th Century Fox fame?
25 How many Warner Brothers were there?

**Answers Pot Luck 22** (see Quiz 55)
**1** Lewis. **2** *Female.* **3** Paltrow. **4** *Oklahoma!.* **5** Eddie Murphy. **6** Peck. **7** *Murder on the Orient Express.* **8** *Five.* **9** Stallone. **10** Barney. **11** Crystal. **12** Gere. **13** 1960s. **14** John Travolta. **15** Innocence. **16** Keaton. **17** Madonna's. **18** *Annie Hall.* **19** Hunter. **20** Steel. **21** 1940s. **22** Seven. **23** Winona Ryder. **24** Bette Davis. **25** Bacon.

## *QUIZ 54* WORLD CINEMA ........ LEVEL 1

*Answers – see page 68*

1 Who did Antonio Banderas play in *Il Giovane Mussolini*?
2 In which part of the UK was *Trainspotting* set?
3 Where was *Farewell My Concubine* banned when it was first released?
4 On which romantic day did the action of *Picnic at Hanging Rock* take place?
5 *Les Enfants du Paradis* was shot at the end of which war?
6 Michelangelo Antonioni hails from which European country?
7 Where were the first Mad Max films with Mel Gibson made?
8 Which French film director Roger died in February 2000?
9 Which 1993 film by New Zealander Jane Campion has the name of a musical instrument as its title?
10 Jacques Tati hails from country?
11 Which British film magnate had the name and initial J. Arthur?
12 What is the first name of Greek actress Mercouri?
13 Which country's film industry is referred to as 'Bollywood'?
14 Which Italian director was Giuseppe Bertolucci's elder brother?
15 Who, with 'Jules', is in the title of the 60s Truffaut classic?
16 Which film with Cate Blanchett about an English queen was directed by Indian Shekhar Kapur?
17 Where does Neil Jordan hail from?
18 Which French actress was often known by her initials B.B.?
19 *Abba the Movie* was a collaboration between Australia and where?
20 Which Italian actress played opposite Marcello Mastroianni 12 times?
21 Where was *The Seven Samurai* made?
22 How was Czech-born actress Hedy Kielser known when she moved to Hollywood?
23 In which capital city were the Cinecitta Studios founded?
24 Ingmar Bergman hails from which Scandinavian country?
25 What is the first name of Finnish-born Hollywood director Harlin?

**Answers 1940s Stars** (see Quiz 56)
**1** Hayworth. **2** England. **3** Ginger Rogers. **4** Bob Hope. **5** Tracy. **6** Henry. **7** Ingrid Bergman. **8** Ronald Reagan. **9** John Wayne. **10** Costello. **11** Davis. **12** Cole Porter. **13** Lombard. **14** Fruit. **15** Cagney. **16** Sweden. **17** Humphrey Bogart. **18** Fred Astaire. **19** Taylor. **20** Priest. **21** Hepburn. **22** Robert. **23** Red. **24** Rooney. **25** Legs.